Think Math!

Teacher Guide

Volume 2

Developed by Education Development Center, Inc.
through National Science Foundation

Grant No. ESI-0099093

EDC

Published and distributed by:

Math

www.Math.SchoolSpecialty.com

Think Math! Teacher Guide

Printing 4 – 6/2010

Webcrafters, Madison, WI

1358057

978-0-15-359414-4

This program was funded in part through the National Science Foundation under Grant No. ESI-0099093. Any opinions, findings, and conclusions or recommendations expressed in this program are those of the authors and do not necessarily reflect the views of the National Science Foundation.

Acknowledgement

We especially want to acknowledge the inspiration we derived from two special works and their visionary authors: *Vision in Elementary Mathematics*, by W. W. Sawyer, and *Math Workshop* by Robert Wirtz and his colleagues.

Sawyer and Wirtz understood the power of puzzlement, curiosity, and surprise—for teachers as well as for children. They crafted problems that provide not only essential practice, but the added bonus of ideas and surprises for the observant child. These discovery opportunities foreshadow later learning, so that when children must master hard ideas in later grades, the ideas are already well underway.

Part of Sawyer's "vision" was literally about vision—the power of graphic images and formats that capture mathematical ideas and processes and that reduce the sole reliance on words. Clear, precise mathematical language is essential, of course, but jumpstarting ideas without words helps not only the English Language Learner, but all children, and builds secure concepts to which they can attach their growing mathematical vocabulary. Both *Vision* and *Math Workshop* introduced a technique of teaching—for occasional use—in which the teacher, playfully, is absolutely silent! This change of pace rivets children's attention as they watch eagerly for clues— after all, there's nothing to listen for—and creates an almost electric charge in the classroom.

Sawyer also recognized children as great language learners, who acquire even the formal language of algebra if it is not just "another thing to learn," but is seen as a convenient "shorthand" for expressing ideas and patterns that the children are eager to describe.

Finally, both works recognized teachers as intelligent, college-educated adults. *Math Workshop* showed the utmost respect for teachers, giving flexibility as well as guidance, and recognizing that only through the teacher's complete engagement, judgment, and thoughtful teaching can a lesson really work.

We gratefully acknowledge what we learned, over many years, from these mentors, and hope that our work lives up to the brilliance and uncanny insight and foresight they brought to mathematics.

E. Paul Goldenberg, Principal Investigator

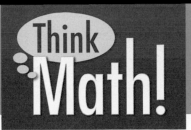

Contents

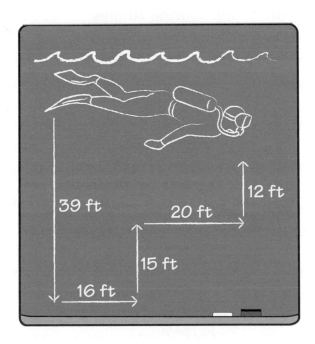

Contents

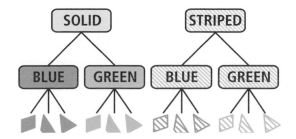

Think Math! Contents

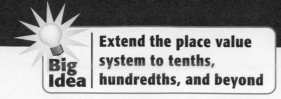

Big Idea Extend the place value system to tenths, hundredths, and beyond

Decimals

About the Chapter

Decimals are often viewed as the beginning of mysterious mathematical territory for the elementary student. In fact, they are simply numbers just like any others. Like fractions, they can represent numbers located *between* whole numbers. Many programs begin by connecting decimals to fractional quantities (tenths and hundredths), using manipulatives to make this connection concrete. *Think Math!*'s approach is designed to build the decimal work on the strongest foundation of understanding that students have available: their understanding of how numbers are ordered. Since students' ideas about fractions are still developing, their understanding of fractions is far too shaky a foundation upon which to build an understanding of a whole new way to write numbers: decimals.

Decimal Notation Decimals are a way of notating "numbers between numbers" The notation, in fact, is not entirely new, but simply an extension of the place value system students have been using since first grade. Since crossing the decimal point involves considering the fractional parts of numbers—tenths and hundredths, and later thousandths and so on—students must learn to connect the notation to ideas that are already in play for them. However, the rules are the same. Every place you move to the right represents a value that is one tenth that of the previous place.

Reading the Notation While the place value rules are the same, learning to read and write decimals, and to become comfortable with differences in magnitude, takes time and practice. Just as the Eraser Store activities helped students look at place value for whole numbers in a new light, crossing the decimal point involves getting reacquainted with the importance of comparing and combining like places.

Developing Concepts Across the Grades

Topic	Prior Learning	Learning in Chapter 8	Later Learning
Place Value	• Label number lines up to 10,000 • Discuss place value up to one million **Grade 3, Chapter 4**	• Read and write numbers through the millions • Use place value to compare and order numbers through millions • Represent decimals using base-10 blocks **Lessons 8.1, 8.7**	• Use place value to read, write, compare, and order whole numbers through the billions place and decimals through the thousandths place **Grade 5, Chapter 7**
Decimals	• Add and subtract money amounts **Grade 3, Chapter 3**	• Locate numbers expressed as decimals on the number line • Connect dollar notation and decimals • Add and subtract decimals **Lessons 8.2–8.10**	• Use rounding to estimate decimals to the nearest whole number, tenth, or hundredth • Add, subtract, and multiply with decimals **Grade 5, Chapter 7**
Fractions	• Use fraction names and symbols to describe fractional parts of whole objects • Construct models of equivalent fractions **Grade 3, Chapter 7**	• Compare decimals to fractions • Understand that fractions and decimals are different ways of representing the same number **Lesson 8.5**	• Connect decimals and fractions that name tenths, hundredths, and thousandths **Grade 5, Chapter 7**

Chapter Planner

Lesson	Objectives	NCTM Standards	Vocabulary	Materials/Resources
CHAPTER 8 World Almanac For Kids • Vocabulary • Games • Challenge Teacher Guide pp. 593A–593F, Student Handbook pp. 124–125, 136–140				
1 **Using Place Value** PACING **1** DAY **Teacher Guide** pp. 594–601 **Lesson Activity Book** pp. 149–150 **Student Handbook** Student Letter p. 123 Review Model p. 126 Game p. 138	• To read and write numbers through the millions • To use place value to compare and order numbers through the millions	1, 2, 6, 7, 8, 10	place place value	**For the students:** ■ School-Home Connection, TR: SHC29–SHC32 ■ TR: AM69 ■ P61, E61, SR61 Literature Connection: **If You Made a Million** **Teacher Guide** p. 592
2 **Introducing Decimals** PACING **1** DAY **Teacher Guide** pp. 602–609 **Lesson Activity Book** pp. 151–152 **Student Handbook** Review Model p. 127	• To understand that decimals represent numbers located between two consecutive whole numbers on a number line • To use a calculator to multiply	1, 2, 6, 7, 8, 9, 10	digits point	**For the students:** ■ calculator ■ P62, E62, SR62
3 **Zooming in on the Number Line** PACING **1** DAY **Teacher Guide** pp. 610–615 **Lesson Activity Book** pp. 153–154 **Student Handbook** Game p. 139	• To explore numbers between decimals • To compare decimals	1, 2, 6, 7, 8, 9, 10	tenths hundredths whole numbers	**For the teacher:** ■ calculator ■ transparency of AM70 (optional) **For the students:** ■ TR: AM70 ■ P63, E63, SR63 Science Connection: **Astronomical Units** **Teacher Guide** p. 592
4 **Decimals on the Number Line** PACING **1** DAY **Teacher Guide** pp. 616–625 **Lesson Activity Book** pp. 155–156 **Student Handbook** Review Model p. 128	• To locate numbers expressed as decimals on the number line • To practice comparing numbers expressed as decimals	1, 2, 6, 7, 8, 9, 10	decimal portion non-decimal portion meter stick metric system	**For the teacher:** ■ transparency of AM71–AM74 (optional) **For the students:** ■ number cube ■ P64, E64, SR64 Art Connection: **Art Auction** **Teacher Guide** p. 592
5 **Connecting Fractions to Decimals** PACING **1** DAY **Teacher Guide** pp. 626–633 **Lesson Activity Book** pp. 157–158 **Student Handbook** Explore p. 129 Review Model p. 130	• To compare fractions to decimals • To understand that fractions and decimals are different ways of representing the same number	1, 2, 6, 7, 8, 9, 10	denominator numerator	**For the teacher:** ■ transparency of AM75 (optional) **For the students:** ■ TR: AM75 ■ P65, E65, SR65

NCTM Standards 2000
1. Number and Operations
2. Algebra
3. Geometry
4. Measurement
5. Data Analysis and Probability
6. Problem Solving
7. Reasoning and Proof
8. Communication
9. Connections
10. Representation

Key
AG: Assessment Guide
E: Extension Book
LAB: Lesson Activity Book
P: Practice Book
SH: Student Handbook
SR: Spiral Review Book
TG: Teacher Guide
TR: Teacher Resource Book

MATH GLOSSARY in **Student Handbook** p. 259

Planner (continued)

Chapter Planner (continued)

Lesson	Objectives	NCTM Standards	Vocabulary	Materials/ Resources
6 **Representing Decimals with Pictures** PACING 1 DAY Teacher Guide pp. 634–641 Lesson Activity Book pp. 159–160	• To use a 10-by-10 grid to represent decimals	1, 2, 6, 7, 8, 9, 10	grid	**For the teacher:** ■ transparency of AM76–AM77 (optional) **For the students:** ■ TR: AM76–AM77 ■ P66, E66, SR66
7 **Representing Decimals Using Base-Ten Blocks** PACING 1 DAY Teacher Guide pp. 642–649 Lesson Activity Book pp. 161–162 Student Handbook Explore p. 131	• To represent decimals using base-ten blocks • To add and subtract decimals without regrouping using base-ten blocks	1, 2, 6, 7, 8, 9, 10	base-ten system	**For the students:** ■ base-ten blocks ■ P67, E67, SR67
8 **Adding Decimals** PACING 1 DAY Teacher Guide pp. 650–657 Lesson Activity Book pp. 163–164 Student Handbook Explore p. 132	• To add decimal numbers • To write addition and subtraction fact teams involving decimal numbers	1, 6, 7, 8, 9, 10	sum decimal sums	**For the students:** ■ base-ten blocks (2 flats, 12 rods, 20 cubes) ■ 3 pieces of paper or cardstock ■ P68, E68, SR68
9 **Subtracting Decimals** PACING 1 DAY Teacher Guide pp. 658–665 Lesson Activity Book pp. 165–166 Student Handbook Explore p. 133	• To subtract decimals • To add and subtract decimals in the context of finding distances	1, 6, 7, 8, 9, 10	diagram distance	**For the teacher:** ■ transparency of AM78 (optional) **For the students:** ■ TR: AM78 ■ grid paper ■ base-ten blocks (1 flat, 15 rods, 20 cubes) ■ P69, E69, SR69
10 **Representing Decimals Using Money** PACING 1 DAY Teacher Guide pp. 666–673 Lesson Activity Book pp. 167–168	• To connect money and decimals • To practice adding and subtracting decimals in the context of money	1, 6, 7, 8, 9, 10	dollar notation	**For the teacher:** ■ transparency of AM79 (optional) **For the students:** ■ TR: AM79 ■ coins, play money ■ base-ten blocks ■ P70, E70, SR70
11 **Problem Solving Strategy and Test Prep** PACING 1 DAY Teacher Guide pp. 674–679 Lesson Activity Book pp. 169–170 Student Handbook Review Models pp. 134–135	• To practice the problem solving strategy *act it out* • To articulate the steps and strategies used to solve problems • To prepare for standardized tests	1, 6, 7, 8, 9, 10		**For the teacher:** ■ transparency of LAB p. 169 (optional) **For the students:** ■ base-ten blocks ■ play money ■ TR: AM77

CHAPTER 8 Review/Assessment
TG pp. 680–683, **LAB** pp. 171–172, **AG** pp. AG77–AG80

For the students:
■ Chapter 8 Test pp. AG77–AG78

Games

Use the following games for skills practice and reinforcement of concepts.

Ordering Numbers

Lesson 8.1 ▶

Ordering Numbers provides an opportunity for students to practice using place value to compare and order numbers

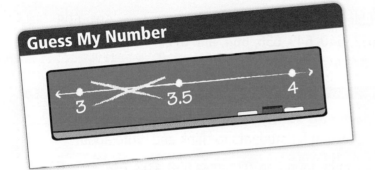

Guess My Number

◀ **Lesson 8.3** *Guess My Number* provides an opportunity for students to practice comparing decimals using a number line

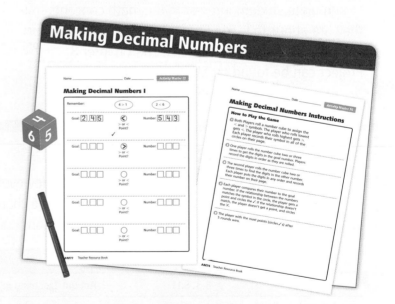

Making Decimal Numbers

Lesson 8.4 ▶

Making Decimal Numbers provides students with additional practice comparing decimals

---

Planning Ahead

In **Lesson 8.1,** students need three sets of cards from Activity Master 69 to play *Ordering Numbers.* You may want to ask a student volunteer to cut out the cards ahead of time.

In **Lesson 8.4,** students will play the *Making Decimal Numbers Game.* Each student will need a number cube. The instructions for this game appear on Activity Master 74. You may wish to give this page to early finishers along with a copy of Activity Master 73 so they can continue working independently.

Developing Problem Solvers

Open-Ended Problem Solving

The Headline Story in the Daily Activities section of every lesson provides an open-ended problem for students to complete. For each story there are many possible responses.

Headline Stories can be found on TG pages 595, 603, 611, 617, 627, 635, 643, 651, 659, and 667.

Headline Story

The World Almanac for Kids feature is designed to stimulate student interest in the math concepts they are about to learn. Students use data to solve problems and explain solutions. The Chapter 8 Project can be found on SH pages 124–125.

Leveled Problem Solving

Leveled Problem Solving provides an opportunity for students to apply learning from the lesson to a real-life situation. Problems are leveled by ability to allow students of all ability levels to become successful problem solvers. Each Leveled Problem Solving begins with a real-life scenario upon which three problems are built.

The levels of problems are:

❶ Basic Level	❷ On Level	❸ Above Level
students needing extra support	students working at grade level	students who are ready for more challenging problems

Leveled Problem Solving can be found on TG pages 601, 608, 615, 624, 632, 640, 649, 656, 664, and 672.

Write Math **Reflect and Summarize the Lesson** poses a problem or question for students to think and write about.

This feature can be found on TG pages 600, 608, 614, 623, 631, 639, 648, 655, 664, 671, and 676. Other opportunities to write about math can be found on LAB pages 150, 152, 157, 158, 164, and 166.

Problem Solving Strategies

The focus of **Lesson 8.11** is the strategy, *act it out.* However, students will use a variety of problem solving strategies as they work through the chapter. The chart below shows strategies that may be useful in completing each lesson.

Strategy	Lesson(s)	Description
✓ Act It Out	8.3, 8.11	Act out "zooming in" to see how numbers fall between other numbers.
Draw a Picture	8.3–8.6	Draw a number line and mark points to compare fractions and decimals.
Guess and Check	8.22	Guess and check to find a number that, when squared, equals another number.
Look for a Pattern	8.3–8.5	Look for a pattern to decide where decimals are located on a number line.
Make a Model	8.6–8.7, 8.10	Make a model to represent decimals to tenths and hundredths, and use it to compare decimals and fractions.
Make an Organized List	8.10	Make an organized list to find the prices of all possible combinations of four items on a price list.
Make a Table	8.1	Make a place-value chart to find the values of digits in numbers.
Work Backward	8.8–8.10	Work backward to find a missing addend in a decimal addition problem.

Meeting the Needs of All Learners

Differentiated Instruction

Extra Support	On Level	Enrichment
Intervention Activities 601, 608, 615, 624, 632, 640, 649, 656, 664, 672	**Practice Book** P61–P70	**Extension Activities** TG pp. 601, 608, 615, 624, 632, 640, 649, 656, 664, 672
	Spiral Review Book SR61–SR70	**Extension Book** E61–E70
	LAB Challenge LAB pp. 150, 152, 154, 156, 158, 160, 162, 164	**LAB Challenge** LAB pp. 150, 152, 154, 156, 158, 160, 162, 164
Lesson Notes Basic Level TG pp. 619, 620	**Lesson Notes** On Level TG pp. 596	**Lesson Notes** Above Level TG pp. 612
Leveled Problem Solving Basic Level 601, 608, 615, 624, 632, 640, 649, 656, 664, 672	**Leveled Problem Solving** On Level 601, 608, 615, 624, 632, 640, 649, 656, 664, 672	**Leveled Problem Solving** Above Level 601, 608, 615, 624, 632, 640, 649, 656, 664, 672

English Language Learners

Suggestions for addressing the needs of students learning English as a second language are included in the Developing Mathematical Language section at the beginning of most lessons.

ELL activities for this chapter can be found on TG pages 595, 603, 611, 617, 627, 635, 643, 651, 659, and 667.

The Multi-Age Classroom

Grade 3	• Students on this level should be able to complete the lessons in Chapter 8 but might need some additional practice with key concepts and skills.	**See Grade 4, Intervention Activities, Lessons 8.1–8.10.**
	• Give students more practice with equivalent fractions to support the connection between fractions and decimals.	**See Grade 3, Lessons 7.2–7.5.**
Grade 4	• Students on this level should be able to complete the lessons in Chapter 8 with minimal adjustments.	**See Grade 4, Practice pages P61–P70.**
Grade 5	• Students on this level should be able to complete the lessons in Chapter 8 and extend decimal concepts and skills.	**See Grade 4, Extension pages E61–E70.**
	• Give students extended work with comparing, adding, and subtracting decimals.	**See Grade 5, Lessons 7.1, 7.2, 7.8–7.10.**

Cross Curricular Connections

Art Connection

Math Concept: understanding decimals

Art Auction

Discuss with students how paintings are often sold at auctions and that the winning bidders might pay millions of dollars for a painting.

- Share the information in the table about the prices paid for paintings at a 2004 auction.

Artist	Price Paid
Monet	$16.8 million
Braque	$2.1 million
Picasso	$11.7 million
Gris	$7.4 million
Matisse	$2.5 million
Renoir	$5.4 million

- Have students order the prices paid from least to greatest. $2.1 million, $2.5 million. $5.4 million, $7.4 million, $11.7 million, $16.8 million

- Have students write the whole number of millions that comes just before and just after the amounts shown. Then have them round the number to the nearest million. 17 million; 2 million; 12 million; 7 million; 3 million; 5 million

Lesson 8.4

Science Connection

Math Concept: understanding decimals

Astronomical Units

- Share with students how distances in space are so large that scientists have simplified them. They call the distance from the sun to the earth 1 A.U., or 1 astronomical unit.

- Have students study the table of the approximate distances in A.U.s of the closest six planets from the sun.

Planet	Approximate Distance from Sun (in A.U.s)
Mercury	0.39
Venus	0.72
Earth	1.00
Mars	1.52
Jupiter	5.20
Saturn	9.54

- Ask students to analyze the information. Have them discuss what information can be learned from reading the table as well as what information cannot be learned from it. Possible answer: you can tell the order of the planets from the sun and about how many times farther one planet is than another from the sun. You cannot tell how many miles each planet is from the sun unless you know how many miles 1 A.U. represents.

Lesson 8.3

Literature Connection

Math Concept: place value

If You Made A Million
By David M. Schwartz
Illustrated by Steven Kellogg

Marvelosissimo the Mathematical Magician helps students understand bigger numbers and money concepts by helping them visualize large quantities of familiar objects.

Lesson 8.1

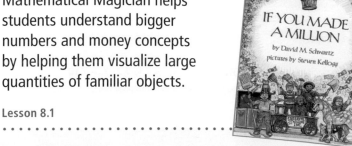

School-Home Connection

Encourage students to play *Guess My Change,* found on the School-Home Connection page, with family members. Students will work with decimals and place value in **Lessons 8.1** and **8.2**.

A reproducible copy of the School-Home Connection letter in English and Spanish can be found in the **Teacher Resource Book,** pages SHC29–SHC32.

Assessment Options

There are many opportunities in *Think Math!* to assess students' understanding of concepts, skills, and problem solving. Learning Goals for Chapter 8 are provided below. The assessment options provide opportunities to evaluate whether or not students have retained learning from prior experiences. Choose the forms of assessment that best meet your needs and the needs of your students.

Chapter 8 Learning Goals

	Learning Goals	Lesson Number
8-A	Compare and order whole numbers	8.1
8-B	Compare and order decimals and locate decimals to hundredths on a number line	8.2–8.4
8-C	Relate decimals to fractions	8.5
8-D	Add and subtract decimals to hundredths, including money	8.6–8.10
8-E	Apply problem solving strategies such as *act it out* to solve problems	8.11

✔ Informal Assessment

Ongoing Assessment
Provides insight into students' thinking to guide instruction (TG pp. 597, 604, 612, 618, 628, 636, 644, 652, 670)

Reflect and Summarize the Lesson
Checks understanding of lesson concepts. (TG pp. 600, 608, 614, 623, 631, 639, 648, 655, 664, 671, 676)

Snapshot Assessment
Mental Math and **Quick Write**
Offers a quick observation of students' progress on chapter concepts and skills (TG pp. 680–681)

Performance Assessment
Provides quarterly assessment of Chapter 8–11 concepts using real-life situations.
Assessment Guide
pp. AG219–AG224

✔ Formal Assessment

Standardized Test Prep
Problem Solving Test Prep
Prepares students for standardized tests.
Lesson Activity Book pp. 170 (TG pp. 677)

Chapter 8 Review/Assessment
Reviews and assesses for the understanding of the chapter.
Lesson Activity Book pp. 171–172 (TG pp. 682)

Chapter 8 Test
Assesses the chapter concepts and skills
Assessment Guide
Form A pp. AG77–AG78
Form B pp. AG79–AG80

Benchmark 3 Assessment
Provides quarterly assessment of Chapters 8–11 concepts and skills
Assessment Guide
Benchmark 3A pp. AG93–AG100
Benchmark 3B pp. AG101–AG108

World Almanac for Kids

Use the World Almanac for Kids feature, *Ready, Set, Down the Hill,* found on pp. 124–125 of the ***Student Handbook,*** to provide students with an opportunity to practice using their problem solving skills by solving real world problems.

FACT•ACTIVITY 1

❶ 200,000 + 10,000 + 0 + 700 + 90 + 5 = 210,795

❷ Check students' answers.

❸ Milford, Montreal, San Juan, San Diego, Salem, Juneau

❹ 1,061 miles is between 991 miles and 1,152 miles.

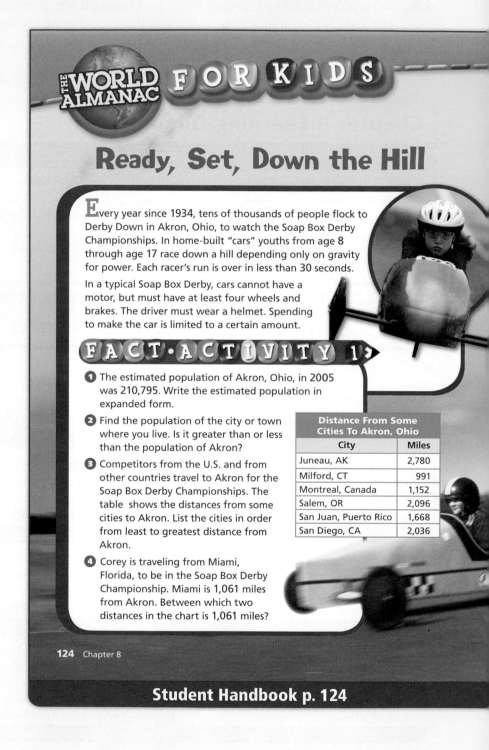

THE WORLD ALMANAC FOR KIDS

Ready, Set, Down the Hill

Every year since 1934, tens of thousands of people flock to Derby Down in Akron, Ohio, to watch the Soap Box Derby Championships. In home-built "cars" youths from age 8 through age 17 race down a hill depending only on gravity for power. Each racer's run is over in less than 30 seconds.

In a typical Soap Box Derby, cars cannot have a motor, but must have at least four wheels and brakes. The driver must wear a helmet. Spending to make the car is limited to a certain amount.

FACT•ACTIVITY 1

❶ The estimated population of Akron, Ohio, in 2005 was 210,795. Write the estimated population in expanded form.

❷ Find the population of the city or town where you live. Is it greater than or less than the population of Akron?

❸ Competitors from the U.S. and from other countries travel to Akron for the Soap Box Derby Championships. The table shows the distances from some cities to Akron. List the cities in order from least to greatest distance from Akron.

❹ Corey is traveling from Miami, Florida, to be in the Soap Box Derby Championship. Miami is 1,061 miles from Akron. Between which two distances in the chart is 1,061 miles?

Distance From Some Cities To Akron, Ohio	
City	Miles
Juneau, AK	2,780
Milford, CT	991
Montreal, Canada	1,152
Salem, OR	2,096
San Juan, Puerto Rico	1,668
San Diego, CA	2,036

124 Chapter 8

Student Handbook p. 124

FACT·ACTIVITY 2

Soap Box Derby racers compete as teams. An adult helps the child build the soap box car and local businesses might help too. The table at the right shows the times of some winners.

Use the table to answer the questions.

❶ Which team had the fastest time? Explain.

❷ What is the difference between Wargo's time and Kimball's time?

❸ Up until 1964, stopwatches only recorded winning times to 1 decimal place. What would Pearson and Wargo's times be if they were only rounded to tenths?

❹ How would you write Pearson's time as a mixed number?

Soap Box Derby Winners		
Year	Team	Time (seconds)
2004	Kimball	27.19
2005	Pearson	26.95
2006	Wargo	26.93

CHAPTER PROJECT

Materials:

stopwatch (with hundredths of a second accuracy); wooden board (to use as ramp); 9 textbooks, close to the same thickness; tennis ball (or any ball that will roll across the classroom floor)

Build a ramp using a board and a textbook as shown. Rest one end of the ramp against the book and the other end on the floor near the wall. Roll the ball down the ramp. Record the time it takes to roll from the top of the ramp (start) to the wall (finish). Repeat four times, each time adding 2 more books.

- When you add more books to the ramp, does the recorded time increase or decrease?

- Which ramp produced the fastest time?

- Find the difference in time for each time you rolled the ball down the ramp.

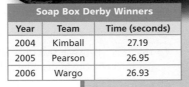

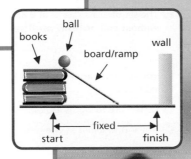

ALMANAC Fact

Soap box cars used to be built from orange crates and roller skate wheels. Today people use lightweight materials like aluminum and fiberglass to build them.

Student Handbook p. 125

FACT·ACTIVITY 2

❶ Wargo; 26.93 seconds is less than 26.95 seconds and less than 27.19 seconds

❷ 0.26 second (27.19 − 26.93 = 0.26)

❸ Pearson: 27.0 seconds; Wargo: 26.9 seconds

❹ $26\frac{95}{100}$

CHAPTER PROJECT

Sample answer:

Number of books	Time (seconds)
1	
3	
5	
7	
9	

- If you add more books, the time decreases.

- The ramp with 9 books produced the fastest time.

- Subtract the time of the ramp with 1 book from 3 books, 3 books from 5 books, etc.

Vocabulary

To reinforce vocabulary concepts, invite students to complete the vocabulary activities on pp. 136–137 of the *Student Handbook.* Encourage students to record their answers in their math journals.

Many responses are possible.

11 Possible response: A 10-by-10 grid has 100 squares on it. Each full grid represents a whole number. The number of columns represents the number of *tenths* in the number, and the number of small squares represents the number of *hundredths.* For example, to represent the number 0.38, shade 3 columns for the 3 *tenths* and 8 additional squares for the 8 *hundredths.*

12 Possible response: Use base-10 blocks to trade 1 whole, the flat, for 10 rods or 100 small cubes. Then remove the number of *tenths* or *hundredths* that are being subtracted. What is left is the difference.

13 Possible response: Think of dimes as *tenths* and pennies as *hundredths.* Add all the pennies, add all the dimes, and add all the dollars. Then trade 10 pennies for 1 dime and 10 dimes for 1 dollar.

Chapter 8 Vocabulary

Choose the best vocabulary term from Word List A for each sentence.

1 The __?__ is the number in a fraction that is below the bar. **denominator**

2 __?__ are symbols, such as 0, 1, 2, 3, 4, 5, 6, 7, 8, and 9, that are used to write numbers. **digits**

3 The answer to an addition problem is called a(n) __?__. **sum**

4 In __?__ the cents are written as a decimal part of a dollar. **dollar notation**

5 The value of a digit in a number is determined by its __?__. **place value**

6 The __?__ between two cities is how far you have to travel to get from one city to the other. **distance**

7 Pennies tell how many __?__ of a dollar there are. **hundredths**

8 The set of __?__ starts at 0 and goes up one unit at a time without end. **whole numbers**

Word List A

base-10 system
denominator
diagram
digits
distance
dollar notation
hundredths
meter stick
metric system
non-decimal portion
numerator
place value
sum
tenths
whole numbers

Complete each analogy using the best term from Word List B.

9 Letters are to words as __?__ are to numbers. **digits**

10 Dollar is to dimes as one is to __?__. **tenths**

Word List B

decimal portion
digits
grid
place value
point
tenths

⟩ Talk Math

Discuss with a partner what you have just learned about decimals. Use the vocabulary terms *tenths* and *hundredths*.

11 How can you use a 10-by-10 grid to represent decimals?

12 How can you subtract a decimal number from a whole number?

13 How can you add money amounts written in dollar notation?

136 Chapter 8

Student Handbook p. 136

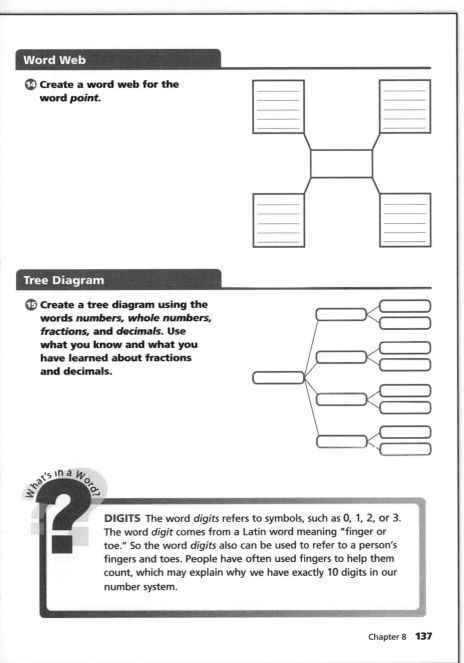

Word Web

⓮ **Create a word web for the word *point*.**

Tree Diagram

⓯ **Create a tree diagram using the words *numbers*, *whole numbers*, *fractions*, and *decimals*. Use what you know and what you have learned about fractions and decimals.**

What's in a Word?

DIGITS The word *digits* refers to symbols, such as 0, 1, 2, or 3. The word *digit* comes from a Latin word meaning "finger or toe." So the word *digits* also can be used to refer to a person's fingers and toes. People have often used fingers to help them count, which may explain why we have exactly 10 digits in our number system.

Chapter 8   **137**

Student Handbook p. 137

⓮ Many answers are possible. One example is provided.

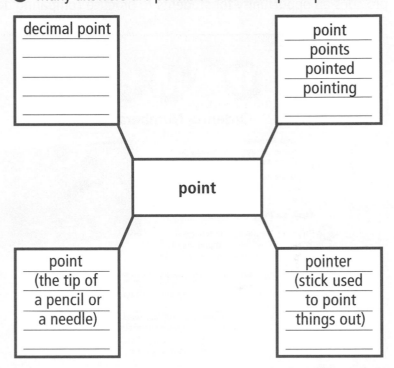

⓯ Many answers are possible. One example is provided.

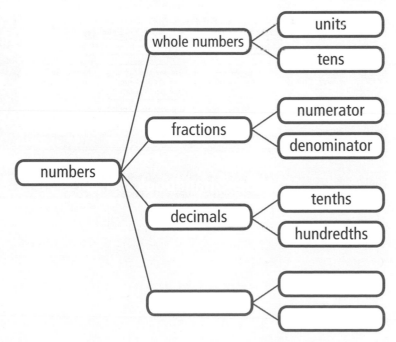

Games

Encourage early finishers and students ready to go beyond the lesson objectives to play the games on pp. 138-139 of the *Student Handbook.* **Lesson 8.1** *Ordering Numbers* provides an opportunity for students to practice using place value to compare and order numbers. **Lesson 8.3** *Guess My Number* provides an opportunity for students to practice comparing decimals using a number line.

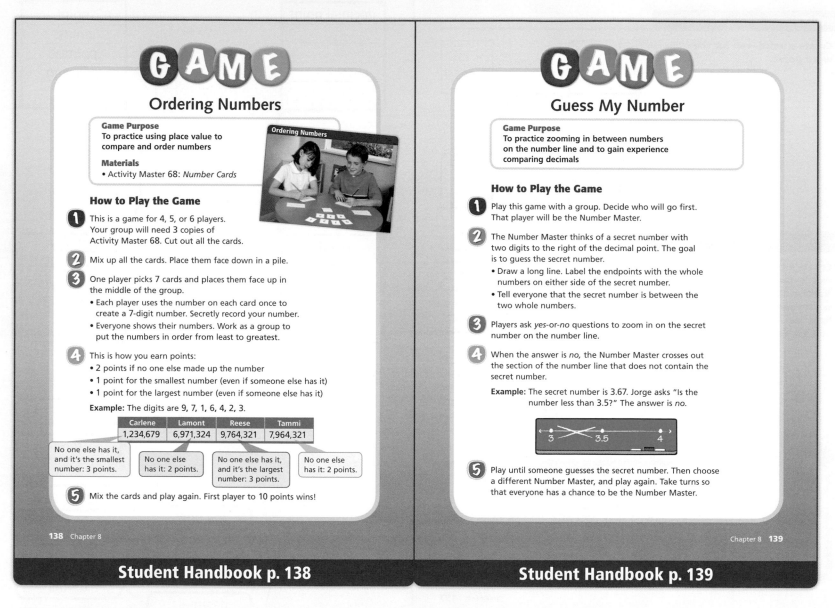

GAME

Ordering Numbers

Game Purpose
To practice using place value to compare and order numbers

Materials
• Activity Master 68: *Number Cards*

How to Play the Game

1. This is a game for 4, 5, or 6 players. Your group will need 3 copies of Activity Master 68. Cut out all the cards.

2. Mix up all the cards. Place them face down in a pile.

3. One player picks 7 cards and places them face up in the middle of the group.
   • Each player uses the number on each card once to create a 7-digit number. Secretly record your number.
   • Everyone shows their numbers. Work as a group to put the numbers in order from least to greatest.

4. This is how you earn points:
   • 2 points if no one else made up the number
   • 1 point for the smallest number (even if someone else has it)
   • 1 point for the largest number (even if someone else has it)

   Example: The digits are 9, 7, 1, 6, 4, 2, 3.

Carlene	Lamont	Reese	Tammi
1,234,679	6,971,324	9,764,321	7,964,321

   No one else has it, and it's the smallest number: 3 points.

   No one else has it: 2 points.

   No one else has it, and it's the largest number: 3 points.

   No one else has it: 2 points.

5. Mix the cards and play again. First player to 10 points wins!

138 Chapter 8

GAME

Guess My Number

Game Purpose
To practice zooming in between numbers on the number line and to gain experience comparing decimals

How to Play the Game

1. Play this game with a group. Decide who will go first. That player will be the Number Master.

2. The Number Master thinks of a secret number with two digits to the right of the decimal point. The goal is to guess the secret number.
   • Draw a long line. Label the endpoints with the whole numbers on either side of the secret number.
   • Tell everyone that the secret number is between the two whole numbers.

3. Players ask *yes-or-no* questions to zoom in on the secret number on the number line.

4. When the answer is *no*, the Number Master crosses out the section of the number line that does not contain the secret number.

   Example: The secret number is 3.67. Jorge asks "Is the number less than 3.5?" The answer is *no*.

5. Play until someone guesses the secret number. Then choose a different Number Master, and play again. Take turns so that everyone has a chance to be the Number Master.

Chapter 8 139

Student Handbook p. 138   **Student Handbook p. 139**

Challenge

This Challenge activity challenges students to answer questions about decimal patterns and to make up their own decimal pattern. This activity can be found on p. 140 of the *Student Handbook.*

Ayesha and her friends created decimal patterns. Then they made up questions about the patterns to challenge each other.

Student	Pattern
Ayesha	0.14, 0.28, 0.42, 0.56
Luke	5.1, 4.8, 4.5, 4.2
Cameron	0.3, 2, 3.7, 5.4
Tanya	4, 3.64, 3.28, 2.92
Erin	2.5, 4.09, 5.68, 7.27
Seth	12, 10.92, 9.84, 8.76

Use the patterns above to answer the questions.

1 Which patterns increase?

2 Which patterns decrease?

3 Find the next number in each student's pattern.

4 Find the rule for each student's pattern.

5 Find the eighth number in each student's pattern.

6 Write the first number of each pattern in order from smallest to largest.

7 Write the eighth number for each pattern in order from smallest to largest.

Now make up your own decimal pattern.

8 What are the first four terms in your pattern?

9 Does your pattern increase or decrease?

10 Explain the rule you used to create the pattern.

140 Chapter 8

Student Handbook p. 140

1 Ayesha, Cameron, and Erin have increasing patterns.

2 Luke, Tanya, and Seth have decreasing patterns.

3 Ayesha: 0.7; Luke: 3.9; Cameron: 7.1; Tanya: 2.56; Erin: 8.86; Seth: 7.68

4 Ayesha: add 0.14; Luke: subtract 0.3; Cameron: add 1.7; Tanya: subtract 1.48; Erin: add 1.59; Seth: subtract 1.08

5 Ayesha: 1.12; Luke: 3; Cameron: 12.2; Tanya: 1.48; Erin: 13.63; Seth: 4.44

6 0.14, 0.3, 2.5, 4, 5.1, 12

7 1.12, 1.48, 3, 4.44, 12.2, 13.63

8 Answers will depend on students' patterns.

9 Answers will depend on students' patterns.

10 Answers will depend on students' patterns.

Lesson 1 Using Place Value

NCTM Standards 1, 2, 6, 7, 8, 9, 10

Lesson Planner

STUDENT OBJECTIVES
- To read and write numbers through the millions
- To use place value to compare and order numbers through the millions

1 | Daily Activities (TG p. 595)

| Open-Ended Problem Solving/Headline Story | Skills Practice and Review—What's My Number? |

2 | Teach and Practice (TG pp. 596–600)

	MATERIALS
Ⓐ **Reading the Student Letter** (TG p. 596)	• TR: Activity Master, AM69
Ⓑ **Reading and Writing Large Numbers** (TG p. 597)	• 📖 LAB pp. 149–150
	• 📖 SH pp. 123, 126, 138
Ⓒ **Playing a Game:** *Ordering Numbers* (TG p. 598)	
Ⓓ **Using Place Value** (TG p. 599)	

3 | Differentiated Instruction (TG p. 601)

Leveled Problem Solving (TG p. 601)	**Practice Book P61**
Intervention Activity (TG p. 601)	**Extension Book E61**
Extension Activity (TG p. 601)	**Spiral Review Book SR61**
Literature Connection (TG p. 592)	

Lesson Notes

About the Lesson

In this first lesson of the chapter on decimals, students focus on place value. They review the values of digits in whole numbers through the millions, seeing how each move to the left is associated with a place value increase to the next larger power of 10. This will help them see that the same property holds for decimal numbers. The heart of the decimal system is this: every time you move a digit one place to the left, its value is multiplied by 10; every time you move it to the right, its value is divided by 10.

Use with Lesson Activity Book pp. 149–150.

Developing Mathematical Language

Vocabulary: place, place value

A digit's *place* is its location in a number. Moving left from the decimal point, the *places* are ones, tens, hundreds, thousands, and so on. Moving right, they are tenths, hundredths, thousandths, and so on. The *place value* of a digit depends on its *place.* The *place value* of 3 in 4,321 is 300. The *place value* of 3 in 26,738 is 30.

Review the terms *place* and *place value* with students.

Beginning Talk about different meanings of the word *place:* space for a particular purpose (a toybox is a *place* for toys), a space or seat (my *place* in line), a substitute (in *place* of), and so on. Point out that digits have *places* in numbers. Write a 3-digit number, and name the digit in each *place.*

Intermediate Use 6 different digits to write a 6-digit number on the board. Point out that each digit is in a different *place* in the number. Have students identify the *place value* of each digit.

Advanced Secretly write a multi-digit number on paper, and then have students guess your number by asking questions. Restrict questions to those involving *place value* only.

Open-Ended Problem Solving

Read the Headline Story to your students. Encourage them to think of creative scenarios that incorporate information from the story.

 Headline Story

> **Mr. Yang found some one dollar bills, some hundred dollar bills, and even some thousand-dollar bills! He didn't find any ten-dollar bills. He called the police to tell them how much money he had found.**

Possible responses: If Mr. Yang found 3 hundred dollar bills, 5 single dollar bills, and 2 thousand dollar bills, he would have found $2,305. If Mr. Yang found more hundred dollar bills than thousand and single dollar bills, he might have found $2,704. The least amount of money that Mr. Yang could have found is $2,202 since he found at least 2 of each bill.

Skills Practice and Review

What's My Number?

Tell students that you're thinking of a number between 1,000 and 2,000 and that they should ask *yes/no* questions to try to find it. They should try to ask as few questions as possible to find the number. To get students started, help them ask questions that eliminate lots of numbers at once. For example, students might ask if the hundreds digit is less than 5, if the number is greater than or less than 1,500, if the number is odd or even, or if the tens digit is greater than 4. In later lessons, students will use this same method to zoom in on larger numbers, so make sure they see how to use place value to do this.

whole class · 5 MIN

NCTM Standards 1, 2, 6, 7, 8, 9, 10

A Reading the Student Letter

Purpose To introduce decimals

Introduce Read the Student Letter with your class. You might briefly discuss your goals for this chapter or have students tell you what they already know about decimals.

Task Ask students to think about the questions asked in the letter. The examples in the letter were chosen to help students think of written prices and how decimals are used to describe temperature. Some students may also recognize decimals from sports statistics, such as batting averages. Students will have opportunities to see decimals used in these contexts as they work through the chapter, so it's not important to bring up examples that they don't mention at this point.

Differentiated Instruction

On Level Students need to pay careful attention to zeros in large numbers. For example, to write the number "three hundred sixty thousand, two hundred nine," students must realize that they need to use a 0 in the thousands and tens digits (360,209). Similarly, to read this number, students must realize that the 0 in the thousands place makes the number "three hundred sixty thousand" rather than "thirty-six thousand." Try to use zeros in different places within numbers so that students get plenty of practice reading and placing them. This will also prepare students to read and use zeros in decimals.

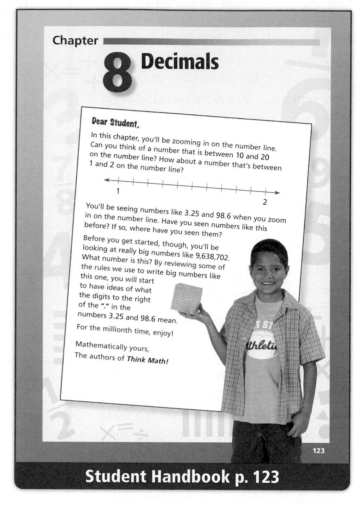

Student Handbook p. 123

Talk Math

❓ Can you think of a number that is between 10 and 20 on the number line? Possible answer: 18 (Be sure students understand that "between" does not mean "in the middle of." The number 15 is halfway between 10 and 20—"in the middle of"—but any number greater than 10 and less than 20 is between 10 and 20.)

❓ Can you think of a number that is between 1 and 2 on the number line? Possible answer: 1.27

❓ Where have you seen a number like 3.25 before? Possible response: $3.25, the price of a box of cereal

❓ Where have you seen a number like 98.6 before? Possible response: 98.6 degrees Fahrenheit, normal human body temperature

❓ What number is this: 9,638,702? nine million, six hundred thirty-eight thousand, seven hundred two

Use with Lesson Activity Book pp. 149–150.

B Reading and Writing Large Numbers

NCTM Standards 1, 2, 6, 7, 8, 9, 10

Purpose To read and write numbers in the millions

Introduce Tell students that numbers in the millions are found in newspapers and magazines every day. As examples, you might mention that Yellowstone National Park, America's first national park, has an area of 2,219,791 acres, and that the population of the United States when the first census was taken, in 1790, was 3,929,214.

Problem Write a seven-digit number on the board, such as 6,380,451. **Ask: What number did I write?** Have a student read the number. Make sure all students understand how to read this number before having students read a few others that you write on the board. Then ask the following questions. To involve the entire class, have students write the numbers on pieces of paper and then hold the papers up to show you.

Talk Math

❓ How would you write the number seven million, five hundred six thousand, eighty four? 7,506,084

❓ How would you write the number nine million, ten thousand, nine? 9,010,009

Problem Write another 7-digit number on the board, such as 3,947,021. **Ask: What is the value of each digit?** Write this information on the board for students to reference as they complete the LAB pages later in the lesson. Continue with other numbers through 999,999,999.

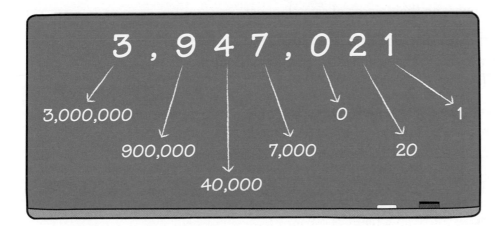

Talk Math

❓ I am thinking of a 4-digit number with 2 zeroes, a 1 in the thousands place, and a 2 in the ones place. What is the number? 1,002 (one thousand, two)

❓ I am thinking of a 5-digit number with 3 zeroes, the same number of ten thousands as 846,295 has, and the same number of tens as 48,672 has. What is the number? 40,070 (forty thousand, seventy)

✓ Ongoing Assessment

• Do students know the values of whole-number places from ones to millions?

• Do students read numbers from 1 to 10 million?

Teacher Story

❝My class wanted to know what numbers come after the millions. I told them that after 999,999,999 comes 1 billion, which is a 1 with 9 zeros after it. Some students had heard of trillions and asked how many zeros 1 trillion has. I told them that after 999,999,999,999 comes 1 trillion. They realized on their own that 1 trillion must therefore have 12 zeros. Some students might even know that a *google* is a 1 with 100 zeros after it!❞

C Playing *Ordering Numbers*

Materials
- For each group of students: cards cut from three copies of AM69
- For each student: piece of scratch paper

NCTM Standards 1, 2, 6, 7, 8, 9, 10

Purpose To practice using place value to compare and order numbers

Goal The goal is to collect points while ordering 7-digit numbers from least to greatest, and to be the first to score 10 points.

Prepare Materials Students play in groups of four to six. Each group will need cards cut from three copies of Activity Master: Number Cards. Each student will need a piece of scratch paper. If you think that students need additional practice with comparing and ordering large numbers before playing, you might write two numbers on the board and ask students how they can decide which one is bigger. Make sure students understand that they could begin by comparing the numbers of digits in the two numbers. If the numbers have the same number of digits, they should then compare the digits of the highest place value where the two numbers differ.

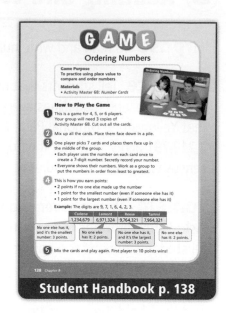

Student Handbook p. 138

How to Play

❶ Students mix the cards and put them in a stack face down.

❷ One player picks seven cards and places them face up in the middle of the group.

❸ Each player uses each card once to create a 7-digit number. Students should secretly record their numbers on their pieces of scratch paper.

❹ Students show their numbers. The group cooperates to put the numbers in order from least to greatest.

❺ Players receive points as follows: Each unique number is worth 2 points. The least and greatest numbers are each worth 1 point (even if it they were written by more than one player).

❻ Students return the cards to the stack and shuffle the cards.

❼ Play continues, beginning with Step 2. A new player chooses seven cards. The first player to get 10 points wins.

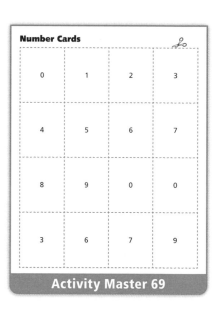

Number Cards

0	1	2	3
4	5	6	7
8	9	0	0
3	6	7	9

Activity Master 69

Purpose To practice reading, writing, and comparing large numbers

NCTM Standards 1, 2, 6, 7, 8, 9, 10

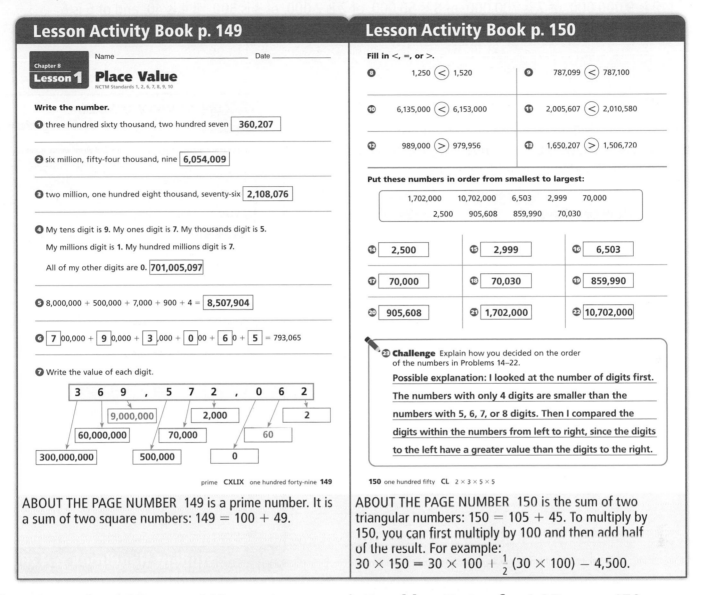

Lesson Activity Book p. 149

Name _____ Date _____

Chapter 8
Lesson 1 **Place Value**
NCTM Standards 1, 2, 6, 7, 8, 9, 10

Write the number.

❶ three hundred sixty thousand, two hundred seven | **360,207** |

❷ six million, fifty-four thousand, nine | **6,054,009** |

❸ two million, one hundred eight thousand, seventy-six | **2,108,076** |

❹ My tens digit is **9**. My ones digit is **7**. My thousands digit is **5**.
My millions digit is **1**. My hundred millions digit is **7**.
All of my other digits are **0**. | **701,005,097** |

❺ 8,000,000 + 500,000 + 7,000 + 900 + 4 = | **8,507,904** |

❻ **7** 00,000 + **9** 0,000 + **3** ,000 + **0** 00 + **6** 0 + **5** = 793,065

❼ Write the value of each digit.

| 3 | 6 | 9 | , | 5 | 7 | 2 | , | 0 | 6 | 2 |

9,000,000   2,000   2
60,000,000   70,000   60
300,000,000   500,000   0

prime **CXLIX** one hundred forty-nine **149**

ABOUT THE PAGE NUMBER 149 is a prime number. It is a sum of two square numbers: 149 = 100 + 49.

Lesson Activity Book p. 150

Fill in <, =, or >.

❽ 1,250 < 1,520   ❾ 787,099 < 787,100

❿ 6,135,000 < 6,153,000   ⓫ 2,005,607 < 2,010,580

⓬ 989,000 > 979,956   ⓭ 1,650,207 > 1,506,720

Put these numbers in order from smallest to largest:

| 1,702,000 | 10,702,000 | 6,503 | 2,999 | 70,000 |
| 2,500 | 905,608 | 859,990 | 70,030 |

⓮ **2,500**	⓯ **2,999**	⓰ **6,503**
⓱ **70,000**	⓲ **70,030**	⓳ **859,990**
⓴ **905,608**	㉑ **1,702,000**	㉒ **10,702,000**

㉓ **Challenge** Explain how you decided on the order of the numbers in Problems 14–22.

Possible explanation: I looked at the number of digits first. The numbers with only 4 digits are smaller than the numbers with 5, 6, 7, or 8 digits. Then I compared the digits within the numbers from left to right, since the digits to the left have a greater value than the digits to the right.

150 one hundred fifty **CL** 2 × 3 × 5 × 5

ABOUT THE PAGE NUMBER 150 is the sum of two triangular numbers: 150 = 105 + 45. To multiply by 150, you can first multiply by 100 and then add half of the result. For example:
30 × 150 = 30 × 100 + $\frac{1}{2}$ (30 × 100) = 4,500.

Teaching Notes for LAB page 149

Have students complete the page individually or with partners.

Students practice reading, writing, and comparing large numbers. On this page, numbers are presented in word form, in expanded form, and by referring to specific digits. At the bottom of the page, students find the value of each digit in a 7-digit number.

All the numbers on the page have at least one zero. This gives students practice using zeros as placeholders in numbers.

Teaching Notes for LAB page 150

On this page, students compare and order numbers. Their strategies for ordering numbers will vary. You might take note of some of their ideas and talk about them when students begin to order decimals in upcoming lessons.

Challenge Problem The Challenge Problem asks students to explain how they ordered the numbers in the preceding section.

Reflect and Summarize the Lesson

 Write Math

> **What is the value of each digit in 9,752,346? What is a number that is greater than this number? What is a number that is less than this number?** Possible responses: The value of 9 is 9,000,000, of 7 is 700,000, of 5 is 50,000, of 2 is 2,000, of 3 is 300, of 4 is 40, and of 6 is 6. One number that is greater than 9,752,346 is 9,752,347. One number that is less is 9,752,345.

Review Model

Refer students to Review Model: Reading and Writing Numbers in the *Student Handbook,* p. 126 to see how they can use a place-value chart to read and write whole numbers.

✔ Check for Understanding

① five million, two hundred thirty-one thousand, six hundred ninety-nine

② three million, seventy-four thousand, five hundred one

③ two hundred sixty thousand, eight

④ 9,108,314

⑤ 6,002,960

⑥ 422,038

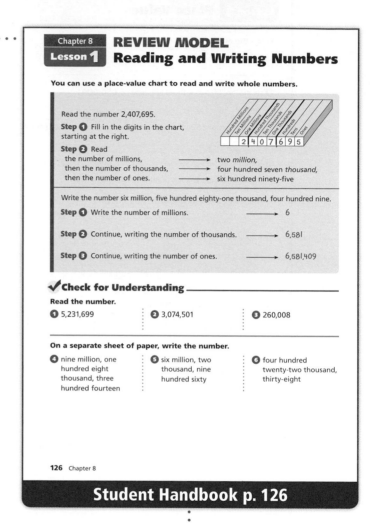

Student Handbook p. 126

Use with Lesson Activity Book pp. 149–150.

3 | Differentiated Instruction

Leveled Problem Solving

The distance between Earth and the sun is about 149,598,000 kilometers.

❶ Basic Level

What is the value of the first 9 in the number? Explain. 9,000,000; Possible explanation: It is the first digit in the millions period.

❷ On Level

How many times greater is the value of the first 9 than the value of the second 9? Explain. 100; Possible explanation: Each place to the left has a value 10 times greater than the place to its right, and 10 × 10 = 100.

❸ Above Level

What would the number be if the final zero were dropped? Explain. 14,949,800; Possible explanation: Dropping a place is the same as dividing the number by 10.

Intervention	Practice	Extension

Activity Digit Shuffle

Provide pairs of students with a set of cards numbered 0–9. Tell students to mix up the cards and place them face down. Have both students select three cards and then use all six cards to make three different 6-digit numbers. Ask students to write the numbers in order and in word form.

Have students repeat the activity using different numbers of cards.

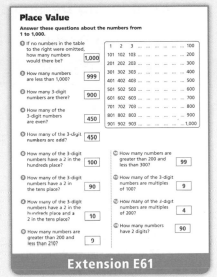

Practice P61

Extension E61

Spiral Review

Spiral Review Book page SR61 provides review of the following previously learned skills and concepts:

• exploring properties of addition in magic squares

• solving problems using the strategy *look for a pattern*

You may wish to have students work with a partner to complete the page.

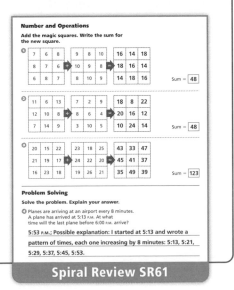

Spiral Review SR61

Extension Activity
Working Backward

Have small groups of students practice counting backward several numbers from 10, 100, and 1,000. Ask them to describe any patterns that they see. For example, students might notice that the first number counting backward has all nines.

Then have students count backward several numbers from 10,000; 100,000; and 1,000,000, applying the pattern that they discovered with smaller numbers.

Lesson 2 Introducing Decimals

NCTM Standards 1, 2, 6, 7, 8, 9, 10

Lesson Planner

STUDENT OBJECTIVES

- To understand that decimals represent numbers located between two consecutive whole numbers on a number line
- To use a calculator to multiply

1 | Daily Activities (TG p. 603)

Open-Ended Problem Solving/Headline Story	Skills Practice and Review— What's My Number?

2 | Teach and Practice (TG pp. 604–608)

	MATERIALS
(A) **Multiplying on a Calculator** (TG p. 604)	• calculator
(B) **Introducing Decimals** (TG pp. 605–606)	• 📖 LAB pp. 151–152
(C) **Exploring Decimals** (TG p. 607)	• 📖 SH p. 127

3 | Differentiated Instruction (TG p. 609)

Leveled Problem Solving (TG p. 609)	Practice Book P62
Intervention Activity (TG p. 609)	Extension Book E62
Extension Activity (TG p. 609)	Spiral Review Book SR62

Lesson Notes

About the Lesson

Students build on their understanding of place value from the previous lesson by interpreting decimals as numbers located between two consecutive whole numbers on the number line. In the previous lesson, students saw that place values decrease from left to right. In this lesson, they apply this observation to digits located to the right of the ones place.

Students use calculators in this lesson. Because calculators show non-whole numbers as decimals (rather than fractions), they provide a natural context for introducing decimals and motivating students to use them.

About the Mathematics

In this lesson, students try to find a number that, when multiplied by itself, equals 40. In later grades, they will learn that this number is called the square root of 40. Exploration of this more advanced idea gives students experience with the problem solving strategy of successive approximation to refine an answer.

Use with Lesson Activity Book pp. 151–152.

Developing Mathematical Language

Vocabulary: digits, point

This lesson introduces students to decimals as numbers between whole numbers. For now, we avoid discussing the place values of the *digits* to the right of the decimal point. Students may use the word *point* when reading a decimal (2.6 is "two *point* six"). Once students start reading decimals beyond tenths, encourage them to say the *digits* rather than the number to the right of the decimal point (2.49 is "two *point* four nine"). This will help students avoid the mistake of thinking that, for example, "*point* six" is less than "*point* forty-nine" because 6 is less than 49.

Review the terms *digits* and *point* with students.

Beginning Write three decimal numbers on the board. Ask students to name the *digits* to the left and to the right of the *point*. Then read aloud the number with students.

Intermediate Write three decimal numbers on the board with only 1 digit to the right of the decimal point. Ask students to order the numbers from least to greatest by comparing the *digits*.

Advanced Have students use three *digits* to write as many different numbers as they can. Have them compare and order their numbers and then read them aloud.

Open-Ended Problem Solving

Read the Headline Story to your students. Encourage them to think of interesting ways to solve the problem.

> **Mari multiplied a whole number by itself. What might her result have been?**

Possible responses: If she multiplied 5 by itself, then her result was 25. Her result must have been 0 or greater. She could have gotten 0, 1, 4, 9, 16, 25, 36, or any other square number.

Skills Practice and Review

What's My Number?

As you did in the last lesson, tell students that you're thinking of a number, but this time choose a number in the hundred thousands. Again, have students ask *yes/no* questions to find your number. The fewer questions they ask before determining the number, the better. To help students keep track of what they know about the number and to encourage them to use place value to narrow down the possible numbers, sketch this diagram for a 6-digit number on the board:

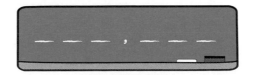

As students ask questions about the digits in the number, keep track of the possibilities below each blank. For example, if a student asks if the number is greater than 500,000 and the answer is *yes,* write 5, 6, 7, 8, and 9 below the blank for the first digit to indicate that these are the possible digits for this position. Similarly, if students ask if the thousands digit is odd and the answer is *no,* write 0, 2, 4, 6, and 8 below the third line from the left. Once all the digits have been found, have the class read the number aloud. Continue with other numbers, including 7- and 8-digit numbers (millions and ten millions).

pairs or
whole class

10 MIN

Materials
• For each student:
  calculator

NCTM Standards 1, 2, 6, 7, 8, 9, 10

✔ **Ongoing Assessment**

• Do students add, subtract,
  multiply, and divide on a
  calculator?

A Multiplying on a Calculator

Purpose To practice using a calculator

Introduce This lesson presents decimals as notation used by
calculators to represent numbers located between whole numbers.
Therefore, you may need to teach students how to use calculators.
Be sure every student has a calculator. Point out that this activity will
serve as a review for students who already know how to use
calculators, and as an introduction for those who do not.

Problem Ask the class to choose a familiar multiplication problem,
such as 7 × 4. Have students find the answer with their calculators.
The fact that students are likely to know the product already will serve as a
self-check that they have found the correct answer. To help students use their
calculators, you might ask questions like the following:

 **Talk Math**

❷ How do you turn the calculator on? How do you clear your calculator?
Answers will depend on the calculators that are used.

❷ What do you press first to perform this multiplication? 7 or 4

❷ What do you see on your display screen? the number pressed

❷ What do you press next? the [×] key

❷ What is on the screen now? the original number

❷ What do you press next? the factor you didn't press the first time

❷ What is the last button you press? the [=] key

❷ What is on the screen now? 28

If necessary, repeat this activity with other problems, like those below. You
may wish to have students work in small groups to help each other get used
to their calculators.

Practice Find the answer.

9 × 6 54	18 + 23 41	63 ÷ 9 7	75 − 48 27
12 × 5 60	55 + 65 120	98 ÷ 7 14	61 − 6 55

Use with Lesson Activity Book pp. 151–152.

B Introducing Decimals

Purpose To explore decimals using a calculator

Introduce Now that students know how to use a calculator, tell them that you want them to choose a number between 1 and 12, multiply it by itself—in other words, *square* the number—and then tell you the product. Explain that you will use this product to figure out what their number was. (If you know the squares of numbers beyond 12 by heart, you might allow students to choose numbers greater than 12.) For example, if a student says his or her product is 121, you would say that the number must be 11. You might wish to mention that 11 is the *square root* of 121, the number which, when multiplied by itself, equals 121. A square with an area of 121 squares inches has four sides each measuring 11 inches.

Problem After finding several students' numbers, switch roles by telling students your product and asking them to find the number you started with. Begin with products that they should already know, such as 25 (5 × 5) or 64 (8 × 8). Then, give them some larger products, such as 625 (25 × 25), so that students must use the calculator to find the answer.

Share You might have students offer some ideas on how to use a calculator to find the number you started with. For example, they might suggest using the *guess and check* strategy, squaring a randomly chosen number, comparing the product with your number, then adjusting up or down and trying again.

Problem Now give students a number that is not a perfect square, such as 40, and ask them to find your number. Students will likely say that 40 is an impossible product because 6 × 6 is too small but 7 × 7 is too big. Tell them that there are numbers between 6 and 7 they can try. To illustrate, write the numbers 6.1, 6.2, 6.3, and so on, through 6.9, on the board. Read the numbers as "six point one," "six point two," and so on.

If students suggest using fractions, tell them that most calculators don't have a way of writing fractions, so students will need to find a different way to write these numbers. Ask students to see if any of the numbers you wrote on the board might be your number. If necessary, show students where the decimal point is on the calculator. Sketch a table on the board like the one at the right, and record the products that students find. Read the numbers aloud as a class.

Numbers between 6 and 7	→ Numbers multiplied by themselves
6	36
6.1	37.21
6.2	38.44
6.3	39.69
6.4	40.96
6.5	42.25
6.6	43.56
6.7	44.89
6.8	46.24
6.9	47.61
7	49

Materials
- For each student: calculator

NCTM Standards 1, 2, 6, 7, 8, 9, 10

Teacher Story

"As I went through this lesson with my students, one of them noted that decimals are like fractions, because, like fractions, decimals are located between whole numbers. I pointed out that decimals are simply a different way of writing fractions. Decimals are especially useful when you work with calculators because you can't input fractions into most calculators."

Finally, ask students what two numbers your number must be between. Students should see from the table that your number must be between 6.3 and 6.4.

Talk Math

❷ How do you know that the number is between 6.3 and 6.4? Possible response: 40 is between 39.69 and 40.96 in the table. The number which, when squared, gives 39.69 is 6.3. The number which, when squared, gives 40.96 is 6.4.

❷ Estimate the number that, when multiplied by itself, gives 45. Explain how you made your estimate. Possible estimate: 6.71; possible explanation: 6.7 squared is 44.89, which is slightly less than 45. So I chose an estimate that is slightly bigger than 6.7.

C Exploring Decimals LAB pp. 151–152

individuals or pairs · 20 MIN

Purpose To locate whole numbers and decimals on a number line

NCTM Standards 1, 2, 6, 7, 8, 9, 10

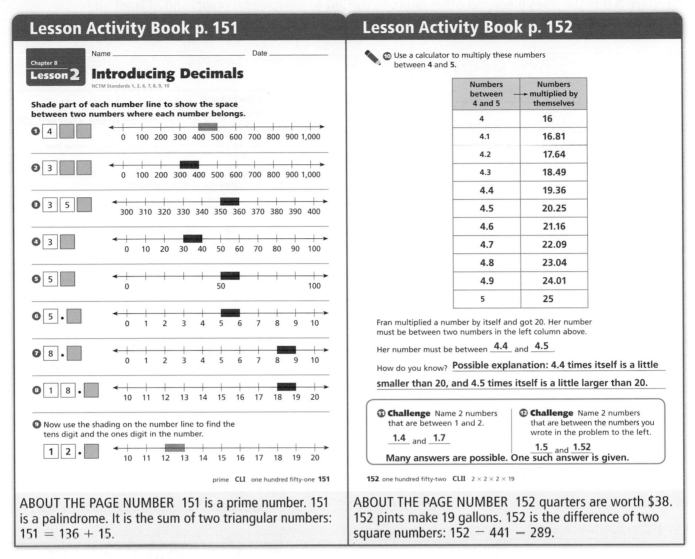

Teaching Notes for LAB page 151

Have students complete the page individually or with partners.

Students explore the idea that decimals are numbers between whole numbers. They shade sections on a number line to show where numbers with certain digits will appear.

Concept Alert When students shade the part of the number line where a number with missing digits must fall, they will likely shade from one marked point line to another. You might want to discuss with students which of the endpoints could actually be the number and which could not. For example, in Problem 1, students should shade from 400 to 500, the region where a number with a 4 in the hundreds place might fall. The number could be 400 but it could not be 500, because the hundreds digit in 500 is 5, not 4. Similarly, in Problem 3, students should shade from 350 to 360, but they should also recognize that 350 is included in the shaded region while 360 is not.

Teaching Notes for LAB page 152

Students use calculators to approximate the number between 4 and 5 which, when squared, gives 20. As in the lesson, this activity illustrates the importance of decimals as numbers which, when squared, produce non-square numbers.

Challenge Problem The Challenge Problem asks students first to name two numbers between 1 and 2, then to find two numbers between the first two.

Reflect and Summarize the Lesson

 Write Math

Find two numbers between 9 and 10. How do you know they are between 9 and 10?
Possible answers: 9.4, 9.7, 9.90, 9.95; possible explanation: A number between 9 and 10 should have a 9 in the ones place, no other digits to the left of the decimal point, and at least one non-zero digit to the right of the decimal point.

Review Model

Refer students to Review Model: Understanding Decimals in the *Student Handbook* p. 127 to practice locating decimals on a number line, naming whole numbers on either side of a decimal, and reading decimals.

✔ Check for Understanding

❶ 2 and 3

❷ 13 and 14

❸ 0 and 1

❹ one point two

❺ twenty point four

❻ six point one seven

❼ Press 9, then 2, then the decimal point key, then 0, then 5.

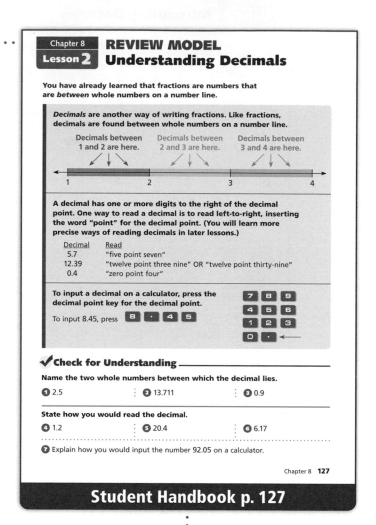

Student Handbook p. 127

Use with Lesson Activity Book pp. 151–152.

Leveled Problem Solving

A spider can travel between 1 and 2 miles an hour.

① Basic Level

Bobbi wrote a spider's speed as 1.■ ■. What are the greatest possible values for ■ and ■? Explain. 9 and 9; Possible explanation: 1.99 is the greatest number with 2 decimal places less than 2.

② On Level

A giant tortoise travels 0.■ ■ miles an hour. What is the greatest possible difference between the speeds of a tortoise and a spider? Explain. 1.98 miles an hour; If the spider is 1.99 and the tortoise is 0.01, the difference is 1.98.

③ Above Level

A mouse travels 8.00 miles an hour. How much faster than a spider does a mouse travel? Explain. between 6.01 and 6.99 miles an hour faster; Possible explanation: 1.99 + 6.01 = 8; 1.01 and 6.99 = 8.

Intervention | Practice | Extension

Activity The Number Between

Provide pairs of students with a set of cards numbered 0–9. Tell students to mix the cards and place them face down. Each student selects one card. Students use the cards to write a decimal number. Students then tell which two whole numbers the decimal lies between. Discuss how the numbers change when the digits are reversed in the decimal. Repeat the activity several times. Vary it by having students select three cards to write the decimal number.

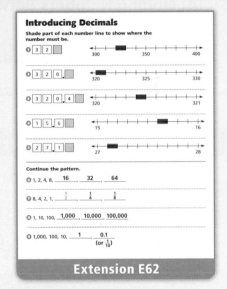

Practice P62

Extension E62

Spiral Review

Spiral Review Book page SR62 provides review of the following previously learned skills and concepts:

- using shapes with known areas to find the area of more complex shapes
- converting between ounces, pounds, and tons

You may wish to have students work with a partner to complete the page.

Spiral Review S62

Extension Activity
Decimal Patterns

Students write several lists of 10 decimal numbers in the form X.X, beginning with X.0. For example, if the first digit is 8, the numbers would be 8.0 through 8.9. Next, ask them to compare the sets and describe any patterns they see. Students might notice that the digits to the right of the decimal point always start at 0 and end at 9, or that the digit to the left of the decimal point always stays the same in each set (you never reach the next whole number).

Lesson 3 Zooming in on the Number Line

NCTM Standards 1, 2, 6, 7, 8, 9, 10

Lesson Planner

STUDENT OBJECTIVES
- To explore numbers between decimals
- To compare decimals

1 | Daily Activities (TG p. 611)

| Open-Ended Problem Solving/Headline Story | Skills Practice and Review— What's My Number? |

2 | Teach and Practice (TG pp. 612–614)

MATERIALS

Ⓐ **Finding Numbers Between Decimals** (TG p. 612)

Ⓑ **Zooming in on the Number Line** (TG p. 613)

Ⓒ **Playing a Game: Guess My Number** (TG p. 614)

- TR: Activity Master, AM70
- transparency of AM70 (optional)
- calculator
- 📖 LAB pp. 153–154
- 📖 SH p. 139

3 | Differentiated Instruction (TG p. 615)

Leveled Problem Solving (TG p. 615)	Practice Book P63
Intervention Activity (TG p. 615)	Extension Book E63
Extension Activity (TG p. 615)	Spiral Review Book SR63
Science Connection (TG p. 592)	

Lesson Notes

About the Lesson

In the previous lesson, students discovered that decimals are numbers between whole numbers. In this lesson, students zoom in closer and look between decimals to find even more numbers. Students conclude this lesson by playing a game where they must compare decimals in order to figure out a secret decimal. By comparing decimals with one or two digits to the right of the decimal point, students begin to explore the relative values of the digits.

Use with Lesson Activity Book pp. 153–154.

Developing Mathematical Language

Vocabulary: tenths, hundredths, whole numbers

The prefix *deci-* means "one tenth." As with *whole numbers,* each successive place to the right in decimal numbers is one tenth the value of the preceding place. The decimal point separates the *whole number* part of a decimal number from the decimal part. The place to the right of the decimal point is the *tenths* place. A *tenth* is one of ten equal parts. The *hundredths* place is to the right of the *tenths* place. A *hundredth* is one of one hundred equal parts.

Review the terms *tenths, hundredths,* and *whole numbers* with students.

Beginning Write 17.25 on the board. Have students underline the *whole numbers.* Then have them name the digits in the *tenths* and *hundredths* places.

Intermediate Have a volunteer write a 4-digit number on the board and place a decimal point between the two middle digits. Have students identify the *whole numbers* and then the digits in the *tenths* and *hundredths* places.

Advanced Have students write numbers as you name digits for *whole numbers* and for *tenths* and *hundredths* places. Then have them read the numbers back to you.

Open-Ended Problem Solving

Read the Headline Story to your students. Encourage them to create problems that can be solved using information from the story.

 **Headline Story**

> Erin had ____ dollars, ____ quarters, and four pennies. She gave Jay three of her coins.

Possible responses: Some amounts she could have had $2.79 or $5.54. She could not have had $2.32 or $3.17. The amount she had must have had a 4 or 9 at the end of it because adding 4 pennies to any number of quarters gives a total that ends in 4 or 9.

Skills Practice and Review

What's My Number?

As you did in the last lesson, tell students that you're thinking of a number, but this time choose a number in the millions. Again, have students ask *yes/no* questions to find your number. To help students keep track of what they know about the number and to encourage them to use place value to narrow down the possible numbers, sketch this diagram for a 7-digit number on the board:

As students ask questions about the digits in the number, keep track of the possibilities below each blank. For example, if a student asks if the number is greater than 5 million and the answer is *yes,* write 5, 6, 7, 8, and 9 below the blank for the first digit to indicate that these are the possible digits for this position. Continue with other numbers, including 8-digit numbers.

pairs

20 MIN

A Finding Numbers Between Decimals

Materials

- For the teacher: transparency of AM70 (optional)
- For each student: AM70

NCTM Standards 1, 2, 6, 7, 8, 9, 10

Purpose To explore numbers between whole numbers and between tenths

Introduce Give each student a copy of Activity Master: Zooming in on the Number Line. Explain that this activity will allow students to look at a specific region of the number line in greater and greater detail.

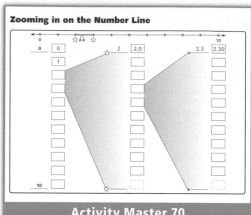

Activity Master 70

Task Direct students to complete the Activity Master with a partner. Students should be able to fill in the numbers between 0 and 10 and between 2 and 3. The numbers between 2.3 and 2.4 will be new to them. Encourage students to look for patterns on the page that can help them fill in these numbers. They may notice, for example, that the number 2 becomes 2.0 in the center column and that the number 2.3 becomes 2.30 in the right column. This suggests they should add an extra digit in each column. Also, the rightmost digit increases by 1 on each step as students move down the column. This suggests they should write 2.31 after 2.30, so that the rightmost digit will be 1 more than 0.

✔ **Ongoing Assessment**

- Do students understand that appending a zero to the right of the decimal portion of a decimal number does not change the number's value? So, 7 = 7.0, 3.4 = 3.40, and 12.96 = 12.960.

Share After most students have finished, have them share their answers and their reasoning. If students don't mention the patterns above, point them out.

Also, call attention to the number line at the top of the page. Make sure students notice that all the numbers in the center and right columns of the page fall between 2 and 3. To be sure students understand this, act out "zooming in" with your class. Give three students cards to hold, one with the number 2 on it, one with the number 3, and one with the number 4. Ask students to arrange themselves in order.

Now give another student a card with 2.4 on it and ask him or her to find the correct place in the line. Continue with other numbers, both tenths and hundredths, as you feel necessary. You can also ask students to compare some numbers in the middle or right column with numbers in the left column.

Differentiated Instruction

Above Level Advanced students may realize that no matter how close two numbers are, other numbers lie between them. To put it another way: there are infinitely many numbers between 1 and 2, between 1.1 and 1.2, between 1.10 and 1.11, and so on. If you think your students are ready for this idea, you might challenge them by asking if they think there are any numbers that are so close together that no other numbers lie between them. **no**

💬 **Talk Math**

❷ Name a number between 7 and 8. Explain how you found your answer. Possible answer: 7.4; possible explanation: I wrote 7 as 7.0. Then I changed the right-hand digit to a number between 0 and 10. I chose 4. So my number was 7.4.

❷ Name a number between 5.4 and 5.5. Explain how you found your answer. Possible answer: 5.48; possible explanation: I wrote 5.4 as 5.40. Then I changed the right-hand digit to a number between 0 and 10. I chose 8. So my number was 5.48.

B **Zooming in on the Number Line** LAB pp. 153–154

Purpose To practice finding numbers between given numbers

NCTM Standards 1, 2, 6, 7, 8, 9, 10

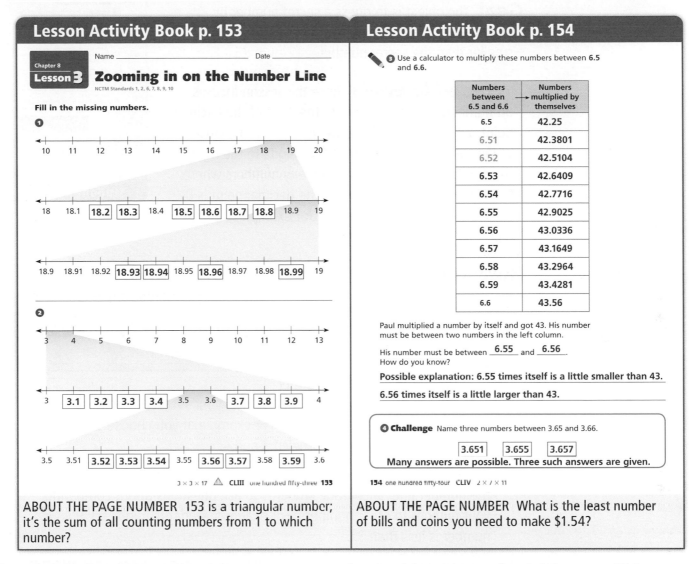

Lesson Activity Book p. 153

Name _____ Date _____

Chapter 8
Lesson 3 **Zooming in on the Number Line**
NCTM Standards 1, 2, 6, 7, 8, 9, 10

Fill in the missing numbers.

❶

10 11 12 13 14 15 16 17 18 19 20

18 18.1 **18.2 18.3** 18.4 **18.5 18.6 18.7 18.8** 18.9 19

18.9 18.91 18.92 **18.93 18.94** 18.95 **18.96** 18.97 18.98 **18.99** 19

❷

3 4 5 6 7 8 9 10 11 12 13

3 **3.1 3.2 3.3 3.4** 3.5 3.6 **3.7 3.8 3.9** 4

3.5 3.51 **3.52 3.53 3.54** 3.55 **3.56 3.57** 3.58 **3.59** 3.6

3 × 3 × 17 ▲ CLIII one hundred fifty-three **153**

ABOUT THE PAGE NUMBER 153 is a triangular number; it's the sum of all counting numbers from 1 to which number?

Lesson Activity Book p. 154

❸ Use a calculator to multiply these numbers between **6.5** and **6.6.**

Numbers between 6.5 and 6.6 →	Numbers multiplied by themselves
6.5	42.25
6.51	42.3801
6.52	42.5104
6.53	42.6409
6.54	42.7716
6.55	42.9025
6.56	43.0336
6.57	43.1649
6.58	43.2964
6.59	43.4281
6.6	43.56

Paul multiplied a number by itself and got 43. His number must be between two numbers in the left column.

His number must be between _**6.55**_ and _**6.56**_. How do you know?

Possible explanation: 6.55 times itself is a little smaller than 43.

6.56 times itself is a little larger than 43.

❹ **Challenge** Name three numbers between 3.65 and 3.66.

3.651   **3.655**   **3.657**

Many answers are possible. Three such answers are given.

154 one hundred fifty-four CLIV 2 × 7 × 11

ABOUT THE PAGE NUMBER What is the least number of bills and coins you need to make $1.54?

Teaching Notes for LAB page 153

Have students work on the page individually or with partners.

This page is similar to Activity A. It gives students additional practice with the idea of zooming in on the number line to find numbers between given numbers. Students first find numbers between 18 and 19, then between 18.9 and 19. At the bottom of the page, students find numbers between 3 and 4 and between 3.5 and 3.6.

Teaching Notes for LAB page 154

This page gives students practice with estimation and refined estimation as they look for a number that, when multiplied by itself, gives 43 (that is, to estimate the square root of 43). Students need calculators to complete the page.

Challenge Problem The Challenge Problem asks students to find three numbers between 3.65 and 3.66. To do so, they can extend the idea they used to find a number between 2.3 and 2.4 in Activity A, first writing 3.65 as 3.650, then changing the final digit to a number between 0 and 10.

C Playing *Guess My Number*

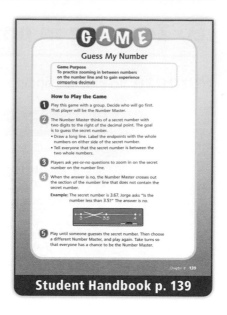

Student Handbook p. 139

NCTM Standards 1, 2, 6, 7, 8, 9, 10

Purpose To practice zooming in between numbers on the number line, and to gain experience with comparing decimals

Goal The object is to guess a secret number by eliminating ranges of numbers that are larger or smaller than the secret number

Prepare Materials Since this lesson focuses on numbers with two digits to the right of the decimal point, tell students that all the numbers you choose today will have no more than two digits to the right of the point. For now, don't include any numbers where the second digit to the right of the decimal point is 0, as students may not yet realize, for example, that 3.3 and 3.30 are the same number.

How to Play

❶ Secretly pick a number with no more than two digits after the decimal point. Draw a long line on the board, label the endpoints with the whole numbers on either side of your number, and tell students that your secret number is between the two whole numbers. For example, if you choose 3.67, draw a line with endpoints labeled 3 and 4.

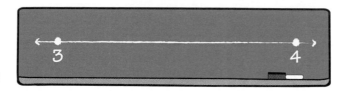

❷ Have students ask *yes/no* questions to zoom in on your secret number on the number line. Encourage students to ask questions about comparing your number to other numbers. For example, students might ask if your number is less than 3.5.

❸ After saying *yes* or *no* to a student's question, invite another student to cross out the section of the number line that does not contain your number. For example, if the secret number were 3.67 and a student asked, "Is the number less than 3.5?" you would say *no,* mark 3.5 on the number line, and ask a student to cross out the section of the number line between 3 and 3.5.

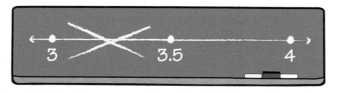

❹ Repeat steps 2 and 3 until a student guesses the secret number.

Reflect and Summarize the Lesson

Write Math
Name a number between 8.6 and 8.7. Explain how you found the number.
Possible answer: 8.62; possible explanation: I wrote 8.6 as 8.60. Then I changed the right-hand digit to a number between 0 and 10. I chose 2. So my number was 8.62.

Leveled Problem Solving

A theme park river ride in Virginia covers an area of more than 3.5 acres but less than 3.6 acres.

❶ Basic Level

The area has 2 digits to the right of the decimal point. What is the least it can be? Explain. 3.51 acres; Possible explanation: 3.51 is the smallest number after 3.5 with two decimal places.

❷ On Level

The area has 2 digits to the right of the decimal point. What is the greatest it can be? Explain. 3.59 acres; This is the largest number before 3.6 with only 2 decimal places.

❸ Above Level

If the area of the ride is exactly halfway between 3.5 and 3.6 acres, what is its area? Explain. 3.55 acres; Between 3.5 and 3.6, there are 4 numbers less than 3.55 and 4 greater.

Intervention

Activity Decimal Chart

Write these numbers on the board: 4.56, 4.62, 4.53. Help students write each number in a place-value chart such as this:

Ones		Tenths	Hundredths
	.		

Have students tell which two numbers lie between 4.5 and 4.6. 4.56, 4.53 Discuss how the chart helps with the identification. Repeat with other decimal numbers.

Practice

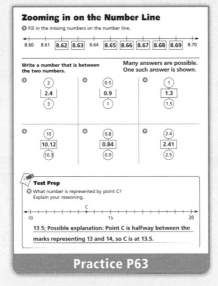

Practice P63

Extension

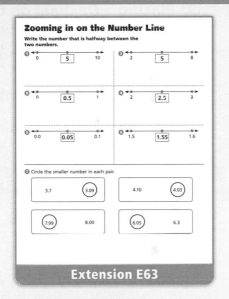

Extension E63

Extension Activity
Numbers Between Decimals

Provide 10 × 10 grids. Have small groups use the grids to display numbers between decimals. For example, students can start by shading 0.7 on one grid and 0.8 on another. Then have them shade other grids to show the numbers between the two— 0.71, 0.72, and so on, through 0.79.

Allow time for students to discuss how the grids show a progression of the numbers between the decimals.

Spiral Review

Spiral Review Book page SR63 provides review of the following previously learned skills and concepts:

- separating arrays into parts to model simpler multiplications that can be used to complete multidigit multiplication
- listing all possible outcomes for an experiment

You may wish to have students work with a partner to complete the page.

Spiral Review SR63

Lesson 4 Decimals on the Number Line

NCTM Standards 1, 2, 6, 7, 8, 9, 10

Lesson Planner

STUDENT OBJECTIVES ....
- To locate numbers expressed as decimals on the number line
- To practice comparing numbers expressed as decimals

1 | Daily Activities (TG p. 617)

Open-Ended Problem Solving/Headline Story	Skills Practice and Review— Ordering Large Numbers

2 | Teach and Practice (TG pp. 618–623)

	MATERIALS
(A) Placing a Decimal on the Number Line (TG pp. 618–619)	• TR: Activity Masters, AM71–AM74
(B) Comparing Decimals (TG p. 620)	• transparency of AM71–AM74 (optional)
(C) Decimals on the Number Line (TG p. 621)	• number cube
(D) Playing a Game: _Making Decimal Numbers_ (TG p. 622)	• LAB pp. 155–156 • SH p. 128

3 | Differentiated Instruction (TG p. 624)

Leveled Problem Solving (TG p. 624)	Practice Book P64
Intervention Activity (TG p. 624)	Extension Book E64
Extension Activity (TG p. 624)	Spiral Review Book SR64
Art Connection (TG p. 592)	

Lesson Notes

About the Lesson

In this lesson, students focus in on and locate decimals on progressively more detailed sections of the number line. Students compare decimals and apply their understanding of decimal notation. These activities prepare students to relate fractions and decimals in the next lesson.

About the Mathematics

Students can use their knowledge of whole numbers to understand decimals. For example, students know that, moving left to right, the place values of digits in whole numbers decrease by a factor of 10 from one place to the next. The same is true of the place values of digits in decimals. Similarly, students know that zeros in whole numbers act as placeholders. So do zeros in decimals.

Numbers can be expressed in a variety of forms, for example as sums of other numbers, as decimals, and as fractions. Expressed in decimal form, numbers are especially convenient, both for showing their magnitudes and for precisely positioning them on the number line.

Use with Lesson Activity Book pp. 155–156.

Developing Mathematical Language

A decimal number has a both a *decimal portion* and a *non-decimal portion*. The *decimal portion* of the number is the part to the right of the decimal point. The value of the *decimal portion* is always less than 1. The *non-decimal portion* is the whole-number part of the number. Because 0 is a whole number, the whole-number part may be 0. The *metric system* is a system of measurement based on the decimal system. Units are related by powers of 10. A *meter stick* is measurement tool that uses a number line based on the decimal system.

Review the terms *decimal portion, non-decimal portion,* and *meter stick* with students.

Beginning Write a decimal number on the board. Have students name the *decimal portion* of the number and then the *non-decimal portion.*

Intermediate Write a decimal number with non-repeating digits on the board. Name a digit, and have students tell you whether it is in the *decimal portion* or the *non-decimal portion* of the number.

Advanced Let students examine a *meter stick* and a yardstick or ruler. Have students compare the two measuring devices.

1 | Daily Activities

Open-Ended Problem Solving

Read the Headline Story to your students. Encourage them to make interesting statements using information from the story.

 Headline Story

> **Jim wrote a decimal number on the board that was between 3 and 5 and had 3 digits.**

Possible responses: The ones digit of Jim's number must be 3 or 4. His number could be 3.81. His number could not be 4.2793 because that number has more than 3 digits.

Skills Practice and Review

Ordering Large Numbers

Begin by asking students to write numbers in the millions on the board, and to say them out loud. The rest of the class should make sure that the numbers students write and the numbers they say are the same. Once you have about ten numbers on the board, ask the class to compare and order these numbers from smallest to biggest. You might first ask for the smallest number and put a 1 next to it to indicate that it's first in order. Then ask for the next smallest number and mark it with a 2, and so on.

whole class 10 MIN

A Placing a Decimal on the Number Line

Materials
- For the teacher: transparency of AM71 (optional)
- For each student: AM71 (optional)

NCTM Standards 1, 2, 6, 7, 8, 9, 10

Purpose To develop strategies for placing decimals on the number line

Introduce Display a transparency of Activity Master: Labeled Number Lines, or draw the number lines on the board. Name a number between 3 and 4 that has 2 digits to the right of the decimal points, such as 3.73.

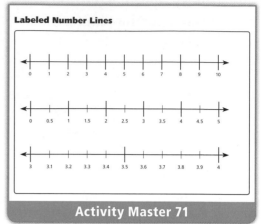

Task **Ask students to place the number in its correct location on each number line, and to explain their reasoning.** You might have students place the number on the overhead or chalkboard number lines, or you might hand out copies of the page and have students work individually before they record the results for the class to see.

✔ **Ongoing Assessment**
- Given a decimal number, do students determine the two nearest whole numbers between which the given number lies?
- Given a decimal number with two decimal places, do students determine the two nearest numbers, each written to tenths, between which the given number lies?

Share Ask students to explain how they knew where to place the decimal between two whole numbers on the first number line. They can use the ones digit to determine the whole numbers on either side of the decimal. The digits to the right of the decimal point indicate that the number is slightly greater than the ones digit, but, because the value of the decimal part is less than one, it's less than the next whole number. In the example 3.73, the number is more than 3 but less than 4. So, it falls between 3 and 4 on the number line.

To place 3.73 on the second number line, students must compare 3.73 to 3.5 in order to decide whether the number is closer to 3 or to 4. Students may remember from previous lessons that when they zoomed in between 3 and 4, they saw that 3.7 was closer to 4 than it was to 3. Students could also reason that 3.7 is more than 3.5, and therefore 3.73 is between 3.5 and 4 on the number line.

To place the number on the third number line, students must reason that 3.73 is between 3.7 and 3.8. If they are confused about this, you might remind them to say each digit in the number separately. For example, they should read 3.73 as "three point seven three" rather than "three point seventy-three." This can help them see that the number is 3.7 plus a little more, and therefore belongs just after 3.7.

Finally, ask a student to name another two-decimal-place number between 3 and 4. Have a second student write this number on the board. Then have the class read the number out loud. Repeat Activity A with this new number.

Talk Math

❓ Between which two whole numbers does 8.04 lie? Explain your reasoning. 8 and 9; Possible explanation: The ones digit, 8, indicates that the number is greater than 8. The decimal part, 04, indicates that the number is less than the next whole number after 8, which is 9. So, 8.04 is between 8 and 9.

❓ Between which two numbers, each with one digit to the right of the decimal point, does 6.58 lie? Explain your reasoning. 6.5 and 6.6; Possible explanation: 6.58 is "six point five eight." So, it is more than "six point five" and less than "six point six."

Differentiated Instruction

Basic Level Some students may look at a decimal number by focusing on the decimal point and considering the digits on either side of it separately. Students who do this might notice that digit values increase as they move away from the decimal point on the left side, but decrease as they move to the right. They may not think of the decimal part of the number as a part that is less than 1. The result is that they may not see a number like 12.6 as a number between 12 and 13 on a number line. To help students see decimal numbers as specific numbers between whole numbers, you might point out that decimal numbers are like whole numbers in that place values decrease as you move from left to right.

B Comparing Decimals

Purpose To compare decimals without using number lines

Introduce In the previous activity, students were asked to place numbers on number lines. This required them to compare given numbers to labeled numbers on number lines. In this activity, students continue to compare decimals, but without the aid of number lines. If students need additional support, you might suggest that they sketch number lines to help them.

Differentiated Instruction

Basic Level Students who are unable to place a decimal between the two nearest whole numbers may lack an understanding of the values of the digits in the decimal. To assist these students, you might cover the decimal part of the number and ask students where they would place the number on the number line. Then uncover the decimal part. Explain that the decimal portion of the number indicates that the number is slightly more than the non-decimal part, but still less than the next whole number.

Problems **Write several pairs of decimal numbers on the board, and ask students which number in each pair is larger.** If, for example, you write 1.3 and 1.8, students should reason that both of these numbers are between 1 and 2, but that 1.3 is closer to 1 and 1.8 is closer to 2. So, 1.8 must be larger.

In choosing pairs of numbers to write, be sure to give some with different numbers of digits to the right of the decimal point, such as 1.26 and 1.8. This will motivate students to think about the place values of the digits beyond the decimal point. That is, students need to realize that they should compare 1.2 and 1.8 to determine that 1.8 is bigger than 1.26.

Practice Here are some other pairs of numbers students might compare:

- 0.7 and 1.2 (0 is less than 1, so 0.7 is less than 1.2.)
- 2.3 and 2.25 (2.3 is "two point three" and 2.25 is "two point two five." So, 2.3 is greater than 2.25.)
- 1.09 and 1.1 (1.1 = 1.10, so 1.09 is less than 1.1.)

Talk Math

❷ Which is greater, 6.8 or 5.9? Why? 6.8; Possible explanation: I compared the whole-number parts. 6 is greater than 5, so 6.8 must be greater than 5.9.

❷ Which is greater, 9.2 or 9.18? Why? 9.2; Possible explanation: 9.2 is "nine point two zero." 9.18 is "nine point one eight." So, 9.2 is greater than 9.18.

Extend Display a meter stick. Remind students that in the metric system, lengths are measured using millimeters, centimeters, and meters. Point out that metric lengths are expressed as decimals. Show that the width of a piece of $8\frac{1}{2} \times 11$ inch paper is about 21.6 centimeters. You may wish to contrast the metric and customary measurement systems by pointing out that in the latter, lengths are *not* written in decimals. A desk that measures 3 feet 9 inches in length is *not* 3.9 feet long.

Decimals on the Number Line LAB pp. 155–156

 individuals or pairs

 20 MIN

Purpose To place decimals on number lines and compare decimals

NCTM Standards 1, 2, 6, 7, 8, 9, 10

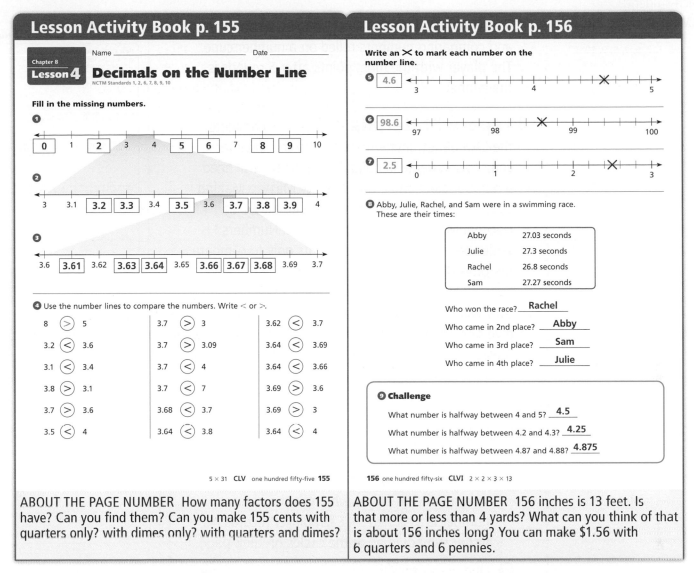

Teaching Notes for LAB page 155

Have students work on the page individually or with partners. Students label the number lines on the page with decimal numbers. They then use these labeled number lines to compare decimals, zooming in to find numbers between whole numbers and numbers between decimals. All of the comparisons involve numbers that appear on the number lines at the top of the page.

Teaching Notes for LAB page 156

In the Problems 6 and 7, students should reason that the each mark on the number line represents an increase of 0.2 (not 0.1) from the previous mark.

To figure out who won the race, students must realize that the smaller the time, the better the result. Students must compare numbers without the use of corresponding number lines.

Challenge Problem The Challenge Problem asks students to name numbers halfway between other numbers. Encourage students to draw number lines to help them find the numbers.

D Playing *Making Decimal Numbers*

Materials

- For each student:
  TR: AM72–AM74

NCTM Standards 1, 2, 6, 7, 8, 9, 10

Purpose To practice comparing decimals

Goal The goal is to collect points by recording and comparing numbers rolled on a number cube. The player with the most points after 5 rounds is the winner.

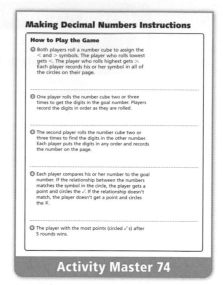

Activity Master 74

Prepare Materials As students complete the LAB pages, invite them to play this decimal comparison game in pairs. Each student will need a number cube and either Activity Master: Making Decimal Numbers I or Activity Master: Making Decimal Numbers II. Making Decimal Numbers I is easier because it requires students only to compare the ones digits of numbers. If they choose Making Decimal Numbers II, which supplies the ones digits, they will need to consider decimal portions of numbers. You might decide to give only the harder version of the game to more advanced students. Activity Master: Making Decimal Numbers Instructions explains how to play the game. You may wish to give this page to students as they finish the LAB pages, instead of explaining the rules to each pair.

How to Play

❶ Each player rolls the number cube. The player who rolls the lowest number is assigned the < symbol. The player who rolls the highest number is assigned >. Each player records his or her symbol in all of the circles on their page.

❷ One player rolls the number cube two or three times, recording each number rolled as a digit in the goal number. Players write the digits in the order they are rolled.

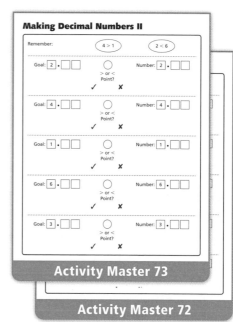

Activity Master 73

Activity Master 72

❸ The second player rolls the number cube two or three times, recording the numbers as digits in the other number. The player may write the digits in any order.

❹ Each player compares his or her number to the goal number. If the relationship between the numbers matches the symbol in the circle, the player gets a point and circles the ✓. If the relationship doesn't match, the player doesn't get a point, and circles the X.

❺ The player with the most points (circled ✓s) after 5 rounds wins.

Reflect and Summarize the Lesson

 Write Math

Which number is larger, 3.7 or 3.65? Explain your reasoning.
3.7; Possible answer: 3.65 is "three point six five." 3.7 is "three point seven." Since 7 is bigger than 6, 3.7 is bigger than 3.65.

Review Model ....

Refer students to Review Model: Placing Decimals in the *Student Handbook* p. 128, to see how they can use the digits in a decimal number to decide where to place the number on the number line.

✔ Check for Understanding

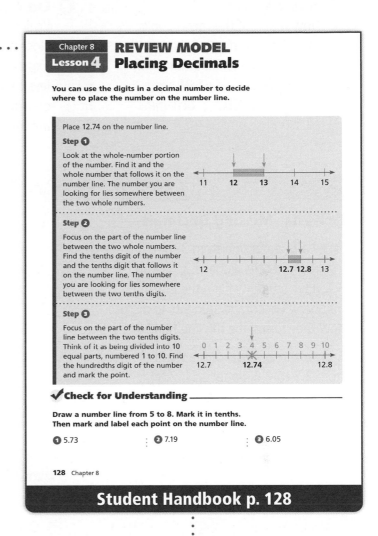

Student Handbook p. 128

Leveled Problem Solving

In a race, Vern's time was 58.79 seconds, Emanuel's time was 59.09 seconds, and Antwan's time was 61.01 seconds.

❶ Basic Level
How many of the racers took more than 1 minute? Explain. one; Possible explanation: Only Antwan's time of 61.01 sec is greater than 60 sec, or 1 min.

❷ On Level
Which racer's time was the closest to exactly 1 minute? Explain. Emanuel; 59.09 sec is less than 1 sec away from 60 sec, or 1 min; 61.01 sec and 58.79 sec are more than 1 sec from 60 sec.

❸ Above Level
Joe was faster than Antwan but slower than Emanuel. What might his time have been? Explain. 59.99 seconds; 59.9 is greater than 59.09 but less than 61.

Intervention	Practice	Extension

Activity Missing Decimals

Draw a number line from 3 to 4 marked in tenths. Label 3.2, 3.5, and 3.7. Have students fill in the missing numbers. Encourage students to discuss how they found the missing numbers.

Repeat the activity with a number line from 2.5 to 2.6. Label 2.51, 2.54, and 2.59.

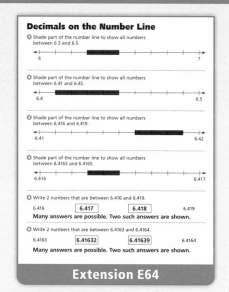

Practice P64

Extension E64

Spiral Review

Spiral Review Book page SR64 provides review of the following previously learned skills and concepts:

- solving problems using the strategy *solve a simpler problem*
- solving magic square puzzles by working backward

You may wish to have students work with a partner to complete the page.

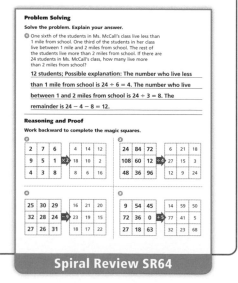

Spiral Review SR64

Extension Activity
Decimal Puzzles

Have small groups make 14 cards—the digits 0–9, $>$, $<$, and two cards each with a decimal point. Challenge students to use the cards to make the following comparisons:

- 1-digit decimals that are greater than 2-digit decimals (for example: $3.9 > 1.87$)
- 2-digit decimals that are greater than other 2-digit decimals (for example: $2.76 < 3.01$)

Have students record their comparisons. Let groups share and discuss their comparisons.

Teacher's Notes 🍎

Daily Notes . . .

Quick Notes

More Ideas

Lesson 5 Connecting Fractions to Decimals

NCTM Standards 1, 2, 6, 7, 8, 9, 10

Lesson Planner

STUDENT OBJECTIVES
- To compare fractions to decimals
- To understand that fractions and decimals are different ways of representing the same number

1 | Daily Activities (TG p. 627)

| Open-Ended Problem Solving/Headline Story | Skills Practice and Review—Comparing and Ordering Decimals |

2 | Teach and Practice (TG pp. 628–631)

Ⓐ **Comparing Fractions and Decimals** (TG p. 628)

Ⓑ **Putting Fractions and Decimals on the Number Line** (TG p. 629)

Ⓒ **Connecting Fractions to Decimals** (TG p. 630)

MATERIALS
- TR: Activity Master, AM75
- transparency of AM75
- 📖 LAB pp. 157–158
- 📖 SH pp. 129–130

3 | Differentiated Instruction (TG p. 632)

Leveled Problem Solving (TG p. 632)	Practice Book P65
Intervention Activity (TG p. 632)	Extension Book E65
Extension Activity (TG p. 632)	Spiral Review Book SR65

Lesson Notes

About the Lesson

In this lesson, students relate fractions to decimals and begin to use what they know about fractions to obtain another view of decimals. They will see that the digit to the right of the decimal point tells "how many tenths." For example, 3 in 0.3 stands for $\frac{3}{10}$. The next digit to the right records hundredths. (Students will further explore this idea in the next two lessons when they use base-ten grids and blocks to represent decimals.) Students also place fractions and decimals on the same number line and notice that both are ways to describe numbers and can therefore name the same point.

About the Mathematics

In this lesson, students see that fractions and decimals are two different ways of naming numbers that may not be whole numbers. The denominator of a fraction indicates the total number of pieces into which a whole is separated. The numerator indicates the number of those pieces. In decimals, the total number of pieces is indicated by the place value of the digit (tenths, hundredths, thousandths, and so on). The number of pieces is indicated by the digit in that position. A fraction can divide the whole into any number of parts, while decimals are restricted to powers of 10.

Use with Lesson Activity Book pp. 157–158.

Developing Mathematical Language

Vocabulary: denominator, numerator

A fraction is a way of representing a part of a whole or of a group. It is the ratio of the part to the whole. The *numerator* is the number above the bar in a fraction that tells how many equal parts are described by the fraction. The *denominator* is the number below the bar that tells the total number of equal parts. In $\frac{3}{8}$, the *numerator* is 3 and the *denominator* is 8.

Review the terms *denominator* and *numerator* with students.

Beginning Write a fraction on the board. Have students name the number in the *numerator,* the top number, and in the *denominator,* the bottom number.

Intermediate Ask students to write a fraction. Name a number for the *numerator* and a different number for the *denominator.*

Advanced Write several fractions on the board, each with a different *numerator* and *denominator.* Name a number that is either the *numerator* or *denominator* of one of the fractions. Ask students to identify its position as either *numerator* or *denominator.*

Open-Ended Problem Solving

Read the Headline Story to your students. Encourage them to use logical reasoning to draw conclusions about the number.

 Headline Story

> **Deepa marked a point on a number line between 8 and 9, and labeled it with a decimal number. The number was closer to 9 than to 8.**

Possible responses: The ones digit of the number must be 8. The number must be greater than 8.5 but less than 9. The number could be 8.8, 8.62, 8.55721, or any other number between 8.5 and 9. The tenths digit could be 5, 6, 7, 8, or 9.

Skills Practice and Review

Comparing and Ordering Decimals

Draw a number line on the board, marking 10 and 11. Write two decimals on the board that are between 10 and 11, for example, 10.5 and 10.8. Have the class read the numbers aloud and tell you which number is larger. Locate the two numbers on the number line. Write another number on the board, for example, 10.12. Ask students to read it aloud and to compare it to each of the other numbers, placing the new number where it belongs on the number line. Continue, inviting students to come to the board to write a number between 10 and 11 and to read it aloud. As each number is added, have the class decide where it belongs on the number line. Once you have about 10 numbers, ask students to read them from smallest to biggest. Finally, repeat the activity, sketching money amounts on the chalkboard, such as $5.80 and $3.82. As before, have students name the amounts, compare them two by two, and order them.

pairs

15 MIN

A Comparing Fractions and Decimals

NCTM Standards 1, 2, 6, 7, 8, 9, 10

Purpose To develop strategies for comparing fractions to decimals

Introduce Remind students of this basic fact about fractions: the denominator of a fraction indicates the total number of equal pieces into which a whole is separated. The numerator indicates the number of those pieces that are being counted.

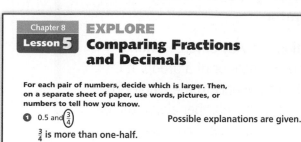

Chapter 8 **EXPLORE**

Lesson 5 **Comparing Fractions and Decimals**

For each pair of numbers, decide which is larger. Then, on a separate sheet of paper, use words, pictures, or numbers to tell how you know.

❶ 0.5 and $\frac{3}{4}$ Possible explanations are given.

$\frac{3}{4}$ is more than one-half.

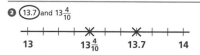

❷ 13.7 and $13\frac{4}{10}$

13    $13\frac{4}{10}$ 13.7   14

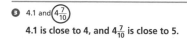

❸ 4.1 and $4\frac{7}{10}$

4.1 is close to 4, and $4\frac{7}{10}$ is close to 5.

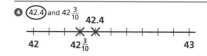

❹ 42.4 and $42\frac{3}{10}$ 42.4

42    $42\frac{3}{10}$ 43

Chapter 8 **129**

Student Handbook, p. 129

✔ Ongoing Assessment

• Do students locate fractions written as halves or tenths on a number line, e.g. $\frac{1}{2}$ or $\frac{7}{10}$?

Task Have students complete Explore: **Comparing Fractions and Decimals.** Possible explanations are given.

❶ 0.5 and $\frac{3}{4}$ $\frac{3}{4}$; 0.5 is one half or two fourths; three fourths is more than two fourths.

❷ 13.7 and $13\frac{4}{10}$ 13.7;

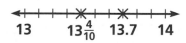

13    $13\frac{4}{10}$ 13.7 14

❸ 4.1 and $4\frac{7}{10}$ $4\frac{7}{10}$; 4.1 is close to 4, and $4\frac{7}{10}$ is close to 5.

❹ 42.4 and $42\frac{3}{10}$ 42.4;

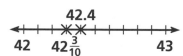

42.4

42    $42\frac{3}{10}$ 43

Share After students have had a chance to answer most of the questions on the page, have them share their answers and strategies. Some students may compare the fractional and decimal parts of both numbers in a pair to a common benchmark. Others may see which number is farther to the right on a number line.

💬 **Talk Math**

❓ Which is larger, 7.5 or $7\frac{1}{4}$? Explain. 7.5; Possible explanation: 0.5 is one half or two fourths; seven and two fourths is larger than seven and one fourth.

❓ Points representing two numbers appear on a number line. Which number is larger? Possible answer: the number represented by the point farther to the right

Putting Fractions and Decimals on the Number Line

Purpose To label a number line with fractions and decimals

Introduce To help students relate decimals to fractions, display Activity Master: Labeling Points on Number Lines. Give each student a copy of the page.

Task Have students complete the page.

Problem 1 is done for students. In Problems 2–4, students review placing fractions on a number line. This prepares them for Problem 5, where they see that decimals and fractions can represent the same number.

Students may remember how to find the fractional pieces into which each line is separated from Chapter 7, but you may need to remind them that the number of pieces into which the line is cut determines the type of fraction. Thus, the fractional pieces in Problem 2 are halves, because there are two pieces (from 2 to $2\frac{1}{2}$ and from $2\frac{1}{2}$ to 3). The pieces in Problem 3 are fourths, because there are four pieces (from 2 to $2\frac{1}{4}$, from $2\frac{1}{4}$ to $2\frac{1}{2}$, from $2\frac{1}{2}$ to $2\frac{3}{4}$, and from $2\frac{3}{4}$ to 3). The pieces in Problem 4 are thirds because there are three pieces, and the fractional pieces in Problem 5 are tenths because there are ten pieces.

❷ The missing number is $2\frac{1}{2}$.

❸ The missing numbers are $2\frac{1}{4}$, $2\frac{1}{2}$ or $2\frac{2}{4}$, and $2\frac{3}{4}$.

❹ The missing numbers are $2\frac{1}{3}$ and $2\frac{2}{3}$.

❺ The missing fractions are $2\frac{1}{10}$, $2\frac{2}{10}$, $2\frac{3}{10}$, $2\frac{4}{10}$, $2\frac{5}{10}$, $2\frac{6}{10}$, $2\frac{7}{10}$, $2\frac{8}{10}$, and $2\frac{9}{10}$. The missing decimals are 2.1, 2.2, 2.4, 2.5, 2.6, 2.7, 2.8, and 2.9.

When students label the number line in Problem 5 with decimals, they should begin to see that the digit immediately to the right of the decimal point represents the number of tenths. You might help students notice this by asking them for the place value of the digit to the right of the ones digit. Students will likely struggle to describe this place value now, but with time they will connect the place value and the fraction that it represents. To help them develop this understanding, begin reading decimal numbers in a way that emphasizes the values of their digits. For example, read 2.3 as "2 and 3 tenths" rather than "2 point 3." As you discuss students' work on the page, have them read decimals this way.

Talk Math

❓ What number is halfway between $5\frac{3}{4}$ and 6? Explain. $5\frac{7}{8}$; Possible explanation: The line is divided into eighths. The number is halfway between $5\frac{6}{8}$ and $5\frac{8}{8}$, or 6.

❓ What number is halfway between 8 and $8\frac{1}{3}$? Explain. $8\frac{1}{6}$; Possible explanation: The line is divided into sixths. The number is halfway between 8 and $8\frac{2}{6}$.

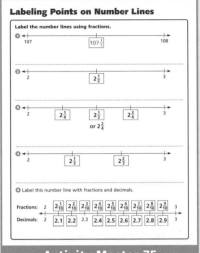

Activity Master 75

Materials

- For the teacher: transparency of AM75 (optional)
- For each student: AM75

NCTM Standards 1, 2, 6, 7, 8, 9, 10

Possible Discussion

Some students may wonder why they are learning about decimals when they already know about fractions, which convey the same information. You might motivate the use of decimals by pointing out ways in which decimals are easier to use than fractions. For example, because decimals follow specific place value rules from the base-ten system, it's easy to compare them by moving digit by digit, left to right. Decimals are easier to add and subtract than fractions with different denominators because they don't need to be converted to equivalent fractions. Still, there are times when fractions are more useful. For example, fractions are convenient for showing relationships: it's easy to see that $\frac{3}{8}$ is half of $\frac{6}{8}$, but it's not obvious that 0.375 is half of 0.75. Also, some fractions don't have convenient decimal forms. For example, $\frac{1}{3}$ is equal to $0.\overline{3}$ (the 3 repeats forever), and you can't easily do precise decimal arithmetic with this repeating decimal. Finally, fractions are useful in probability, as students will discover in Chapter 10.

individuals
or pairs

  20 MIN

Purpose To practice relating fractions and decimals

NCTM Standards 1, 2, 6, 7, 8, 9, 10

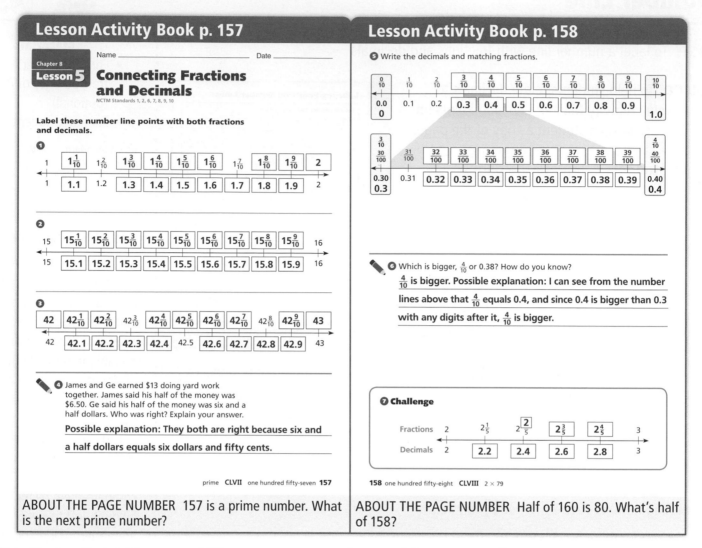

Lesson Activity Book p. 157

Chapter 8
Lesson 5 **Connecting Fractions and Decimals**
NCTM Standards 1, 2, 6, 7, 8, 9, 10

Label these number line points with both fractions and decimals.

❶

❷

❸

❹ James and Ge earned $13 doing yard work together. James said his half of the money was $6.50. Ge said his half of the money was six and a half dollars. Who was right? Explain your answer.

Possible explanation: They both are right because six and a half dollars equals six dollars and fifty cents.

prime **CLVII** one hundred fifty-seven **157**

Lesson Activity Book p. 158

❺ Write the decimals and matching fractions.

❻ Which is bigger, $\frac{4}{10}$ or 0.38? How do you know?

$\frac{4}{10}$ is bigger. Possible explanation: I can see from the number lines above that $\frac{4}{10}$ equals 0.4, and since 0.4 is bigger than 0.3 with any digits after it, $\frac{4}{10}$ is bigger.

❼ **Challenge**

158 one hundred fifty-eight **CLVIII** 2 × 79

ABOUT THE PAGE NUMBER 157 is a prime number. What is the next prime number?

ABOUT THE PAGE NUMBER Half of 160 is 80. What's half of 158?

Teaching Notes for LAB page 157

Have students complete the page individually or with partners. The page gives students additional practice connecting fractions and decimals. Students label each number line with both decimals and fractions. Only decimals with one digit after the decimal point are used.

To answer the last question, students must reason that 6.50 and $6\frac{1}{2}$ represent the same number.

Teaching Notes for LAB page 158

This page challenges students to relate fractions to decimals through hundredths. As students zoom in on the number line to label some of the numbers between 0.3 and 0.4, they may be surprised to find that the line is separated into 10 pieces but that the fractions have denominators of 100. If students ask, you might explain that had you zoomed in on each piece of the number line at the top of the page, there would be 100 pieces; they are simply looking at one section of that number line.

Challenge Problem The Challenge problem asks students to relate decimals to fractions when the denominator of the fraction is not a power of 10. The problem requires students to relate fractions with denominators other than 10 or 100 to decimals.

Reflect and Summarize the Lesson

Write Math

Which is larger, $2\frac{4}{9}$ or 2.5? Explain your reasoning. 2.5; Possible explanation: 4 is less than half of 9, so $2\frac{4}{9} < 2\frac{1}{2}$. Since $2.5 = 2\frac{1}{2}$, $2\frac{4}{9} < 2.5$, or $2.5 > 2\frac{4}{9}$.

Review Model

Refer students to Review Model: Comparing Fractions with Decimals in the *Student Handbook,* p. 130 to see how they can use a common benchmark or a number line to compare a fraction with a decimal.

✔ Check for Understanding

❶ $2\frac{9}{10}$

❷ $6\frac{3}{10}$

❸ $1\frac{7}{10}$

❹ 9.9

❺ 4.6

❻ 8.6

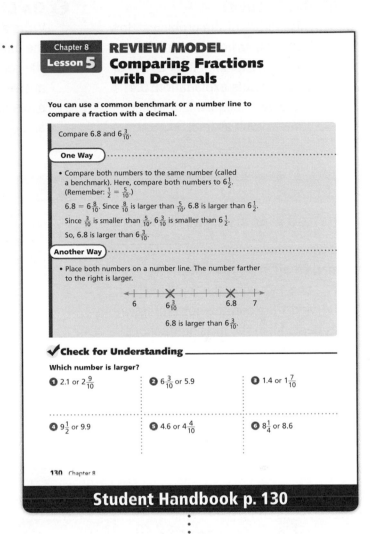

Chapter 8
Lesson 5
REVIEW MODEL
Comparing Fractions with Decimals

You can use a common benchmark or a number line to compare a fraction with a decimal.

Compare 6.8 and $6\frac{3}{10}$.

One Way

• Compare both numbers to the same number (called a benchmark). Here, compare both numbers to $6\frac{1}{2}$. (Remember: $\frac{1}{2} = \frac{5}{10}$.)

$6.8 = 6\frac{8}{10}$. Since $\frac{8}{10}$ is larger than $\frac{5}{10}$, 6.8 is larger than $6\frac{1}{2}$.

Since $\frac{3}{10}$ is smaller than $\frac{5}{10}$, $6\frac{3}{10}$ is smaller than $6\frac{1}{2}$.

So, 6.8 is larger than $6\frac{3}{10}$.

Another Way

• Place both numbers on a number line. The number farther to the right is larger.

6.8 is larger than $6\frac{3}{10}$.

✔ **Check for Understanding**

Which number is larger?

❶ 2.1 or $2\frac{9}{10}$ **❷** $6\frac{3}{10}$ or 5.9   **❸** 1.4 or $1\frac{7}{10}$

❹ $9\frac{1}{2}$ or 9.9   **❺** 4.6 or $4\frac{4}{10}$ **❻** $8\frac{1}{4}$ or 8.6

130 Chapter 8

Student Handbook p. 130

3 | Differentiated Instruction

Leveled Problem Solving

Luisa finished about half of her homework problems before dinner.

❶ Basic Level
Luisa did $\frac{4}{10}$ of the problems. How could you write what she did as a decimal? Explain. **either as 0.4 or 0.40; Possible explanation: 0.4 and 0.40 are equivalent to each other as well as to $\frac{4}{10}$.**

❷ On Level
Write a decimal and a fraction for the part of her homework that she could have done. **Possible answer: 0.3, $\frac{3}{10}$; Possible explanation: 0.3 is less than 0.5, and $\frac{3}{10}$ is the same as 0.3.**

❸ Above Level
She told a friend she had done $\frac{1}{3}$, or 0.3, of the problems. Do $\frac{1}{3}$ and 0.3 represent the same number? Explain. **No; $\frac{1}{3}$ means 1 out of 3 equal parts, and 0.3 means 3 out of 10 equal parts. $\frac{1}{3}$ of 10 is not 3.**

Intervention	Practice	Extension

Activity Equivalent Numbers

Draw a number line from 1 to 2 marked off in tenths. Label $1\frac{1}{10}$, $1\frac{3}{10}$, and $1\frac{9}{10}$ along the top. Label 1.1, 1.4, and 1.8 along the bottom. Have students fill in the missing fractions and decimals.

Ask students to identify pairs of equivalent fractions and decimals. Then have students compare pairs of the decimals and fractions.

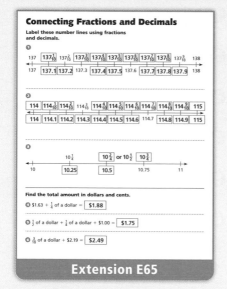

Practice P65

Extension E65

Spiral Review

Spiral Review Book page SR65 provides review of the following previously learned skills and concepts:

- classifying triangles as acute, right, or obtuse
- finding changes between temperatures

You may wish to have students work with a partner to complete the page.

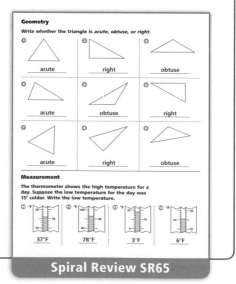

Spiral Review SR65

Extension Activity
Mixed-Up Sounds

Give a total of 10 different color cubes to each group. Have students write a decimal and a fraction to describe the part of the group that each color represents. Then give each group 1 more cube, and challenge them to do the same with 11 cubes. Discuss why decimals could be easily written for the first group but not for the second group. 11 is not a factor of 100, so 11 as a denominator does not translate into an exact decimal.

Teacher's Notes 🍎

Daily Notes . . .

Quick Notes

More Ideas

Lesson 6 Representing Decimals with Pictures

NCTM Standards 1, 2, 6, 7, 8, 9, 10

Lesson Planner

STUDENT OBJECTIVE ·
- To use a 10-by-10 grid to represent decimals

1 | Daily Activities (TG p. 635)

Open-Ended Problem Solving/Headline Story	Skills Practice and Review—Ordering Decimals

2 | Teach and Practice (TG pp. 636–639)

Ⓐ **Representing Tenths on a Grid** (TG p. 636)

Ⓑ **Representing Hundredths on a Grid** (TG pp. 637–638)

Ⓒ **Representing Decimals with Pictures** (TG p. 639)

MATERIALS

- TR: Activity Masters, AM76–AM77
- transparencies of AM76–AM77 (optional)
- 📖 LAB pp. 159–160

3 | Differentiated Instruction (TG p. 640)

Leveled Problem Solving (TG p. 640)	Practice Book P66
Intervention Activity (TG p. 640)	Extension Book E66
Extension Activity (TG p. 640)	Spiral Review Book SR66

Lesson Notes

About the Lesson

In the last lesson, students explored the relation between fractions and decimals. In this lesson they continue to explore this connection by visually representing decimals as they represented fractions in **Chapter 7.** Students use a 10-by-10 grid to represent 1, and then shade the grid to represent various decimals. These grid representations will help when students add and subtract decimals in later lessons.

In the next lesson, students use base-ten blocks. Students begin with grids rather than with blocks because they are used to a base-ten flat representing 100, not 1 whole. The grids help them transition to the new block values.

Use with Lesson Activity Book pp. 159–160.

Developing Mathematical Language

Vocabulary: grid

A *grid* is a pattern of horizontal and vertical lines. The lines intersect to form congruent squares. Ten-by-ten *grids* have 100 equal-size squares. Ten-by-ten *grids* can represent hundreds, or they can represent hundredths. When a section of a 10 × 10 *grid* is shaded, the shaded section can be thought of as a part of the whole. When modeling decimals, the *grid* can be used to represent hundredths. Each section is one hundredth of the whole.

Review the term *grid* with students.

Beginning Show students notebook paper and *grid* paper. Have them point to the *grid*.

Intermediate Have students describe how to make a *grid*, or have them draw one on the board.

Advanced Have students name *grids* that they have seen or know about. Students might suggest window panes, latitude and longitude lines, streets on a city map, floor or ceiling tiles, and other similar *grids*.

Open-Ended Problem Solving

Read the Headline Story to your students. Encourage them to think of interesting scenarios that incorporate information from the story.

 **Headline Story**

> **Lin found her favorite movie at the video store. It cost ____ dollars and ____ cents, but she had a coupon for 5 dollars off.**

Possible responses: If the video cost $12.50, Lin would have to pay $7.50 for the movie. If the video cost less than 5 dollars, Lin didn't have to pay anything for the movie. If Lin paid $6.25, the movie must have cost $11.25.

Skills Practice and Review

Ordering Decimals

As in the previous lesson, draw a number line on the board, marking as endpoints two consecutive whole numbers. Have students suggest various decimal numbers between these two; make sure some of numbers have 1 decimal place and some have two. Invite students to write the numbers on the board and to read them aloud. The class should check that the number the student reads is the same as the written number. Once you have about 10 numbers, ask students to order the numbers from smallest to biggest. Write the numbers in a column.

Sketch the above money amounts on the chalkboard. Have students read the amounts. Then have the class order the amounts from smallest to biggest.

whole class · 10 MIN

A Representing Tenths on a Grid

Materials

- For the teacher: transparency of AM76 (optional)

NCTM Standards 1, 2, 6, 7, 8, 9, 10

Purpose To use pictures of decimals to relate fractions and decimals and to understand the place value of the first digit to the right of the decimal point

Introduce Display the top of Activity Master: Grids for Shading or sketch a similar picture on the board. Shade a few columns in the grid.

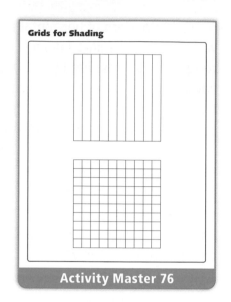

Grids for Shading

Activity Master 76

Problem Ask students to name the fraction that the picture represents. For example, if you shaded three columns, the corresponding fraction is $\frac{3}{10}$.

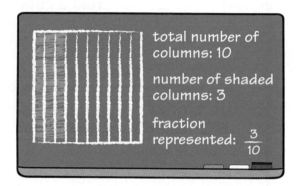

total number of columns: 10

number of shaded columns: 3

fraction represented: $\frac{3}{10}$

✔ **Ongoing Assessment**

- The Skills Practice and Review activity on the previous page provides you with an opportunity to assess students' understanding of the relative sizes of decimals. Try to keep this activity fast-paced so that every student has a chance to correctly place a decimal in an ordered list. You can see which students continue to have difficulty recognizing the values of the digits.

Next, ask students to name the decimal that the picture represents. If necessary, you might sketch a number line from 0 to 1 that is separated into ten pieces. Have a student mark where $\frac{3}{10}$ falls on this number line. Then ask students to use the number line to figure out the decimal that marks this same point (0.3), just as they did in the previous lesson.

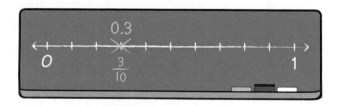

0.3

0      $\frac{3}{10}$ 1

Repeat this activity by shading different portions of the grid. When you think students are ready, ask them to write and read the decimal represented by the picture.

💬 **Talk Math**

❷ In a 10-column grid, every other column, beginning with Column 1, is shaded. What decimal does the grid represent? Explain your reasoning. 0.5; Possible explanation: 5 columns are shaded, so the grid represents five tenths, or 0.5.

❷ Brianna shaded a 10-column grid to represent 1. How did she shade the grid? She shaded all 10 columns, or the entire grid.

B **Representing Hundredths on a Grid**

whole class **20 MIN**

Purpose To represent tenths and hundredths on a grid

Introduce Display the bottom of Activity Master: Grids for Shading or sketch a similar picture on the board. Make sure that students understand that the grid has 100 squares. Shade the same portion of the grid that you shaded in Activity A (such as 0.3).

Problem **Ask students to write and read the decimal that the picture represents.** Students will likely recognize that although there are more grid lines in this picture than there were in the previous activity, the number of shaded columns remains unchanged. As a result, the decimal represented by the picture (0.3 or three tenths) remains unchanged as well.

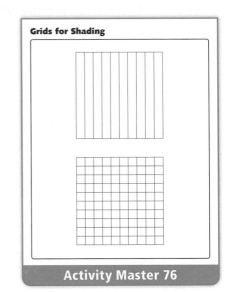

Grids for Shading

Activity Master 76

🗨 **Talk Math**

❓ What fraction, in tenths, is represented by the picture? Explain your reasoning. $\frac{3}{10}$; Possible explanation: There are 10 columns, so each column represents one tenth of the picture. Three of the columns are shaded, so 3 tenths of the picture are shaded.

❓ What fraction, in hundredths, is represented by the picture? Explain your reasoning. $\frac{30}{100}$; Possible explanation: There are 100 squares, so each square represents one hundredth of the picture. Thirty of the squares are shaded, so 30 hundredths of the picture are shaded.

Blank Grids

Activity Master 77

Share Ask students for ideas on how they can write a decimal to show that 30 hundredths of the grid are shaded. Help them to reason that 0.30 shows this. (See Possible Discussion.)

Problem **Now shade a portion of the grid with one column that is only partially shaded. Ask students to name the fraction and decimal represented by the picture.** For example, this grid represents $\frac{58}{100}$ or 0.58:

Materials
* For the teacher: transparency of AM76–AM77 (optional)
* For each student: TR: AM76–AM77

NCTM Standards 1, 2, 6, 7, 8, 9, 10

Possible Discussion

The grids in this lesson are intended to help students see why 0.3 and 0.30 are equivalent. In the lesson, you shade 3 of the tenths bars in a 10-column grid, then 30 of the hundredths squares (or 3 columns) in a 10 by 10 grid. Students write a decimal for each of these shadings. You might then have students describe what they notice about the two decimals. (They both describe the same portion of the grid and therefore must be equivalent.) Advanced students may even extend their discovery to equivalent fractions: the same portion of the grid is shaded in both instances, but the number of shaded pieces and the number of total pieces were scaled by the same number (10). Conclusion: $\frac{3}{10}$ and $\frac{30}{100}$ are equivalent fractions.

Use with Lesson Activity Book pp. 159–160.

If students don't make the connection, point out that of the 100 squares in the grid, 58 are shaded. So, 58 hundredths are shaded. Just as we regroup 10 ones into a group of ten, we group a full column here (representing 10 hundredths) into a group of tenths. When we write that amount as a decimal, we indicate 5 full columns by writing 5 in the tenths place; we indicate the 8 remaining squares by writing 8 in the hundredths place. So, the decimal is 0.58.

Repeat this activity for a few other examples, such as 16 squares (0.16), 81 squares (0.81), or 7 squares (0.07). If you have time and feel students are ready, ask them to use AM76: Blank Grids to represent decimals that you name. For example, you might ask students to shade their grids to represent 0.36, 0.06, 0.9, or 0.40.

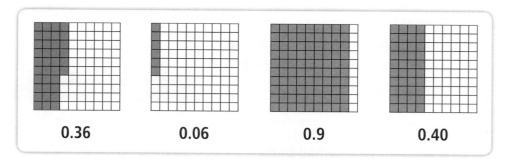

| 0.36 | 0.06 | 0.9 | 0.40 |

To provide additional practice, ask students to name the decimal that describes the part of a given grid that is *not* shaded. For example, in the first grid above, 0.36 is shaded and 0.64 is not shaded.

Students will have further opportunities to explore the place values of decimal digits on the LAB pages and in subsequent lessons. Don't expect mastery of these ideas yet.

Problem Read, Compare and Order Tenths and Hundredths Using Money

Provide students with dimes. Have them combine multiple groups of 2-9 dimes and read aloud the amounts as tenths. For example: For 2 dimes students would say two tenths and for 4 dimes the students would say 4 tenths. Have students choose two groups and compare them using the terms *is greater than, is less than* and *is equal to.* Then have students choose three groups of dimes and order the amounts from least to greatest and greatest to least. Repeat the activity with pennies and dimes having students say the amounts in hundredths. For example: For 3 dimes and 2 pennies students would say thirty-two hundredths and for 8 dimes and 6 pennies students would say eighty-six hundredths. Continue the activity having students compare two amounts and then compare and order three or more amounts.

Purpose To write decimals that represent shaded portions of grids

NCTM Standards 1, 2, 6, 7, 8, 9, 10

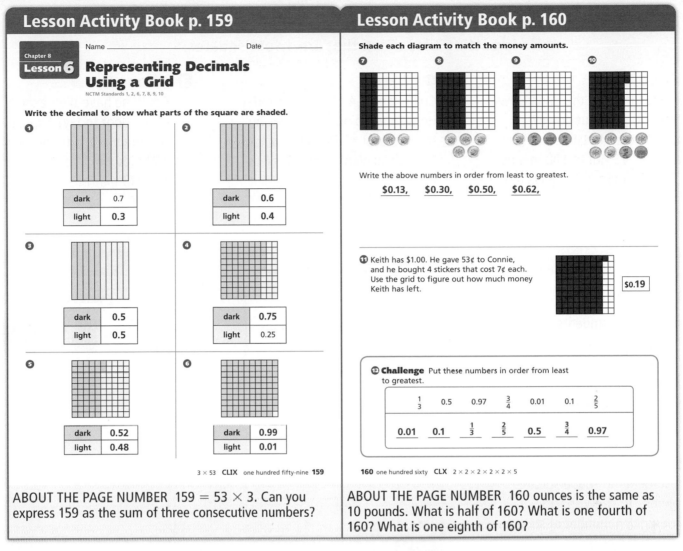

Lesson Activity Book p. 159

Chapter 8
Lesson 6 **Representing Decimals Using a Grid**
NCTM Standards 1, 2, 6, 7, 8, 9, 10

Write the decimal to show what parts of the square are shaded.

①	②
dark 0.7 / light 0.3	dark 0.6 / light 0.4
③	④
dark 0.5 / light 0.5	dark 0.75 / light 0.25
⑤	⑥
dark 0.52 / light 0.48	dark 0.99 / light 0.01

3 × 53 **CLIX** one hundred fifty-nine **159**

ABOUT THE PAGE NUMBER 159 = 53 × 3. Can you express 159 as the sum of three consecutive numbers?

Lesson Activity Book p. 160

Shade each diagram to match the money amounts.

⑦ ⑧ ⑨ ⑩

Write the above numbers in order from least to greatest.

$0.13, **$0.30,** **$0.50,** **$0.62,**

⑪ Keith has $1.00. He gave 53¢ to Connie, and he bought 4 stickers that cost 7¢ each. Use the grid to figure out how much money Keith has left.

$0.19

⑫ **Challenge** Put these numbers in order from least to greatest.

| $\frac{1}{3}$ | 0.5 | 0.97 | $\frac{3}{4}$ | 0.01 | 0.1 | $\frac{2}{5}$ |

| 0.01 | 0.1 | $\frac{1}{3}$ | $\frac{2}{5}$ | 0.5 | $\frac{3}{4}$ | 0.97 |

160 one hundred sixty **CLX** 2 × 2 × 2 × 2 × 2 × 5

ABOUT THE PAGE NUMBER 160 ounces is the same as 10 pounds. What is half of 160? What is one fourth of 160? What is one eighth of 160?

Teaching Notes for LAB page 159

Have students complete the page individually or with partners. LAB page 159 gives students more practice with writing decimals to match shaded parts of a grid. Some of the grids are cut into 10 pieces, while others are cut into 100 pieces.

Some students may notice that the decimals for the shaded and unshaded portions add to 1.

Teaching Notes for LAB page 160

Students shade grids to match given decimals and then order the decimals. They also use a grid to help them answer a question about money. For Problems 7–11, ask students to read the amounts represented on the grids as money amounts. For example, the Problem 7 grid represents thirty cents or thirty hundredths of a dollar. The Problem 11 grid represents nineteen cents or nineteen hundredths of a dollar.

Challenge Problem The Challenge problem asks students to order a collection of fractions and decimals from least to greatest.

Reflect and Summarize the Lesson

 Write Math

A grid contains 100 small squares. What decimal is represented when 40 of those squares are shaded? when 47 squares are shaded? when 100 squares are shaded? Explain your reasoning. 0.40; 0.47; 1; Possible explanations: Each square represents 1 hundredth of the grid. If 40 squares are shaded, 40 hundredths, or 0.40, are shaded. If 47 squares are shaded, 47 hundredths, or 0.47, are shaded. If 100 squares are shaded, one whole grid, or 1, is shaded.

Leveled Problem Solving

**Collin's kitchen floor is a square 10 feet on each side.
He is putting tiles down that are 1-foot squares.**

❶ Basic Level

Collin has tiled $\frac{3}{4}$ of the floor. How many tiles has he put down? Explain. 75 tiles; Possible explanation: 75 out of 100 means 0.75, or $\frac{75}{100}$, and $\frac{75}{100}$ is equivalent to $\frac{3}{4}$.

❷ On Level

Collin tiled 0.4 of the floor today. He wanted to do $\frac{3}{5}$ of it. Has he tiled at least $\frac{3}{5}$? Explain. No; Possible explanation: 0.4 is less than 0.5, or $\frac{1}{2}$; $\frac{3}{5}$ is greater than 0.5; so, he has done less than $\frac{3}{5}$.

❸ Above Level

Could he have tiled exactly $\frac{1}{3}$ of the floor today? Explain. No; There are 100 tiles, and $\frac{1}{3}$ of 100 tiles would be a little more than 33 tiles but not as much as 34 tiles.

Intervention	Practice	Extension

Activity Fill the Grid

Display and provide students with a 10 × 10 grid. Demonstrate how to shade one hundredth, or 0.01 of the grid. Have students shade the first column and tell what part is shaded. 0.10 Next, have students shade the top 4 squares in the second column and tell what part is shaded. 0.14 Continue by asking students to shade squares and fill columns to show specific decimals or a given number of squares until the grid is fully shaded.

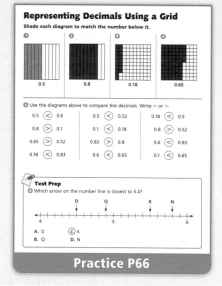

Practice P66

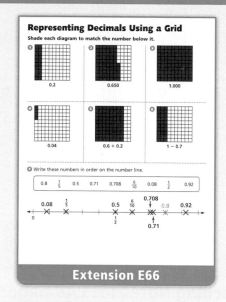

Extension E66

Spiral Review

Spiral Review Book page SR66 provides review of the following previously learned skills and concepts:

- writing fractions that are equivalent to one half
- solving problems using the strategy *make a table*

You many wish to have students work with a partner to complete the page.

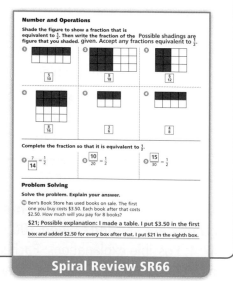

Spiral Review SR66

Extension Activity
The Last Hundredth

Give pairs of students a 10 × 10 grid. Have them play this game, and then discuss whether it is better to go first or last. Players take turns shading small squares, naming the amount they shade. A player may shade no more than 0.09 on a turn. The player who must shade the final small square loses the game. You may wish to have students vary the maximum number of squares to be shaded and discuss whether that changes any strategy they may have found.

Teacher's Notes 🍎

Daily Notes . . .

Quick Notes

Lesson 7 Representing Decimals Using Base-Ten Blocks

NCTM Standards 1, 2, 6, 7, 8, 9, 10

Lesson Planner

STUDENT OBJECTIVES
- To represent decimals using base-ten blocks
- To add and subtract decimals without regrouping using base-ten blocks

1 | Daily Activities (TG p. 643)

| Open-Ended Problem Solving/Headline Story | Skills Practice and Review—Reading and Writing Decimals |

2 | Teach and Practice (TG pp. 644–648)

MATERIALS

(A) **Representing Decimals with Blocks** (TG pp. 644–645)

(B) **Using Blocks to Model Addition and Subtraction of Decimals** (TG pp. 646–647)

(C) **Representing Decimals Using Base-Ten Blocks** (TG p. 648)

- base-ten blocks (2 flats, 10 rods, 10 cubes)
- 📖 LAB pp. 161–162
- 📖 SH p. 131

3 | Differentiated Instruction (TG p. 649)

Leveled Problem Solving (TG p. 649)	Practice Book P67
Intervention Activity (TG p. 649)	Extension Book E67
Extension Activity (TG p. 649)	Spiral Review Book SR67

Lesson Notes

About the Lesson

Students use base-ten blocks to represent decimals and to add and subtract decimals that have one or two digits after the decimal point. Base-ten blocks allow students to deepen their understanding of the relation between tenths and hundredths. Through their previous experiences with base-ten blocks, students know that 10 cubes equal 1 rod and that 10 rods (100 cubes) equal 1 flat. Students now assign the value of 1 to a flat (just as the 10-by-10 grids in the previous lesson had a value of 1). Consequently, each rod has a value of 0.1, or 1 tenth, and each small cube has a value of 0.01, or 1 hundredth. Students then use their understanding of how cubes relate to rods and flats to see that 10 hundredths equal 1 tenth, 10 tenths equal 1, and 100 hundredths equal 1.

About the Mathematics

Base-ten blocks, as their name suggests, were designed to mirror the base-ten system. The small cube, rod, flat, and big cube model four successive place values in the base-ten number system. However, the four place values they represent are flexible. Until now, students have used these blocks in the obvious way, using 1 small cube to represent 1, 10 small cubes as a rod to represent 10, 100 small cubes as a flat to represent

(continued on page R4)

Use with Lesson Activity Book pp. 161–162.

Developing Mathematical Language

Vocabulary: base-ten system

The *base-ten system* is a place value system in which numbers are expressed using the numerals 0 to 9 and successive powers of 10. Each successive place to the left and right of the ones place (10^0) indicates a multiple of a power of 10. This means each successive place to the left is 10 times greater than the preceding place. Each successive place to the right is one tenth (0.1) the preceding place. The numerals 0–9 and the powers of 10 can be used to generate all of the numbers in the *base-ten system*.

Review the term *base-ten system* with students.

Beginning Draw 10 tally marks on the board. Ask students to write the corresponding number in the *base-ten system*. Add 10 more tally marks and repeat.

Intermediate Write the following numbers on the board in a row: 1, 10, 100. Ask students to read each number. Discuss how the numbers are related in the the *base-ten system*. Elicit that 100 is 10 times 10, and 1,000 is 10 times 100.

Advanced List measures that do and do not represent the *base-ten system,* such as octaves, time, and liquid measures like cups, pints, quarts, and gallons. Have students identify those measures that represent the *base-ten system,* such as centimeters or liters.

Open-Ended Problem Solving

Read the Headline Story to your students. Encourage them to make creative statements using information from the story.

 Headline Story

Edward noticed that he has 43 hundredths of a dollar. He has fewer than 10 coins.

Sample responses: Edward has 43¢. He might have 4 dimes and 3 pennies. He might have 1 quarter, 3 nickels, and 3 pennies. He might have 1 quarter, 1 dime, 1 nickel, and 3 pennies. The fewest number of coins he could have is 6 coins. He must have 3 pennies.

Skills Practice and Review

Reading and Writing Decimals

Sketch a 10 × 10 grid and tell students that the whole grid represents 1. Shade in some of the grid and ask them to write the decimal for the amount shaded. Ask a student to come to the board and write the amount; the whole class can read the number and agree (or disagree) that the number correctly represents the shaded amount. Students may correctly read the number in several ways. If, for example, you shade in 6 columns and 5 extra cells, students may correctly read the number as "sixty-five hundredths," "six tenths and five hundredths," or "point six five." Repeat with several other numbers, using both tenths and hundredths. Finally, ask students to read and write the amounts represented by models of dollar amounts that you sketch on the chalkboard. For example, if you draw 4 dimes and 3 pennies, students may read "forty-three cents" or "forty-three hundredths of a dollar," and write $0.43. Include some amounts in tenths of a dollar, such as 2 dimes (twenty cents or two tenths of a dollar).

2 | Teach and Practice

pairs ⏱ 15 MIN

A Representing Decimals with Blocks

Materials

• For each student: base-ten blocks (2 flats, 10 rods, 10 cubes)

NCTM Standards 1, 2, 6, 7, 8, 9, 10

✔ Ongoing Assessment

• Do students demonstrate an understanding that when the value of a base-ten flat is 1, the value of a rod is 0.1 ($\frac{1}{10}$), and the value of a cube is 0.01 ($\frac{1}{100}$)?

Purpose To use base-ten blocks to represent whole numbers, tenths, and hundredths

Introduce Give each student a copy of Explore: Representing Decimals with Blocks. Each pair of students will also need a supply of base-ten blocks. Remind students that in the last lesson they used grids to represent decimals. Now they will use base-ten blocks for the same purpose.

Task Have students work with partners to complete the Explore page. As students work on the page, check in with each pair to make sure they were able to answer the first two questions about the value of the rod and the cube. If necessary, place ten rods on the flat to help students reason that each rod is one tenth ($\frac{1}{10}$, 0.1) of the flat. Similarly, you might ask students how many cubes make up a flat to help them see that each cube is worth one hundredth ($\frac{1}{100}$) of the flat.

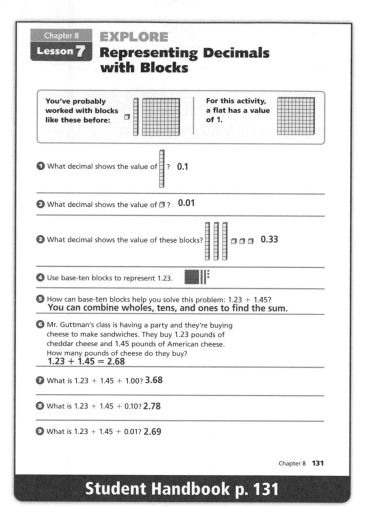

Student Handbook p. 131

❶ What decimal shows the value of a rod? 0.1

❷ What decimal shows the value of a cube? 0.01

❸ What decimal shows the value of

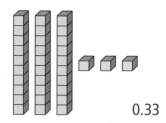

0.33

4 Use base-ten blocks to represent 1.23.

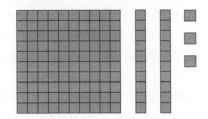

5 How can base-ten blocks help you solve this problem: 1.23 + 1.45?
You can combine wholes, tens, and ones to find the sum.

6 Mr. Guttman's class is having a party and they're buying cheese to make sandwiches. They buy 1.23 pounds of cheddar cheese and 1.45 pounds of American cheese. How many pounds of cheese do they buy?
1.23 + 1.45 = 2.68

7 What is 1.23 + 1.45 + 1.00? 3.68

8 What is 1.23 + 1.45 + 0.10? 2.78

9 What is 1.23 + 1.45 + 0.01? 2.69

Share Once students have had a chance to work through the page, have them share their answers. As they do so, make sure they understand that the rod represents the tenths digit of a decimal and that the cube represents the hundredths digit. This is emphasized by Problems 6, 7, and 8, where students determine the new decimal when only a flat, a rod, or a cube is added to a number. As part of the next activity, students will discuss their strategies for adding the decimals at the bottom of the page.

Talk Math

? How many base-ten cubes would you need to represent the number represented by 6 rods? Explain your reasoning. 60; Possible explanation: Each rod represents 10 cubes, so 6 rods represent 6 × 10 = 60 cubes.

? How many base-ten rods would you need to represent the number represented by 6 flats? Explain your reasoning. 60; Possible explanation: Each flat represents 10 rods, so 6 flats represent 6 × 10 = 60 rods.

B Using Blocks to Model Addition and Subtraction of Decimals

Materials

- For each student: base-ten blocks (2 flats, 10 rods, 10 cubes)

NCTM Standards 1, 2, 6, 7, 8, 9, 10

Purpose To explore addition and subtraction of decimals

Introduce At the bottom of the Activity A Explore page, students are asked to add decimals. As you begin your discussion of students' strategies for solving these problems, mention the context for the problems. Problem 6 (1.23 + 1.45) is about making a purchase of two items weighing 1.23 pounds and 1.45 pounds. Problem 7 (1.23 + 1.45 + 1.00) could be about the combined purchase of three items in a grocery store.

Share Have students share their strategies for solving the problems. Most students probably combined their models of the addends, then translated the results into decimals. So (Problem 6), they might have combined the blocks representing 1.23 and 1.45, obtaining 2 flats, 6 rods, and 8 cubes. This represents the decimal 2.68.

To help students prepare for subtracting decimals, ask them to give a number sentence that describes removing 1 flat, 4 rods, and 5 cubes from 2 flats, 6 rods, and 8 cubes. Students should see that 2.68 − 1.45 = 1.23 does this. If students don't mention that these two number sentences are members of the same fact family, point it out, for it may provide students with a strategy for completing other sums or differences of decimals.

Problem Now write on the board a subtraction problem that does not involve decomposing a tenth into 10 hundredths. Ask students to use base-ten blocks to model and solve the problem.

For example, write 0.82 − 0.40 = _____. Students should represent the larger decimal with base-ten blocks and then remove blocks that represent the number being subtracted. The remaining blocks are the difference.

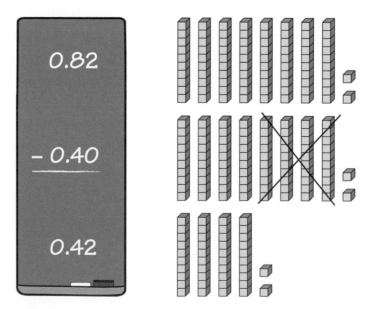

So, 0.82 − 0.40 = 0.42.

Use with Lesson Activity Book pp. 161–162.

Practice If you have time, ask students to work in pairs to solve a few more addition and subtraction problems. Include examples like $0.53 - 0.2 = $ _____, where one number has tenths and hundredths digits while the other number has only a tenths digit. For now, avoid problems that require regrouping. Students will focus on regrouping in the next two lessons.

Talk Math

❷ What number sentence describes removing 2 flats, 3 rods, and 7 cubes from 3 flats, 7 rods, and 9 cubes? $3.79 - 2.37 = 1.42$

❷ What number sentence describes adding 1 flat, 5 rods, and 4 cubes to 2 flats, 3 rods, and 4 cubes? $1.54 + 2.34 = 3.88$

C Representing Decimals Using Base-Ten Blocks LAB pp. 161–162

individuals or pairs

 20 MIN

Purpose To practice using tenths and hundredths

NCTM Standards 1, 2, 6, 7, 8, 9, 10

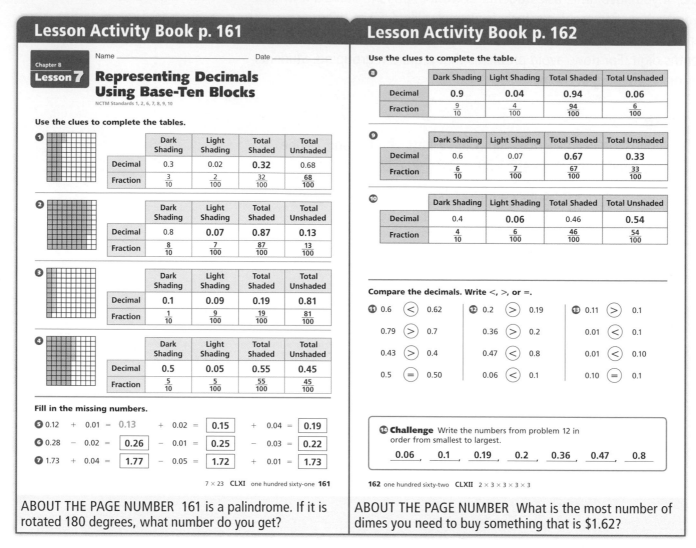

Lesson Activity Book p. 161

Name _____ Date _____

Chapter 8
Lesson 7 Representing Decimals Using Base-Ten Blocks
NCTM Standards 1, 2, 6, 7, 8, 9, 10

Use the clues to complete the tables.

1

	Dark Shading	Light Shading	Total Shaded	Total Unshaded
Decimal	0.3	0.02	**0.32**	0.68
Fraction	$\frac{3}{10}$	$\frac{2}{100}$	$\frac{32}{100}$	$\frac{68}{100}$

2

	Dark Shading	Light Shading	Total Shaded	Total Unshaded
Decimal	0.8	**0.07**	**0.87**	**0.13**
Fraction	$\frac{8}{10}$	$\frac{7}{100}$	$\frac{87}{100}$	$\frac{13}{100}$

3

	Dark Shading	Light Shading	Total Shaded	Total Unshaded
Decimal	0.1	0.09	0.19	0.81
Fraction	$\frac{1}{10}$	$\frac{9}{100}$	$\frac{19}{100}$	$\frac{81}{100}$

4

	Dark Shading	Light Shading	Total Shaded	Total Unshaded
Decimal	0.5	0.05	0.55	0.45
Fraction	$\frac{5}{10}$	$\frac{5}{100}$	$\frac{55}{100}$	$\frac{45}{100}$

Fill in the missing numbers.

5 $0.12 + 0.01 = 0.13 + 0.02 = \boxed{0.15} + 0.04 = \boxed{0.19}$

6 $0.28 - 0.02 = \boxed{0.26} - 0.01 = \boxed{0.25} - 0.03 = \boxed{0.22}$

7 $1.73 + 0.04 = \boxed{1.77} - 0.05 = \boxed{1.72} + 0.01 = \boxed{1.73}$

7 × 23 **CLXI** one hundred sixty-one **161**

ABOUT THE PAGE NUMBER 161 is a palindrome. If it is rotated 180 degrees, what number do you get?

Lesson Activity Book p. 162

Use the clues to complete the table.

8

	Dark Shading	Light Shading	Total Shaded	Total Unshaded
Decimal	0.9	0.04	0.94	0.06
Fraction	$\frac{9}{10}$	$\frac{4}{100}$	$\frac{94}{100}$	$\frac{6}{100}$

9

	Dark Shading	Light Shading	Total Shaded	Total Unshaded
Decimal	0.6	0.07	**0.67**	**0.33**
Fraction	$\frac{6}{10}$	$\frac{7}{100}$	$\frac{67}{100}$	$\frac{33}{100}$

10

	Dark Shading	Light Shading	Total Shaded	Total Unshaded
Decimal	0.4	**0.06**	0.46	**0.54**
Fraction	$\frac{4}{10}$	$\frac{6}{100}$	$\frac{46}{100}$	$\frac{54}{100}$

Compare the decimals. Write <, >, or =.

11 $0.6 < 0.62$ **12** $0.2 > 0.19$ **13** $0.11 > 0.1$

$0.79 > 0.7$ $0.36 > 0.2$ $0.01 < 0.1$

$0.43 > 0.4$ $0.47 < 0.8$ $0.01 < 0.10$

$0.5 = 0.50$ $0.06 < 0.1$ $0.10 = 0.1$

14 Challenge Write the numbers from problem 12 in order from smallest to largest.

0.06 , 0.1 , 0.19 , 0.2 , 0.36 , 0.47 , 0.8

162 one hundred sixty-two **CLXII** 2 × 3 × 3 × 3 × 3

ABOUT THE PAGE NUMBER What is the most number of dimes you need to buy something that is $1.62?

Teaching Notes for LAB page 161

Have students work on the page individually or with partners. The page combines many of the ideas students have been working on during this chapter. It is intended to prepare students for adding and subtracting tenths and hundredths in upcoming lessons. Problems 1–4 focus on decomposing numbers into tenths and hundredths as students write the numbers in both fraction and decimal form. The problems at the bottom of the page give students practice with simple additions and subtractions of tenths and hundredths.

Teaching Notes for LAB page 162

The top of the page presents problems like those on the previous page. Students are asked to decompose numbers into tenths and hundredths and to write them in both fraction and decimal form. Students solve these problems without the aid of grids, motivating them to begin to think more abstractly about tenths and hundredths. However, students may use base-ten blocks to represent each number concretely if they need them.

Challenge Problem The Challenge problem asks students to order the numbers in Problem 12. Since 0.2 appears twice in the problem, students order seven numbers.

Reflect and Summarize the Lesson

 Write Math What number sentence describes adding 1 flat, 4 rods, and 2 cubes to 1 flat, 3 rods, and 6 cubes? $1.42 + 1.36 = 2.78$

Use with Lesson Activity Book pp. 161–162.

3 | Differentiated Instruction

Leveled Problem Solving

A chef has 1.58 pounds of flour.

1 Basic Level

The chef makes a cake using 1 pound of flour. How much flour is left? Explain. 0.58 pound; Possible explanation: 1.58 − 1 = 0.58, or 1.58 − 1.00 = 0.58.

2 On Level

The chef makes some cookies using $\frac{1}{2}$ pound of flour. How much flour is left? Explain. 1.08 pounds; Possible explanation: 1.58 − 0.5 = 1.08.

3 Above Level

The chef makes pizza dough using $1\frac{1}{2}$ pounds of flour. How much flour is left? Explain. 0.08 pounds; Possible explanation: 1.58 − 1.5 = 0.08 or 1.58 − 1.50 = 0.08.

Intervention

Activity Squares, Lines, and Xs

Have students use squares, lines, and Xs to represent decimal blocks:

$$\square = 1 \qquad | = 0.1 \qquad \times = 0.01$$

Then have students draw squares, lines, and Xs to find each of the following sums and differences:

1.2 + 1.4 2.6

2.11 + 1.35 3.46

3.4 − 1.1 2.3

2.53 − 1.21 1.32

Practice

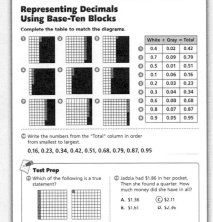

Practice P67

Extension

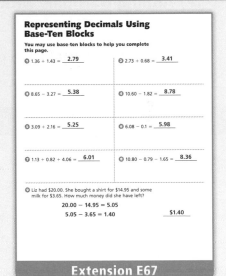

Extension E67

Spiral Review

Spiral Review Book page SR67 provides review of the following previously learned skills and concepts:

- using patterns to develop strategies for learning multiplication facts
- exploring congruence as a way to verify area

You may wish to have students work with a partner to complete the page.

Spiral Review SR67

Extension Activity
New Unit

Have small groups of students model various numbers of tenths and hundredths, using the flat to represent 0.1 and the rod to represent 0.01. For example, to model 0.83, they would show 8 flats and 3 rods.

When students are comfortable with the new unit model, have them quiz one another with numbers of their own choice.

Lesson 8 Adding Decimals

NCTM Standards 1, 2, 6, 7, 8, 9, 10

Lesson Planner

STUDENT OBJECTIVES
- To add decimal numbers
- To write addition and subtraction fact teams involving decimal numbers

1 Daily Activities (TG p. 651)

| Open-Ended Problem Solving/Headline Story | Skills Practice and Review— Reading Decimals |

2 Teach and Practice (TG pp. 652–655)

	MATERIALS
ⓐ **Adding Decimals with Base-Ten Blocks** (TG pp. 652–653)	• base-ten blocks (2 flats, 12 rods, 20 cubes)
ⓑ **Adding Decimals** (TG p. 654)	• 3 pieces of paper or cardstock
ⓒ **Making a Fact Family** (TG p. 655)	• 📖 LAB pp. 163–164 • 📖 SH p. 132

3 Differentiated Instruction (TG p. 656)

Leveled Problem Solving (TG p. 656)	Practice Book P68
Intervention Activity (TG p. 656)	Extension Book E68
Extension Activity (TG p. 656)	Spiral Review Book SR68

Lesson Notes

About the Lesson

In the previous lesson, students performed simple additions and subtractions of decimals involving only tenths or only hundredths. In this lesson, students continue to add decimals and begin to regroup hundredths, tenths, and wholes. They continue to use base-ten blocks to illustrate addition and to help with regrouping. In the next lesson students will regroup to subtract decimals.

About the Mathematics

Like whole numbers, decimals and fractions can be used to create fact families. For example:

- Addition and subtraction are inverse operations. Just as the number sentence $2 + 3 = 5$ tells us that $5 - 3 = 2$, the number sentence $1.67 + 2.58 = 4.25$ tells us that $4.25 - 2.58 = 1.67$.
- The order of the addends doesn't affect the sum. Just as $3 + 4 = 4 + 3$, $2.59 + 10.82 = 10.82 + 2.59$.

Use with Lesson Activity Book pp. 163–164.

Developing Mathematical Language

Vocabulary: decimal sums, sum

A *sum* is the result of the addition of numbers. Place-value models, diagrams, or place-value charts can be used to help compute *decimal sums.* As with whole numbers, it is important to align place values before adding and to regroup when necessary. Lining up the decimal points in addends helps one recognize like place values. The decimal point must also be recorded in the *sum.*

Review the terms *sum* and *decimal sums* with students.

Beginning Have students add 2 and 2. Ask them what the *sum* is. Then talk about what they think *decimal sums* are—the answer when you add decimals.

Intermediate Have students write an addition fact and circle the *sum.* Have students use a 10-by-10 grid to represent a *decimal sum.*

Advanced Have students describe the difference between a *sum* and a *decimal sum.*

Open-Ended Problem Solving

Read the Headline Story to your students. Encourage them to use logical reasoning to draw conclusions about Joe's hikes.

 Headline Story

> Joe hiked 2.7 miles before lunch. After lunch, he hiked 2.56 miles. Tomorrow he will hike 5. ____ more miles.

Possible responses: He hiked 5.26 miles today. He hiked 0.14 more miles before lunch than he did after lunch. He hiked more than two-and-a-half miles both before and after lunch. He hiked fewer than three miles both before and after lunch. If he hikes the same distance tomorrow, he will hike a total of 10.52 miles. If he hikes 5.02 miles tomorrow, he will have hiked a shorter distance than he hiked today.

Skills Practice and Review

Reading Decimals

Write a three-digit number on the board and ask students to read it aloud. Then place a decimal point somewhere in the number and ask students to read the number again. Continue to move the decimal point in the number until it has been placed in every possible position. For example, if the number is 123, you can write .123, 1.23, or 12.3. Ask students how they would build 1.23 and 12.3 with base-ten blocks. Hold up the blocks as students describe the numbers. Ask students to order the numbers from smallest to largest. Say which is bigger. Repeat this activity with a three-digit number that contains a zero, such as 401 or 520, inviting students to build the numbers that have one or two decimal places. Finally, write money amounts such as $2.60 and $4.73. Ask students to read the amounts and to represent the amounts using play money.

pairs · 20 MIN

A Adding Decimals with Base-Ten Blocks

Materials
- For each student: base-ten blocks (2 flats, 12 rods, 20 cubes)

NCTM Standards 1, 2, 6, 7, 8, 9, 10

✓ **Ongoing Assessment**

- Do students understand that addition of decimals with base-ten blocks is similar to whole number addition with blocks? Just as students would trade in 10 cubes for 1 rod when the cubes represented 1 and the rods represented 10, they trade 10 cubes for 1 rod when the cubes represent hundredths and the rods represent tenths. Students might be encouraged by the fact that they have already explored strategies for adding with base-ten blocks. This may increase their confidence when computing with decimals. However, watch for students who fall back into the more familiar process and record their answers as whole numbers instead of decimals. You may need to remind students several times throughout the lesson that they are working with decimals and that the flat now represents 1, not 100.

Purpose To explore addition of decimals

Introduce See that each student has a copy of Explore: Adding Decimals with Blocks. Each pair of students will also need a supply of base-ten blocks. Remind students of the process they used in the last lesson, when they combined block representations of decimals to find decimal sums. In this activity, they will extend the process to sums whose representations have more than ten cubes or rods. Students will need to trade blocks in order to minimize the numbers of flats, rods, and small cubes in their sums.

Task Have students work with partners to complete the Explore page.

Before students begin, be sure they understand the process of trading:

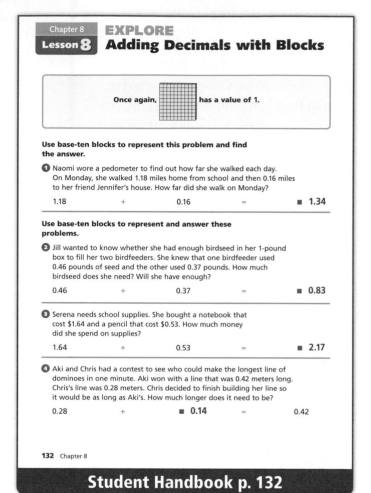

Student Handbook p. 132

If you have 10 cubes, trade them for 1 rod.

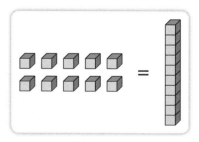

If you have 10 rods, trade them for 1 flat.

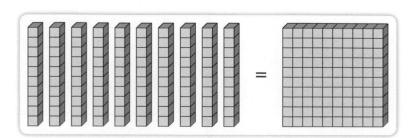

Use with Lesson Activity Book pp. 163–164.

Share After students have completed their work, bring them together to discuss their strategies for solving the problems.

❶ $1.18 + 0.16 = 1.34$

When 8 cubes in 1.18 are added to 6 cubes in 0.16, the result is 14 cubes. Students should trade 10 of the 14 cubes for 1 rod, leaving 4 cubes. The sum is 1 flat, 3 rods, and 4 cubes, or 1.34.

❷ $0.46 + 0.37 = 0.83$

When 6 cubes in 0.46 are added to 7 cubes in 0.37, the result is 13 cubes. Students should trade 10 of the 13 cubes for 1 rod, leaving 3 cubes. The sum is 0 flats, 8 rods, and 3 cubes, or 0.83.

❸ $1.64 + 0.53 = 2.17$

When 6 rods in 1.64 are added to 5 rods in 0.53, the result is 11 rods. Students should trade 10 of the 11 rods for 1 flat, leaving 1 rod. The sum is 2 flats, 1 rod, and 7 cubes, or 2.17.

❹ $0.28 + 0.14 = 0.42$

A common strategy for solving problems like this is to count on from the first addend until reaching the sum. For example, students might have modeled 0.28 with 2 rods and 8 cubes. Then they could add 1 rod to represent 0.38. Adding another rod would result in 0.48, which is too much, so students should use cubes to add hundredths until they reach 0.42.

Talk Math

❓ Marcus used base-ten blocks to add two decimals. The sum was 1 flat, 15 rods, 9 cubes. What was the sum, written as a decimal? Explain your reasoning. 2.59; Possible explanation: I traded 10 of the 15 rods for 1 flat, with 5 rods left over. I added the new flat to the one that I already had. The result was 2 flats, 5 rods, and 9 cubes, which represents 2.59.

❓ Val used base-ten blocks to add two decimals. The sum was 1 flat, 8 rods, 17 cubes. What was the sum, written as a decimal? Explain your reasoning. 1.97; Possible explanation: I traded 10 of the 17 cubes for 1 rod, with 7 cubes left over. I added the new rod to the 8 that I already had. The result was 1 flat, 9 rods, 7 cubes, which represents 1.97.

individuals or pairs

20 MIN

Purpose To practice addition of decimals

NCTM Standards 1, 2, 6, 7, 8, 9, 10

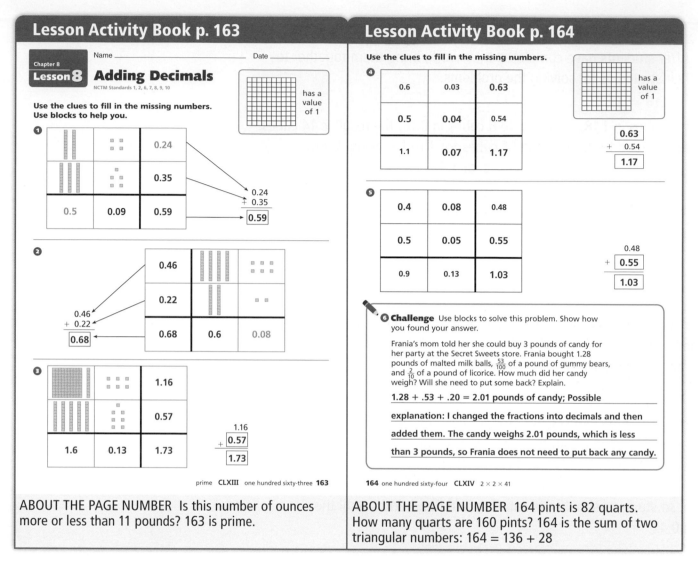

Lesson Activity Book p. 163

Chapter 8
Lesson 8 **Adding Decimals**
NCTM Standards 1, 2, 6, 7, 8, 9, 10

Name _____ Date _____

Use the clues to fill in the missing numbers.
Use blocks to help you.

has a value of 1

❶
		0.24
		0.35
0.5	0.09	0.59

  0.24
+ 0.35
  0.59

❷
0.46		
0.22		
0.68	0.6	0.08

  0.46
+ 0.22
  0.68

❸
		1.16
		0.57
1.6	0.13	1.73

  1.16
+ 0.57
  1.73

prime **CLXIII** one hundred sixty-three **163**

Lesson Activity Book p. 164

Use the clues to fill in the missing numbers.

has a value of 1

❹
0.6	0.03	0.63
0.5	0.04	0.54
1.1	0.07	1.17

  0.63
+ 0.54
  1.17

❺
0.4	0.08	0.48
0.5	0.05	0.55
0.9	0.13	1.03

  0.48
+ 0.55
  1.03

❻ **Challenge** Use blocks to solve this problem. Show how you found your answer.

Frania's mom told her she could buy 3 pounds of candy for her party at the Secret Sweets store. Frania bought 1.28 pounds of malted milk balls, $\frac{53}{100}$ of a pound of gummy bears, and $\frac{2}{10}$ of a pound of licorice. How much did her candy weigh? Will she need to put some back? Explain.

1.28 + .53 + .20 = 2.01 pounds of candy; Possible

explanation: I changed the fractions into decimals and then

added them. The candy weighs 2.01 pounds, which is less

than 3 pounds, so Frania does not need to put back any candy.

164 one hundred sixty-four **CLXIV** 2 × 2 × 41

ABOUT THE PAGE NUMBER Is this number of ounces more or less than 11 pounds? 163 is prime.

ABOUT THE PAGE NUMBER 164 pints is 82 quarts. How many quarts are 160 pints? 164 is the sum of two triangular numbers: 164 = 136 + 28

Teaching Notes for LAB page 163

Have students complete the page individually or with partners. Students are encouraged to add tenths and hundredths separately as they find decimal sums. Drawings of base-ten blocks are provided to help students complete the additions.

The problems on the page gradually increase in difficulty. Problems 1 and 2 do not require regrouping, but Problem 3 does.

Teaching Notes for LAB page 164

Problems 4 and 5 require regrouping. No drawings of base-ten blocks are provided on this page, but if students want to use base-ten blocks to help solve the problems, they should be encouraged to do so.

Challenge Problem The Challenge Problem requires students to translate fractions into decimals before performing their calculations.

C Making a Fact Family

Purpose To relate decimal addition and subtraction

Introduce In preparation for **Lesson 8.9:** Subtracting Decimals, this activity will help students relate decimal addition and subtraction through the use of a fact family for a decimal addition sentence. The activity will also help students see that decimals behave like other numbers. Choose an addition problem from earlier in this lesson, for example 1.18 + 0.16 = 1.34, from Explore: Adding Decimals with Blocks. Write the numbers on three large cards or pieces of paper, one number to a card. Ask three students to hold the cards up in front of the class. Line up the students in any order.

Task **Ask the class to think of a number sentence that could be written using the numbers in the order they see them.** For example, if the numbers were ordered 0.16, 1.18, 1.34, students could suggest the number sentence 0.16 + 1.18 = 1.34. Record the sentence on the board. Then ask three new students to hold the cards and to stand in a different order. Again, have the class think of a number sentence for the arrangement.

Repeat this activity until the class has found all four sentences in the fact family for the three numbers. You might point out that more than one number sentence is possible for some of the arrangements, depending on the location of the equal sign. For example, if the numbers were ordered 1.34, 1.18, and 0.16, students could suggest either 1.34 − 1.18 = 0.16 or 1.34 = 1.18 + 0.16. Of course, 1.18 + 0.16 = 1.34 is equivalent to 1.34 = 1.18 + 0.16. The two sentences should be considered as one member of the fact family.

Note that not all arrangements will yield fact family members. In this example, students will not be able to make a number sentence from 1.18, 1.34, and 0.16.

 Talk Math

❷ What fact family can you write using the numbers 0.56, 0.15, and 0.41?

0.41 + 0.15 = 0.56	0.56 − 0.15 = 0.41
0.15 + 0.41 = 0.56	0.56 − 0.41 = 0.15

❷ What number sentence can you write using the numbers 1.84, 0.43, and 1.41 in the order they are written here? 1.84 − 0.43 = 1.41 or 1.84 = 0.43 + 1.41

❷ What subtraction problem can you write using the same numbers that appear in the addition problem 1.56 + 0.23 = 1.79? 1.79 − 1.56 = 0.23 or 1.79 − 0.23 = 1.56

Materials
• For the teacher: 3 pieces of paper or cardstock

NCTM Standards 1, 2, 6, 7, 8, 9, 10

Reflect and Summarize the Lesson

Write Math **Find the sum of 1.43 and 0.85 and explain your reasoning.** 2.28; Possible explanation: I added 1 flat, 4 rods, 3 cubes to 8 rods, 5 cubes, to obtain a total of 1 flat, 12 rods, 8 cubes. I traded 10 of the 12 rods for 1 flat, with 2 rods left over. I now had 1 + 1 = 2 flats. The final sum was 2 flats, 2 rods, 8 cubes, which represented 2.28.

Leveled Problem Solving

The Bright Angel trail is 0.8 kilometers long.
Cape Final Trail is 6.4 kilometers long.

❶ Basic Level

If you hike both trails, how far will you have hiked? Explain. 7.2 km; 6.4 + 0.8 = 7.2.

❷ On Level

If you hike 3.5 kilometers of Cape Final Trail before lunch, how far will you have to hike after lunch? Explain. 2.9 km; 6.4 − 3.5 = 2.9.

❸ Above Level

If you hike 9.3 kilometers in all, how much more than the length of both trails have you hiked? Explain. 2.1 km; 0.8 + 6.4 = 7.2; 9.3 − 7.2 = 2.1.

Intervention

Activity Picturing Addition

☐ = 1 | = 0.1   ✗ = 0.01

Have students draw pictures of squares, lines, and Xs to find these sums:

1.23 + 1.45 2.68   1.57 + 3.92 5.49

2.16 + 1.38 3.54   1.73 + 1.68 3.41

Remind students to regroup as needed. Discuss how the drawings help them find the sums.

Practice

Adding Decimals
Compare. Write <, >, or =.

① 1.34 < 1.4	② 0.6 + 0.5 > 1	③ 1.3 + 0.07 < 1.6 + 0.04
④ 0.08 < 0.3	⑤ 0.3 + 0.6 < 1	⑥ 2.6 + 0.01 < 2.6 + 0.05
⑦ 0.4 = 0.40	⑧ 0.92 + 0.37 > 1	⑨ 3.8 + 0.02 > 1.8 + 0.02
⑩ 0.61 < 0.9	⑪ 0.29 + 0.18 < 1	⑫ 1.7 + 0.05 < 1.9 + 0.04
⑬ 0.95 < 1.06	⑭ 0.38 + 0.62 = 1	⑮ 0.9 + 0.08 < 3.1 + 0.06
⑯ 2.70 = 2.7	⑰ 0.59 + 0.54 > 1	⑱ 0.3 + 0.04 = 0.2 + 0.14
⑲ 0.88 < 1.3	⑳ 0.72 + 0.16 < 1	㉑ 0.6 + 0.09 > 0.3 + 0.07

Test Prep

㉒ If ▦ is worth 1, which decimal is represented by the model? Explain your reasoning.

1.3; Possible explanation: The first square is worth 1. Three of the 10 columns in the second square are shaded, so it is worth three-tenths. Total: 1.3.

Practice P68

Extension

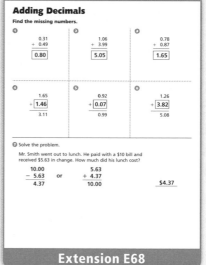

Adding Decimals
Find the missing numbers.

①
| 0.31 + 0.49 = 0.80 | 1.06 + 3.99 = 5.05 | 0.78 + 0.87 = 1.65 |

②
| 1.65 + 1.46 = 3.11 | 0.92 + 0.07 = 0.99 | 1.26 + 3.82 = 5.08 |

③ Solve the problem.
Mr. Smith went out to lunch. He paid with a $10 bill and received $5.63 in change. How much did his lunch cost?

10.00 − 5.63 = 4.37   or   5.63 + 4.37 = 10.00 $4.37

Extension E68

Spiral Review

Spiral Review Book page SR68 provides review of the following previously learned skills and concepts:

- multiplying 2-digit numbers by multiples of 10
- reading and interpreting bar graphs

You may wish to have students work with a partner to complete the page.

Number and Operations
Find the product.

① 26 × 10 = 260	② 51 × 20 = 1,020	③ 78 × 40 = 3,120	④ 17 × 60 = 1,020
⑤ 41 × 30 = 1,230	⑥ 55 × 10 = 550	⑦ 87 × 70 = 6,090	⑧ 82 × 90 = 7,380
⑨ 93 × 50 = 4,650	⑩ 15 × 40 = 600	⑪ 67 × 70 = 4,690	⑫ 62 × 30 = 1,860
⑬ 48 × 90 = 4,320	⑭ 91 × 40 = 3,640	⑮ 59 × 60 = 3,540	⑯ 77 × 80 = 6,160

Data Analysis and Probability
For 17–19, use the bar graph. It shows the results of a class survey.

⑰ How much greater is the total number of students who went to the movies than the number who did not go at all?
12

⑱ How many more students went to the movies once than went three or more times?
2

⑲ There are 27 students in the class. How many of them did NOT take part in the survey?
7 students

HOW MANY TIMES HAVE YOU GONE TO THE MOVIES THIS MONTH?

(bar graph: Number of Students vs Number of Times — None, Once, Twice, Three or more)

Spiral Review SR68

Extension Activity
Decimal Families

Have pairs of students create decimal fact families by generating decimal numbers with number cubes. Each student rolls a number cube three times—the first result represents a whole number, the second a number of tenths, and the third a number of hundredths. Have students work together to write two addition sentences and two subtraction sentences that make a fact family for their numbers.

Use with Lesson Activity Book pp. 163–164.

Teacher's Notes 🍎

Daily Notes . . .

Quick Notes

More Ideas

Lesson 9 Subtracting Decimals

NCTM Standards 1, 2, 6, 7, 8, 9, 10

Lesson Planner

STUDENT OBJECTIVES
- To subtract decimals
- To add and subtract decimals in the context of finding distances

1 Daily Activities (TG p. 659)

Open-Ended Problem Solving/Headline Story	**Skills Practice and Review**—Comparing and Ordering Decimals with Base-Ten Blocks

2 Teach and Practice (TG pp. 660–664)

MATERIALS

A Subtracting Decimals With Base-Ten Blocks (TG pp. 660–661)	• TR: Activity Master, AM78
	• transparency of AM78 (optional)
B Subtracting Decimals (TG p. 662)	• base-ten blocks (1 flat, 15 rods, 20 cubes)
	• grid paper
C Finding Distances (TG pp. 663–664)	• 📖 LAB pp. 165–166
	• 📖 SH p. 133

3 Differentiated Instruction (TG p. 665)

Leveled Problem Solving (TG p. 665)	**Practice Book P69**
Intervention Activity (TG p. 665)	**Extension Book E69**
Extension Activity (TG p. 665)	**Spiral Review Book SR69**

Lesson Notes

About the Lesson

Students continue to develop their understanding of decimals and place value as they begin subtracting decimals that require decomposing 1 whole into 10 tenths or 1 tenth into 10 hundredths. Students use base-ten blocks to model the subtractions and to aid with regrouping. At the end of the lesson, students apply decimals to the problem of finding distances between towns.

Use with Lesson Activity Book pp. 165–166.

Developing Mathematical Language

Vocabulary: diagram, distance

A *diagram* is a drawing that can be used to represent a situation. *Diagrams* are useful in Mathematics because they provide a pictorial summary of information. A *diagram* can help clarify information or make it easier to recognize relationships. This can be especially true when *distances* are involved. *Distance* is a measure of the length between two points. A *diagram* may show how the points are related.

Review the terms *diagram* and *distance* with students.

Beginning Draw a simple *diagram* of the room on the board. Discuss what the *diagram* represents with the students.

Intermediate Have students use a meter stick to measure the *distance* between two points on the *diagram*.

Advanced Have students create their own *diagrams* showing different *distances* between points in the classroom.

Open-Ended Problem Solving

Read the Headline Story to your students. Encourage them to make creative statements using information from the story.

 Headline Story

> Heidi picked 3.1 pounds of strawberries on Saturday. On Sunday, she picked 2.58 pounds. She picked strawberries again on Monday.

Possible responses: Heidi picked 5.68 pounds of strawberries over the weekend. She picked 0.52 pounds more on Saturday than she did on Sunday. She picked more than $2\frac{1}{2}$ pounds each day. If she picks 2.5 pounds on Monday, then she'll have picked more than 8 pounds during the 3 days.

Skills Practice and Review

Comparing and Ordering Decimals Amounts Using Money

Materials
• play money

Provide students with play money. First have students use dimes only to represent amounts between $0.10 and $1.00. Ask volunteers to read the numbers and write them on the board; other students can verify that each is written correctly. Repeat with two more amounts. Have students compare and order the amounts using play money. Repeat with three more amounts, but this time write the numbers on the board and have students represent them with the play money. After students have ordered them from smallest to largest, have them read the numbers as a class. Repeat the activity using amounts between $1.00 and $5.00, such as $2.47.

pairs · 15 MIN

Ⓐ Subtracting Decimals with Base-Ten Blocks

Materials
- For each student: base-ten blocks (1 flat, 15 rods, 20 cubes)

NCTM Standards 1, 2, 6, 7, 8, 9, 10

Purpose To explore subtraction of decimals

Introduce Each student should have a copy of Explore: Subtracting Decimals with Blocks. Each pair of students will also need a supply of base-ten blocks. Students should solve each problem using a process similar to the one they used in the last lesson to add decimals. First, they should represent the larger number with base-ten blocks. Then they should remove blocks representing the decimal being subtracted. New in this lesson is the fact that students will have to trade blocks in order to have enough cubes or rods to perform the subtractions.

Task Have students work with partners to complete the Explore page.

Share After students have completed their work, bring them together to discuss their strategies for solving the problems.

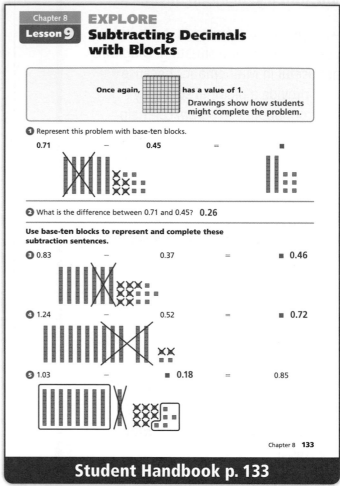

Student Handbook p. 133

❶ First, represent 0.71 with base-10 blocks.

Because there aren't enough hundredths to remove 5 of them, trade 1 tenth for 10 hundredths.

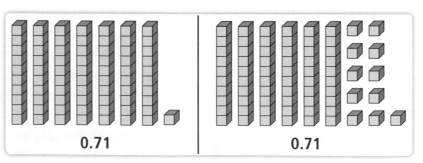

0.71   0.71

② Next, subtract 4 tenths and 5 hundredths.

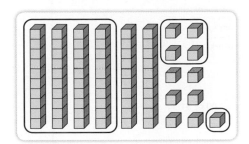

Now there are
2 tenths and
6 hundredths
left, so the
difference is
0.26.

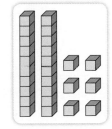

Teacher Story

"One of my students noticed that adding decimals involves trading blocks at the very end of the addition process, in order to use the fewest blocks to represent the sum. By contrast, the student noticed that when subtracting decimals, blocks are traded *before* performing calculations, and that trading results in more, rather than fewer, blocks."

❸ $0.83 - 0.37 = 0.46$
Trade one of the 8 rods in 0.83 for 10 cubes. That leaves 7 rods and gives you 10 cubes to add to the 3 you started with, for $10 + 3 = 13$ cubes.

7 rods, 13 cubes $-$ 3 rods, 7 cubes $=$ 4 rods, 6 cubes, or 0.46.

❹ $1.24 - 0.52 = 0.72$
Trade the flat in 1.24 for 10 rods. That leaves 0 flats and gives you 10 rods to add to the 2 you started with, for $10 + 2 = 12$ rods.

0 flats, 12 rods, 4 cubes $-$ 0 flats, 5 rods, 2 cubes $=$ 7 rods, 2 cubes, or 0.72.

❺ $1.03 - 0.18 = 0.85$
Represent 1.03 with 1 flat, 3 cubes. Trade the flat for 10 rods, leaving 10 rods, 3 cubes. Trade one of the rods for 10 cubes, leaving 9 rods, 13 cubes. Now remove as many rods and cubes as necessary to leave 0.85, or 8 rods, 5 cubes. To do this, you must remove 1 rod, 8 cubes, or 0.18.

💬 Talk Math

❓ How would you subtract 0.01 from 0.10 using base-10 blocks? Possible response: I would represent 0.10 with a rod. I would trade the rod for 10 cubes, then remove 1 cube to represent subtracting 0.01. There would be 9 cubes left, so $0.10 - 0.01 = 0.09$.

❓ How would you subtract 0.1 from 1 using base-10 blocks? Possible response: I would represent 1 with a flat. I would trade the flat for 10 rods, then remove 1 rod to represent subtracting 0.1. There would be 9 rods left, so $1 - 0.1 = 0.9$.

individuals or pairs

 20 MIN

Purpose To practice subtraction of decimals

NCTM Standards 1, 2, 6, 7, 8, 9, 10

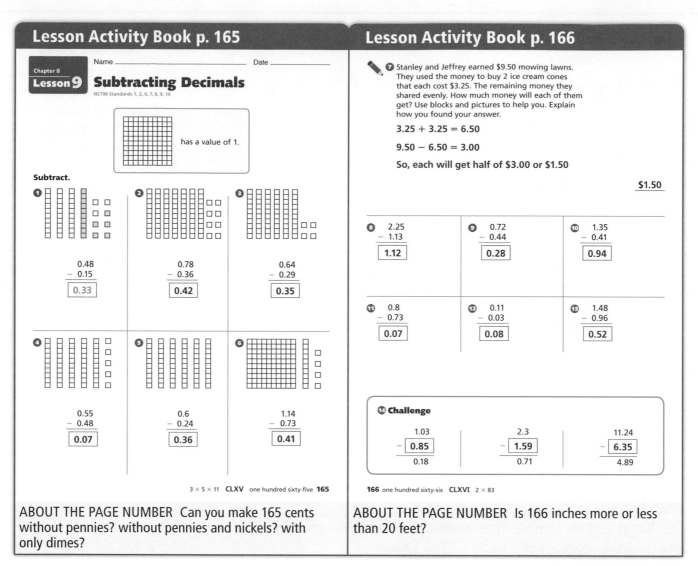

Lesson Activity Book p. 165

Chapter 8
Lesson 9 **Subtracting Decimals**
NCTM Standards 1, 2, 6, 7, 8, 9, 10

has a value of 1.

Subtract.

❶
0.48
− 0.15
0.33

❷
0.78
− 0.36
0.42

❸
0.64
− 0.29
0.35

❹
0.55
− 0.48
0.07

❺
0.6
− 0.24
0.36

❻
1.14
− 0.73
0.41

3 × 5 × 11 **CLXV** one hundred sixty-five **165**

ABOUT THE PAGE NUMBER Can you make 165 cents without pennies? without pennies and nickels? with only dimes?

Lesson Activity Book p. 166

❼ Stanley and Jeffrey earned $9.50 mowing lawns. They used the money to buy 2 ice cream cones that each cost $3.25. The remaining money they shared evenly. How much money will each of them get? Use blocks and pictures to help you. Explain how you found your answer.

3.25 + 3.25 = 6.50

9.50 − 6.50 = 3.00

So, each will get half of $3.00 or $1.50

$1.50

❽
2.25
− 1.13
1.12

❾
0.72
− 0.44
0.28

❿
1.35
− 0.41
0.94

⓫
0.8
− 0.73
0.07

⓬
0.11
− 0.03
0.08

⓭
1.48
− 0.96
0.52

⓮ Challenge

1.03
− **0.85**
0.18

2.3
− **1.59**
0.71

11.24
− **6.35**
4.89

166 one hundred sixty-six **CLXVI** 2 × 83

ABOUT THE PAGE NUMBER Is 166 inches more or less than 20 feet?

Teaching Notes for LAB page 165

Have students complete the page individually or with partners. The problems provide practice in subtracting decimals in standard vertical format. In each problem, the larger number is represented with a picture of base-ten blocks. Students might shade or cross out parts of the picture to indicate the decimal amount being subtracted. They could then count the remaining blocks to find the answer.

Teaching Notes for LAB page 166

To help students transition away from concrete models of decimals, this page doesn't provide pictures of base-ten blocks. Nevertheless, have blocks available for students who want to use them to model the problems.

Challenge Problem Students are given the larger numbers and the differences in three subtraction problems. They must find the smaller numbers, the numbers that were subtracted from the larger numbers.

C **Finding Distances**

Purpose To add and subtract decimals in the context of finding distances

Introduce Display a transparency of Activity Master: Distances Between Towns or draw a similar figure on the board. Pass out grid paper so that students can draw diagrams to help them solve the three problems on the page.

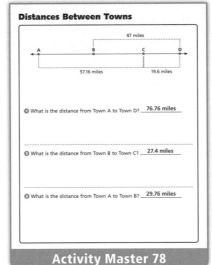

Activity Master 78

Problems **Have students study the diagram at the top of the page, and then find the distances in Problems 1–3.** Give students a few minutes to solve the problems.

Share Bring the class together and ask students to share their strategies for solving the problems. In Problem 1, students can find the distance from A to D by adding the distance between A and C to the distance between C and D. Students may find it helpful to add the whole-number parts of the distances and then deal with the decimal portions, modeling with pictures of blocks, if necessary.

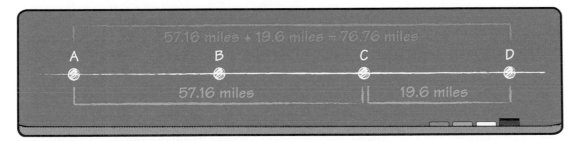

In Problem 2, students can find the distance between B and C by subtracting the distance between C and D from the distance between B and D.

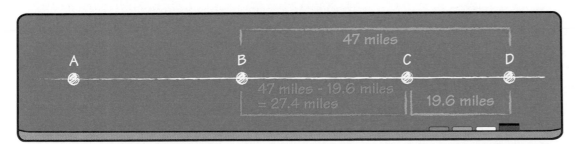

In Problem 3, students can find the distance between A and B by subtracting the distance between B and C (from Problem 2) from the distance between A and C.

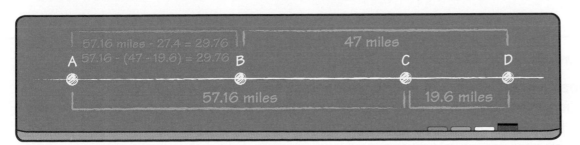

Materials
- For the teacher: transparency of AM78 (optional)
- For each student: grid paper

NCTM Standards 1, 2, 6, 7, 8, 9, 10

 **Talk Math**

Allenburg, Barkerville, and Cranston are all on Highway 47, and in the order they are listed here.

❷ If you know the distance between Allenburg and Barkerville and the distance between Barkerville and Cranston, how can you find the distance from Allenburg to Cranston? Find the sum of the two distances.

❷ If you know the distance between Allenburg and Cranston and the distance between Allenburg and Barkerville, how can you find the distance between Barkerville and Cranston? Subtract the smaller distance from the larger distance.

Reflect and Summarize the Lesson

 Write Math

Complete this number sentence and explain your reasoning: 4 − 2.93 = _____. 1.07; Possible explanation: Imagine trading one of the 4 flats for 100 cubes, leaving 3 flats, 100 cubes; 3 flats, 100 cubes − 2 flats, 93 cubes = 1 flat, 7 cubes, or 1.07.

Leveled Problem Solving

It is 11.87 miles from Kennedy Airport to LaGuardia Airport.
It is 24.85 miles from LaGuardia Airport to Newark Liberty Airport.

❶ Basic Level

If you drive from Kennedy Airport to LaGuardia Airport and then to Newark Liberty Airport, how far will you drive in all? Explain. 36.72 mi; 11.87 + 24.85 = 36.72.

❷ On Level

If you drive from Kennedy Airport to LaGuardia Airport and back again, how far will you drive? Explain. 23.74 mi; 11.87 + 11.87 = 23.74.

❸ Above Level

How much farther is it from LaGuardia Airport to Newark Liberty Airport than from LaGuardia Airport to Kennedy Airport? Explain. 12.98 mi; 24.85 − 11.87 = 12.98.

Intervention

Activity Picturing Subtraction

Have students use squares, lines, and Xs to represent decimal blocks:

$\square$ = 1 | = 0.1   ✗ = 0.01

Have students draw pictures to model the first number and cross out blocks for the second number to find each difference:

3.4 − 1.7 1.7   2.35 − 1.18 1.17

2.7 − 1.88 0.82   3.5 − 1.94 1.56

Practice

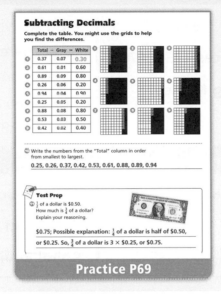

Subtracting Decimals

Complete the table. You might use the grids to help you find the differences.

Total	− Gray	= White
0.37	0.07	0.30
0.61	0.01	0.60
0.89	0.09	0.80
0.26	0.06	0.20
0.94	0.04	0.90
0.25	0.05	0.20
0.88	0.08	0.80
0.53	0.03	0.50
0.42	0.02	0.40

⑩ Write the numbers from the "Total" column in order from smallest to largest.

0.25, 0.26, 0.37, 0.42, 0.53, 0.61, 0.88, 0.89, 0.94

Test Prep

⑪ ½ of a dollar is $0.50. How much is ¾ of a dollar? Explain your reasoning.

$0.75; Possible explanation: ¼ of a dollar is half of $0.50, or $0.25. So, ¾ of a dollar is 3 × $0.25, or $0.75.

Practice P69

Extension

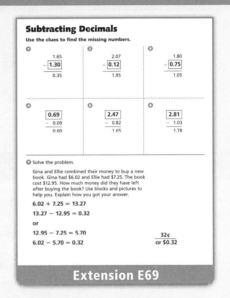

Subtracting Decimals

Use the clues to find the missing numbers.

| 1.65 − 1.30 = 0.35 | 2.07 − 0.12 = 1.95 | 1.80 − 0.75 = 1.05 |
| 0.69 − 0.09 = 0.60 | 2.47 − 0.82 = 1.65 | 2.81 − 1.03 = 1.78 |

⑦ Solve the problem.

Gina and Ellie combined their money to buy a new book. Gina had $6.02 and Ellie had $7.25. The book cost $12.95. How much money did they have left after buying the book? Use blocks and pictures to help you. Explain how you got your answer.

6.02 + 7.25 = 13.27

13.27 − 12.95 = 0.32

or

12.95 − 7.25 = 5.70

6.02 − 5.70 = 0.32

32¢ or $0.32

Extension E69

Spiral Review

Spiral Review Book page SR69 provides review of the following previously learned skills and concepts:

- measuring lengths to the nearest quarter unit
- solving problems using the strategy *guess and check*

You may wish to have students work with a partner to complete the page.

Measurement

Measure the line segment to the nearest quarter inch.

① ____ 3¼ inches
② ____ 4¼ inches
③ ____ 2 inches
④ ____ 2½ inches
⑤ ____ 4 inches
⑥ ____ 3¾ inches
⑦ ____ 2¼ inches
⑧ ____ 3¼ inches

Problem Solving

Solve the problem. Explain your answer.

⑨ Vicki weighs her dog Buster on her home scale. Then she weighs herself. When she stands on the scale with her dog, it reads 127 pounds. Vicki weighs 53 pounds more than her dog. How much do they each weigh?

Vicki: 90 pounds; Buster: 37 pounds; I used the strategy guess and check to solve. I guessed pairs of numbers that differed by 53. Then I added them and checked to see if the sum was 127. If it was not, I adjusted my guess and tried again until I found the answer.

Spiral Review SR69

Extension Activity
Skip a Place

Have students explore subtractions of a decimal number from a whole number. Present students with a subtraction such as 3 − 0.48. Ask: *What number must be displayed with blocks?* 3 *What trades must be made?* 1 unit for 10 tenths and 1 tenth for 10 hundredths *What does the new problem look like?* 2 units, 9 tenths, 10 hundredths minus 4 tenths, 8 hundredths *What is the difference?* 2.52 Repeat with other subtractions.

Lesson 10 Representing Decimals Using Money

NCTM Standards 1, 2, 6, 7, 8, 9, 10

Lesson Planner

STUDENT OBJECTIVES
- To connect money and decimals
- To practice adding and subtracting decimals in the context of money

1 | Daily Activities (TG p. 667)

| Open-Ended Problem Solving/Headline Story | Skills Practice and Review— Comparing and Ordering Decimals with Base-Ten Blocks |

2 | Teach and Practice (TG pp. 668–671)

MATERIALS

(A) **Decimals and Money** (TG pp. 668–669)

(B) **Finding Combinations of Prices** (TG p. 670)

(C) **Representing Decimals Using Money** (TG p. 671)

- TR: Activity Master, AM79
- transparency of AM79 (optional)
- play money
- base-ten blocks or coins
- LAB pp. 167–168

3 | Differentiated Instruction (TG p. 672)

Leveled Problem Solving (TG p. 672)	Practice Book P70
Intervention Activity (TG p. 672)	Extension Book E70
Extension Activity (TG p. 672)	Spiral Review Book SR70

Lesson Notes

About the Lesson

Students solidify their understanding of decimals by representing decimals with money. As they practice addition and subtraction of decimals in this familiar context, students deepen their understanding of price notation. Most students probably already know that a penny is 1 hundredth of a dollar, but now they are able to understand why $0.01 indicates this value. This allows them to see why a nickel (or 5¢) is written as $0.05, a dime (or 10¢) as $0.10, and a quarter (or 25¢) as $0.25.

Use with Lesson Activity Book pp. 167–168.

Developing Mathematical Language

Vocabulary: dollar notation

A dollar sign, $, signifies the use of *dollar notation*. *Dollar notation* is an example of an application of the decimal system. In *dollar notation*, places have the same value as in the decimal system, although they are read differently. You read *dollar notation* in dollars and cents. For example, $4.25 is "four dollars and twenty-five cents."

Review the term *dollar notation* with students.

Beginning Write different money amounts on the board, some using a cent sign and some in *dollar notation*. Have students identify the amounts written in *dollar notation*.

Intermediate Write 50¢ and $0.50 on the board. Point out that both terms mean the same thing—fifty cents. Have students identify which is written in *dollar notation*.

Advanced Have students describe the difference between writing an amount less than one dollar using a cent sign and using *dollar notation*.

Open-Ended Problem Solving

Read the Headline Story to your students. Encourage them to draw logical conclusions based on information in the story.

 Headline Story

> **Manju bought a ruler for $0.37. She paid with a bill. How much change might she have received?**

Posible responses: If she paid with a $1 bill, then she would have received $0.63 in change. If she paid with a $5 bill, then she would have received $4.63. If she received $9.63 in change, then she paid with a $10 bill.

Skills Practice and Review

Comparing and Ordering Decimals with Base-Ten Blocks and Money

Materials
- base-ten blocks
- play money

Provide students with base-ten blocks, reminding them that a flat has a value of 1. Ask students to put out 1 flat and 3 rods and ask them to write down the number it represents. Ask a volunteer to write the number on the board and have other students verify that it is written correctly. Read the number as a class. Repeat with two more numbers, for example, 1 flat, 3 rods, and 1 cube, or 2 rods and 4 cubes. Have students order the three numbers, referring to their base-ten models as needed. Repeat with three more numbers, but this time use dollar amounts in tenths of dollars, such as $1.30. Write them on the board. Have students read them and represent them with play money. Repeat with three more numbers, but this time use dollar amounts in hundredths, such as $4.81. Write them on the board. Have students read them and represent them with play money.

whole class · 15 MIN

A Decimals and Money

Materials
- For the teacher: coins
- For the students: play money

NCTM Standards 1, 2, 6, 7, 8, 9, 10

Purpose To use the context of money to give further meaning to the tenths and hundredths digits in decimals.

Introduce Review the process for writing decimals to represent amounts of money. Show students a group of coins and ask them to write the value in dollar notation (for example, $0.30 instead of 30¢). Repeat two or three times with other amounts, for example 1 dime ($0.10), 1 penny ($0.01), 2 dimes and 3 pennies ($0.23), 1 quarter and 1 nickel ($0.30), or 4 pennies ($0.04).

Possible Discussion

Because students are already comfortable with money, it can be used as a familiar context for reinforcing ideas about decimals. Discussions about money can clarify the relation between common decimals such as 0.25, 0.50, and 0.75 and fractions. Previous lessons showed that decimals like 0.25 can easily be written as fractions ($\frac{25}{100}$). Even students who are already comfortable simplifying fractions will benefit from thinking about parallels between fractions and coins. The fact that a quarter is one-fourth of a dollar, for example, makes it easy to see that 0.25 is equivalent to $\frac{1}{4}$. Similarly, 0.5 is equivalent to $\frac{1}{2}$ and 0.75 is equiivalent to $\frac{3}{4}$. If you think your students are ready, you might take some time during this lesson to discuss relations between decimals and their corresponding fractions.

Problem Ask students how many dimes there are in 1 dollar. Then ask them to name the portion of a dollar that a dime represents.

Because 10 dimes equal 1 dollar, 1 dime is one-tenth of a dollar. Show students 10 dimes and count by tens with them to see that the value of the coins is 1 dollar. Ask students for the fraction and the decimal that represent one-tenth. $\frac{1}{10}$ and 0.10 Next, hold up two of the dimes and ask students to name the fraction and the decimal that these 2 coins represent. $\frac{2}{10}$ and 0.20 Continue holding up various numbers of dimes (including at least one example of more than 9 dimes). Each time, ask students how to write the corresponding decimal notation and dollar notation. Write at least five of these amounts in decimal and dollar notations, and ask students to order the amounts.

Repeat this activity with pennies. Since 100 pennies equal 1 dollar, 1 penny is one-hundredth of a dollar. Again, ask students to name the fraction and the decimal that represent one-hundredth. $\frac{1}{100}$ and 0.01 Hold up various numbers of pennies. Each time, ask students how to write the corresponding decimal notation. Include an example with 10 pennies to help students see that because 10 pennies equals 1 dime, the decimals representing 10 pennies and 1 dime are equivalent (0.10).

So far, you have been asking students to write the values of groups of coins as decimals. Now reverse the process. First tell them to let D represent dimes and to let P represent pennies. Ask the following questions.

💬 Talk Math

❷ Using only dimes and pennies, name a group of coins whose value, written as a decimal, is 0.25. DDPPPPP

❷ Using only dimes and pennies, name a group of coins whose value, written as a decimal, is 0.63. DDDDDDPPP

Now ask students to use shorthand for the answers they have been giving. Instead of writing DDDDDDPPP for 0.63, for example, they should write 6D + 3P.

💬 Talk Math

❓ Name a group of coins whose value, written as a decimal, is 0.49. 4D + 9P

❓ Name a group of coins whose value, written as a decimal, is 0.87. 8D + 7P

❓ What relationship do you see between the value of a group of coins, written as a decimal, and the number of dimes and pennies in a group that has the same value? Possible response: The tenths digit of the decimal is the number of dimes. The hundredths digit is the number of pennies.

Finally, write three decimals on the board. Ask students to write the amounts, as before, using D to represent dimes and P to represent pennies. Invite a volunteer to the board to order the three decimals. Repeat, writing three decimals on the board but this time asking students to model the decimals with play money. Begin by having students use only dimes and write the values they can model with dimes. Then have students compare two amounts, then three amounts before ordering the amounts from least to greatest. Once students can do this with tenths, have them do it with money amounts using hundredths such as $3.42. Again, invite a volunteer to the board to order the three decimals.

Teacher Story

❝I didn't have real or play coins available, so I wrote each coin combination on the board before asking students for the corresponding decimal. This worked out well because it gave the class a record of both the coins and their corresponding decimals.**❞**

B Finding Combinations of Prices

Materials
- For each student: AM79; play money

NCTM Standards 1, 2, 6, 7, 8, 9, 10

✓ Ongoing Assessment
- Do students add and subtract decimal amounts written to the tenths and hundredths places?

Purpose To practice adding money amounts

Introduce This activity gives students practice with decimal computation while also encouraging them to use problem solving strategies such as *make an organized list*. Give each student a supply of play money and a copy of Activity Master: Store Prices.

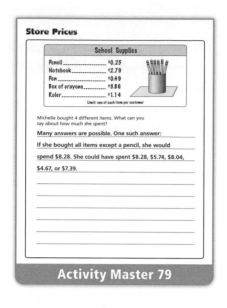

Activity Master 79

Task Have students work in small groups to answer the question about Michelle's purchases. If necessary, you might help students get started by asking questions like the following:

💬 Talk Math

❓ If Michelle bought one of each item, how much money would she have spent? $8.53

❓ If Michelle bought one of each item except a pencil, how much would she have spent? $8.28

❓ If Michelle bought one of each item except a notebook, how much would she have spent? $5.74

Share After a few minutes, have students share their answers and strategies for answering the question. Students may recognize that, for each purchase of four items, one of the five items is omitted. Since there are five items, there are five different amounts Michelle could have spent. The straightforward way to find them is to find the sums of all possible combinations of four items. Another way is to find the total of the five items, then, from it, to subtract the price of each item. For example, to find the cost of all the items except the pencil, students could subtract the price of a pencil from the total price of all the items. Once the total price of all five items is known, this strategy is simpler than adding the prices of four items each time.

Practice If you have extra time, have students think about the amounts that Michelle might have spent had she bought just two items. For example, the least she could have spent was $0.74 and the most she could have spent was $6.65. There are ten different amounts she could have spent.

individuals or pairs

 20 MIN

Purpose To practice relating money and decimals

NCTM Standards 1, 2, 6, 7, 8, 9, 10

Lesson Activity Book p. 167

Name _____ Date _____

Chapter 8
Lesson 10 **Representing Decimals Using Money**
NCTM Standards 1, 2, 6, 7, 8, 9, 10

Use the clues to fill in the missing numbers.

1

Number of dimes	1	3	9	8	4	11	13	19	27	36
Decimal	0.10	**0.30**	0.90	0.80	**0.40**	**1.10**	1.30	**1.90**	**2.70**	**3.60**

2

Number of pennies	37	**49**	**18**	1	8	**36**	119	**193**	207	**635**
Decimal	0.37	0.49	0.18	**0.01**	**0.08**	0.36	**1.19**	1.93	**2.07**	6.35

3

Number of nickels	1	**5**	**9**	15	20	21	**30**	**33**	49	59
Decimal	0.05	0.25	0.45	**0.75**	1	**1.05**	1.50	1.65	**2.45**	**2.95**

4
```
  $0.51
+ $0.49
───────
 $1.00
```

5
```
  $0.96
+ $0.04
───────
 $1.00
```

6
```
  $0.83
  $0.17
───────
 $1.00
```

prime **CLXVII** one hundred sixty-seven **167**

Lesson Activity Book p. 168

7
```
  $1.00
- $0.73
───────
 $0.27
```

8
```
  $1.00
- $0.89
───────
 $0.11
```

9
```
  $1.00
- $0.92
───────
 $0.08
```

10
```
  $1.30
+ $0.70
───────
 $2.00
```

11
```
  $1.03
+ $0.97
───────
 $2.00
```

12
```
  $0.71
+ $1.29
───────
 $2.00
```

13
```
  $10.00
- $2.72
───────
  $7.28
```

14
```
  $20.00
- $7.28
────────
 $12.72
```

Challenge Use words, pictures, and numbers to show how you found your answers.

15 Letitia is collecting money for her youth group. Her goal is to have $13.50 by Sunday. She's set aside $6.73 of her own money, and her brother said he'd contribute the rest. How much will he need to give her? **$6.77**

16 Joneau and Sonya are having a contest to see who can save the most money. Joneau has $15.68 saved up. When Sonya counts her money, she finds out that Joneau has $3.29 more than she does. How much money has Sonya saved? **$12.39**

168 one hundred sixty-eight **CLXVIII** $2 \times 2 \times 2 \times 2 \times 3 \times 7$

ABOUT THE PAGE NUMBER How many quarters would you need to buy something for $1.67? 167 is a prime number.

ABOUT THE PAGE NUMBER 168 inches is 14 feet. How many inches are in 15 feet?

Teaching Notes for LAB page 167

Have students complete the page individually or with partners. The page gives students more practice with relating money and decimals, and with adding and subtracting decimals. They may recognize that they can use previous entries in each table to find larger decimals or numbers of coins.

When recording a decimal for 1 or 8 pennies in Problem 2, students may forget to write a zero placeholder in the tenths place. If students mistakenly record 0.10 as their answer, you might point out that 0.10 is the decimal that represents the value of 1 dime (as they can see in Problem 1).

Teaching Notes for LAB page 168

Students find missing addends or subtrahends in problems about money. You may wish to provide students with base-ten blocks and/or coins to model the problems.

Challenge Problems These problems require students to apply to larger numbers the same skills they used in earlier problems.

 Write Math

Reflect and Summarize the Lesson

What decimal represents the total value of two dollars, one quarter, four dimes, and three pennies? Explain how you found the answer. 2.68 or $2.68; Possible explanation: I wrote two dollars as $2.00, one quarter as $0.25, four dimes as $0.40, and three pennies as $0.03. Then I added the amounts: $2.00 + $0.25 + $0.40 + $0.03 = $2.68.

Leveled Problem Solving

A backpack costs $18.79.

❶ Basic Level

Carlos buys a notebook for $5.99 and a backpack. How much does he spend? Explain. $24.78; $5.99 + $18.79 = $24.78.

❷ On Level

Carlos pays for a backpack with a $20 bill. How much change does he get? Explain. $1.21; $20.00 − $18.79 = $1.21.

❸ Above Level

After buying a backpack, Carlos gets $0.21 in change. If he paid with bills, what is the least number of bills He could have used? Explain. 6 bills; He gave the clerk $19: 1 ten, 1 five, 4 ones.

Intervention	Practice	Extension

Activity Money Table

Have students make money tables similar to a place-value chart, to add and subtract money amounts.

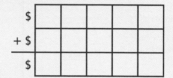

Have students find these sums and differences:

$0.79 + $3.45, $2.83 + $4.50, and $10 − $0.92. $4.24, $7.33, $9.08

Representing Decimals Using Money

Watch the signs!

❶ 23.78 − 9.81	❷ 8.92 + 3.45	❸ 2.4 − 0.75	❹ 3.07 − 1.82
13.97	**12.37**	**1.65**	**1.25**

❺ 26.32 + 19.64	❻ 3.6 − 1.43	❼ 4.19 + 2.80	❽ 5.27 + 6.08
45.96	**2.17**	**6.99**	**11.35**

❾ 2.83 + **0.06** = 2.89	❿ 4.31 − **0.04** = 4.27	⓫ 5.48 − **0.42** = 5.06	⓬ 1.96 + **0.07** = 2.03

⓭ 1.24 − **0.04** = 1.2	⓮ 3.14 + **0.4** = 3.54	⓯ 2.22 − **0.3** = 1.92	⓰ 0.68 + **0.02** = 0.7

Test Prep

⓱ Bryanna's family bought two packages of ground beef. One package weighed 0.68 lbs. The other package weighed 1.32 lbs. If ground beef cost $2.50 a pound, what was the total cost? Explain.

$5; Possible explanation: The total weight was 0.68 + 1.32 = 2 lbs; 2 × $2.50 = $5.

Practice P70

Representing Decimals Using Money

Use this price chart to answer the questions.

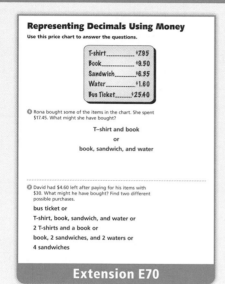

T-shirt	$7.95
Book	$9.50
Sandwich	$6.35
Water	$1.60
Bus Ticket	$25.40

❶ Rona bought some of the items in the chart. She spent $17.45. What might she have bought?

T-shirt and book
or
book, sandwich, and water

❷ David had $4.60 left after paying for his items with $30. What might he have bought? Find two different possible purchases.

bus ticket or

T-shirt, book, sandwich, and water or

2 T-shirts and a book or

book, 2 sandwiches, and 2 waters or

4 sandwiches

Extension E70

Spiral Review

Spiral Review Book page SR70 provides review of the following previously learned skills and concepts:

- identifying and extending a rule using tables
- describing attributes of rectangles, rhombuses, and squares

You may wish to have students work with a partner to complete the page.

Algebra

Write the rule for the table. Then write the missing numbers.

Input	Output		Input	Output		Input	Output		Input	Output
4	12		3	9		13	7		20	10
7	21		5	11		11	5		12	6
1	3		9	15		7	1		14	7
6	**18**		2	**8**		9	**3**		16	**8**
10	**30**		11	**17**		12	**6**		2	**1**

Multiply by 3.   Add 6.   Subtract 6.   Divide by 2.

Geometry

Write the letters of the figures that are examples of the quadrilateral named.

❺ Squares

A   B   C   D

B, D

❻ Rectangles

A   B   C   D

A, B, C

❼ What name describes all the figures in Problems 5 and 6?
Possible answers: quadrilaterals, parallelograms

Spiral Review SR70

Extension Activity
Time for Change

Have pairs of students make change and check their results by subtracting. Have one student make up a price between $1.00 and $5.00. The other student chooses to pay with a $5, $10, or $20 bill. The first student finds the change by counting on from the price to the bill used to pay. The other student checks by subtracting the price from the bill used to pay. Partners switch roles and repeat the activity with other numbers.

Teacher's Notes 🍎

Daily Notes . . .

Quick Notes

More Ideas

Lesson 11 Problem Solving Strategy and Test Prep

NCTM Standards 1, 2, 6, 7, 8, 9, 10

Lesson Planner

- To practice the problem solving strategy *act it out*.
- To articulate the steps and strategies used to solve problems
- To prepare for standardized tests

Problem Solving Strategy: Act it Out (TG pp. 675–676, 678–679)

MATERIALS

Ⓐ **Discussing the Problem Solving Strategy: Act it Out** (TG p. 675)

Ⓑ **Solving Problems by Applying the Strategy** (TG p. 676)

- transparency of LAB p. 169 (optional)
- base-ten blocks, play money, or TR: AM77
- 📖 LAB p. 169
- 📖 SH pp. 134–135

Problem Solving Test Prep (TG p. 677)

Ⓒ **Getting Ready for Standardized Tests** (TG p. 677)

- 📖 LAB p. 170

Lesson Notes

About Problem Solving

Problem Solving Strategy: Act it Out

Throughout this chapter, students have been studying decimal numbers. In some of the lessons, students modeled decimals with manipulatives. Therefore, this lesson focuses on the problem solving strategy *act it out* in the context of decimals. The LAB pages assess students' understanding of place value and decimal numbers.

Skills Practice and Review

Guess My Number

Play this game from **Lesson 8.3** to review skills students have been learning in this chapter. Draw a number line. Label the endpoints with consecutive whole numbers. Secretly choose a number between the endpoints. Tell students the number of digits that follow the decimal point of your number. Have students ask *yes/no* questions until they guess your number. You may wish to cross out the section of the number line eliminated by each answer. For the greatest difficulty, use numbers with zeroes in the tenths place and non-zero numbers in the hundredths place, such as 2.03 or 17.09.

Problem Solving Strategy

(A) Discussing the Problem Solving Strategy: Act it Out

whole class 15 MIN

Purpose To share strategies for solving problems and focus on the problem solving strategy *act it out.*

NCTM Standards 1, 2, 6, 7, 8, 9, 10

Introduce Ask students to recall when they used the strategy *act it out* to solve problems in this chapter. Students may recall using play money to act out the process of buying items in a store and receiving change, and base-ten blocks to act out the process of adding and subtracting decimals.

Introduce the following problem.

Problem **The area of the lawn in front of City Hall is 1.37 acres.** The area of the lawn beside the library is 0.47 acres. Mr. Clyde mowed half of the total area of the two lawns in the morning and the rest in the afternoon. What area did he mow in the morning?

Share **Ask students to share their strategies for solving the problem.** One way is to use base-ten blocks to represent the areas of the two lawns and to *act out* the problem.

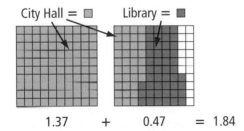

City Hall = ▢   Library = ▪

1.37   +   0.47   =   1.84

Next, trade for rods and cubes, and separate the total into two equal groups.

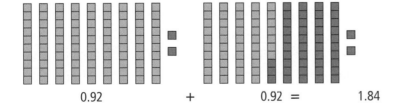

0.92   +   0.92 =   1.84

💬 Talk Math

❷ How many acres did Mr. Clyde mow in the morning? Explain. 0.92 acres; Possible explanation: When base-ten blocks representing 1.84 are divided into two groups, the blocks in each group represent 0.92.

❷ The total area of the lawns at City Hall, the library, and the fire station is 2 acres. What is the area of the fire station lawn? Explain. 0.16 acres; Possible explanation: Base-ten blocks representing the totals of the other two lawns are 0.16 less than 2 flats.

Solving Problems by Applying the Strategy LAB p. 169

NCTM Standards 1, 2, 6, 7, 8, 9, 10

Purpose To share strategies for solving problems and focus on the problem solving strategy *act it out*

Teaching Notes for LAB page 169

Students practice the problem solving strategy *act it out* by solving the problems independently or in pairs. Help students get started by asking questions such as the following:

 Read to Understand

What do you know? Andy gave the cashier a $5 bill for items costing $1.18 and $0.97.

What do you need to find out? the amount of change Andy received.

 Plan

How can you solve this problem? Think about the strategies you might use.

How could you act it out? Use base-ten blocks or play money to represent the decimal numbers and act out the computations.

 Solve

How might you model the situation? Students could use base-ten blocks to represent $5.20 as the decimal 5.20. They could remove 1.18 and 0.97 from the representation, trading rods for cubes as necessary. The remaining blocks would represent the answer.

 Check

Look back at the original problem. Did you answer the question that was asked? Does your answer make sense? How do you know?

Students can use this method to solve the other problems on LAB page 169. Supplement these questions with ones that are specifically tailored to the individual problems.

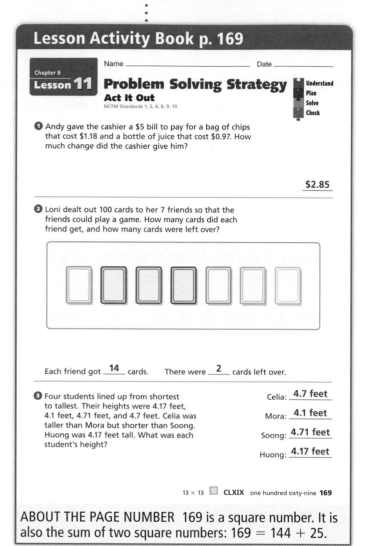

Lesson Activity Book p. 169

Name _____ Date _____

Chapter 8
Lesson 11 **Problem Solving Strategy**
Act It Out
NCTM Standards 1, 2, 6, 8, 9, 10

Understand
Plan
Solve
Check

❶ Andy gave the cashier a $5 bill to pay for a bag of chips that cost $1.18 and a bottle of juice that cost $0.97. How much change did the cashier give him?

$2.85

❷ Loni dealt out 100 cards to her 7 friends so that the friends could play a game. How many cards did each friend get, and how many cards were left over?

Each friend got **14** cards.   There were **2** cards left over.

❸ Four students lined up from shortest to tallest. Their heights were 4.17 feet, 4.1 feet, 4.71 feet, and 4.7 feet. Celia was taller than Mora but shorter than Soong. Huong was 4.17 feet tall. What was each student's height?

Celia: **4.7 feet**
Mora: **4.1 feet**
Soong: **4.71 feet**
Huong: **4.17 feet**

13 × 13 ☐ **CLXIX** one hundred sixty-nine **169**

ABOUT THE PAGE NUMBER 169 is a square number. It is also the sum of two square numbers: $169 = 144 + 25$.

Reflect and Summarize the Lesson

 Write Math **When might the strategy *act it out* be a good one to try to solve a problem?** Possible response: when you can use a model or play activities to represent the situation in the problem and look for relationships among its parts

(C) Getting Ready for Standardized Tests LAB p. 170

individuals

20 MIN

Purpose To prepare students for standardized tests

NCTM Standards 1, 2, 6, 7, 8, 9, 10

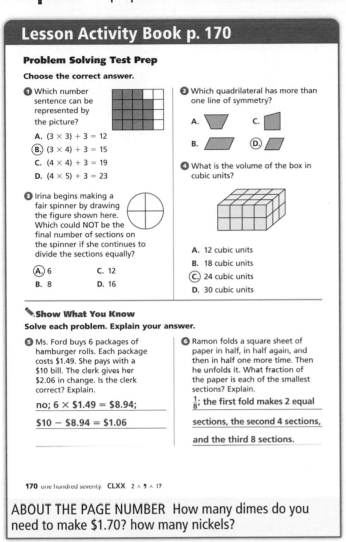

Lesson Activity Book p. 170

Problem Solving Test Prep

Choose the correct answer.

1 Which number sentence can be represented by the picture?

A. $(3 \times 3) + 3 = 12$
B. $(3 \times 4) + 3 = 15$
C. $(4 \times 4) + 3 = 19$
D. $(4 \times 5) + 3 = 23$

3 Irina begins making a fair spinner by drawing the figure shown here. Which could NOT be the final number of sections on the spinner if she continues to divide the sections equally?

A. 6
B. 8
C. 12
D. 16

2 Which quadrilateral has more than one line of symmetry?

A.
B.
C.
D.

4 What is the volume of the box in cubic units?

A. 12 cubic units
B. 18 cubic units
C. 24 cubic units
D. 30 cubic units

Show What You Know

Solve each problem. Explain your answer.

5 Ms. Ford buys 6 packages of hamburger rolls. Each package costs $1.49. She pays with a $10 bill. The clerk gives her $2.06 in change. Is the clerk correct? Explain.

no; $6 \times \$1.49 = \$8.94$;

$\$10 - \$8.94 = \$1.06$

6 Ramon folds a square sheet of paper in half, in half again, and then in half one more time. Then he unfolds it. What fraction of the paper is each of the smallest sections? Explain.

$\frac{1}{8}$; the first fold makes 2 equal

sections, the second 4 sections,

and the third 8 sections.

170 one hundred seventy CLXX 2 × 5 × 17

ABOUT THE PAGE NUMBER How many dimes do you need to make $1.70? how many nickels?

Teaching Notes for LAB page 170

The test items on this page are written in the same style and arranged in the same format as those on many state assessments. The page is cumulative and is designed for students to apply a variety of problem solving strategies, including *act it out.* Students might share the strategies they use.

The Item Analysis Chart below highlights some of the possible strategies that may be used for each item.

Show What You Know

Written Response

Direct students' attention to Problems 5 and 6. Explain that they can solve both problems by acting them out. Then have them write explanations of how they know their answers are correct. To provide more space for students to communicate their thinking about these problems, you may wish to have them write their responses and explanations on a separate sheet of paper. Use the Scoring Rubric below to evaluate their understanding.

Item Analysis Chart

Item	Strategy
1	Act it out, write an equation
2	Make a model
3	Draw a picture, use logical reasoning
4	Make a model, write an equation
5	Act it out, write an equation
6	Act it out

Scoring Rubric

2	• Demonstrates complete understanding of the problem and chooses an appropriate strategy to determine the solution
1	• Demonstrates a partial understanding of the problem and chooses a strategy that does not lead to a complete and accurate solution
0	• Demonstrates little understanding of the problem and shows little evidence of using any strategy to determine a solution

Review Model...

Refer students to Problem Solving Review Model: Act It Out to review a model of the four steps they can use with the problem solving strategy *act it out*.

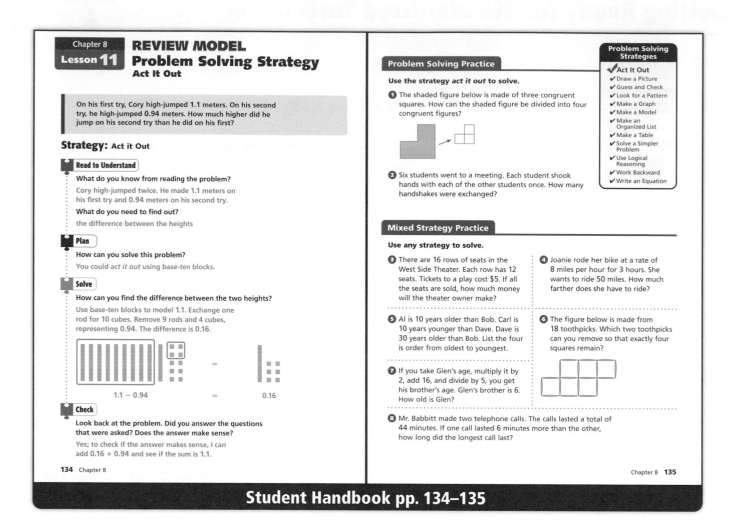

Student Handbook pp. 134–135

Task Have students read the problem at the top of the Review Model page.

💬 Talk Math

❓ What do you need to find out? the difference in heights between Cory's two high-jumps

❓ On which jump did Cory jump higher? his first jump

❓ What strategy can you use to solve the problem? You could *act it out*.

❓ What materials could you use to *act it out*? Possible answers: grids, coins, or base-ten blocks

❓ Using base-ten blocks, if you start with 11 rods to model 1.1, how can you subtract 0.94? Exchange 1 rod for 10 cubes. Then remove 9 rods and 4 cubes.

❓ How can you find the answer? After I remove 1 rod and 6 cubes, 1 rod and 6 cubes remain. They represent 0.16. So, Cory jumped 0.16 meter higher on his first jump than he did on his second.

❓ What other strategy could you use to solve the problem? Possible answers: *work backward* or *guess and check*

Use with Lesson Activity Book pp. 169–170.

1 Possible explanation: You can *act it out* to solve the problem. You can draw a picture of the figure on a piece of paper, then try various congruent shapes until you find the one that works. It makes sense to try shapes that are similar to the shape of the shaded figure.

2 15; Possible explanation: You can *act it out* with five classmates to solve the problem. Each of the six students could shake hands with each of the others exactly once. The six of you could keep track of the total number of handshakes.

3 $960; Possible explanation: You can *use logical reasoning* to solve the problem. The total cost is the number of seats times the cost per seat. So find the product: $16 \times 12 \times \$5$.

4 26 miles; Possible explanation: You can *write an equation* to solve the problem. Think: The distance remaining is 50 miles minus the distance Joanie has gone. So, distance $= 50 - 8 - 8 - 8 = 26$ miles.

5 Dave, Carol, Al, Bob; Possible explanation: You can *use logical reasoning* to solve the problem.

Al is 10 years older than Bob, so Al = Bob + 10.

Carl is 10 years younger than Dave, and Dave is 30 years older than Bob. So Dave = Bob + 30 and Carl = Bob + 30 − 10.

Therefore Dave is the oldest, then Carl, then Al, and then Bob.

6 Possible explanation: You can use *logical reasoning* to solve the problem. If two toothpicks are removed from 18, 16 remain. If 16 toothpicks form 4 squares, the squares cannot share any sides. So, look for a way to have 4 squares with no common sides.

7 7; Possible explanation: You can *work backward* to solve the problem. $6 \times 5 = 30$; $30 - 16 = 14$; $14 \div 2 = 7$.

8 25 minutes; Possible explanation: You can *guess and check* to solve the problem. Guess a pair of numbers that differ by 6. Check their sum. If it is not 44, adjust the numbers and guess again. Continue until you find a pair with a sum of 44.

Decimals

NCTM Standards 1, 2, 6, 7, 8, 9, 10

Purpose To provide students with an opportunity to demonstrate understanding of Chapter 8 concepts and skills

MATERIALS
- LAB pp. 171–172
- Chapter 8 Test (Assessment Guide pp. AG77–AG78)

Chapter 8 Learning Goals and Assessment Options

These learning goals are assessed in many ways throughout the chapter. The chart below correlates each learning goal to specific formal and informal assessment options.

	Learning Goals	Lesson Number	Snapshot Assessment	Chapter Review Item Numbers	Chapter Test Item Numbers
				LAB pp. 171–172	Assessment Guide pp. AG77–AG78
8-A	Compare and order whole numbers	8.1	1, 5	12, 13	1, 2
8-B	Compare and order decimals and locate decimals to hundredths on a number line	8.2–8.4	2, 6, 7	1–4, 10, 14, 15	3–8
8-C	Relate decimals to fractions	8.5	3, 8	5–7	9, 10
8-D	Add and subtract decimals to hundredths, including money	8.6–8.10	4, 10	8, 9, 11, 16	11–14
8-E	Apply problem solving strategies such as *act it out* to solve problems	8.11	9	17	15

📷 Snapshot Assessment

The following Mental Math and Quick Write questions and tasks provide a quick, informal assessment of students' understanding of Chapter 8 concepts, skills, and problem solving strategies.

whole class 🕐 **10 MIN**

Mental Math This oral assessment uses mental math strategies and can be used with the whole class.

❶ Use the digits 2, 2, 4, 4, 6, 6, 8, and 8.
Build the smallest whole number possible.
22,446,688 or twenty-two million, four hundred forty-six thousand, six hundred eighty-eight
Build the largest whole number possible.
88, 664, 422 or eighty-eight million, six hundred sixty-four thousand, four hundred twenty-two
(Learning Goal 8-A)

❷ Name a number between 12 and 12.5. Explain how you found your answer. Possible answer: 12.3
Name a number between 13.5 and 13.6. Explain how you found your answer, Possible answer: 13.52
Which is greater, 39.45 or 38.99? 39.45
(Learning Goal 8-B)

③ What number is halfway between 12.4 and $12\frac{1}{2}$?
Explain. 12.45; Possible explanation: 12.4 = 12.40
and $12\frac{1}{2}$ = 12.50; 12.45 is halfway between
12.40 and 12.50.

Which is smaller, 1.7 or $1\frac{1}{2}$? $1\frac{1}{2}$

Which is smaller, $8\frac{3}{4}$ or 8.25? 8.25
(Learning Goal 8-C)

④ Add: 1.12 + 2.12 + 3.12 6.36

Add: 10.55 + 10.44 20.99

Add: $1.23 + $4.56 $5.79

Subtract: 18.67 − 10.65 8.02

Subtract: 20.05 − 10.55 9.5

Subtract: $4.90 − $1.75 $3.15
(Learning Goal 8-D)

Quick Write This informal written assessment can be administered to small groups or the whole class. Read each question and have the students record response on their write-on boards. Encourage students to listen and think about the questions before responding.

⑤ Place in order from smallest to largest:

    a. 53,076,918

    b. 35,760,819

    c. 53,760,918

    d. 35,076,819 d, b, a, c

Place in order from largest to smallest:

    e. 112,096,002

    f. 9,999,990

    g. 52,043,876

    h. 89,845,899 e, h, g, f
(Learning Goal 8-A)

⑥ Build the number:

    Place a 0 in the ones place.

    Place a 3 in the tens place.

    Place a 5 in the tenths place.

    Place a 2 in the hundreds place.

    Place a 1 in the hundredths place. 230.51

    Write the number which is 0.3 greater than the number you just built. 230.81
(Learning Goal 8-B)

---

⑦ Between which two whole numbers on a number line would you find the following:

    7.36 7 and 8

    24.08 24 and 25
(Learning Goal 8-B)

⑧ Write as a decimal:

    $6\frac{3}{10}$ 6.3

    $17\frac{78}{100}$ 17.78

    $62\frac{1}{2}$ 62.5

    $43\frac{8}{100}$ 43.08
(Learning Goal 8-C)

---

⑨ The cafeteria is selling snacks. Each bag of raisins costs 25¢, each apple costs 15¢, and each orange costs 20¢. Spencer purchases the snacks for his group of friends at the table. He spends exactly $1.50. He bought 1 of one snack, 2 of another snack, and 4 of another snack. What snacks did he buy? Show your work.

25¢ + 25¢ + 25¢ + 25¢ = $1.00 (4 bags of raisins)

15¢ + 15¢ = 30¢ (2 apples)

20¢ (1 orange)

$1.00 + $0.30 + $0.20 = $1.50
(Learning Goal 8-E)

⑩ Josh bought 3 items at the school store. Each one cost 15¢. How much did he spend and how much change did he get back from a dollar? Show your work. 15¢ + 15¢ + 15¢ = 45¢ spent;
$1.00 − 0.45 = $0.55 change

Hillary bought 4 cookies. Each cookie cost 75¢. How much did she spend, and how much change did she get back from a five dollar bill? Show your work.
75¢ + 75¢ + 75¢ + 75¢ = $3.00 spent;
$5.00 − $3.00 = $2.00 change
(Learning Goal 8-D)

Formal Assessment

Chapter Review/Assessment The Chapter 8 Review/Assessment on *Lesson Activity Book* pages 171–172 assesses students' understanding of decimals. Students should be able to complete these pages independently.

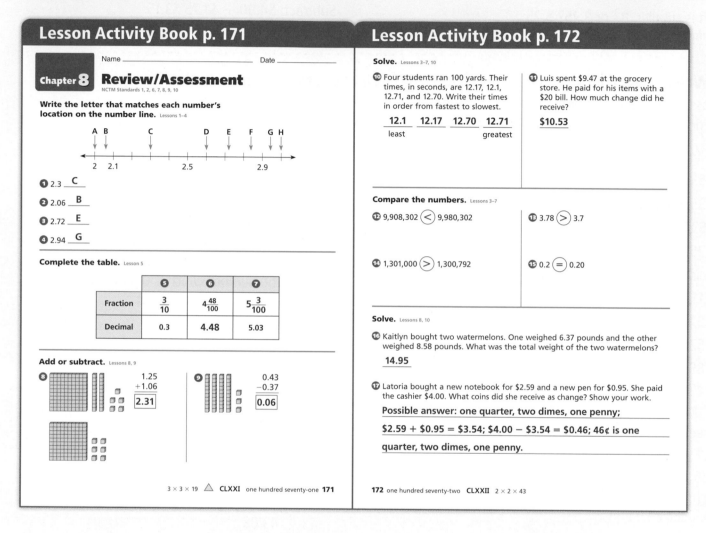

Extra Support Students who have difficulty with items on the Chapter 8 Review/Assessment may need review of the lesson where development of the concept was provided. You can use the Intervention Activity to increase students' understanding before the Chapter Test is given.

Chapter Test Use the Chapter 8 Test in the *Assessment Guide* to assess concepts, skills, and problem solving from the chapter and to prepare students for standardized tests. The Chapter Test and other test items are also available online.

Chapter Notes

Quick Notes

More Ideas

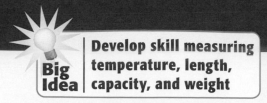

Measurement

About the Chapter

In this chapter, students will deepen their knowledge of measurement as they work with time, temperature, length, capacity, and weight. Students gain experience estimating and measuring each of these, and in converting among different units for measuring length, capacity, and weight.

Reasons for Measurement

The purpose of measurement—and particularly, measurement using standard units—is to describe the physical nature of the world. One can use such information to answer questions concerning the length, weight, temperature, and other properties of matter. Measurement is also used to compare objects to decide which is longer, heavier, slower, colder, and so on. Measurement allows scientists to collect research data and to test observations.

Choosing Units Thoughtfully

When measuring, it is important to choose the units of measure thoughtfully, so they are sensible and useful. For example, while it's possible to measure how far it is from home to school in inches, it doesn't really provide useful information about the distance between the two (unless you perform some conversions). Similarly, it's not practical (though sometimes fun!) to describe your age in seconds, or your weight in milligrams.

> 1 foot = 12 inches
> 1 yard = 3 feet
> 1 yard = 36 inches

Estimation and Familiarity

A sense of the size of a standard unit, such as an inch or a square centimeter, takes time and experience to build. Such a sense is essential, however, if students are to become skilled estimators. Allow students to estimate various measurements. In this chapter, students will develop benchmarks and gain experience in making useful estimates.

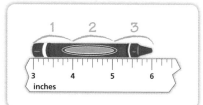

Developing Concepts Across the Grades

Topic	Prior Learning	Learning in Chapter 9	Later Learning
Measure Lengths	• Measure to the nearest quarter-inch • Measure to the nearest centimeter **Grade 3, Chapter 10**	• Use a ruler to measure lengths • Measure length in centimeters using Cuisenaire® Rods • Convert among inches, feet, and yards **Lessons 9.3–9.5**	• Select and use appropriate units and formulas to find length, perimeter, and area **Grade 5, Chapter 10**
Measure Capacity, Weight, Time, Temperature	• Measure and compare time • Measure and compare weights • Analyze temperature data **Grade 3, Chapter 13**	• Measure capacity, weight, temperature • Use minutes or days for computations involving time • Convert between measurement units **Lessons 9.1, 9.2, 9.6–9.10**	• Understand the difference between volume and capacity **Grade 4, Chapter 15**
Estimate Measurements	• Use benchmarks to estimate measurements in centimeters **Grade 3, Chapter 8**	• Estimate length, capacity, and weight **Lessons 9.3, 9.5, 9.6, 9.7, 9.9, 9.10**	• Estimate perimeters and areas on floor plans **Grade 4, Chapter 15**

Chapter Planner

Lesson	Objectives	NCTM Standards	Vocabulary	Materials/Resources

CHAPTER 9 World Almanac For Kids • Vocabulary • Games • Challenge
Teacher Guide pp. 691A–691F, Student Handbook pp. 142–143, 154–158

1 Computing with Time and Money

PACING 1 DAY

Teacher Guide pp. 692–701
Lesson Activity Book pp. 173–174
Student Handbook
Student Letter p. 141
Review Model p. 144

- To use cents for computations involving money
- To use minutes or days for computations involving time

1, 2, 6, 7, 8, 9, 10

unit

For the teacher:
- demonstration clock (optional)
- transparency of AM80 (optional)

For the students:
- School-Home Connection, TR: SHC33–SHC36
- TR: AM80
- small clocks (optional)
- P71, E71, SR71

Social Studies Connection:
Changing Currency
Teacher Guide p. 690

2 Measuring Temperature

PACING 1 DAY

Teacher Guide pp. 702–709
Lesson Activity Book pp. 175–176
Student Handbook
Game p. 156

- To measure changes in temperature in degrees Fahrenheit

1, 2, 6, 7, 8, 9, 10

degree

For the teacher:
- transparency of AM81 (optional)

For the students:
- TR: AM82–AM83
- centimeter cubes or other game pieces, number cubes
- P72, E72, SR27

Science Connection:
Degree Days
Teacher Guide p. 690

3 Measuring Length

PACING 1 DAY

Teacher Guide pp. 710–719
Lesson Activity Book pp. 177–178
Student Handbook
Review Model p. 145

- To review measuring with a ruler
- To estimate, measure, and compare lengths

1, 2, 6, 7, 8, 9, 10

length

For the students:
- TR: AM84
- inch ruler
- centimeter ruler
- P73, E73, SR73

4 Measuring in Inches, Feet, and Yards

PACING 1 DAY

Teacher Guide pp. 720–729
Lesson Activity Book pp. 179–180
Student Handbook
Explore p. 146
Review Model p. 147

- To practice using a ruler to measure length
- To convert among inches, feet, and yards
- To practice multiplication and division

1, 2, 6, 7, 8, 9, 10

inch

foot

yard

For the teacher:
- 3 foot-long rulers
- yard stick

For the students:
- TR: AM85
- P74, E74, SR74

Literature Connection:
How Tall, How Short, How Far Away
Teacher Guide p. 690

NCTM Standards 2000
1. Number and Operations
2. Algebra
3. Geometry
4. Measurement
5. Data Analysis and Probability
6. Problem Solving
7. Reasoning and Proof
8. Communication
9. Connections
10. Representation

Key
AG: Assessment Guide
E: Extension Book
LAB: Lesson Activity Book
P: Practice Book
SH: Student Handbook
SR: Spiral Review Book
TG: Teacher Guide
TR: Teacher Resource Book

MATH GLOSSARY in Student Handbook p. 259

Planner (continued) ➡

Chapter Planner (continued)

Lesson	Objectives	NCTM Standards	Vocabulary	Materials/Resources
5 **Measuring Length in Centimeters** PACING 1 DAY **Teacher Guide** pp. 730–737 **Lesson Activity Book** pp. 181–182 **Student Handbook** Explore p. 148 Review Model p. 149 Game p. 157	• To measure length in centimeters using Cuisenaire® Rods • To estimate and measure length using multiple copies of a unit, or by comparing an unknown length to a known length	1, 2, 6, 7, 8, 9, 10	centimeter	**For the students:** ■ centimeter rulers ■ Cuisenaire® Rods ■ TR: AM86 ■ inch rulers ■ paper clips ■ pencils ■ Review Model ■ P75, E75, SR75
6 **Measuring Capacity in Cups, Pints, and Quarts** PACING 1 DAY **Teacher Guide** pp. 738–743 **Lesson Activity Book** pp. 183–184 **Student Handbook** Explore p. 150	• To estimate and measure capacity using standard and non-standard units • To convert among cups, pints, and quarts	1, 2, 6, 7, 8, 9, 10	cup pint quart	**For the teacher:** ■ standard cup, pint, and quart measures ■ substance to measure (e.g., rice, dried beans, corn kernels) **For the students:** ■ standard measuring cups ■ drinking cups ■ substance to measure (e.g., rice, dried beans, corn kernels) ■ P76, E76, SR76
7 **Measuring Capacity in Gallons and Liters** PACING 1 DAY **Teacher Guide** pp. 744–751 **Lesson Activity Book** pp. 185–186	• To estimate and measure capacity • To convert among cups, pints, quarts, and gallons • To compare customary and metric units of capacity	1, 2, 6, 7, 8, 9, 10	liter milliliter	**For the teacher:** ■ cup, pint, quart, gallon, and liter containers ■ substance to measure (e.g., rice, dried beans, corn kernels) ■ teaspoon (optional) **For the students:** ■ cup, pint, quart, gallon, and liter containers ■ substance to measure (e.g., rice, dried beans, corn kernels) ■ P77, E77, SR77
8 **Computing Amounts of Liquid** PACING 1 DAY **Teacher Guide** pp. 752–759 **Lesson Activity Book** pp. 187–188	• To complete tables and solve problems involving conversions among units of capacity	1, 2, 6, 7, 8, 9, 10	gallon	**For the teacher:** ■ transparency of AM87 (optional) ■ transparency of AM88 (optional) **For the students:** ■ TR: AM87 (optional) ■ TR: AM88 ■ P78, E78, SR78
9 **Measuring Weight in Ounces, Pounds, and Tons** PACING 1 DAY **Teacher Guide** pp. 760–767 **Lesson Activity Book** pp. 189–190 **Student Handbook** Explore p. 151	• To estimate, measure, and compare weights in ounces, pounds, and tons • To convert among ounces, pounds, and tons	1, 2, 6, 7, 8, 9, 10	pound ton	**For the teacher:** ■ scale (balancing scale and bathroom scale recommended) ■ objects that weigh about 1 ounce and 1 pound **For the students:** ■ objects to weigh (e.g., cereal, water, rice, books) ■ P79, E79, SR79

Planner (continued) ➤

Chapter Planner (continued)

Lesson	Objectives	NCTM Standards	Vocabulary	Materials/ Resources
10 **Measuring Weight in Grams and Kilograms** PACING 1 DAY **Teacher Guide** pp. 768–775 **Lesson Activity Book** pp. 191–192	• To estimate, measure, and compare weight in grams and kilograms • To understand the difference between weight and mass • To practice converting between measurement units	1, 2, 6, 7, 8, 9, 10	mass weight	**For the teacher:** ▪ gram scale ▪ paper clip ▪ liter of water ▪ objects to weigh (e.g., quart of milk, pint of rice, can of tomatoes) **For the students:** ▪ P80, E80, SR80
11 **Problem Solving Strategy and Test Prep** PACING 1 DAY **Teacher Guide** pp. 776–781 **Lesson Activity Book** pp. 193–194 **Student Handbook** Review Model pp. 152–153	• To use the problem solving strategy *look for a pattern* • To articulate the steps and strategies used to solve problems • To prepare for standardized tests	1, 2, 6, 7, 8, 9, 10		
CHAPTER 9 Assessment TG pp. 784–785, **LAB** pp. 195–196, **AG** pp. AG81–AG84				**For the students:** ▪ Chapter 9 Test pp. AG81–AG84

Planning Ahead

In **Lesson 9.2,** students will be playing the *Target Temperatures* game. Each pair of students will need a copy of AM83: Target Temperature.

Starting in **Lesson 9.6,** students will need substances to measure (e.g. rice, dried beans, corn kernels).

Games

Use the following games for skills practice and reinforcement of concepts.

Lesson 9.2 *Target Temperatures* provides students practice with adding and subtracting temperatures.

Lesson 9.5 ▶
Build-a-Foot provides students practice using Cuisenaire® Rods to find lengths in centimeters, and to relate centimeters to inches.

Build-a-Foot

Developing Problem Solvers

Open-Ended Problem Solving

The Headline Story in the Daily Activities section provides an open-ended situation where students can pose and solve problems. For each story, there are many possible responses.

Headline Stories can be found on TG pages 693, 703, 711, 721, 731, 739, 745, 753, 761, and 769.

 Headline Story

Leveled Problem Solving

Leveled Problem Solving provides an opportunity for students to apply learning from the lesson to a real-life situation. Problems are leveled by ability to allow students of all ability levels to become successful problem solvers. Each Leveled Problem Solving begins with a real-life scenario upon which three problems are built.

The levels of problems are:

❶ Basic Level	❷ On Level	❸ Above Level
students who need extra support	students working at grade level	students who are ready for more challenging problems

Leveled Problem Solving can be found on TG pages 700, 708, 718, 729, 737, 743, 751, 758, 766, and 774.

 **WORLD ALMANAC FOR KIDS**

The World Almanac for Kids feature is designed to stimulate student interest in the math concepts they are about to learn. Students use data to solve problems and explain solutions. The Chapter 9 Project can be found on SH pages 142–143.

Write Math **Reflect and Summarize the Lesson** poses a problem or question for students to think and write about. This feature can be found on TG pages 699, 707, 717, 728, 736, 742, 750, 757, 765, 773, and 778.

Other opportunities to write about math can be found on LAB pages 188, 190, and 194.

Problem Solving Strategies

The focus of **Lesson 9.11** is the strategy *look for a pattern.* However, students will use a variety of problem solving strategies as they work through the chapter. The chart below shows strategies that may be useful in completing each lesson.

Strategy	Lesson(s)	Description
Act It Out	9.3, 9.6	Act it out to decide which of several lines is the longest or the shortest.
Draw a Picture	9.6	Draw a picture to solve problems involving capacity.
Guess and Check	9.3, 9.8	Guess and check by measuring to find the longest of several given lines.
✓ Look for a Pattern	9.4, 9.9	Look for a pattern to convert among inches, feet, and yards in a table.
Make a Table	9.4, 9.7, 9.8, 9.9	Make a table to find the number of one unit of measure in another.
Make an Organized List	9.7, 9.8, 9.9	Make an organized list to convert among units of capacity.
Use Logical Reasoning	9.1, 9.4, 9.6, 9.7, 9.9	Use logical reasoning to find the sum of amounts expressed in different units.
Write an Equation	9.2	Write and solve an equation to find the difference between two temperatures.

Meeting the Needs of All Learners

Differentiated Instruction		
Extra Support	**On Level**	**Enrichment**
Intervention Activities TG pp. 700, 708, 718, 729, 737, 743, 751, 758, 766, 774	**Practice Book** pp. P71–P80	**Extension Activities** TG pp. 700, 708, 718, 729, 737, 743, 751, 758, 766, 774
	Spiral Review Book pp. SR71–SR80	**Extension Book** pp. E71–E80
	LAB Challenge LAB pp. 174, 176, 178, 180, 182, 184, 186, 188, 190, 192	**LAB Challenge** LAB pp. 174, 176, 178, 180, 182, 184, 186, 188, 190, 192,
Lesson Notes **Basic Level** TG pp. 714, 722, 742	**Lesson Notes** **On Level** TG pp. 741, 749	**Lesson Notes** **Above Level** TG pp. 704, 705
Leveled Problem Solving **Basic Level** TG pp. 700, 708, 718, 729, 737, 743, 751, 758, 766, 774	**Leveled Problem Solving** **On Level** TG pp. 700, 708, 718, 729, 737, 743, 751, 758, 766, 774	**Leveled Problem Solving** **Above Level** TG pp. 700, 708, 718, 729, 737, 743, 751, 758, 766, 774

English Language Learners

Suggestions for addressing the needs of children learning English as a second language are included in the Developing Mathematical Language section at the beginning of most lessons.

ELL activities for this chapter can be found on TG pages 693, 703, 711, 721, 731, 739, 745, 753, 761, and 769.

The Multi-Age Classroom

Grade 3	• Students on this level should be able to complete the lessons in Chapter 9 but might need some additional practice with key concepts and skills. • Give students more practice with measuring capacity and weight.	See Grade 4, Intervention Activities, Lesson 9.1–9.10. See Grade 3, Lessons 13.4, 13.5, 13.6, 13.7.
Grade 4	• Students on this level should be able to complete the lessons in Chapter 9 with minimal adjustments.	See Grade 4, Practice pages P71–P80.
Grade 5	• Students on this level should be able to complete the lessons in Chapter 9 and to extend measurement and estimation concepts and skills. • Give students extended work measuring volume.	See Grade 4, Extension pages E71–E80. See Grade 5, Lessons 13.4, 13.5.

Cross Curricular Connections

Social Studies Connection

Math Concept: converting money amounts

Changing Currency

- Tell students that different countries have different units of money and that the units have different values. Ask students who have traveled to other countries to share their knowledge of those countries' money systems.

- Tell students that twelve countries in Europe have agreed to use the same money unit, the euro. Two of the countries are France and Italy. You may wish to have students research which other countries use the euro.

- Explain that although its value varies, the euro is worth about 1.2 U.S. dollars. Have students use whatever problem solving strategy they choose to complete the table below.

Euros	1	2	3	4	5	6
U.S. Dollars	1.2	2.4	3.6	4.8	6.0	7.2

Lesson 9.1

Science Connection

Math Concept: temperature in degrees Fahrenheit

Degree Days

Explain to students that meteorologists (weather forecasters) use the idea of "degree days" to measure the demand for heating or cooling. Below 65°F, there are heating degree days; above 65°F, there are cooling degree days. The number of degree days for a date is the difference between 65°F and the average temperature for that date.

Have students calculate the degree days for their location yesterday. Have them:

- find the low temperature and the high temperature;

- add the two temperatures and divide the total by 2. If the result is greater than 65, the degree days will represent cooling; if the result is less than 65, it will represent heating;

- find the difference between the result and 65. That number is the number of "degree days."

Students can compare their findings with information given in newspapers or in weather forecasts.

Lesson 9.2

Literature Connection

Math Concept: measuring

How Tall, How Short, How Far Away
By David Adler
Illustrated by Nancy Tobin

In this book, students will see how units of measurement have changed through time. Fascinating facts and colorful illustrations will captivate students' attention as they learn about ancient and modern methods of measurement.

Lesson 9.4

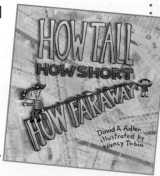

School-Home Connection

Encourage students to do the *Treasure Hunt* activity, found on the School-Home Connection page, with a family member. Students will work with the concepts of comparing measurements and converting between units in **Lessons 9.1** through **9.11**.

A reproducible copy of the School-Home Connection letter in English and in Spanish can be found in the *Teacher Resource Book,* pages SHC33–SHC36.

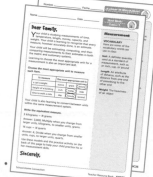

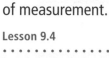

Assessment Options

There are many opportunities in *Think Math!* to assess students' understanding of concepts, skills, and problem solving. Learning Goals for Chapter 9 are provided below. The assessment options provide opportunities to evaluate whether or not students have retained learning from prior experiences. Choose the forms of assessment that best meet the needs of your students.

Chapter 9 Learning Goals

	Learning Goals	Lesson Number
9-A	Compute with time and money	9.1
9-B	Measure and compute changes in temperature	9.2
9-C	Use customary units to measure length, capacity, and weight, and convert among units	9.3, 9.4, 9.6, 9.8
9-D	Use metric units to measure length, capacity, and mass/weight, and convert among units	9.5, 9.7, 9.10
9-E	Apply problem solving strategies such as *look for a pattern* to solve problems	9.11

✔ Informal Assessment

Ongoing Assessment
Provides insight into students' thinking to guide instruction (TG pp. 695, 714, 716, 724, 727, 740, 746, 748, 754, 762, 770)

Reflect and Summarize the Lesson
Checks understanding of lesson concepts (TG pp. 699, 707, 717, 728, 736, 742, 750, 757, 765, 773, 778)

Snapshot Assessment
Mental Math and Quick Write
Offers a quick observation of students' progress on chapter concepts and skills (TG pp. 782–783)

Performance Assessment
Provides quarterly assessment of Chapters 8–11 concepts using real-life situations
Assessment Guide
pp. AG219–AG224

✔ Formal Assessment

Standardized Test Prep
Problem Solving Test Prep
Prepares students for standardized tests
Lesson Activity Book p. 194 (TG p. 779)

Chapter 9 Review/Assessment
Reviews and assesses students' understanding of the chapter
Lesson Activity Book pp. 195–196 (TG p. 784)

Chapter 9 Test
Assesses the chapter concepts and skills
Assessment Guide
Form A pp. AG81–AG82
Form B pp. AG83–AG84

Benchmark 3 Assessment
Provides quarterly assessment of Chapters 8–11 concepts and skills
Assessment Guide
Benchmark 3A pp. AG93–AG100
Benchmark 3B pp. AG101–AG108

World Almanac for Kids

Use the World Almanac for Kids feature, *Ready for Summer,* found on pp. 142–143 of the **Student Handbook,** to provide students with an opportunity to practice using their problem solving skills by solving real world problems.

FACT•ACTIVITY 1

❶ 14 days; 2 weeks

❷ 105 minutes

❸ 2 hours, 40 minutes

❹ 9 days; $9 \times 24 = 216$ hours

WORLD ALMANAC FOR KIDS

Ready for Summer!

What is your favorite season: fall, winter, spring, or summer? For many people, summer is the best time of the year. Many families plan summer activities from taking trips to jumping into a backyard pool.

FACT•ACTIVITY 1

❶ Noshi's trip will begin on the first day of summer. On June 7th, he begins counting the days until his trip. How many more days until Noshi's trip? How many weeks?

❷ Noshi's plane departs at 2:30 P.M. He arrives at the airport at 12:45 P.M. How many minutes until the plane takes off?

❸ If the flight is 160 minutes long, how many hours and minutes is the flight?

❹ Noshi's return flight from vacation arrives on June 30th at 2:30 P.M. How many days and hours have passed since his plane took off on June 21st?

JUNE

sunday	monday	tuesday	wednesday	thursday	friday	saturday
1	2	3	4	5	6	7
8	9	10	11	12	13	14
15	16	17	18	19	20	21 Summer Begins!
22	23	24	25	26	27	28
29	30					

142 Chapter 9

Student Handbook p. 142

FACT·ACTIVITY 2

How do you keep cool in hot weather? There are simple things many families do at home. Some set up sprinklers or use hoses and sheets of plastic to make homemade water slides. Some families set up shallow pools to keep cool.

A family looks at the following two plastic inflatable pools.

Family Swimming Pools			
Name	Length	Width	Height
Blue Lagoon	10 feet	6 feet	1 foot, 10 inches
Clear Blue	5 feet	5 feet	$1\frac{1}{2}$ feet

1. Katia is 4 feet tall. How many inches taller is she than the top of the Clear Blue pool?

2. The Blue Lagoon pool is filled up to 6 inches below its height. What will be the height in inches of the water in the pool?

3. Erik's family wants to enclose the Blue Lagoon pool with fencing. If they have 360 inches of fencing, do they have enough to enclose the pool? Explain why or why not.

CHAPTER PROJECT

Some kids sell lemonade on hot summer days. Plan a lemonade stand. Find a recipe that uses lemons. List the ingredients. How many servings does the recipe make? Suppose you are going to make 5 times the number of servings. Determine how much of each ingredient you will need and list the amounts.

- Weigh one lemon. How many ounces does one lemon weigh? How many total ounces and pounds of lemons will you need?

- How much water does your recipe require? Express the total amount of water you will need in cups, pints, and quarts.

- Fix a price and make a price chart for the cost of 1 to 10 cups of your lemonade.

ALMANAC
Fact

Even though Florida is surrounded by the ocean, there are more than 1,000,000 swimming pools in the state.

Student Handbook p. 143

FACT·ACTIVITY 2

1. 48 inches − 18 inches = 30 inches taller

2. 22 inches − 6 inches = 16 inches of water

3. No; Possible explanation: They need at least 10 + 10 + 6 + 6 = 32 feet of fence to enclose the pool. 32 × 12 = 384 inches of fence, so 360 inches is not enough.

CHAPTER PROJECT

Sample recipe: makes 6 servings

6 lemons
$\frac{1}{2}$ cup sugar
4 cups cold water
1 cup crushed ice

If I make 5 times the recipe, I will use:

6 × 5 = 30 lemons; $\frac{1}{2}$ × 5 = $2\frac{1}{2}$ cups sugar; 4 × 5 = 20 cups cold water; 1 × 5 = 5 cups crushed ice

- 1 lemon weighs about 2 oz, so 2 × 6 = 12 oz for 1 recipe; 12 × 5 = 60 oz needed for 5 times the recipe; 60 oz = 3 lb 12 oz

- 4 cups water = 2 pt = 1 qt needed for 1 recipe; so 20 cups = 10 pts = 5 quarts needed for 5 times the recipe.

- Price at $0.50 a cup

Cups	1	2	3	4	5	6	7	8	9	10
Cost ($)	0.50	1.00	1.50	2.00	2.50	3.00	3.50	4.00	4.50	5.00

Vocabulary

To reinforce vocabulary concepts, invite students to complete the vocabulary activities on pp. 154–155 of the *Student Handbook.* Encourage students to record their answers in their math journals.

Many responses are possible.

13 Possible response: There are 2 *cups* in a *pint.* Each *quart* contains 2 *pints,* so there are 4 *cups* in a *quart.* A *gallon* holds 4 *quarts,* so there are 16 *cups* in a *gallon.*

14 Possible response: If I have 3 *gallons,* for example, then I have 12 *quarts,* because each *gallon* has 4 *quarts* and $3 \times 4 = 12$. I can multiply 12×2 to get 24 *pints.* Then I can multiply 24×2 to get 48 *cups.*

Chapter 9 Vocabulary

Choose the best vocabulary term from Word List A for each sentence.

Word List A
centimeter
cup
degree
foot
gallon
inch
length
liter
milliliter
pint
pound
quart
ton
unit
weight
yard

1 A(n) __?__ is the unit used for measuring temperature. **degree**

2 You can measure __?__ in ounces, pounds, or tons. **weight**

3 The measurement of an object from end to end is its __?__. **length**

4 The __?__ is a customary unit for measuring capacity equal to 16 cups. **gallon**

5 One __?__ is exactly 3 feet long. **yard**

6 A fish tank holding 240 gallons of water weighs about 1 __?__. **ton**

7 One __?__ in the metric system is about the same as 1 quart in the customary system. **liter**

8 One hundredth of a meter is 1 __?__. **centimeter**

9 A(n) __?__ is one twelfth of a foot. **inch**

10 Four cups are the same as 1 __?__. **quart**

Complete each analogy. Use the best term from Word List B.

Word List B
gallon
inch
liter
pound
quart
yard

11 Foot is to length as __?__ is to weight. **pound**

12 Cup is to pint as half-gallon is to __?__. **gallon**

Talk Math

Discuss with a partner what you have learned about measurement. Use the vocabulary terms *cup, gallon, pint,* and *quart.*

13 How can you find the number of cups in a gallon?

14 Suppose you know the number of gallons you have. How can you find how many cups you have?

154 Chapter 9

Student Handbook p. 154

Analysis Chart

15 Create an analysis chart for the terms *inch, foot, yard,* and *centimeter*. Use what you know and what you have learned about measures of length.

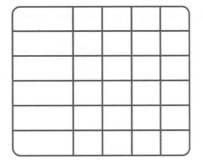

Word Web

16 Create a word web using the term *pound*.

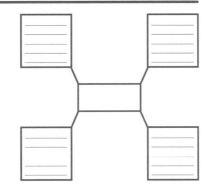

Chapter 9   **155**

Student Handbook p. 155

---

15 Many answers are possible. One example is provided.

	inch	foot	yard	centimeter
A spoon is longer.	true	false	false	true
A stair step is higher.	true	false	false	true
My shoe is shorter.	false	true	true	false
My notebook paper is wider.	true	false	false	true
I could easily carry a stack of books this high.	true	true	false	true

16 Many answers are possible. One example is provided.

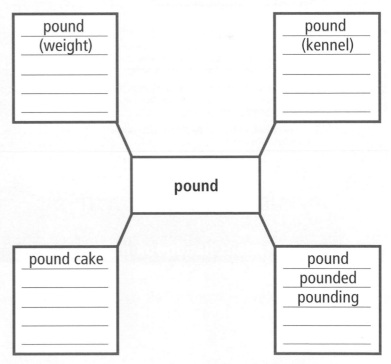

Games

Target Temperatures in **Lesson 9.2** provides an opportunity for students to learn common temperature benchmarks, and to practice adding and subtracting temperatures. *Build-a-Foot* in **Lesson 9.5** provides an opportunity for students to practice using Cuisenaire® Rods to find lengths in centimeters, and to relate centimeters to inches.

These games can be found in the *Student Handbook* on pp. 156–157.

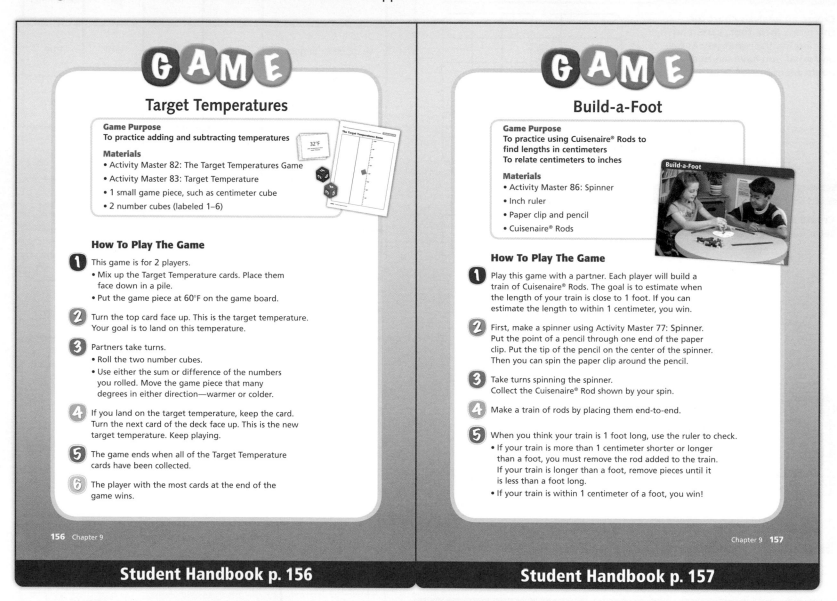

Target Temperatures

Game Purpose
To practice adding and subtracting temperatures

Materials
• Activity Master 82: The Target Temperatures Game
• Activity Master 83: Target Temperature
• 1 small game piece, such as centimeter cube
• 2 number cubes (labeled 1–6)

How To Play The Game

1 This game is for 2 players.
• Mix up the Target Temperature cards. Place them face down in a pile.
• Put the game piece at 60°F on the game board.

2 Turn the top card face up. This is the target temperature. Your goal is to land on this temperature.

3 Partners take turns.
• Roll the two number cubes.
• Use either the sum or difference of the numbers you rolled. Move the game piece that many degrees in either direction—warmer or colder.

4 If you land on the target temperature, keep the card. Turn the next card of the deck face up. This is the new target temperature. Keep playing.

5 The game ends when all of the Target Temperature cards have been collected.

6 The player with the most cards at the end of the game wins.

156 Chapter 9

Build-a-Foot

Game Purpose
To practice using Cuisenaire® Rods to find lengths in centimeters
To relate centimeters to inches

Materials
• Activity Master 86: Spinner
• Inch ruler
• Paper clip and pencil
• Cuisenaire® Rods

How To Play The Game

1 Play this game with a partner. Each player will build a train of Cuisenaire® Rods. The goal is to estimate when the length of your train is close to 1 foot. If you can estimate the length to within 1 centimeter, you win.

2 First, make a spinner using Activity Master 77: Spinner. Put the point of a pencil through one end of the paper clip. Put the tip of the pencil on the center of the spinner. Then you can spin the paper clip around the pencil.

3 Take turns spinning the spinner. Collect the Cuisenaire® Rod shown by your spin.

4 Make a train of rods by placing them end-to-end.

5 When you think your train is 1 foot long, use the ruler to check.
• If your train is more than 1 centimeter shorter or longer than a foot, you must remove the rod added to the train. If your train is longer than a foot, remove pieces until it is less than a foot long.
• If your train is within 1 centimeter of a foot, you win!

Chapter 9 157

Student Handbook p. 156

Student Handbook p. 157

Challenge

This activity challenges students to measure distances around a curve by using a string to measure the curve and then measuring the string. This activity can be found on p. 158 of the *Student Handbook.*

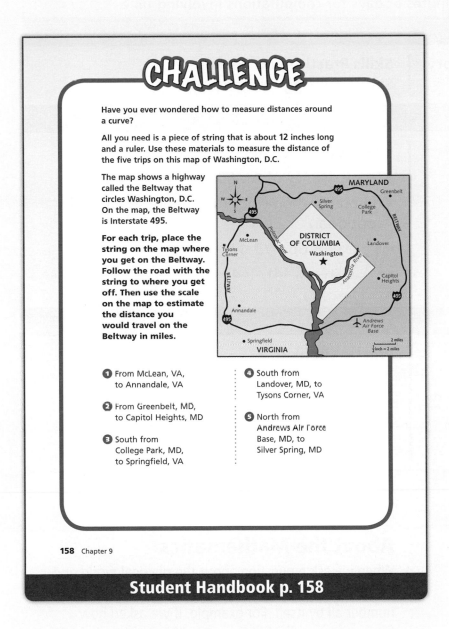

Many estimates are possible. One is given.

❶ about 8 miles

❷ about 8 miles

❸ about 27 miles

❹ about 28 miles

❺ about 20 miles

Lesson 1 Computing with Time and Money

NCTM Standards 1, 2, 6, 7, 8, 9, 10

Lesson Planner

STUDENT OBJECTIVES
- To use cents for computations involving money
- To use minutes or days for computations involving time

1 Daily Activities (TG p. 693)

Open-Ended Problem Solving/Headline Story	Skills Practice and Review— Skip-Counting by 7 and 15

2 Teach and Practice (TG pp. 694–699)

	MATERIALS
Ⓐ **Introducing Measurement** (TG p. 694)	• TR: Activity Master, AM80
Ⓑ **Adding 2 + 6 with Different Units** (TG p. 695)	• transparency of AM80 (optional)
Ⓒ **Computing Time Intervals** (TG pp. 696–697)	• demonstration clock (optional), small clocks (optional)
Ⓓ **Computing with Time and Money** (TG p. 698)	• 📖 LAB pp. 173–174 • 📖 SH pp. 141, 144

3 Differentiated Instruction (TG p. 700)

Leveled Problem Solving (TG p. 700)	Practice Book P71
Intervention Activity (TG p. 700)	Extension Book E71
Extension Activity (TG p. 700)	Spiral Review Book SR71
Social Studies Connection (TG p. 690)	

Lesson Notes

About the Lesson

Students begin the measurement chapter by focusing on the importance of specifying units of measurement. By seeing that an open number sentence can be completed in many ways, depending on the units, students are motivated to explore units of measurement as a tool for conveying what the numbers in the sentence refer to. As students measure intervals of time, they use clocks and timelines. Working with timelines is related to measuring length as an interval on a ruler, which appears in later lessons.

About the Mathematics

When we ask a question about the physical world and expect a number as an answer, we rarely expect the number all by itself. For example, if we asked how far someone walked, the answer "3" does not help, unless we know whether it is "3 miles," "3 blocks," or "3 yards". Still, in everyday language we often omit the units because they are implied. In addition to providing a context, units also can indicate a type of measurement, such as time (e.g., minutes) or length (e.g., inches). We can add two measurements only if the quantities are of the same type, allowing us to convert to common units.

Use with Lesson Activity Book pp. 173–174.

Developing Mathematical Language

Vocabulary: unit

It isn't easy to define the term *unit* formally in a way that will make sense to fourth graders. However, students should understand the term when it is used in context. If you want them to learn the word itself, have them remember examples and uses of the term, not definitions. By the end of the chapter, students should know the types of measurement that are associated with standard *units*—for example, that inches are used to measure length.

Review the term *unit* with students.

Beginning List several measurements on the board, such as 10 inches, 42¢, and 8 minutes. For one of the measurements, point out the *unit*. Have students work in pairs to identify the *unit* for each remaining measurement.

Intermediate Have students stand in a circle around the classroom. Have one student call out a measurement, such as 7 bicycles, and then name a student to call out its *unit*. Repeat until all students have had a chance to call out a measurement and *unit.*

Advanced On notebook paper, have students write a sentence that uses at least one *unit,* such as, "Art paid 27¢ for 3 pens." Have students trade papers with a partner and identify the *units.* In this example, the *units* are cent and pen.

Open-Ended Problem Solving

Read the Headline Story to the students. Encourage them to think of interesting scenarios and make a table of possible times that incorporate information from the story.

Headline Story

> Susan finished lunch 15 minutes before Juan.

Possible responses: If Susan finished at 1:15, Juan finished at 1:30. If Juan finished at 1:55, Susan finished at 1:40. I can make a table with possible finishing times:

Susan	12:00	11:15	11:32	12:50	11:04	11:28
Juan	12:15	11:30	11:47	1:05	11:19	11:43

Skills Practice and Review

Skip-Counting by 7 and 15

This activity prepares students to use multiples of 7 when making calculations involving days and weeks, and to use multiples of 15 when making calculations involving minutes and hours. Have students count by 7s from zero to 126 in unison. Then have them count backwards by 7s from 126 to zero, saying 126, 119, 112, and so on.

Repeat this activity, this time pointing to individual students and having them call out the next number in the sequence. To provide students with visual help, draw a horizontal line on the board and, as students call out the numbers, represent them on the line. The line must reach to 126, so be sure there is enough space.

Repeat this activity, counting by 15s from zero to 165.

 whole class | 5 MIN

Ⓐ Introducing Measurement

NCTM Standards 1, 2, 6, 7, 8, 9, 10

Purpose To introduce measurement

Introduce The Student Letter introduces students to key concepts of measurement. Read the letter aloud with the class.

Problem Ask the following question:

• **What does "somethings" mean in the sum "10 somethings + 2 somethings"?** Possible answer: It means a thing you use to measure the size of an object, like feet or pounds.

Share Briefly discuss the range of topics students will see in this chapter. Then ask students to share some of the important ideas they remember about measurement. For example, students may remember that you can measure the amount of water that a container can hold, or how heavy something is. Students are likely to remember basic equivalents such as 7 days in a week, 12 inches in a foot, and 60 minutes in an hour.

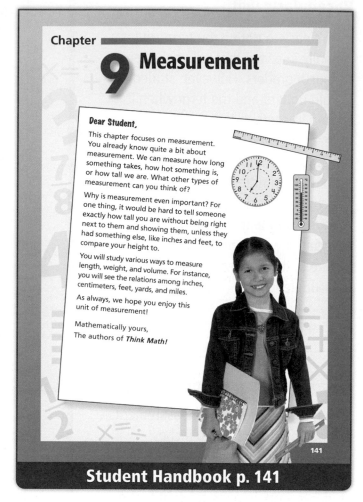

Student Handbook p. 141

💬 **Talk Math**

❷ What is the sum of 10 cents and 2 cents? 12 cents

❷ Is the sum of 10 cents and 2 nickels equal to 12 cents, 12 nickels, or something else? Explain. something else; Possible explanation: To add cents and nickels, you first have to think of each nickel as 5 cents. So, the sum is 10 cents plus 5 cents plus 5 cents, or 20 cents.

Use with Lesson Activity Book pp. 173–174.

B Adding 2 + 6 with Different Units

NCTM Standards 1, 2, 6, 7, 8, 9, 10

Purpose To see how measurement units provide a context for numbers

Introduce Write the following number sentence on the board, leaving spaces after the 2, the 6, and the 20:

Pause to give students a chance to think about how this sentence could possibly make sense before writing the word *days* after the 20.

Problem Ask this question:

- **What could you write after 2 and after 6 that would make the sentence true?**

  If necessary, prompt students by writing the word *weeks* after the 2. Help students to see that 2 *weeks* + 6 *days* = 20 *days*.

Share Ask students to find other ways to complete the sentence 2 ____ + 6 ____ = _____. After students have had a chance to give a few of their own examples, write any of the following problems on the board that students have not already given:

2 stars + 6 stars = ____ 8 stars

2 dimes + 6 nickels = ____ Possible answers: 8 coins, 50¢, 10 nickels, or 2 quarters

2 feet + 6 inches = ____ Possible answers: 30 inches or $2\frac{1}{2}$ feet

2 hours + 6 minutes = ____ 126 minutes

Conclude by asking students what to do with a problem like 2 miles + 6 gallons. Students should reason that this makes no sense, because we cannot add completely unlike things: miles measure distance and gallons measure capacity, so they cannot be added. (See About the Mathematics.)

🗨 Talk Math

❓ How can you find the sum of 2 minutes + 6 seconds? Possible answer: There are 60 seconds in a minute, so 2 minutes = 2 × 60 = 120 seconds. So, 2 minutes + 6 seconds = 120 seconds + 6 seconds = 126 seconds.

❓ What word can you write in the space to make a true sentence: 3 dimes + 4 nickels = 2 _____? quarters

✅ Ongoing Assessment

- Do students know basic measurement equivalents such as 12 inches in a foot, 60 minutes in an hour, and 10 cents in a dime?

Computing Time Intervals

Materials

- For the teacher: demonstration clock (optional), AM80 transparency (optional)
- For each student: AM80, small clock (optional)

NCTM Standards 1, 2, 6, 7, 8, 9, 10

Possible Discussion

Your students might enjoy learning the curious origins of some of the familiar and not so familiar measurement units.

You might use a discussion of the history of measurement units to point out the importance of having a common standard to refer to, no matter what that standard is. A "foot" is a useful measure, so long as everyone agrees to use the same foot as the standard, and not his or her own feet. Below are some facts that might interest your students:

- The first known units of measure seem to have been created more than 4,000 years ago by the ancient peoples of Mesopotamia and Egypt.
- The first units of measure were based on parts of the human body (hand or foot), the dimensions of common items, the distances one could walk in a day, and other everyday lengths and distances.

(continued on page 697)

Purpose To measure intervals of time

Introduce Write the following number sentence on the board. Challenge students to think of units that will make the sentence true.

$$1\underline{\quad} - 40\underline{\quad} = 20\underline{\quad}$$

If students need help, write the word *hour* after the 1.
1 hour − 40 minutes = 20 minutes

Task **For the following problems, choose times that match your students time-telling skills. Invite a student to set a demonstration clock to a time that you whisper to them (for example, a quarter past four or two forty-five). Ask another student to read the time.** Then ask a question like one of the following:

- How long is it until six o'clock?
- If I started my homework at the time shown on the clock and did not stop until six o'clock, how long would I have worked?

Students should say how many hours or minutes will pass from the time shown on the clock until the other time you have given. After students answer, move the hands on the clock to show the passing time, and have students check their answers by counting the hours and minutes as you do this.

After finding a few other time intervals this way, display the transparency of Activity Master: Timelines, or sketch a timeline on the board. Ask a student to choose a time shown on the timeline and to mark it. Then ask another student to choose and mark another time on the same timeline. Finally, ask students to find the number of hours and/or minutes between the two times, as they did with the clocks. Again, you might show how to count the hour intervals between the markings separately from the minutes.

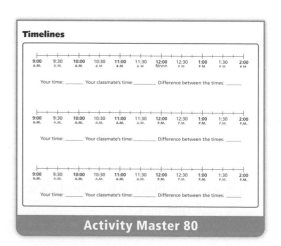

Use with Lesson Activity Book pp. 173–174.

Once students are comfortable with finding time intervals in this way, give each a copy of Activity Master: Timelines. Ask them to mark a different time on each of the three timelines. Students should then find someone who chose a different time for the first timeline. They should each mark the other's time on the timeline, determine the time interval between these two times, and record it on their paper. They should do the same for each of their timelines.

Talk Math

❷ A movie started at 11:30 A.M. and was over at 2 P.M. How long did the movie last? Explain your reasoning. 2 hours 30 minutes; Possible explanation: It is 2 hours from 11:30 A.M. to 1:30 P.M. and 30 minutes from 1:30 P.M. to 2 P.M., for a total of 2 hours 30 minutes.

❷ What words can you write in the following sentence to make the sentence true: 30 ____ + 45 ____ + 45 ____ = 2 ____ ? minutes; minutes; minutes; hours

Possible Discussion
(continued from page 696)

- In Finland, a *pennikuuluma* was used as a measure of distance equal to 10 kilometers. This was the distance at which hunters could hear their barking dogs.

- Ancient Egyptians measured the smallest things with a hair taken from the muzzle of a donkey. They measured bigger things with *palms* (1 palm = 4 fingers) and *ells* (1 ell = 6 palms).

- The unit of length *mile* was created by the Romans; it was equal to 1000 *paces* (or double steps). The word *mile* is related to *mille* (one thousand in Latin).

individuals
or pairs
  20 MIN

Purpose To convert money and time amounts

NCTM Standards 1, 2, 6, 7, 8, 9, 10

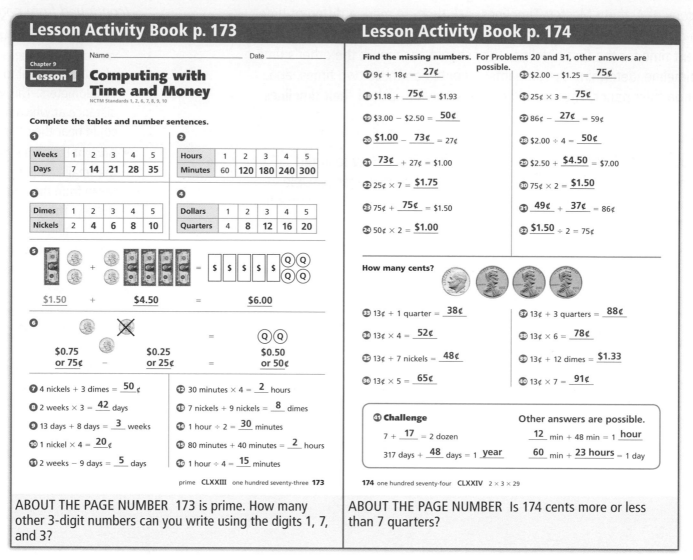

Lesson Activity Book p. 173

Chapter 9
Lesson 1 **Computing with Time and Money**
NCTM Standards 1, 2, 6, 7, 8, 9, 10

Name _____ Date _____

Complete the tables and number sentences.

1

Weeks	1	2	3	4	5
Days	7	**14**	**21**	**28**	**35**

2

Hours	1	2	3	4	5
Minutes	60	**120**	**180**	**240**	**300**

3

Dimes	1	2	3	4	5
Nickels	2	**4**	**6**	**8**	**10**

4

Dollars	1	2	3	4	5
Quarters	4	**8**	**12**	**16**	**20**

5 $1.50 + $4.50 = $6.00

6 $0.75 or 75¢ − $0.25 or 25¢ = $0.50 or 50¢

7 4 nickels + 3 dimes = **50** ¢
8 2 weeks × 3 = **42** days
9 13 days + 8 days = **3** weeks
10 1 nickel × 4 = **20** ¢
11 2 weeks − 9 days = **5** days

12 30 minutes × 4 = **2** hours
13 7 nickels + 9 nickels = **8** dimes
14 1 hour ÷ 2 = **30** minutes
15 80 minutes + 40 minutes = **2** hours
16 1 hour ÷ 4 = **15** minutes

prime **CLXXIII** one hundred seventy-three **173**

ABOUT THE PAGE NUMBER 173 is prime. How many other 3-digit numbers can you write using the digits 1, 7, and 3?

Lesson Activity Book p. 174

Find the missing numbers. For Problems 20 and 31, other answers are possible.

17 9¢ + 18¢ = **27¢**
18 $1.18 + **75¢** = $1.93
19 $3.00 − $2.50 = **50¢**
20 **$1.00** − **73¢** = 27¢
31 **73¢** + 27¢ = $1.00
22 25¢ × 7 = **$1.75**
23 75¢ + **75¢** = $1.50
24 50¢ × 2 = **$1.00**

25 $2.00 − $1.25 = **75¢**
26 25¢ × 3 = **75¢**
27 86¢ − **27¢** = 59¢
28 $2.00 ÷ 4 = **50¢**
29 $2.50 + **$4.50** = $7.00
30 75¢ × 2 = **$1.50**
31 **49¢** + **37¢** = 86¢
32 **$1.50** ÷ 2 = 75¢

How many cents?

33 13¢ + 1 quarter = **38¢**
34 13¢ × 4 = **52¢**
35 13¢ + 7 nickels = **48¢**
36 13¢ × 5 = **65¢**

37 13¢ + 3 quarters = **88¢**
38 13¢ × 6 = **78¢**
39 13¢ + 12 dimes = **$1.33**
40 13¢ × 7 = **91¢**

41 Challenge Other answers are possible.

7 + **17** = 2 dozen
317 days + **48** days = 1 year

12 min + 48 min = 1 **hour**
60 min + **23 hours** = 1 day

174 one hundred seventy-four **CLXXIV** 2 × 3 × 29

ABOUT THE PAGE NUMBER Is 174 cents more or less than 7 quarters?

Teaching Notes for LAB page 173

Have students complete the page individually or with partners.

Remind students to pay careful attention to the units in each problem. All of the problems involve money or time, but the units vary from problem to problem and within each problem. In future lessons, students will complete similar problems involving other units of measurement, such as feet and inches, pounds and ounces, and quarts and gallons.

Teaching Notes for LAB page 174

These problems are more difficult than those on LAB p. 173 because the computations involve larger amounts of money or amounts that are not always multiples of 5¢. Students may answer using cent (¢) or dollar ($) notation.

Challenge Problems These problems require students to find missing values in number sentences each of which involves two different units. Students may need to be reminded that there are 12 in a dozen and 365 days in a year.

Write Math

Find two different ways to complete this number sentence: 3 ____ + 9 ____ = ____.
Possible answers: 3 eggs + 9 eggs = 1 dozen eggs; 3 inches + 9 inches = 1 foot; 3 hours +
9 minutes = 189 minutes; 3 pennies + 9 dimes = 93¢

Review Model . . . .

Refer students to the Review Model: Adding Different Units in
the *Student Handbook* p. 144 to practice adding units.

✔ Check for Understanding

1 6 dimes or 12 nickels or 60¢

2 8 dimes or 16 nickels or 80¢

3 $3\frac{1}{2}$ feet or 42 inches

4 $4\frac{1}{4}$ feet or 51 inches

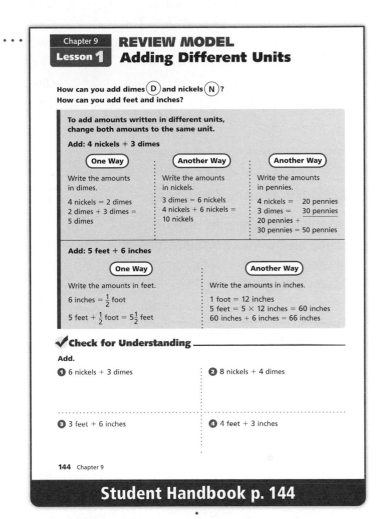

Chapter 9
Lesson 1
REVIEW MODEL
Adding Different Units

How can you add dimes (D) and nickels (N)?
How can you add feet and inches?

To add amounts written in different units,
change both amounts to the same unit.

Add: 4 nickels + 3 dimes

One Way	Another Way	Another Way
Write the amounts in dimes.	Write the amounts in nickels.	Write the amounts in pennies.
4 nickels = 2 dimes 2 dimes + 3 dimes = 5 dimes	3 dimes = 6 nickels 4 nickels + 6 nickels = 10 nickels	4 nickels = 20 pennies 3 dimes = 30 pennies 20 pennies + 30 pennies = 50 pennies

Add: 5 feet + 6 inches

One Way	Another Way
Write the amounts in feet.	Write the amounts in inches.
6 inches = $\frac{1}{2}$ foot 5 feet + $\frac{1}{2}$ foot = $5\frac{1}{2}$ feet	1 foot = 12 inches 5 feet = 5 × 12 inches = 60 inches 60 inches + 6 inches = 66 inches

✔ Check for Understanding

Add.

1 6 nickels + 3 dimes   **2** 8 nickels + 4 dimes

3 3 feet + 6 inches   **4** 4 feet + 3 inches

144 Chapter 9

Student Handbook p. 144

Leveled Problem Solving

Monica spends 2 weeks and 5 days at sleep-away camp.

❶ Basic Level
How many days is Monica at camp? Explain. 19 days; 2 × 7 + 5 = 19 days.

❷ On Level
On her way home, she visits her cousin for 2 days. How long is she away from home? Explain. 21 days, or 3 weeks; length of camp is 2 × 7 + 5 = 19 days; 19 + 2 = 21.

❸ Above Level
Cornell spends 1 week at one camp and 10 days at another camp. Who spends more time at camp? Explain. Monica; Monica: 2 × 7 + 5 = 19 days, Cornell: 7 + 10 = 17 days; 19 > 17.

| Intervention | Practice | Extension |

Activity Money Changing

List coin denominations in a column on the board. Ask two students each to choose a number from 1 to 5. Assign those numbers to two different denominations, and have students make the combination using play or real coins. Have them trade coins to give only one kind of coin, then ask for the total amount.

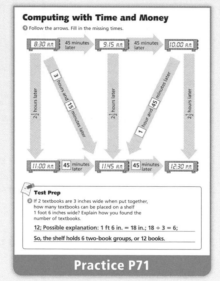

Practice P71

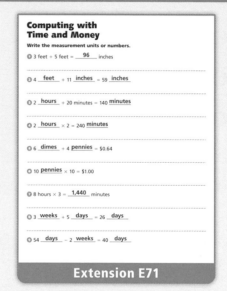

Extension E71

Spiral Review

Spiral Review Book page SR71 provides review of the following previously learned skills and concepts:

- finding different rectangles with the same perimeter
- solving problems using the problem solving strategy *look for a pattern*

You may wish to have students work with partners to complete the page.

Spiral Review SR71

Extension Activity
Money Matters

Have students work in pairs. Ask them to try to list all the different ways they can make 60¢ using only nickels, dimes, and quarters. Encourage students to organize their lists from greatest number of coins to least number of coins. Have students compare their lists to see whether they missed any combinations. 13 combinations are possible.

Teacher's Notes 🍎

Daily Notes . . .

🗒️ **Quick Notes**

More Ideas

Lesson 2 Measuring Temperature

NCTM Standards 1, 2, 6, 7, 8, 9, 10

Lesson Planner

STUDENT OBJECTIVE ·
- To measure changes in temperature in degrees Fahrenheit

1 Daily Activities (TG p. 703)

Open-Ended Problem Solving/Headline Story	Skills Practice and Review— Adding and Subtracting Decimals

2 Teach and Practice (TG pp. 704–707)

	MATERIALS
Ⓐ **Reading a Thermometer** (TG p. 704) Ⓑ **Discussing Changes in Temperature** (TG p.705) Ⓒ **Measuring Temperature** (TG p. 706) Ⓓ **Playing a Game:** *Target Temperatures* (TG p. 707)	• transparency of AM81 (optional) • thermometer • TR: Activity Masters, AM82–AM83 • centimeter cubes or other game pieces, number cubes • 📖 LAB pp. 175–176 • 📖 SH p. 156

3 Differentiated Instruction (TG p. 708)

Leveled Problem Solving (TG p. 708)	**Practice Book P72**
Intervention Activity (TG p. 708)	**Extension Book E72**
Extension Activity (TG p. 708)	**Spiral Review Book SR72**
Science Connection (TG p. 690)	

Lesson Notes

About the Lesson

Standard thermometers show temperatures the same way number lines show numbers. In this lesson, students focus on measuring temperature. They practice adding and subtracting multi-digit numbers as they compute changes in temperature. They also gain familiarity with some commonly used temperatures by playing the *Target Temperatures* game.

Use with Lesson Activity Book pp. 175–176.

Developing Mathematical Language

Vocabulary: degree

On both the Fahrenheit and Celsius temperature scales, the temperatures at which water freezes and boils are defining benchmarks. On the Fahrenheit scale, the spread between the freezing and boiling points is divided into 180 equal *degrees.* On the Celsius scale, the spread between the same two points is divided into 100 equal *degrees.* Because more Fahrenheit than Celsius *degrees* are crowded into the same space, a rise of 1 *degree* Fahrenheit represents a smaller temperature change than a rise of 1 *degree* Celsius.

Review the term *degree* with students.

Beginning Draw or provide pictures of items that are hot and cold. Write a probable temperature on each and point out to students what the temperature is for one item. Have the students say what the temperature is for the remaining items, using the item name and the term *degree* in a sentence.

Intermediate Have students work in small groups to list things that could be measured in *degrees.* Display the lists in the classroom.

Advanced Have students work in small groups to create two lists of things that could be measured in *degrees,* one list for cold things and another list for hot things.

Open-Ended Problem Solving

Read the Headline Story to the students. Encourage them to think of creative scenarios and write two equations with different values that incorporate information from the story.

 Headline Story

> This year, the highest temperature in the summer was ____°F. The lowest temperature in the winter was 53° colder than the warmest summer temperature.

Possible responses: If the temperature on the hottest summer day was 90°F, then the temperature on the coldest winter day was 37°F. If the temperature on the coldest winter day was 22°F, then the temperature on the hottest summer day was 75°F.

Skills Practice and Review

Adding and Subtracting Decimals

Materials
• coins, paper bag

Put a collection of coins in a paper bag. Ask a student to reach in and grab a handful of coins. Count the money with the class. Then ask students to write the amount in dollar notation. For example, if a student grabbed 5 quarters, 2 dimes, and 4 pennies, students should write $1.49. Set the coins aside and ask another student to grab a handful of coins. Again, record the amount in dollar notation. Finally, ask students to find the sum and the difference of the two amounts. After writing answers on the board, use the coins to model the sum and difference. To check the sum, combine the coins and find their total value; to check the difference, remove coins representing the lesser amount from coins representing the greater amount.

whole class **5 MIN**

A Reading a Thermometer

Materials

- For the teacher: AM81 transparency (optional), thermometer

NCTM Standards 1, 2, 6, 7, 8, 9, 10

Differentiated Instruction

Above Level Motivated students may wish to collect information about weather changes over a period of a month. Encourage them to collect temperature data and to record sky conditions such as "sunny," "cloudy," or "rainy." During the month, students can describe trends they observe and make predictions. At the end of the month they can make a bar graph of the temperature data and another one showing the sky conditions.

Teacher Story

❝Since we were going to be collecting temperature for several lessons, our class decided to graph the data too. We plotted both morning and afternoon readings on the same bar graph, using different colors to distinguish the two. This allowed us to also see the differences between the morning and afternoon temperature by looking at the differences in the heights.❞

Purpose To introduce the thermometer to students

Introduce Display Activity Master: Blank Thermometer or sketch a thermometer on the board.

Task Use the thermometer to help students understand the following facts about thermometers:

- The numbers on a thermometer are like the numbers on a number line: they increase in order from bottom to top (for a thermometer oriented vertically), just as numbers on a number line increase from left to right.

- Most thermometers do not label every degree. Each mark on Activity Master: Blank Thermometer indicates a change of 2 degrees.

- Thermometers contain a liquid that expands when the temperature rises and contracts when the temperature falls. This causes the liquid to rise or fall to the mark representing the new temperature.

Share Have a real thermometer available. Ask students to come up in small groups, read the temperature, and record it. Hang the thermometer outside the window and have students record the temperature at the end of the day. (For the next few days, the class will be reading the temperature at the beginning and end of the school day, and calculating the temperature change.)

 Talk Math

❓ On Jason's thermometer, there are 4 marks between 20°F and 45°F. What is the temperature change from one mark to the next?
5 degrees

❓ On Denise's thermometer, there are 9 marks between 10°F and 30°F. How many marks are there between 30°F and 38°F? Explain your reasoning.
3 marks: Possible explanation: There are 9 marks in the 20 degrees between 10°F and 30°F, or 1 mark every 2 degrees. So, between 30°F and 38°F, there must be marks at 32°, 34°, and 36°.

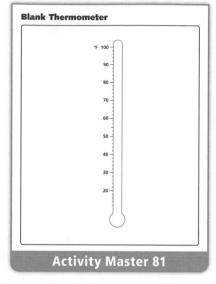

Blank Thermometer

°F 100
90
80
70
60
50
40
30
20

Activity Master 81

B Discussing Changes in Temperature

Purpose To find the difference between two temperatures

Introduce Ask students to describe trends or patterns in the weather they are familiar with. A simple example might be the fact that temperatures are warmer in the summer than they are in the winter, or that in your area of the country, the greatest precipitation occurs in the spring. Point out that to discover trends or patterns in the weather, or to make predictions about weather in the future, we need to keep accurate temperature records, to see how temperatures vary from night to day, from season to season, or from year to year.

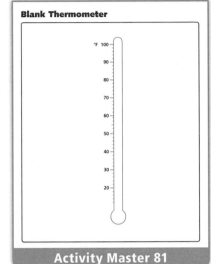

Blank Thermometer

Activity Master 81

Problem Display the blank thermometer from Activity A. Name two different temperatures and ask a student to label the temperatures on the thermometer. Then ask students to state which temperature is hotter and which is colder. Finally, ask them to find the difference between the two temperatures.

Practice Repeat the above activity with other temperature pairs. Be sure students are comfortable finding changes in temperatures, associating higher numbers on the thermometer with hotter temperatures, and associating lower numbers on the thermometer with colder temperatures.

Share Ask students to describe real-life questions they're familiar with that might be answered by keeping accurate temperature records. As examples, students might mention questions relating to possible global warming, human body temperatures, or temperatures on other planets.

Talk Math

❷ Between 6 A.M. and noon, the temperature in Cody, Wyoming, rose from 38°F to 77°F. What was the temperature change during that 6-hour period? 39°F

❷ The temperature in Middleton started at 45°F, rose 28 degrees, then fell 33 degrees. What was the final temperature? Explain your reasoning. 40°F; Possible explanation: I saw that the temperature fell 5 degrees more than it rose. So I subtracted 5 degrees from the starting temperature. 45°F − 5°F = 40°F.

Materials

• For the teacher: AM81 transparency (optional)

NCTM Standards 1, 2, 6, 7, 8, 9, 10

Possible Discussion

Just as length can be measured in feet and inches (sometimes referred to as "English" units), or in meters and centimeters (metric units), temperature can also be measured on two different scales: degrees Fahrenheit (English units), or degrees Celsius (metric units). On the Celsius scale, water freezes at 0 degrees and boils at 100 degrees. On the Fahrenheit scale, more familiar in the U.S., water freezes at 32 degrees and boils at 212 degrees. In other words, 0° Celsius is the same as 32° Fahrenheit. This again points out the importance of specifying units of measurement, because 0° Fahrenheit is much colder than 0° Celsius. In a later chapter, students will explore Celsius degrees as a context for working with negative numbers.

Differentiated Instruction

Above Level For motivated students, have two glasses of water, one cold and the other warm. Have the students measure the temperature in each glass every 2 minutes as it approaches room temperature, then make and compare graphs.

Purpose To practice finding changes in temperature and reading a chart

NCTM Standards 1, 2, 6, 7, 8, 9, 10

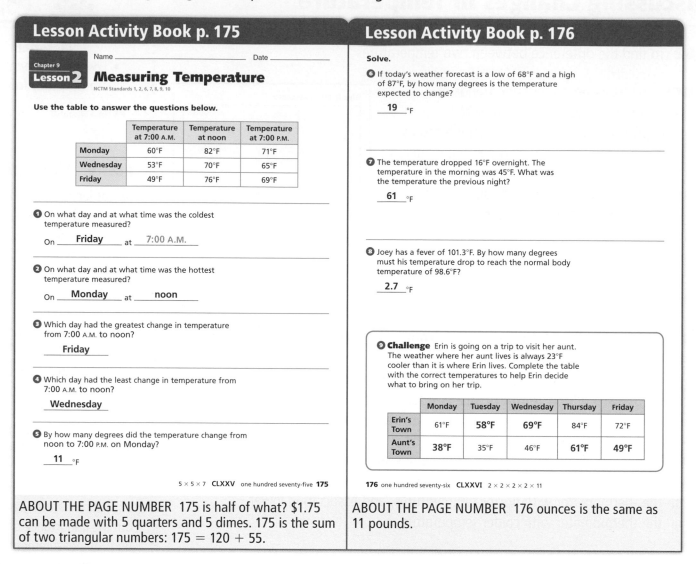

Lesson Activity Book p. 175

Chapter 9
Lesson 2 **Measuring Temperature**
NCTM Standards 1, 2, 6, 7, 8, 9, 10

Use the table to answer the questions below.

	Temperature at 7:00 A.M.	Temperature at noon	Temperature at 7:00 P.M.
Monday	60°F	82°F	71°F
Wednesday	53°F	70°F	65°F
Friday	49°F	76°F	69°F

❶ On what day and at what time was the coldest temperature measured?

On __Friday__ at __7:00 A.M.__

❷ On what day and at what time was the hottest temperature measured?

On __Monday__ at __noon__

❸ Which day had the greatest change in temperature from 7:00 A.M. to noon?

__Friday__

❹ Which day had the least change in temperature from 7:00 A.M. to noon?

__Wednesday__

❺ By how many degrees did the temperature change from noon to 7:00 P.M. on Monday?

__11__ °F

5 × 5 × 7 **CLXXV** one hundred seventy-five **175**

Lesson Activity Book p. 176

Solve.

❻ If today's weather forecast is a low of 68°F and a high of 87°F, by how many degrees is the temperature expected to change?

__19__ °F

❼ The temperature dropped 16°F overnight. The temperature in the morning was 45°F. What was the temperature the previous night?

__61__ °F

❽ Joey has a fever of 101.3°F. By how many degrees must his temperature drop to reach the normal body temperature of 98.6°F?

__2.7__ °F

❾ **Challenge** Erin is going on a trip to visit her aunt. The weather where her aunt lives is always 23°F cooler than it is where Erin lives. Complete the table with the correct temperatures to help Erin decide what to bring on her trip.

	Monday	Tuesday	Wednesday	Thursday	Friday
Erin's Town	61°F	**58°F**	69°F	84°F	72°F
Aunt's Town	**38°F**	35°F	46°F	**61°F**	49°F

176 one hundred seventy-six **CLXXVI** 2 × 2 × 2 × 2 × 2 × 11

ABOUT THE PAGE NUMBER 175 is half of what? $1.75 can be made with 5 quarters and 5 dimes. 175 is the sum of two triangular numbers: 175 = 120 + 55.

ABOUT THE PAGE NUMBER 176 ounces is the same as 11 pounds.

Teaching Notes for LAB page 175

Have students complete the page individually or with partners. Students use the table at the top of the page to answer the questions that follow.

After students have completed this page, introduce the game *Target Temperatures* in Activity D.

Teaching Notes for LAB page 176

Problem 8 requires students to find a change in temperature from one non-whole number of degrees to another non-whole number of degrees. This problem allows students to practice working with decimals, which they studied in the previous chapter.

Challenge Problem To complete the table, students must decide whether to add or subtract 23°F to the given temperature, and then find the sum or difference.

D Playing *Target Temperatures*

Purpose To learn common temperature benchmarks, and to practice adding and subtracting temperatures

Goal The object of this game *Target Temperatures* is for players to collect cards by adding and subtracting temperatures that will allow them to land on benchmark temperatures on the game board. The winner is the player with the most cards when play ends.

Prepare Materials Each pair of students will need a copy of Activity Master: The Target Temperatures Game, a centimeter cube or other small game piece, two number cubes, and the Target Temperature cards cut from Activity Master: Target Temperature.

Materials
- For each pair: AM82, cards cut from AM83, centimeter cube or other small game piece, two number cubes

NCTM Standards 1, 2, 6, 7, 8, 9, 10

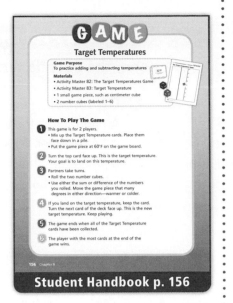

Student Handbook p. 156

How to Play

❶ Players place the Target Temperature cards face down in a pile, and the centimeter cube at 60°F on the thermometer of Activity Master: The Target Temperatures Game.

❷ One player turns the top card face up. This is the "target temperature," the temperature players are trying to land on.

❸ Players alternate turns. On each turn, a player rolls two number cubes. The player may move the game piece either the sum or the difference of the numbers on the cubes, and in either the warmer or colder direction.

❹ If a player lands on the target temperature, that player keeps the Target Temperature card and turns a new card face up as the new target temperature.

❺ Play ends when players have collected all of the Target Temperature cards.

❻ The player with the most cards at the end of the game wins.

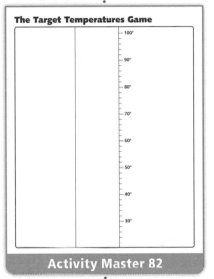

The Target Temperatures Game

Activity Master 82

Target Temperature

32°F	98°F
(the temperature when water freezes)	(about the temperature inside our bodies)
72°F	100°F
(room temperature)	(a body temperature that indicates a fever)
31°F	28°F
(about the temperature when skim milk freezes)	(about the temperature when sea water freezes)

Activity Master 83

Reflect and Summarize the Lesson

Write Math Which is hotter, 98°F or 32°F? How much hotter? 98°F; 66°F

3 | Differentiated Instruction

Leveled Problem Solving

At noon, the outside temperature is 54°F.

❶ Basic Level

Inside, the temperature is 72°F. Is it warmer inside or outside? Explain how you know. inside; The higher the temperature, the warmer it is; 72 > 54.

❷ On Level

An hour later, the temperature is 14° warmer. What is the temperature then? Explain. 68°F; 54 + 14 = 68.

❸ Above Level

At 1:00 P.M., it is 59°F. In the next hour it falls 8°. What is the change in temperature from noon to 2:00 P.M.? Explain. 3° less; 59 − 8 = 51; 54 − 51 = 3.

Intervention	Practice	Extension

Activity Hot or Cold

Have pairs of students play this game. Have each student secretly write a temperature in degrees Fahrenheit on notebook paper. Then have students take turns guessing the other student's temperature. If the temperature is higher than the one guessed, the other student replies "colder." If the temperature is lower than the guess, the other student replies "hotter." Have students play until a student guesses the correct temperature.

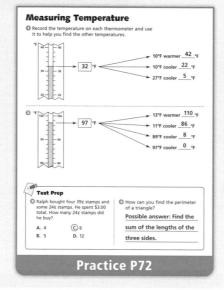

Practice P72

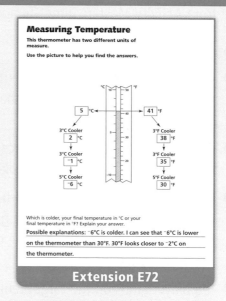

Extension E72

Spiral Review

Spiral Review Book page SR72 provides review of the following previously learned skills and concepts:

• practicing addition and subtraction skills

• recording and interpreting data on a bar graph

You may wish to have students work with partners to complete the page.

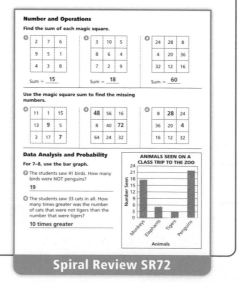

Spiral Review SR72

Extension Activity
Seasons by Degrees

Organize students into groups of four. Have each group make four drawings, one for each season of the year. Tell students to draw a thermometer on each drawing showing a typical temperature for that season. Display the drawings of the seasons and thermometers around the classroom.

Teacher's Notes 🍎

Daily Notes . . .

Quick Notes

More Ideas

Lesson 3 Measuring Length

NCTM Standards 1, 2, 6, 7, 8, 9, 10

Lesson Planner

STUDENT OBJECTIVES ·
- To review measuring with a ruler
- To estimate, measure, and compare lengths

1 | Daily Activities (TG p. 711)

Open-Ended Problem Solving/Headline Story	Skills Practice and Review—Reading a Thermometer

2 | Teach and Practice (TG pp. 712–717)

MATERIALS

Ⓐ **Comparing and Ordering Lengths** (TG pp. 712–713)

Ⓑ **Measuring with a Ruler** (TG p. 714)

Ⓒ **Measuring Length** (TG p. 715)

Ⓓ **Discussing Measurement Strategies** (TG p. 716)

- TR: Activity Master, AM84
- inch rulers, centimeter rulers
- 📖 LAB pp. 177–178
- 📖 SH p. 145

3 | Differentiated Instruction (TG p. 718)

Leveled Problem Solving (TG p. 718)	Practice Book P73
Intervention Activity (TG p. 718)	Extension Book E73
Extension Activity (TG p. 718)	Spiral Review Book SR73

Lesson Notes

About the Lesson

In this lesson, students measure lengths using both standard units (such as centimeters, inches, and feet) and non-standard units (such as finger lengths). They first compare and order the lengths of lines without the use of a ruler, an activity that involves estimating lengths. Then they review how to use a ruler and refresh their skills by measuring lengths. Finally, students explore strategies for approximating lengths, such as comparing an item to another item of known length. Students continue to measure length in **Lesson 9.4** and **Lesson 9.5**. This lesson serves as an exploration and review, and does not expect mastery.

Developing Mathematical Language

Vocabulary: length

The term *length* usually refers to a physical distance, such as the distance from one end of an object to the other.

- The *length* of the table is 4 feet.
- The bookshelf has a *length* of 2 yards.

Length also can be used in reference to the passage of time: "The *length* of time for the flight will be 3 hours."

Familiarize students with the term *length.*

Beginning Write and label on the board something measured by *length.* Then, have small groups of students create lists of things measured by *length.* Encourage them to have 5 items on their lists.

Intermediate Have students work in pairs. Ask each pair to write a sentence that uses the word *length.* Let each pair share their sentence with another pair.

Advanced Write on the board the heading *Length.* Ask students to think of situations when they would need to measure or know a *length.* Record the situations under the heading.

Open-Ended Problem Solving

Read the Headline Story to the students. Encourage them to think of interesting ways to solve the problem.

 Headline Story

> **Nancy is 8 inches taller than her younger sister and 5 inches shorter than her older brother. What can you say about the heights of the three children?**

Possible responses: If Nancy is 4 feet 5 inches tall, then her sister is 3 feet 9 inches tall and her brother is 4 feet 10 inches tall. If her brother is 5 feet tall, then Nancy is 4 feet 7 inches tall, and her sister is 3 feet 11 inches tall. Her brother is 13 inches taller than her sister.

Skills Practice and Review

Reading a Thermometer

Have students use the outside thermometer to read and record temperature data at the beginning and end of school. Add the data to your class table. Have students calculate the changes in temperature from yesterday, using yesterday's temperature data.

Materials
- AM81 transparency (optional) or large thermometer

To provide additional practice in reading a Fahrenheit thermometer, display Activity Master: Blank Thermometer from **Lesson 9.2,** or sketch a thermometer on the board. If you have a large enough thermometer for students to see the markings from their seats, you might use that instead. Point to various marks on the thermometer and ask students to state the temperatures that the marks indicate. Students should realize that only even numbers of degrees are marked and that the numbers increase from bottom to top. Be sure to point to some of the spaces between marks so that students have practice reading odd numbers of degrees as well.

pairs or
whole class

⏱ **10 MIN**

Materials
- For each pair: AM84

NCTM Standards 1, 2, 6, 7, 8, 9, 10

(A) Comparing and Ordering Lengths

Purpose To compare and order lengths without a ruler

Introduce Have students work in pairs on Activity Master: Measuring Lines. Explain that students will be exploring strategies for comparing and ordering lengths of lines without using a ruler.

Task Direct students to the following challenges, which appear on Activity Master: Measuring Lines.

❶ Which line is the longest? A

How do you know? Possible answer: I thought that A looked the longest. To check my guess, I placed my pencil point beside A and held the pencil at the other end of the line. Then I compared the length with the lengths of the other lines. All of them were shorter than A.

❷ Which line is the shortest? C

How do you know? Possible answer: I thought that C looked the shortest. To test my guess, I placed my hand beside C and noted how long the line was compared to my hand. Then I placed my hand beside the other lines. All of them were longer than C.

❸ Put the lines in order from shortest to longest. C, E, G, F, D, B, A

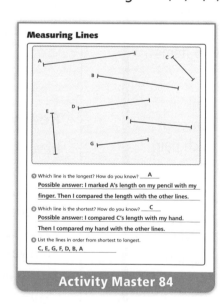

Measuring Lines

❶ Which line is the longest? How do you know? ___A___
Possible answer: I marked A's length on my pencil with my finger. Then I compared the length with the other lines.

❷ Which line is the shortest? How do you know? ___C___
Possible answer: I compared C's length with my hand. Then I compared my hand with the other lines.

❸ List the lines in order from shortest to longest.
C, E, G, F, D, B, A

Activity Master 84

Share After students have finished the page, have them share the strategies for finding the longest and shortest lines, and for putting the lengths in order.

In the next activity, students will use rulers to check their answers.

Talk Math

❷ Line M is longer than Line N. Line P is shorter than Line N. Which is longer, Line M or Line P? Explain your reasoning. **Line M is longer; Possible answer: M is longer than N, and N is longer than P. So, M is longer than P.**

❷ Line R is longer than Line S. Line S is shorter than Line T. Can you tell which is longer, Line R or Line T? Explain your reasoning. **no; Possible answer: Both R and T are longer than S, but there is no way of comparing the lengths of R and T to each other.**

Materials

- For each student: AM84 from Activity A, inch ruler, centimeter ruler

NCTM Standards 1, 2, 6, 7, 8, 9, 10

✔ **Ongoing Assessment**

- Do students measure the length of a line using an inch ruler?
- Do students measure the length of a line using a centimeter ruler?

Differentiated Instruction

Basic Level Watch for students who fail to align the zero mark of the ruler with one end of a line when they set out to measure the length of the line. Point out that this is the most practical method for measuring the line's length, as all it requires is for students to read the ruler mark at the other end of the line.

Teacher Story

❝When I mentioned the ruler as a measurement tool, I also named a few other devices for measuring length, such as an odometer (length of a car trip) and a pedometer (distance one walks). One student mentioned a trundle wheel, a device that is rolled along the ground to measure long distances like the perimeter of a pond.❞

Ⓑ Measuring with a Ruler

Purpose To measure length using a ruler

Introduce Pass out inch and centimeter rulers to the students.

Task **Direct students to measure the lengths of the lines on Activity Master: Measuring Lines from Activity A.** If necessary, remind students that the easiest way to measure a line with a ruler is to align the zero mark of the ruler with one end of the line, then to read the mark on the ruler at the other end of the line. Also, you might remind students that they can find the length by counting the intervals between marks, but not by counting the marks themselves.

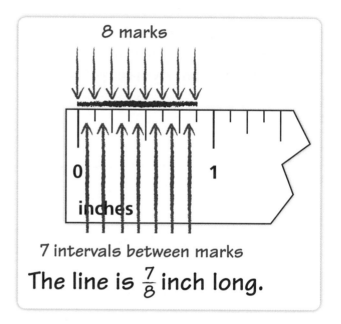

8 marks

0   1

inches

7 intervals between marks

The line is $\frac{7}{8}$ inch long.

Share After they measure the lines, have students share their results. They should see that the order of the lines from shortest to longest is C, E, G, F, D, B, A.

Ask students to measure one of the lines with both a centimeter ruler and an inch ruler. Students will find that, because centimeters are smaller than inches, a given length measures a greater number of centimeters than inches. Students will have further opportunity to compare inches and centimeters as they complete LAB pages 177 and 178.

💬 **Talk Math**

❓ Line M is $1\frac{3}{4}$ inches long. Line N is $2\frac{1}{4}$ inches long. Which line is longer? Explain your reasoning. line N is longer; Possible explanation: $2 > 1$, so $2\frac{1}{4} > 1\frac{3}{4}$.

❓ Line P is $1\frac{3}{4}$ inches long. Line Q is $1\frac{3}{8}$ inches long. Which line is longer? Explain your reasoning. line P is longer; Possible explanation: $\frac{3}{4} > \frac{3}{8}$, so $1\frac{3}{4} > 1\frac{3}{8}$.

C Measuring Length LAB pp. 177–178

Purpose To find objects of given lengths

NCTM Standards 1, 2, 6, 7, 8, 9, 10

Lesson Activity Book p. 177

Name _____ Date _____

Chapter 9
Lesson 3 **Measuring Length**
NCTM Standards 1, 2, 6, 7, 8, 9, 10

Measurement Scavenger Hunt   Many answers are possible.

Use a ruler to find things in your classroom that match these descriptions. Write the length of each object below its name.

❶ something longer than your foot

Object: _____

Length: _____

❷ something shorter than 2 inches

Object: _____

Length: _____

❸ something a little longer than 6 inches

Object: _____

Length: _____

❹ something about 1 inch wide

Object: _____

Length: _____

❺ something about 2.5 centimeters wide

Object: _____

Length: _____

❻ something shorter than your pinkie finger

Object: _____

Length: _____

❼ something longer than 1 foot but shorter than 2 feet

Object: _____

Length: _____

❽ something longer than 20 centimeters but shorter than 25 centimeters

Object: _____

Length: _____

❾ something about the length of your thumb

Object: _____

Length: _____

3 × 59 **CLXXVII** one hundred seventy-seven **177**

ABOUT THE PAGE NUMBER 3 × 59 = 177, and that's the only way to write it as a product, unless you switch the order, or use 1 or a fraction.

Lesson Activity Book p. 178

Use a ruler and estimate to find things in your classroom that match these descriptions. Many answers are possible.

❿ something taller than you

Object: _____

⓫ something taller than your teacher

Object: _____

⓬ something a little shorter than 2 feet

Object: _____

⓭ something about 10 centimeters long

Object: _____

⓮ something about 1 foot long

Object: _____

⓯ something longer than 5 feet

Object: _____

⓰ something about 1 yard long

Object: _____

⓱ something about 100 centimeters long

Object: _____

⓲ something about 3 feet long

Object: _____

⓳ Challenge

something longer than 1 foot but shorter than 100 centimeters

Object: _____

⓴ Challenge

something longer than 2 centimeters but shorter than 1 foot

Object: _____

㉑ Challenge

something longer than 1 meter but shorter than 3 yards

Object: _____

178 one hundred seventy-eight **CLXXVIII** 2 × 89

ABOUT THE PAGE NUMBER Half of 180 is 90. What is half of 178?

Teaching Notes for LAB page 177

Have students work individually or in pairs to search the classroom for items that match the descriptions on the page. As students find items, they should write the names and lengths in the boxes, the latter of which they can find by measuring with their rulers. Problems 4–5 and others allow students to become familiar with and compare the U.S. customary system and the metric systems of measurement.

Teaching Notes for LAB page 178

To find most of the objects on this page, students will probably approximate rather than measure exactly. Because of this, students are not required to record the dimensions of the items as they did on LAB page 177.

Challenge Problems To find these objects, students will need to compare measurements given in the customary and metric measurement systems.

D Discussing Measurement Strategies

NCTM Standards 1, 2, 6, 7, 8, 9, 10

Purpose To discuss strategies for completing LAB pages 177–178

Introduce After students have completed the LAB pages, gather the class together.

Task Have students discuss their strategies for finding objects in the scavenger hunt. Start by pointing out that some of the tasks on the LAB pages—for example, finding something shorter than 2 inches or something about 10 centimeters long—can be completed using a ruler. Others like finding something longer than 1 foot but shorter than 2 feet cannot be found directly with an inch ruler. For such measurements, students may need to lay out several ruler lengths or use another strategy, such as directly comparing objects.

Share Stimulate class discussion by asking questions like the following:

- **How did you find something longer than your foot?** Students may have directly compared the lengths of their feet with those of items around the classroom, or they may have measured the lengths of their feet with rulers and then found objects greater in length. They might also have cut strips of paper the lengths of their feet and compared them to other objects.

- **How did you find something longer than 5 feet without a 5-foot long ruler?** Students may have used knowledge of their own heights to help them estimate lengths or heights of 5 feet, or they may have placed five rulers end-to-end and used them as 5-foot rulers. A third method would have been to place an inch ruler at one end of an object, then move it four times, marking the end-point each time with a finger or pencil mark, creating, in effect, a 5-foot ruler.

- **How did you find something about 2 centimeters long?** Since 1 inch equals approximately 2.5 centimeters, a 2-centimeter-long object would be slightly shorter than 1 inch in length.

💬 Talk Math

❷ A stool is 1 yard tall. A table is 34 inches tall. Which is taller? Explain. **the stool; Possible explanation: There are 36 inches in a yard. Since 36 > 34, a yard is greater than 34 inches.**

❷ A baseball bat is 1 yard long. A softball bat is 1 meter long. Which is longer? Explain. **the softball bat; Possible explanation: A meter is slightly longer than a yard.**

✓ Ongoing Assessment

- Do students know very general relationships between U.S. customary system units and metric system units? (1 inch equals about 2.5 centimeters and 1 yard is slightly shorter than 1 meter.)

Reflect and Summarize the Lesson

Write Math **How could you tell someone who cannot see you how tall you are in a way that they would understand?** Possible answers: You could state your height using standard units such as inches or feet that the person is familiar with. You could compare your height with that of a common object with which the person is familiar, saying, for example, "I am twice the height of a desk."

Review Model

Refer students to the Review Model: Reading an Inch Ruler in the **Student Handbook** p. 145 to practice reading a ruler in increments of one-eighth inch.

✔ Check for Understanding

❶ $2\frac{1}{4}$ inches

❷ $1\frac{1}{2}$ inches

❸ $\frac{7}{8}$ inch

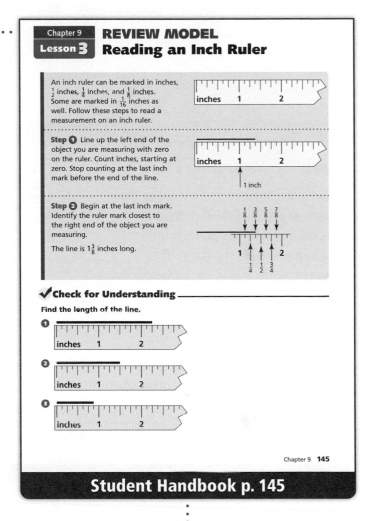

Student Handbook p. 145

Leveled Problem Solving

Randy measures a red pencil, a blue pencil, and a green pencil.

❶ Basic Level

The red pencil measures $4\frac{3}{4}$ inches. The blue pencil measures 5 inches. Which pencil is longer? Explain. blue pencil; $5 > 4$

❷ On Level

The red pencil measures $4\frac{3}{4}$ inches, and the green pencil measures $4\frac{5}{8}$ inches. Which pencil is longer? Explain. red pencil; $\frac{3}{4} > \frac{5}{8}$

❸ Above Level

The red pencil measures $4\frac{3}{4}$ inches, the blue pencil measures 5 inches, and the green pencil measures $4\frac{5}{8}$ inches. Which is the shortest pencil? Explain. green pencil; $4\frac{5}{8} < 4\frac{3}{4} < 5$

Intervention

Activity Measuring Lines

Have each student use a ruler to draw a line of any length on notebook paper, measure it, and record the measurement on the page. Then have students exchange papers with partners. Have students verify their partners' measurements.

Students might benefit by placing a book at the end of the line. Then they can place the ruler against the book to keep the ruler from sliding.

Practice

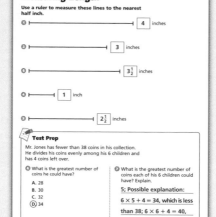

Practice P73

Extension

Extension E73

Spiral Review

Spiral Review Book page SR73 provides review of the following previously learned skills and concepts:

- finding missing digits in related multiplication and division sentences
- solving problems using the strategy *act it out*

You may wish to have students work with partners to complete the page.

Spiral Review SR73

Extension Activity
Lines and Number Sentences

Have students use a ruler to draw a line of any length. Then have them place a dot on the line. Have students measure from each end to the dot. Then have them measure the length of the entire line. Ask students to write a number sentence that includes all three measures.

Use with Lesson Activity Book pp. 177–178.

Teacher's Notes 🍎

Daily Notes . . .

Quick Notes

More Ideas

Lesson 4 Measuring in Inches, Feet, and Yards

NCTM Standards 1, 2, 6, 7, 8, 9, 10

Lesson Planner

STUDENT OBJECTIVES
- To practice using a ruler to measure length
- To convert among inches, feet, and yards
- To practice multiplication and division

1 Daily Activities (TG p. 721)

Open-Ended Problem Solving/Headline Story	Skills Practice and Review— Finding Changes in Temperature

2 Teach and Practice (TG pp. 722–728)

	MATERIALS
Ⓐ **Measuring with a "Broken Ruler"** (TG pp. 722–723) Ⓑ **Converting Among Inches, Feet, and Yards** (TG pp. 724–725) Ⓒ **Measuring in Inches, Feet, and Yards** (TG p. 726) Ⓓ **Discussing Conversion Strategies** (TG p. 727)	• TR: Activity Master, AM85 • 3 foot-long rulers, yard stick • 📖 LAB pp. 179–180 • 📖 SH pp. 146–147

3 Differentiated Instruction (TG p. 729)

Leveled Problem Solving (TG p. 729)	Practice Book P74
Intervention Activity (TG p. 729)	Extension Book E74
Extension Activity (TG p. 729)	Spiral Review Book SR74
Literature Connection (TG p. 690)	

Lesson Notes

About the Lesson

Students continue to measure length in this lesson. They focus on measuring in inches as they work with "broken rulers," rulers that are missing the starting or "zero" end. This approach assesses and enhances students' understanding of using and reading a ruler, since they cannot follow the usual procedure of lining up the ruler with the object they are measuring.

In this situation, they cannot use a single mark on the ruler as the measure of length, but must instead determine the length by computing the distance between two marks on the ruler. Students also explore the relationships among inches, feet, and yards, and use these relationships to simplify computations with measurements.

Use with Lesson Activity Book pp. 179–180.

Developing Mathematical Language

Vocabulary: inch, foot, yard

An *inch* originally was the width of a man's thumb. A *foot* was the length of a foot. A *yard* was the distance from the tip of a man's nose to the end of his outstretched arm. Since thumbs, feet, and arms varied greatly in length and width, the system was very approximate and not very useful. It wasn't until the 13th Century that King Edward I of England took the first step toward standardizing measures. Edward ordered that a permanent measuring stick made of iron, very close in length to our present-day *yard,* would serve as a master standard yardstick for the entire kingdom.

Review the terms *inch, foot,* and *yard* with students.

Beginning Display objects that are 1 *inch* long, 1 *foot* long and 1 *yard* long with their lengths labeled. Have students name more items that are about 1 *inch* long, 1 *foot* long, and 1 *yard* long.

Intermediate Have students work in small groups to list items usually measured in *inches.* Then have them repeat the exercise for *feet* and for *yards.*

Advanced Have students work in pairs. Tell one student to name an object. The other student then names the most appropriate unit, *inch, foot,* or *yard,* for measuring the length of the object and gives a reason for their choice. Have students alternate roles.

---

1 | Daily Activities

Open-Ended Problem Solving

Read the Headline Story to the students. Encourage them to make a model as a reference to guide them, and to think of creative scenarios that incorporate information from the story.

 Headline Story

> **Marcia, Shirley, and Joshua were talking in the hallway at school. Joshua's classroom was at the very end of the hall, twice as far from where they were standing as Marcia's classroom. Shirley's classroom was 50 feet away from them. Marcia's classroom was twice as far as Shirley's.**

Possible responses: All three students are in different classrooms. Marcia's classroom is 100 feet away from where the kids were standing. Marcia's classroom and Shirley's classroom could be 150 feet apart, but they could also be only 50 feet apart. Joshua's classroom is 200 feet away from where the kids are standing.

Skills Practice and Review

Finding Changes in Temperature

Display Activity Master: Blank Thermometer from **Lesson 9.2,** or sketch a thermometer on the board. Have students read various temperatures on the thermometer, record those temperatures, and find the differences between various pairs of temperatures.

Materials
• AM81 transparency (optional)

whole class **10 MIN**

A Measuring with a "Broken Ruler"

Materials
- For each student: AM85

NCTM Standards 1, 2, 6, 7, 8, 9, 10

Purpose To practice measuring with a ruler

Introduce Have students work on Explore: Measuring with a Broken Ruler individually or with partners. Each student will need a ruler cut from Activity Master: Broken Rulers. Draw attention to the fact that the rulers have purposely been "broken" at both ends, so that the zero mark students might normally use when they measure line lengths is not available to them.

Differentiated Instruction

Basic Level When students are using the broken ruler, watch for students who continue to assume that the length of an object is the mark on the ruler where the object ends, even though the mark where the object started was not zero. Also watch for students who reason that since 1 and 2 are missing from the ruler, they should subtract 2 from the reading at the right end of an object they are measuring. Help students to notice that an interval 3 inches in length is missing from the ruler, so they need to subtract 3 inches from the right-end mark. A drawing like the one below may help some students.

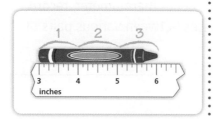

Task To begin, have students verify the lengths of the first three lines on the Explore page, as a self-check that they are properly using the rulers.

Use the broken ruler to check the lengths of these lines:

❶ $2\frac{3}{4}$ inches

❷ 4 inches

❸ $1\frac{1}{4}$ inches

Now use a broken ruler to find the lengths of these lines:

❹ $2\frac{1}{2}$ inches

❺ 3 inches

❻ $2\frac{1}{4}$ inches

❼ $3\frac{1}{2}$ inches

❽ $1\frac{3}{4}$ inches

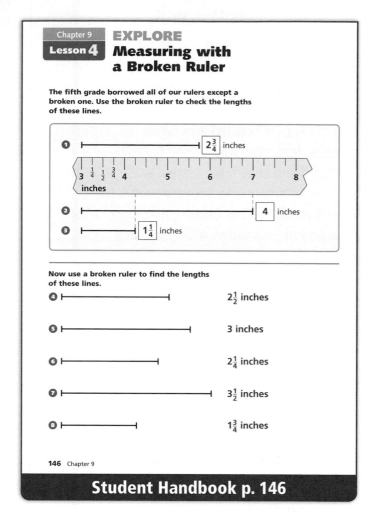

Student Handbook p. 146

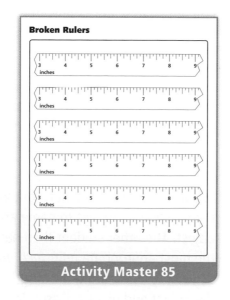

Activity Master 85

Use with Lesson Activity Book pp. 179–180.

Share Once most students have completed the page, go over the answers as a class and have students share their strategies for finding lengths with broken rulers.

Talk Math

❷ The left end of a line is at the 2-inch mark on a ruler. The right end is at $5\frac{1}{4}$ inches. How long is the line? $3\frac{1}{4}$ inches

❷ The right end of a $2\frac{3}{4}$-inch line is at the $4\frac{1}{2}$-inch mark on a ruler. Where is the left end? Explain your reasoning. the $1\frac{3}{4}$-inch mark on the ruler; Possible explanation: I started at the $4\frac{1}{2}$-inch mark. Moving left 2 inches got me to the $2\frac{1}{2}$-inch mark. Moving left another $\frac{1}{2}$ inch got me to the 2-inch mark. Since $2\frac{1}{2} + \frac{1}{4} = 2\frac{3}{4}$, I needed to go another $\frac{1}{4}$ inch. I ended at the $1\frac{3}{4}$-inch mark.

Possible Discussion

In using the broken ruler to find the lengths of lines on Explore: Measuring with a Broken Ruler, students cannot simply read lengths from one mark on the ruler; they must either subtract or count to determine lengths. Consider the example of measuring the crayon on the previous page with a broken ruler by lining up one end of the crayon at the 3. If the other end lines up with the 6, the length of the crayon is the distance between the two marks. To find the distance, we can either count the 1-inch intervals or subtract 3 inches from 6 inches.

B Converting Among Inches, Feet, and Yards

Materials
- For the teacher:
  3 foot-long rulers,
  yard stick

NCTM Standards 1, 2, 6, 7, 8, 9, 10

Purpose To convert among inches, feet, and yards

Introduce Before beginning this activity, decide which parts, if any, are new material for your students, which parts might be useful review, and which parts are so familiar that you can skip over them. Most likely, few of your students will need to review the relationship between feet and inches, but the mental computation of doing it can be valuable to them all. Explain that in this activity, students will be expressing measurements in inches, feet, and yards, and converting among the three units.

Task Ask students to help you complete a table, but without being told how to do so. Draw a table on the board with a row for feet and a row for inches.

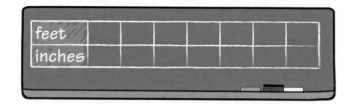

Write a number in the row for feet and silently invite a student to fill in the corresponding number of inches. For example, if you write 3 (feet), the student should write 36 (inches). Doing this activity silently will allow students who do not remember that there are 12 inches in a foot to recall this fact by finding a pattern in the table entries.

Continue with different numbers of feet, silently inviting students to fill in the corresponding numbers of inches. Then begin writing numbers in the row for inches and invite students to fill in the corresponding numbers of feet.

- As a challenge (and to build in review of fractions and decimals), depending on the level of your students, you might include numbers of feet expressed as simple mixed numbers and decimals, such as $2\frac{1}{3}$, $4\frac{1}{2}$, and 1.5. For example, you might write $4\frac{1}{2}$ (or 4.5) feet. A student should respond with 54 inches. Similarly, if you write 30 inches, a student should write $2\frac{1}{2}$ (or 2.5) feet. If you write $2\frac{2}{3}$ feet, a student should write 32 inches.

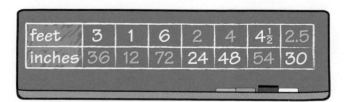

feet	3	1	6	2	4	$4\frac{1}{2}$	2.5
inches	36	12	72	24	48	54	30

Use with Lesson Activity Book pp. 179–180.

Repeat this activity using a table with a row for yards and a row for feet. (If you have students who do not know that there are 3 feet in a yard, you may need to fill in one or two pairs of numbers to get them started.)

- For further review of fractions, again include halves and thirds in the table. For example, if you write $1\frac{1}{2}$ (or 1.5) yards, a student should write $4\frac{1}{2}$ feet. If you write $7\frac{1}{2}$ feet, a student should write $2\frac{1}{2}$ yards. If you write $2\frac{1}{3}$ yards, a student should write 7 feet. For advanced groups, you may want to include half-feet in the table.

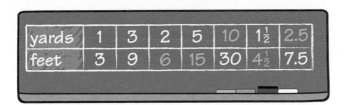

yards	1	3	2	5	10	$1\frac{1}{2}$	2.5
feet	3	9	6	15	30	$4\frac{1}{2}$	7.5

Share After completing the tables, show students a yardstick with three foot-long rulers lined up below it. This will allow students to see that a yard is the same length as 3 feet.

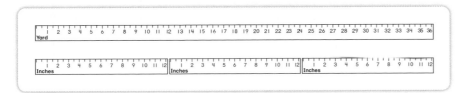

Ask these questions:

- **How many inches are there in a yard? How do you know?** 36; There are 12 inches in a foot and 3 feet in a yard, and $12 \times 3 = 36$.

Finally, ask students to help you make a table of equivalents, summarizing the relationships among inches, feet, and yards.

> 1 foot = 12 inches
> 1 yard = 3 feet
> 1 yard = 36 inches

Talk Math

❷ If you know the length of an object in feet, how can you find its length in inches? Possible answer: Multiply the length in feet by 12.

❷ If you know the length of an object in feet, how can you find its length in yards? Possible answer: Divide the length in feet by 3.

C Measuring in Inches, Feet, and Yards LAB pp. 179–180

individuals or pairs · 20 MIN

Purpose To practice converting among inches, feet, and yards

NCTM Standards 1, 2, 6, 7, 8, 9, 10

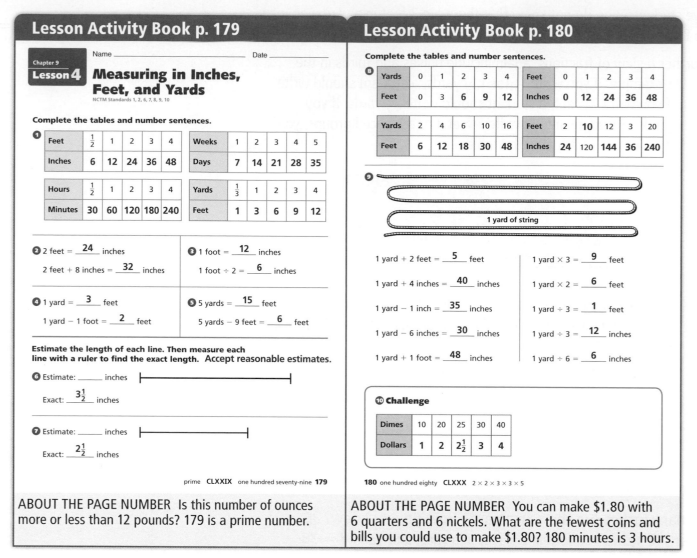

Lesson Activity Book p. 179

Name _____ Date _____

Chapter 9
Lesson 4 **Measuring in Inches, Feet, and Yards**
NCTM Standards 1, 2, 6, 7, 8, 9, 10

Complete the tables and number sentences.

1

Feet	$\frac{1}{2}$	1	2	3	4
Inches	6	12	24	36	48

Weeks	1	2	3	4	5
Days	7	14	21	28	35

Hours	$\frac{1}{2}$	1	2	3	4
Minutes	30	60	120	180	240

Yards	$\frac{1}{3}$	1	2	3	4
Feet	1	3	6	9	12

2 2 feet = __24__ inches
2 feet + 8 inches = __32__ inches

3 1 foot = __12__ inches
1 foot ÷ 2 = __6__ inches

4 1 yard = __3__ feet
1 yard − 1 foot = __2__ feet

5 5 yards = __15__ feet
5 yards − 9 feet = __6__ feet

Estimate the length of each line. Then measure each line with a ruler to find the exact length. **Accept reasonable estimates.**

6 Estimate: _____ inches
Exact: __$3\frac{1}{2}$__ inches

7 Estimate: _____ inches
Exact: __$2\frac{1}{2}$__ inches

prime **CLXXIX** one hundred seventy-nine **179**

Lesson Activity Book p. 180

Complete the tables and number sentences.

8

Yards	0	1	2	3	4
Feet	0	3	6	9	12

Feet	0	1	2	3	4
Inches	0	12	24	36	48

Yards	2	4	6	10	16
Feet	6	12	18	30	48

Feet	2	10	12	3	20
Inches	24	120	144	36	240

9

1 yard of string

1 yard + 2 feet = __5__ feet
1 yard + 4 inches = __40__ inches
1 yard − 1 inch = __35__ inches
1 yard − 6 inches = __30__ inches
1 yard + 1 foot = __48__ inches

1 yard × 3 = __9__ feet
1 yard × 2 = __6__ feet
1 yard ÷ 3 = __1__ feet
1 yard ÷ 3 = __12__ inches
1 yard ÷ 6 = __6__ inches

10 Challenge

Dimes	10	20	25	30	40
Dollars	1	2	$2\frac{1}{2}$	3	4

180 one hundred eighty **CLXXX** $2 \times 2 \times 2 \times 3 \times 3 \times 5$

ABOUT THE PAGE NUMBER Is this number of ounces more or less than 12 pounds? 179 is a prime number.

ABOUT THE PAGE NUMBER You can make $1.80 with 6 quarters and 6 nickels. What are the fewest coins and bills you could use to make $1.80? 180 minutes is 3 hours.

Teaching Notes for LAB page 179

Have students complete the page individually or with partners. They will need rulers for Problems 6–7.

Students may use a variety of strategies to solve the problems on this page. To find 1 foot ÷ 2 in Problem 3, students might first figure out that 1 foot = 12 inches, and then use this conversion to find 12 inches ÷ 2. Alternatively, students might reason that 1 foot ÷ 2 = half a foot, which is 6 inches.

Teaching Notes for LAB page 180

Students can use the tables at the top of the page to help them complete the problems below.

Challenge Problems In these problems, students make conversions between dimes and dollars as they did between inches and feet. First they determine the numerical relationship between the units (1 dollar = 10 dimes). Then they multiply or divide, as required, by the appropriate factor (10).

D Discussing Conversion Strategies

Purpose To discuss strategies for converting between units

NCTM Standards 1, 2, 6, 7, 8, 9, 10

Introduce Point out that computations involving measurements can sometimes be simplified by first converting the measurements to other units.

Problem Write the following problem on the board:

123 inches x 7 = ?

Explain that the problem can be simplified by first converting the measurement in inches to feet. Because there are 12 inches in a foot, 120 inches = 10 feet. Therefore, 123 inches = 10 feet 3 inches. To solve, multiply 10 feet × 7 (70 feet) and 3 inches × 7 (21 inches), and add the products to find the total (70 feet 21 inches, or 70 feet + 1 foot 9 inches, or 71 feet 9 inches). (Before adding, students could also convert 3 inches × 7 from inches to feet and inches.)

As another example of how conversions can simplify problems involving measurements, show that students can use what they know about the number of inches or feet in one measurement to find the number of inches or feet in a larger measurement. For example, because there are 6 feet in 2 yards, students can reason that in 5 times as many yards, there must be 5 times as many feet: 30 feet in 10 yards.

Practice Solve the following problems:

- 54 inches × 5 = ? 22 feet 6 inches, or 270 inches
- 244 inches × 6 = ? 122 feet, or 1,464 inches
- 126 inches × 9 = ? 94 feet 6 inches, or 1,134 inches
- How many feet are there in 20 yards? 60 feet
- How many inches are there in 8 feet? 96 inches

💬 Talk Math

❷ How can you use the fact that there are 10 nickels in 2 quarters to find the number of nickels in 6 quarters? Possible answer: Since 6 = 2 × 3, the number of nickels must be 10 × 3 = 30 nickels.

❷ How can you use the fact that there are 60 inches in 5 feet to find the number of feet in 180 inches? Possible answer: Since 180 = 60 × 3, the number of feet must be 5 × 3 = 15 feet.

✓ Ongoing Assessment

- Do students correctly simplify a measurement in feet and inches, where the number of inches is greater than 12? For example, can they write 5 feet 17 inches = 5 feet + 1 foot 5 inches = 6 feet 5 inches?

- Do students correctly simplify a measurement in yards and feet, where the number of inches is greater than 3? For example, can they write 8 yards 7 feet = 8 yards + 2 yards 1 foot = 10 yards 1 foot?

Reflect and Summarize the Lesson

Write Math

Write 67 inches in yards, feet, and inches. Explain your method. 1 yard, 2 feet, 7 inches; Possible explanation: 67 inches is 5 feet 7 inches and 5 feet is 1 yard 2 feet. So, 67 inches is 1 yard, 2 feet, 7 inches. Another method: 67 inches is 5 inches less than 2 yards, which is 5 inches less than 1 yard 3 feet, which is 1 yard, 2 feet, 7 inches.

Review Model

Refer students to the Review Model: Converting Inches and Feet in the *Student Handbook* p. 147 to practice converting units.

✔ **Check for Understanding**

① 84 inches

② 3 feet

③ 60 inches

④ 8 feet

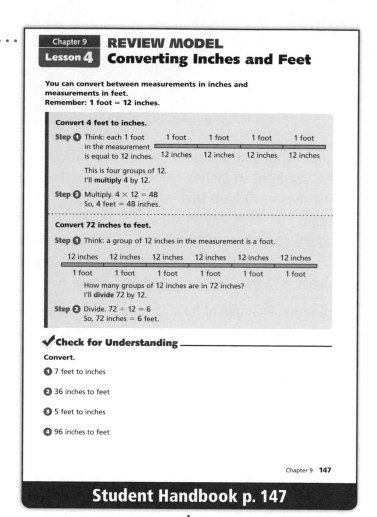

Student Handbook p. 147

3 | Differentiated Instruction

Leveled Problem Solving

Nadia is 10 inches taller than her sister Ally.

❶ Basic Level

Ally is 3 feet 11 inches tall. How tall is Nadia? Explain.
4 ft 9 in.; 3 ft 11 in. + 10 in. = 3 ft 21 in.; 21 in. = 1 ft 9 in.; 3 ft + 1 ft 9 in. = 4 ft 9 in.

❷ On Level

Nadia is 4 feet 9 inches tall. How tall is Ally? Explain.
3 ft 11 in.; 4 ft 9 in. − 10 in. = 3 ft 21 in. − 10 in. = 3 ft 11 in.

❸ Above Level

Ally is 1 foot 3 inches shorter than Ed. Ed is 5 feet 2 inches tall. How tall is Nadia? Explain. 4 ft 9 in.; 5 ft 2 in. − 1 ft 3 in. = 4 ft 14 in. − 1 ft 3 in. = 3 ft 11 in. (Ally); 3 ft 11 in. + 10 in. = 3 ft 21 in. = 4 ft 9 in.

Intervention	Practice	Extension

Intervention

Activity Circle Game

Have students stand in a circle to count off measures one inch at a time. Choose a student to start, who says "1 inch." Then the student to the left says "2 inches." When the count gets to 12 inches, that student says "1 foot." The student at 24 inches will say "2 feet," the student at 36 inches will say "1 yard," and so on. To be sure more than one student does the conversions, a prime number of students (>3) is needed.

Practice

Measuring in Inches, Feet, and Yards
Measure the lengths.

❶ 5 in. 6 7 8 9 10

❷ $4\frac{1}{2}$ inches

❸ $2\frac{1}{4}$ inches

Use one of the measurements listed to make each statement true.

1 ft	1 yd	6 in.	2 ft	7 in.	19 in.	18 in.

1 ft = 12 inches   1 ft 6 in. = **18 in.**   **2 ft** + 1 ft = 1 yd
1 yd − 3 feet   3 in. + 4 in. = **7 in.**   **6 in.** × 2 = 1 ft
1 yd = 36 inches   7 in. + 1 ft = **19 in.**   1 ft × 3 = 1 yd
2 ft = 24 inches   18 in. ÷ 3 = **6 in.**   6 in. + **18 in.** = 2 ft

Test Prep

❶ Eric has between 45 and 75 photos. When he puts them in groups of 2, 3, 4, 5, or 6, there are none left over. When he puts them in groups of 7, there are some left over. Find the number of photos Eric has. Show your reasoning.

Possible answer: The number must be a multiple of 10 because placed in groups of 2 or 5, no photos are left over. Of the numbers 50, 60, and 70, only 60 is a multiple of 3, 4, and 6.

Practice P74

Extension

Measuring in Inches, Feet, and Yards
Write the measurement numbers or units.

❶ $2\frac{2}{3}$ feet = **32** inches   ❷ $3\frac{1}{2}$ yards = $10\frac{1}{2}$ **feet**

❸ 1.5 yards = **54** inches   ❹ $4\frac{1}{2}$ yards = **$13\frac{1}{2}$** or 13.5 feet

❺ $3\frac{1}{4}$ feet = **39** inches   ❻ 5 feet = $1\frac{2}{3}$ yards

❼ 50 inches = **$4\frac{1}{6}$** feet   ❽ $3\frac{3}{4}$ yards = **$11\frac{1}{4}$** or 11.25 feet

❾ $1\frac{1}{3}$ feet = 16 **inches**   ❿ 6.5 feet = **78** inches

⓫ $2\frac{1}{4}$ yards = **$6\frac{3}{4}$** or 6.75 feet   ⓬ 42 inches = $1\frac{1}{6}$ **yards**

⓭ 54 inches = **$4\frac{1}{2}$** or 4.5 feet   ⓮ 7 feet 6 inches = **2.5** yards

Extension E74

Spiral Review

Spiral Review Book page SR74 provides review of the following previously learned skills and concepts:

- identifying perpendicular and parallel lines
- adding and subtracting decimals

You may wish to have students work with partners to complete the page.

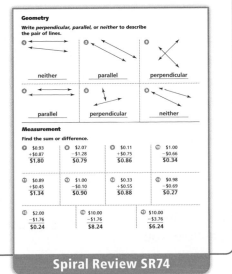

Geometry
Write perpendicular, parallel, or neither to describe the pair of lines.

❶ neither   ❷ parallel   ❸ perpendicular

❹ parallel   ❺ perpendicular   ❻ neither

Measurement
Find the sum or difference.

❼ $0.93 + $0.87 = $1.80   ❽ $2.07 − $1.28 = $0.79   ❾ $0.11 + $0.75 = $0.86   ❿ $1.00 − $0.66 = $0.34

⓫ $0.89 + $0.45 = $1.34   ⓬ $1.00 − $0.10 = $0.90   ⓭ $0.33 + $0.55 = $0.88   ⓮ $0.98 − $0.69 = $0.27

⓯ $2.00 − $1.76 = $0.24   ⓰ $10.00 − $1.76 = $8.24   ⓱ $10.00 − $3.76 = $6.24

Spiral Review SR74

Extension Activity
How Many of Me Are There?

Have pairs of students use yardsticks to measure each other's arm span—the distance from fingertip to fingertip when both arms are level with the shoulders. Then ask students to find the total length of 10; 100; 1,000; and 2,000 arm spans, computing with their own arm-span lengths. Tell students to convert the lengths to appropriate measures including miles (5,280 feet or 1,760 yards).

Lesson 5 Measuring Length in Centimeters

NCTM Standards 1, 2, 6, 7, 8, 9, 10

Lesson Planner

STUDENT OBJECTIVES
- To measure length in centimeters using Cuisenaire® Rods
- To estimate and measure length using multiple copies of a unit, or by comparing an unknown length to a known length

1 Daily Activities (TG p. 731)

Open-Ended Problem Solving/Headline Story	Skills Practice and Review— Calculating Temperature Change and Elapsed Time

2 Teach and Practice (TG pp. 732–736)

	MATERIALS
(A) **Estimating Length with Cuisenaire® Rods** (TG pp. 732–733)	• TR: Activity Master, AM86
(B) **Measuring Length in Centimeters** (TG p. 734)	• Cuisenaire® Rods
(C) **Playing a Game: *Build-a-Foot*** (TG p. 735)	• centimeter rulers, inch rulers, paper clips, pencils
	• 📖 LAB pp. 181–182
	• 📖 SH pp. 148–149, 157

3 Differentiated Instruction (TG p. 737)

Leveled Problem Solving (TG p. 737)	Practice Book P75
Intervention Activity (TG p. 737)	Extension Book E75
Extension Activity (TG p. 737)	Spiral Review Book SR75

Lesson Notes

About the Lesson

Students use a white Cuisenaire® Rod, which measures 1 centimeter along any edge, to find the lengths of other rods. This is an example of using multiple copies of a unit to measure a longer length. Students also continue to develop strategies for using known lengths to estimate unknown lengths, by comparing Cuisenaire® Rods with other lines and objects.

About the Mathematics

One way to estimate unknown lengths is to compare them with personal measurements. For example, you can use your own height to estimate the height of a ceiling, or your hand to estimate the width of a desk. But when you need to measure something precisely and share that measurement with others, you must use standard units. Telling someone that the doorway is about a foot and a half taller than you are is only partial information, unless the person happens to know your height. If you know your height, you can estimate the height of the doorway in a unit that everyone has access to, and report that measurement.

Developing Mathematical Language

Vocabulary: centimeter

The word *centimeter* consists of two parts, *centi,* which means "hundredth," and *meter.* Therefore, 1 *centimeter* is 1 hundredth of a meter (and 100 *centimeters* make 1 meter). Mention related words that can help students remember the meaning of *centimeter.* For example, century means 100 years and cents are hundredths of a dollar.

A meter was originally defined as one-ten millionth of the distance from the equator to the North Pole.

Review the term *centimeter* with students.

Beginning Give students *centimeter* rulers. Have each student measure parts of his or her hand to discover which part measures about 1 *centimeter.* Have students share their findings.

Intermediate Ask students to list several objects in the room that can be measured in *centimeters.*

Advanced Have pairs of students choose a pencil and guess its length in *centimeters.* Then have them measure the pencil with a *centimeter* ruler to determine whether the estimate is reasonable. Encourage them to repeat the exercise with other classroom objects.

Open-Ended Problem Solving

Read the Headline Story to the students. Encourage them to create questions that Lucy's observation might suggest.

 Headline Story

> **When one of Lucy's friends was standing next to his desk, Lucy noticed that the desk seemed to be about half as tall as he was.**

Possible responses: If Lucy's friend is about $4\frac{1}{2}$ feet tall, then the desk is about 2 feet 3 inches high. Lucy's own desk is probably about half Lucy's height, though it could be a bit higher or lower. If Lucy's friend is in 4th grade, what height might we expect him to be? What other heights might be reasonable to estimate in relation to our own heights? Can we judge the height of the classroom ceiling by estimating how many times our height it might be?

Skills Practice and Review

Calculating Temperature Change and Elapsed Time

Materials
- demonstration clock, train or plane schedule

Have students use temperature data from yesterday to calculate the change in temperature. You may wish to have them continue to collect temperature data, adding data to your class table. Students will not measure temperature again until a later chapter.

To give students practice with another kind of measurement—finding time intervals—set the demonstration clock to a time and say that is when an airplane took off. Then give the time the plane landed, and ask students to find how long the flight was. Repeat the activity with different take-off or landing times. For added interest, download a train or plane schedule from the Internet and have students use it to calculate trip times.

individuals or whole class **15 MIN**

Materials
- For each student: centimeter ruler
- For each pair: Cuisenaire® Rods

NCTM Standards 1, 2, 6, 7, 8, 9, 10

A Estimating Length with Cuisenaire® Rods

Purpose To use Cuisenaire® Rods to estimate measurements

Introduce Provide each student with a copy of Explore: Measuring Length with Cuisenaire® Rods and a centimeter ruler, and each pair of students with Cuisenaire® Rods. Explain that students are going to be using Cuisenaire® Rods to estimate certain lengths. They will need to devise their own strategies for making these estimates. Be sure students understand that the white rod measures 1 centimeter along each edge.

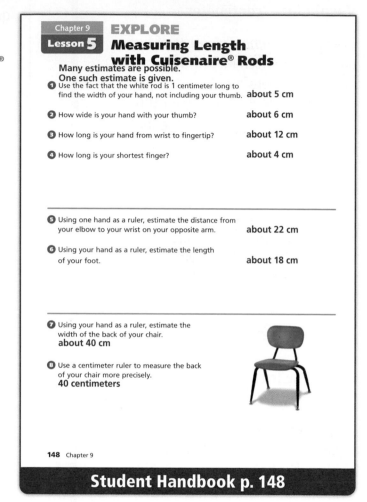

Chapter 9
Lesson 5

EXPLORE
Measuring Length with Cuisenaire® Rods
Many estimates are possible.
One such estimate is given.

1. Use the fact that the white rod is 1 centimeter long to find the width of your hand, not including your thumb. **about 5 cm**

2. How wide is your hand with your thumb? **about 6 cm**

3. How long is your hand from wrist to fingertip? **about 12 cm**

4. How long is your shortest finger? **about 4 cm**

5. Using one hand as a ruler, estimate the distance from your elbow to your wrist on your opposite arm. **about 22 cm**

6. Using your hand as a ruler, estimate the length of your foot. **about 18 cm**

7. Using your hand as a ruler, estimate the width of the back of your chair. **about 40 cm**

8. Use a centimeter ruler to measure the back of your chair more precisely. **40 centimeters**

148   Chapter 9

Student Handbook p. 148

Task Direct students to the following challenges, which appear on Explore: Measuring Length with Cuisenaire® Rods:

1. Use the fact that the white rod is 1 centimeter long to find the width of your hand, not including your thumb. Possible estimate: 5 centimeters

2. How wide is your hand with your thumb? Possible estimate: 6 centimeters

3. How long is your hand from wrist to fingertip? Possible estimate: 12 centimeters

4. How long is your shortest finger? Possible estimate: 4 centimeters

5. Using one hand as a ruler, estimate the distance from your elbow to your wrist on your opposite arm. Possible estimate: 22 centimeters

6. Using your hand as a ruler, estimate the length of your foot. Possible estimate: 18 centimeters

7. Using your hand as a ruler, estimate the width of the back of your chair. Possible estimate: 40 centimeters

8. Use a centimeter ruler to measure the back of your chair more precisely. Possible answer: 40 centimeters

Use with Lesson Activity Book pp. 181–182.

Share Ask students to share their strategies for making their estimates. To make the initial measurements of their hands, students may decide to use rows of white rods, a strategy that uses multiple copies of a single unit. Or they may use the white rod to measure other rods and then use those greater lengths to make their estimates. For example, students can use the purple rod in place of four white blocks, thereby simplifying the estimation process. Once students find some useful measurements of their hands, they can then use their hands as rulers for estimating the lengths in Problems 5 and 6.

For the last two problems, students use their informal "hand rulers" to estimate the widths of the backs of their chairs. They then make more precise measurements with rulers (or with their Cuisenaire® Rods). (See Possible Discussion for more on estimation.)

Once students have completed the page, briefly check their answers. Have them make a table of the lengths of all the Cuisenaire® Rods, in centimeters. Students will need to know correct lengths for the rods before completing LAB page 181.

Talk Math

? Jason's hands are about 6 centimeters wide. He measured the table to be about 12 hands wide. About how wide is the table? How did you find your answer? about 72 cm; Possible explanation: 10 hand widths would be 60 centimeters, and another 2 hand widths would be another 12 centimeters.

? If everyone in your class used their hand-ruler to measure the width of the door to the classroom, would everyone get the same measurement? Explain. Possible answer: no; possible explanation: to get the same measurements, all of the hands would have to be the same size. They are not.

Possible Discussion

Many students struggle to understand what it means to estimate. Instead of evaluating their estimates based on how reasonable they are, these students may feel successful only if their estimates precisely equal the value they are attempting to estimate. To change this perception, you may wish to compliment students on the reasonableness of their estimates rather than on the precision of their estimates.

Purpose To estimate and measure the lengths of lines

NCTM Standards 1, 2, 6, 7, 8, 9, 10

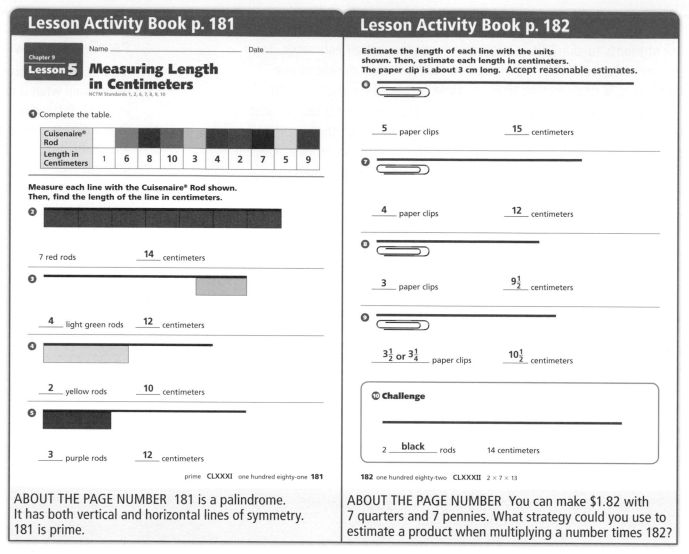

Teaching Notes for LAB page 181

Have students complete the page individually or with partners. On this page, students use Cuisenaire® Rods to find the lengths of lines in centimeters. Each length is an exact multiple of the length of the rod shown. If necessary, you might draw a picture of the Cuisenaire® Rods in order from shortest to longest on the board to help students find the lengths the rods.

Teaching Notes for LAB page 182

To estimate the lengths of the lines on this page, students use the fact that the paper clip shown is about 3 centimeters long. Not all of the lengths are exact multiples of the paper clip unit.

Challenge Problem This problem asks students to estimate the length of a line without a picture of a rod of a given length to compare it with. This will challenge their visual estimation abilities.

Playing *Build-a-Foot*

Purpose To practice using Cuisenaire® Rods to find lengths in centimeters, and to relate centimeters to inches

Goal The object of this game, *Build-a-Foot,* is for players to estimate when the lengths of trains of Cuisenaire® Rods are close to 1 foot. The winner is the first player to correctly estimate the length to within 1 centimeter.

Prepare Materials Each pair of students will need Activity Master: Spinner, Cuisenaire® Rods, an inch ruler, a paper clip, and a pencil to play this game.

Each pair will need to make a spinner. To do so, students should hold the pencil with its tip in the center of the spinner, and then place a paper clip around the pencil so that it lays flush against the paper.

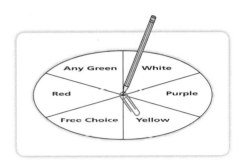

How to Play

❶ Players alternate turns. The player whose turn it is spins the spinner and collects the Cuisenaire® Rod indicated.

❷ Players use their rods to make "trains" of rods by placing them end-to-end.

❸ When a player thinks his or her train is 1 foot long, the player may ask for a ruler to check its length.

❹ If the train is more than 1 centimeter shorter or longer than a foot, the player must remove the last piece added to the train. If the train is still longer than a foot, keep removing pieces until it is less than a foot long. If the train is within 1 centimeter of a foot, that player is the winner.

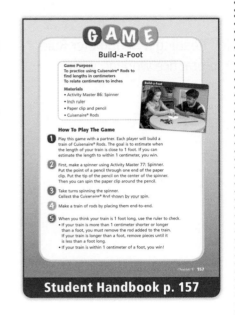

Student Handbook p. 157

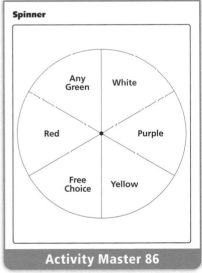

Activity Master 86

Materials
• For each pair: AM86, Cuisenaire® Rods, inch ruler, paper clip, pencil

NCTM Standards 1, 2, 6, 7, 8, 9, 10

Teacher Story

"Some of my students were curious about the exact relationship between inches and centimeters. We looked at a ruler and saw that there are about $2\frac{1}{2}$ centimeters in each inch. Because students had worked with decimals, I told them that the relationship is close to 2.54 centimeters in every inch. Because 2.54 is close to 2.5, we agreed to use 2.5 when estimating the number of centimeters in a given number of inches. One of my students used this information to figure out that if there are about 2.5 centimeters in 1 inch, there must be about 5 centimeters in 2 inches, 10 in 4 inches, and 30 centimeters in 1 foot. When the students played *Build-a-Foot,* the ones who remembered this relationship always knew when to compare their trains to the ruler."

Write Math

How might you use a ruler that is 8 centimeters long to find the length of a line that is much longer? Possible answers: You might line up multiple copies of the ruler end-to-end till they approximate the length of the line. You might estimate that the line appeared to be a certain number times the length of the ruler. You might mark the end of the ruler, then move the other end of the ruler to the mark, continuing in this way until you have measured the entire line.

Review Model...

Refer students to the Review Model: Reading a Centimeter Ruler in the **Student Handbook** p. 149 to practice working with centimeter rulers.

✓ Check for Understanding

❶ 1.9 centimeters

❷ 0.5 centimeters

❸ 1.0 centimeters

❹ 2.3 centimeters

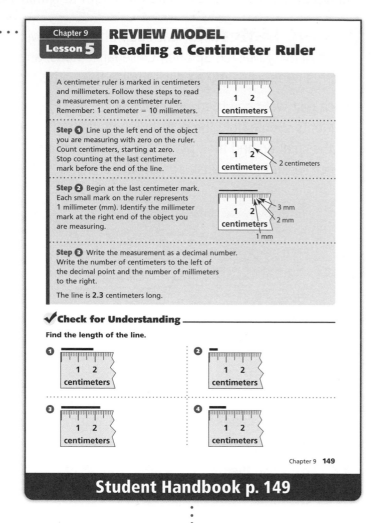

Use with Lesson Activity Book pp. 181–182.

Leveled Problem Solving

The width of Cal's hand is about 6 centimeters. He uses his hand to measure the width of a library book.

❶ Basic Level
The book is about 4 hands wide. About how wide is the book in centimeters? Explain. about 24 centimeters; $4 \times 6 = 24$

❷ On Level
The book is about 3.5 hands wide. About how wide is the book in centimeters? Explain. about 21 centimeters; $3.5 \times 6 = 21$

❸ Above Level
Cal knows that 1 inch is about 2.5 centimeters. About how many inches long is his book if it is about 5 hands long? Explain. about 12 inches; $6 \times 5 = 30$ cm; $30 \div 2.5 = 12$

Intervention	Practice	Extension

Activity Benchmarks

Have small groups choose a classroom item, such as a paper clip or a pen, to use as a unit of measurement. Tell each group to use the unit to measure the length of a larger classroom item. List all the units on the board. One at a time, have each group tell the class what item they measured and the number of units but not which unit was used. The other students guess what unit was used to make the measurement.

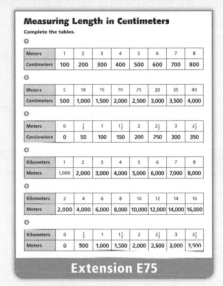

Practice P75

Extension E75

Spiral Review

Spiral Review Book page SR75 provides review of the following previously learned skills and concepts:

- splitting arrays into smaller parts to simplify finding the total number of squares
- solving problems using the strategy *solve a simpler problem*

You may wish to have students work with partners to complete the page.

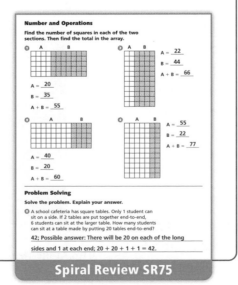

Spiral Review SR75

Extension Activity
Centimeters to Meters

Show students a meter stick. Tell them that 1 meter is 100 centimeters and have them verify that on the meter stick. Then ask students to identify classroom items that are about 1 meter long. Have students check their estimates using a meter stick.

Lesson 6 Measuring Capacity in Cups, Pints, and Quarts

NCTM Standards 1, 2, 6, 7, 8, 9, 10

Lesson Planner

STUDENT OBJECTIVES
- To estimate and measure capacity using standard and non-standard units
- To convert among cups, pints, and quarts

1 | Daily Activities (TG p. 739)

Open-Ended Problem Solving/Headline Story	Skills Practice and Review— Doubling Elapsed Times

2 | Teach and Practice (TG pp. 740–742)

MATERIALS

Ⓐ **Exploring the Capacity of a Paper Cup** (TG p. 740)

Ⓑ **Comparing Cups, Pints, and Quarts** (TG p. 741)

Ⓒ **Measuring Capacity in Cups, Pints, and Quarts** (TG p. 742)

- standard measuring cups, drinking cups, substance to measure (e.g., rice, dried beans, corn kernels)
- standard pint and quart measures
- 📖 LAB pp. 183–184
- 📖 SH p. 150

3 | Differentiated Instruction (TG p. 743)

Leveled Problem Solving (TG p. 743)	Practice Book P76
Intervention Activity (TG p. 743)	Extension Book E76
Extension Activity (TG p. 743)	Spiral Review Book SR76

Lesson Notes

About the Lesson

In this lesson, students measure the capacities of various containers, using cups, pints, and quarts as units. Then they compare these units, finding that 2 cups equal 1 pint and 2 pints equal 1 quart. From this they conclude that 4 cups equal 1 quart. In the next lesson, as they continue to work with cups, pints, and quarts, students will be introduced to an even larger unit, the gallon.

About the Mathematics

The measuring units introduced in this lesson are related by a doubling pattern. Students do not see the entire system in this lesson, but it starts with tablespoons.

> 2 tablespoons = 1 fl oz
> 2 fl oz has no commonly used name, but if we double twice more...
>
> 8 fl oz = 1 cup
> 2 cups = 1 pint
> 2 pints = 1 quart
> 2 quarts = 1 half-gallon
> 2 half-gallons = 1 gallon

The Skills Practice and Review provides students with practice doubling.

Use with Lesson Activity Book pp. 183–184.

Developing Mathematical Language

Vocabulary: cup, pint, quart

Unlike units in the customary systems for measuring length, weight, time, and others, customary capacity units are consistently related by a factor of 2. In this lesson students learn that 2 *cups* = 1 *pint* and 2 *pints* = 1 *quart.*

Review the terms *cup* and *quart* with students.

Beginning Show students a *cup* measure and a *quart* measure. Use each term in a sentence and write it on the board. Then, ask each student to write a sentence using both words. Let students take turns reading their sentences aloud.

Intermediate Ask students to name things they would measure with a *cup* and a *quart.* Then have volunteers share cooking experiences in which they have used cups or quarts to measure liquids.

Advanced Have students work in pairs. Have one student name a container that holds liquid, such as a pitcher of lemonade, and ask the other student to identify the most appropriate unit for measuring how much the container holds. Have students alternate roles.

Open-Ended Problem Solving

Read the Headline Story to the students. Encourage them to think of creative ways to solve the problem.

 Headline Story

Lavar has a restaurant with 9 seats at the counter and 2 small tables. He uses 3 eggs to make an omelet. How many dozen eggs might he need in a morning to serve omelets to his customers?

Possible responses: If he cooked 4 omelets, he would need 1 dozen eggs. If he beat 5 dozen eggs, then he could make 20 omelets. If he made 2 omelets, then he would use half a dozen eggs. If he had 17 customers in his restaurant at once and they all ordered an omelet, he would need 51 eggs, which is 4 dozen 3 eggs, or 4 and a quarter dozen.

Skills Practice and Review

Doubling Elapsed Times

Materials
• demonstration clock

Set the demonstration clock to 1:00. Ask students to read the time.

Move the minute hand 1 minute forward, say that 1 minute has passed, and ask what time the clock now says. 1:01 Reset the clock to 1:00 and ask what time it would be if twice as much time had passed as before. 1:02 Continue in this way, moving the clock back to 1:00 each time, and asking what the time would be if twice as much time passed as in the previous example. Next four answers: 1:04, 1:08, 1:16, 1:32 Note that when 1:64 and subsequent times are reached, the hour as well as the minutes will change. Continue to at least 1:256 (5:16). If you have time, you might challenge students to repeat this activity starting at a time that is not an exact hour.

pairs · 20 MIN

(A) Exploring the Capacity of a Paper Cup

Materials

- For each student: standard measuring cup, drinking cup, substance to measure (e.g., rice, dried beans, corn kernels)

NCTM Standards 1, 2, 6, 7, 8, 9, 10

✔ Ongoing Assessment

- Do students understand that a "standard" measure like 1 foot or 1 cup has a fixed size, so that the number of units in a measurement will be the same no matter who is measuring?

Teacher Story

❝So that students had enough time to explore capacity, I had them physically measure capacity one day and complete the lesson on a second day.

Also, to offer students additional practice with measurement, I set up a measurement center with different containers and materials for individual students to use. I also made several laminated cards, each listing objects for students to measure. This seemed to help students become more familiar with the different types of measures and measuring instruments. I included rulers, tape measures, and yardsticks, along with cup, pint, and quart measures.❞

Purpose To introduce capacity

Introduce Set up a measurement area where students can explore capacity, or distribute something for groups of students to measure, for example, rice, dry beans, or corn kernels. Each student should have access to a standard measuring cup. Give each student a drinking cup, or use drinking cups that students brought from home. Then give students Explore: What is a Cup? to complete in pairs.

Task Direct students to the following challenges, which appear on Explore: What is a Cup?

❶ Can your own cup hold more or less than a standard measuring cup? Answers will depend on sizes of students' cups.

❷ Pick up a handful of rice, beans, or whatever your teacher supplies. Estimate how many of your handfuls make a standard cup. Then measure to check your estimate. Answers will depend on sizes of students' hands.

❸ Use a standard measuring cup to find out how much your cup will hold. Answers will depend on sizes of students' cups.

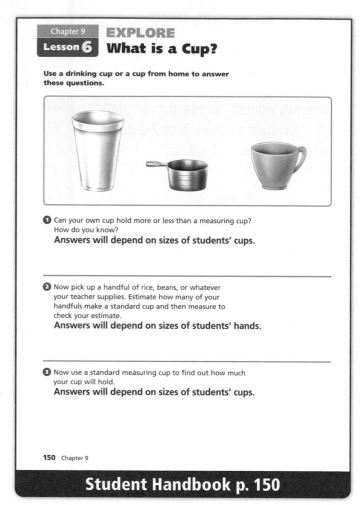

Student Handbook p. 150

To judge whether a student's drinking cup is larger or smaller than a measuring cup, he or she will likely just look at the two cups. The second question asks the student first to *estimate* how many handfuls it will take to fill the measuring cup, then actually to try it out. A good enough measurement can be found by filling a cup using handfuls, then emptying it into the measuring cup, being careful not to go beyond the highest mark on the measuring cup.

💬 Talk Math

❓ Will all students use the same number of handfuls of rice to fill a standard measuring cup? Explain your reasoning. no; Possible explanation: All students' hands are not the same size.

❓ Joey's drinking cup has half the capacity of a standard measuring cup. How many times must Joey fill his cup to fill a measuring cup? 2 times

Use with Lesson Activity Book pp. 183–184.

B Comparing Cups, Pints, and Quarts

Purpose To introduce pints and quarts

Introduce Display standard cup, pint, and quart measures. State that the two larger containers have capacities of 1 pint and 1 quart, and mention that, like cups, pints and quarts are widely used standard measures.

Problem Ask students to make the following estimates:

- How many cups do you think it would take to fill the pint container? Possible estimate: about 2 cups

- How many cups do you think it would take to fill the quart container? Possible estimate: about 4 cups

After students make their estimates, repeatedly fill the cup with rice or dried beans and pour it into the pint container until it is filled. After showing that 2 cups fill the pint container, write 2 cups = 1 pint on the board.

Repeat the demonstration, using the quart container this time. After showing that 4 cups fill the quart container, write 4 cups = 1 quart on the board.

Share Challenge students with the following question:

- Based on what you have seen, how many pints do you think there are in 1 quart? 2 pints

Ask students to explain how they found the answer. If no one can explain clearly or easily how they found the answer, write the equations at the right on the board:

> 4 cups = 1 quart
> (2 cups) + (2 cups) = 1 quart
> (1 pint) + (1 pint) = 1 quart
> 2 pints = 1 quart

Fill the pint container and pour it into the quart container to show that, in fact, 2 pints = 1 quart. Write 2 pints = 1 quart on the board. Leave all three equivalencies on the board for students to reference while completing LAB pages 183–184:

> 2 cups = 1 pint
> 4 cups = 1 quart
> 2 pints = 1 quart

Talk Math

❓ What fraction can you write to express the portion of 1 pint that is represented by 1 cup? $\frac{1}{2}$

❓ What fraction can you write to express the portion of 1 quart that is represented by 1 cup? $\frac{1}{4}$

Materials
- For the teacher: standard cup, pint, and quart measures; substance to measure (e.g., rice, dried beans, corn kernels)

NCTM Standards 1, 2, 6, 7, 8, 9, 10

Differentiated Instruction

On Level In Activity B, students find out that 2 cups = 1 pint, 4 cups = 1 quart, and 2 pints = 1 quart. If you would prefer to have students discover these equivalencies on their own, without your demonstrating the equivalencies for them, you might split the class into groups. Ask some groups to find how many cups are in a pint, some to find how many cups are in a quart, and some to find how many pints are in a quart. Then have the groups share what they have found. Record the results on the board for everyone to use as they complete the LAB pages.

Measuring Capacity in Cups, Pints, and Quarts LAB pp. 183–184

 individuals or pairs

 20 MIN

Purpose To compare cups, pints, and quarts

NCTM Standards 1, 2, 6, 7, 8, 9, 10

Lesson Activity Book p. 183

Name _____ Date _____

Chapter 9
Lesson 6 **Measuring Capacity in Cups, Pints, and Quarts**
NCTM Standards 1, 2, 6, 7, 8, 9, 10

Compare the amounts. Write <, >, or = in each ◯.

❶ 1 quart ⟩ 1 pint   ❷ 2 cups = 1 pint

❸ 1 cup ⟨ 1 quart   ❹ 1 quart ⟨ 3 pints

❺ 1 pint ⟩ 1 cup   ❻ 3 cups ⟨ 1 quart

Write the missing number to make each statement true.

❼ 1 pint = __2__ cups   ❽ 1 quart = __2__ pints

❾ 1 quart = __4__ cups   ❿ __2__ pints = 4 cups

⓫ 6 pints = __3__ quarts   ⓬ __6__ cups = 3 pints

3 × 61   **CLXXXIII**   one hundred eighty-three **183**

Lesson Activity Book p. 184

Solve.

⓭ Howie filled a pint container halfway. How many more cups does he need to fill the container completely?

__1__ cup(s)

⓮ Sharon poured 3 cups of water out of a filled 2-pint container. How many cups were left?

__1__ cup(s)

⓯ Rebecca used a pint container to fill a quart container with water. How many times did she fill the pint container?

__2__ times

⓰ Carl needed a quart of milk for his special smoothies. He had 3 cups of milk. Did he have enough?

yes   (no)

⓱ Jen bought a pint of juice at the store and shared it equally with a friend. How much did each child get?

__½__ pint or 1 cup

⓲ Lizzie gave each of her 6 friends a cup of milk. How many pints is that?

__3__ pints

⓳ **Challenge** Peter poured 6 cups of water into a 2-quart container. Did he fill the container?

yes   (no)

⓴ **Challenge** James emptied half of a 2-quart container into pint containers. He poured the rest into cups. How many cups did he fill?

__4__ cups

184 one hundred eighty-four   **CLXXXIV**   2 × 2 × 2 × 23

ABOUT THE PAGE NUMBER Is 183 ounces more or less than 12 pounds?

ABOUT THE PAGE NUMBER Is 8 quarters enough to make $1.84?

Teaching Notes for LAB page 183

Have students complete the page individually or with partners.

The relationships in Problems 1–6 should be clear if cup, pint, and quart containers are in view. The equivalencies written on the board should also help.

Differentiated Instruction **Basic Level** If students are unclear about how to use the equivalencies developed in the previous activities, you might have them actually measure some of the amounts on this page to help them find the answers.

Teaching Notes for LAB page 184

This page requires students to compare units of capacity in real-life contexts. Remind students that they know a number of problem solving strategies that can help them (e.g., *act it out, draw a picture,* and *make a table*).

Challenge Problems These problems require students to compare cups and quarts. Converting from one amount to the other involves multiplying or dividing by 4 rather than by 2, as in the other problems.

Reflect and Summarize the Lesson

Write Math

How many cups equal 3 quarts? How many pints? Explain your reasoning using pictures, numbers, or words. Possible answer: There are 4 cups in a quart. In 3 quarts, therefore, there are 4 × 3 = 12 cups. There are 2 pints in a quart. In 3 quarts, therefore, there are 2 × 3 = 6 pints.

3 | Differentiated Instruction

Leveled Problem Solving

A recipe for ice cream cake calls for 4 quarts of ice cream.

❶ Basic Level

How many pints of ice cream should Melody buy to make one cake? Explain. 8 pints; 1 quart = 2 pints; $2 \times 4 = 8$

❷ On Level

Melody has 10 pints of ice cream. Can she make the cake? Explain. Yes; The recipe requires 4 quarts, which is the same as 8 pints; $8 < 10$.

❸ Above Level

Each serving of cake will contain 1 cup of ice cream. How many servings will there be? Explain. 16 servings; 1 quart = 2 pints, 1 pint = 2 cups. The cake has 4 quarts of ice cream: $4 \times 2 \times 2 = 16$.

| Intervention | Practice | Extension |

Activity Count Off

Have students work in groups of four to count off measures, one cup at a time, starting with 1 cup. Tell students to switch units when appropriate so that the counting is as follows: 1 cup, 1 pint, 3 cups, 1 quart, 5 cups, 3 pints, 7 cups, 2 quarts, and so on. When the groups reach 5 quarts, have them start over with a different student starting the count off.

Practice

Measuring Capacity in Cups, Pints, and Quarts

Fill in the missing amounts.

❶
| 2 years | + | 3 years | = | **5** years |
| 24 months | + | 36 months | = | **60** months |

❷
| 1 quart | + | 2 quarts | = | 3 quarts |
| 4 cups | + | **8** cups | = | **12** cups |

❸
| 2 yards | + | 6 yards | = | **8** yards |
| **6** feet | + | 18 feet | = | 24 feet |

❹
| 10 quarts | + | **9** quarts | = | 19 quarts |
| **20** pints | + | 18 pints | = | **38** pints |

❺
| 3 feet | + | **2** yards | = | 3 yards |
| **36** inches | + | 6 feet | = | **9** feet |

Test Prep

❻ Which expression does NOT have the same value as 36×42?

A. $(30 \times 42) + (6 \times 42)$ C. $(30 \times 40) + (6 \times 40) + (2 \times 30) + (6 \times 2)$
B. $(36 \times 40) + (36 \times 2)$ **D.** $(30 \times 40) + (6 \times 2)$

Practice P76

Extension

Measuring Capacity in Cups, Pints, and Quarts

Andre is trying to measure various amounts, but he has only the following containers:

a bowl that holds exactly 3 cups of liquid
a 1-pint container
a $1\frac{1}{2}$-cup mug   Many answers are possible. One such answer is given.

❶ How can Andre accurately measure 1 cup of milk?

Possible answer: He could fill the bowl with milk and then pour as much as he could into the pint container. 1 cup of milk would be left in the bowl.

❷ How can Andre accurately measure $2\frac{1}{2}$ cups of milk?

Possible answer: He could fill the pint container and then pour it into the bowl. Then he could fill the pint container again and pour as much as he could into the mug. $\frac{1}{2}$ cup of milk would remain in the pint container. He could add it to the bowl to make $2\frac{1}{2}$ cups of milk.

Extension E76

Spiral Review

Spiral Review Book page SR76 provides review of the following previously learned skills and concepts:

- comparing and ordering fractions
- finding missing dimensions in an array of tiles

You may wish to have students work with partners to complete the page.

Number and Operations

Write < or > to compare the fractions. Use the diagrams at the top of each column to help you.

❶ $\frac{7}{10} < \frac{5}{10}$ ❷ $\frac{1}{3} > \frac{5}{12}$ ❸ $\frac{3}{6} < \frac{10}{12}$

❹ $\frac{2}{5} < \frac{1}{3}$ ❺ $\frac{3}{8} > \frac{2}{3}$ ❻ $\frac{7}{12} > \frac{1}{3}$

❼ $\frac{3}{10} > \frac{4}{5}$ ❽ $\frac{5}{6} < \frac{5}{12}$ ❾ $\frac{2}{3} > \frac{2}{3}$

Write the fractions in order from least to greatest.

❿ $\frac{1}{4} \frac{1}{3} \frac{1}{8}$ ⓫ $\frac{5}{3} \frac{7}{6} \frac{2}{8}$ ⓬ $\frac{2}{9} \frac{5}{7} \frac{3}{12}$
   $\frac{1}{4} \frac{1}{3} \frac{1}{8}$ $\frac{2}{3} \frac{5}{6} \frac{7}{8}$ $\frac{2}{3} \frac{3}{9} \frac{9}{12}$

Algebra

Complete the fact family. Use the pictures if needed.

⓭ $5 \times \underline{6} = 30$ ⓮ $4 \times \underline{7} = 28$
$\underline{6} \times 5 = 30$ $\underline{7} \times 4 = 28$
$30 \div 5 = \underline{6}$ $28 \div 4 = \underline{7}$
$30 \div \underline{6} = 5$ $28 \div \underline{7} = 4$

Spiral Review SR76

Extension Activity
Race to Convert

Write a number, such as 10, on the board. Have students convert 10 cups to quarts and pints, 10 pints to cups and quarts, and 10 quarts to cups and pints.

Have students form two teams. Write a different number on the board, and have the teams race to correctly complete the conversions. Repeat with other numbers.

Lesson 7 Measuring Capacity in Gallons and Liters

NCTM Standards 1, 2, 6, 7, 8, 9, 10

Lesson Planner

STUDENT OBJECTIVES
- To estimate and measure capacity
- To convert among cups, pints, quarts, and gallons
- To compare customary and metric units of capacity

1 | Daily Activities (TG p. 745)

Open-Ended Problem Solving/Headline Story	Skills Practice and Review— Doubling

2 | Teach and Practice (TG pp. 746–750)

	MATERIALS
(A) **Comparing Cups, Pints, Quarts, and Gallons** (TG pp. 746–747) (B) **Comparing Customary and Metric Units of Capacity** (TG pp. 748–749) (C) **Measuring Capacity in Gallons and Liters** (TG p. 750)	• cup, pint, quart, gallon, and liter containers; substance to measure (e.g., rice, dried beans, corn kernels); teaspoon (optional) • 📖 LAB pp. 185–186

3 | Differentiated Instruction (TG p. 751)

Leveled Problem Solving (TG p. 751)	Practice Book P77
Intervention Activity (TG p. 751)	Extension Book E77
Extension Activity (TG p. 751)	Spiral Review Book SR77

Lesson Notes

About the Lesson

Students continue to measure capacity, working with cups, pints, and quarts. They are introduced to gallons, and discover that 1 gallon = 4 quarts = 8 pints = 16 cups.

Then they work with liters, a metric unit of capacity. To get a sense of the size of a liter, students compare customary units to liters. They practice converting among various units within the two systems, customary and metric, and make approximate comparisons across systems (e.g., 7 cups > 1 liter).

In the metric system, units are related by a factor of 10.

> 10 milliliters = 1 centiliter
> 10 centiliters = 1 deciliter
> 10 deciliters = 1 liter

In practice, despite the fact that this system so perfectly matches our place-value system, most people ignore the complicated terminology and refer only to liters and milliliters. Half a liter, then, is equated with 0.5 liters or 500 milliliters, rather than 5 deciliters.

Use with Lesson Activity Book pp. 185–186.

Developing Mathematical Language

Vocabulary: liter, milliliter

One *milliliter* takes up the same space as a white Cuisenaire® Rod (or a small base-10 cube). A *liter* is 1,000 *milliliters,* so it takes up the same space as a 10 × 10 × 10 cube (the large base-10 cube).

If you have students who speak Spanish, Portuguese, French, or Italian, they may be able to contribute the word for 1,000 in their languages. In Spanish and Portuguese, 1,000 is *mil,* in French it's *mille* (pronounced "meal"), and in Italian it's *mille* (pronounced "mee-lay"). A millipede is a "thousand legger," though it does not really have a thousand legs. A millennium is 1,000 years.

Review the term *liter* with students.

Beginning Show students a *liter* container. Have students identify items that are sold by the *liter.*

Intermediate Write various units of capacities on the board. Have students tell whether each is less than a *liter,* about a *liter,* or more than a *liter.*

Advanced Have students work in groups to make three lists of three different types of containers: those that contain less than a *liter,* about a *liter,* and more than a *liter.*

Open-Ended Problem Solving

Read the Headline Story to the students. To help students get started, you might openly wonder how many quarts of milk the entire class drinks in a day, or how long it would take one student to drink what a cow produces each day.

 Headline Story

Milk cows in the United States produce an average of 26 quarts of milk per day. How much milk do you drink each day? What can you conclude from these facts?

Possible responses: I drink 3 glasses of milk each day. I think each is about a cup of milk. In 4 days, I drink 12 cups of milk, or 3 quarts. By making a table, I can see that it would take me over a month to drink all the milk a cow gives in a day!

Days	4	8	12	16	32	36
Quarts	3	6	9	12	24	27

Skills Practice and Review

Doubling

This activity prepares students to work with equivalencies among cups, pints, and quarts. Point to individual students and have each double the previous number, starting with 1: 1, 2, 4, 8, 16, and so on. Continue to at least 512. As students say the numbers, write them in a vertical list on the board. Repeat, starting at 5. Write the new list of numbers next to the first.

1	5
2	10
4	20
8	40
16	80
32	160
64	320
128	640
256	1,280
512	2,560
1,024	5,120
2,048	10,240

small groups

20 MIN

A Comparing Cups, Pints, Quarts, and Gallons

Materials

- For each group: cup, pint, quart, and gallon containers; substance to measure (e.g., rice, dried beans, corn kernels)

NCTM Standards 1, 2, 6, 7, 8, 9, 10

Purpose To compare customary units of capacity

Introduce Show standard cup, pint, and quart containers to the class. Remind students of the relationships they found among cups, pints, and quarts in the previous lesson by asking how many cups fill a pint 2, how many pints fill a quart 2, and how many cups fill a quart 4. Record these facts on the board.

Problems Display the gallon container. Ask students to estimate how many quarts they think would fill a gallon. Then ask them to predict the number of pints or cups there are in a gallon.

To allow students to check their estimates and predictions, divide them into small groups. Try to have six groups, if possible, because that will allow you to assign two groups to each key relationship (the number of cups in a gallon, the number of pints in a gallon, and the number of quarts in a gallon).

Each group will need appropriate containers and a substance to measure, such as water, rice, or beans. To enumerate the relationship between two units, students should repeatedly fill the smaller-unit container and pour it into the larger-unit container, counting the number of fillings. Assigning two groups to each relationship helps assure more accurate measurements. (See Ongoing Assessment for ideas on how to help students measure accurately and find correct equivalencies.)

✓ Ongoing Assessment

- Do students reach incorrect conclusions when measuring to compare cups with gallons because their measurements are not precise. For example, do they count more than 16 cups in a gallon if they do not fill each cup to the 8-ounce line, or fewer than 16 if they stop below the gallon line? For students who get incorrect results, you might ask them to show you how they measured. This will give you a chance to see students' measuring techniques and help them find their errors.

Share Gather the class to share their results. It's likely that the quart and pint groups will get the correct results: 4 quarts = 1 gallon, 8 pints = 1 gallon. However, because so much measuring is involved for the gallon groups, one or more of them may fail to obtain the correct result of 16 cups = 1 gallon. If that happens, you might have group members check to see if their results make sense by asking them to convert the other groups' results into cups:

quart groups

1 gallon = 4 quarts
1 quart = 4 cups
So, 1 gallon = 4 x 4 = 16 cups.

pint groups

1 gallon = 8 pints
1 pint = 2 cups
So, 1 gallon = 8 x 2 = 16 cups.

Write the equivalencies on the board for students to refer to during the rest of the lesson.

Talk Math

❷ How many quarts are there in 5 gallons? Explain your reasoning.
20 quarts; Possible explanation: 1 gallon = 4 quarts, so 5 gallons =
5 × 4 = 20 quarts.

❷ How many cups are there in 3 gallons? Explain your reasoning.
48 cups; Possible explanation: 1 gallon = 16 cups, so 3 gallons =
3 × 16 = 48 cups.

B Comparing Customary and Metric Units of Capacity

Materials

- For each group: cup, pint, quart, and liter containers; funnel; substance to measure (e.g., rice, dried beans, corn kernels); teaspoon (optional)

NCTM Standards 1, 2, 6, 7, 8, 9, 10

Ongoing Assessment

- Do students know the basic equivalencies relating cups, pints, quarts, and gallons?

Purpose To introduce the liter

Introduce Ask students whether they have heard the word *liter* before. If any have, ask them where they heard the word, or what items are sold by the liter. Most students will have seen soda sold in 2-liter containers, though not all will have noticed the units. Students who have been to or lived in other countries may know of gasoline being sold by the liter. Some may know that scientists measure liquids in liters.

Task **Hand out a 1-liter container to each group of students. Ask:**

- How does this container compare with cup, pint, quart, and gallon containers? (If you cannot obtain a one-liter container, use a two-liter bottle and note the changes below.) Possible answer: the container appears bigger than a cup and a pint, smaller than a gallon, and about the same size as a quart.

Students will probably find that the quart and liter containers (or half-gallon and two-liter containers) are hard to compare visually. Have them fill the quart container with rice, sand, or beans, and then carefully pour it into the liter container. (They may want to use a funnel.) When finished, there should be a small bit of room left at the top of the liter container. This direct comparison shows that a quart is slightly smaller than a liter. (For more on metric units of capacity, see Developing Mathematical Language.)

Have the groups repeat this, filling the liter bottle with cups and pints. Students will see that quantities equivalent to a quart—4 cups and 2 pints—are also slightly smaller than a liter.

To help students relate customary units and liters, suggest that they first relate the given units to quarts, then use the fact that a quart is slightly less than a liter. For example, you might ask:

- Which is the larger measure, 3 cups or 1 liter? Why? 1 liter; Possible answer: 3 cups is less than a quart, and a quart is less than a liter.

- Which is the larger measure, 5 pints or 2 liters? Why? 5 pints; Possible answer: 5 pints is a lot more than 2 quarts, and 2 liters is only a bit more than 2 quarts.

- Which is the larger measure, 4 liters or 1 gallon? Why? 4 liters; Possible answer: A quart is less than a liter, so 4 quarts (or 1 gallon) is less than 4 liters.

Finally, tell students that there are 1,000 milliliters in 1 liter. (See Developing Mathematical Language for suggestions on how to help students remember this relationship.) If you have a teaspoon, you might tell students that the spoon holds about 5 milliliters of liquid.

Talk Math

❷ Which is more, 500 milliliters or 1 quart? Explain your reasoning.
1 quart; Possible explanation: 500 milliliters is half a liter and therefore less than 1 quart, which is almost 1 liter.

❷ Which is more, 1,000 milliliters or 7 cups? Explain your reasoning. 7 cups; Possible explanation: 7 cups is almost 2 quarts and 1,000 milliliters is just slightly more than 1 quart.

Differentiated Instruction

On Level As in the previous lesson, you may choose to give students additional practice with measuring by having them physically compare the units in Activity B. Split the class into groups, have each group make a different comparison (e.g., cups to liters, pints to liters, quarts to liters, gallons to liters), and then have students share their discoveries. Write the relationships they find on the board. Unlike cups, pints, and quarts, however, customary and metric units are not related by whole numbers. Instead, students should find that a quart is slightly less than a liter, and that a gallon is therefore a little less than 4 liters.

Measuring Capacity in Gallons and Liters LAB pp. 185–186

Purpose To relate cups, pints, quarts, gallons, and liters

NCTM Standards 1, 2, 6, 7, 8, 9, 10

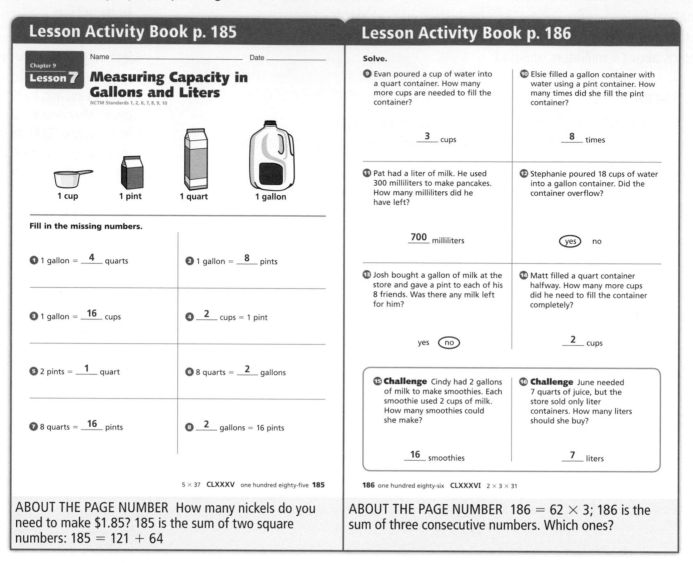

Lesson Activity Book p. 185

Name _____ Date _____

Chapter 9
Lesson 7

Measuring Capacity in Gallons and Liters
NCTM Standards 1, 2, 6, 7, 8, 9, 10

1 cup   1 pint   1 quart   1 gallon

Fill in the missing numbers.

1. 1 gallon = __4__ quarts
2. 1 gallon = __8__ pints
3. 1 gallon = __16__ cups
4. __2__ cups = 1 pint
5. 2 pints = __1__ quart
6. 8 quarts = __2__ gallons
7. 8 quarts = __16__ pints
8. __2__ gallons = 16 pints

5 × 37 CLXXXV one hundred eighty-five **185**

ABOUT THE PAGE NUMBER How many nickels do you need to make $1.85? 185 is the sum of two square numbers: 185 = 121 + 64

Lesson Activity Book p. 186

Solve.

9. Evan poured a cup of water into a quart container. How many more cups are needed to fill the container?

__3__ cups

10. Elsie filled a gallon container with water using a pint container. How many times did she fill the pint container?

__8__ times

11. Pat had a liter of milk. He used 300 milliliters to make pancakes. How many milliliters did he have left?

__700__ milliliters

12. Stephanie poured 18 cups of water into a gallon container. Did the container overflow?

(yes) no

13. Josh bought a gallon of milk at the store and gave a pint to each of his 8 friends. Was there any milk left for him?

yes (no)

14. Matt filled a quart container halfway. How many more cups did he need to fill the container completely?

__2__ cups

15. **Challenge** Cindy had 2 gallons of milk to make smoothies. Each smoothie used 2 cups of milk. How many smoothies could she make?

__16__ smoothies

16. **Challenge** June needed 7 quarts of juice, but the store sold only liter containers. How many liters should she buy?

__7__ liters

186 one hundred eighty-six CLXXXVI 2 × 3 × 31

ABOUT THE PAGE NUMBER 186 = 62 × 3; 186 is the sum of three consecutive numbers. Which ones?

Teaching Notes for LAB page 185

Have students complete the page individually or with partners. On this page, students relate customary units for measuring capacity—cups, pints, quarts, and gallons.

They should use the equivalencies they found in the lesson. That is, if 4 quarts = 1 gallon, then 8 pints = 1 gallon, and 16 cups = 1 gallon.

Teaching Notes for LAB page 186

On this page, students reason about both customary and metric units of capacity in real-life contexts.

Challenge Problems Each of these problems requires students to make two conversions and then to carry out a computation.

Reflect and Summarize the Lesson

 Write Math

About how many cups are in a liter? About how many liters are in a gallon? Explain, using pictures, numbers, or words. Possible answers: Since there are 4 cups in a quart, and a quart is a little less than a liter, there are a little more than 4 cups in a liter. Similarly, since there are 4 quarts in a gallon and a quart is a little less than a liter, there are a little less than 4 liters in a gallon.

Use with Lesson Activity Book pp. 185–186.

3 | Differentiated Instruction

Leveled Problem Solving

Celia's bucket holds 2 liters of water.

❶ Basic Level

Ken's bucket holds 2 gallons of water. Whose bucket holds more? Explain. Ken's; 1 L is a little more than 1 qt, and there are 4 qt in 1 gal, so there are about 8 L in 2 gal. 8 L is much more than 2 L.

❷ On Level

Anya's bucket holds 4 quarts of water. Whose bucket holds more? Explain Anya's; 1 L is a little more than 1 qt, so 2 L is a little more than 2 qt. 4 qt is much more than 2 qt.

❸ Above Level

Ben's bucket holds 12 cups of water. Whose bucket holds more? Explain Ben's; 12 c is the same as 3 qt, and 2 L is a little more than 2 qt. 3 qt is much more than 2 qt.

Intervention	Practice	Extension

Activity Marking Comparisons

Give students different translucent containers that are close to, if not exactly, standard measurement units in capacity. Have them repeatedly pour all water from a full, smaller container into a larger one, marking the level of the water each time. Then have them record how many marks are on the larger container and write an equivalence, such as 4 quarts = 1 gallon.

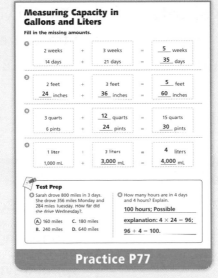

Practice P77

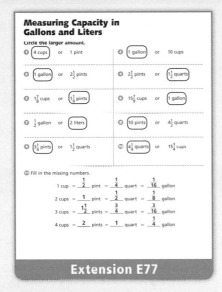

Extension E77

Extension Activity
Estimation Counts!

Fill a liter container with beans or corn kernels. Show students the filled liter container and an empty quart container. Give each group a portion of beans or kernels from the liter container, and ask them to count the items. Have each group share their count and determine the total for the liter container. Then place as many items into the quart container as will fit. Have groups estimate the number of items in the quart container. Have groups count the items to check their estimates.

Spiral Review

Spiral Review Book page SR77 provides review of the following previously learned skills and concepts:

- comparing and ordering angles
- classifying events as possible, impossible, more, or less likely

You may wish to have students work with partners to complete the page.

Geometry

Which angle is larger?

Write the angles in order from smallest to largest.

P, N, M   T, R, S   M, L, N

Data Analysis and Probability

For 7–8, write *impossible* or *possible*.

A new student will come into your class before the end of the year.   possible

Next week, there will be no Friday.   impossible

Choose the event that is the more likely of the two.

getting an even number or getting a number less than 3 when you roll a 1–6 number cube

getting an even number

getting an even number or getting a number greater than 3 when you draw one of 8 cards marked 1–8

getting a number greater than 3

Spiral Review SR77

Lesson 8 Computing Amounts of Liquid

NCTM Standards 1, 2, 6, 7, 8, 9, 10

Lesson Planner

STUDENT OBJECTIVE ....
▪ To complete tables and solve problems involving conversions among units of capacity

1 Daily Activities (TG p. 753)

Open-Ended Problem Solving/Headline Story	Skills Practice and Review— Doubling

2 Teach and Practice (TG pp. 754–757)

MATERIALS

Ⓐ **Converting Among Units of Capacity** (TG pp. 754–755)

Ⓑ **Solving Problems Through Unit Conversions** (TG p. 756)

Ⓒ **Computing Amounts of Liquid** (TG p. 757)

- TR: Activity Masters, AM87–AM88 (optional)
- transparencies of AM87–AM88 (optional)
- 📖 LAB pp. 187–188

3 Differentiated Instruction (TG p. 758)

Leveled Problem Solving (TG p. 758)	Practice Book P78
Intervention Activity (TG p. 758)	Extension Book E78
Extension Activity (TG p. 758)	Spiral Review Book SR78

Lesson Notes

About the Lesson

In **Lesson 9.6** and **Lesson 9.7,** students estimated and measured volume, or capacity. In this lesson, students use what they have learned about measurement to compute using various units of capacity. They then solve word problems involving conversions between units, connecting their computations to everyday situations.

Use with Lesson Activity Book pp. 187–188.

Developing Mathematical Language

Vocabulary: gallon

Like other units discussed in this chapter, a *gallon* once meant different things to different people. The unit was standardized in the United States in 1832. Since then, an American *gallon* has been equivalent to 231 cubic inches or 3.785 liters. Internationally, however, confusion still reigns. The British *gallon* is larger than an American *gallon,* the equivalent of 277.5 cubic inches or 4.546 liters. The majority of nations do not use *gallons* at all but measure capacity in liters.

Review the term *gallon* with students.

Beginning Give each student an index card, and ask them to write *1 quart* on the card. Have 4 students tape their cards together. Then tell them to turn over the taped cards and write *1 gallon* across all 4 cards.

Intermediate Have students name items sold by the quart. Then help them determine whether those items are also sold by the *gallon.*

Advanced Have students work in small groups. Have each group make three lists: one of containers that hold less than a *gallon,* one of containers that hold about a *gallon,* and another of containers that hold more than a *gallon.* Invite students to share their lists with the class.

Open-Ended Problem Solving

Read the Headline Story to the students. To get students started, suggest that they think about how many gallons of milk a cow produces in a day, a week, or a year, or how much water it drinks in the same amounts of time.

 Headline Story

Milk cows in the United States produce an average of 26 quarts of milk per day. To produce that amount of milk, a cow drinks almost 33 gallons of water! It takes 1 gallon of milk to make 1 pound of cheese. What can you conclude from these facts?

Possible responses: 4 quarts equals 1 gallon, so 26 quarts of milk equals $6\frac{1}{2}$ gallons in a day. That is 13 gallons in 2 days, 26 in 4 days, 39 in 6 days, and 45.5 in a week. Since 1 gallon of milk makes 1 pound of cheese, 45.5 pounds of cheese can be made with a week's worth of the cow's milk. A cow drinks about 3,700 cups of water each week.

Skills Practice and Review

Doubling

Say a number less than 10 and then choose a student to double it. Then choose another student to double the result, and so on, each time doubling the current number. As students say the numbers, make a vertical list on the board. For example, if you said 3, the list would be 3, 6, 12, 24, 48, and so on. Try to make a list that is about ten steps long. Repeat, starting with other numbers less than 10.

individuals, pairs, or whole class

15 MIN

Materials

- For the teacher: AM87 transparency (optional)
- For each student: AM87 (optional)

NCTM Standards 1, 2, 6, 7, 8, 9, 10

✔ **Ongoing Assessment**

- Do students know the basic equivalencies relating cups, pints, quarts, gallons, liters, and milliliters?

A Converting Among Units of Capacity

Purpose To convert among cups, pints, quarts, liters, and milliliters

Introduce Display the first table on Activity Master: Comparing Units of Capacity or draw a similar table on the board. Explain that students will be converting back and forth between various pairs of units of capacity that they have studied.

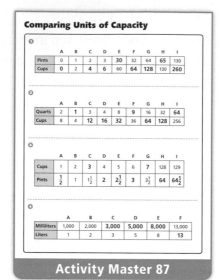

Comparing Units of Capacity

	A	B	C	D	E	F	G	H	I
Pints	0	1	2	3	30	32	64	65	130
Cups	0	2	4	6	60	64	128	130	260

	A	B	C	D	E	F	G	H	I
Quarts	2	1	3	4	8	9	16	32	64
Cups	8	4	12	16	32	36	64	128	256

	A	B	C	D	E	F	G	H	I
Cups	1	2	3	4	5	6	7	128	129
Pints	$\frac{1}{2}$	1	$1\frac{1}{2}$	2	$2\frac{1}{2}$	3	$3\frac{1}{2}$	64	$64\frac{1}{2}$

	A	B	C	D	E	F
Milliliters	1,000	2,000	3,000	5,000	8,000	13,000
Liters	1	2	3	5	8	13

Activity Master 87

Task Direct students to complete the four tables on the page. You may wish to have students complete the first table as a silent class activity. To do this, silently invite a student to fill in one of the missing numbers. If the number is correct, motion for another student to fill in another missing number. If the answer is incorrect, erase the number and invite a new student to fill in the number. Completing the chart as a silent activity ensures that students' thinking is not interrupted by other students' ideas.

Once the table is complete, ask students to describe the patterns in the chart. For example, students should realize that the number of cups is double the number of pints. Similarly, students may notice that they can add together entries in certain columns to complete other columns. For example, to complete entry F in the first table, students can add entries E and C.

Practice Continue completing the tables on the page, either as a silent activity or by having students work with partners to fill in the table entries. If you complete the charts as a class, be sure to leave them on display for the remainder of the lesson.

Share Once the page is complete, go over some of the answers to make sure that students know that the number of cups is always 4 times the number of quarts, and that the number of milliliters is 1,000 times the number of liters. You might spend a few extra minutes discussing the third table, which contains half-units. Once students figure out that 1 cup equals $\frac{1}{2}$ pint, they can use this to find the other values in the chart. For example, to find entry E, students can add together entries A and D.

Talk Math

❷ Jessica knows how many cups of milk she drinks in a month. How can she find the number of quarts she drinks in a month? **by dividing the number of cups by 4**

❷ A large container of fruit juice has the number of milliliters of juice that it contains written on its label. How could you find the number of liters of juice in the container? **by dividing the number of milliliters by 1,000**

Teacher Story

❝I put large labels on cup, pint, quart, gallon, and liter containers, and left these out for students to look at during the lesson. This helped students to see which containers are smaller than others and which are bigger. It even seemed to remind students of some of the relationships among the units. One student said she remembered that 16 of one of the units equaled 1 gallon, but she could not remember which one. Because the cup was the smallest container, she figured that must be the one.❞

Materials

- For the teacher: AM88 transparency (optional)
- For each student: AM88

NCTM Standards 1, 2, 6, 7, 8, 9, 10

B Solving Problems Through Unit Conversions

Purpose To solve real-life problems involving quantities of liquid

Introduce Display a transparency of Activity Master: Solving Problems or distribute copies of the page to students. Tell students that the problems on the page describe everyday situations involving liquid capacities.

Problem Direct students to solve the problems on Activity Master: Solving Problems. Depending on your class, you might work through one or two problems together or you might have students complete the page working in pairs. As you go over the problems, help students to see how they can refer to the tables from Activity A to solve the problems. This will prepare them to use the tables when they work on LAB pages 187–188 in Activity C.

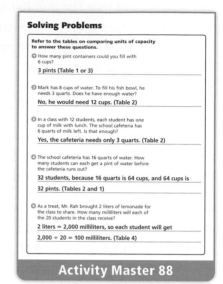

Activity Master 88

❶ How many pint containers could you fill with 6 cups? 3 pints; Students can read the answer by referring to the relevant entry in Table 12 or Table 3.

❷ Mark has 8 cups of water. To fill his fish bowl, he needs 3 quarts. Does he have enough water? No. Table 2 shows that he needs 12 cups of water, 4 more cups than he has.

❸ In a class with 12 students, each student has 1 cup of milk with lunch. The school cafeteria has 6 quarts of milk left. Is that enough? Yes. Table 2 shows that the cafeteria needs only 3 quarts of milk to provide 12 cups of milk for students.

❹ The school cafeteria has 16 quarts of water. How many students can each get a pint of water before the cafeteria runs out? 32 students; Table 2 shows that 16 quarts equals 64 cups, and Table 1 shows that 64 cups equals 32 pints.

❺ As a treat, Mr. Rah brought 2 liters of lemonade for the class to share. How many milliliters will each of the 20 students in the class receive? 100 milliliters; Table 4 shows that 2 liters equals 2,000 milliliters, and 2,000 ÷ 20 = 100.

💬 **Talk Math**

❓ How can you use Tables 1–2 to find the number of pints in 32 quarts? Possible answer: Table 2 shows that 32 quarts equals 128 cups. Table 1 shows that 128 cups equals 64 pints.

❓ Blair wants to make a table comparing cups and gallons. For each number of gallons in the table, how can he find the number of cups? by multiplying the number of gallons by 16

Use with Lesson Activity Book pp. 187–188.

individuals or pairs   **20 MIN**

Purpose To practice converting among capacity units

NCTM Standards 1, 2, 6, 7, 8, 9, 10

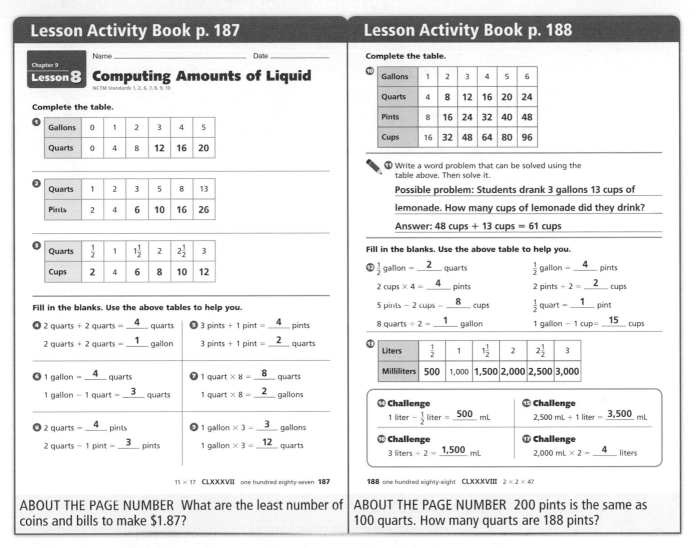

Lesson Activity Book p. 187

Chapter 9
Lesson 8 **Computing Amounts of Liquid**
NCTM Standards 1, 2, 6, 7, 8, 9, 10

Name _____ Date _____

Complete the table.

❶
Gallons	0	1	2	3	4	5
Quarts	0	4	8	**12**	**16**	**20**

❷
Quarts	1	2	3	5	8	13
Pints	2	4	**6**	**10**	**16**	**26**

❸
Quarts	$\frac{1}{2}$	1	$1\frac{1}{2}$	2	$2\frac{1}{2}$	3
Cups	2	4	**6**	**8**	**10**	**12**

Fill in the blanks. Use the above tables to help you.

❹ 2 quarts + 2 quarts = **4** quarts

2 quarts + 2 quarts = **1** gallon

❺ 3 pints + 1 pint = **4** pints

3 pints + 1 pint = **2** quarts

❻ 1 gallon = **4** quarts

1 gallon − 1 quart = **3** quarts

❼ 1 quart × 8 = **8** quarts

1 quart × 8 = **2** gallons

❽ 2 quarts = **4** pints

2 quarts − 1 pint = **3** pints

❾ 1 gallon × 3 = **3** gallons

1 gallon × 3 = **12** quarts

11 × 17 **CLXXXVII** one hundred eighty-seven **187**

Lesson Activity Book p. 188

Complete the table.

❿
Gallons	1	2	3	4	5	6
Quarts	4	8	12	16	20	24
Pints	8	16	24	32	40	48
Cups	16	32	48	64	80	96

⓫ Write a word problem that can be solved using the table above. Then solve it.

Possible problem: **Students drank 3 gallons 13 cups of lemonade. How many cups of lemonade did they drink?**

Answer: **48 cups + 13 cups = 61 cups**

Fill in the blanks. Use the above table to help you.

⓬ $\frac{1}{2}$ gallon = **2** quarts

2 cups × 4 = **4** pints

5 pints − 2 cups = **8** cups

8 quarts ÷ 2 = **1** gallon

$\frac{1}{2}$ gallon = **4** pints

2 pints ÷ 2 = **2** cups

$\frac{1}{2}$ quart = **1** pint

1 gallon − 1 cup = **15** cups

⓭
Liters	$\frac{1}{2}$	1	$1\frac{1}{2}$	2	$2\frac{1}{2}$	3
Milliliters	500	1,000	1,500	2,000	2,500	3,000

⓮ **Challenge**
1 liter − $\frac{1}{2}$ liter = **500** mL

⓯ **Challenge**
2,500 mL + 1 liter = **3,500** mL

⓰ **Challenge**
3 liters ÷ 2 = **1,500** mL

⓱ **Challenge**
2,000 mL × 2 = **4** liters

188 one hundred eighty-eight **CLXXXVIII** 2 × 2 × 47

ABOUT THE PAGE NUMBER What are the least number of coins and bills to make $1.87?

ABOUT THE PAGE NUMBER 200 pints is the same as 100 quarts. How many quarts are 188 pints?

Teaching Notes for LAB page 187
Have students complete the page individually or with partners.

The page includes tables similar to those in Activity A. As in the activity, the tables can be used to complete the number sentences that follow. The number sentences are in pairs. The first sentence can be used to complete the second one.

Teaching Notes for LAB page 188
The number sentences on this page are more difficult than those on LAB p. 187, because each involves two conceptual steps. For example, in Problem 12, students must first multiply 2 cups by 4, then convert the product, 8 cups, into pints.

Challenge Problems These problems involve computations with metric units of capacity, which students are likely to be less comfortable with than they are with customary units.

Reflect and Summarize the Lesson

 Write Math

You have five 2-liter bottles of juice. How could you figure out if you have enough drinks for each of 10 people to have 4 cups of juice? Use pictures, numbers, or words.
Possible answers: Since you need 4 cups for each of 10 people, you need 4 × 10 = 40 cups. Since there are 4 cups in a quart, you need 40 ÷ 4 = 10 quarts. Since a quart is almost a liter, you need a little less than 10 liters. Since you have five 2-liter bottles, you have 10 liters of juice. So you have enough juice.

Leveled Problem Solving

A bowl holds 1 gallon of juice.

❶ Basic Level

How many cups do 2 bowls hold? Explain. 32 cups; 1 gal = 16 c; 16 × 2 = 32.

❷ On Level

Karen estimates that each person at her party will drink about 2 cups of juice. How many people will the juice bowl serve? Explain. 8 people; 1 gal = 16 c; 16 ÷ 2 = 8.

❸ Above Level

How many quarts of juice should Mike make if he wants to fill the bowl three times? Explain. 12 quarts; 1 gal = 4 qt; 3 gal = 3 × 4 qt = 12 qt.

Intervention

Activity Counter Conversions

Have students recall and record the equivalences from one unit to the next larger (2 cups = 1 pint, 2 pints = 1 quart, etc.). Use four colors of counters and assign a unit to each color (e.g. blue = gallon). Have students create the table at the top of LAB page 188, using the counters to help them make the conversions. (Trade each gallon counter for 4 quart counters, etc.)

Practice

Computing Amounts of Liquid

Quarts	$\frac{1}{2}$	1	2	3	4	7	10	5	6	9
Pints	1	2	4	6	8	14	20	10	12	18
Cups	2	4	8	12	16	28	40	20	24	36

Karen drinks 6 cups of water a day. How many quarts does she drink? $1\frac{1}{2}$ quarts

Michael needs 3 pints of juice to make punch. He has 9 cups of juice. Does he have enough? (yes) no

John bought 4 quarts of milk at the store. He gave a cup to each of his 5 friends. How many cups does he have left? 11 cups

Kelly had 4 pints of tomato juice, and then she bought another quart at the store. How much tomato juice does she have? 6 pints or 3 quarts

Test Prep

Hallie has these cards.

8	6	4	1

How many different 4-digit numbers can she make? Explain how she can be sure that she has included every possible number in her list. 24 different numbers; Possible answer: Hallie can make all possible numbers beginning with 1, then beginning with 4, then with 6, and finally with 8.

Practice P78

Extension

Computing Amounts of Liquid

Convert this recipe so that the amounts are in cups.

1 quart orange juice = **4** cups orange juice

3 pints grapefruit juice = **6** cups grapefruit juice

$\frac{1}{2}$ quart pineapple juice = **2** cups pineapple juice

$\frac{1}{2}$ pint papaya juice = **1** cup papaya juice

Complete this table so that each column contains equivalent amounts.

Cups	1	2	3	4	5	6	7	8	40
Pints	$\frac{1}{2}$	1	$1\frac{1}{2}$	2	$2\frac{1}{2}$	3	$3\frac{1}{2}$	4	20
Quarts	$\frac{1}{4}$	$\frac{1}{2}$	$\frac{3}{4}$	1	$1\frac{1}{4}$	$1\frac{1}{2}$	$1\frac{3}{4}$	2	10

Solve.

Allen drank 1 liter of water, Josh drank 2 pints of water, and Alex drank 3 cups of water. Praveen drank the least water and Ross drank the most. How much water might Ross and Praveen have had?

Ross:
Possible answer: any amount more than 1 liter, such as $1\frac{1}{2}$ liters, 1 gallon, 6 cups, 3 pints, or $2\frac{1}{2}$ pints

Praveen:
Possible answer: any amount less than 3 cups, such as $\frac{1}{2}$ quart, 1 pint, 1 cup, or $\frac{1}{8}$ gallon

Extension E78

Spiral Review

Spiral Review Book page SR78 provides review of the following previously learned skills and concepts:

- measuring changes in temperature in degrees Fahrenheit
- using logical reasoning to complete magic squares

You may wish to have students work with partners to complete the page.

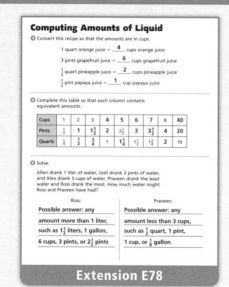

Measurement

For 1–5, use the table, which shows the high temperatures in selected cities on one autumn day.

City	High Temperature
New York City	54°F
Dallas	71°F
Anchorage	19°F
San Francisco	47°F
Kansas City	67°F
Honolulu	81°F

What is the difference in temperatures between the warmest and coolest cities? 62°F

What is the difference in temperatures between San Francisco and New York City? 7°F

What is the difference in temperatures between the two warmest cities? 10°F

What is the difference in temperatures between the two coolest cities? 28°F

The day after these temperatures were recorded, the temperature in Dallas was 87°F. How many degrees warmer was Dallas than it had been the day before? 16°F

Reasoning and Proof

Complete the magic square. Then write the sum.

7	12	11
14	10	6
9	8	13

Sum = 30

6	20	10
16	12	8
14	4	18

Sum = 36

21	25	5
1	17	33
29	9	13

Sum = 51

Spiral Review SR78

Extension Activity What Am I?

Have students work in small groups to determine how many ways they can write units in the blanks to make this a true number sentence:

2 _____ = 1 _____
  pints   quart
  cups   pint

Then ask them to repeat the activity with this number sentence:

4 _____ = 1 _____
  quarts   gallon
  cups   quart

Use with Lesson Activity Book pp. 187–188.

Teacher's Notes 🍎

Daily Notes . . .

Quick Notes

More Ideas

Lesson 9 Measuring Weight in Ounces, Pounds, and Tons

NCTM Standards 1, 2, 6, 7, 8, 9, 10

Lesson Planner

STUDENT OBJECTIVES ··································
- To estimate, measure, and compare weights in ounces, pounds, and tons
- To convert among ounces, pounds, and tons

1 Daily Activities (TG p. 761)

Open-Ended Problem Solving/Headline Story	Skills Practice and Review— Skip-Counting by 4, 8, and 16

2 Teach and Practice (TG pp. 762–765)

	MATERIALS
(A) **Measuring in Ounces, Pounds, and Tons** (TG pp. 762–763) (B) **Estimating Weights** (TG p. 764) (C) **Measuring Weight in Ounces, Pounds, and Tons** (TG p. 765)	• scale (balancing scale and bathroom scale recommended), objects that weigh about 1 ounce and 1 pound, objects to weigh (e.g., cereal, water, rice, books) • 📖 LAB pp. 189–190 • 📖 SH p. 151

3 Differentiated Instruction (TG p. 766)

Leveled Problem Solving (TG p. 766)	Practice Book P79
Intervention Activity (TG p. 766)	Extension Book E79
Extension Activity (TG p. 766)	Spiral Review Book SR79

Lesson Notes

About the Lesson

Students begin measuring, estimating, and comparing weights. They also develop a sense of the sizes of ounces, pounds, and tons as they estimate and compare the weights of various items. In the next lesson, students will continue to explore the measurement of weight as they are introduced to grams and kilograms.

About the Mathematics

When comparing the weights of objects, it is important to choose the quantities of each item thoughtfully. For example, to compare the weight of corn flakes to corn kernels you might compare 1 pint of each or even one corn kernel to one corn flake. Each comparison would tell you something different, but each would provide some information. If, however, you compared 1 cup of kernels to 2 pints of corn flakes, it is less clear that there would be much you could say about the relative weights of corn kernels to corn flakes.

Use with Lesson Activity Book pp. 189–190.

Developing Mathematical Language

Vocabulary: pound, ton

Students may wonder why the abbreviation for *pound* is lb. In Latin, the term for a *pound* of weight is *libra pondo,* the word *libra* (the origin of the abbreviation) meaning *pound,* the word *pondo* meaning weight. People commonly say that something weighs a *ton* when it is very heavy, without regard to its actual weight. Examples of objects whose weights might be given in *tons,* and typical weights for each: blue whale (150 *tons*); African elephant (7–8 *tons*); compact car ($1\frac{1}{2}$ *tons*).

Review the terms *pound* and *ton* with students.

Beginning Name an object. Tell whether the object is light enough to be weighed in *pounds* or heavy enough to be weighed in *tons.* Name more objects. Have students tell whether the object is weighed in *pounds* or in *tons.*

Intermediate Have students take turns naming an item that weighs about 1 *pound.* Repeat for items that weigh about 1 *ton.*

Advanced Have students work in small groups. Have each group make three lists: one of items that weigh less than a *pound,* another of items that weigh about a *pound,* and another of items that weigh more than a *pound.* Ask students to circle any items that might weigh a *ton* or more.

1 | Daily Activities

Open-Ended Problem Solving

Read the Headline Story to the students. Encourage them to think of interesting ways to complete the sentences.

Headline Story

> Nancy's pet weighs ___?___.
> Her pet could be a ___?___.

Possible responses: Nancy's pet weighs <u>20 lb.</u> Her pet could be <u>a big cat</u>; <u>a small dog</u>; Nancy's pet weighs <u>3 lb.</u> Her pet could be <u>a kitten</u>; <u>a large parrot</u>; <u>a guinea pig</u>.

Skills Practice and Review

Skip-Counting by 4, 8, and 16

To prepare students for using multiples of 16 as they convert between ounces and pounds, begin at 0 and have students count by 4s. Point to individual students as you go along so that the first student says 0, the second says 4, the third says 8, and so on, to at least 96. As students say the numbers, write the numbers on a number line on the board. There will be at least 25 numbers to label, so be sure there is enough space.

Repeat this activity, having students count by 8s and then by 16s. Rather than writing the numbers on a new number line, encourage students to see if they can use the number line already on the board. Since 8 and 16 are both multiples of 4, all the numbers that students say will already be on the line. Leave the number line on the board for students to refer to during the lesson.

pairs or whole class

20 MIN

(A) Measuring in Ounces, Pounds, and Tons

Materials

- For the teacher: scale (balancing scale and bathroom scale recommended), objects that weigh about 1 ounce and 1 pound
- For each student: objects to weigh (e.g., cereal, water, rice, books)

NCTM Standards 1, 2, 6, 7, 8, 9, 10

✔ Ongoing Assessment

- Do students know how to multiply 1- and 2-digit whole numbers?
- Do students know how to multiply by 1,000 mentally?

Teacher Story

❝Some of my students noticed that the number of ounces in a pound is the same as the number of cups in a gallon: 16 ounces in 1 pound, 16 cups in 1 gallon. I thought this was a helpful observation that might allow the class to better remember both relationships, so I asked the students to share it with the class.❞

Purpose To introduce ounces, pounds, and tons

Introduce Have students work on Explore: Weight with partners. Explain that to answer the questions, students will need to think carefully about the weights of objects. Call attention to the examples at the top of the page:

- A birthday card weighs about 1 ounce.
- A loaf of bread weighs about 1 pound.
- A 2-year old elephant weighs about 1 ton.

Task Direct students to the following challenges, which appear on Explore: Weight:

1. How many ounces are in a ton? Each of the 2,000 pounds in a ton consists of 16 ounces, so there are $16 \times 2,000 = 32,000$ ounces in a ton.

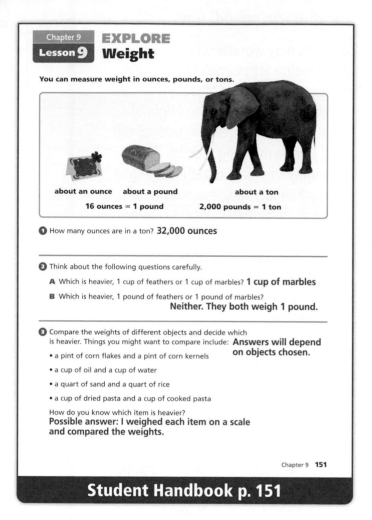

Chapter 9
Lesson 9

EXPLORE
Weight

You can measure weight in ounces, pounds, or tons.

about an ounce   about a pound   about a ton
16 ounces = 1 pound   2,000 pounds = 1 ton

1. How many ounces are in a ton? **32,000 ounces**

2. Think about the following questions carefully.
   A. Which is heavier, 1 cup of feathers or 1 cup of marbles? **1 cup of marbles**
   B. Which is heavier, 1 pound of feathers or 1 pound of marbles?
      Neither. They both weigh 1 pound.

3. Compare the weights of different objects and decide which is heavier. Things you might want to compare include: **Answers will depend on objects chosen.**
   - a pint of corn flakes and a pint of corn kernels
   - a cup of oil and a cup of water
   - a quart of sand and a quart of rice
   - a cup of dried pasta and a cup of cooked pasta
   How do you know which item is heavier?
   Possible answer: I weighed each item on a scale and compared the weights.

Chapter 9   151

Student Handbook p. 151

2. A. Which is heavier, 1 cup of feathers or 1 cup of marbles? Both cups are the same size, so the cup of marbles is heavier.

   B. Which is heavier, 1 pound of feathers or 1 pound of marbles? Both weigh 1 pound, so neither is heavier. However, a pound of feathers takes up a much greater space than a pound of marbles.

To allow students to complete the third question on the page, you might set up one or more scales for students to use to compare weights. Alternatively, you might simply allow students to develop their own strategies for comparing weights, without the use of scales. Similarly, you might have pre-measured amounts of materials whose weights students can compare, or you might allow students to find objects in the room to compare. (See the Teacher Story on the next page for an idea of how to set up your class for this activity.)

❸ Compare the weights of different objects and decide which is heavier. Things you might want to compare include:

a pint of corn flakes and a pint of corn kernels A pint of corn kernels is heavier.

a cup of oil and a cup of water A cup of water is heavier.

a quart of sand and a quart of rice A quart of sand is heavier.

a cup of dried pasta and a cup of cooked pasta A cup of cooked pasta is heavier.

How do you know which item is heavier? Possible answer: I weighed each item on a bathroom scale and compared the weights.

Share When students have completed the page, have them share their answers and strategies for answering the questions. For example, in Problem 1, students may have simplified 16 × 2,000 by first finding 16 × 2, then multiplying the result by 1,000.

In Problem 2A, students should realize that having the same volume does not necessarily mean that the weights are equal. In Problem 2B, they should realize that the volumes of the two items are very different. A pound of feathers takes up a very large space compared to a pound of marbles. Nevertheless, both weigh 1 pound.

In Problem 3, students may have put the two items being compared on scales, they may have held the items in different hands, or they might have compared the items to standard weights such as a 1-pound weight or a loaf of bread.

Talk Math

❷ Greg's dog weighs 50 pounds. How many ounces does it weigh? Explain your reasoning. 800 ounces; 50 × 16 = 800

❷ If you knew the weight of an object in ounces, how could you find its weight in pounds? Divide the weight in ounces by 16.

B Estimating Weights

Materials
- For the teacher: scale (balancing scale and bathroom scale recommended)

NCTM Standards 1, 2, 6, 7, 8, 9, 10

Purpose To estimate weights

Introduce Explain that in this activity, students will need to estimate weights, then use their estimates to solve word problems.

Problems Present problems like the following to the class. Ask students to solve the problems and to explain their methods.

- Would you measure the weight of your chair in ounces, pounds, or tons? pounds; Possible explanation: if a loaf of bread weighs about a pound and an elephant weighs about a ton, then the chair is likely to weigh a few pounds.

- About how much do the chairs in your class weigh in all? Possible answer: about 150 pounds; possible explanation: I multiplied my estimate for the weight of a chair, 5 pounds, by the number of chairs in the class, 30; 5 pounds $\times$ 30 = 150 pounds.

- About how many chairs would you need for all of them to weigh a ton? Possible answer: about 400 chairs; possible explanation: I divided 2,000, the number of pounds in 1 ton, by 5, the estimated weight of each chair in pounds; 2,000 $\div$ 5 = 400.

- Do all of the chairs in your school weigh more or less than a ton? Possible answer: more; possible explanation: I multiplied the estimated number of classrooms in the school, 20, by the estimated weight of all the chairs in this classroom, 150 pounds; 20 $\times$ 150 = 3,000; the product, 3,000 pounds, is greater than 1 ton, 2,000 pounds.

Share Ask students to estimate how many fourth graders it would take for their combined weights to equal a ton. Record students' guesses. Then, assuming that an average fourth-grader weighs about 60 pounds, use a calculator or estimate to find an answer. See how close initial guesses were to the estimate.

Finally, ask students for suggestions on how you could use a bathroom scale to weigh a chair or some other object too large to fit on the scale. If no student mentions it, demonstrate the following method. First, ask a volunteer to stand on the scale. Record the volunteer's weight. Then record the total weight when the student is holding the chair. The difference between the two readings is the weight of the chair.

Talk Math

❷ Would you measure the weight of a piece of toast in ounces, pounds, or tons? Explain your reasoning. ounces; Possible explanation: A loaf of bread weighs about a pound. Since there are 16 ounces in a pound, the small fraction of a loaf represented by a piece of toast would best be weighed in ounces.

❷ Give an example of something that might well be measured in either ounces or pounds. Explain your reasoning. Possible answer: a grapefruit; Possible explanation: I tried to think of something that weighed about half a pound. It would make sense to record such a weight as $\frac{1}{2}$ pound or 8 ounces.

Use with Lesson Activity Book pp. 189–190.

Measuring Weight in Ounces, Pounds, and Tons LAB pp. 189–190

 individuals or pairs **20 MIN**

Purpose To practice converting among units of weights

NCTM Standards 1, 2, 6, 7, 8, 9, 10

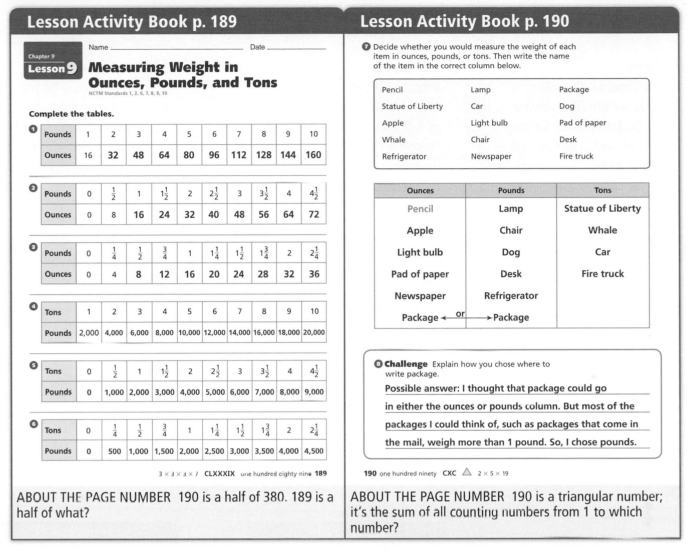

Lesson Activity Book p. 189

Name _____ Date _____

Chapter 9
Lesson 9 **Measuring Weight in Ounces, Pounds, and Tons**
NCTM Standards 1, 2, 6, 7, 8, 9, 10

Complete the tables.

①

Pounds	1	2	3	4	5	6	7	8	9	10
Ounces	16	32	48	64	80	96	112	128	144	160

②

Pounds	0	$\frac{1}{2}$	1	$1\frac{1}{2}$	2	$2\frac{1}{2}$	3	$3\frac{1}{2}$	4	$4\frac{1}{2}$
Ounces	0	8	16	24	32	40	48	56	64	72

③

Pounds	0	$\frac{1}{4}$	$\frac{1}{2}$	$\frac{3}{4}$	1	$1\frac{1}{4}$	$1\frac{1}{2}$	$1\frac{3}{4}$	2	$2\frac{1}{4}$
Ounces	0	4	8	12	16	20	24	28	32	36

④

Tons	1	2	3	4	5	6	7	8	9	10
Pounds	2,000	4,000	6,000	8,000	10,000	12,000	14,000	16,000	18,000	20,000

⑤

Tons	0	$\frac{1}{2}$	1	$1\frac{1}{2}$	2	$2\frac{1}{2}$	3	$3\frac{1}{2}$	4	$4\frac{1}{2}$
Pounds	0	1,000	2,000	3,000	4,000	5,000	6,000	7,000	8,000	9,000

⑥

Tons	0	$\frac{1}{4}$	$\frac{1}{2}$	$\frac{3}{4}$	1	$1\frac{1}{4}$	$1\frac{1}{2}$	$1\frac{3}{4}$	2	$2\frac{1}{4}$
Pounds	0	500	1,000	1,500	2,000	2,500	3,000	3,500	4,000	4,500

3 × 3 × 3 × 7 CLXXXIX one hundred eighty-nine **189**

ABOUT THE PAGE NUMBER 190 is a half of 380. 189 is a half of what?

Lesson Activity Book p. 190

⑦ Decide whether you would measure the weight of each item in ounces, pounds, or tons. Then write the name of the item in the correct column below.

Pencil	Lamp	Package
Statue of Liberty	Car	Dog
Apple	Light bulb	Pad of paper
Whale	Chair	Desk
Refrigerator	Newspaper	Fire truck

Ounces	Pounds	Tons
Pencil	Lamp	Statue of Liberty
Apple	Chair	Whale
Light bulb	Dog	Car
Pad of paper	Desk	Fire truck
Newspaper	Refrigerator	
Package ←—or—→ Package		

⑧ Challenge Explain how you chose where to write package.

Possible answer: I thought that package could go in either the ounces or pounds column. But most of the packages I could think of, such as packages that come in the mail, weigh more than 1 pound. So, I chose pounds.

190 one hundred ninety CXC △ 2 × 5 × 19

ABOUT THE PAGE NUMBER 190 is a triangular number; it's the sum of all counting numbers from 1 to which number?

Teaching Notes for LAB page 189

Have students complete the page individually or with partners.

As students complete the tables on this page, you might encourage them to look for patterns. For example, if students know that 1 pound is 16 ounces and $\frac{1}{2}$ pound is 8 ounces, then $1\frac{1}{2}$ pounds is the sum of 16 ounces and 8 ounces, or 24 ounces.

Teaching Notes for LAB page 190

Students use their understanding of ounces, pounds, and tons to decide the best units for measuring the weights of various items. The goal is for students to have an idea of the relative weights of those units.

Challenge Problem This question focuses on the fact that certain items can reasonably be measured using either of two different units. Student are asked to choose one of the two units and to explain why they think it is a better choice than the other.

Reflect and Summarize the Lesson

Write Math Which of the following items are closest in weight to 1 ounce, 1 pound, and 1 ton: piece of paper, carton of milk, penny, truck, magazine, airplane? Possible answers: a piece of paper and a penny are probably closest to an ounce. A carton of milk and a magazine are probably closest to a pound. A truck is probably closest to a ton.

Leveled Problem Solving

Jay is considering whether the weights of different objects should be measured in ounces, pounds, or tons.

❶ Basic Level

Which unit should he use to measure the weight of a serving of yogurt? Explain your reasoning. ounce; A serving of yogurt weighs less than a pound.

❷ On Level

Which unit should he use to measure the combined weights of 6 fire trucks? Explain your reasoning. ton; A fire truck weighs more than a ton, and a ton is the greatest unit of measure.

❸ Above Level

Which unit should he use to measure the weight of a classroom fish tank full of water? Explain your reasoning. pound; A full fish tank weighs more than a pound and much less than a ton.

Intervention	Practice	Extension

Activity Weight Ways

Organize small groups of students. Tell everyone that 5 quarters weigh 1 ounce, a large grapefruit weighs about 1 pound, and a pickup truck weighs about 1 ton. Have students take turns naming a common item while the others in the group use the equivalent weights to determine which unit—ounce, pound, or ton—could be used to measure it.

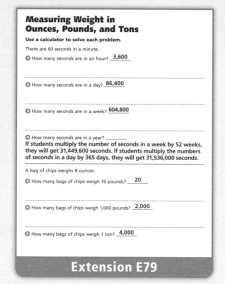

Measuring Weight in Ounces, Pounds, and Tons

Fill in the missing amounts.

① 1 lb + 2 lb = 3 lb
   16 oz + 32 oz = **48** oz

② 1 meter + 4 meters = 5 meters
   100 cm + **400** cm = **500** cm

③ 4 tons + 2 tons = **6** tons
   8,000 pounds + 4,000 pounds = 12,000 pounds

④ 4 quarts + **5** quarts = 9 quarts
   16 cups + **20** cups = 36 cups

Test Prep

⑤ The scale shows how much 6 apples weigh. How much would 10 apples of the same size weigh?

A. 5 pounds   C. 10 pounds
B. 6 pounds   D. 12 pounds

Practice P79

Measuring Weight in Ounces, Pounds, and Tons

Use a calculator to solve each problem.

There are 60 seconds in a minute.

❶ How many seconds are in an hour? **3,600**

❷ How many seconds are in a day? **86,400**

❸ How many seconds are in a week? **604,800**

❹ How many seconds are in a year? _____
If students multiply the number of seconds in a week by 52 weeks, they will get 31,449,600 seconds. If students multiply the numbers of seconds in a day by 365 days, they will get 31,536,000 seconds.

A bag of chips weighs 8 ounces.

❺ How many bags of chips weigh 10 pounds? **20**

❻ How many bags of chips weigh 1,000 pounds? **2,000**

❼ How many bags of chips weigh 1 ton? **4,000**

Extension E79

Spiral Review

Spiral Review Book page SR79 provides review of the following previously learned skills and concepts:

- verifying symmetry with reflections
- using the problem solving strategy *guess and check*

You may wish to have students work with partners to complete the page.

Geometry

Decide whether the line is a line of symmetry. Write *yes* or *no*.

① yes   ② no   ③ no

④ no   ⑤ yes   ⑥ yes

⑦ yes   ⑧ yes   ⑨ no

Problem Solving

Solve the problem. Explain your answer.

⑩ Together, John and Andrea make 92 cards to give to friends. John makes 16 more cards than Andrea. How many cards do they make?
John 54, Andrea 38; Possible explanation: I guessed numbers, adjusting each guess, until I found two whose sum was 92 and whose difference was 16.

⑪ Kyle has $2.55 in his pocket. If he has only quarters and nickels and has 3 more quarters than nickels, how many of each coin does he have?
9 quarters, 6 nickels; Possible explanation: I guessed numbers of coins, adjusting each guess, until I found a total value of $2.55.

Spiral Review SR79

Extension Activity
A Pint's A Pound!

Tell students that a common folk saying is, "A pint's a pound the world around." Let them know that a pint of water actually weighs 1.04375 pounds but that it is common to use 1 pound as an approximation of its weight. Have students use that equivalence to estimate the weights of 1 cup, 1 quart, and 1 gallon of water. $1 \text{ c} = \frac{1}{2}$ lb, or 8 oz; 1 qt = 2 lb; 1 gal = 8 lb

Use with Lesson Activity Book pp. 189–190.

Teacher's Notes 🍎

Daily Notes . . .

More Ideas

Quick Notes

Lesson 10 Measuring Weight in Grams and Kilograms

NCTM Standards 1, 2, 6, 7, 8, 9, 10

Lesson Planner

STUDENT OBJECTIVES
- To estimate, measure, and compare weight in grams and kilograms
- To understand the difference between weight and mass
- To practice converting between measurement units

1 | Daily Activities (TG p. 769)

Open-Ended Problem Solving/Headline Story	Skills Practice and Review— Ounces, Pounds, and Tons

2 | Teach and Practice (TG pp. 770–773)

Ⓐ **Introducing Grams and Kilograms** (TG pp. 770–771)

Ⓑ **Weight Versus Mass** (TG p. 772)

Ⓒ **Measuring Weight in Grams and Kilograms** (TG p. 773)

MATERIALS

- gram scale, paper clip, liter of water, objects to weigh (e.g., quart of milk, pint of rice, can of tomatoes)
- 📖 LAB pp. 191–192

3 | Differentiated Instruction (TG p. 774)

Leveled Problem Solving (TG p. 774)	Practice Book P80
Intervention Activity (TG p. 774)	Extension Book E80
Extension Activity (TG p. 774)	Spiral Review Book SR80

Lesson Notes

About the Lesson

Students continue their exploration of weight in this lesson, but now focus on the metric units of gram and kilogram. Students gain a sense of these units by noticing that a paper clip weighs about a gram and that a liter of water weighs about a kilogram (in fact, it weighs exactly 1 kilogram). Students also practice converting between units of measurement on the LAB pages. Finally, students discuss the difference between weight and mass, as required in some states. (See About the Mathematics for an explanation of this distinction.)

About the Mathematics

The distinction between weight and mass is easy to describe but not so easy to understand. Imagine that you precisely measured 1 pound of meat and then took it to the moon. You would no longer have 1 pound of meat because the *weight* of an object— the thing that scales measure—depends on the pull of gravity. Because gravity is less strong on the moon than it is on Earth, the weight of the meat on the moon would be about one-sixth of a pound. The meat clearly contains the same amount of stuff on the moon as it does on Earth. So, you would be just as full from eating the meat on the moon as you would be on Earth, even though it weighed less. This is because the *mass* of the meat remains constant no matter where it is.

Use with Lesson Activity Book pp. 191–192.

Developing Mathematical Language

Vocabulary: mass, weight

The U.S. customary units of tons, pounds, and ounces are measures of *weight.* The metric units of grams and kilograms are measures of *mass.* (See About the Mathematics for a discussion of the difference between *mass* and *weight.*) Because there is a straightforward relationship between *mass* and *weight,* we will use the terms interchangeably.

Review the term *weight* with students.

Beginning Name two different measurements, one of which is a measurement of *weight,* such as 1 yard of fabric and 10 pounds of apples. Have students tell which one is a measurement of *weight.* Repeat with several examples.

Intermediate Give an example of an item that is sold or packaged by *weight.* Then, ask students to name more things that are sold or packaged by *weight.* Be sure everyone gets a chance to name something different.

Advanced Have students name different units of *weight.* Have a volunteer write a list of the units on the board.

Open-Ended Problem Solving

Read the Headline Story to the students. Encourage them to think of creative scenarios that incorporate information from the story.

 Headline Story

> In Jasmine's set of building blocks, a brick is heavier than 2 cylinders, but 2 bricks are lighter than 5 cylinders. What can you say?

Possible responses: 2 bricks are heavier than 4 cylinders; 3 bricks are heavier than 6 cylinders but lighter than 8 cylinders.

Skills Practice and Review

Ounces, Pounds, and Tons

State some measurements in tons and ask students for the corresponding measurements in pounds. Then ask for conversions from pounds to ounces. You might write 2,000 pounds = 1 ton and 16 ounces = 1 pound on the board to help students with these conversions. Continue, asking for other conversions that students can perform mentally. Here are some examples:

2 lbs to oz 32 oz	3 tons to lbs 6,000 lbs
16,000 oz to lbs 1,000 lbs	10,000 lbs to tons 5 tons
10 lbs to oz 160 oz	10 tons to lbs 20,000 lbs
32,000 oz to lbs 2,000 lbs	4,000 lbs to tons 2 tons

Depending on your students, give values like these:

$\frac{1}{2}$ lb to oz 8 oz

$10\frac{1}{2}$ lbs to oz 160 oz for 10 lbs, and 8 oz for $\frac{1}{2}$ lb, so 168 oz

A few students may be ready for the challenge of converting to half-units. For example, you might ask how many pounds are in 56 ounces. $3\frac{1}{2}$ pounds

whole class · 25 MIN

A Introducing Grams and Kilograms

Materials
- For the teacher: gram scale; paper clip; liter of water; objects to weigh (e.g., quart of milk, pint of rice, can of tomatoes)

NCTM Standards 1, 2, 6, 7, 8, 9, 10

 **Ongoing Assessment**
- Do students multiply and divide by 1,000 mentally?

Purpose To introduce metric units of weight

Introduce Tell students that, just as there are two sets of units that can be used to measure capacity (cups, pints, quarts, gallons/milliliters, liters), there are also two sets that can be used to measure weight. Students learned one set of units in the previous lesson—ounces, pounds, and tons. They will learn the other set in this lesson—grams and kilograms. Ask students if they have heard of these units before. Some may have heard of the units in scientific contexts, as scientists generally measure in grams and kilograms. Others may have family or friends in other countries who use grams and kilograms.

Task Direct students' attention to the following demonstrations:

- Using a gram scale, weigh a paper clip.
- Using the same scale, weigh something much heavier, such as a quart of milk.

(If you do not have a gram scale, tell students that a paper clip weighs about 1 gram and a quart of milk weighs about 1 kilogram.)

Let students feel the weights of the items. Then choose, or let students choose, other items to weigh. First, have students estimate the weights based on what they already know from the demonstrations. Then have them weigh the items on the scale. This will help students test and refine their sense of the approximate weights of a gram and a kilogram.

Before students make their estimates, you might let them hold a paper clip or quart of milk in one hand and the new item in the other, to facilitate comparison. Some objects you might choose to weigh include a liter of water, a can of tomatoes, an index card, or a pencil.

Finally, tell students that 1 kilogram is equal to 1,000 grams, and write this equivalency on the board.

Practice Give students a few measurements in each unit and ask them to convert to another unit. This will ensure that students are prepared to convert between grams and kilograms on the LAB pages. Possible examples:

How many grams are in 5 kilograms? 5,000

How many kilograms are in 2,000 grams? 2

How many grams are in 9 kilograms? 9,000

How many kilograms are in 14,000 grams? 14

How many grams are in 2.5 kilograms? 2,500

How many kilograms are in 6,500 grams? 6.5

Talk Math

❷ If you know the weight of an object in kilograms, how can you find its weight in grams? Multiply the weight in kilograms by 1,000.

❷ If you know the weight of an object in grams, how can you find its weight in kilograms? Divide the weight in grams by 1,000.

B Weight Versus Mass

Possible Discussion

Gravity is the pull that makes things fall down. Gravity remains roughly constant on the surface of the Earth. As you move farther away from the planet, gravity's pull decreases in the same way that a magnet's pull decreases as you move farther away. This makes the weight decrease, but does not change the mass of an object. Students may have seen pictures of astronauts walking on the moon. An astronaut is the same height and size on the moon as on Earth (and thus has the same mass), but weighs less on the moon than on Earth. To help students understand that, you might point out how easily astronauts bounce around on the moon.

If students show continued curiosity about gravity, you might explain that all objects exert a gravitational pull on other objects. The mass of an object determines the strength of the gravitational pull that it exerts. The moon exerts a gravitational pull but not as strong as Earth's, because the moon is smaller than Earth. Because Jupiter is bigger than Earth, its gravitational pull is greater than Earth's. You might ask students whether their weight would be more or less on Jupiter than it is on Earth. (It would be more, because Jupiter's gravitational pull is stronger.)

Purpose To distinguish between weight and mass

Introduce Tell students that a typical fourth grader would weigh about 10 pounds on the moon. Say that this activity will help students understand why that is.

Task Ask students to describe what they have heard about "weightlessness" in space, or whether they have seen pictures of astronauts in space. Look for what students can bring to the discussion that will help them understand the idea that an object might have different weights elsewhere in the universe—on the moon or on Mars, for example— than it does on Earth. Exactly what its weight will be will depend on the strength of the object's pull of gravity. Earth's gravity is all that we experience directly (unless we have been in outer space). The moon, which is much smaller than Earth, has only about one sixth of Earth's gravitational pull. As a result, on the moon an object weighs only about one sixth of what it weighs on Earth. A fourth grader who weighs 60 pounds on Earth will weigh about 10 pounds on the moon. The student has the same *mass* in both places, since he or she does not lose or gain any substance in traveling between the two places. But the *weights* are different, because the strengths of the gravitational pulls are different.

It might be easier for students to think about mass if they think about the quantity of clay that goes into a model. More clay is more mass. If a sculptor made a clay statue, the amount of clay would not change if the statue were taken to the moon. However, the statue's weight would change. Students may find it interesting to figure out their weights or the weights of familiar objects on the moon or Jupiter. On the moon, objects weigh one sixth of what they weigh on Earth. On Jupiter, they would weigh about $2\frac{1}{2}$ times what they weigh here. Ask this question:

- If you were on Jupiter, how do think Jupiter's gravity would affect you compared with the way Earth's gravity affects you? Possible answer: It would be harder to walk and to jump on Jupiter than it is on Earth.

The main idea to convey is that weight depends on where we do the weighing, but mass, which is the amount of stuff that makes up an object, is constant.

Talk Math

❓ Marci weighs 50 pounds on Earth. How much would she weigh on Jupiter? about 125 pounds

❓ Ilya weighs 20 pounds on the moon. How much would he weigh on Jupiter? about 300 pounds

❓ What is the difference between weight and mass? Possible answer: Mass is the amount of substance in an object and weight is based on the strength of the gravitational pull of an object.

Measuring Weight in Grams and Kilograms LAB pp. 191–192

Purpose To convert among units of weight

NCTM Standards 1, 2, 6, 7, 8, 9, 10

Lesson Activity Book p. 191

Chapter 9 Lesson 10 **Measuring Weight in Grams and Kilograms**

NCTM Standards 1, 2, 6, 7, 8, 9, 10

Name _____ Date _____

Complete the tables.

①

Kilograms	1	2	3	5	8	10	12	15
Grams	1,000	2,000	3,000	5,000	8,000	10,000	12,000	15,000

②

Kilograms	0	$\frac{1}{2}$	1	$1\frac{1}{2}$	2	$2\frac{1}{2}$	3	$3\frac{1}{2}$
Grams	0	500	1,000	1,500	2,000	2,500	3,000	3,500

③

Kilograms	0	$\frac{1}{4}$	$\frac{1}{2}$	$\frac{3}{4}$	1	$2\frac{1}{4}$	$3\frac{3}{4}$	$5\frac{1}{2}$
Grams	0	250	500	750	1,000	2,250	3,750	5,500

④

Yards	1	2	3	5	10	$1\frac{1}{2}$	$\frac{5}{6}$	$1\frac{1}{6}$
Feet	3	6	9	15	30	$4\frac{1}{2}$	$2\frac{1}{2}$	$3\frac{1}{2}$
Inches	36	72	108	180	360	54	30	42

⑤

Hours	0	$\frac{1}{2}$	1	$1\frac{1}{2}$	2	$2\frac{1}{2}$	3	$3\frac{1}{2}$
Minutes	0	30	60	90	120	150	180	210
Seconds	0	1,800	3,600	5,400	7,200	9,000	10,800	12,600

prime **CXCI** one hundred ninety-one **191**

ABOUT THE PAGE NUMBER 191 is a palindrome. Do you know what the next one will be? 191 is prime.

Lesson Activity Book p. 192

Solve.

⑥ If a paper clip weighs about 1 gram, about how much do 273 paper clips weigh?

__273 grams__

⑦ If 3,016 large paper clips weigh about 6 kilograms, about how much does 1 large paper clip weigh?

__2 grams__

⑧ There are 250 paper clips in a box. Each box weighs $\frac{1}{4}$ of a kilogram.

How many boxes weigh $3\frac{1}{2}$ kilograms? __14 boxes__

How many boxes weigh 7 kilograms? __28 boxes__

How many boxes weigh 70 kilograms? __280 boxes__

⑨ Could a car weigh 5 kilograms?

__no__

⑩ Could a book weigh 5 kilograms?

__yes__

⑪ Challenge A kilogram is a little heavier than 2 pounds. Write <, >, or =.

2 kilograms $>$ 4 pounds   3 kilograms $<$ 10 pounds

3 kilograms $>$ 3 pounds $5\frac{1}{2}$ kilograms $>$ 10 pounds

192 one hundred ninety-two **CXCII** $2 \times 2 \times 2 \times 2 \times 2 \times 6$

ABOUT THE PAGE NUMBER There are 192 ounces in 12 pounds. There are 192 months in 16 years.

Teaching Notes for LAB page 191

Have students complete the page individually or with partners.

Encourage students to look for patterns in the tables, and to use earlier answers in the tables to find later ones. For example, to find the number of grams in $2\frac{1}{2}$ kilograms, students could add the number of grams in 2 kilograms to the number of grams in $\frac{1}{2}$ kilogram.

Teaching Notes for LAB page 192

Students use weight measurements to solve word problems, then use their understanding of the size of a gram and a kilogram to determine the reasonableness of two weight measurements.

Challenge Problems These problems require students to compare customary and metric units of weight measurement. Students should use the fact that a kilogram is a little heavier than 2 pounds to help with these comparisons.

Reflect and Summarize the Lesson

Write Math How many grams are in $5\frac{1}{2}$ kilograms? How do you know? 5,500 grams; Possible explanation: Since there are 1,000 grams in 1 kilogram, there are $5 \times 1,000 = 5,000$ grams in 5 kilograms. There are 500 grams in $\frac{1}{2}$ kilogram, so $5\frac{1}{2}$ kilograms $= 5$ kilograms $+ \frac{1}{2}$ kilogram $= 5,000$ grams $+ 500$ grams $= 5,500$ grams.

Leveled Problem Solving

Lorelei's baby brother weighs 4 kilograms.

❶ Basic Level

How many grams does the baby weigh? Explain. 4,000 g; 1 kg = 1,000 grams; 1,000 × 4 = 4,000.

❷ On Level

John's baby sister weighs 3,600 grams. Who weighs more? Explain. Lorelei's baby brother; 4 kg = 4 × 1,000, or 4,000 grams; 4,000 > 3,600.

❸ Above Level

Greg's puppy weighs 1,830 grams. Who weighs more? How much more? Explain. Lorelei's baby brother weighs 2,170 g more; 4 kg = 4,000 g; 4,000 > 1,830; 4,000 − 1,830 = 2,170.

Intervention

Activity Conversions

Have students work in pairs. Tell students that to convert from a larger unit to a smaller unit, you multiply, and to convert from a smaller unit to a larger unit, you divide. Write this sentence on the board: "How many grams are in _____ kilograms?" Have a student write a number in the blank. Allow pairs to help each other with the conversion. Continue the activity using other numbers.

Practice

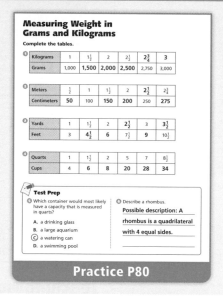

Practice P80

Extension

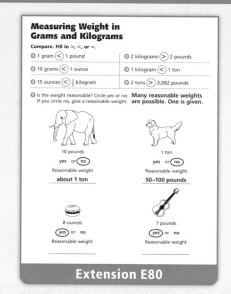

Extension E80

Spiral Review

Spiral Review Book page SR80 provides review of the following previously learned skills and concepts:

- adding decimal numbers
- converting between cups, pints, and quarts

You may wish to have students work with partners to complete the page.

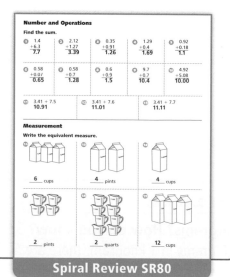

Spiral Review SR80

Extension Activity
Kilograms to Milligrams

Tell students that there are 1,000 milligrams in 1 gram and 1,000 grams in a kilogram. Divide the class into two teams. Write a number on the board, and have students convert that many kilograms to grams, that many grams to milligrams, or that many kilograms to milligrams. The first student to make the conversion correctly wins a point for his or her team. Play until one team wins 7 points.

Use with Lesson Activity Book pp. 191–192.

Teacher's Notes 🍎

Daily Notes . . .

Quick Notes

More Ideas

Lesson 11 Problem Solving Strategy and Test Prep

NCTM Standards 1, 2, 6, 7, 8, 9, 10

Lesson Planner

- To use the problem solving strategy *look for a pattern*
- To articulate the steps and strategies used to solve problems
- To prepare for standardized tests

Problem Solving Strategy:
Look For a Pattern (TG pp. 777–778, 780–781)

MATERIALS

Ⓐ **Discussing the Problem Solving Strategy: Look For a Pattern** (TG p. 777)

Ⓑ **Solving Problems by Applying the Strategy** (TG p. 778)

-  LAB p. 193
- SH pp. 152–153

Problem Solving Test Prep (TG p. 779)

Ⓒ **Getting Ready for Standardized Tests** (TG p. 779)

- LAB p. 194

Lesson Notes

About Problem Solving

Problem Solving Strategy: Look For a Pattern

Throughout this chapter, students have been studying measurement. In some of the lessons, students converted between units of measurement by completing tables. They were encouraged to look for patterns in the tables to help them make the conversions. This lesson focuses on the problem solving strategy *look for a pattern*. The LAB pages assess students' understanding of measurement.

Skills Practice and Review

Weight Versus Mass

Ask students to explain the difference between weight and mass that they explored in **Lesson 9.10.** Mass is a measure of the amount of stuff that makes up an object. Weight is a measure of how heavy an object is. Ask questions about these two concepts to help students distinguish between weight and mass. Here are some possible questions:

- Is an astronaut heavier on Earth or on the moon? on Earth

- Is the mass of an astronaut more or less on Earth than it is on the moon, or are they the same? They are the same.

- Where is the weight of an astronaut greater, on Earth or on the moon? on Earth

- Does a book have less weight or less mass on the moon than it does on Earth? less weight

(A) Discussing the Problem Solving Strategy: Look For a Pattern

whole class 🕐 15 MIN

NCTM Standards 1, 2, 6, 7, 8, 9, 10

Purpose To share strategies for solving problems and focus on the problem solving strategy *look for a pattern*

Introduce Remind students that throughout this chapter they have seen patterns in the tables they have used to convert between units of measurement. Sketch the table shown at the right to illustrate what you are talking about.

gallons	1	2	3	4
quarts	4	8	12	16

Ask students to describe some of the patterns they see in the table. Possible answer: The numbers in the top row increase by 1. The numbers in the bottom row increase by 4. The numbers in the bottom row are 4 times the numbers in the top row.

Point out that problems of many varieties can be solved by finding and extending patterns. Introduce the following problem.

Problem Junior League footballs weigh 12 ounces. A carton of the balls weighs 6 pounds. How many Junior League footballs are there in a carton?

Share Have students share their strategies for solving the problem. If no one mentions it, point out that two different units are mentioned in the problem. A good first step, then, regardless of the strategy used, will be to convert the weights to a single unit. Since there are 16 ounces in a pound, a carton of footballs weighs 6 × 16, or 96 ounces.

A good strategy to use to find the number of footballs that weigh 96 ounces is *look for a pattern.* One football weighs 12 ounces. Each additional football adds 12 ounces to the weight of the carton. We can show the pattern in a table:

Number of footballs	1	2	3	4	5	6	7	8
Weight of footballs (oz)	12	24	36	48	60	72	84	96

💬 Talk Math

❓ How much do 5 footballs weigh? 60 ounces

❓ Twenty-eight footballs weigh 336 ounces. How much do 27 footballs weigh? 29 footballs? Explain. 324 ounces; 348 ounces; Possible explanation: 27 balls weigh 12 ounces less than 28 balls, and 336 − 12 = 324; 29 balls weigh 12 ounces more than 28 balls, and 336 + 12 = 348.

❓ How many Junior League footballs are in a carton? Explain. 8; In the table, 8, the number of footballs, is above 96, the number of ounces.

B Solving Problems by Applying the Strategy LAB p. 193

 individuals or pairs **15 MIN**

Purpose To practice the problem solving strategy *look for a pattern*

NCTM Standards 1, 2, 6, 7, 8, 9, 10

Teaching Notes for LAB page 193

Students practice the problem solving strategy *look for a pattern* by solving each of the problems working independently or in pairs. Help students get started with Problem 1 by asking questions such as the following:

 Read to Understand

What do you need to find out? the pattern for degrees Fahrenheit (°F) and the pattern for degrees Zonk (°Z)

 Plan

How can you solve this problem? Possible answer: Think about the strategies you might use.

How could you look for a pattern in the data? Possible answer: I could look for relationships among the numbers in the rows and columns of the table.

 Solve

What patterns can you find in the numbers in the table? Possible answers: Left to right, the numbers in the top row increase by 18, the numbers in the bottom row increase by 10.

How can you use the patterns to answer the question? Possible answer: by filling in the missing numbers in the patterns

 Check

Look back at the original problem. Did you answer the questions that were asked? Does your answer make sense? How do you know?

Students can look for a pattern to solve the last problem on LAB page 193. Supplement the questions above with ones that are tailored to that problem.

Lesson Activity Book p. 193

Chapter 9
Lesson 11 **Problem Solving Strategy**
Look for a Pattern
NCTM Standards 1, 2, 6, 7, 8, 9, 10

Name _____ Date _____

Understand
Plan
Solve
Check

❶ Rita measured the temperature in degrees Fahrenheit (°F) for several days. Her teacher, Mr. Chang, changed her measurements to a made-up unit called degrees Zonk (°Z). Complete the table.

°F	32	50	68	86	**104**
°Z	0	10	20	**30**	40

How did you complete the table?

Possible answer: I noticed that the numbers increased
by 18 in the top row and 10 in the bottom row.

❷ Wendy invented her own unit of measurement called the gool. She made a table of some measurements, and then converted them into inches. Complete the table.

	Paper	Crayon	Pencil	Water Bottle	Finger
Gools	104	52	65	**117**	39
Inches	8	**4**	5	9	3

prime CXCIII one hundred ninety-three **193**

ABOUT THE PAGE NUMBER 193 is prime. It is the sum of two squares: 193 = 144 + 49

Reflect and Summarize the Lesson

Write Math **When might the strategy *look for a pattern* be a good one to use to solve a problem?** Possible answer: *Look for a pattern* might be a good strategy to use when you know three or four numbers that appear to be related to one another, and when you are asked to find another number that is related to the ones you know.

Use with Lesson Activity Book pp. 193–194.

C **Getting Ready for Standardized Tests** LAB p. 194

individuals **20** MIN

Purpose To prepare students for standardized tests

NCTM Standards 1, 2, 6, 7, 8, 9, 10

Lesson Activity Book p. 194

Problem Solving Test Prep

Choose the correct answer.

1 Rolls at the bakery are priced as shown in the table. If the pattern continues, how much would 10 rolls cost?

Rolls	1	2	3	4
Cost	$0.50	$0.75	$1.00	$1.25

A. $2.00   C. $2.50
B. $2.25   **(D.) $2.75**

2 How many more faces does a rectangular prism with a square base have than a pyramid with a square base?

(A.) 1
B. 2
C. 3
D. 4

Show What You Know

Solve each problem. Explain your answer.

3 There are 10 sandwiches on a plate. They have either turkey or salami or both. Four of the sandwiches have turkey, and 8 have salami. How many have both? Explain how you found your answer.

2 sandwiches; Possible explanation: Use guess and check. Guess that 2 sandwiches have both, so 2 more must have only turkey, and 6 more must have only salami; 2 + 2 + 6 = 10.

4 In the pattern shown below, you can find the sum of each row.

```
        1          Row 1
      1   1        Row 2
    1   2   1      Row 3
  1   3   3   1    Row 4
```

Describe the pattern you see in the sums of the first 4 rows. If the pattern continues, what will be the sum of Row 8? Explain how you decided.

128; The sum of each row is double the sum of the row above it. So, the sums are 16 (Row 5), 32 (Row 6), 64 (Row 7), and 128 (Row 8).

194 one hundred ninety-four **CXCIV** 2 × 97

ABOUT THE PAGE NUMBER 194 is the sum of two square numbers: 194 = 169 + 25

Teaching Notes for LAB page 194

The test items on this page were written in the same style and are arranged in the same format as those on many state assessments. The test is cumulative and is designed for students to apply a variety of problem solving strategies, including *look for a pattern, make a model,* and *use logical reasoning.* Students might share the strategies they use.

The Item Analysis Chart indicates one of the possible strategies that may be used for each test item.

Show What You Know

Written Response

Direct students' attention to Problems 2 and 3. For Problem 2, remind students that all the faces of a rectangular prism are rectangles. All the faces of a pyramid are triangles, except the base, which may be a polygon. For Problem 3, suggest that, if students don't see a straightforward solution, they try guessing the number of sandwiches that have both turkey and salami, then checking to see if their guesses makes sense. Then have students write explanations describing how they know their answers are correct. To provide more space for students to communicate their thinking about these problems, you may wish to have them write their responses and explanations on a separate sheet of paper. Use the Scoring Rubric below to evaluate their understanding.

Item Analysis Chart

Item	Strategy
1	Look for a pattern
2	Make a model
3	Guess and check
4	Look for a pattern

Scoring Rubric

2	• Demonstrates complete understanding of the problem and chooses an appropriate strategy to determine the solution
1	• Demonstrates a partial understanding of the problem and chooses a strategy that does not lead to a complete and accurate solution
0	• Demonstrates little understanding of the problem and shows little evidence of using any strategy to determine a solution

---

Review Model

Refer students to Problem Solving Review Model: Look for a Pattern found on *Student Handbook* pp. 152–153 to review a model of the four steps they can use with the problem solving strategy *look for a pattern*. Additional problem solving practice is also provided.

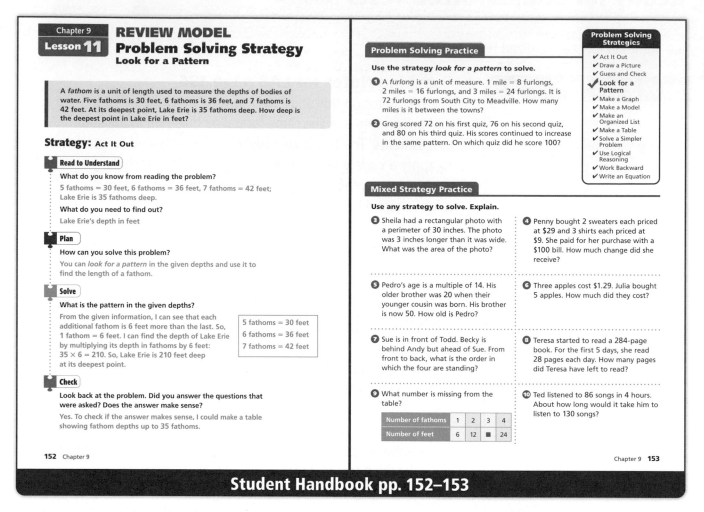

Student Handbook pp. 152–153

Task Have students read the problem at the top of the Review Model page. Then discuss.

🗨 Talk Math

❓ What do you know from reading the problem? information about a unit called a fathom and about Lake Erie's depth in fathoms

❓ What do you need to find out? Lake Erie's depth in feet

❓ What strategy can you use to solve the problem? You could *look for a pattern.*

❓ How could you find a pattern in the given examples of lengths written in fathoms? Possible answer: You could see how much each length differs from the next.

❓ What is the difference in length between 5 fathoms and 6 fathoms? between 6 fathoms and 7 fathoms? 6 feet; 6 feet

❓ How long is a fathom? 6 feet

❓ How can you find the depth of Lake Erie in feet? How deep is it? Multiply its depth in fathoms by 6 feet; $35 \times 6 = 210$, so it is 210 feet deep.

1 9 miles; Possible explanation: You can use the problem solving strategy *look for a pattern* by noticing that for each mile the equivalent number of furlongs is the number of miles times 8. So, to find how many miles are in 72 furlongs, divide 72 by 8. 72 ÷ 8 = 9 miles

2 eighth quiz; Possible explanation: You can use the problem solving strategy *look for a pattern* by seeing that his scores increased by 4 points each time. I counted from 80, which was Greg's third quiz, to 100, which was Greg's eighth quiz.

Mixed Strategy Practice

3 54 square inches; Possible explanation: You can use the problem solving strategies *draw a picture* and *guess and check.* I drew the photo and labeled the sides with the measurements that I guessed. Then I checked to see if I was correct by adding all of the sides. I found that the length of the photo must be 6 inches and the width 9 inches for the perimeter to be 30 inches. The area is length × width: 6 × 9 = 54 square inches.

4 $15; Possible explanation: You can use the problem solving strategy *solve a simpler problem.* I found the total amount of the purchases by first multiplying the number of each item by its price: 2 × $29 = $58; 3 × $9 = $27. Then I added the products together: $58 + $27 = $85. Last, I subtracted: $100 − $85 = $15.

5 42; Possible explanation: You can use the problem solving strategies *make an organized list* and *use logical reasoning.* The first few multiples of 14 are 0, 14, 28, 42, 56, and 70. Since Pedro's older brother is 50, Pedro can't be 56 or 70. If the brother was 20 when the cousin was born, the cousin must be 30. Since the cousin is younger, Pedro must be 42.

6 $2.15; Possible explanation: You can use the problem solving strategy *act it out.* I got coins worth $1.29 and put them into three piles so each pile had the same amount, 43¢. Then I made two more piles just like that, and found the total amount, $2.15.

7 Andy, Becky, Sue, Todd; Possible explanation: You can use the problem solving strategies *use logical reasoning* and *draw a diagram.* I used logical reasoning and the information given to me in the problem to draw a diagram of the order they were in. Andy had to be first because he was ahead of Becky who was ahead of Sue. Sue was ahead of Todd.

8 144 pages; Possible explanation: You can use the problem solving strategy *solve a simpler problem.* First, I multiplied: 5 days × 28 pages per day = 140 pages. Then I subtracted: 284-page book − 140 pages read = 144 pages left to read.

9 18 feet; Possible explanation: You can use the problem solving strategy *find a pattern.* I noticed that every fathom multiplied by six gave me the number of feet. So, I multiplied 3 × 6 = 18 feet.

10 about 6 hours; Possible explanation: You can use the problem solving strategy *solve a simpler problem.* First I estimated 86 songs in 4 hours is a bit more than 20 songs an hour. Since 130 songs is between 120 songs (6 × 20) and 140 songs (7 × 20), it would take a bit more than 6 hours.

Measurement

NCTM Standards 1, 2, 3, 4, 5, 6, 7, 8, 9, 10

Purpose To provide students with an opportunity to demonstrate understanding of Chapter 9 concepts and skills

MATERIALS

• LAB pp. 195–196
• Chapter 9 Test
  (Assessment Guide
  pp. AG81–AG82)

Chapter 9 Learning Goals and Assessment Options

These learning goals are assessed in many ways throughout the chapter. The chart below correlates each learning goal to specific formal and informal assessment options.

	Learning Goals	Lesson Number	Snapshot Assessment	Chapter Review Item Numbers	Chapter Test Item Numbers
			Item Number	LAB pp. 195–196	Assessment Guide pp. AG81–AG82
9-A	Compute with time and money	9.1	1, 3, 7, 11	6, 7, 13	11, 12, 16, 17
9-B	Measure and compute changes in temperature	9.2	5, 8	1, 12	1–3
9-C	Use customary units to measure length, capacity, and weight, and convert among units	9.3, 9.4, 9.6, 9.8, 9.9	2, 4, 9	2–4, 8, 9	4, 9, 10, 13–15, 18
9-D	Use metric units to measure length, capacity, and mass/weight, and convert among units	9.5, 9.7–9.10	6, 10	5, 10, 11	5–8
9-E	Apply problem solving strategies such as *look for a pattern* to solve problems	9.11	12	14	19, 20

Snapshot Assessment

The following Mental Math and Quick Write questions and tasks provide a quick, informal assessment of students' understanding of Chapter 9 concepts, skills, and problem solving strategies.

whole class   **10 MIN**

Mental Math This oral assessment uses mental math strategies and can be used with the whole class.

❶ You have 3 dimes, 1 nickel, and 2 pennies. How much money do you have? 37¢

You have 3 dollars in quarters. How many quarters do you have? 12
(Learning Goal 9-A)

❷ What customary unit is best used to measure:
  • length of your fingers? inch
  • weight of your little sister? pounds
  • the milk you drink at lunch? cup
(Learning Goal 9-C)

❸ How many seconds are in 4 minutes? 240

How many days are in 5 weeks? 35

How many weeks are in 70 days? 10
(Learning Goal 9-A)

❹ How many inches are in a yard? 36

How many feet are in 2 yards? 6

How many ounces are in 2 pounds? 32
(Learning Goal 9-C)

5 The temperature was 66°F this morning; now it is 86°F. What was the temperature change from this morning? 20°

Was that an increase or decrease in temperature? increase

The outside temperature is 56°F. The temperature falls 13°. What is the temperature now? 43°F
(Learning Goal 9-B)

6 What metric unit is best used to measure:
- length of a sheet of note paper? centimeter
- weight of your paperback book? gram
- the distance between Miami and Orlando? kilometer
(Learning Goal 9-D)

Quick Write This informal written assessment can be administered to small groups or the whole class. Read each question and have the students record responses on their write-on boards. Encourage students to listen and think about the questions before responding.

7 Find the missing values in the tables.

Days	7	21	35	14	49
Weeks	1	3	5	2	7

Hours	2	3	1	5	4
Minutes	120	180	60	300	240

3 weeks − 11 days = ____ days 10

2 hours − 30 minutes = ____ minutes 90

2 minutes + 3 minutes = ____ seconds 300

5 quarters + 5 dimes = $____ 1.75
(Learning Goal 9-A)

8 At 8:00 a.m., the temperature was 64°F. The temperature rises 12° by noon, and falls 5° by 6:00 p.m. What is the temperature at 6:00 p.m.? 71°F
- The temperature was 15°C when Hal woke up at 7:30 a.m. The temperature rises 7° by noon. By 3:00 p.m., the temperature was 2° higher than it was at noon. What is the temperature at 3:00 p.m.? 24°C.
- If the outdoor temperature was 84° in Memphis, was it measured in Fahrenheit(F) or Celsius(C)? F
(Learning Goal 9-B)

9 2 feet + 5 inches = ____ inches 29

2 yards − 30 inches = ____ inches 42

8 cups = ____ quarts 2

3 gallons − 5 quarts = ____ quarts 7

3 pounds = ____ ounces 48

5 pounds − 48 ounces = ____ ounces 32

8,000 pounds = ____ tons 4
(Learning Goal 9-C)

10 1 liter − 250 milliliters = ____ milliliters 750

3 meters + 50 centimeters = ____ centimeters 350

1,000 meters + 6,000 meters = ____ kilometers 7

42 grams + 1 kilogram = ____ grams 1,042

1 gram − 600 milligrams = ____ milligrams 400
(Learning Goal 9-D)

11 Evan has $5.00 in coins in his bank. Half of his money is in quarters. The other half is all in dimes. How many quarters does Evan have in his bank? 10 quarters How many dimes does he have in his bank? 25 dimes
(Learning Goal 9-A)

12 Roger has a puzzle for his classmates. When he says 1, the answer is 12. When he says 2, the answer is 24. When he says 4, the answer is 48. What is the possible pattern? multiply by 12

What measurement is he converting? feet to inches
(Learning Goal 9-E)

Chapter 9 ASSESSMENT

Formal Assessment

Chapter Review/Assessment The Chapter 9 Review/Assessment on *Lesson Activity Book* pages 195–196 assesses students' understanding of measurement. Students should be able to complete these pages independently.

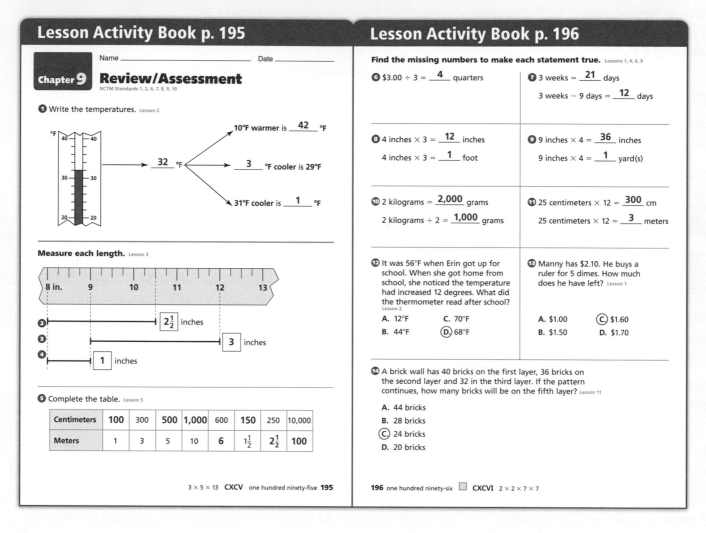

Extra Support Students who have difficulty with items on the Chapter 9 Review/Assessment may need to review the lesson where development of the concept was provided. You can use the Intervention Activity in that lesson to increase students' understanding before the Chapter Test is given.

Chapter Test Use the Chapter 9 Test in the *Assessment Guide* to assess concepts, skills, and problem solving from the chapter and to prepare students for standardized tests. The Chapter Test and other test items are also available online.

Chapter Notes

 Quick Notes

More Ideas

Data and Probability

About the Chapter

Your students have been working with data since first grade, gaining experience with collecting, organizing, displaying, and interpreting information. When interpreting data, students have largely focused on describing characteristics of data sets. In this chapter, students begin to develop mathematical tools to help them analyze data and answer questions about the probability that a particular event will occur.

Finding All Possible Outcomes Students begin the chapter drawing on their intuitive ideas about the likelihood of events. They work with a set of attribute cards that represent all 12 possible combinations of 3 shapes, 2 colors, and 2 patterns, using logical reasoning and informal language such as *certain, likely, unlikely,* and *impossible* to describe the likelihood of drawing certain kinds of cards from the deck. For example, since all the cards are either blue or green, it's certain they will draw a card that's one of these two colors. On the other hand, it's impossible to draw a red card. Students also begin to express likelihood as a fraction, comparing the number of favorable outcomes to the number of all possible outcomes.

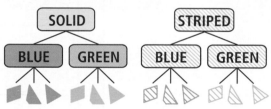

Probability Experiments When we can identify all possible outcomes for a certain set of events, we can do experiments to see how closely actual results agree with the predicted results. Students perform experiments and draw bar graphs to analyze the data they generate.

Using Data to Generate Probability

In the second half of the chapter, students collect and graph data about themselves. They use graphs to look for patterns and ways to generalize about the data.

Developing Concepts Across the Grades

Topic	Prior Learning	Learning in Chapter 10	Later Learning
Probability	• List all possible outcomes for an experiment **Grade 3, Chapter 8**	• Describe the likelihood of an event • Compare probabilities of events • Predict the results of an experiment by calculating probabilities **Lessons 10.1–10.5**	• List possible outcomes of a probability experiment • Use experimental results to make predictions **Grade 5, Chapter 14**
Graphing Data	• Collect, organize, and interpret data in a pictograph • Interpret a bar graph **Grade 3, Chapter 13**	• Graph and analyze survey data • Analyze and compare data using bar graphs • Graph measurement data **Lessons 10.4, 10.6–10.8**	• Make and read scatter plots, pictographs, line plots, and stem-and-leaf plots • Graph a given set of data using a circle graph **Grade 5, Chapter 14**
Fractions	• Use fraction names and symbols to describe fractional parts of whole objects • Compare fractions **Grade 3, Chapter 7**	• Relate a fraction of items with given attributes to the likelihood of choosing an item with those attributes • Express probability as a fraction **Lessons 10.2, 10.3**	• Use fractions to describe the results of an experiment • Compare whole numbers, fractions, decimals, and percents **Grade 5, Chapter 14**

Chapter Planner

Lesson	Objectives	NCTM Standards	Vocabulary	Materials/Resources

CHAPTER 10 World Almanac For Kids • Vocabulary • Games • Challenge
Teacher Guide pp. 793A–793F, **Student Handbook** pp. 160–161, 170–174

1 Finding Combinations of Attributes

PACING 1 DAY

Teacher Guide pp. 794–801
Lesson Activity Book pp. 197–198
Student Handbook
Student Letter p. 159
Game p. 172

- To find combinations of attributes
- To determine the portion of all possible combinations that match a given description

1, 2, 6, 7, 8, 9, 10

attribute

For the teacher:
- transparency of AM89 (optional)

For the students:
- School Home Connection, TR: SHC37–SHC40
- TR: AM90, AM91
- blue pencil
- green pencil
- scissors
- P81, E81, SR81

Social Studies Connection
Secret Codes
Teacher Guide p. 792

---

2 Describing the Likelihood of an Event

PACING 1 DAY

Teacher Guide pp. 802–809
Lesson Activity Book pp. 199–200
Student Handbook
Explore p. 162

- To describe the likelihood of an event as *impossible, unlikely, likely,* or *certain*
- To relate a fraction of items with given attributes to the likelihood of choosing an item with those attributes

1, 2, 6, 7, 8, 9, 10

certain

likely

unlikely

impossible

For the students:
- set of 12 attribute cards from Lesson 10.1
- P82, E82, SR82

Science Connection:
Need an Umbrella?
Teacher Guide p. 792

---

3 Introducing Probability

PACING 1 DAY

Teacher Guide pp. 810–817
Lesson Activity Book pp. 201–202
Student Handbook
Review Model p. 163
Game p. 173

- To express probability as a fraction
- To compare the probabilities of events

1, 2, 6, 7, 8, 9, 10

probability

For the teacher:
- set of 12 attribute cards from Lesson 10.1
- TR: AM92–AM94
- P83, E83, SR83

Literature Connection:
Do You Wanna Bet? Your Chance to Find Out About Probability
Teacher Guide p. 792

---

4 Drawing From a Deck of Attribute Cards

PACING 1 DAY

Teacher Guide pp. 818–827
Lesson Activity Book pp. 203–204
Student Handbook
Explore p. 164
Review Model p. 165

- To predict the result of an experiment
- To conduct an experiment, organize data in a bar graph, and analyze the results

1, 2, 6, 7, 8, 9, 10

mode

range

For the teacher:
- transparency of AM95 (optional)
- extra copies of LAB p. 203
- graph created in Activity C

For the students:
- P84, E84, SR84

NCTM Standards 2000

1. Number and Operations
2. Algebra
3. Geometry
4. Measurement
5. Data Analysis and Probability
6. Problem Solving
7. Reasoning and Proof
8. Communication
9. Connections
10. Representation

Key

AG: Assessment Guide
E: Extension Book
LAB: Lesson Activity Book
P: Practice Book

SH: Student Handbook
SR: Spiral Review Book
TG: Teacher Guide
TR: Teacher Resource Book

MATH GLOSSARY in **Student Handbook** p. 259

Planner (continued)

Chapter 10 Data and Probability

Chapter Planner (continued)

Lesson	Objectives	NCTM Standards	Vocabulary	Materials/Resources
5 Drawing Blocks PACING 1 DAY **Teacher Guide** pp. 828–837 **Lesson Activity Book** pp. 205–206 **Student Handbook** Explore p. 166 Review Model p. 167	• To predict the results of an experiment by calculating probabilities • To conduct an experiment, organize the data, and interpret the results • To compare predictions with experimental results	1, 2, 6, 7, 8, 9, 10	**outcome**	**For the teacher:** ▪ transparency of AM96 (optional) ▪ transparency marker ▪ coins, blocks, or cards numbered 1–9 ▪ opaque bag ▪ completed graph from Activity B **For the students:** ▪ coins ▪ completed LAB pp. 205–206 ▪ completed SH p. 166 ▪ P85, E85, SR85
6 Collecting and Analyzing Survey Data PACING 1 DAY **Teacher Guide** pp. 838–845 **Lesson Activity Book** pp. 207–208	• To create survey questions and to collect survey responses • To graph and analyze survey data	1, 2, 6, 7, 8, 9, 10	**data**	**For the students:** ▪ graph paper ▪ rulers ▪ P86, E86, SR86
7 Collecting Measurement Data PACING 1 DAY **Teacher Guide** pp. 846–853 **Lesson Activity Book** pp. 209–210	• To collect data by measuring arm lengths • To interpret bar graphs	1, 2, 6, 7, 8, 9, 10	**precision**	**For the teacher:** ▪ sample measuring tools (such as measuring tape or string and a ruler) ▪ transparency of AM97 (optional) **For the students:** ▪ measuring tool (such as measuring tape or string and ruler) ▪ P87, E87, SR87
8 Analyzing Measurement Data PACING 1 DAY **Teacher Guide** pp. 854–859 **Lesson Activity Book** pp. 211–212	• To graph measurement data • To analyze and compare data using bar graphs	1, 2, 6, 7, 8, 9, 10	**median**	**For the teacher:** ▪ bar graph of arm-length data from Lesson 10.7 ▪ transparency of AM98 (optional) **For the students:** ▪ P88, E88, SR88
9 Problem Solving Strategy and Test Prep PACING 1 DAY **Teacher Guide** pp. 860–865 **Lesson Activity Book** pp. 213–214 **Student Handbook** Review Models pp. 168–169	• To apply the problem solving strategy *make a graph* • To articulate the steps and strategies used to solve problems • To prepare for standardized tests	1, 2, 6, 7, 8, 9, 10		**For the teacher:** ▪ transparency of LAB p. 213 (optional)

CHAPTER 10 Assessment **TG** pp. 866–869, **LAB** pp. 215–216, **AG** pp. AG85–AG88				**For the students:** ▪ Chapter 10 Test pp. AG85–AG86

Games..

Use the following games for skills practice and reinforcement of concepts.

Lesson 10.1 ▶
Attribute Memory provides an opportunity for students to practice identifying common attributes.

Attribute Memory

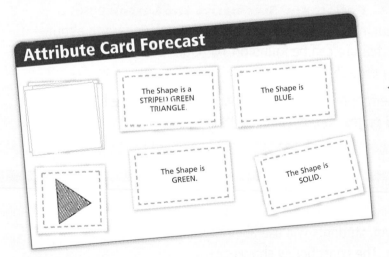

Attribute Card Forecast

The Shape is a STRIPED GREEN TRIANGLE.

The Shape is BLUE.

The Shape is GREEN.

The Shape is SOLID.

◀ Lesson 10.3 *Attribute Card Forecast* provides an opportunity for students to practice calculating simple probabilities.

Planning Ahead

In **Lesson 10.1,** each group of students needs two copies of Activity Master 91: Blank Cards. Students will need colored pencils to color the attribute cards blue and green.

In **Lessons 10.2** and **10.3,** you will be using attribute cards that were used in **Lesson 10.1.**

In **Lesson 10.7,** you will be completing a bar graph of arm lengths. Keep this graph for use in **Lesson 10.8.**

Developing Problem Solvers

Open-Ended Problem Solving

The Headline Story in the Daily Activities section provides an open-ended situation where students can pose and solve problems. For each story, there are many possible responses.

Headline Stories can be found on TG pages 795, 803, 811, 819, 829, 839, 847, and 855.

Headline Story

Leveled Problem Solving

Leveled Problem Solving provides an opportunity for students to apply learning from the lesson to a real-life situation. Problems are leveled by ability to allow students of all ability levels to become successful problem solvers. Each Leveled Problem Solving begins with a real-life scenario upon which three problems are built.

The levels of problems are:

❶ Basic Level	❷ On Level	❸ Above Level
students who need extra support	students working at grade level	students who are ready for more challenging problems

Leveled Problem Solving can be found on TG pages 801, 808, 817, 827, 836, 844, 852, and 859.

THE WORLD ALMANAC FOR KIDS

The World Almanac for Kids feature is designed to stimulate student interest in the math concepts they are about to learn. Students use data to solve problems and explain solutions. The Chapter 10 Project can be found on SH pages 160–161.

Write Math **Reflect and Summarize the Lesson** poses a problem or question for students to think and write about. This feature can be found on TG pages 800, 807, 816, 826, 835, 843, 851, 858, and 862.

Other opportunities to write about math can be found on LAB pages 200, 202, 206, 208, and 211.

Problem Solving Strategies

The focus of **Lesson 10.9** is the strategy *make a graph*. However, students will use a variety of problem solving strategies as they work through the chapter. The chart below shows strategies that may be useful in completing each lesson.

Strategy	Lesson(s)	Description
Act It Out	10.4	Act it out to find the results of a probability experiment.
Draw a Picture	10.1, 10.2	Draw a tree diagram to find combinations of attributes.
Look for a Pattern	10.4–10.6	Look for a pattern to analyze experimental data.
Make a Graph	10.4–10.6, 10.9	Make a graph to display and analyze the result of a probability experiment.
Make a Organized List	10.1–10.2, 10.5	Make an organized list of shapes to find combinations of attributes.
Use Logical Reasoning	10.1, 10.2, 10.5, 10.6	Use logical reasoning to find combination of attributes.
Write an Equation	10.3	Write and solve an equation to find the probability of *not* choosing a particular card.

Meeting the Needs of All Learners

Differentiated Instruction		
Extra Support	**On Level**	**Enrichment**
Intervention Activities TG pp. 801, 808, 817, 827, 836, 844, 852, 859	**Practice Book** pp. P81–P88	**Extension Activities** TG pp. 801, 808, 817, 827, 836, 844, 852, 859
	Spiral Review Book pp. SR81–SR88	**Extension Book** pp. E81–E88
	LAB Challenge LAB pp. 198, 200, 201, 203, 206, 208 210, 212	**LAB Challenge** LAB pp. 198, 200, 201, 203, 206, 208 210, 212
Lesson Notes Basic Level TG p. 797	**Lesson Notes** On Level TG p. 813	**Lesson Notes** Above Level TG p. 851
Leveled Problem Solving Basic Level TG pp. 801, 808, 817, 827, 836, 844, 852, 859	**Leveled Problem Solving** On Level TG pp. 801, 808, 817, 827, 836, 844, 852, 859	**Leveled Problem Solving** Above Level TG pp. 801, 808, 817, 827, 836, 844, 852, 859

English Language Learners

Suggestions for addressing the needs of children learning English as a second language are included in the Developing Mathematical Language section at the beginning of most lessons.

ELL activities for this chapter can be found on TG pages 795, 803, 811, 819, 829, 839, 847, and 855.

The Multi-Age Classroom

Grade 3	• Students on this level should be able to complete the lessons in Chapter 10, but might need some additional practice with key concepts and skills. • Give students more practice with charts, graphs, and probability.	See Grade 4, Intervention Activities, Lessons 10.1–10.8. See Grade 3, Lessons 8.1–8.5.
Grade 4	• Students on this level should be able to complete the lessons in Chapter 10 with minimal adjustments.	See Grade 4, Practice pages P81–P88.
Grade 5	• Students on this level should be able to complete the lessons in Chapter 10 and to extend data and probability concepts and skills. • Give students extended work with probability.	See Grade 4, Extension pages E81–E88. See Grade 5, Lessons 14.1–14.4.

Cross Curricular Connections

Social Studies Connection

Math Concept: listing possible outcomes

Secret Codes

- Tell students that throughout history, people have used codes to send messages that others could not read. Discuss Enigma, the machine used by Germany during World War II. This machine produced a code by using several different alphabet substitutions.

- To demonstrate how complex Enigma's codes were, show students that by using just 5 letters of the alphabet there are 120 possible arrangements of the letters. This total comes from 5 possible substitutions for the first letter, 4 for the next letter, 3 for the next, 2 for the next, and 1 for the last ($5 \times 4 \times 3 \times 2 \times 1 = 120$).

- Have students use the same idea to see how many different code "words" are possible for a 4-letter word. Ask them to find all the 4-letter arrangements for the word STOP. There are $4 \times 3 \times 2 \times 1$, or 24 possible arrangements of the letters in STOP: STOP, STPO, SPTO, SPOT, SOPT, SOTP, TSOP, TSPO, TOSP, TOPS, TPSO, TPOS, OSTP, OSPT, OTSP, OTPS, OPST, OPTS, PSTO, PSOT, PTSO, PTOS, POST, POTS.

Lesson 10.1

Science Connection

Math Concept: describing likelihoods

Need an Umbrella?

- Explain to students that weather forecasting is an everyday use of probabilities. Forecasters describe the likelihood of rain or snow using a fraction in the form of a percent.

- Have students study the table below for an 8-day period in Chicago, Illinois.

- For each day, ask students to describe the chance of rain or snow as more or less likely than the day before. Sunday, Tuesday, Wednesday and Thursday are more likely to have rain or snow than the day before; Monday and Friday are less likely; Friday and Saturday are equally likely.

Day	Chance of Rain/Snow
Saturday	$\frac{10}{100}$
Sunday	$\frac{80}{100}$
Monday	$\frac{10}{100}$
Tuesday	$\frac{20}{100}$
Wednesday	$\frac{30}{100}$
Thursday	$\frac{70}{100}$
Friday	$\frac{20}{100}$
Saturday	$\frac{20}{100}$

Lesson 10.2

Literature Connection

Math Concept: probability

Do You Wanna Bet?
Your Chance to Find Out About Probability

By Jean Cushman
Illustrated by Martha Weston

In this book, students will follow Danny and Brian as they learn how data and probability can be used in breaking codes, playing games, and other fun situations.

Lesson 10.3

School-Home Connection

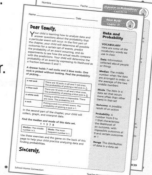

A reproducible copy of the School-Home Connection letter in English and in Spanish can be found in the *Teacher Resource Book*, pages SHC37–SHC40.

Encourage students to play *The ABC Game,* found on the School-Home Connection page, with a family member. Students will work with the concept of predicting the outcome of an experiment in **Lessons 10.4** and **10.5.**

Assessment Options

There are many opportunities in *Think Math!* to assess students' understanding of concepts, skills, and problem solving. Learning Goals for Chapter 10 are provided below. The assessment options provide opportunities to evaluate whether or not students have retained learning from prior experiences. Choose the forms of assessment that best meet the needs of your students.

Chapter 10 Learning Goals

	Learning Goals	Lesson Number
10-A	Determine the number of combinations possible for a set of objects	10.1
10-B	Describe, predict, and compare likelihoods using certain, likely, unlikely, or impossible	10.2, 10.3
10-C	Find probabilities	10.4–10.6
10-D	Interpret a bar graph	10.5–10.8
10-E	Apply problem solving strategies such as *make a graph* to solve problems	10.9

✔ Informal Assessment

Ongoing Assessment
Provides insight into students' thinking to guide instruction (TG pp. 796, 799, 804, 806, 812, 814, 820, 830, 832, 841, 848, 850, 856)

Reflect and Summarize the Lesson
Checks understanding of lesson concepts (TG pp. 800, 807, 816, 826, 835, 843, 851, 858, 862)

Snapshot Assessment
Mental Math and **Quick Write**
Offers a quick observation of students' progress on chapter concepts and skills (TG pp. 866–867)

Performance Assessment
Provides quarterly assessment of Chapters 8–11 concepts using real-life situations
Assessment Guide
pp. AG219–AG224

✔ Formal Assessment

Standardized Test Prep
Problem Solving Test Prep
Prepares students for standardized tests
Lesson Activity Book pp. 214 (TG p. 863)

Chapter 10 Review/Assessment
Reviews and assesses students' understanding of the chapter
Lesson Activity Book pp. 215–216 (TG p. 868)

Chapter 10 Test
Assesses the chapter concepts and skills
Assessment Guide
Form A pp. AG85–AG86
Form B pp. AG87–AG88

Benchmark 3 Assessment
Provides quarterly assessment of Chapters 8–11 concepts and skills
Assessment Guide
Benchmark 3A pp. AG93–AG100
Benchmark 3B pp. AG101–AG108

World Almanac for Kids

Use the World Almanac for Kids feature, *You Quack Me Up!,* found on pp. 160–161 of the ***Student Handbook,*** to provide students with an opportunity to practice using their problem solving skills by solving real world problems.

FACT•ACTIVITY 1

❶ star, 2 out of 12; $\frac{2}{12}$

circle, 4 out of 12; $\frac{4}{12}$

triangle, 6 out of 12; $\frac{6}{12}$

❷ smile face, triangle, 6 out of 12; $\frac{6}{12}$

❸ 1 star out of 12 ducks

THE WORLD ALMANAC FOR KIDS

You Quack Me Up!

Whether it is a state fair, a county fair, or a school fair, there is something for everyone to smile about at a fair.

There is a children's duck pond game at Center Elementary School Fair. Twelve plastic ducks are in the pond and each duck has a star, circle, or triangle hidden on its bottom. You pick a duck at random from the pond. You will win a pencil top eraser prize depending on which symbol is on the bottom of the duck you pick. The table shows how many ducks have each symbol, and which pencil top eraser you will receive.

Duck Pond Game		
Symbol	**Pencil Top Eraser**	**Number of Ducks**
☆	dinosaur	2
○	train	4
△	smile face	6

FACT•ACTIVITY 1

❶ What portion of the plastic ducks have a star? a circle? a triangle? Write each portion as a fraction.

❷ If you pick a plastic duck at random, which pencil top eraser are you most likely to receive?

❸ How many ducks with stars would there have to be to make the likelihood of receiving a dinosaur pencil top eraser $\frac{1}{12}$?

160 Chapter 10

Student Handbook p. 160

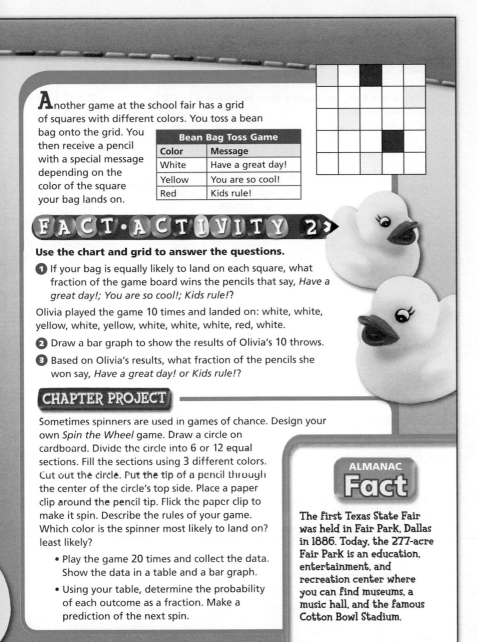

Another game at the school fair has a grid of squares with different colors. You toss a bean bag onto the grid. You then receive a pencil with a special message depending on the color of the square your bag lands on.

Bean Bag Toss Game

Color	Message
White	Have a great day!
Yellow	You are so cool!
Red	Kids rule!

FACT·ACTIVITY 2

Use the chart and grid to answer the questions.

1 If your bag is equally likely to land on each square, what fraction of the game board wins the pencils that say, *Have a great day!; You are so cool!; Kids rule!*?

Olivia played the game 10 times and landed on: white, white, yellow, white, yellow, white, white, white, red, white.

2 Draw a bar graph to show the results of Olivia's 10 throws.

3 Based on Olivia's results, what fraction of the pencils she won say, *Have a great day! or Kids rule!*?

CHAPTER PROJECT

Sometimes spinners are used in games of chance. Design your own *Spin the Wheel* game. Draw a circle on cardboard. Divide the circle into 6 or 12 equal sections. Fill the sections using 3 different colors. Cut out the circle. Put the tip of a pencil through the center of the circle's top side. Place a paper clip around the pencil tip. Flick the paper clip to make it spin. Describe the rules of your game. Which color is the spinner most likely to land on? least likely?

- Play the game 20 times and collect the data. Show the data in a table and a bar graph.
- Using your table, determine the probability of each outcome as a fraction. Make a prediction of the next spin.

ALMANAC Fact

The first Texas State Fair was held in Fair Park, Dallas in 1886. Today, the 277-acre Fair Park is an education, entertainment, and recreation center where you can find museums, a music hall, and the famous Cotton Bowl Stadium.

Student Handbook p. 161

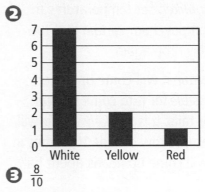

FACT·ACTIVITY 2

1 *Have a great day!:* $\frac{19}{25}$

You are so cool!: $\frac{4}{25}$

Kids rule!: $\frac{2}{25}$

2

[Bar graph: White = 7, Yellow = 2, Red = 1]

3 $\frac{8}{10}$

CHAPTER PROJECT:

Sample answer:

- Spinner: 6 equal sections: 3 sections in green, 2 in blue, 1 in red.

- Rule: To win the game, the spinner must land on red.

- Play this game 20 times. Show the data on a bar graph.

- Green: $\frac{12}{20}$ (most likely)

- Blue: $\frac{5}{20}$

- Red: $\frac{3}{20}$ (least likely)

- Prediction of the 21st spin: the spinner will land on green.

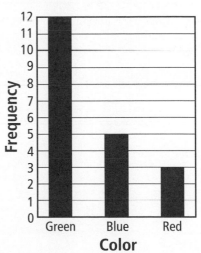

[Bar graph: Green = 12, Blue = 5, Red = 3; y-axis labeled Frequency, x-axis labeled Color]

Vocabulary

To reinforce vocabulary concepts, invite students to complete the vocabulary activities on pp. 170–171 of the *Student Handbook.* Encourage students to record their answers in their math journals.

Many answers are possible.

12 Possible answer: It would be *impossible* for the temperatures to keep going up forever. They are *likely* to stop rising soon. It is *unlikely* for temperatures to go up 20 degrees the next day. I am *certain* that the temperatures will someday drop again.

13 Possible answer: I am *certain* it will come up either heads or tails. It is *impossible* for it to come up with anything except heads or tails. It is *unlikely* that it will come up heads 100 times in a row or tails 100 times in a row. It is *likely* that it will come up heads about half the time.

Chapter **10** Vocabulary

Choose the best vocabulary term from Word List A for each sentence.

Word List A
- attribute
- certain
- data
- impossible
- likely
- median
- mode
- outcome
- precision
- probability
- range
- unlikely

1 A(n) __?__ is often stated as some number from 0 to 1. **probability**

2 Information can also be called __?__. **data**

3 An event with a probability of less than $\frac{1}{2}$ is a(n) __?__ event. **unlikely**

4 To find the __?__ of a set of data, subtract the smallest number from the largest number. **range**

5 An event with a probability of 1 is a(n) __?__ event. **certain**

6 An event with a probability of 0 is a(n) __?__ event. **impossible**

7 A measurement of 1 hour has less __?__ than a measurement of 54 minutes. **precision**

8 A(n) __?__ is a possible result of an action. **outcome**

9 The __?__ of a set of data is the item that appears more often than any of the other items. **mode**

Complete each analogy. Use the best term from Word List B.

Word List B
- likely
- median
- probability

10 Usually is to __?__ as always is to certain. **likely**

11 *B* is to *ABC* as __?__ is to a set of data. **median**

Talk Math

Discuss with a partner what you have just learned about data and probability. Use the vocabulary terms *certain, impossible, likely,* and *unlikely.*

12 Suppose temperatures increased 2 degrees each day last week. How can you describe temperatures for the next day?

13 A coin is flipped 100 times. How can you describe the outcomes?

170 Chapter 10

Student Handbook p. 170

Word Line

14 Create a word line for the terms *certain*, *impossible*, *likely*, and *unlikely*. Arrange the words from 0 to 1.

Words:

Sequence:

_____

Concept Map

15 Create a concept map for *Describe Data*. Use what you have learned about ways to describe a set of data.

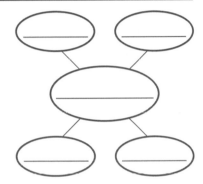

What's in a Word?

DATA Ancient Romans did not have e-mail, so they wrote messages by hand. At the end of a message, they wrote "*datum*," meaning "given" and the month and day. More than one *datum* is *data*. The Romans used *data* to mean "the time and place stated."

Today, we use the word *data* to mean information collected about people or things. Weights, heights, lengths, dates, and populations are all *data*.

Chapter 10 **171**

14 Many answers are possible. One example is given.

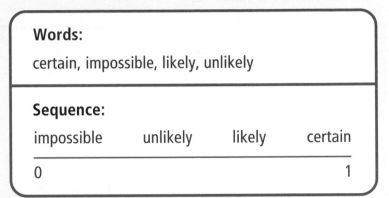

Words:

certain, impossible, likely, unlikely

Sequence:

| impossible | unlikely | likely | certain |

0   1

15 Many answers are possible. One example is given.

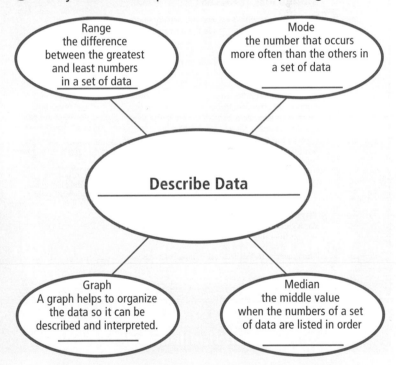

Range
the difference between the greatest and least numbers in a set of data

Mode
the number that occurs more often than the others in a set of data

Describe Data

Graph
A graph helps to organize the data so it can be described and interpreted.

Median
the middle value when the numbers of a set of data are listed in order

Games

These games can be found in the *Student Handbook* on pp. 172–173. *Attribute Memory* in **Lesson 10.1** provides an opportunity for students to practice identifying common attributes. *Attribute Card Forecast* in **Lesson 10.3** provides an opportunity for students to practice calculating simple probabilities.

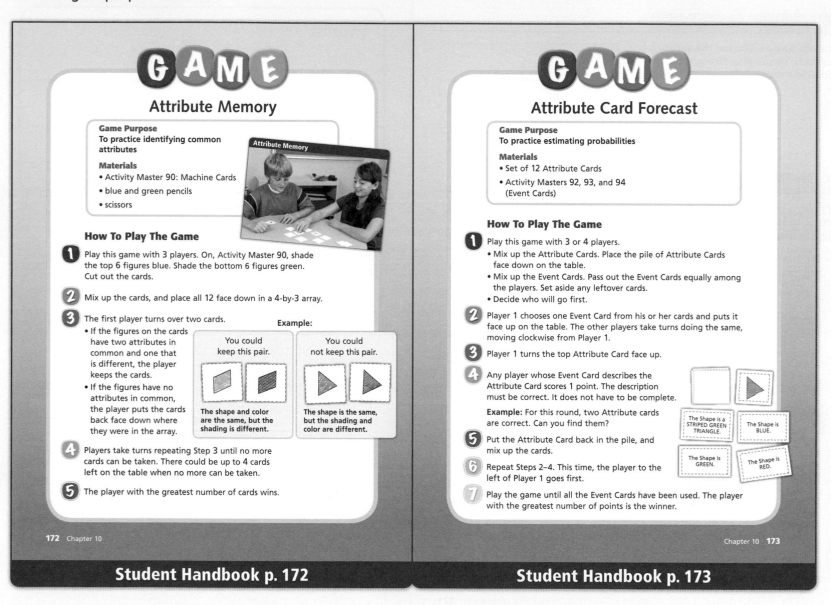

GAME

Attribute Memory

Game Purpose
To practice identifying common attributes

Materials
• Activity Master 90: Machine Cards
• blue and green pencils
• scissors

How To Play The Game

1 Play this game with 3 players. On, Activity Master 90, shade the top 6 figures blue. Shade the bottom 6 figures green. Cut out the cards.

2 Mix up the cards, and place all 12 face down in a 4-by-3 array.

3 The first player turns over two cards.
• If the figures on the cards have two attributes in common and one that is different, the player keeps the cards.
• If the figures have no attributes in common, the player puts the cards back face down where they were in the array.

Example:

You could keep this pair.	You could not keep this pair.
The shape and color are the same, but the shading is different.	The shape is the same, but the shading and color are different.

4 Players take turns repeating Step 3 until no more cards can be taken. There could be up to 4 cards left on the table when no more can be taken.

5 The player with the greatest number of cards wins.

172 Chapter 10

Student Handbook p. 172

GAME

Attribute Card Forecast

Game Purpose
To practice estimating probabilities

Materials
• Set of 12 Attribute Cards
• Activity Masters 92, 93, and 94 (Event Cards)

How To Play The Game

1 Play this game with 3 or 4 players.
• Mix up the Attribute Cards. Place the pile of Attribute Cards face down on the table.
• Mix up the Event Cards. Pass out the Event Cards equally among the players. Set aside any leftover cards.
• Decide who will go first.

2 Player 1 chooses one Event Card from his or her cards and puts it face up on the table. The other players take turns doing the same, moving clockwise from Player 1.

3 Player 1 turns the top Attribute Card face up.

4 Any player whose Event Card describes the Attribute Card scores 1 point. The description must be correct. It does not have to be complete.

Example: For this round, two Attribute cards are correct. Can you find them?

The Shape is a STRIPED GREEN TRIANGLE.	The Shape is BLUE.
The Shape is GREEN.	The Shape is RED.

5 Put the Attribute Card back in the pile, and mix up the cards.

6 Repeat Steps 2–4. This time, the player to the left of Player 1 goes first.

7 Play the game until all the Event Cards have been used. The player with the greatest number of points is the winner.

Chapter 10 173

Student Handbook p. 173

Challenge

This activity challenges students to play games and then use what they know about probability to decide whether each is a fair game. This activity can be found on p. 174 of the *Student Handbook.*

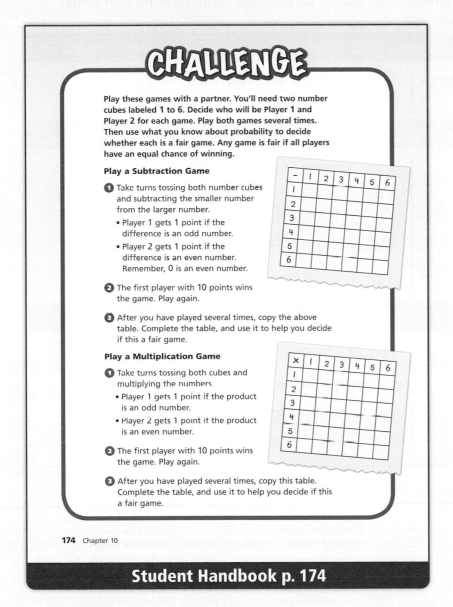

Student Handbook p. 174

Subtraction Game: The game is fair. There are 36 possible outcomes, as shown in the tables below. Each player wins on 18 out of the 36; $\frac{18}{36} = \frac{1}{2}$, so each player has an equal chance of winning.

−	1	2	3	4	5	6
1	0	1	2	3	4	5
2	1	0	1	2	3	4
3	2	1	0	1	2	3
4	3	2	1	0	1	2
5	4	3	2	1	0	1
6	5	4	3	2	1	0

or

−	1	2	3	4	5	6
1	E	O	E	O	E	O
2	O	E	O	E	O	E
3	E	O	E	O	E	O
4	O	E	O	E	O	E
5	E	O	E	O	E	O
6	O	E	O	E	O	E

Multiplication Game: The game is not fair. There are 36 possible outcomes, as shown in the tables below. The player with even products has 27 out of 36 ways of winning; the player with odd products has 9 out of 36 ways. So, the probability of an even product is $\frac{27}{36}$, or $\frac{3}{4}$; the probability of an odd product is $\frac{9}{36}$, or $\frac{1}{4}$.

×	1	2	3	4	5	6
1	1	2	3	4	5	6
2	2	4	6	8	10	12
3	3	6	9	12	15	18
4	4	8	12	16	20	24
5	5	10	15	20	25	30
6	6	12	18	24	30	36

or

×	1	2	3	4	5	6
1	O	E	O	E	O	E
2	E	E	E	E	E	E
3	O	E	O	E	O	E
4	E	E	E	E	E	E
5	O	E	O	E	O	E
6	E	E	E	E	E	E

Lesson 1 Finding Combinations of Attributes

NCTM Standards 1, 2, 6, 7, 8, 9, 10

Lesson Planner

STUDENT OBJECTIVES
- To find combinations of attributes
- To determine the portion of all possible combinations that match a given description

1 | Daily Activities (TG p. 795)

Open-Ended Problem Solving/Headline Story	Skills Practice and Review— Finding Fractions That Add to 1

2 | Teach and Practice (TG pp. 796–800)

	MATERIALS
Ⓐ **Introducing Probability** (TG pp. 796–797)	• TR: Activity Masters, AM89–AM91
Ⓑ **Creating Attribute Cards** (TG p. 798)	• blue pencils, green pencils, scissors
Ⓒ **Playing *Attribute Memory*** (TG p. 799)	• 📖 LAB pp. 197–198
Ⓓ **Finding Combinations of Attributes** (TG p. 800)	• 📖 SH pp. 159, 172

3 | Differentiated Instruction (TG p. 801)

Leveled Problem Solving (TG p. 801)	Practice Book P81
Intervention Activity (TG p. 801)	Extension Book E81
Extension Activity (TG p. 801)	Spiral Review Book SR81
Social Studies Connection (TG p. 792)	

Lesson Notes

About the Lesson

In this lesson, students make a deck of cards that vary according to three attributes: shape, color, and shading. They will use the deck to explore probability in subsequent lessons. To prepare for these explorations, students find cards that match a given description.

About the Mathematics

There are several ways for students to use their cards to find combinations of attributes. One is to make a systematic list of shapes, changing one attribute on each card to get the next related card:

Solid blue parallelogram	⇨	Striped blue parallelogram
Solid blue trapezoid	⇨	Striped blue trapezoid
Solid blue triangle	CHANGE THE SHADING	Striped blue triangle
⬇ CHANGE THE COLOR		⬇ CHANGE THE COLOR
Solid green parallelogram	⇨	Striped green parallelogram
Solid green trapezoid	⇨	Striped green trapezoid
Solid green triangle	CHANGE THE SHADING	Striped green triangle

A second way is to draw a tree diagram:

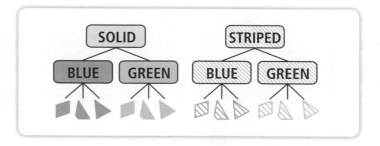

Use with Lesson Activity Book pp. 197–198.

Developing Mathematical Language

Vocabulary: attribute

An *attribute* is a quality or feature of someone or something. To clarify the meaning of *attribute,* ask students to use one word to describe objects that you name or show. Each word is an *attribute.* Examples, with possible *attributes:* penny (round, copper, lightweight); piece of paper (rectangular, white, thin); basketball (hollow, spherical, bouncy)

Familiarize students with the term *attribute.*

Beginning Show any object and describe it to the students. Then repeat the description using the word *attribute.* For example, "This pen is red, thin, and long. These are all *attributes* of the pen." Have students do the same for other objects.

Intermediate Display several geometric figures such as a square, a rectangle, and a trapezoid. For each figure, make a list on the board of its *attributes.* Ask students to match the figure to the list of its *attributes* and to describe the figure using the *attributes.*

Advanced Display several geometric figures such as a square, a rectangle, and a trapezoid. Ask students to choose one of them and make a list of the figure's *attributes.* Have volunteers read their lists to the class, and have others match each list to the correct figure.

---

1 Daily Activities

Open-Ended Problem Solving

Read the Headline Story to the students. Encourage them to make an organized list to keep track of the combinations and think of inventive problems that can be solved using information from the story.

 Headline Story

What can you say about the number of sundaes you could make with the following ingredients?

ICE CREAM	SAUCE	TOPPING
Chocolate	Hot Fudge	Strawberries
Vanilla	Caramel	Nuts
		Chocolate Chips

Choose one of each.

Possible response: For each choice of ice cream you could make 6 different sundaes: 3 with hot fudge and 3 with caramel sauce. Since there are 2 types of ice cream, you could make $2 \times 6 = 12$ different sundaes.

Skills Practice and Review

Finding Fractions That Add to 1

Write the following number sentence on the board. Ask students to name numbers that could go in the triangle and the square:

$$\triangle + \square = 1$$

If students say $1 + 0$, ask for other numbers that would make the sentence true.

Record pairs of fractions on the board as students name them. Accept all correct fraction combinations. For example, if the triangle is $\frac{1}{4}$, then both $\frac{3}{4}$ and $\frac{6}{8}$ are correct values for the square.

If students have difficulty finding fractions, ask questions like, "If the triangle is $\frac{1}{8}$, what is the square?" $\frac{7}{8}$
Repeat with other fractions less than 1.

individuals or whole class · 10 MIN

Materials
- For the teacher: AM89 transparency (optional)

NCTM Standards 1, 2, 6, 7, 8, 9, 10

A Introducing Probability

Purpose To introduce probability

Introduce The Student Letter introduces students to key concepts of probability. Have students read the letter individually or together as a class.

Task The Student Letter asks several questions about tossing a coin. Then it describes a machine that prints cards with figures on them. This machine has three sets of knobs: color, shape, and shading. Ask students to discuss the questions in the letter with a partner.

- If you toss a coin, how likely is it that the coin will come up heads? Possible answer: It is equally likely that the coin will come up heads and that it will come up tails.

- If you toss a coin 10 times in a row, about how many times would you expect to get heads? Possible answer: about 5 times

- Could you get 10 heads in a row? Would it surprise you if that happened? Possible answer: You could get 10 heads in a row but it's not likely, and I would be very surprised if it happened.

Chapter

10 Data and Probability

Dear Student,

If you toss a coin, how likely is it that the coin will come up heads? If you toss a coin 10 times in a row, about how many times would you expect to get heads? Could you get 10 heads in a row? Would it surprise you if that happened?

These are all questions about probability: how likely it is that some particular thing will happen.

Imagine a machine that prints out cards with figures on them. There are three possible figures: a parallelogram, a trapezoid, and a triangle. The figures can be either blue or green, and either striped or solid-colored. You can set each of the levers separately to pick the color, shape, and pattern that the machine will print on a card. In this picture, the machine has been set to print a solid blue trapezoid.

How many different combinations of color, shape, and pattern do you think the machine can make? How many of those combinations would be blue figures?

If you set the switches without looking, how likely is it that the machine will print a blue figure? You'll be talking about questions like this as you learn about probability.

Mathematically yours,
The authors of *Think Math!*

159

Student Handbook p. 159

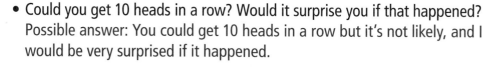

✔ Ongoing Assessment

- Do students recognize triangles, trapezoids, and parallelograms when presented in different orientations?

Share To facilitate discussion about the card deck, ask students to name the specific figures shown on the machine. parallelogram, trapezoid, triangle The diagrams on the machine show non-standard orientations of the three figures, in order to give students more practice in identifying geometric figures.

Use with Lesson Activity Book pp. 197–198.

You may find it convenient to sketch a picture of the machine on the board or to use a transparency of Activity Master: Unusual Machine. Refer to the figure as you talk with the class. Choose a setting for the machine. Then sketch the card that the machine would print. Be sure students can identify all three attributes of the card. For example, the card shown beside the machine in the Student Letter is blue, it is a trapezoid, and it has solid shading.

Finally, pose this question to the class: "How many different cards can the machine make?" Students may think that you are asking how many cards can be made with the machine on a single setting, in which case the answer would be one card. Encourage students to think about *all* possible settings on the machine. Record students' hypotheses on the board so that they may check them after the next activity.

Unusual Machine
BLUE · GREEN · SOLID · STRIPED

Activity Master 89

💬 Talk Math

❷ If you had a deck of all the different cards the machine could make, would the number of blue cards and the number of green cards be the same or different? Explain your reasoning. the same; Possible explanation: There are only two colors, so half of the cards will be green and half will be blue.

❷ If you had a deck of all the different cards the machine could make, would the number of blue cards and the number of trapezoids be the same or different? Explain your reasoning. different; Possible explanation: One-half of the cards would be blue, but only one-third of them would be trapezoids.

Differentiated Instruction

Basic Level For students having difficulty distinguishing among the three figures, cut out and label models of the figures from cardboard:

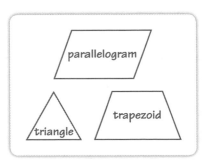
parallelogram
triangle
trapezoid

Show the figures one at a time, in various orientations, first with the labels showing, then with the figures turned upside-down. Have students name the figures as you display them.

B Creating Attribute Cards

Materials
- For each student: AM91 (two copies), blue pencil, green pencil, scissors

NCTM Standards 1, 2, 6, 7, 8, 9, 10

Purpose To find all combinations of three attributes

Introduce Have students cut cards from two copies of Activity Master: Blank Cards. The cards from one copy of the page are exactly enough for one student or group, but give each student or working group two copies, so that students must figure out how many cards to use.

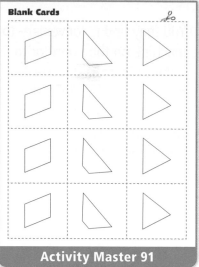

Blank Cards

Activity Master 91

Task Have each student use blue and green pencils to make all possible cards the machine can produce. Ask students to compare the number of cards they made with their hypotheses from the previous activity.

Share When students have created their cards, discuss strategies they used to make sure they had a complete deck. Make sure students see the benefit of being systematic. For example:

    blue *solid* parallelogram

    blue *striped* parallelogram

    blue *solid* trapezoid

    blue *striped* trapezoid

    blue *solid* triangle

    blue *striped* triangle

    . . . and so on.

Students will use their cards in this and subsequent lessons, so be sure all students have the same cards. Make sure the class agrees that the machine can make 12 different cards.

💬 Talk Math

❷ If the machine also had a "red" setting, how many red triangles could it make? Explain your reasoning. 2; Possible explanation: It could make a red solid triangle and a red striped triangle.

❷ If the machine also had a "red" setting, how many striped parallelograms could it make? Explain your reasoning. 3; Possible explanation: It could make a blue striped parallelogram, a green striped parallelogram, and a red striped parallelogram.

Purpose To practice identifying common attributes

Goal The object of this game, *Attribute Memory,* is for players to recognize when two figures differ by exactly one attribute, and to remember where the cards showing those figures are on the table. The winner is the player with the most cards when no more cards can be taken.

Prepare Materials Each group should have a set of 12 attribute cards from Activity B. Make sure they have a complete set of all 12 figures. (As an alternative, you may wish to have them color and cut out cards from Activity Master: Machine Cards.)

How to Play

1 Players place all 12 attribute cards face down in a 4-by-3 array.

2 One player turns over two cards. If the cards have two attributes in common, the player takes both cards. If the player cannot take the cards, the player turns the cards over and replaces them where they were picked up.

3 All players take turns repeating Step 2 until no more pairs can be taken. (Up to 4 cards may be left.) The player with the most cards wins.

When demonstrating the game, show examples of pairs of cards students might draw. The following are pairs that a player could keep:

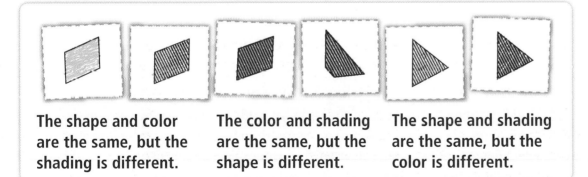

The shape and color are the same, but the shading is different.

The color and shading are the same, but the shape is different.

The shape and shading are the same, but the color is different.

These are pairs that a player could not keep:

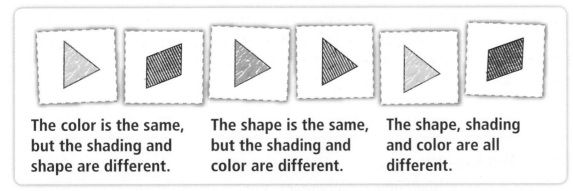

The color is the same, but the shading and shape are different.

The shape is the same, but the shading and color are different.

The shape, shading and color are all different.

Remind students that they are looking for cards with two attributes in common. Point out that two cards cannot have three attributes in common, because such cards would have to be identical.

Materials
• For each group: Attribute cards from Activity B; AM 90 (optional)

NCTM Standards 1, 2, 6, 7, 8, 9, 10

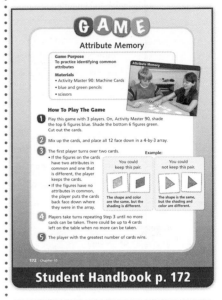

Student Handbook p. 172

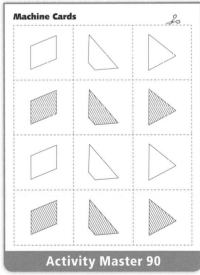

Activity Master 90

✓ Ongoing Assessment

• Do students identify triangles, trapezoids, and parallelograms, regardless of the orientations of the figures?

• Do students identify attributes of a figure?

• Do students consider two attributes together?

Purpose To identify cards with given attributes

NCTM Standards 1, 2, 6, 7, 8, 9, 10

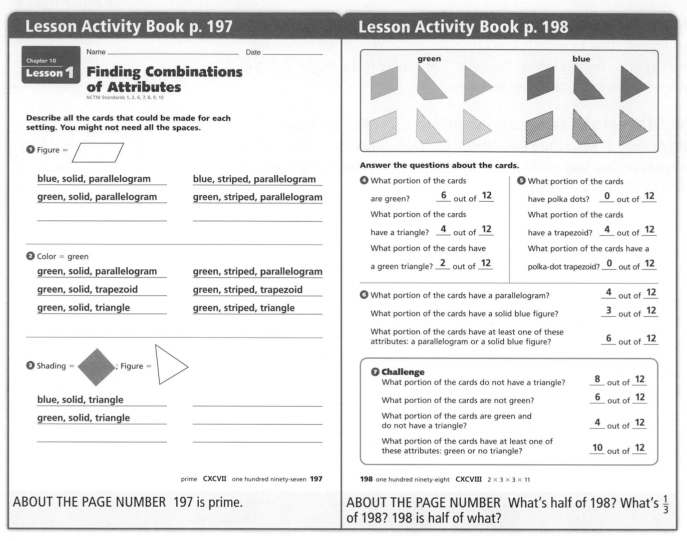

Teaching Notes for LAB page 197

Have students complete the page individually or with partners. Of the three problems on the page, Problem 2 leads to the greatest number of possibilities, because 3 different figures and 2 different colors are used to vary the combinations. Problem 3 leads to the fewest number of possibilities because two attributes are fixed. For all three problems, there is space for students to describe the cards in words, but they may draw pictures of the figures if they wish.

Teaching Notes for LAB page 198

In the next lesson, students will express probabilities as fractions. You may wish to have students write fractions that are equivalent to their answers on this page.

Challenge Problems In these problems, students must look for cards that do *not* carry a particular attribute. Some students may simply count to find the number of cards that carry the attribute. Others may notice that they can find the answer by subtracting from 12 the number of cards that *do* carry the attribute.

Reflect and Summarize the Lesson

Write Math

If the machine made cards in 3 colors, blue, green, and orange, how many different cards could it make? Use pictures, numbers, or words, and explain how you found your answer. 18; Possible explanation: I reasoned that since there are 6 blue cards and 6 green cards, there would be 6 orange cards; 6 + 6 + 6 = 18.

Leveled Problem Solving

Jason has 7 lunch picture cards. There is a glass of orange juice, a bottle of water, a carton of milk, a tuna sandwich, a cheese sandwich, and two types of fruit. A meal is a drink, a sandwich, and a fruit.

❶ **Basic Level**
How many meals will have a tuna sandwich and a glass of orange juice? Explain. 2 meals; one meal with each type of fruit

❷ **On Level**
How many different meals will have a tuna sandwich, a drink, and a fruit? Explain. 6 meals; 3 meals with a drink and 2 meals with a fruit; $3 \times 2 = 6$

❸ **Above Level**
How many different meals can Jason make if a meal has a drink, a sandwich, and a fruit? Explain. 12 meals; 4 meals with each drink; $3 \times 4 = 12$

Intervention	Practice	Extension

Intervention

Activity What's Missing?

Display a collection of about 5 plastic cups, using ones with different attributes, including size, material, and design. With students not looking, remove one of the cups. Ask students to describe it, naming it by its attributes. Repeat several times, having students practice naming objects using as many attributes as needed to identify it.

Practice

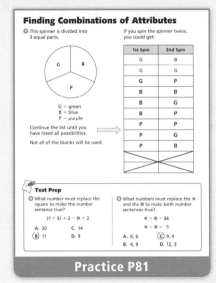

Practice P81

Extension

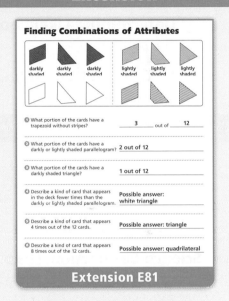

Extension E81

Spiral Review

Spiral Review Book page SR81 provides review of the following previously learned skills and concepts:

- locating numbers expressed as decimals on the number line
- solving problems using the strategy *work backward*

You may wish to have students work with a partner to complete the page.

Spiral Review SR81

Extension Activity
Attribute Match Game

Display the 12 attribute cards face up on the table.

Challenge pairs of students to play the following game. The first student chooses any card. The other chooses a card that differs from the first by exactly one attribute and stacks it on top of the first. Play continues until all cards are used or it is impossible to make another move.

Lesson 2 Describing the Likelihood of an Event

NCTM Standards 1, 2, 6, 7, 8, 9, 10

Lesson Planner

STUDENT OBJECTIVES
- To describe the likelihood of an event as *impossible, unlikely, likely,* or *certain*
- To relate a fraction of items with given attributes to the likelihood of choosing an item with those attributes

1 Daily Activities (TG p. 803)

Open-Ended Problem Solving/Headline Story	Skills Practice and Review— Finding Fractions That Add to 1

2 Teach and Practice (TG pp. 804–807)

	MATERIALS
(A) **Exploring Likelihood** (TG pp. 804–805)	• Set of 12 attribute cards from Lesson 10.1
(B) **Determining Likelihood More Precisely** (TG p. 806)	• 📖 LAB pp. 199–200
(C) **Describing the Likelihood of an Event** (TG p. 807)	• 📖 SH p. 162

3 Differentiated Instruction (TG p. 808)

Leveled Problem Solving (TG p. 808)	**Practice Book P82**
Intervention Activity (TG p. 808)	**Extension Book E82**
Extension Activity (TG p. 808)	**Spiral Review Book SR82**
Science Connection (TG p. 792)	

Lesson Notes

About the Lesson

Students use the cards created in **Lesson 10.1** to predict the likelihood of drawing cards with particular attributes. They use the words *impossible, unlikely, likely,* and *certain* to describe the likelihood of these events. This work prepares students to express probabilities as fractions in **Lesson 10.3.**

About the Mathematics

If you toss a coin, there are two possible events, heads or tails. There is 1 chance in 2 that you will toss heads, so the probability of tossing heads is $\frac{1}{2}$. Saying that the probability is $\frac{1}{2}$ is a way of saying that if you tossed a coin many times, you would expect

to get heads about half of those times. (In **Lessons 10.4–10.5,** students will investigate this phenomenon by performing experiments to test the frequencies of particular events.)

When drawing cards, we assume that no card has a greater likelihood of being drawn than any other. So, when we say that the likelihood of drawing a trapezoid from a deck of attribute cards is 4 out of 12, we mean that out of 12 equally likely events, 4 will give the result we're looking for, a trapezoid. Thus, the probability of drawing a trapezoid is 4 chances out of 12, or $\frac{1}{3}$.

Developing Mathematical Language

Vocabulary: certain, likely, unlikely, impossible

In this lesson, students use the terms *certain*, *likely*, *unlikely*, and *impossible* to describe likelihoods of events. While *certain* and *impossible* have precise mathematical definitions (a *certain* event has a probability of 1, an *impossible* event has a probability of 0), *likely* and *unlikely* do not; they describe events generally, not mathematically. The class will need to agree on meanings for these terms. One useful approach is to apply *likely* to an event that is more likely than not to happen; that is, an event with a probability greater than $\frac{1}{2}$.

Familiarize students with the terms *certain*, *likely*, *unlikely*, and *impossible*.

Beginning Describe some simple, nonmathematical events for the class. For one event, say whether the event is *certain*, *likely*, *unlikely*, or *impossible* to happen. Ask students to tell whether the other events are *certain*, *likely*, *unlikely* or *impossible*.

Intermediate Ask volunteers to name a nonmathematical event that they believe is *certain* to occur. Repeat with *likely*, *unlikely* and *impossible* events.

Advanced Have students make a 4-column table, using each term as a heading for a column. Ask students to write a simple event for each column, and then have partners compare their tables.

Open-Ended Problem Solving

Read the Headline Story to the students. Encourage them to think of interesting ways to answer the question.

 Headline Story

Andrew tossed a number cube twice and then found the sum of the two numbers he tossed. What can you say about the sum?

Possible responses: The sum must have been at least 2. He could have gotten 2 only by tossing 1 twice. The sum could not have been greater than 12. He could have gotten 12 only by tossing 6 twice. There are 4 different ways he could have gotten a sum of 5: tossing 1 and 4, 2 and 3, 3 and 2, or 4 and 1.

Skills Practice and Review

Finding Fractions That Add to 1

Repeat this activity from **Lesson 10.1.** Write the following number sentence on the board. Ask students to name numbers that could go in the triangle and the square:

$$\triangle + \square = 1$$

If students say $1 + 0$, ask for other numbers that would make the sentence true.

Record pairs of fractions on the board as students name them. Accept all correct fraction combinations. For example, if the triangle is $\frac{1}{4}$, then both $\frac{3}{4}$ and $\frac{6}{8}$ are correct values for the square.

If students have difficulty finding fractions, ask questions like, "If the triangle is $\frac{1}{8}$, what is the square?" $\frac{7}{8}$ Repeat with other fractions less than 1.

individuals, small groups,
or whole class

20 MIN

Materials

- For each student: set of 12 attribute cards from Lesson 10.1

NCTM Standards 1, 2, 6, 7, 8, 9, 10

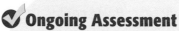

Ongoing Assessment

- Do students identify and distinguish among parallelograms, trapezoids, and triangles?

(A) Exploring Likelihood

Purpose To explore the likelihoods of drawing cards with given attributes

Introduce Have students work independently on Explore: How Likely Is It? Explain that they will be judging the likelihoods of choosing particular cards from their decks of attribute cards, assuming that they choose randomly. Point out that choosing *randomly* means to choose with no knowledge of the card they are choosing, as though they were blindfolded.

Task Direct students to the following questions, which appear on Explore: How Likely Is It? Encourage students to refer to their decks of attribute cards to help them answer the questions. Did students have systematic ways to find all the possible combinations of shapes for question 1? How did they make decisions about whether it was *certain, likely,*

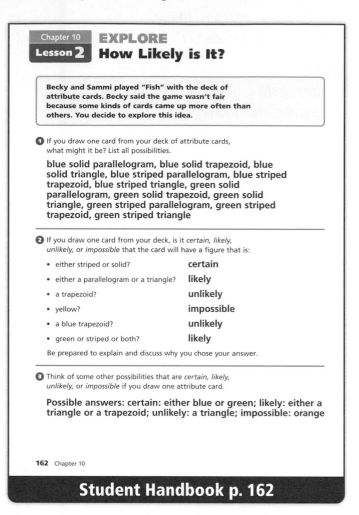

Student Handbook p. 162

unlikely, and *impossible* to draw a particular kind of card from the attribute card deck?

❶ If you draw one card from your deck of attribute cards, what might it be? List all the possibilities. It could be any of the 12 cards in the deck

❷ If you draw one card from your deck, is it certain, likely, unlikely, or impossible that the card will have a shape that is:

- either striped or solid? certain, because every card is either striped or solid
- either a parallelogram or a triangle? likely, because more than half the cards (8 out of 12) are either parallelograms or triangles
- a trapezoid? unlikely, because less than half the cards (4 out of 12) are trapezoids
- yellow? impossible, because no cards are yellow

- a blue trapezoid? unlikely, because less than half the cards (2 out of 12) are blue trapezoids
- green or striped or both? likely, because more than half the cards (9 out of 12) are green or striped or both

❸ Think of some other possibilities that are certain, likely, unlikely, or impossible if you draw one attribute card. Possible answers: certain: either blue or green; likely: either blue or a triangle; unlikely: a parallelogram; impossible: a circle

Share Reconvene the class to discuss the meanings of the terms *certain, likely, unlikely,* and *impossible. Certain* and *impossible* are easy to define. An event is certain if it must always happen. An event is impossible if it can never happen. *Likely* and *unlikely* don't have such obvious meanings, and there is no mathematical definition of either. If students aren't sure whether to call an event *likely* or *unlikely,* ask them to think about whether the event is more likely than not to happen. This suggests that it makes sense to classify events that occur more than half the time as *likely,* and events that occur less than half the time as *unlikely.*

Practice **You draw a card from your deck of attribute cards. Classify the given event as *certain, likely, unlikely, or impossible:***

- checkered impossible
- a triangle unlikely
- a parallelogram, a trapezoid, or a triangle certain
- either green or a parallelogram likely

💬 **Talk Math**

❓ Jessica tossed a penny 10 times. Give an example of each of the following, and explain your reasoning for each:

- a certain event a head or a tail on every toss; Possible explanation: Only heads or tails are possible.
- a likely event at least 1 head; Possible explanation: Heads and tails are equally likely, so you would expect to get around 5 heads. Getting at least 1 head, then, seems likely.
- an unlikely event 10 heads; Possible explanation: Heads and tails are equally likely, so you would expect to get around 5 heads. Getting more than 5 heads, then, seems unlikely.
- an impossible event 11 heads; Possible explanation: Since she tossed the coin 10 times, there must be exactly 10 events.

Teacher Story

❝I introduced 'likelihood' in a more interactive way than that described in the lesson. I wrote examples on the board but omitted the key words *certain, likely, unlikely,* and *impossible.* Students had to choose the word for each example that made each sentence true for our deck of cards. For example, students matched 'unlikely' with 'It is _____ that I will pick a card with a triangle on it.' I then made other statements using the new terms, and asked my students to decide whether the statements were true or not. For example, my students decided that the statement, 'It is likely that I will draw a red card' was incorrect for our deck. In fact, it would be impossible to draw a red card. To wrap up, I started a sentence using one of the terms and asked students to finish it. An example was: 'It is certain that . . . I will draw a card that is either blue or green.'❞

B Determining Likelihood More Precisely

Materials
- For each student: set of 12 attribute cards from Lesson 10.1

NCTM Standards 1, 2, 6, 7, 8, 9, 10

✓ **Ongoing Assessment**
- Do students write simple fractions in simplest form?
- Do students reason that "4 out of 12" is equivalent to "1 out of 3"?

Possible Discussion

Students may think that an event is *likely* if it happens nearly all the time, and *unlikely* if it almost never happens. But they may not be sure what to call an event that happens some of the time. By suggesting that an event is likely if it happens more often than not, you can help students understand likelihood as something that can have a number associated with it, and some events as more likely than others.

In later lessons, students will begin comparing likelihoods by describing events as more likely or less likely. For example, if one event occurs $\frac{1}{12}$ of the time, and another occurs $\frac{3}{12}$ of the time, then neither event is likely, but the second is *more* likely than the first. If three events each occur $\frac{1}{3}$ of the time, we say that all three are *equally* likely.

Purpose To explore how likelihood can be stated numerically

Introduce Explain that so far, students have been classifying events that are possible but not certain as *likely* or *unlikely.* Both of these are very general terms. Explain that in this activity, students will explore a method they can use to classify likely and unlikely events more precisely.

Problem Ask students how likely it is that, in one draw, they would draw a triangle card from their deck of attribute cards. If they say "unlikely," ask them to be more precise: "But how unlikely?"

Prompt students by asking if they would draw a triangle more or less than half the time. Students should be comfortable saying that drawing a triangle is unlikely but not impossible: it should happen less than half the time. To explain why, students might say that less than half the cards have triangles on them.

Now ask: **Can you predict how often you should expect to draw a triangle?**

Students should be able to reason that since 4 out of the 12 cards show a triangle, they have 4 chances out of 12 to draw a triangle. So, they should expect to draw a triangle about $\frac{4}{12}$, or $\frac{1}{3}$, of the time.

They might also reason that since the cards show three shapes, with equal numbers of each, students could expect to draw a triangle (and each of the other two shapes) about a third of the time.

In **Lesson 10.3,** students will work more extensively with expressing probabilities as fractions, so it is not necessary for them to spend too much time with this idea now. However, students should understand that they can figure out the likelihood of drawing a particular kind of card by determining the fractional portion of the deck that matches the description.

💬 **Talk Math**

❷ How often should you expect to get a blue card if you draw a card from the deck? Explain your reasoning. 6 times out of 12, or $\frac{1}{2}$ of the time; Possible explanation: 6 out of 12 cards are blue.

❷ A number cube is numbered 1–6. If you toss the cube, how often should you expect to toss a 1 or a 2? Explain your reasoning. 2 times out of 6, or $\frac{1}{3}$ of the time; Possible explanation: 2 out of the 6 possible events are either 1 or 2.

Purpose To practice assessing the likelihood of an event

NCTM Standards 1, 2, 6, 7, 8, 9, 10

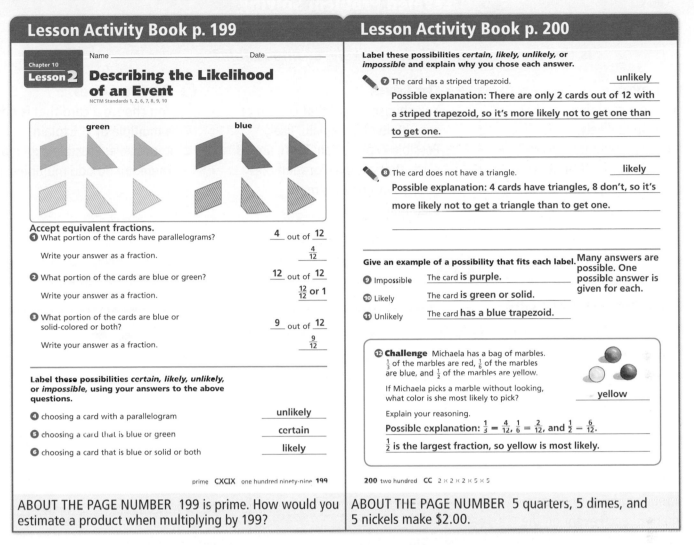

Lesson Activity Book p. 199

Chapter 10
Lesson 2 **Describing the Likelihood of an Event**
NCTM Standards 1, 2, 6, 7, 8, 9, 10

green   blue

Accept equivalent fractions.
❶ What portion of the cards have parallelograms? ___**4**___ out of ___**12**___

Write your answer as a fraction. $\frac{4}{12}$

❷ What portion of the cards are blue or green? ___**12**___ out of ___**12**___

Write your answer as a fraction. $\frac{12}{12}$ or 1

❸ What portion of the cards are blue or solid-colored or both? ___**9**___ out of ___**12**___

Write your answer as a fraction. $\frac{9}{12}$

Label these possibilities *certain, likely, unlikely,* **or** *impossible,* **using your answers to the above questions.**
❹ choosing a card with a parallelogram — unlikely
❺ choosing a card that is blue or green — certain
❻ choosing a card that is blue or solid or both — likely

prime **CXCIX** one hundred ninety-nine **199**

Lesson Activity Book p. 200

Label these possibilities *certain, likely, unlikely,* **or** *impossible* **and explain why you chose each answer.**
❼ The card has a striped trapezoid. — unlikely

Possible explanation: There are only 2 cards out of 12 with a striped trapezoid, so it's more likely not to get one than to get one.

❽ The card does not have a triangle. — likely

Possible explanation: 4 cards have triangles, 8 don't, so it's more likely not to get a triangle than to get one.

Give an example of a possibility that fits each label.
❾ Impossible — The card **is purple.**
❿ Likely — The card **is green or solid.**
⓫ Unlikely — The card **has a blue trapezoid.**

Many answers are possible. One possible answer is given for each.

⓬ **Challenge** Michaela has a bag of marbles. $\frac{1}{3}$ of the marbles are red, $\frac{1}{6}$ of the marbles are blue, and $\frac{1}{2}$ of the marbles are yellow.

If Michaela picks a marble without looking, what color is she most likely to pick? — yellow

Explain your reasoning.
Possible explanation: $\frac{1}{3} = \frac{4}{12}$, $\frac{1}{6} = \frac{2}{12}$, and $\frac{1}{2} = \frac{6}{12}$.
$\frac{1}{2}$ is the largest fraction, so yellow is most likely.

200 two hundred **CC** 2 × 2 × 2 × 5 × 5

ABOUT THE PAGE NUMBER 199 is prime. How would you estimate a product when multiplying by 199?

ABOUT THE PAGE NUMBER 5 quarters, 5 dimes, and 5 nickels make $2.00.

Teaching Notes for LAB page 199

Have students complete the page individually or with partners. Problems 1–3 review fractions and prepare students for writing probabilities in fractional notation. Accept equivalent fractions as well as $\frac{12}{12}$ and $\frac{0}{12}$ for 1 and 0 respectively.

Some students may recognize that they can use their answers to Problems 1–3 to help find the answers to Problems 4–6.

Teaching Notes for LAB page 200

Challenge Problem Students may recognize that they can answer the question by deciding which of the three fractions is largest. They could reason that for the fraction $\frac{1}{6}$, the whole is divided into 6 parts. For the fraction $\frac{1}{3}$, the whole is divided into 3 parts. For the fraction $\frac{1}{2}$, the whole is divided into just 2 parts. Each of the 2 parts must be bigger than each of the 3 parts and each of the 6 parts. So, $\frac{1}{2}$ is largest, and the most likely color is yellow.

Reflect and Summarize the Lesson

 Write Math

You choose a card from your deck of attribute cards. Give an example of a card that you would be *likely* **to choose and one that you would be** *unlikely* **to choose. Explain.** Possible answer: likely: a card that is green or a trapezoid; unlikely: a triangle; possible explanations: More than half (8 out of 12) of the cards show green or a trapezoid. Less than half (4 out of 12) show a triangle.

Leveled Problem Solving

You randomly choose a card from a deck of cards numbered 1–20.
Is the event *certain*, *likely*, *unlikely*, or *impossible*?

❶ Basic Level

You choose a card that is a 1, 2, or 3. Explain. unlikely; Possible explanation: There are only 3 cards out of 20 that are 1, 2, or 3.

❷ On Level

You choose a card that is even or a multiple of 3. Explain. likely; Possible explanation: There are 13 cards that are even or multiples of 3; 13 out of 20 is more than half.

❸ Above Level

You choose a card that is odd and a multiple of 2. Explain. impossible; Possible explanation: There are no odd multiples of 2.

Intervention	Practice	Extension

Activity Using a Number Line

Draw a segment on the board. Label the ends *impossible* and *certain.* Mark the halfway point on the line. Write *unlikely* below the left half of the line and *likely* below the right half.

Present students with various events. Ask students to place a dot where they think the probability of the event lies. Encourage students to discuss the placement of each event on the number line.

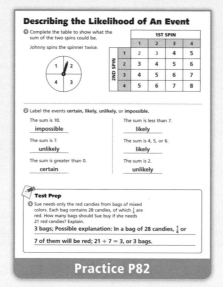

Practice P82

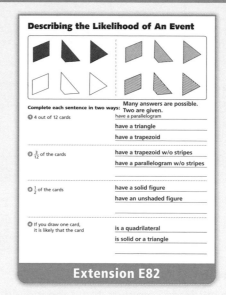

Extension E82

Spiral Review

Spiral Review Book page SR82 provides review of the following previously learned skills and concepts:

• finding the area of complex shapes by breaking them down into pieces of known area

• identifying and extending a rule using tables

You may wish to have students work with a partner to complete the page.

Spiral Review SR82

Extension Activity
Likely or Unlikely Fractions

Draw a two-column table on the board with *Likely* and *Unlikely* as headings. Display various fractions, and ask students to place each in the column that describes the likelihood of an event with that probability. Discuss the attributes of the fractions in each column. The dividing line should be $\frac{1}{2}$; fractions with a probability of less than $\frac{1}{2}$ can be described as "unlikely", and those with a probability of greater than $\frac{1}{2}$ can be described as "likely."

Teacher's Notes 🍎

Daily Notes . . .

Quick Notes

More Ideas

Lesson 3 Introducing Probability

NCTM Standards 1, 2, 6, 7, 8, 9, 10

Lesson Planner

STUDENT OBJECTIVES ·
- To express probability as a fraction
- To compare the probabilities of events

1 | Daily Activities (TG p. 811)

Open-Ended Problem Solving/Headline Story	Skills Practice and Review— Comparing Fractions to $\frac{1}{2}$

2 | Teach and Practice (TG pp. 812–816)

MATERIALS

(A) **Expressing and Comparing Likelihoods Using Fractions** (TG pp. 812–813)

(B) **Playing a Game: Attribute Card Forecast** (TG p. 814)

(C) **Introducing Probability** (TG p. 815)

- Set of 12 attribute cards from Lesson 10.1
- TR: Activity Masters, AM92–AM94
- 📖 LAB pp. 201–202
- 📖 SH pp. 163, 173

3 | Differentiated Instruction (TG p. 817)

Leveled Problem Solving (TG p. 817)	Practice Book P83
Intervention Activity (TG p. 817)	Extension Book E83
Extension Activity (TG p. 817)	Spiral Review Book SR83
Literature Connection (TG p. 792)	

Lesson Notes

About the Lesson

In **Lesson 10.2**, students used informal language to talk about the likelihoods of various events. In this lesson, they learn to express likelihood mathematically, using probability. Probability, being a number, allows for easier comparisons of the likelihoods of events than is possible with words alone.

About the Mathematics

The probability of an event is a number from 0 to 1. If the event is impossible, its probability is 0; if the event is certain to occur, its probability is 1. To express a probability as a fraction, first determine the number of possible *outcomes* of the event. In the case of drawing a card at random from a 12-card attribute deck, there are 12 possible outcomes. Then determine the number of possible outcomes that are favorable. For example, to find the probability of drawing a trapezoid from the deck, note that 4 of the 12 cards show a trapezoid. There are 4 favorable outcomes out of 12 possible outcomes, so the probability of drawing a trapezoid is $\frac{4}{12}$, or $\frac{1}{3}$.

To compare likelihoods of events, express their probabilities as fractions and then compare the fractions.

Use with Lesson Activity Book pp. 201–202.

Developing Mathematical Language

Vocabulary: probability

The preceding lessons used informal language to talk about the likelihood of events. This lesson introduces the mathematical term *probability,* with which your students may or may not be familiar. In casual language, we sometimes say things like, "There's a 30% chance of rain," but *probabilities* are most commonly stated as fractions or decimals from 0 to 1. An impossible event has a *probability* of 0. A certain event has a *probability* of 1. In the above example, the *probability* that it will rain is 0.3, or $\frac{3}{10}$.

Familiarize students with the term *probability.*

Beginning Describe several non-mathematical events, using the term *likelihood.* Have students repeat the description using the term *probability.*

Intermediate Have students make up *probability* statements about events for which they know the total number of outcomes and the number of favorable outcomes. For example, ask students to tell the *probability* of tossing an even number with a number cube.

Advanced Use an 8-section spinner (numbered 1–8) to have students generate *probability* statements. Have a student make a statement, such as "the *probability* of an even number is 4 out of 8, or $\frac{4}{8}$" and explain why that is the probability. Repeat with other possible outcomes.

Open-Ended Problem Solving

Read the Headline Story to the students. Encourage students to make an organized list to keep track of all the combinations and to think of creative ways to solve the problem.

 Headline Story

I have 3 different shirts, orange, striped, and blue. I have 4 different skirts, orange, striped, checkered, and polka dotted. Of all the possible shirt-skirt outfits I can make, how many have an orange shirt? How may have stripes? How many total outfits can I make?

orange shirt: 4; stripes: 6; total: 12

Skills Practice and Review

Comparing Fractions to $\frac{1}{2}$

To prepare students for expressing probabilities as fractions, write fractions on the board and ask students if each is greater than $\frac{1}{2}$, equal to $\frac{1}{2}$, or less than $\frac{1}{2}$. Here are some fractions you might use:

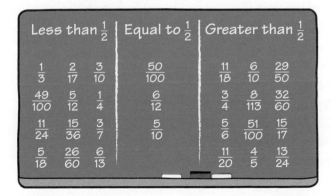

Less than $\frac{1}{2}$			Equal to $\frac{1}{2}$	Greater than $\frac{1}{2}$		
$\frac{1}{3}$	$\frac{2}{17}$	$\frac{3}{10}$	$\frac{50}{100}$	$\frac{11}{18}$	$\frac{6}{10}$	$\frac{29}{50}$
$\frac{49}{100}$	$\frac{5}{12}$	$\frac{1}{4}$	$\frac{6}{12}$	$\frac{3}{4}$	$\frac{8}{113}$	$\frac{32}{60}$
$\frac{11}{24}$	$\frac{15}{36}$	$\frac{3}{7}$	$\frac{5}{10}$	$\frac{5}{6}$	$\frac{51}{100}$	$\frac{15}{17}$
$\frac{5}{18}$	$\frac{26}{60}$	$\frac{6}{13}$		$\frac{11}{20}$	$\frac{4}{5}$	$\frac{13}{24}$

whole class

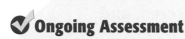
15 MIN

Materials

• For each student: set of 12 attribute cards from Lesson 10.1

NCTM Standards 1, 2, 6, 7, 8, 9, 10

✔ **Ongoing Assessment**

• Do students compare fractions with like denominators?

Purpose To use fractions to express and compare probabilities

Introduce Have students take out their sets of attribute cards. Remind students that in the last lesson, they found the likelihoods of many events involving the drawing of cards from their decks. State that now they're going to explore a way to decide which of several events is the *most* or *least* likely. This might be a good time to mention that the word *probability* means *likelihood,* and that in later math classes students will take, probability will be the preferred term.

Problem Ask the following question:

• If you're playing "Fish" with your attribute cards and you pick a card from your deck without looking, what is the probability that it will be green?

Share By now, students should be comfortable with the idea that since 6 cards out of 12 are green, there are 6 chances in 12 that the card will be green. Write the fraction $\frac{6}{12}$ on the board, and tell students that the probability of picking a green card is six twelfths. (Some students may recognize that the probability could also be written as $\frac{1}{2}$.) Ask students to explain why the probability is six twelfths. If no one comes up with the explanation, write this equation on the board:

Concept Alert

Some students may find it puzzling that an event that is certain has a probability of 1. It may help them to think of 1 as the "whole": if something has a probability of $\frac{1}{2}$, that means it happens half of the time; if something has a probability of 1, it happens all of the time. A probability cannot be greater than 1, because something can't happen more often than "all the time." Similarly, a probability cannot be less than 0, because an event can't happen less often than "none of the time."

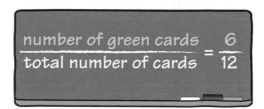

$$\frac{\text{number of green cards}}{\text{total number of cards}} = \frac{6}{12}$$

Practice Ask students to find the following:

• the probability of picking a blue card $\frac{6}{12}$
• the probability of picking a card with a trapezoid $\frac{4}{12}$
• the probability of picking a card that is either green or blue $\frac{12}{12}$, or 1
• the probability of picking a red card $\frac{0}{12}$, or 0

Use with Lesson Activity Book pp. 201–202.

Problem Once students seem comfortable talking about likelihoods in terms of fractions, ask them to decide which of two events is *more* likely. **For example, are they more likely to pick a blue card or a card with a trapezoid?** Students might reason in two ways:

- They might directly compare the probability of picking a blue card ($\frac{6}{12}$) to the probability of picking a trapezoid ($\frac{4}{12}$). Because $\frac{6}{12}$ is greater than $\frac{4}{12}$, it is more likely that someone will pick a blue card.

- They might indirectly compare the probabilities by comparing the number of cards that fit each event. Because 6 of the cards are blue but only 4 of the cards have trapezoids, it is more likely that someone will pick a blue card.

The first method described above, the direct method of comparing probabilities, is the better general strategy. If students use the second method, have them check their conclusions using fractions. Point out that when the events being compared have different numbers of possible outcomes, the second method will not work.

Talk Math

❷ Are you more likely to choose a card with a striped triangle or a card with a trapezoid? Explain your reasoning. trapezoid; Possible explanation: Probability of choosing a striped triangle $= \frac{2}{12}$; probability of choosing a trapezoid $= \frac{4}{12}$; $\frac{4}{12} > \frac{2}{12}$.

❷ Are you more likely to choose a card that is either green or blue or a card with a parallelogram? Explain your reasoning. green or blue; Possible explanation: Probability of choosing green or blue = 1; probability of choosing a parallelogram $= \frac{4}{12}$; $1 > \frac{4}{12}$.

On Level If students need additional work writing probabilities as fractions, sketch these numbered cards on the board:

Ask questions like the following:

If you turned the cards face down and chose one without looking, what is that probability that you would choose:

- the number 2? $\frac{2}{10}$ or $\frac{1}{5}$
- the number 3? $\frac{3}{10}$
- an odd number? $\frac{4}{10}$ or $\frac{2}{5}$
- a 3 or a 4? $\frac{7}{10}$

B Playing a Game: *Attribute Card Forecast*

Materials
- For each group:
  set of 12 attribute
  cards from Lesson 10.1,
  AM92–AM94

NCTM Standards 1, 2, 6, 7, 8, 9, 10

Purpose To calculate probabilities of events

Goal The object of this game, *Attribute Card Forecast,* is for players to choose cards from their hands that they believe will have the best chances of matching randomly chosen attribute cards. The winner is the player who does this most successfully.

Prepare Materials Provide each group with a deck of attribute cards and a deck of Event Cards cut from Activity Master: Event Cards 1, Activity Master: Event Cards 2, and Activity Master: Event Cards 3.

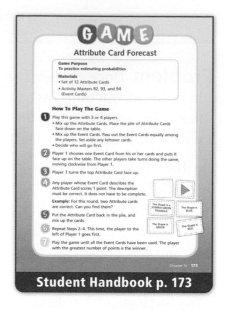

Student Handbook p. 173

How to Play

❶ Shuffle each deck separately. Place the deck of attribute cards face down on the table.

❷ Deal the Event Cards equally among the players. If cards are left over, set them aside; these cards will not be used.

❸ The first player chooses an Event Card from his or her hand and lays it face up on the table. The rest of the players do the same in turn, moving clockwise from the first player.

❹ The first player turns the top card of the attribute card deck face up.

❺ Any player whose Event Card correctly describes the attribute card scores a point. The description must be correct, but it does not have to be complete. For example, if the attribute card is the striped green trapezoid, then an event card that says "the card is green" or "the card is a striped trapezoid" scores a point; a card that says "the card is a blue striped trapezoid" or "the card is not green" would not score.

❻ The attribute card is replaced in the deck, and the attribute card deck is shuffled.

❼ Repeat steps 3–5. This time, the "first player" is the person to the left of the player who went first in the previous round.

❽ The game continues until all the Event Cards have been used. The winner is the player who scores the most points.

❾ For a longer game, shuffle and deal the Event Cards again after they have been used. Players should specify that they are playing a certain number of times through the Event Card deck, or until someone reaches a specific number of points.

✔ **Ongoing Assessment**

- Do your students make connections between their Event Cards and the likelihood they will earn a point when the attribute card is turned over as they play *Attribute Card Forecast*?

- Do they read everyone's Event Cards and discuss who is likely to receive a point when the attribute card is turned over?

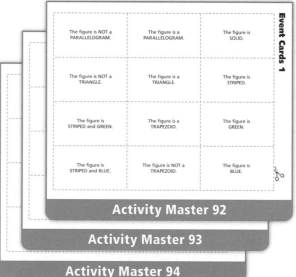

Activity Master 92

Activity Master 93

Activity Master 94

Purpose To find the probabilities of given events

NCTM Standards 1, 2, 6, 7, 8, 9, 10

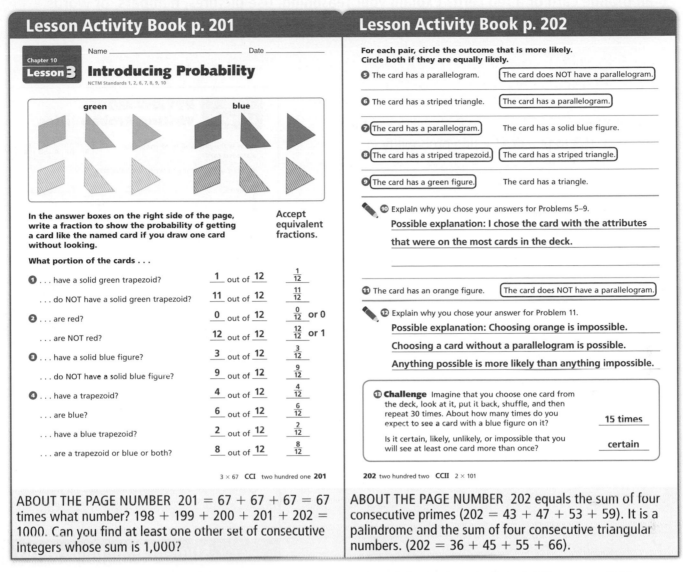

Lesson Activity Book p. 201

Chapter 10 Lesson **3** **Introducing Probability**
NCTM Standards 1, 2, 6, 7, 8, 9, 10

green   blue

In the answer boxes on the right side of the page, write a fraction to show the probability of getting a card like the named card if you draw one card without looking.

Accept equivalent fractions.

What portion of the cards . . .

1 . . . have a solid green trapezoid? **1** out of **12** $\frac{1}{12}$

. . . do NOT have a solid green trapezoid? **11** out of **12** $\frac{11}{12}$

2 . . . are red? **0** out of **12** $\frac{0}{12}$ or 0

. . . are NOT red? **12** out of **12** $\frac{12}{12}$ or 1

3 . . . have a solid blue figure? **3** out of **12** $\frac{3}{12}$

. . . do NOT have a solid blue figure? **9** out of **12** $\frac{9}{12}$

4 . . . have a trapezoid? **4** out of **12** $\frac{4}{12}$

. . . are blue? **6** out of **12** $\frac{6}{12}$

. . . have a blue trapezoid? **2** out of **12** $\frac{2}{12}$

. . . are a trapezoid or blue or both? **8** out of **12** $\frac{8}{12}$

3 × 67 **CCI** two hundred one **201**

ABOUT THE PAGE NUMBER 201 = 67 + 67 + 67 = 67 times what number? 198 + 199 + 200 + 201 + 202 = 1000. Can you find at least one other set of consecutive integers whose sum is 1,000?

Lesson Activity Book p. 202

For each pair, circle the outcome that is more likely. Circle both if they are equally likely.

5 The card has a parallelogram. [The card does NOT have a parallelogram.]

6 The card has a striped triangle. [The card has a parallelogram.]

7 [The card has a parallelogram.] The card has a solid blue figure.

8 [The card has a striped trapezoid.] [The card has a striped triangle.]

9 [The card has a green figure.] The card has a triangle.

10 Explain why you chose your answers for Problems 5–9.
Possible explanation: I chose the card with the attributes that were on the most cards in the deck.

11 The card has an orange figure. [The card does NOT have a parallelogram.]

12 Explain why you chose your answer for Problem 11.
Possible explanation: Choosing orange is impossible.
Choosing a card without a parallelogram is possible.
Anything possible is more likely than anything impossible.

13 Challenge Imagine that you choose one card from the deck, look at it, put it back, shuffle, and then repeat 30 times. About how many times do you expect to see a card with a blue figure on it? **15 times**

Is it certain, likely, unlikely, or impossible that you will see at least one card more than once? **certain**

202 two hundred two **CCII** 2 × 101

ABOUT THE PAGE NUMBER 202 equals the sum of four consecutive primes (202 = 43 + 47 + 53 + 59). It is a palindrome and the sum of four consecutive triangular numbers. (202 = 36 + 45 + 55 + 66).

Teaching Notes for LAB page 201

Have students complete the page individually or with partners.

On this page, allow students to answer using any fraction equivalent to the given answer, so that they can focus on the meaning of the fractions rather than on making sure they have found the simplest fraction possible. In Problems 1–3, the pairs of events are related. If one event does not happen, the other must happen. As a result, the sum of the two probabilities in each problem equals 1.

Teaching Notes for LAB page 202

Challenge Problem This problem previews work students will do in **Lesson 10.4.** Some students may recognize that, because the probability of picking a blue card is $\frac{1}{2}$, it should turn up about half the time (or 15 times).

The second part of the Challenge Problem involves critical thinking rather than probability. Even if the first 12 cards that are picked are all different, the thirteenth card must repeat one of them. Therefore, it is certain that students will see at least one card more than once.

Reflect and Summarize the Lesson

Write Math The probability of picking an orange card from Jody's deck of attribute cards is $\frac{1}{5}$. The probability of choosing a red card is $\frac{1}{4}$. If you draw a card, are you more likely to draw an orange card or a red card? Explain your reasoning. Use pictures, numbers, or words.

a red card; Possible explanation: $\frac{1}{4} > \frac{1}{5}$, so it's more likely that I will draw a red card.

Review Model ....

Refer students to the Review Model: Writing Probabilities in the *Student Handbook* p. 163 to practice writing probability in fraction form.

✔ Check for Understanding

❶ $\frac{2}{6}$ (or $\frac{1}{3}$)

❷ $\frac{3}{6}$ or ($\frac{1}{2}$)

❸ $\frac{1}{6}$

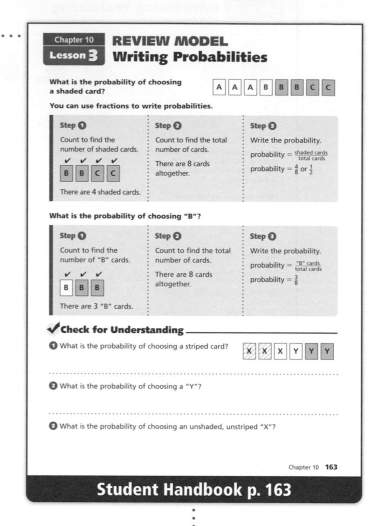

Use with Lesson Activity Book pp. 201–202.

Leveled Problem Solving

**Cards in a deck are numbered from 1 through 20.
You randomly choose one card from the deck.**

❶ Basic Level

Are you more likely to choose an even card or a multiple of 3? Explain using probability. an even card; The probability of an even card is $\frac{10}{20}$, that of a multiple of 3 is $\frac{6}{20}$; $\frac{10}{20} > \frac{6}{20}$.

❷ On Level

Are you more likely to choose a number less than 8 or a number greater than 14? Explain using probability. a number less than 8; The probability of a number less than 8 is $\frac{7}{20}$; that of a number greater than 14 is $\frac{6}{20}$; $\frac{7}{20} > \frac{6}{20}$.

❸ Above Level

Compare the probability of choosing a multiple of 3 and the probability of choosing a multiple of 5. Explain which is more likely using probabilities. A multiple of 3 is more likely to be chosen than a multiple of 5; $\frac{6}{20} > \frac{4}{20}$.

Intervention

Activity How Many Outcomes?

Reinforce the idea that the denominator of a probability fraction is the total number of possible outcomes, so long as the fraction has not been reduced. Have students sketch several spinners with different numbers of equal sections. Ask them to label each section. Then, for each spinner, have students list all possible outcomes for a single-spin experiment with that spinner.

Practice

Introducing Probability

If Laura spins the spinner once, what is the probability that the spinner . . . Accept equivalent fractions.

27	30
49	6
55	14
18	35

❶ lands on a multiple of 3?	$\frac{4}{8}$	❻ lands on an even number?	$\frac{4}{8}$
does not land on a multiple of 3?	$\frac{4}{8}$	lands on an odd number?	$\frac{4}{8}$
❷ lands on a multiple of 5?	$\frac{3}{8}$	❼ lands on a one-digit number?	$\frac{1}{8}$
lands on a multiple of 10?	$\frac{1}{8}$	lands on a two-digit number?	$\frac{7}{8}$
❸ lands on a three-digit number?	0	❽ lands on a number less than 100?	$\frac{8}{8} = 1$
lands on a number with a 1 in the ones place?	0	lands on a number greater than 5?	$\frac{8}{8} = 1$

Test Prep

❾ How many pairs of parallel lines does this figure have?

A. 0
B. 1
C. 2
D. 3

❿ How many lines of symmetry can be drawn on this square?

A. 0
B. 1
C. 2
D. 4

Practice P83

Extension

Introducing Probability

Use your deck of attribute cards to follow these steps and answer each question.

❶ What portion of the cards are striped blue? 3 out of 12

❷ If you draw one card, what is the probability that it will be striped blue? $\frac{3}{12}$

Remove the solid blue triangle from the deck and put it aside.

❸ What portion of the remaining cards are striped blue? 3 out of 11

❹ If you draw one card now, what is the probability that it will be striped blue? $\frac{3}{11}$

Now, remove the green striped parallelogram and the solid green trapezoid and put them aside.

❺ Now what portion of the cards are striped blue? 3 out of 9

❻ If you draw one card now, what is the probability that it will be striped blue? $\frac{3}{9}$

❼ Which is more likely: drawing a striped blue card from the deck as it is now, or drawing a striped blue card from the full deck you started with? Explain your answer.
Possible explanation: $\frac{3}{9}$ ($\frac{1}{3}$) is greater than $\frac{3}{12}$ ($\frac{1}{4}$), so the likelihood of drawing a striped blue card is greater now.

Extension E83

Spiral Review

Spiral Review Book page SR83 provides review of the following previously learned skills and concepts:

- estimating, measuring, and comparing lengths
- graphing, analyzing, and drawing conclusions from temperature data

You may wish to have students work with a partner to complete the page.

Measurement

Circle the larger measurement.

❶ 17 inches or 1½ feet	❷ 1 yard or 2 feet 15 inches
❸ 2 yards or 5 feet	❹ 31 inches or 2 feet 6 inches
❺ 51 inches or 2½ yards	❻ 1¼ feet or 19 inches

Reasoning and Proof

For 7–11, use the graph.

❼ Which was the warmest day of the week?
Saturday

❽ On how many days was the high temperature above 50°F?
3

HIGH TEMPERATURES DURING ONE WEEK

❾ At which two days would you look to find the difference between the warmest high temperature and the coolest?
Wednesday and Saturday

❿ Estimate the difference between the warmest high temperature and the coolest.
about 16–18°F

⓫ Describe the changes in the high temperatures for the week.
Possible answers: They moved up and down from one day to the next; it seemed to be getting warmer overall.

Spiral Review SR83

Extension Activity
Designing a Spinner

Challenge students to draw a spinner for which all of these hold:

- The probability of spinning an even number is $\frac{3}{6}$.
- The probability of spinning an odd number is also $\frac{3}{6}$.
- The probability of spinning an odd number greater than 5 is 0.
- The probability of spinning an even number less than 6 or greater than 10 is 0.

a 6-part spinner labeled 1, 3, 5, 6, 8, 10

Lesson 4 Drawing From a Deck of Attribute Cards

NCTM Standards 1, 2, 6, 7, 8, 9, 10

Lesson Planner

STUDENT OBJECTIVES ·
■ To predict the result of an experiment
■ To conduct an experiment, organize data in a bar graph, and analyze the results

1 | Daily Activities (TG p. 819)

Open-Ended Problem Solving/Headline Story	Skills Practice and Review— Comparing Fractions to $\frac{1}{2}$

2 | Teach and Practice (TG pp. 820–826)

	MATERIALS
Ⓐ **Predicting the Results of an Experiment** (TG pp. 820–821)	• transparency of AM95 (optional)
Ⓑ **Drawing From a Deck of Attribute Cards** (TG p. 822)	• 📖 LAB pp. 203–204
Ⓒ **Recording the Results of the Experiment** (TG p. 823)	• 📖 SH pp. 164–165
Ⓓ **Discussing the Results of the Experiment** (TG pp. 824–825)	

3 | Differentiated Instruction (TG p. 827)

Leveled Problem Solving (TG p. 827)	Practice Book P84
Intervention Activity (TG p. 827)	Extension Book E84
Extension Activity (TG p. 827)	Spiral Review Book SR84

Lesson Notes

About the Lesson

Students make predictions about how often they are likely to draw one type of card from their decks of attribute cards. Then they conduct an experiment, comparing their results with their predictions.

About the Mathematics

In this lesson, students find and interpret the mode (the most frequently observed value in a set of data), and the range (the spread in the data). Students draw cards from their decks and record the number of trapezoids they get in 30 draws. Suppose that in one classroom the number of trapezoids students drew ranged from 5 to 13 and in a second classroom the number ranged from 5 to 25. The data would be more tightly clustered in the first classroom. But relying on only the range to describe data can be limiting. What if all the draws from the second class ranged from 5 to 13 trapezoids except one—that is, the "outlier" 25? How different, in fact, would the data from the two classrooms be?

Use with Lesson Activity Book pp. 203–204.

Developing Mathematical Language

Vocabulary: mode, range

The *mode* of a set of data is the most commonly occurring value. The *range* is the spread of the values. In the set {3, 5, 6, 6, 10}, 6 is the *mode* and 7 (= 10 − 3) is the *range*. Your students do not need to use these terms, but if they ask about them, use the terms in context. As long as students understand the conceptual ideas behind the terms, they will be prepared to analyze data in this and later lessons.

Familiarize students with the term *range.*

Beginning Use the term *range* in context with students, for example, mentioning that for recess they could choose a *range* of activities—baseball, kickball, tag, or the climbing structure. Ask students to give examples of other kinds of *ranges.*

Intermediate Display a set of data and ask students to identify the *range* of values: What is the smallest value? the largest? Continue with other data sets.

Advanced Ask students to create a set of data and to identify the *range.* What is the smallest value? the largest? the difference between the two?

Open-Ended Problem Solving

Read the Headline Story to the students. Encourage them to think of imaginative scenarios that incorporate information from the story.

 Headline Story

> Margot picked a marble out of a bag of marbles, recorded its color, and returned it to the bag. She shook up the bag and then repeated the process several times. She drew a red marble $\frac{1}{3}$ of the time.

Possible responses: If Margot drew 9 marbles in all, she must have picked a red marble 3 times. If Margot drew 7 red marbles, she must have repeated the drawing process 21 times. The number of marbles Margot drew is a multiple of 3, because one-third of that number is a whole number. Margot must have drawn at least 3 marbles, at least 1 of which was red.

Skills Practice and Review

Comparing Fractions to $\frac{1}{2}$

Repeat the Skills Practice activity from **Lesson 10.3.** Write a fraction on the board and ask students if the fraction is greater than $\frac{1}{2}$, equal to $\frac{1}{2}$, or less than $\frac{1}{2}$. Here are some fractions you might use:

Less than $\frac{1}{2}$			Equal to $\frac{1}{2}$	Greater than $\frac{1}{2}$		
$\frac{1}{3}$	$\frac{2}{17}$	$\frac{3}{10}$	$\frac{50}{100}$	$\frac{11}{18}$	$\frac{6}{10}$	$\frac{29}{50}$
$\frac{49}{100}$	$\frac{5}{12}$	$\frac{1}{4}$	$\frac{6}{12}$	$\frac{3}{4}$	$\frac{81}{113}$	$\frac{32}{60}$
$\frac{11}{24}$	$\frac{15}{36}$	$\frac{3}{7}$	$\frac{5}{10}$	$\frac{5}{6}$	$\frac{51}{100}$	$\frac{15}{17}$
$\frac{5}{18}$	$\frac{26}{60}$	$\frac{6}{13}$		$\frac{11}{20}$	$\frac{4}{5}$	$\frac{13}{24}$

individuals or whole class **15 MIN**

NCTM Standards 1, 2, 6, 7, 8, 9, 10

A Predicting the Results of an Experiment

Purpose To predict the results of a probability experiment

Introduce Have students work independently on Explore: How Likely is Drawing a Trapezoid? Explain that in this activity, students will predict the results of an experiment involving attribute cards. In the next activity, they will perform the experiment. Finally, they will have an opportunity to look back and compare their predictions with the actual results.

The exploration page asks students to predict how many times in 30 draws they would draw a trapezoid from a deck of attribute cards. Students are asked to express their predictions as fractions. So, if they think that 10 cards out of 30 will be trapezoids, that's $\frac{10}{30}$ or $\frac{1}{3}$ of the cards.

✔ Ongoing Assessment

- Do students write a fraction to express their results? For example, can they write that drawing 3 trapezoids out of 10 draws means that they drew a trapezoid $\frac{3}{10}$ of the time?

- Do students write fractions that are equivalent to a given fraction? For example, do they recognize that fractions such as $\frac{2}{3}$ and $\frac{6}{9}$ that are equivalent to $\frac{4}{6}$?

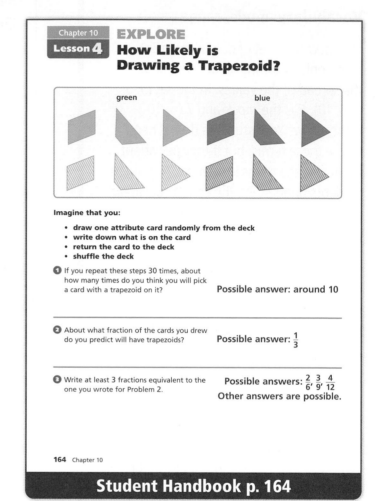

Student Handbook p. 164

Task Direct students to the following challenges, which appear on Explore: How Likely is Drawing a Trapezoid?

Imagine that you draw one attribute card randomly from the deck, write down what is on the card, return the card to the deck, and shuffle the deck.

- If you repeat these steps 30 times, about how many times do you think you will pick a card with a trapezoid on it?

  Possible answer: around 10; Students may reason that since $\frac{1}{3}$ of the cards show trapezoids, they will draw trapezoids about $\frac{1}{3}$ of the time. $30 \div 3 = 10$. Students should see that although 10 is a good prediction, the actual number may be different from 10.

- What fraction of the cards you drew do you predict will have trapezoids?

  Possible answer: $\frac{1}{3}$; Students may reason that since $\frac{1}{3}$ of the cards in the deck show trapezoids, it is reasonable to predict that they will draw trapezoids about $\frac{1}{3}$ of the time.

Use with Lesson Activity Book pp. 203–204.

- Write at least 3 fractions equivalent to the one you wrote for Problem 1. Possible answers: $\frac{2}{6}$, $\frac{3}{9}$, $\frac{4}{12}$; Students may reason that the numerator (top number) of the fraction should be one-third the denominator (bottom number).

Share Once students have worked on the page independently, ask them to share their predictions with the class and to explain and justify their reasoning. Write some of the predictions on the board. You will be comparing these predictions with actual results later in the lesson.

Some students may expect that, because one third of the cards *are* trapezoids, $\frac{1}{3}$ of the cards that are picked at random will be trapezoids. The reality is a bit more complicated. What the $\frac{1}{3}$ tells us is not what will happen, or even what will happen most often, but that over many trials, the number of trapezoids drawn will tend to cluster around $\frac{1}{3}$ (some going over, some under, and a few exactly $\frac{1}{3}$).

Although students have not done much work finding the simplest form of a fraction, they should be comfortable finding a variety of fractions equivalent to their predictions. Equivalent fractions will help them to compare one prediction with another, and to compare their predictions with the results of the experiment, once they have gathered their data.

Talk Math

❷ If you drew a card 40 times from your deck, replacing the card each time, how many of the cards that you drew would be blue? Explain your reasoning. about 20; Possible explanation: Half of the cards in the attribute deck are blue. So it would be reasonable to expect that about half of the 40 draws would result in blue cards. $40 \div 2 = 20$.

❷ Is the fraction $\frac{1}{4}$ equivalent to the fraction $\frac{3}{12}$? How do you know? yes; Possible explanation: The bottom number of each fraction is 4 times the top number.

Purpose To record and analyze the results of an experiment

NCTM Standards 1, 2, 6, 7, 8, 9, 10

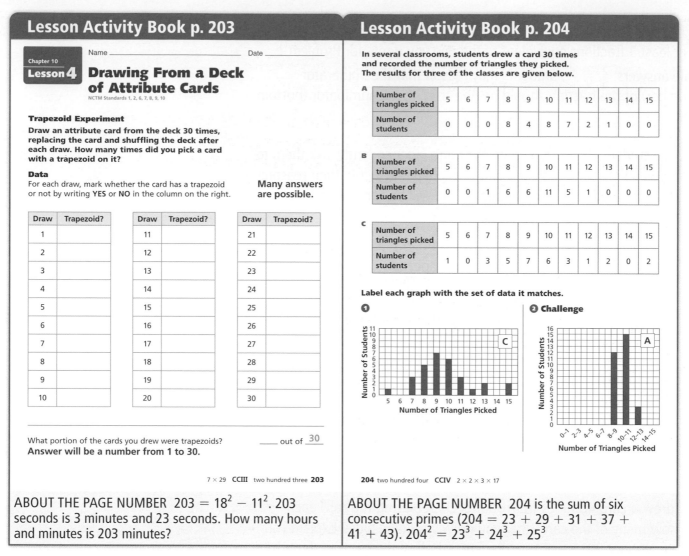

Lesson Activity Book p. 203

Name _____ Date _____

Chapter 10
Lesson 4 **Drawing From a Deck of Attribute Cards**
NCTM Standards 1, 2, 6, 7, 8, 9, 10

Trapezoid Experiment
Draw an attribute card from the deck 30 times, replacing the card and shuffling the deck after each draw. How many times did you pick a card with a trapezoid on it?

Data
For each draw, mark whether the card has a trapezoid or not by writing **YES** or **NO** in the column on the right.

Many answers are possible.

Draw	Trapezoid?
1	
2	
3	
4	
5	
6	
7	
8	
9	
10	

Draw	Trapezoid?
11	
12	
13	
14	
15	
16	
17	
18	
19	
20	

Draw	Trapezoid?
21	
22	
23	
24	
25	
26	
27	
28	
29	
30	

What portion of the cards you drew were trapezoids? _____ out of _30_
Answer will be a number from 1 to 30.

7 × 29 **CCIII** two hundred three **203**

ABOUT THE PAGE NUMBER $203 = 18^2 - 11^2$. 203 seconds is 3 minutes and 23 seconds. How many hours and minutes is 203 minutes?

Lesson Activity Book p. 204

In several classrooms, students drew a card 30 times and recorded the number of triangles they picked. The results for three of the classes are given below.

A

Number of triangles picked	5	6	7	8	9	10	11	12	13	14	15
Number of students	0	0	0	8	4	8	7	2	1	0	0

B

Number of triangles picked	5	6	7	8	9	10	11	12	13	14	15
Number of students	0	0	1	6	6	11	5	1	0	0	0

C

Number of triangles picked	5	6	7	8	9	10	11	12	13	14	15
Number of students	1	0	3	5	7	6	3	1	2	0	2

Label each graph with the set of data it matches.

❶

❷ Challenge

204 two hundred four **CCIV** 2 × 2 × 3 × 17

ABOUT THE PAGE NUMBER 204 is the sum of six consecutive primes ($204 = 23 + 29 + 31 + 37 + 41 + 43$). $204^2 = 23^3 + 24^3 + 25^3$

Teaching Notes for LAB page 203

Students should draw a card from the deck, record on LAB page 203 whether or not it is a trapezoid, replace the card, and shuffle the deck. They should repeat this process 30 times. In the next activity, students will combine their results on a class graph or discussion.

The probability of drawing a trapezoid is $\frac{1}{3}$, which means we should expect about 10 out of 30 cards drawn to be trapezoids. However, as students will discover, this does not mean they will actually pick 10 trapezoids.

Teaching Notes for LAB page 204

Students should not work on this page until the class has finished recording the results of the trapezoid experiment on LAB page 203.

Challenge Problem The first graph breaks the data down, assigning a single number of triangles to each column. The second graph displays data in clusters. The first column with shaded rectangles represents 8 or 9 triangles, the second column 10 or 11 rectangles, and the third column 12 or 13 triangles.

C **Recording the Results of the Experiment**

Purpose To record the results of the trapezoid experiment

Introduce Gather students for a class discussion. They should have their completed LAB page 203 with them.

Task Direct students to record the numbers of times they picked cards with trapezoids on a class bar graph. Use Activity Master: Experimental Results for recording the data, or draw a graph on the board.

For example, if one student reports drawing 8 cards with a trapezoid, that student would shade the lowest square in the "8" column. Another student who drew 8 cards with a trapezoid would shade the next higher box in the column. The shading would show that two people obtained the same results in their experiments.

Materials
- For the teacher: transparency of AM95 (optional), extra copies of LAB p. 203
- For each student: LAB pp. 203–204

NCTM Standards 1, 2, 6, 7, 8, 9, 10

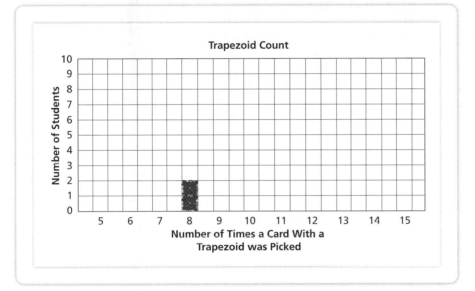

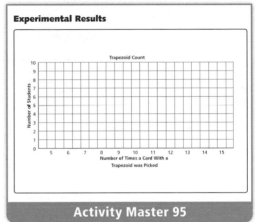

Give each student who records a result a second copy of LAB page 203. Ask the student to repeat the experiment, drawing a card from the deck 30 more times and then recording the result on the class graph. Remind students to replace the card and shuffle the deck after each draw.

Talk Math

❓ One-third of the cards in the deck are trapezoids, and one-third of 30 is 10. Did everyone who completed the experiment turn up exactly 10 trapezoids? Why or why not? Explain your answer. Possible answer: no; possible explanation: 10 is a number of trapezoids it is reasonable to expect will turn up. But other numbers of trapezoids are possible as well.

❓ Is it possible for a student to draw a trapezoid on each of his or her 30 tries? Explain. yes; Possible explanation: It is possible to draw a trapezoid 30 times because there will always be trapezoids in the deck to draw, but very unlikely.

D Discussing the Results of the Experiment

Materials
- For the teacher: graph created in Activity C

NCTM Standards 1, 2, 6, 7, 8, 9, 10

Purpose To summarize the results of the trapezoid experiment

Introduce Direct students' attention to the graph showing the combined results of all the trapezoid experiments.

Task Ask students to answer the following questions. Answers will vary, depending on your students' results.

- Which number of trapezoids occurred the most? (The number will likely be 10 or a number close to 10.)

- How many students drew more than 8 trapezoids but less than 12 trapezoids?

- How many students drew exactly 10 cards with trapezoids?

Use the terms *mode* and *range* in context, asking students to find the most frequent response (mode) and the spread of data (the range). If you would like, you can tell students that they can calculate the range by subtracting the smallest value from the largest one. For example, if the least value on the graph is 6 and the greatest is 13, the range is $13 - 6 = 7$.

Ask students to compare their results with the predictions they made in Activity A. Then use the following questions to draw attention to the experimental results:

- What was the smallest number of trapezoids drawn? (This is the number that appears farthest left on the graph.)

- What was the largest number of trapezoids drawn? (This is the number that appears farthest right on the graph.)

- Why did many students draw about 10 cards with a trapezoid? Possible answer: Because one-third of the cards are trapezoids, it is most likely that the number of trapezoids drawn will be close to one-third of the total number of cards drawn, about 10.

- Why are there few students (or none) who drew more than 15 cards with trapezoids? Possible answer: The most likely number of cards with trapezoids that students will draw is 10. It is far less likely, though not impossible, that students will draw a number of trapezoid cards much larger than 10.

Use with Lesson Activity Book pp. 203–204.

Are you surprised that not all groups drew 10 trapezoids? (Students may respond to this question in many different ways. Although they may be surprised that the actual results were different from the predicted results, the discussion should help them see that probabilities are not certainties. If the class continued the experiment, most, but not all, of the results would be very close to 10 trapezoids. This idea will be explored further in the next lesson.)

Talk Math

❷ How could you compare the total number of trapezoids drawn by all the students to the total number of cards drawn? Possible answer: I could count the number of trapezoids drawn by using the fact that each shaded section in the "8" column represents 8 trapezoids, each shaded section in the "9" column represents 9 trapezoids, and so on. I could count the total number of cards drawn by counting the number of shaded squares and multiplying the result by 30. I expect the latter number to be about 3 times larger than the former.

❷ If you had conducted the experiment with a card other than the trapezoid, which card or cards would have been best to choose if you wanted the results to be clustered around 10? Explain. triangle or parallelogram; Possible explanation: Like the trapezoid, one-third of the cards are triangles and one-third are parallelograms.

Write Math

If you drew a card from the set of attribute cards 60 times, about how many times would you expect to draw a card with a green triangle on it? Explain your reasoning. about 10: Possible explanation: One-sixth of the cards in the deck show green triangles, so it would be reasonable to expect that about one-sixth of the 60 cards, or 10 cards, would show green triangles.

Review Model . . . .

Refer students to the Review Model: Finding Equivalent Fractions Using Patterns in the **Student Handbook** p. 165 to practice looking for a relationship between the numerator and denominator of a fraction or set of fractions.

❶ Many answers are possible, including
$\frac{1}{4}$, $\frac{3}{12}$, and $\frac{4}{16}$

❷ Many answers are possible, including
$\frac{3}{5}$, $\frac{9}{15}$, and $\frac{12}{20}$

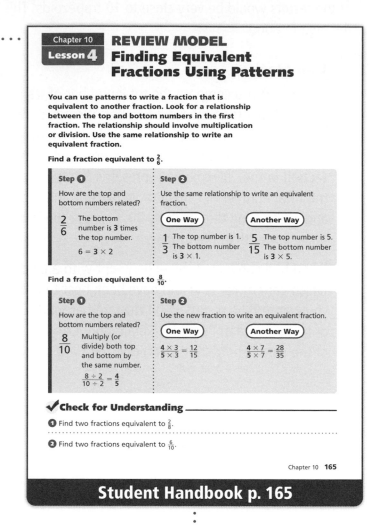

Student Handbook p. 165

Use with Lesson Activity Book pp. 203–204.

Leveled Problem Solving

In an experiment, you toss a number cube labeled 1–6.

❶ Basic Level

If you do the experiment 60 times, about how many times would you expect to toss a number less than 4? Explain. about 30 times; $\frac{3}{6}$, or $\frac{1}{2}$, of the possible outcomes are less than 4; $\frac{1}{2}$ of 60 is 30.

❷ On Level

If you make 60 tosses, about how many times would you expect to toss a number that is even or less than 4? Explain. about 50 times; 5 of the 6 numbers (1, 2, 3, 4, 6) fit the description, $\frac{5}{6} = \frac{50}{60}$.

❸ Above Level

If you do make 60 tosses, about how many times would you expect to toss a number that is less than 3 or greater than 4? Explain. about 40 times; $\frac{4}{6}$ of the numbers fit the description (1, 2, 5, 6); $\frac{4}{6} = \frac{40}{60}$

Intervention

Activity Predicting Outcomes

Show students a spinner labeled 2–9.

- What is the probability that you will spin a 7 in one spin? $\frac{1}{8}$
- If you spin the spinner 40 times, about how many times would you expect to spin 7? about 5 times
- Write the probability of spinning a 7 as a fraction if you spin 40 times. $\frac{5}{40}$

Have students choose a different outcome and answer the questions for that outcome.

Practice

Practice P84

Extension

Extension E84

Spiral Review

Spiral Review Book page SR84 provides review of the following previously learned skills and concepts:

- making equivalent fractions with or without a model or picture
- seeing that shapes that have been translated, reflected, or rotated are congruent to the original shape

You may wish to have students work with a partner to complete the page.

Spiral Review SR84

Extension Activity
Extending Probabilities

Have students draw an "unfair" spinner (i.e., one for which the probability of landing on some sections is greater than that of landing on others). Have students calculate the probability of landing on each section.

Lesson 5 Drawing Blocks

NCTM Standards 1, 2, 6, 7, 8, 9, 10

Lesson Planner

STUDENT OBJECTIVES
- To predict the results of an experiment by calculating probabilities
- To conduct an experiment, organize the data, and interpret the results
- To compare predictions with experimental results

1 Daily Activities (TG p. 829)

Open-Ended Problem Solving/Headline Story	Skills Practice and Review— Listing Possible Outcomes

2 Teach and Practice (TG pp. 830–835)

	MATERIALS
Ⓐ Introducing the 9-Block Experiment (TG pp. 830–831)	• transparency of AM96 (optional), transparency marker
Ⓑ Collecting and Graphing Results (TG p. 832)	• coins, blocks, or cards numbered 1–9, opaque bag
Ⓒ Drawing Blocks (TG p. 833)	• 📖 LAB pp. 205–206
Ⓓ Comparing Results to Predictions (TG p. 834)	• 📖 SH pp. 166–167

3 Differentiated Instruction (TG p. 836)

Leveled Problem Solving (TG p. 836)	Practice Book P85
Intervention Activity (TG p. 836)	Extension Book E85
Extension Activity (TG p. 836)	Spiral Review Book SR85

Lesson Notes

About the Lesson

In this lesson, students continue to explore the relationship between predictions and experimental results. Students deepen their understanding of how to interpret bar graphs as they record and analyze data.

About the Mathematics

Let's say we want to know the likelihood of drawing a green trapezoid from our deck of attribute cards. There are two ways to think about calculating the probability of this event.

We could predict the probability theoretically by listing all the possible outcomes (there are 12 different cards that can be drawn, each equally likely) and noting how many of them are green trapezoids (2: the solid green trapezoid and the striped green trapezoid). The *theoretical* probability of drawing a green trapezoid is therefore $\frac{2}{12}$, or $\frac{1}{6}$.

Alternatively, we could design an experiment in which we repeatedly draw cards from our deck (replacing the card after each draw), record each outcome, and then calculate the fraction of all the outcomes that are green trapezoids. This *experimental* probability of drawing a green trapezoid may not match exactly the theoretical probability of $\frac{2}{12}$. The more times we repeat the experiment, however, the closer we should expect the theoretical and experimental probabilities to come to each other.

Use with Lesson Activity Book pp. 205–206.

Developing Mathematical Language

Vocabulary: outcome

An *outcome* is a possible result of an action. This is true in everyday life as well as in mathematics. If Smith and Jones are the two candidates for mayor, then there are two possible *outcomes* to the mayoral election, a victory by Smith or a victory by Jones. Likewise, if you flip a dime, there are two possible *outcomes,* heads or tails. Probabilities are the same in the real world and in mathematics: the probabilities that you will randomly pick the winner of a two-candidate mayoral race or the result of the coin toss are both $\frac{1}{2}$.

Familiarize students with the term *outcome.*

Beginning Display various devices that lead to different *outcomes* in probability experiments, including a spinner, number cube, set of cards, and paper cup for tossing. For one device, name an *outcome* of using the device. Then, ask students to name an *outcome* of using the remaining devices.

Intermediate Display a spinner, a number cube and a set of cards. Have students choose one and list all the possible *outcomes* from it. Let students share their lists, identifying each result as an *outcome.*

Advanced Provide students with blank spinners with 8 equal sections. Ask them to fill in the sections any way they want, trade spinners with a partner, and name all possible *outcomes* for their partner's spinner.

Open-Ended Problem Solving

Read the Headline Story to the students. Encourage them to think in terms of likelihood. Actual experimentation with multiple draws (replacing the candy each time before trying again) should accompany class discussion to show that anything can happen on any one trial, but that the more trials, the "more likely" the predicted outcome will occur. This will assure that students are not merely asserting the probabilities and thinking that they dictate results of one-time events.

 Headline Story

> Jenise bought a package of assorted candies. $\frac{1}{6}$ of the candies were strawberry flavored, $\frac{1}{3}$ were lemon, and the rest were orange. Jenise took a candy from the bag without looking. What can you say about the candy she took?

Possible responses: $\frac{1}{2}$ of the candies must have been orange, so the candy she took was more likely to have been orange than lemon. Strawberry was the least likely flavor, so there was a better chance that she got lemon than that she got strawberry. She had the same chance of getting orange as getting either lemon or strawberry.

Skills Practice and Review

Listing Possible Outcomes

Ask students to imagine tossing three coins, a penny, a nickel, and a dime. Call on students to provide possible outcomes. Ask the class how they can be sure they have listed all the possible outcomes and no duplicates. You can help them organize their work systematically by making a table or an organized list. Provide play money for those students who need help visualizing the outcomes. Provide play money for those students who need help visualizing the outcomes. The possible outcomes are HHH, HHT, HTH, HTT, THH, THT, TTH, and TTT.

individuals or
whole class

⏱ **10** MIN

Materials
• For each student: coin

NCTM Standards 1, 2, 6, 7, 8, 9, 10

✔ **Ongoing Assessment**

• Do students find two-ninths, three-ninths, or any other number of ninths of a number, if they know the value of one-ninth of the number?

Ⓐ Introducing the 9-Block Experiment

Purpose To predict the outcome of an experiment

Introduce Ask students to predict how many heads will turn up if every student tosses a coin. Record the predictions. Then have students toss coins. (If the number of students is uneven, you can toss a coin too.) Ask students to compare the predictions with the results. Ask: Was the number of heads exactly half the total number of tosses?

Now have students work independently on Explore: 9-Block Experiment. Explain that the page introduces an experiment that students will perform in the next activity, and asks them to predict the outcome of the experiment.

Task Direct students to the following challenges, which appear on Explore: 9-Block Experiment. Draw their attention to the figure at the top of the page, which represents 9 blocks numbered 1–9.

❶ If you put these blocks into a bag and drew one without looking, what is the probability that the number on your block would be:

  • even? $\frac{4}{9}$; 4 of 9 blocks (2, 4, 6, and 8) have even numbers.

  • a multiple of 3? $\frac{3}{9}$ or $\frac{1}{3}$; 3 of 9 blocks (3, 6, and 9) have numbers that are multiples of 3.

  • a square number? $\frac{3}{9}$ or $\frac{1}{3}$; 3 of 9 blocks (1, 4, and 9) have numbers that are square numbers.

  • at least 5? $\frac{5}{9}$; 5 of 9 blocks (5, 6, 7, 8, and 9) have numbers 5 or greater.

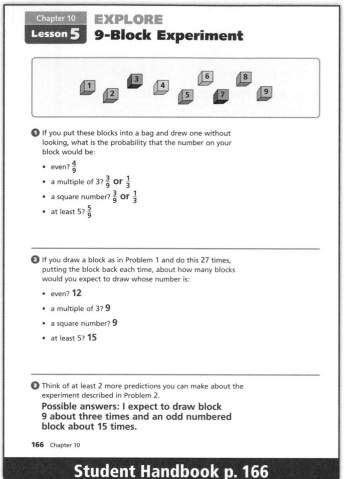

Chapter 10 **EXPLORE**
Lesson **5** **9-Block Experiment**

❶ If you put these blocks into a bag and drew one without looking, what is the probability that the number on your block would be:

  • even? $\frac{4}{9}$
  • a multiple of 3? $\frac{3}{9}$ or $\frac{1}{3}$
  • a square number? $\frac{3}{9}$ or $\frac{1}{3}$
  • at least 5? $\frac{5}{9}$

❷ If you draw a block as in Problem 1 and do this 27 times, putting the block back each time, about how many blocks would you expect to draw whose number is:

  • even? **12**
  • a multiple of 3? **9**
  • a square number? **9**
  • at least 5? **15**

❸ Think of at least 2 more predictions you can make about the experiment described in Problem 2.
Possible answers: I expect to draw block 9 about three times and an odd numbered block about 15 times.

166 Chapter 10

Student Handbook p. 166

Use with Lesson Activity Book pp. 205–206.

❷ If you draw a block as in Problem 1 and do this 27 times, each time replacing the block, about how many blocks would you expect to draw whose number is:

- even? 12; Possible explanation: I would expect to draw an even number about 4 times out of 9 draws, so I'd expect about 3 times as many for 27 draws; $3 \times 4 = 12$.

- a multiple of 3? 9; Possible explanation: There are 3 multiples of 3 (3, 6, 9), so I'd expect to draw a multiple of 3 about 3 times out of 9 draws. I'd expect about 3 times as many for 27 draws; $3 \times 3 = 9$.

- a square number? 9; There are 3 square numbers (1, 4, 9), so I'd expect to draw a square number about 3 times out of 9 draws. I'd expect about 3 times as many for 27 draws; $3 \times 3 = 9$.

- at least 5? 15; Possible explanation: There are 5 blocks that have numbers that are at least 5, so I'd expect to get a 5, 6, 7, 8, or 9 about 5 times out of 9 draws. I'd expect about 3 times as many for 27 draws; $3 \times 5 = 15$.

❸ Think of at least two more predictions you can make about the experiment described in Problem 2. Possible predictions: I would expect to draw about 6 blocks whose numbers are multiples of 4, because 2 of the 9 blocks show numbers that are multiples of 4 (4 and 8), and $\frac{2}{9} \times 27 = 6$. I would expect to draw 21 blocks whose numbers are between 1 and 9, because 7 of the 9 blocks show numbers that are between 1 and 9 (2, 3, 4, 5, 6, 7, and 8), and $\frac{7}{9} \times 27 = 21$.

Share After students have worked on the Explore page, gather them to discuss and justify their predictions.

The page also asks students to come up with other predictions they can make about the experiment. Ask students to share some of their predictions and record them for later reference. (Some types of questions that students may come up with in addition to ones like those on the exploration page include "How many blocks will be numbered 1, 2, or 3?" or "How many times will block 7 be drawn?")

Talk Math

❷ If you draw a block without looking, what is the probability that it will be a 7? Explain your reasoning. $\frac{1}{9}$; 1 of the blocks shows a 7.

❷ If you draw a block 27 times, how many blocks would you expect to draw with the number 7 on it? Explain your reasoning. about 3; $\frac{1}{9}$ of 27 is 3.

B Collecting and Graphing Results

Materials

- For the teacher: transparency of AM96 (optional), transparency marker, blocks or cards numbered 1–9, opaque bag

NCTM Standards 1, 2, 6, 7, 8, 9, 10

✓ Ongoing Assessment

- Do students understand how to record class data on a bar graph?

Purpose To prepare a graph to record the results of an experiment, and to conduct the experiment

Introduce Project a transparency of AM96: Bar Graph of Class Data or sketch the graph on the board. Explain that you are going to draw a graph that students can use to record the results of the experiment they are about to perform. Remind them that they will be drawing blocks numbered 1–9 twenty-seven times.

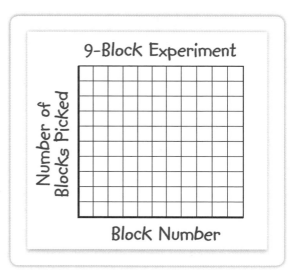

Bar Graph of Class Data

Activity Master 96

Task Ask students to help you label the graph. If necessary, review how to label and number the axes. The horizontal axis needs a column for each possible outcome (blocks 1–9), and an appropriate label, such as "Block Number." The vertical axis will indicate the number of times each block is chosen; it needs an appropriate label, such as "Number of Blocks Picked." Have students suggest a title, such as "9-Block Experiment."

The rows should be numbered, but there is no way to tell in advance how many rows will be needed. The class may want to estimate a likely number of rows, leaving space at the top of the graph to add more rows if necessary.

9-Block Experiment

Number of Blocks Picked

Block Number

Briefly describe the experiment. You will put blocks or cards numbered from 1 to 9 into an opaque bag. Each student in turn will draw one block at random from the bag and return it to the bag before the next student's turn. A total of 27 blocks will be drawn. (This total will make calculations easier for the students. If necessary, you can draw the extras yourself, or have some students take a second turn.)

Next, perform the experiment. After students draw blocks at random, they should record the number on the graph. For example, if a student drew block #5, the student would shade one square in the column for block #5. The student would then replace the block in the bag and mix the blocks well. Make sure that, in the end, the class has drawn a block 27 times.

Use with Lesson Activity Book pp. 205–206.

Purpose To analyze the results of the 9-block experiment

NCTM Standards 1, 2, 6, 7, 8, 9, 10

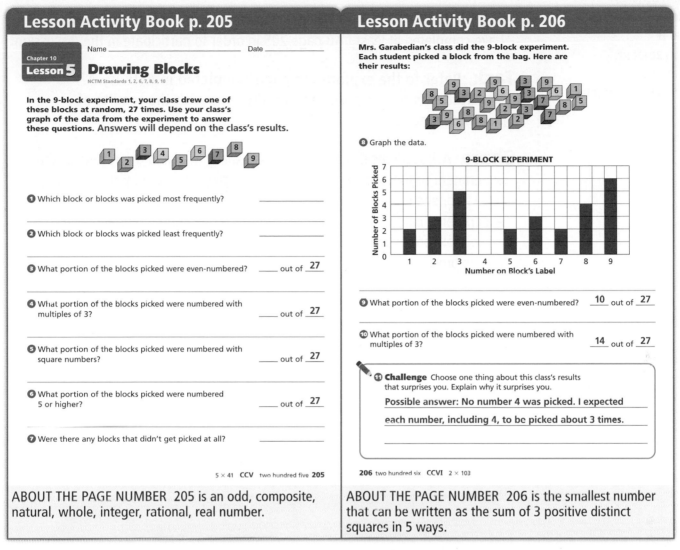

Lesson Activity Book p. 205

Chapter 10
Lesson 5 **Drawing Blocks**
NCTM Standards 1, 2, 6, 7, 8, 9, 10

In the 9-block experiment, your class drew one of these blocks at random, 27 times. Use your class's graph of the data from the experiment to answer these questions. Answers will depend on the class's results.

❶ Which block or blocks was picked most frequently? _____

❷ Which block or blocks was picked least frequently? _____

❸ What portion of the blocks picked were even-numbered? ____ out of **27**

❹ What portion of the blocks picked were numbered with multiples of 3? ____ out of **27**

❺ What portion of the blocks picked were numbered with square numbers? ____ out of **27**

❻ What portion of the blocks picked were numbered 5 or higher? ____ out of **27**

❼ Were there any blocks that didn't get picked at all? _____

5 × 41 **CCV** two hundred five **205**

ABOUT THE PAGE NUMBER 205 is an odd, composite, natural, whole, integer, rational, real number.

Lesson Activity Book p. 206

Mrs. Garabedian's class did the 9-block experiment. Each student picked a block from the bag. Here are their results:

❽ Graph the data.

9-BLOCK EXPERIMENT

❾ What portion of the blocks picked were even-numbered? **10** out of **27**

❿ What portion of the blocks picked were numbered with multiples of 3? **14** out of **27**

⓫ **Challenge** Choose one thing about this class's results that surprises you. Explain why it surprises you.

Possible answer: No number 4 was picked. I expected each number, including 4, to be picked about 3 times.

206 two hundred six **CCVI** 2 × 103

ABOUT THE PAGE NUMBER 206 is the smallest number that can be written as the sum of 3 positive distinct squares in 5 ways.

Teaching Notes for LAB page 205

Have students complete the page individually or with partners.

On this page, students use the class's bar graph to answer questions about the results of the experiment. Be sure that the graph is displayed so that everyone can refer to it. Problems 3–7 are the questions students considered in Activity A. Students are likely to find that some of the class results failed to match the results they predicted.

Teaching Notes for LAB page 206

On this page, students are asked to graph and analyze data from a 9-block experiment different from the one they conducted.

Challenge Problem Students are asked to write about something in the data they find surprising. As with any such experiment, there are many ways in which the results might not match the prediction. Here, for example, an even-numbered block was drawn 10 times, not the predicted 12 times.

D Comparing Results to Predictions

Materials
- For the teacher: completed graph from Activity B
- For each student: completed LAB pp. 205–206; completed Explore SH p. 166

NCTM Standards 1, 2, 6, 7, 8, 9, 10

Purpose To review the results of the 9-block experiment

Introduce Show the completed graph from Activity B. Students should have completed at least LAB page 205 in order to participate in the discussion.

Task Refer to the exploration page completed in Activity A. Ask students to compare their predictions with the results of the experiment.

Share Ask students if their predictions exactly matched the results of the experiment. If they did not, ask students to give reasons why that might have happened. Be sure students understand that the results of probability experiments can differ from what might have been predicted, and that a reasonable prediction is not "wrong" if it fails to anticipate experimental results precisely.

Use with Lesson Activity Book pp. 205–206.

Reflect and Summarize the Lesson

Write Math

> **In the 9-block experiment, is it possible that a block with an even number would not be picked at all in 27 draws? Is it likely? Explain your answer.** It is possible that an even number block wouldn't be picked, but it's unlikely; Possible explanation: Since there are 4 even-numbered blocks; I would expect to draw an even number about $\frac{4}{9}$ of the time. In 27 draws, that would be about 12 times. So it would be unusual to have 0 draws if I'm expecting about 12.

Review Model ....

Refer students to Review Model: Making a Bar Graph in the *Student Handbook* p. 167 to practice displaying data in a bar graph.

✔ Check for Understanding

1

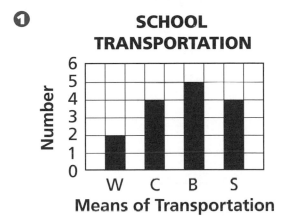

SCHOOL TRANSPORTATION

Sample labels are shown. Others are possible, as are other orders for displaying the columns.

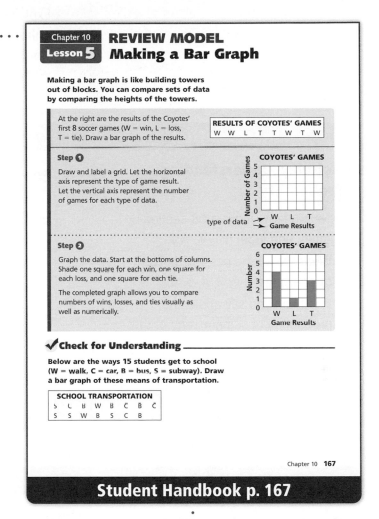

Student Handbook p. 167

Leveled Problem Solving

A bag holds cards numbered from 1 to 10. Sam chooses a card, looks at the number, and puts the card back. He does this 30 times and graphs the results.

❶ Basic Level
In a graph of the data, what could the vertical axis represent? the number of times each card was picked

❷ On Level
If the vertical axis is "number of cards drawn," what is the biggest number he needs to have? Explain. 30; Even though it is unlikely, it is possible that the same card will be picked 30 times.

❸ Above Level
About how many times would you expect an even number to be drawn? Explain. About 15; You are doing the experiment 30 times, $\frac{1}{2}$ of the numbers are even, and $\frac{1}{2}$ of 30 is 15.

Intervention	Practice	Extension

Activity Understanding Probability

Have students make an 8-section spinner, and label it 1–8. Ask:

- What are all the possible outcomes of one spin? 1, 2, 3, 4, 5, 6, 7, 8

- What can you say about the probability of spinning any of these outcomes? They are all equally likely.

- If you get three 5s in a row, what is the probability that you will get a 5 on the next spin? $\frac{1}{8}$

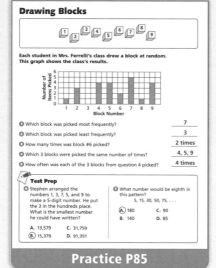

Practice P85

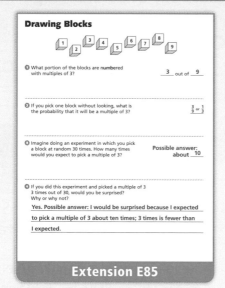

Extension E85

Spiral Review

Spiral Review Book page SR85 provides review of the following previously learned skills and concepts:

- practicing adding, subtracting, multiplying, and dividing multidigit numbers

- solving problems using the strategy *draw a picture*

You may wish to have students work with a partner to complete the page.

Number and Operations

Find the sum.

❶ 381 + 219	❷ 745 + 89	❸ 422 + 199	❹ 611 + 928
600	834	621	1,539

❺ 86 + 85 + 21	❻ 108 + 98 + 85	❼ 47 + 76 + 754	❽ 96 + 175 + 36
192	291	877	307

Find the difference.

❾ 351 − 194	❿ 520 − 359	⓫ 792 − 225	⓬ 905 − 689
157	161	567	216

Find the product.

⓭ 32 × 41	⓮ 63 × 19	⓯ 107 × 96	⓰ 229 × 35
1,312	1,197	10,272	8,015

Find the quotient.

⓱ 96 ÷ 8	⓲ 119 ÷ 7	⓳ 504 ÷ 9	⓴ 221 ÷ 17
12	17	56	13

Problem Solving

Solve the problem. Explain your answer.

㉑ Andrew has 3 new books to put on his shelf. In how many different orders can he put the books?

6 different orders; Possible explanation: I made an organized list of the possible orders. There are 6: 123, 132, 213, 231, 312, 321.

Spiral Review SR85

Extension Activity
Extending Probabilities

Have students make a bar graph for predicted results of spinning a 1–6 spinner 40 times. For their graphs, ask them to answer these questions:

- What is the range of outcomes?

- What is the mode outcome?

- Why do you think your predictions make sense? Students should see that if each outcome is equally likely, it would make sense to predict results that are reasonably close to one another.

Teacher's Notes 🍎

Daily Notes . . .

Quick Notes

More Ideas

Lesson 6 Collecting and Analyzing Survey Data

NCTM Standards 1, 2, 6, 7, 8, 9, 10

Lesson Planner

- To create survey questions and to collect survey responses
- To graph and analyze survey data

1 Daily Activities (TG p. 839)

Open-Ended Problem Solving/Headline Story	Skills Practice and Review—Multiplying by 7

2 Teach and Practice (TG pp. 840–843)

	MATERIALS
(A) **Surveying the Class** (TG p. 840)	• graph paper, rulers
(B) **Graphing Survey Data** (TG pp. 841–842)	• 📖 LAB pp. 207–208
(C) **Collecting and Analyzing Survey Data** (TG p. 843)	

3 Differentiated Instruction (TG p. 844)

Leveled Problem Solving (TG p. 844)	Practice Book P86
Intervention Activity (TG p. 844)	Extension Book E86
Extension Activity (TG p. 844)	Spiral Review Book SR86

Lesson Notes

About the Lesson

In this lesson, students are likely to encounter different types of data in their graphs of responses to survey questions. Some questions have numerical answers (for example, "How many siblings do you have?"); others do not (for example "What's your favorite ice cream flavor?"). Both types of information can be usefully displayed in a bar graph; the types of questions we ask about the data may be quite different. (See About the Mathematics.)

About the Mathematics

When data are numerical, we can look for patterns in the numbers, by asking questions such as: What range of values do the responses fall into? Are there clusters of responses around particular values, or are the responses scattered randomly? For non-numerical data, we can make the data numerical by counting them, perhaps looking at how many responses fall into each category and then analyzing their relative frequencies.

One way to think about differences between numerical and non-numerical data is to ask whether you could rearrange the order of the columns of a graph displaying the data. It doesn't make any difference whether you place the column representing strawberry ice cream preferences next to the column representing chocolate preferences or the one representing vanilla preferences. It doesn't make sense, though, to place the column representing students who have 1 sibling next to the column representing students who have 4 siblings.

(continued on page R5)

Developing Mathematical Language

Vocabulary: data

Your students may be surprised to learn that the word *data* is a plural noun, and that the statement "My *data* is accurate" is not, strictly speaking, grammatically correct. The correct statement is "My *data* are accurate." (The singular form of the word *data* is the awkward and rarely used "datum.") In common usage the distinction is blurred. What is important is that your students hear the word in context.

Familiarize students with the term *data.*

Beginning Display the results of any survey or display a graph on the board or on a transparency. Tell students that all the information shown are facts or *data.* Ask a student to identify a piece of data from the display.

Intermediate Describe a survey that your students might conduct, such as finding the number of hours of reading students do on the weekend. Ask students to name examples of *data* that they would expect to collect from the survey you describe.

Advanced Provide pairs of students with a copy of a graph from a newspaper or magazine. Ask them to describe the *data* that the graph displays. Have pairs share their findings in groups.

Open-Ended Problem Solving

Read the Headline Story to the students. Encourage them to draw diagrams of possible spinners and to think of other creative ways to solve the problem.

 Headline Story

Hannah made a spinner with sections colored red, yellow, and blue, but it wasn't a fair spinner. The spinner was most likely to land on blue and least likely to land on red. The probability of landing on yellow was $\frac{1}{4}$. What can you say about the probability of landing on blue?

Possible responses: The probability of landing on yellow is $\frac{1}{4}$, so the probability of *not* landing on yellow is $\frac{3}{4}$. The probability of landing on blue is greater than $\frac{1}{4}$, because blue is more likely than yellow. The probability of landing on blue must also be less than $\frac{3}{4}$, because there's at least a small chance of landing on red.

Skills Practice and Review

Multiplying by 7

Say a number from 3 to 12. Ask a student to name the number that is 7 times the number you named. Explain that students should say *only* the answer, and no other words such as "Seven times three is . . . ." Repeat, using other initial numbers.

2 | Teach and Practice

Ⓐ Surveying the Class

Purpose To conduct a survey

Introduce Take a minute or two to make sure your students understand what a survey is. You might ask them to think of examples of situations in which a survey might be used in real life, or occasions when they have conducted or participated in surveys for school.

Task Ask students to suggest survey questions they could ask each other to learn something interesting about the class. Write the suggestions on the board. Some examples:

- How many pets do you have?
- What month were you born in?

When you have collected 4–6 questions, survey the students for their responses to the questions. One way to do this would be to have each student write down his or her response to each question. For each question in turn, ask a student to read his or her response. Then ask all who responded the same way to raise their hands. Next, ask someone with a different response to read it, and ask for a show of hands from those whose responses match. Repeat the process until you have counted the entire class. (Make sure students understand that they can raise their hands for only one response.) For each question, keep a record of how many students chose each response. Students will graph this data in Activity B.

💬 Talk Math

❓ Why should you choose only one response to each survey question? Possible answer: The purpose of the survey is to collect data on each person's favorite response, of all the possible responses, or the most common response, of all those possible. You can have only one "favorite," and there can be only one "most common."

❓ How do possible responses to the question, "How many pets do you have" differ from possible responses to the question, "What is your favorite color?" Possible answer: Responses to the first question are numbers. Responses to the second question are words.

Teacher Story

❝I extended this lesson into a second class period, to allow the students to conduct the surveys themselves. This took time and a moderate amount of organization, but students enjoyed the activity and learned a good deal from it. It also sparked some good discussion about how to make sure you've counted everyone in the class once and only once, and about how to handle unusual responses to survey questions.❞

Purpose To draw a bar graph to display survey results

Introduce Display the tallies of student responses to the questions you posed in Activity A.

Task Divide the class into groups. Assign a survey question to each group. Direct each group to make a bar graph of the class's responses to its question.

Students must decide how they will label and number their axes. Most groups will let their horizontal axis represent the various responses to their survey question, and the vertical axis the number of votes each response received. This is the customary method, but if a group interchanges the axis labels, its graph is not "wrong." The bars will extend horizontally rather than vertically. During later class discussions, draw attention to any such graphs groups may have made, and ask students to discuss the similarities and differences with respect to the more conventional orientation.

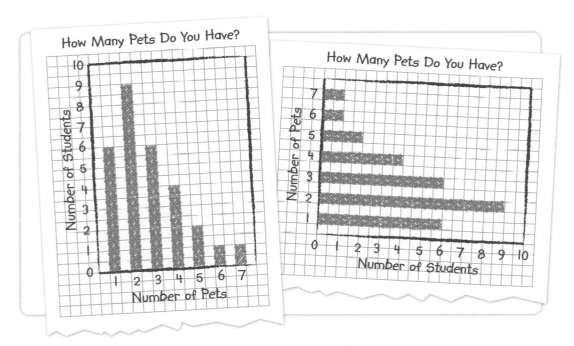

Share After students have completed their graphs, bring the class together to discuss its results. Ask questions like the following:

- What responses to your question were given? Were those all the possible responses, or if you had questioned more students, might one or more have given a response you don't have on your graph? (For an open-ended question like "What's your favorite ice cream flavor?" it's always possible that someone will pick a flavor no one else has thought of. For questions like "How many siblings do you have?" or "What's your birth month?" it's always possible that someone might have a different number of siblings or a different birth month than anyone whose response has already been recorded, but at some point these possibilities start to get pretty unlikely.

Materials
- For each group: graph paper, ruler

NCTM Standards 1, 2, 6, 7, 8, 9, 10

✓ **Ongoing Assessment**
- Do students know how to number and label the axes of a bar graph?
- Do students know how record data on a bar graph?

Concept Alert

Some surveys provide specific answers to questions for respondents to choose from. When students create graphs of such surveys, it's not uncommon for them to omit answers that no one chose. Suppose a survey question asked, "Of the following ice cream flavors, which is your favorite: vanilla, chocolate, strawberry, cherry?" If no one chose, say, cherry, students might create a graph that only listed vanilla, chocolate, and strawberry. In fact, they should include cherry on their graph, and show it collecting zero votes. Otherwise, a person looking at the graph wouldn't know whether cherry was omitted because no one voted for it or because it wasn't a choice. The difference is subtle, but important.

- What was the most/least common response? (For questions with a pre-defined set of possible responses, this may raise the question of whether a response that was chosen 0 times counts as "least common," or should even be on the graph at all.)

- Were all the responses chosen about the same number of times, or are there some that were chosen a lot and others that were chosen very little?

- Were most responses clustered around some particular value, or were they scattered? (This question makes sense only for questions with numerical answers, since for a question like "What's your favorite ice cream flavor?" no response is "close" to any other. However, the ice cream question might get students thinking about differences between the types of survey questions that were asked.)

- For questions with numerical answers, you can ask about the range of responses. For example, "What is the largest/smallest number of siblings anyone has?"

Talk Math

❷ How can you find the number of students who participated in your survey? Possible answer: Since each shaded square on my graph represents one person, I can simply count to find the total number of shaded squares.

❷ If the results of a survey are displayed on a bar graph, how can you tell the most common response to the survey question simply by looking at the bars of the graph? Possible answer: The most common response will be represented by the longest bar.

Collecting and Analyzing Survey Data LAB pp. 207–208

individuals or pairs   **20 MIN**

Purpose To draw and interpret bar graphs

NCTM Standards 1, 2, 6, 7, 8, 9, 10

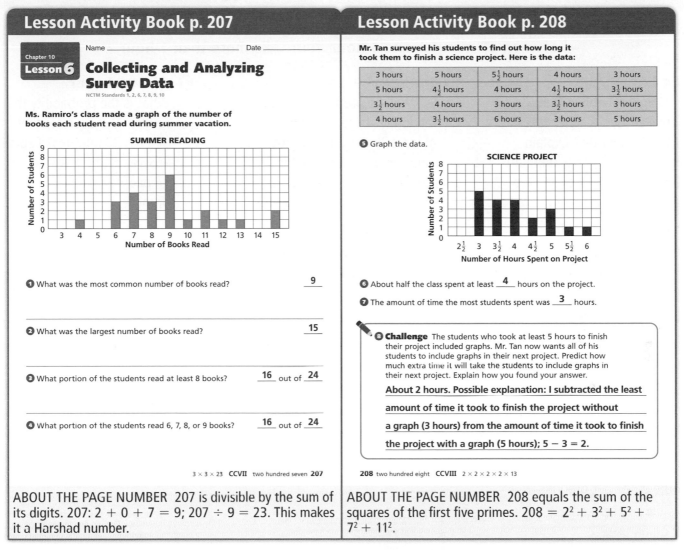

Lesson Activity Book p. 207

Name _____ Date _____

Chapter 10
Lesson 6 **Collecting and Analyzing Survey Data**
NCTM Standards 1, 2, 6, 7, 8, 9, 10

Ms. Ramiro's class made a graph of the number of books each student read during summer vacation.

SUMMER READING

(bar graph: Number of Students vs Number of Books Read)

❶ What was the most common number of books read? **9**

❷ What was the largest number of books read? **15**

❸ What portion of the students read at least 8 books? **16** out of **24**

❹ What portion of the students read 6, 7, 8, or 9 books? **16** out of **24**

3 × 3 × 23 CCVII two hundred seven **207**

Lesson Activity Book p. 208

Mr. Tan surveyed his students to find out how long it took them to finish a science project. Here is the data:

3 hours	5 hours	$5\frac{1}{2}$ hours	4 hours	3 hours
5 hours	$4\frac{1}{2}$ hours	4 hours	$4\frac{1}{2}$ hours	$3\frac{1}{2}$ hours
$3\frac{1}{2}$ hours	4 hours	3 hours	$3\frac{1}{2}$ hours	3 hours
4 hours	$3\frac{1}{2}$ hours	6 hours	3 hours	5 hours

❺ Graph the data.

SCIENCE PROJECT

(bar graph: Number of Students vs Number of Hours Spent on Project)

❻ About half the class spent at least **4** hours on the project.

❼ The amount of time the most students spent was **3** hours.

❽ **Challenge** The students who took at least 5 hours to finish their project included graphs. Mr. Tan now wants all of his students to include graphs in their next project. Predict how much extra time it will take the students to include graphs in their next project. Explain how you found your answer.
About 2 hours. Possible explanation: I subtracted the least amount of time it took to finish the project without a graph (3 hours) from the amount of time it took to finish the project with a graph (5 hours); 5 − 3 = 2.

208 two hundred eight CCVIII 2 × 2 × 2 × 2 × 13

ABOUT THE PAGE NUMBER 207 is divisible by the sum of its digits. 207: 2 + 0 + 7 = 9; 207 ÷ 9 = 23. This makes it a Harshad number.

ABOUT THE PAGE NUMBER 208 equals the sum of the squares of the first five primes. $208 = 2^2 + 3^2 + 5^2 + 7^2 + 11^2$.

Teaching Notes for LAB page 207

Have students complete the page individually or with partners. Students analyze data from a bar graph and think about what questions can and cannot be answered by looking at the graph. Problems 3 and 4 illustrate two ways of thinking about the range of values "most" of the data falls into. Problem 4 draws attention to the central "hump" of the graph.

Teaching Notes for LAB page 208

Students graph survey results and interpret the data.

Challenge Problem This problem provides an example of how data from a survey might be used in a real-life situation. To answer Mr. Tan's question, students will need to think about what the graph tells them about the time spent by a "typical student" or by "most students" in Mr. Tan's class.

Reflect and Summarize the Lesson

Write Math Jonathan recorded these responses to his survey question "How many cars does your family own?": 0 cars (1 vote), 1 car (6 votes), 2 cars (14 votes), 3 cars (4 votes). Explain how he could display the data in a bar graph. Possible answer: He could label the horizontal axis "Number of Cars" and list choices of 0, 1, 2, and 3 cars. He could label the vertical axis "Number of Votes" and write numbers from 0 to 14. Finally, he could shade the appropriate number of boxes above each of the 4 horizontal choices, using the vertical axis as a guide.

Use with Lesson Activity Book pp. 207–208.

Chapter 10 • Lesson 6 **843**

Leveled Problem Solving

Eight teachers get to school in less than 30 minutes; 20 take between 30 minutes and 1 hour; four take more than 1 hour.

❶ Basic Level

What is the probability that a randomly chosen teacher takes less than 30 minutes? Explain how you know. $\frac{8}{32}$, or $\frac{1}{4}$; There are 32 teachers, and 8 of them take less than 30 minutes.

❷ On Level

What is the probability that a randomly chosen teacher takes at least 30 minutes but not more than 1 hour? Explain your answer. $\frac{20}{32}$, or $\frac{5}{8}$; Out of 32 teachers, 20 take more than 30 minutes but less than 1 hour.

❸ Above Level

What is the probability that a randomly chosen teacher takes at least 30 minutes? Explain your answer. $\frac{24}{32}$, or $\frac{3}{4}$; A total of 24 people take 30 minutes or more.

Intervention	Practice	Extension

Activity Displaying Data

Display these data and ask the questions below.

Favorite Fruit	Students
Orange	6
Banana	5
Apple	7
Peach	3

- What type of graph would you use to display the data? bar graph
- What would be the greatest number on an axis? 7

Have pairs of students make a graph of the data in the table.

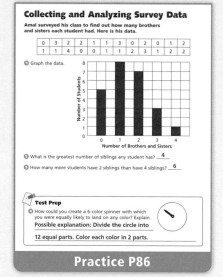

Practice P86

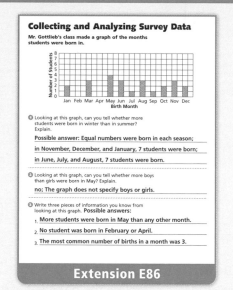

Extension E86

Spiral Review

Spiral Review Book page SR86 provides review of the following previously learned skills and concepts:

- using patterns to develop strategies for learning multiplication facts
- estimating and measuring capacity

You may wish to have students work with a partner to complete the page.

Spiral Review SR86

Extension Activity
Analyzing Data

Have students make a bar graph of the data. Then ask them to explain

Biggest Animal I Ever Saw	Number of Students
Whale	4
Elephant	12
Giraffe	2
Horse	1
Alligator	3

whether this question makes sense:

- Can we use a table to decide which is the biggest animal ever seen by those surveyed? No; The data do not show the sizes of the animals.

Teacher's Notes 🍎

Daily Notes . . .

Quick Notes

More Ideas

Lesson 7 Collecting Measurement Data

NCTM Standards 1, 2, 6, 7, 8, 9, 10

Lesson Planner

STUDENT OBJECTIVES
- To collect data by measuring arm lengths
- To interpret bar graphs

1 Daily Activities (TG p. 847)

Open-Ended Problem Solving/Headline Story	Skills Practice and Review—Multiplying by 8

2 Teach and Practice (TG pp. 848–851)

	MATERIALS
(A) **Introducing a Measuring Experiment** (TG p. 848)	• transparency of AM97 (optional), transparency marker
(B) **Discussing Measuring Technique** (TG pp. 849–850)	• measuring tools (such as measuring tapes or string and rulers)
(C) **Collecting Measurement Data** (TG p. 851)	• 📖 LAB pp. 209–210

3 Differentiated Instruction (TG p. 852)

Leveled Problem Solving (TG p. 852)	Practice Book P87
Intervention Activity (TG p. 852)	Extension Book E87
Extension Activity (TG p. 852)	Spiral Review Book SR87

Lesson Notes

About the Lesson

Students collect data to help answer the question, "If I am to measure a fourth grader's arm, what can I predict about how long it would be?" Students practice measuring skills and prepare data they will analyze in the next lesson. They will see that collecting and graphing data can help to answer questions related to probability.

Use with Lesson Activity Book pp. 209–210.

Developing Mathematical Language

Vocabulary: precision

The *precision* of a measurement is related to the unit of measurement chosen. The smaller the unit of measure, the greater the *precision* of the measurement. A measurement of $5\frac{3}{8}$ inches is more *precise* than a measurement of $5\frac{1}{4}$ inches, because $\frac{1}{8}$ inch is smaller than $\frac{1}{4}$ inch. A measurement of 4 feet is more precise than a measurement of 1 yard. Students may prefer measuring with larger units because it is easier to do so. Help them to see the importance of obtaining the most *precise* measurements possible.

Familiarize students with the terms *precision* and *precise.*

Beginning Write several pairs of measurements on the board, such as "3 cups" and "about 1 quart." Tell which measurement is more *precise* and why by completing the sentence " _____ is more *precise* because _____." Then ask students to do the same for the other measurements.

Intermediate Name several measurements. For each measurement, ask a volunteer to give a more *precise* measurement close to the given one. For example, if you say "about 1 yard", students might answer "35 inches" or "3 feet."

Advanced Have partners write several pairs of measurements of approximately the same value. For each pair of measurements, have partners decide which is more *precise.*

Open-Ended Problem Solving

Read the Headline Story to the students. Encourage them to think how they could collect and record data to answer the question, and what they could predict about the results.

 Headline Story

> **How many siblings do the students in this class have?**

Possible responses: The class might collect data using tallies. The class might make a histogram. Students might also find the average number of siblings, the most common number of siblings, or the different numbers of siblings that students have. Or they might make a chart like this:

Number of siblings	0	1	2	3	4	5	6
Number of students	3	8	6	5	0	1	2

Skills Practice and Review

Multiplying by 8

Say a number from 3 to 12. Ask a student to name the number that is 8 times the number you named. Explain that students should say *only* the answer, and no other words such as "Eight times three is . . . ." Repeat, using other initial numbers.

whole class **10 MIN**

A Introducing a Measuring Experiment

NCTM Standards 1, 2, 6, 7, 8, 9, 10

Purpose To introduce the measurement experiment students will do in Activity C

Introduce Ask this question: "If I measured the length of a fourth grader's arm, how long do you think it would be?"

Task **Engage your students in a discussion of your question. See that some of the following points are made during the discussion:**

- Not all students' arm lengths are the same.

- Students can *estimate* the answer, but they can't be *certain* of the answer without collecting data.

- If you knew which student had the shortest arm and which student had the longest arm, and if you measured their arms, you would know that everyone else's arm length would be somewhere between those two values.

- For experiments or events like this, you need to collect data before you can reach any conclusions.

- Students will need to gather some actual measurements before they can answer the question.

💬 Talk Math

❓ When in everyday life might someone want to collect data about a group of students? Possible answer: The school principal might collect data to answer the question, "How many days are fourth graders absent each year?" or "How far do fourth graders live from school?"

❓ If we collect data about arm lengths for our class, what kinds of questions might we be able to answer? Possible answers: We could ask about the longest and shortest arms, or the most common arm length. Depending on how we collect the data, we might be able to tell who has the longest (or shortest) arm length.

✔ Ongoing Assessment

- Do students understand the difference between an estimate and a calculated answer?

Teacher Story

❝I wanted my students to make connections between the work we were doing to collect and analyze data in class and the use of data in everyday life. So I assigned a homework project that involved looking for charts, graphs, or discussions of statistics. We live in a big sports town, so a lot of kids brought in information about batting averages, free throw statistics, and yards rushed. Other students brought in pie charts and bar graphs from the newspaper. One girl's mom remembered old TV commercials which claimed that "9 out of 10 doctors agree" with something the sponsors wanted viewers to agree with. We had a good discussion about the kinds of data we run into every day.❞

Purpose To discuss details of how to conduct the arm-measuring experiment

Introduce If, in Grade 3 *Think Math!,* students made measurements similar to those they will make in this lesson, remind them of this fact.

Task Explain that before students can answer the question, "How long is a fourth grader's arm?" they should think about some of the issues that are involved in measuring lengths.

Share Pose the following questions to the class:

- **What do we mean when we say "arm length?" How can we make sure that we're all measuring the same thing?** Students should realize that it is important for everyone to measure the same way, so students can compare their measurements. Since the initial question didn't specify what "arm length" means, the class may decide to measure their arms from the fingertips or from the wrist, to the neck or to the armpit.

- **Does it matter which arm (left or right) we measure?** Most people's arms are about the same length, but not exactly. For the purpose of this experiment, the difference probably doesn't matter. Nevertheless, your class may feel that measuring the same arm will keep the measurements as consistent as possible

- **How can we make sure our measurements are accurate? What tools will help us measure accurately? Should we somehow check our measurements after we've made them?** Measuring tape, adding-machine tape, and string are good options for measuring tools. String or adding-machine tape can be marked at arm length and then measured with a ruler on a flat surface. One way to obtain an accurate measurement is to have a partner hold the string or tape measure at the tips of the fingers of the student being measured, while the student pulls the measuring tool tight to his or her body. With a volunteer, briefly demonstrate how the class has agreed to measure arm lengths.

- **How precisely should we measure?** At this point, students should be comfortable measuring to the nearest inch, half-inch, and quarter-inch. The instructions on LAB page 209 ask them to measure to the nearest quarter-inch and then round to the nearest inch. This is so that the number of different data points students must graph is reduced. If necessary, discuss with students how to round these measurements to the nearest inch. Students may suggest a general rule that a measurement showing a quarter-inch ($21\frac{1}{4}$) should be rounded down (21), while a measurement showing three quarter-inches ($18\frac{3}{4}$) should be rounded up (19). Measurements showing half-inches are more complicated because they are equidistant from two surrounding whole inches. As a class, decide how you will deal with half-inch measures. (See Possible Discussion.)

Materials
- For the teacher: sample measuring tools, such as a measuring tape or string and a ruler, transparency of AM97 (optional), transparency marker
- For each pair: measuring tool (such as measuring tape or string and ruler)

NCTM Standards 1, 2, 6, 7, 8, 9, 10

Possible Discussion

Rounding to whole numbers can pose a challenge when working with halves. Since halves are literally halfway between the two nearest wholes, some sort of convention must be agreed upon to decide which whole is considered the nearest. A widely used rule is always to round to the larger whole, but you might just as reasonably choose to round to the smaller whole. If you always round up, you will slightly but systematically inflate your data; if you round down, you will introduce a systematic underestimation. Some conventions call for rounding up some of the time and rounding down the rest of the time. Such halfway conventions can also be applied to rounding to the nearest tens, hundreds, and so on.

While students are working on Activity C, prepare a large chart-size grid paper graph or project a transparency of Activity Master: Class Arm Lengths, so that students can to record their arm-length measurements. Have students come forward one at a time to shade the appropriate squares on the graph. Show arm lengths in inches on the horizontal axis and numbers of students with given arm lengths on the vertical axis.

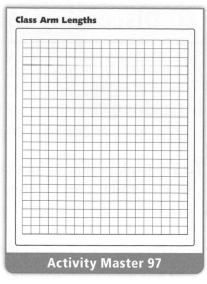

Class Arm Lengths

Activity Master 97

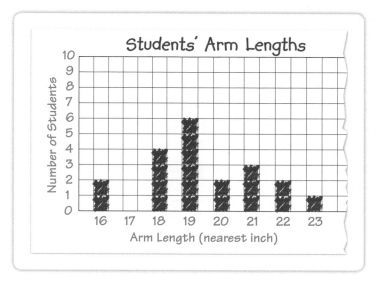

Students' Arm Lengths

✔ Ongoing Assessment

- Do students accurately measure lengths using rulers and string, measuring tapes, or other measuring tools?

- Do students understand how to round a measurement in inches to the nearest inch?

💬 Talk Math

❷ Give two measurements, neither with the number 18 in them, that both round to 18 inches. Possible answers: $17\frac{1}{2}$ inches and $17\frac{3}{4}$ inches.

❷ If three different students each measured a fourth student's arm-length, would they all get the same result? Explain your reasoning. Possible answer: not necessarily; possible explanation: If they measured from slightly different places at each end of the arm, if the student being measured held his or her arm slightly differently for each measurement, or if any other differences among the ways the arm was measured occurred, the measurements might not be the same.

individuals or pairs   **20 MIN**

Purpose To conduct the arm-measuring experiment

NCTM Standards 1, 2, 6, 7, 8, 9, 10

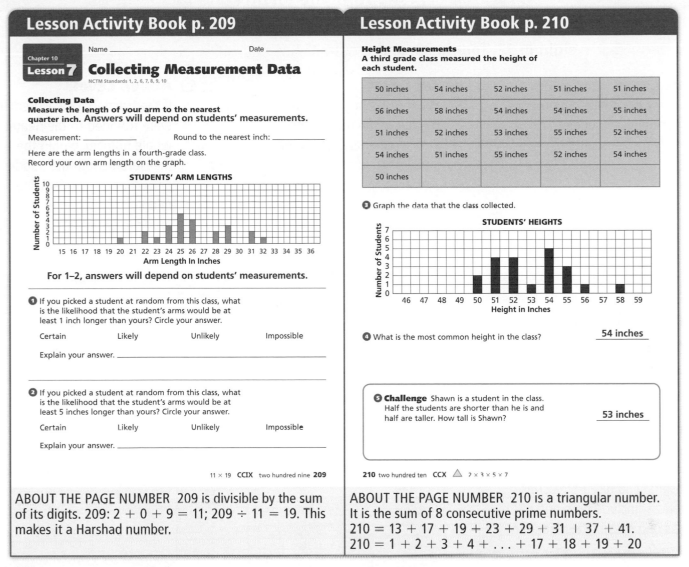

Lesson Activity Book p. 209

Chapter 10
Lesson 7 **Collecting Measurement Data**
NCTM Standards 1, 2, 6, 7, 8, 9, 10

Collecting Data
Measure the length of your arm to the nearest quarter inch. Answers will depend on students' measurements.

Measurement: _____ Round to the nearest inch: _____

Here are the arm lengths in a fourth-grade class. Record your own arm length on the graph.

STUDENTS' ARM LENGTHS

For 1–2, answers will depend on students' measurements.

1 If you picked a student at random from this class, what is the likelihood that the student's arms would be at least 1 inch longer than yours? Circle your answer.

Certain   Likely   Unlikely   Impossible

Explain your answer. _____

2 If you picked a student at random from this class, what is the likelihood that the student's arms would be at least 5 inches longer than yours? Circle your answer.

Certain   Likely   Unlikely   Impossible

Explain your answer. _____

11 × 19   CCIX   two hundred nine **209**

Lesson Activity Book p. 210

Height Measurements
A third grade class measured the height of each student.

50 inches	54 inches	52 inches	51 inches	51 inches
56 inches	58 inches	54 inches	54 inches	55 inches
51 inches	52 inches	53 inches	55 inches	52 inches
54 inches	51 inches	55 inches	52 inches	54 inches
50 inches				

3 Graph the data that the class collected.

STUDENTS' HEIGHTS

4 What is the most common height in the class?   **54 inches**

5 Challenge Shawn is a student in the class. Half the students are shorter than he is and half are taller. How tall is Shawn?   **53 inches**

210 two hundred ten   CCX   △   2 × 3 × 5 × 7

ABOUT THE PAGE NUMBER 209 is divisible by the sum of its digits. 209: 2 + 0 + 9 = 11; 209 ÷ 11 = 19. This makes it a Harshad number.

ABOUT THE PAGE NUMBER 210 is a triangular number. It is the sum of 8 consecutive prime numbers.
210 = 13 + 17 + 19 + 23 + 29 + 31 + 37 + 41.
210 = 1 + 2 + 3 + 4 + … + 17 + 18 + 19 + 20

Teaching Notes for LAB page 209

Have students work with partners. Be sure each pair has measuring tools. Students should measure each other's arm lengths, and then record their measurements to the nearest whole inch on the grid paper or transparency graph that you have prepared (see Activity B). After students have recorded their measurements, they should complete the LAB pages.

Differentiated Instruction Above Level You may want to challenge some or all of your students to answer Problems 1 and 2 using probability (fractions) in addition to words.

Teaching Notes for LAB page 210

Students graph a set of arm-length data.

Challenge Problems Students find the *mode* of the data (the most common item) and the *median* (half the data is greater than the median, half is less). The problems illustrate the fact that the most common measurement is not necessarily representative of the data as a whole.

Reflect and Summarize the Lesson

 Write Math **What would the arm-length graph look like if every measurement were rounded to the nearest foot?** Possible answer: Every measurement would round to either 1 foot or 2 feet. As a result, all the data would be crowded into one or two vertical bars.

Leveled Problem Solving

Three students crossed the room in $27\frac{1}{2}$ paces, six in 30 paces, eight in 32, four in 33, and two in $35\frac{1}{4}$.

❶ Basic Level

What was the most common number of paces needed?

32 paces by 8 students

❷ On Level

What measurement is in the middle of the data, if the measurements are ordered smallest to largest?

32 paces

❸ Above Level

If the fractional measurements were rounded to the nearest whole number, would the measurement in the middle of the data change? Explain. No; The middle is 32 whether the data are rounded or not.

Intervention

Activity Standardizing Measurement

Provide students with various measuring tools, such as rulers, adding machine tape, string, and pencils of known length. Ask students to measure across their desks using one or more measuring tools. Collect results, and discuss reasons for differences. Include precision of measure as one possible explanation.

Practice

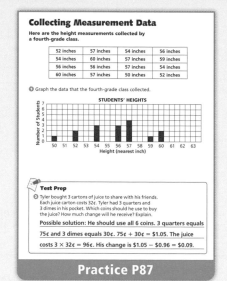

Practice P87

Extension

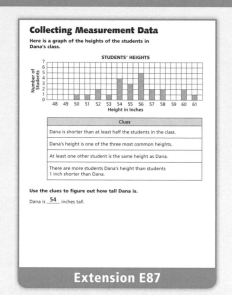

Extension E87

Spiral Review

Spiral Review Book page SR87 provides review of the following previously learned skills and concepts:

- connecting arrays with multiplication
- solving problems using the strategy *solve a simpler problem*

You may wish to have students work with a partner to complete the page.

Spiral Review SR87

Extension Activity
Graph and Analyze Data

Provide pairs of students with a ruler. Have them collect all their books and measure the height of each to the nearest inch.

Have partners graph the data using the horizontal axis for the lengths and the vertical axis for the numbers of books. Then ask students to find the middle height and most common height (if there is one).

Use with Lesson Activity Book pp. 209–210.

Teacher's Notes 🍎

Daily Notes . . .

Quick Notes

More Ideas

Lesson 8 Analyzing Measurement Data

NCTM Standards 1, 2, 6, 7, 8, 9, 10

Lesson Planner

STUDENT OBJECTIVES ···
- To graph measurement data
- To analyze and compare data using bar graphs

1 | Daily Activities (TG p. 855)

Open-Ended Problem Solving/Headline Story	Skills Practice and Review— Calculating Probabilities of Events

2 | Teach and Practice (TG pp. 856–858)

	MATERIALS
Ⓐ **Analyzing Class Arm-Length Data** (TG p. 856)	• bar graph of arm-length data from Lesson 10.7
Ⓑ **Comparing Two Sets of Data** (TG p. 857)	• transparency of AM98 (optional)
Ⓒ **Analyzing Measurement Data** (TG p. 858)	• 📖 LAB pp. 211–212

3 | Differentiated Instruction (TG p. 859)

Leveled Problem Solving (TG p. 859)	Practice Book P88
Intervention Activity (TG p. 859)	Extension Book E88
Extension Activity (TG p. 859)	Spiral Review Book SR88

Lesson Notes

About the Lesson

Students draw bar graphs of the data they collected in **Lesson 10.7** and use the graphs to draw conclusions about arm lengths in the class. They consider the probabilities of choosing a student at random with a certain arm length. The class also uses bar graphs to compare different sets of data.

About the Mathematics

Several measures may be used to help analyze sets of data, including the *range, mode, median,* and *mean.* See About the Mathematics in **Lesson 10.4** and **Lesson 10.6** for further discussion of these measures. Each of these measures provides a generalization of the data; depending on what we want to know, one or another may be the most appropriate measure.

The *mode* is the most common (or most frequent) value in a set of data. The mode is not always a meaningful or representative measure of the data because it may be far from the main cluster of values in the set, or it may be only slightly more common than other values in the set. The *mean* or arithmetic average of the data can be affected by outliers—extreme values in the set—and, as a result may not characterize the data as a whole. The *median* (the value in the middle when the data are listed in order) is likely to be less affected by extreme data points.

Use with Lesson Activity Book pp. 211–212.

Developing Mathematical Language

Vocabulary: median

The *median* is the middle number when the data are arranged in order, or the average of the two middle numbers if there are an even number of items. In the set 2, 7, and 9, the *median* is 7, the middle number. Your students do not need to use these terms but you may wish to describe their meanings in a general way.

Familiarize students with the term *middle.*

Beginning Put an odd number of objects in a line, or draw them on the board, and ask students to find the one in the *middle.*

Intermediate Write the numbers 2, 4, 6, 8, and 10 on the board and ask students to find the number in the *middle* of the series. Continue with other examples.

Advanced Write 5 or 7 numbers on the board. Ask students to order the numbers from smallest to largest and to find the number in the middle of the series.

Open-Ended Problem Solving

Read the Headline Story to the students. Encourage them to think of interesting ways to solve the problem. Invite different students to contribute different parts of the information.

 Headline Story

> Lena is in charge of buying juice for a school party. How can she estimate the total cost?

Possible responses: She can estimate how many people will be at the party and how many cups of juice, on average, each person will want. She will need to know how many cups are in a bottle of juice, the number of bottles she will need, the cost of one bottle, and the total cost of all the bottles.

Skills Practice and Review

Calculating Probabilities of Events

Describe various attribute cards. For each, ask students to give the probability of randomly drawing the card from the deck. Some possible descriptions:

- green striped parallelogram (or any card with three attributes specified) $\frac{1}{12}$
- green (or blue or solid or striped) $\frac{6}{12}$ or $\frac{1}{2}$
- not striped (or not solid or not blue or not green) $\frac{6}{12}$ or $\frac{1}{2}$
- green or striped $\frac{9}{12}$ or $\frac{3}{4}$
- blue or triangle $\frac{8}{12}$ or $\frac{2}{3}$
- not a blue trapezoid $\frac{10}{12}$ or $\frac{5}{6}$

For an additional challenge, give a probability and ask students to name a type of card that has that probability of being drawn.

whole class   15 MIN

(A) Analyzing Class Arm-Length Data

Materials

- For the teacher:
  bar graph of arm-length
  data from Lesson 10.7

NCTM Standards 1, 2, 6, 7, 8, 9, 10

Purpose To discuss the results of the class arm-length experiment

Introduce Display the bar graph of arm-length data that students created in **Lesson 10.7.**

Task Ask students to describe any patterns or peculiarities that they notice in the graph. Ask questions like the following to facilitate the discussion:

- How many students are represented in the graph? (This is the number of shaded squares in the bar graph.)

- What is the longest arm length in the class? (This is the length corresponding to the farthest right shaded square on the graph.)

- What is the shortest arm length in the class? (This is the length corresponding to the farthest left shaded square on the graph.)

- Between which two lengths is about half the class clustered? (You might ask students to look for a "natural" clustering in the middle. You also might ask if students can find a "middle half," with about a quarter of the class above and a quarter below.)

- If everyone in the class lined up in order of arm length, how long would the arm of the person in the middle of the line be? (This question concerns the *median* of the data, although students do not need to use that term.)

- What arm lengths aren't found in the class?

✔ Ongoing Assessment

- Do students distinguish between the meanings of the numbers on the horizontal axis of a bar graph and those on the vertical axis?

💬 Talk Math

❓ If you chose an arm length at random from the data, which length, if any, would you be most likely to choose? the length that occurs most frequently on the graph

❓ Can you use the graph in this activity to draw conclusions about the arm lengths of fourth graders who are not in this class? Explain. possibly; Possible explanation: Fourth graders in other classrooms are probably similar in size to students in my class (and, for example, first graders are generally smaller). So, the length of the arm of a fourth grader from a different class is likely to fit with our class's data.

B Comparing Two Sets of Data

Purpose To compare sets of similar data

Introduce Display Activity Master: Grade 3 Arm Lengths or sketch the graph on the board.

Task Ask students to compare the graph of Grade 3 data with their own data and graph.

You might begin by asking for ideas on how to compare the two graphs. If your students need help getting started, ask questions similar to those you asked in Activity A, this time focusing on the Grade 3 graph. That way, students can compare the way the data are distributed for each graph.

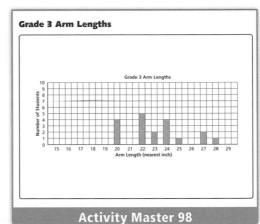

Activity Master 98

Next, have your students compare the graphs. Some questions you might ask to facilitate discussion:

- Are you more likely to find a student with 27-inch arms in the Grade 3 class or in our class?

- Would you say the data are similar in the two classes, or are the data for one class generally greater than those for the other?

- In which class, if any, is there more variation in arm lengths?

Talk Math

❓ We've looked at data for third and fourth graders. How do you think a graph of seventh-grade arm lengths differ from the graph for your class? Possible answer: The data would probably appear farther to the right, in general, because seventh graders' arms are likely to be longer than fourth graders' arms.

❓ If you drew a bar graph showing the number of arms that your classmates have, and a second graph showing the number of arms that the students in a seventh-grade class have, would the graphs be similar or different? Possible answer: they would look exactly alike, with every data point on both graphs representing 2, the number of arms that people have.

Materials
- For the teacher: transparency of AM98 (optional)

NCTM Standards 1, 2, 6, 7, 8, 9, 10

Teacher Story

❝Graphs are extremely helpful tools for interpreting sets of data. Details can become more obvious when data are represented in an organized, visual manner. To highlight this for students, I presented them with a random list of data and asked questions similar to those on LAB page 211. Then I asked students to graph the data and consider the questions again. They saw that using the graph to answer the questions was easier, thanks to the visual organization provided by the graph.❞

individuals or pairs **20 MIN**

Purpose To review the principal results of the arm-length experiment

NCTM Standards 1, 2, 6, 7, 8, 9, 10

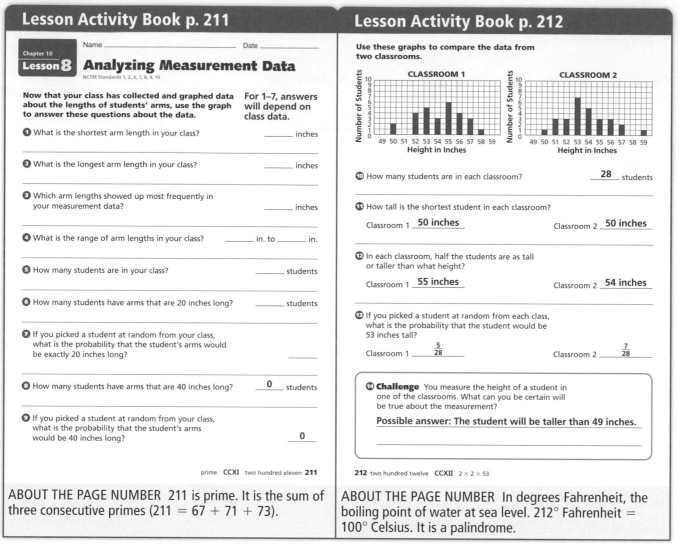

Lesson Activity Book p. 211

Chapter 10
Lesson 8 **Analyzing Measurement Data**
NCTM Standards 1, 2, 6, 7, 8, 9, 10

Name _____ Date _____

Now that your class has collected and graphed data about the lengths of students' arms, use the graph to answer these questions about the data.

For 1–7, answers will depend on class data.

① What is the shortest arm length in your class? _____ inches

② What is the longest arm length in your class? _____ inches

③ Which arm lengths showed up most frequently in your measurement data? _____ inches

④ What is the range of arm lengths in your class? _____ in. to _____ in.

⑤ How many students are in your class? _____ students

⑥ How many students have arms that are 20 inches long? _____ students

⑦ If you picked a student at random from your class, what is the probability that the student's arms would be exactly 20 inches long? _____

⑧ How many students have arms that are 40 inches long? **0** students

⑨ If you picked a student at random from your class, what is the probability that the student's arms would be 40 inches long? **0**

prime **CCXI** two hundred eleven **211**

ABOUT THE PAGE NUMBER 211 is prime. It is the sum of three consecutive primes (211 = 67 + 71 + 73).

Lesson Activity Book p. 212

Use these graphs to compare the data from two classrooms.

CLASSROOM 1 — Number of Students / Height in Inches

CLASSROOM 2 — Number of Students / Height in Inches

⑩ How many students are in each classroom? **28** students

⑪ How tall is the shortest student in each classroom?
Classroom 1 **50 inches**   Classroom 2 **50 inches**

⑫ In each classroom, half the students are as tall or taller than what height?
Classroom 1 **55 inches**   Classroom 2 **54 inches**

⑬ If you picked a student at random from each class, what is the probability that the student would be 53 inches tall?
Classroom 1 **$\frac{5}{28}$**   Classroom 2 **$\frac{7}{28}$**

⑭ **Challenge** You measure the height of a student in one of the classrooms. What can you be certain will be true about the measurement?
Possible answer: The student will be taller than 49 inches.

212 two hundred twelve **CCXII** 2 × 2 × 53

ABOUT THE PAGE NUMBER In degrees Fahrenheit, the boiling point of water at sea level. 212° Fahrenheit = 100° Celsius. It is a palindrome.

Teaching Notes for LAB page 211

Have students complete the page individually or with partners. This page will help students solidify their understanding of the arm-length graph, and also some of the terms used to describe data. It may also serve as an informal assessment of students' skills interpreting graphs. If students find the problems repetitious, have them skip to LAB page 212.

Teaching Notes for LAB page 212

Challenge Problem This problem requires students to draw a conclusion about a student's height that will be true for an arbitrary student chosen from one of the classrooms. Students cannot say, for example, that the student will be less than 59 inches tall, for one student is exactly that height. They could say, however, that the student will be shorter than 5 feet tall or taller than 49 inches.

Reflect and Summarize the Lesson

Write Math Using a graph of arm-length data, how could you find the most common of all the lengths? Possible answer: Look for the tallest bar on the graph. Find the number written below the bar. This is the most common arm length, in inches.

Leveled Problem Solving

A fourth-grade class and an eighth-grade class each made graphs of their ages, heights, favorite foods, and distances they live from school.

① Basic Level

For which graph or graphs would it be difficult to tell which class it represented? Explain. Distance from school and favorite foods; these data are not related to students' ages or sizes.

② On Level

Which graph for the eighth graders would probably have the greatest range? Explain. Heights; ages will be close, and most students will probably live no more than several miles from school.

③ Above Level

Which graph or graphs would have no middle value? Explain. Favorite foods; it does not make sense to try to find foods between other foods.

Intervention

Activity Estimating the Average

Have students add the smallest and largest arm measurements in the group and divide that number by 2. Ask them how the quotient compares to the most common and the middle measures. Help students recognize that if the data are all clustered closely, the quotient will be a good approximation of the middle number but perhaps not of the most common number.

Practice

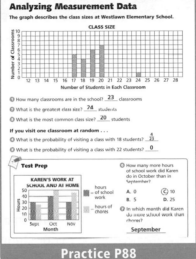

Practice P88

Extension

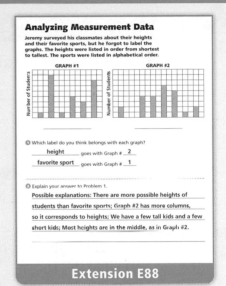

Extension E88

Spiral Review

Spiral Review Book page SR88 provides review of the following previously learned skills and concepts:

- classifying triangles by the number of sides of equal length
- using the terms *impossible, unlikely, likely,* and *certain* to describe the probability of drawing a card with particular attributes

You may wish to have students work with a partner to complete the page.

Spiral Review SR88

Extension Activity
Finding Probabilities

Have pairs complete each statement below and write probabilities for it.

The probability of choosing a student whose arm length is

- at most _____ inches is _____.
- greater than 23 inches is _____.
- between _____ and _____ inches is _____.
- less than _____ inches is _____.
- exactly 17 inches is _____.

Lesson 9 Problem Solving Strategy and Test Prep

NCTM Standards 1, 2, 6, 7, 8, 9, 10

Lesson Planner

STUDENT OBJECTIVES
- To apply the problem-solving strategy *make a graph*
- To articulate the steps and strategies used to solve problems
- To prepare for standardized tests

Problem Solving Strategy:
Make a Graph (TG pp. 861–862, 864–865)

MATERIALS

(A) Discussing the Problem Solving Strategy: Make a Graph (TG p. 861)

(B) Solving Problems by Applying the Strategy (TG p. 862)

- transparency of LAB p. 213 (optional)
- LAB p. 213
- SH pp. 168–169

Problem Solving Test Prep (TG p. 863)

(C) Getting Ready for Standardized Tests (TG p. 863)

- LAB p. 214

Lesson Notes

About Problem Solving

Problem Solving Strategy: Make a Graph

This lesson focuses on the problem solving strategy *make a graph,* which students have used throughout the second half of this chapter. The strategy has widespread applications beyond the study of data and probability, but that topic provides an excellent context for practicing the strategy. Also in this lesson, students have an opportunity to demonstrate their understanding of several key ideas presented in the chapter: identifying all the possible outcomes of an event, describing likelihoods of events using the words *certain, likely, unlikely,* and *impossible,* expressing probabilities as fractions and comparing them, and interpreting graphs.

Skills Practice and Review

Classifying Polygons

Draw shapes on the board one at a time, and ask your students to state whether or not the shape is a polygon. Circle the polygons to record students' conclusions. If students have difficulty remembering the definition of polygon, draw several examples and counterexamples on the board to help students recall the definition. (Polygons are closed shapes with straight sides, no extra lines, and only one inside region.) Here are some shapes you could draw:

When the shapes have been sorted, ask students if they can use other words to describe each type of polygon. Students might use words like quadrilateral, triangle, parallelogram, or trapezoid.

polygons

not polygons

Problem Solving Strategy

A Discussing the Problem Solving Strategy: Make a Graph

whole class · 15 MIN

NCTM Standards 1, 2, 6, 7, 8, 9, 10

Purpose To share strategies for solving problems and focus on the problem solving strategy *make a graph*

Introduce Remind students that they have been making graphs to analyze data in the last few lessons. Point out that graphs present data in an organized way that allows problem solvers to "see" the data. This gives solvers an added tool they did not have when the data were merely a random collection of numbers or items.

Introduce the following problem.

Problem A number cube was numbered from 1 to 6. Jessie knew that the probability of tossing a 2 was $\frac{1}{6}$. She did an experiment to see if she tossed 2's one-sixth of the time. Her results are shown at the right.

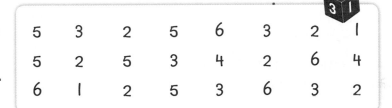

Did Jessie's experimental results match the expected probability?

Share Have students share their strategies for solving the problem. Making a graph allows the data to be analyzed easily. Sketch a graph on the board showing Jessie's number cube tosses.

Each shaded square represents one toss, so Jessie tossed 24 times. She tossed six 2s. According to her experimental results, the probability of tossing a 2 is $\frac{6}{24}$, or $\frac{1}{4}$. Since the expected probability is $\frac{1}{6}$, her results did not match the expected probability.

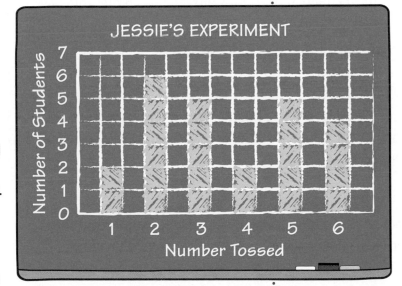

Talk Math

❓ Why is the expected probability of tossing a 2 one-sixth? There are 6 numbers on the cube and 1 of them is 2.

❓ One of the numbers Jessie tossed turned up one-sixth of the time, just as expected. Which number was it? Explain your reasoning. 6; Possible explanation: One-sixth of 24 is 4, so I looked for the number that Jessie tossed 4 times. That number was 6.

B Solving Problems by Applying the Strategy LAB p. 213

individuals or pairs

15 MIN

NCTM Standards 1, 2, 6, 7, 8, 9 10

Purpose To practice the problem solving strategy *make a graph*

Teaching Notes for LAB page 213

Students practice the problem solving strategy *make a graph* by solving each of the problems independently or in pairs. Help students get started with the problems by asking questions such as the following:

Read to Understand

What do you need to find out? the most common hat sizes

Plan

How can you solve this problem? Possible answer: Think about the strategies you might use.

How might you organize the data to help you solve the problem? Possible answer: I could make a graph to display the data visually.

Solve

How can the graph help you determine the most common head sizes? The most common head sizes are the ones represented by the tallest bars on the graph.

What do you need to know in order to answer the last question? You need to know the fraction of the customers who have one of those three hat sizes.

How can the graph help you figure this out? By counting squares on the graph, you can determine how many customers have the indicated sizes.

Check

Look back at the original problem. Did you answer the questions that were asked? Does your answer make sense? How do you know?

Students can use the graph to solve the last problem on LAB page 213. Supplement the questions above with ones that are tailored to that problem.

Lesson Activity Book p. 213

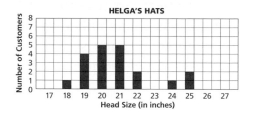

Name _____ Date _____

Chapter 10
Lesson 9 **Problem Solving Strategy**
Make a Graph
NCTM Standards 1, 2, 6, 7, 8, 9, 10

Understand
Plan
Solve
Check

Solve each problem. Helga's Hat Shop can afford to keep only 3 sizes of hats in stock. Helga measured the heads of 20 customers to get an idea of which sizes are most common.

❶ Graph the data to find the 3 most common sizes.

18 inches	24 inches	22 inches	25 inches	19 inches
22 inches	20 inches	19 inches	20 inches	19 inches
21 inches	19 inches	21 inches	21 inches	20 inches
21 inches	20 inches	25 inches	21 inches	20 inches

HELGA'S HATS

(bar graph: Number of Customers vs. Head Size (in inches))

❷ The 3 most common head sizes are: 19 inches, 20 inches, 21 inches

❸ One of the 20 customers wants to buy a hat. What is the probability that one of the 3 sizes you chose will fit the customer? **Accept equivalent fractions.** $\frac{14}{20}$

3 × 71 **CCXIII** two hundred thirteen **213**

ABOUT THE PAGE NUMBER 213 is a number whose product of digits is equal to its sum of digits. 213: 2 × 1 × 3 = 2 + 1 + 3

Reflect and Summarize the Lesson

Write Math **How does making a graph help you solve a problem?** Possible answer: A graph provides a visual image of the data in the problem. It organizes the data in a way that makes them easier to understand, and allows relationships among the data to be seen easily.

Problem Solving Test Prep

C **Getting Ready for Standardized Tests** LAB p. 214

 individuals

 20 MIN

NCTM Standards 1, 2, 6, 7, 8, 9, 10

Purpose To prepare students for standardized tests

Lesson Activity Book p. 214

Problem Solving Test Prep

Choose the correct answer.

1 Samantha glues 8 cubes together to make a larger cube and paints the outside. When she takes the large cube apart, how many of the original 8 cubes will have exactly 3 faces painted?

A. 0   C. 4
B. 2   **(D.)** 8

2 In a board game, Tim begins at 0. He moves forward 3 spaces and back 1. If he makes that move a total of 12 times, how many spaces will he have advanced after the 12 moves?

A. 6   C. 9
B. 8   **(D.)** 24

Show What You Know

Solve each problem. Explain your answer.

3 Jenny brought 36 pieces of fruit to class. Of the 36 pieces of fruit, $\frac{1}{3}$ are oranges, $\frac{1}{3}$ are apples, and the rest are bananas. At the end of the school day, there are 5 bananas. How many bananas were eaten? Explain how you solved the problem.

7 bananas; Possible answer: I used cubes as a model of 36 ÷ 3 = 12. Then I subtracted the 5 that were left and found that 7 had been eaten.

4 Four girls compare their heights. Only one girl is shorter than Abby. Halley is shorter than Ellen. Jesse is shorter than Halley. From this information, can the girls be put in order from shortest to tallest? If so, explain your solution. If not, explain what other information you would need.

Yes; Jesse, Abby, Halley, Ellen; Possible answer: Abby is the second shortest. Nobody is taller than Ellen, so she is the tallest. Jesse is shorter than Halley, so she must be the shortest. Halley must be the second tallest.

214 two hundred fourteen **CCXIV** 2 × 107

ABOUT THE PAGE NUMBER 214 is an even, composite, natural, whole, integer, rational, real number. It is the sum of 5 triangular numbers: 214 = 15 + 21 + 45 + 55 + 78

Teaching Notes for LAB page 214

The test items on this page were written in the same style and are arranged in the same format as those on many state assessments. The test is cumulative and is designed for students to apply a variety of problem solving strategies, including *draw a picture, make a model,* and *use logical reasoning.* Students might share the strategies they use.

The Item Analysis Chart indicates one of the possible strategies that may be used for each test item.

Show What You Know

Written Response

Direct students' attention to Problems 3 and 4. For Problem 3, one way to begin is to find the number of each type of fruit that Jenny brought to class. For Problem 4, explain that students can solve the problem by using objects to represent the four friends' heights. Then have students write explanations describing how they know their answers are correct. To provide more space for students to communicate their thinking about these problems, you may wish to have them write their responses and explanations on a separate sheet of paper. Use the Scoring Rubric below to evaluate their understanding.

Item Analysis Chart

Item	Strategy
1	Make a model
2	Draw a picture
3	Make a model
4	Draw a picture

Scoring Rubric

2	• Demonstrates complete understanding of the problem and chooses an appropriate strategy to determine the solution
1	• Demonstrates a partial understanding of the problem and chooses a strategy that does not lead to a complete and accurate solution
0	• Demonstrates little understanding of the problem and shows little evidence of using any strategy to determine a solution

---

Review Model

Refer students to Problem Solving Review Model: Make a Graph in SH pp. 168–169 to review a model of the four steps they can use with the problem solving strategy *make a graph*. Additional problem solving practice is also provided.

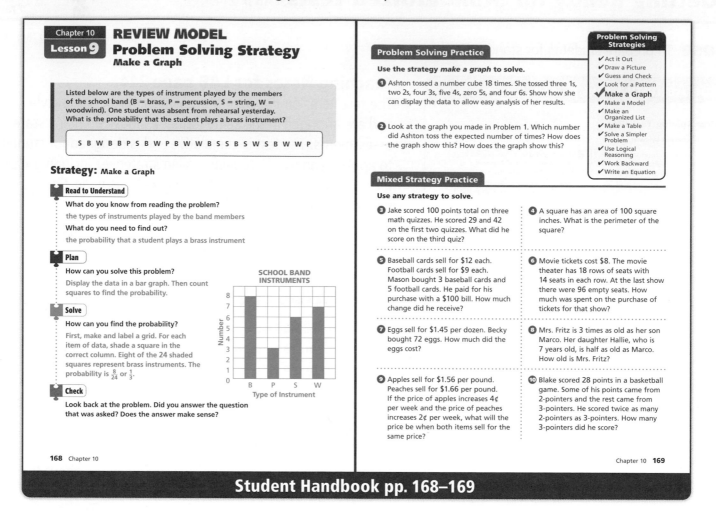

Student Handbook pp. 168–169

Task
Have students read the problem at the top of the Review Model page. Then discuss.

Talk Math

❓ What do you know from reading the problem? the type of instrument played by each band member

❓ What do you need to find out? the probability that a student who missed rehearsal plays a brass instrument

❓ What strategy can you use to solve the problem? You can *make a graph* and analyze the data on the graph

❓ How can you find the probability that the absent band member plays a brass instrument? Compare the number of students who play brass instruments with the number of students in the band

❓ What is the probability? Explain. $\frac{8}{24}$ or $\frac{1}{3}$; There are 8 brass players and 24 total band members, so the probability is $\frac{8}{24}$ or $\frac{1}{3}$.

Use with Lesson Activity Book pp. 213–214.

1

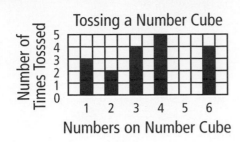

Tossing a Number Cube

Number of Times Tossed

Numbers on Number Cube

Possible explanation: You can use the problem solving strategy *make a graph* to display the data. I made a bar graph. The horizontal axis is the numbers on the sides of the number cube. The vertical axis is the number of times each side occurred for each of the 18 tosses.

2 1; Possible explanation: You can use the problem solving strategies *make a graph* and *use logical reasoning* by figuring out that the expected number of times a side of a number cube should occur is one-sixth of the time. If there are 18 tosses, then each side has a probability of occurring three times. The side, 1, occurred three times.

Mixed Strategy Practice

3 29; Possible explanation: You can use the problem solving strategy *work backward.* First, I found the total number of points Jake scored on the first two quizzes: 29 + 42 = 71. Then I subtracted the total from 100: 100 − 71 = 29.

4 40 inches: Possible explanation: You can use the problem solving strategy *use logical reasoning*. I know that a square has four equal sides. I needed to know a number that when multiplied by itself equals 100. The number is 10. The perimeter of a square with sides of 10 inches each is 40 inches.

5 $19; Possible explanation: You can use the problem solving strategy *solve a simpler problem*. I found the total amount of the purchases by first multiplying the number of each item by its price: 3 × $12 = $36; 5 × $9 = $45. Then I added those products together: $36 + $45 = $81. Last, I subtracted: $100 − $81 = $19.

6 $1,248; Possible explanation: You can use the problem solving strategy *work backward*. I found the total number of seats in the theater by multiplying: 18 rows × 14 seats in each row = 252 seats. Next, I subtracted the number of empty seats: 252 seats − 96 empty seats = 156 full seats. Last, I multiplied the number of full seats by $8, the cost of each ticket: 156 seats × $8 = $1,248.

7 $8.70; Possible explanation: You can use the problem solving strategy *solve a simpler problem*. First, I divided 72 eggs by 12 to find out how many dozen eggs there are: 72 ÷ 12 = 6 dozen eggs. Then, I multiplied 6 dozen by the cost of eggs per dozen: 6 dozen × $1.45 = $8.70.

8 42 years old; Possible explanation: You can use the problem solving strategy *use logical reasoning*. If Hallie is half as old as Marco, then Marco is 14 years old. If Mrs. Fritz is three times as old as Marco, she is 42 years old.

9 $1.76 per pound; Possible explanation: You can use the problem solving strategy *make a table*. I put in the amounts that apples and peaches cost per pound and increased them each week. I increased the price of apples by 4¢ per week and the price of peaches by 2¢ per week until the prices became equal to each other.

10 4; Possible explanation: You can use the problem solving strategy *guess and check*. I guessed two numbers. One number needed to be twice the other. To check, I multiplied the larger of the two numbers by 2 and the other number by 3. When the total equaled 28 points, I knew that Blake scored four 3-pointers and eight 2-pointers.

Data and Probability

NCTM Standards 1, 2, 6, 7, 8, 9, 10

Purpose To provide students with an opportunity to demonstrate understanding of Chapter 10 concepts and skills

MATERIALS

• LAB pp. 215–216
• Chapter 10 Test
  (Assessment Guide pp. AG85–AG86)

Chapter 10 Learning Goals and Assessment Options

These learning goals are assessed in many ways throughout the chapter. The chart below correlates each learning goal to specific formal and informal assessment options.

	Learning Goals	Lesson Number	Snapshot Assessment	Chapter Review Item Numbers	Chapter Test Item Numbers
				LAB pp. 215–216	Assessment Guide pp. AG85–AG86
10-A	Determine the number of combinations possible for a set of objects	10.1	1, 6	1	1–4
10-B	Describe, predict, and compare likelihoods using certain, likely, unlikely, or impossible	10.2, 10.3	2, 7, 8	2, 3	5–7
10-C	Find probabilities	10.4–10.6	3, 5, 9	4, 5	8, 9
10-D	Interpret a bar graph	10.5–10.8	4, 10	17–20	10–13
10-E	Apply problem solving strategies such as *make a graph* to solve problems	10.9	4, 10	6–16	14

📷 Snapshot Assessment

The following Mental Math and Quick Write questions and tasks provide a quick, informal assessment of students' understanding of Chapter 10 concepts, skills, and problem solving strategies.

whole class   **10 MIN**

Mental Math This oral assessment uses mental math strategies and can be used with the whole class.

❶ Name all possible sandwiches you could make using one bread, rye or wheat, and one meat, ham, turkey, or beef. How many different sandwiches are there? rye/ham, rye/turkey, rye/beef, wheat/ham, wheat/turkey, wheat/beef; 6 different sandwiches
(Learning Goal 10-A)

❷ A spinner has 5 equal sections, 4 blue and 1 red. Use **certain, likely, unlikely, impossible** to describe the likelihood of:
  • spinning blue likely
  • spinning red unlikely
  • spinning a color certain
  • spinning a number impossible
  (Learning Goal 10-B)

3 In a deck of 12 cards, 5 are purple, the rest are green.

- State as a fraction the probability of drawing a purple card at random. $\frac{5}{12}$
- State as a fraction the probability of drawing a green card. $\frac{7}{12}$
- Which color is more likely to occur? green
  (Learning Goal 10-C)

4 How can you tell what data item occurs most often in a bar graph? Look for the bar that is the tallest.

How can you determine if two items occurred at the same frequency? Check to see if the bars are the same height.
(Learning Goals 10-D, 10-E)

Quick Write This informal written assessment can be administered to small groups or the whole class. Read each question and have the students write responses on their write-on boards. Encourage students to listen and think about the questions before responding.

5 You have a number cube, labeled 1–6. Write the probability of:

- rolling a 5 $\frac{1}{6}$
- rolling an even number $\frac{3}{6}$ or $\frac{1}{2}$
- rolling a multiple of 3 $\frac{2}{6}$ or $\frac{1}{3}$
  (Learning Goal 10-C)

6 Stacey has 3 shirts: red, blue and white. She has 4 skirts: black, green, purple, and orange. How many different outfits can she make using 1 shirt and 1 skirt? 12
(Learning Goal 10-A)

7 You have a bag with 10 coins: 2 dimes, 3 quarters, 5 pennies. Write the likelihood using **certain, likely, unlikely, impossible.**

- drawing a nickel impossible
- drawing a penny likely
- drawing a dime unlikely
- drawing a coin certain
  (Learning Goal 10-B)

8 A bag has 10 coins: 2 dimes, 3 quarters, 5 pennies.

- Which coin are you most likely to pull out of the bag? penny
- Which coin are you least likely to pull out? dime
  (Learning Goal 10-B)

9 You have 20 cards, numbered from 1 to 20.

- Write in fraction form the probability of drawing an odd number. $\frac{10}{20}$ or $\frac{1}{2}$
- Write in fraction form the probability of drawing a multiple of 2. $\frac{10}{20}$ or $\frac{1}{2}$
- Write in fraction form the probability of drawing a multiple of 5. $\frac{4}{20}$ or $\frac{1}{5}$
- Write the probability of drawing a letter. 0 or impossible
- Write in fraction form the probability of drawing a card with 8 on it. $\frac{1}{20}$
- Write in fraction form the probability of drawing a multiple of 10. $\frac{2}{10}$ or $\frac{1}{5}$
  (Learning Goal 10-C)

10 Draw a bar graph to show how many books each student read. Bob read 2 books, Sue read 4 books, Leah read 5 books, Darrin 4 books, Joe read 6 books and Amy read 3 books.
Check students bar graphs.

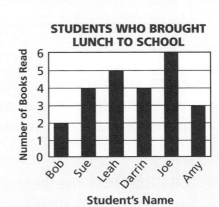

- Who read the most books? Joe
- Who read the same number of books? Sue and Darrin
- Who read 5 books? Leah
- What is the difference between the *most* number of books read and the *least* number of books read? 4
  (Learning Goals 10-D, 10-E)

Formal Assessment

Chapter Review/Assessment The Chapter 10 Review/Assessment on *Lesson Activity Book* pages 215–216 assesses students' understanding of data, probability and problem solving. Students should be able to complete these pages independently.

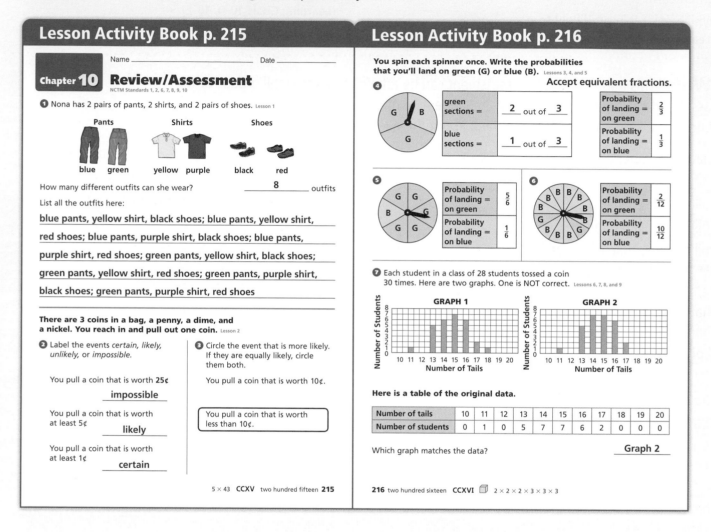

Lesson Activity Book p. 215

Name _____ Date _____

Chapter 10 Review/Assessment
NCTM Standards 1, 2, 6, 7, 8, 9, 10

❶ Nona has 2 pairs of pants, 2 shirts, and 2 pairs of shoes. Lesson 1

Pants — blue green
Shirts — yellow purple
Shoes — black red

How many different outfits can she wear? _____8_____ outfits

List all the outfits here:

blue pants, yellow shirt, black shoes; blue pants, yellow shirt, red shoes; blue pants, purple shirt, black shoes; blue pants, purple shirt, red shoes; green pants, yellow shirt, black shoes; green pants, yellow shirt, red shoes; green pants, purple shirt, black shoes; green pants, purple shirt, red shoes

There are 3 coins in a bag, a penny, a dime, and a nickel. You reach in and pull out one coin. Lesson 2

❷ Label the events *certain, likely, unlikely,* or *impossible.*

You pull a coin that is worth **25¢**.
impossible

You pull a coin that is worth at least 5¢.
likely

You pull a coin that is worth at least 1¢.
certain

❸ Circle the event that is more likely. If they are equally likely, circle them both.

You pull a coin that is worth 10¢.

You pull a coin that is worth less than 10¢.

5 × 43 CCXV two hundred fifteen **215**

Lesson Activity Book p. 216

You spin each spinner once. Write the probabilities that you'll land on green (G) or blue (B). Lessons 3, 4, and 5

Accept equivalent fractions.

❹ green sections = __2__ out of __3__   Probability of landing on green = $\frac{2}{3}$

blue sections = __1__ out of __3__   Probability of landing on blue = $\frac{1}{3}$

❺ Probability of landing on green = $\frac{5}{6}$
Probability of landing on blue = $\frac{1}{6}$

❻ Probability of landing on green = $\frac{2}{12}$
Probability of landing on blue = $\frac{10}{12}$

❼ Each student in a class of 28 students tossed a coin 30 times. Here are two graphs. One is NOT correct. Lessons 6, 7, 8, and 9

GRAPH 1 — Number of Students / Number of Tails

GRAPH 2 — Number of Students / Number of Tails

Here is a table of the original data.

Number of tails	10	11	12	13	14	15	16	17	18	19	20
Number of students	0	1	0	5	7	7	6	2	0	0	0

Which graph matches the data? **Graph 2**

216 two hundred sixteen CCXVI   2 × 2 × 2 × 3 × 3 × 3

Extra Support Students who have difficulty with items on the Chapter 10 Review/Assessment may need review of the lesson where development of the concept was provided. You can use the Intervention Activity to increase students' understanding before the Chapter Test is given.

Chapter Test Use the Chapter 10 Test in the *Assessment Guide* to assess concepts, skills, and problem solving from the chapter and to prepare students for standardized tests. The Chapter Test and other test items are also available online.

Chapter Notes

Quick Notes

More Ideas

_____

_____

_____

_____

_____

_____

_____

_____

_____

_____

_____

_____

_____

_____

_____

_____

_____

_____

_____

_____

_____

_____

_____

_____

Three-Dimensional Geometry

About the Chapter

In this chapter, students use what they already know from their work with two-dimensional figures in Chapter 4 to explore characteristics of three-dimensional figures. They build a variety of interesting and unusual three-dimensional figures and learn to describe and use important attributes of these figures to describe them.

Describing Three-Dimensional Figures
Students extend their understanding of the attributes of two-dimensional figures to three-dimensional figures. They see this connection when they build the figures they study by cutting out and assembling "flat" nets. As they assemble the figures, students can use their imaginations to visualize and predict what they will look like; sometimes the results are surprising!

Classifying Figures
Once the class has built all the figures, they have a "Figure Safari" to explore and sort. As they consider different ways to classify the figures, they explore relationships among the faces, edges, and vertices. The ability to observe and classify figures lays the groundwork for the further development of geometric reasoning.

Measuring Three-Dimensional Figures
While two-dimensional figures are measured in terms of perimeter and area, three-dimensional figures are measured in terms of surface area and volume. Working with the Figure Safari, students explore ways to measure solids, building a strong connection to the formulas for calculating these measures.

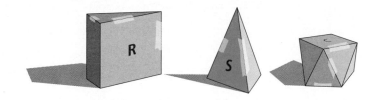

Developing Concepts Across the Grades

Topic	Prior Learning	Learning in Chapter 11	Later Learning
Two-Dimensional Geometry	• Identify congruent figures • Classify polygons using right angles and parallel sides **Grade 3, Chapter 11**	• Use attributes of two-dimensional figures to describe the faces of three-dimensional figures **Lessons 11.1, 11.4**	• Classify triangles and quadrilaterals • Recognize that the sum of the angle measures in a triangle is 180° **Grade 5, Chapter 9**
Three-Dimensional Geometry	• Identify prisms and pyramids • Classify three-dimensional figures **Grade 3, Chapter 11**	• Make three-dimensional figures from nets • Sort three-dimensional figures into prisms and pyramids • Identify three-dimensional figures according to their attributes **Lessons 11.1–11.3**	• Describe the faces, vertices, and edges of three-dimensional figures • Define prisms, pyramids, cones, cylinders, and spheres **Grade 5, Chapter 13**
Measurement	• Measure area in square centimeters • Measure the volume of a box in cubic centimeters **Grade 3, Chapter 10**	• Estimate and find the areas of the faces of prisms with rectangular faces • Find the volume of rectangular prisms **Lessons 11.4–11.6**	• Use appropriate units and formulas to measure length, area, and volume of prisms **Grade 5, Chapter 13**

Chapter Planner

Lesson	Objectives	NCTM Standards	Vocabulary	Materials/ Resources

CHAPTER 11 World Almanac For Kids • Vocabulary • Games • Challenge
Teacher Guide pp. 877A–877F, Student Handbook pp. 176–177, 186–190

1 Making a Figure Zoo

PACING 1 DAY

Teacher Guide
pp. 878–885
Lesson Activity Book
pp. 217–218
Student Handbook
Student Letter p. 175

- To make three-dimensional figures from nets
- To use attributes of two-dimensional figures to describe the faces of three-dimensional figures

3, 6, 7, 8, 9, 10

polyhedra
polyhedron

For the students:
- School-Home Connection, pp. SHC41–SHC44
- TR: AM99–AM122
- scissors, tape
- P89, E89, SR89

2 Describing Three-Dimensional Figures

PACING 1 DAY

Teacher Guide
pp. 886–893
Lesson Activity Book
pp. 219–220

- To sort three-dimensional figures into prisms and pyramids
- To describe the attributes of prisms and pyramids

3, 6 , 7, 8, 9, 10

prisms
pyramid

For the teacher:
- three-dimensional figures from Lesson 11.1
- small nets of figures from Lesson 11.1
- cylinder (e.g., paper towel roll, straw, unsharpened pencil); cone (e.g., party hat, ice cream cone)

For the students:
- P90, E90, SR90

Science Connection:
Show Crystals
Teachers Guide p. 876

3 Going On a Figure Safari

PACING 1 DAY

Teacher Guide
pp. 894–901
Lesson Activity Book
pp. 221–222
Student Handbook
Review Model p. 178
Game p. 188

- To identify three-dimensional figures according to their attributes

3, 6, 7, 8, 9, 10

edge
face
side
vertex
vertices

For the teacher:
- three-dimensional figures from Lesson 11.1

For the students:
- three-dimensional figures from Lesson 11.1
- P91, E91, SR91

Social Studies Connection:
The Best Number Cube
Teachers Guide p. 876

4 Finding the Areas of Faces on Three-Dimensional Figures

PACING 1 DAY

Teacher Guide
pp. 902–909
Lesson Activity Book
pp. 223–224
Student Handbook
Explore p. 179
Review Model p. 180

- To estimate and find the areas of the faces of prisms with rectangular faces

1, 3, 4, 6, 7, 8, 9, 10

net
total area

For the teacher:
- transparency of AM123 (optional)

For the students:
- inch ruler
- three-dimensional figures from Lesson 11.1
- TR: AM123–AM129
- P92, E92, SR92

NCTM Standards 2000

1. Number and Operations
2. Algebra
3. Geometry
4. Measurement
5. Data Analysis and Probability
6. Problem Solving
7. Reasoning and Proof
8. Communication
9. Connections
10. Representation

Key

AG: Assessment Guide
E: Extension Book
LAB: Lesson Activity Book
P: Practice Book

SH: Student Handbook
SR: Spiral Review Book
TG: Teacher Guide
TR: Teacher Resource Book

MATH GLOSSARY in **Student Handbook** p. 259

Planner (continued)

Chapter Planner *(continued)*

Lesson	Objectives	NCTM Standards	Vocabulary	Materials/Resources
5 **Finding Volumes of Three-Dimensional Figures** PACING 1 DAY **Teacher Guide** pp. 910–917 **Lesson Activity Book** pp. 225–226 **Student Handbook** Explore p. 181 Review Model p. 182	• To find the volumes of three-dimensional figures by building them with inch cubes • To explore using the dimensions of three-dimensional figures to compute their volumes	1, 3, 4, 6, 7, 8, 9, 10	area cubic volume	**For the teacher:** ▪ 3 copies of TR: AM99 **For the students:** ▪ TR: AM99–AM122 ▪ Inch cubes ▪ Inch rules (optional) ▪ P93, E93, SR93 **Literature Connection:** **Mummy Math: An Adventure in Geometry** **Teacher Guide** p. 876
6 **More Volumes of Three-Dimensional Figures** PACING 1 DAY **Teacher Guide** pp. 918–925 **Lesson Activity Book** pp. 227–228 **Student Handbook** Explore p. 183 Game p. 189	• To find the volume of a rectangular prism by multiplying its three dimensions • To describe a rectangular prism using its dimensions in $l \times w \times h$ format	1, 3, 4, 6, 7, 8, 9, 10	height length width	**For the students:** ▪ inch cubes, coins, scrap paper ▪ P94, E94, SR94
7 **Problem Solving Strategy and Test Prep** PACING 1 DAY **Teacher Guide** pp. 926–931 **Lesson Activity Book** pp. 229–230 **Student Handbook** Review Model pp. 184–185	• To practice the problem solving strategy *act it out.* • To articulate the steps and strategies used to solve problems • To prepare for standardized tests	1, 3, 4, 6, 7, 8, 9, 10		

CHAPTER 11 Assessment
TG pp. 932–935, **LAB** pp. 231–232, **AG** pp. AG89–AG92

For the students:
▪ Chapter 11 Test pp. AG89–AG90

Games

Use the following games for skills practice
and reinforcement of concepts.

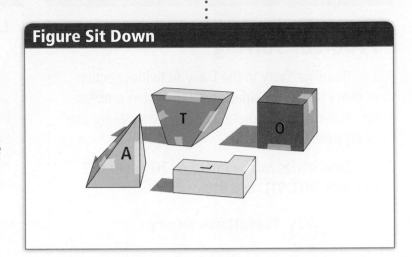

Lesson 11.3 ▶

Figure Sit Down provides an
opportunity for students to practice
identifying attributes of three-
dimensional figures.

Volume Builder

◀ Lesson 11.6 *Volume Builder*
provides opportunity for students to
practice estimating and finding volume.

Planning Ahead

In **Lesson 11.1,** students begin their exploration of polyhedra by
constructing them. Each student will need one of the 25 Figure
Zoo Activity Masters, AM99–AM123, along with scissors
and tape.

In **Lesson 11.3,** students will use the Figure Zoo figures from
Lesson 11.1 to play *Figure Sit Down.* Each student will need one
Figure Zoo polyhedron.

In **Lessons 11.4** and **11.5,** students will examine area and
volume for figures that can be made from cubes. You will need to
construct Figure Y, AM123, for them to explore along with some of
the figures they will make in **Lesson 11.1.**

In **Lesson 11.6,** students will play the *Volume Builder.* Each pair
of players will need a supply of inch cubes, a coin, and a piece of
scratch paper.

Developing Problem Solvers

Open-Ended Problem Solving

The Headline Story in the Daily Activities section of every lesson provides an open-ended problem for students to complete. For each story there are many possible responses.

Headline Stories can be found on TG pages 879, 887, 895, 903, 911, and 919.

 **Headline Story**

Leveled Problem Solving

Leveled Problem Solving provides an opportunity for students to apply learning from the lesson to a real-life situation. Problems are leveled by ability to allow students of all ability levels to become successful problem solvers. Each Leveled Problem Solving begins with a real-life scenario upon which three problems are built.

The levels of problems are:

❶ Basic Level	❷ On Level	❸ Above Level
students needing extra support	students working at grade level	students who are ready for more challenging problems

Leveled Problem Solving can be found on TG pages 884, 892, 900, 909, 917, and 924.

 **FOR KIDS**

The World Almanac for Kids feature is designed to stimulate student interest for the math concepts they are about to learn. Students use data to solve problems and explain solutions. The Chapter 11 Project can be found on SH pages 176–177.

Write Math **Reflect and Summarize the Lesson** poses a problem or question for students to think and write about. This feature can be found on TG pages 884, 891, 899, 908, 916, 923, and 928.

Other opportunities to write about math can be found on LAB pages 218, 219, and 227.

Problem Solving Strategies

The focus of **Lesson 11.7** is the strategy, *act it out.* However, students will use a variety of problem solving strategies as they work through the chapter. The chart below shows strategies that may be useful in completing each lesson.

Strategy	Lesson(s)	Description
✓ Act It Out	11.1, 11.2, 11.3, 11.5, 11.6, 11.7	Act it out to create models of polygons in order to find and describe their attributes.
Look for a Pattern	11.4	To simplify finding areas of nets, look for a pattern of congruent equal-area figures on a net.
Make a Model	11.1, 11.5, 11.6	Make a model to discover the properties of polyhedra.
Make an Organized List	11.2, 11.6	Make an organized list to sort prisms, pyramids, and other polyhedra.
Solve a Simpler Problem	11.5	To find the volume of a pyramid, solve the simpler problem of finding the volume of a prism; then divide by 3.
Use Logical Reasoning	11.1, 11.3	Use logical reasoning to decide which polyhedra display a given set of characteristics.
Write an Equation	11.6	Write an equation Volume = length × width × height to find the volume of a rectangular prism.

Meeting the Needs of All Learners

Differentiated Instruction

Extra Support	Activities For All	Enrichment
Intervention Activities TG pp. 884, 892, 900, 909, 917, and 924	**Practice Book** pp. P89–P94	**Extension Activities** TG pp. 884, 892, 900, 909, 917, and 924
	Spiral Review Book pp. SR89–SR94	**Extension Book** pp. E89–E94
	LAB Challenge LAB pp. 218, 220, 222, 224, 226, 228	**LAB Challenge** LAB pp. 218, 220, 222, 224, 226, 228
Lesson Notes Basic Level TG pp. 883, 897, 923	**Lesson Notes** On Level TG pp. 889, 922	**Lesson Notes** Above Level TG pp. 914
Leveled Problem Solving Basic Level TG pp. 884, 892, 900, 909, 917, and 924	**Leveled Problem Solving** On Level TG pp. 884, 892, 900, 909, 917, and 924	**Leveled Problem Solving** Above Level TG pp. 884, 892, 900, 909, 917, and 924

English Language Learners

Suggestions for addressing the needs of students learning English as a second language are included in the Developing Mathematical Language section at the beginning of most lessons.	ELL activities for this chapter can be found on TG pages 879, 887, 895, 903, 911, and 919.

The Multi-Age Classroom

Grade 3	• Students on this level should be able to complete the lessons in Chapter 11 but might need some additional practice with key concepts and skills.	**See Grade 4, Intervention Activities, Lessons 11.1–11.6.**
	• Give students more practice classifying two-dimensional and three-dimensional figures.	**See Grade 3, Lessons 11.5–11.9.**
Grade 4	• Students on this level should be able to complete the lessons in Chapter 11 with minimal adjustments.	**See Grade 4, Practice pages P89–P94.**
Grade 5	• Students on this level should be able to complete the lessons in Chapter 11 and to extend three-dimensional geometry concepts and skills.	**See Grade 4, Extension pages E89–E94.**
	• Give students extended work with three-dimensional figures.	**See Grade 5, Lessons 13.1–13.3.**

Cross Curricular Connections

Social Studies Connection

Math Concept: attributes of 3-D figures

The Best Number Cube

- Share with students how number cubes have been used for thousands of years to play games. Game cubes have been found in ancient Egyptian tombs. Sometimes solid figures other than cubes were used.

- Discuss with students what must be true for dice to be fair. Students should see that each possible outcome must have a fair chance of coming up.

- Share how the five Platonic solids—tetrahedron, cube, octahedron, icosahedron, and dodecahedron—meet this criteria. Each figure is made up of regular polygons.

- If possible, display models of the five figures and discuss the shapes of the polygons that make up the faces of each figure.

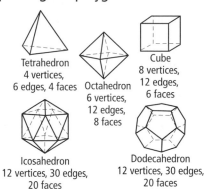

Tetrahedron
4 vertices,
6 edges, 4 faces

Octahedron
6 vertices,
12 edges,
8 faces

Cube
8 vertices,
12 edges,
6 faces

Icosahedron
12 vertices, 30 edges,
20 faces

Dodecahedron
12 vertices, 30 edges,
20 faces

Lesson 11.3

Science Connection

Math Concept: comparing 3-D figures

Snow Crystals

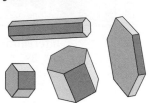

- Share with students how snow crystals look like hexagonal prisms. The shape and thickness of the prism depends on how long it takes the crystal to form. So, the shape of a snowflake is determined, in large part, by the temperature.

- Ask students whether they have heard that no two snowflakes look the same. While it is probably true that no two are identical, it is not mathematically certain.

- Direct students to draw a hexagon and then to extend and join the sides to make a design. When students have finished, ask them to display and compare their figures. Are any of them identical? It is possible that two or more of the "snowflakes" will be identical, but it is not likely, just as in nature.

Lesson 11.2

Literature Connection

Math Concept: Geometry

Mummy Math: An Adventure in Geometry
By Cindy Neuschwander
Illustrated by Bryan Langdo

As students learn to sort their three-dimensional geometric figures into pyramids and prisms, they will enjoy Matt and Bibi's adventure inside an ancient pyramid. The twins must use their knowledge about geometric figures to locate the pharaoh's burial chamber and the way out.
Lesson 11.5

School-Home Connection

Encourage students to build the *Pyramid Puzzle,* found on the School-Home Connection page, with a family member. Students will work with the concept of classifying solids in **Lessons 11.1, 11.2,** and **11.3.**

A reproducible copy of the School-Home Connection letter in English and in Spanish can be found in the *Teacher Resource Book,* pages SHC41–SHC44.

Assessment Options

There are many opportunities in *Think Math!* to assess students' understanding of concepts, skills, and problem solving. Learning Goals for Chapter 11 are provided below. The assessment options provide opportunities to evaluate whether or not students have retained learning from prior experiences. Choose the forms of assessment that best meet the needs of your students.

Chapter 11 Learning Goals

	Learning Goals	Lesson Number
11-A	Identify, sort, and describe three-dimensional figures by their attributes	11.1–11.3
11-B	Find the areas of faces on three-dimensional figures	11.4
11-C	Find volumes of three-dimensional figures	11.5, 11.6
11-D	Apply problem solving strategies such as *act it out* to solve problems	11.7

✔ Informal Assessment

Ongoing Assessment
Provides insight into students' thinking to guide instruction (TG pp. 897, 920, 922)

Reflect and Summarize the Lesson
Checks understanding of lesson concepts
(TG pp. 884, 891, 899, 908, 916, 923, 928)

Snapshot Assessment
Mental Math and **Quick Write**
Offers a quick observation of students' progress on chapters concept and skills
(TG pp. 932–933)

Performance Assessment
Provides quarterly assessment of Chapter 8–11 concepts using real-life situations.
Assessment Guide
pp. AG219–AG225

✔ Formal Assessment

Standardized Test Prep
Problem Solving Test Prep
Prepares students for standardized tests
Lesson Activity Book p. 230 (TG p. 929)

Chapter 11 Review/Assessment
Reviews and assesses students' understanding of the chapter
Lesson Activity Book pp. 231–232 (TG p. 934)

Chapter 11 Test
Assesses the chapter concepts and skills
Assessment Guide
Form A pp. AG89–AG90
Form B pp. AG91–AG92

Benchmark 3 Assessment
Provides quarterly assessment of Chapters 8–11 concepts and skills
Assessment Guide
Benchmark 3A pp. AG93–AG100
Benchmark 3B pp. AG101–AG108

World Almanac for Kids

Use the World Almanac for Kids feature, *Wrapping It Up!*, found on pp. 176–177 of the **Student Handbook,** to provide students with an opportunity to practice using their problem solving skills by solving real world problems.

FACT•ACTIVITY 1

❶ Luka: cylinder; Megan: square pyramid; Nate: cube; Olivia: triangular prism

❷ Possible answer: Megan's toy box has 5 faces—4 triangles and 1 square base. The 4 triangular faces are congruent to each other.

❸ Nate; all of the angles are right angles.

❹ Net B

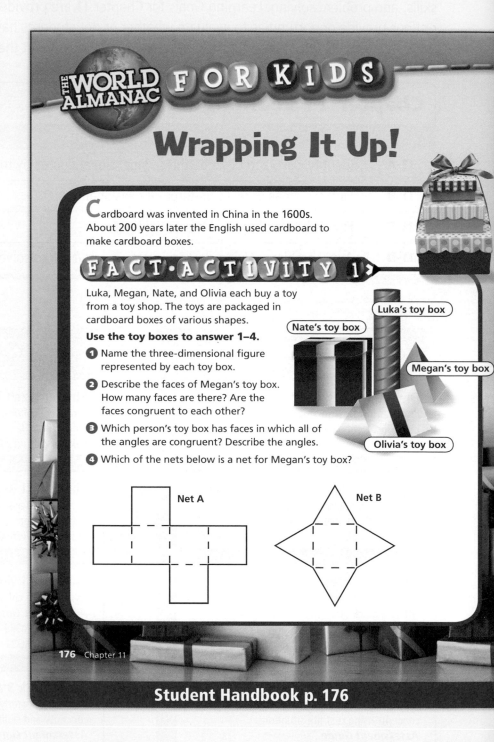

THE WORLD ALMANAC FOR KIDS

Wrapping It Up!

Cardboard was invented in China in the 1600s. About 200 years later the English used cardboard to make cardboard boxes.

FACT•ACTIVITY 1

Luka, Megan, Nate, and Olivia each buy a toy from a toy shop. The toys are packaged in cardboard boxes of various shapes.

Nate's toy box

Luka's toy box

Megan's toy box

Olivia's toy box

Use the toy boxes to answer 1–4.

❶ Name the three-dimensional figure represented by each toy box.

❷ Describe the faces of Megan's toy box. How many faces are there? Are the faces congruent to each other?

❸ Which person's toy box has faces in which all of the angles are congruent? Describe the angles.

❹ Which of the nets below is a net for Megan's toy box?

Net A

Net B

176 Chapter 11

Student Handbook p. 176

FACT·ACTIVITY 2

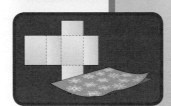

People have been wrapping gifts for almost 2,000 years when paper was invented in China. Today, you can buy all sorts of fancy gift wrap.

Max needs to wrap this gift box.

❶ Trace the net below on a piece of paper. Label the net with the measurements of each edge using the box drawing at the right.

❷ Find the total area of the faces of the box.

❸ Suppose Max's gift wrap measures 5 in. × 10 in. Does he have enough to wrap the box? Explain.

❹ Max wants to fill the box with candy that originally filled a box that was 6 in. long, 2 in. wide, and 2 in. high. Will the candy fit in the box? Explain.

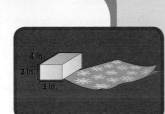

CHAPTER PROJECT

Materials: empty boxes, one-inch cubes, inch ruler

How good are you at estimating volume? Work in groups of 3 or more. Gather a collection of empty boxes shaped like rectangular prisms, such as cereal boxes, shoe boxes, or tissue boxes. Use various sizes.

- Write down the number of one-inch cubes you think will fit in each box. Carefully place as many cubes as you can in each box. Record your results. Compare your estimates to the number of cubes that actually fit in the boxes.

- Then, measure to the nearest inch the length, width, and height of each box and find the volume for each box. Record your results.

- How do you explain the difference between the volume found by placing the cubes in the box and the volume found using the formula?

ALMANAC Fact

Edwin Binney and C. Harold Smith made their first box of crayons in 1903. There were only 8 colors back then. They now make bigger boxes with as many as 120 colors.

Student Handbook p. 177

FACT·ACTIVITY 2

❶ Check students' nets.

❷ $(4 \times 3) + (4 \times 2) + (4 \times 3) + (4 \times 2) + (3 \times 2) + (3 \times 2) = 12 + 8 + 12 + 8 + 6 + 6 = 52$ square inches

❸ No; the total area of the gift wrap is only 50 square inches, which is less than the total area of the faces of the box.

❹ Yes; the original box had 24 cubic inches and this box is 24 cubic inches.

CHAPTER PROJECT

Check students' work. Possible answers:

Tissue box in the shape of a cube:

- Estimate: 100 one-inch cubes; actual: 96 one-inch cubes; $V = lwh = 4 \times 4 \times 6 = 96$; 96 cubic inches

- To explain the difference between the actual number of cubes that fit in a box and the volume found using the formula, students may note that there is some space inside the cube, but not enough to fit in more one-inch cubes (when measurements are not whole numbers).

Vocabulary

To reinforce vocabulary concepts, invite students to complete the vocabulary activities on pp. 186–187 of the *Student Handbook.* Encourage students to record their answers in their math journals.

Many responses are possible.

10 Possible answer: A polyhedron is a *three-dimensional* figure with *faces* that are all polygons. If a *three-dimensional figure* includes faces that are not polygons, the figure is not a polyhedron. You can use a *net* to make a two-dimensional model of a polyhedron. The *net* will be made of figures that are all polygons. Each polygon of the net will be a *face* of the polyhedron.

11 Possible answer: Prisms and pyramids are both *three-dimensional figures* that are polyhedra. Both types of figures have *faces* that are polygons. When you make a *net* of a prism, at most two *faces* may not be rectangles. When you make a *net* of a pyramid, at most one *face* may not be a triangle.

12 Possible answer: You can find the surface area of a polyhedron by making a *net* of the figure. Then you can find the area of each *face* of the figure. Add the areas of the *faces* represented on the *net* to find the total surface area of the polyhedron.

Chapter 11 **Vocabulary**

Choose the best vocabulary term from Word List A for each sentence.

1 A polygon that is one side of a polyhedron is called a(n) __?__. **face**

2 A polyhedron with a polygon base and other faces that are triangles is a(n) __?__. **pyramid**

3 The place where three or more edges of a polyhedron intersect is called a(n) __?__. **vertex**

4 A three-dimensional figure with polygonal faces is called a(n) __?__. **polyhedron**

5 A polyhedron with two congruent polygonal bases and other faces that are rectangles is a(n) __?__. **prism**

6 A line segment that forms the boundary of a face of a polyhedron is called a(n) __?__. **edge**

7 A(n) __?__ is a two-dimensional pattern of a three-dimensional figure. **net**

Word List A

area
edge
face
height
net
polyhedron
prism
pyramid
side
vertex
volume
width

Complete each analogy using the best term from Word List B.

8 Square is to area as __?__ is to volume. **cube**

9 __?__ is to vertices as polyhedron is to polyhedra. **vertex**

Word List B

cube
length
total area
vertex

Talk Math

Discuss with a partner what you have learned about polyhedra. Use the vocabulary terms *face, net,* and *three-dimensional figure.*

10 How can you recognize a polyhedron?

11 How are prisms and pyramids similar? How are they different?

12 How can you find the surface area of a polyhedron?

186 Chapter 11

Student Handbook p. 186

Venn Diagram

13 Create a Venn diagram for the words *area, cubic, face, length, height, nets, polyhedron, total area, volume,* and *width.*

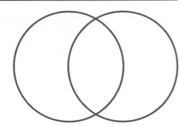

Tree Diagram

14 Create a tree diagram using the word *polyhedra.* Use what you know and what you have learned about three-dimensional figures.

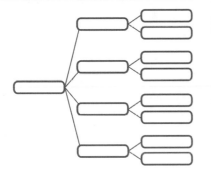

FACE *Face* usually means the front of something. The front of your head from your chin to your forehead is your *face*. Other fronts are the *face* of a building, the *face* of a clock, and the *face* of the moon. *Face* is also an action, such as "face the board," which means "turn toward the board." In math, *face* has a meaning similar to "front." A *face* is any of the plane surfaces of a polyhedron.

Chapter 11 **187**

Student Handbook p. 187

13

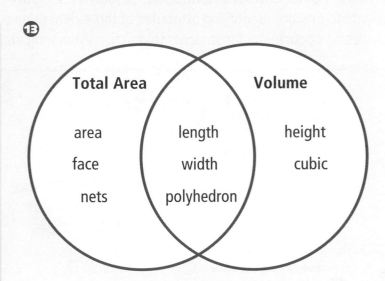

14 Many answers are possible. One example is provided.

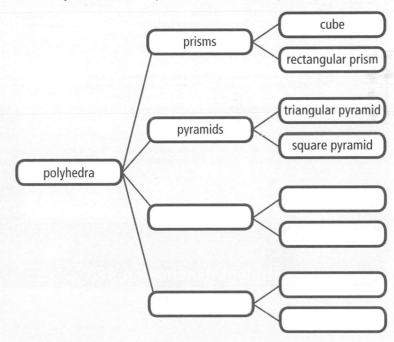

Games

Encourage early finishers and students ready to go beyond the lesson objectives to play the games on pp. 188-189 of the *Student Handbook*. **Lesson 11.3** *Figure Sit Down* provides an opportunity for students to practice identifying attributes of three-dimensional figures. **Lesson 11.6** *Volume Builder* provides an opportunity for students to practice estimating and finding volumes.

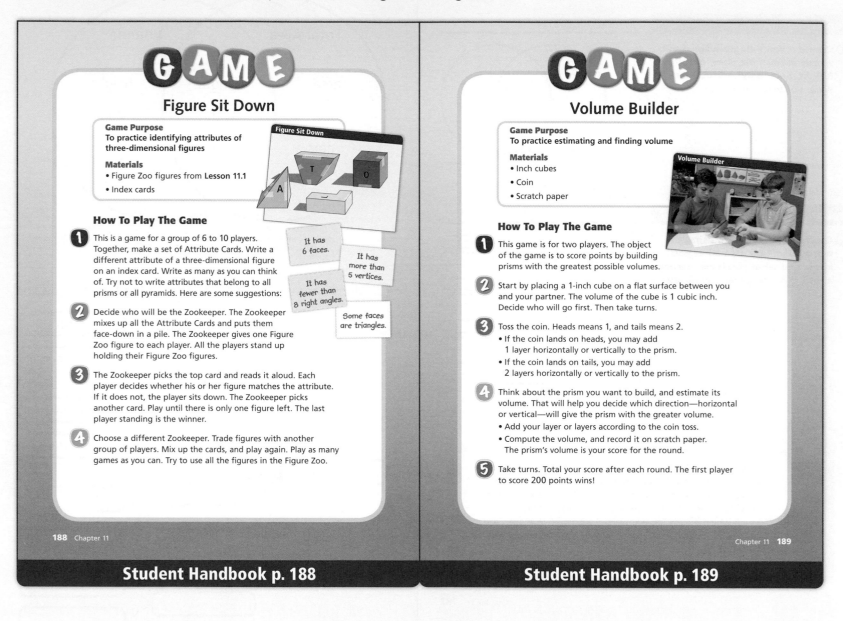

GAME

Figure Sit Down

Game Purpose
To practice identifying attributes of three-dimensional figures

Materials
• Figure Zoo figures from **Lesson 11.1**
• Index cards

How To Play The Game

1 This is a game for a group of 6 to 10 players. Together, make a set of Attribute Cards. Write a different attribute of a three-dimensional figure on an index card. Write as many as you can think of. Try not to write attributes that belong to all prisms or all pyramids. Here are some suggestions:

> It has 6 faces.
> It has more than 5 vertices.
> It has fewer than 8 right angles.
> Some faces are triangles.

2 Decide who will be the Zookeeper. The Zookeeper mixes up all the Attribute Cards and puts them face-down in a pile. The Zookeeper gives one Figure Zoo figure to each player. All the players stand up holding their Figure Zoo figures.

3 The Zookeeper picks the top card and reads it aloud. Each player decides whether his or her figure matches the attribute. If it does not, the player sits down. The Zookeeper picks another card. Play until there is only one figure left. The last player standing is the winner.

4 Choose a different Zookeeper. Trade figures with another group of players. Mix up the cards, and play again. Play as many games as you can. Try to use all the figures in the Figure Zoo.

GAME

Volume Builder

Game Purpose
To practice estimating and finding volume

Materials
• Inch cubes
• Coin
• Scratch paper

How To Play The Game

1 This game is for two players. The object of the game is to score points by building prisms with the greatest possible volumes.

2 Start by placing a 1-inch cube on a flat surface between you and your partner. The volume of the cube is 1 cubic inch. Decide who will go first. Then take turns.

3 Toss the coin. Heads means 1, and tails means 2.
• If the coin lands on heads, you may add 1 layer horizontally or vertically to the prism.
• If the coin lands on tails, you may add 2 layers horizontally or vertically to the prism.

4 Think about the prism you want to build, and estimate its volume. That will help you decide which direction—horizontal or vertical—will give the prism with the greater volume.
• Add your layer or layers according to the coin toss.
• Compute the volume, and record it on scratch paper. The prism's volume is your score for the round.

5 Take turns. Total your score after each round. The first player to score 200 points wins!

Student Handbook p. 188

Student Handbook p. 189

Challenge

This activity challenges students to play games and then use what they know about probability to decide whether each is a fair game. This activity can be found on p. 190 of the *Student Handbook*.

❶ yes; side 2

❷ no

❸ yes; side 1

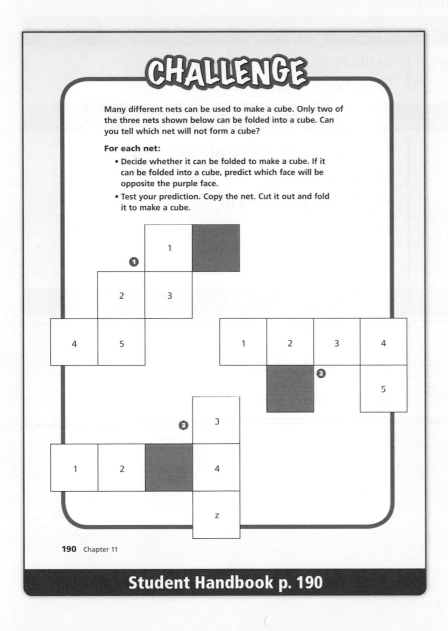

Student Handbook p. 190

Lesson 1 | Making a Figure Zoo

NCTM Standards 3, 6, 7, 8, 9, 10

Lesson Planner

STUDENT OBJECTIVES ·
- To make three-dimensional figures from nets
- To use attributes of two-dimensional figures to describe the faces of three-dimensional figures

1 | Daily Activities (TG p. 879)

Open-Ended Problem Solving/Headline Story	Skills Practice and Review— Classifying Polygons

2 | Teach and Practice (TG pp. 880–884)

	MATERIALS
A Reading the Student Letter (TG p. 880)	• TR: Activity Masters, AM99–AM122
B Building a Figure Zoo (TG pp. 881)	• scissors, tape
C Describing Polyhedra in the Zoo (TG p. 882–883)	• LAB pp. 217–218
D Making a Figure Zoo (TG p. 884)	• SH p. 175

3 | Differentiated Instruction (TG p. 885)

Leveled Problem Solving (TG p. 885)	Practice Book P89
Intervention Activity (TG p. 885)	Extension Book E89
Extension Activity (TG p. 885)	Spiral Review Book SR89

Lesson Notes

About the Lesson

In this first lesson on three-dimensional geometry, students construct three-dimensional figures, then use terms they already know to describe their attributes. Being able to physically manipulate the figures when discussing their attributes will help students to identify features of such figures. Students explore three-dimensional figures generally in this lesson. In the next lesson, they will begin to identify types of polyhedra.

Use with Lesson Activity Book pp. 217–218.

Developing Mathematical Language

Vocabulary: polyhedron, polyhedra

Polyhedron is the precise term for a three-dimensional figure with planar (not curved) faces. (The plural is *polyhedra*.) Explain that *-hedron* means "faces" and ask students to speculate on the meaning of *poly*. You may wish to remind them of the polygons ("many-angled" figures) in Chapter 3. When students understand that *polyhedron* means many-faces, ask them to name other words with the prefix *poly-* meaning "many." Possible answers: polysyllabic (many syllables); Polynesia (many islands)

Familiarize students with the terms *polyhedron* and *polyhedra*

Beginning Tell students that a *polyhedron* has faces that are polygons. Name the faces of a box as you show each face—rectangle and square. Have students tell whether each face is a polygon. Then discuss why the box is a *polyhedron*.

Intermediate Show students a box and a can. Have them tell which figure is a *polyhedron* and why. The box has faces that are polygons, so it is a *polyhedron*. The can has a curved surface, so it is not a *polyhedron*.

Advanced To help students differentiate between the singular and plural forms, point out that students can remember the singular form because it ends in *-on,* which is similar to *one.*

Open-Ended Problem Solving

Read the Headline Story to the students. Encourage them to think of attributes that Figure C has that the others do not.

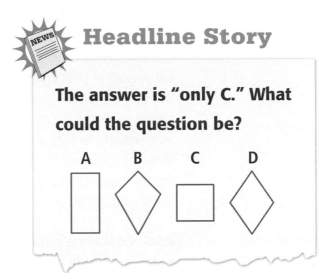

Headline Story

The answer is "only C." What could the question be?

A   B   C   D

Possible responses: In which figure are all the angles equal and all the sides equal? Which figure is a rectangle with four equal sides?

Skills Practice and Review

Classifying Polygons

Draw figures on the board one at a time, and ask your students whether each figure is a polygon. (Polygons are closed figures with straight sides, no extra lines, and only one inside region.) If the figure is a polygon, circle it. If students have difficulty remembering the requirements for polygons, draw several examples and counter-examples on the board to help them recall the definition.

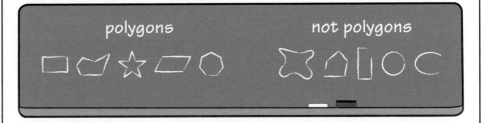

polygons   not polygons

When the figures have been sorted, ask students to give the specific name for each polygon. They might say "quadrilateral," "triangle," "parallelogram," or "trapezoid." Some polygons might not have names.

whole class   5 MIN

NCTM Standards 3, 6, 7, 8, 9, 10

A Reading the Student Letter

Purpose To introduce three-dimensional geometry

Introduce Read the Student Letter with your class. You might briefly discuss your goals for this chapter, or have students tell you what they know about three-dimensional geometry from earlier grades. For example, they may remember that a cube is a three-dimensional figure with six square faces, or that a pyramid has triangular faces.

Task **Challenge students to name everyday objects that have six parallelogram-shaped faces.** Use this challenge to point out the great variety of objects that match this description. Possible answers: shoe box, juice box, cereal box, number cube, filing cabinet

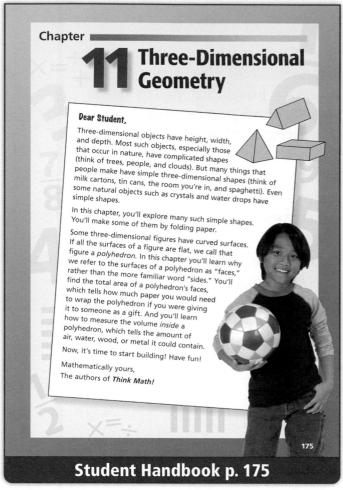

Chapter

11 Three-Dimensional Geometry

Dear Student,

Three-dimensional objects have height, width, and depth. Most such objects, especially those that occur in nature, have complicated shapes (think of trees, people, and clouds). But many things that people make have simple three-dimensional shapes (think of milk cartons, tin cans, the room you're in, and spaghetti). Even some natural objects such as crystals and water drops have simple shapes.

In this chapter, you'll explore many such simple shapes. You'll make some of them by folding paper.

Some three-dimensional figures have curved surfaces. If all the surfaces of a figure are flat, we call that figure a *polyhedron*. In this chapter you'll learn why we refer to the surfaces of a polyhedron as "faces," rather than the more familiar word "sides." You'll find the total area of a polyhedron's faces, which tells how much paper you would need to wrap the polyhedron if you were giving it to someone as a gift. And you'll learn how to measure the volume *inside* a polyhedron, which tells the amount of air, water, wood, or metal it could contain.

Now, it's time to start building! Have fun!

Mathematically yours,
The authors of *Think Math!*

175

Student Handbook p. 175

 Talk Math

❓ The word "polyhedron" is sometimes translated as "many-seated." What does that definition tell you about the possibility that you could place a polyhedron on a table in such a way that it would not topple over? Possible answer: It has many seats, so there should be a number of ways you could set it on a table so that it wouldn't topple.

❓ Which has a larger volume, a baseball or a basketball? Explain your reasoning. a basketball; Possible explanation: The volume of an object is a measure of its interior. Since the interior of a basketball is larger than that of a baseball, a basketball must have a larger volume than a baseball.

Use with Lesson Activity Book pp. 217–218.

B Building a Figure Zoo

Purpose To build models of polyhedra

Introduce Students begin their exploration of polyhedra by constructing them. To do this, each student will need one of the 24 Figure Zoo Activity Masters AM99–AM122, along with scissors and tape. Make sure that each of the figures A through X is assigned to at least one student before you repeat figures.

Task Direct students to use scissors, tape, and the *larger* shapes on their Activity Masters to make three-dimensional shapes. Students should cut along the solid lines, then fold along the dotted lines. Explain that, for easy reference, students should be sure that the letter labels (and the dotted lines) are on the *outside* of the figures.

You may want to demonstrate some strategies for cutting, folding, and taping Activity Master figures. For example, to help students deal with V-shaped inside corners, you might suggest that they make two separate cuts into the corner, rather than attempt to execute a single cut along the full length of the V. This will ensure that they don't have to manipulate their scissors in the tight corner of the V.

Encourage students to use only as much tape as they need to stabilize their figures. If students finish quickly, you might give them additional figures to cut, fold, and tape into polyhedra. (You might want to ask students to make multiple copies of the rectangular box-type shapes B, G, K, L, O, and P, because these polyhedra will be the focus of lessons later in the chapter.) Don't expect students' models to be perfect.

Have each student keep one figure for the next activity. Put the remaining figures in a part of the classroom where they can be seen and handled. For the next lesson, students will need the *smaller* figures that appears on their Activity Masters, so have them cut out the figures, write their names on the backs, and give them to you. Save them for **Lesson 11.2.**

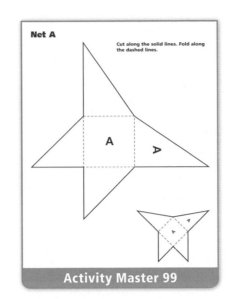

Net A

Cut along the solid lines. Fold along the dashed lines.

A

Activity Master 99

Materials

- For each student: one of the AM99–AM122
- scissors, tape

NCTM Standards 3, 6, 7, 8, 9, 10

Possible Discussion

Students may intuitively understand what two-dimensional and three-dimensional refer to but have trouble describing the differences. For that matter, they may be surprised to hear that something may be one-dimensional. You might explain that one dimension is something with only one direction, such as a straight line. Two dimensions require 2 directions. A rectangle is 2-dimensional because it has both length and width. A cube is 3-dimensional because in addition to length and width it also has height.

 **Talk Math**

❷ Which of the figures shown below could you cut out, fold, and tape to make a cube? A and D

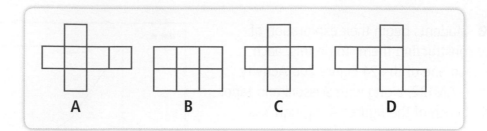

A   B   C   D

❷ Brittany looked at a pattern for a polyhedron and saw at once that it could not be a pattern for a cube. What might she have seen that told her that? Possible answers: more or fewer than 6 faces; faces that were not squares; faces that were not congruent

Describing Polyhedra in the Zoo

Purpose To use geometric terms to identify attributes of polyhedra

Introduce Begin by asking students to focus on one face of their three-dimensional figures. Point to the face labeled A on Polyhedron A as you do this, to help students understand the terms you are using. Have students share something they notice about this face. To prompt them, you might ask questions like the following:

💬 **Talk Math**

❓ What is the shape of the face? square

❓ How many angles does the face have? four

❓ What kind of angles are they? right angles

❓ How many pairs of parallel sides does the face have? two

❓ How many pairs of perpendicular sides does the face have? four

Task **Have students look at the lettered faces on their polyhedra and describe their attributes.** To let all students participate in this activity, have students turn to neighbors and share two things they notice about their figures. Then have a few students share their observations with the class.

Try to have students use as many of the following terms in their observations as possible, so that they will be prepared for the LAB pages: triangle, parallelogram, rectangle, rhombus, square, acute angle, right angle, obtuse angle, parallel, perpendicular.

Share Encourage students to name any of the above terms whose meanings they're not sure of. For each, ask a volunteer to define the term. Then have another volunteer go to the board and draw a sketch to illustrate the meaning of the term.

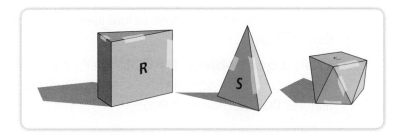

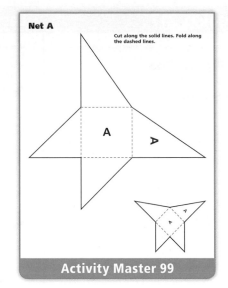

Net A

Cut along the solid lines. Fold along the dashed lines.

A

Activity Master 99

Materials
• For each student: 3-D shape from Activity B; small shape pattern from Activity B

NCTM Standards 3, 6, 7, 8, 9, 10

Differentiated Instruction

Basic Level Students draw upon a variety of skills throughout this chapter. Some of your students, including those who do not usually excel in computation, may display an aptitude for working with spatial problems. This chapter can increase their confidence even as it challenges them. Other students who excel at computation may lack fine motor skills or spatial sense. These students may enjoy geometry once the numerical aspects, such as the computation of volume, are emphasized. Whatever the case, due to the inherently varied skills that are needed to understand geometry, it is important to listen to the way students reason through problems in this chapter to inform your support of them. For example, students who struggle with spatial reasoning may benefit from putting together and taking apart three-dimensional figures as they answer questions about the faces, edges, and vertices.

D Making a Figure Zoo LAB pp. 217–218

20 MIN

Purpose To describe attributes of geometric figures

NCTM Standards 1, 3, 6, 7, 8, 9, 10

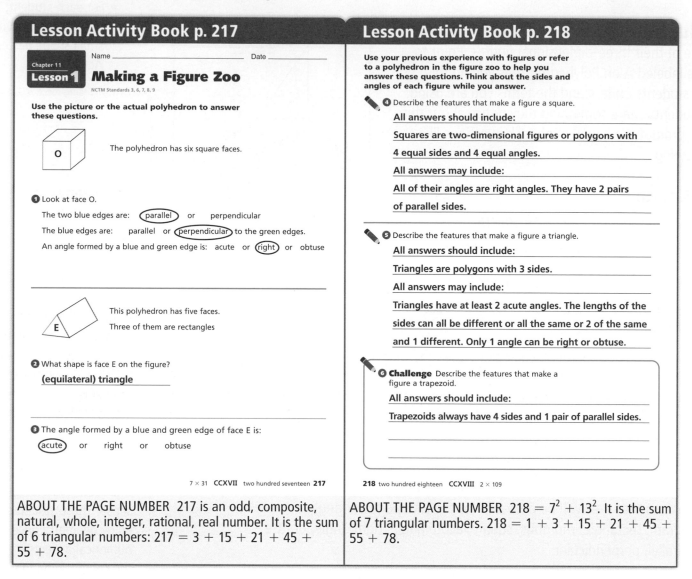

Lesson Activity Book p. 217

Chapter 11
Lesson 1 **Making a Figure Zoo**
NCTM Standards 3, 6, 7, 8, 9

Name _____ Date _____

Use the picture or the actual polyhedron to answer these questions.

O

The polyhedron has six square faces.

❶ Look at face O.

The two blue edges are: (parallel) or perpendicular

The blue edges are: parallel or (perpendicular) to the green edges.

An angle formed by a blue and green edge is: acute or (right) or obtuse

E

This polyhedron has five faces.

Three of them are rectangles

❷ What shape is face E on the figure?

(equilateral) triangle

❸ The angle formed by a blue and green edge of face E is:

(acute) or right or obtuse

7 × 31 CCXVII two hundred seventeen **217**

ABOUT THE PAGE NUMBER 217 is an odd, composite, natural, whole, integer, rational, real number. It is the sum of 6 triangular numbers: 217 = 3 + 15 + 21 + 45 + 55 + 78.

Lesson Activity Book p. 218

Use your previous experience with figures or refer to a polyhedron in the figure zoo to help you answer these questions. Think about the sides and angles of each figure while you answer.

❹ Describe the features that make a figure a square.

All answers should include:

Squares are two-dimensional figures or polygons with 4 equal sides and 4 equal angles.

All answers may include:

All of their angles are right angles. They have 2 pairs of parallel sides.

❺ Describe the features that make a figure a triangle.

All answers should include:

Triangles are polygons with 3 sides.

All answers may include:

Triangles have at least 2 acute angles. The lengths of the sides can all be different or all the same or 2 of the same and 1 different. Only 1 angle can be right or obtuse.

❻ **Challenge** Describe the features that make a figure a trapezoid.

All answers should include:

Trapezoids always have 4 sides and 1 pair of parallel sides.

218 two hundred eighteen CCXVIII 2 × 109

ABOUT THE PAGE NUMBER $218 = 7^2 + 13^2$. It is the sum of 7 triangular numbers. 218 = 1 + 3 + 15 + 21 + 45 + 55 + 78.

Teaching Notes for LAB page 217

Have students complete the page individually or in pairs.

In Problem 1, students answer questions about a cube. In Problem 2, they answer questions about a triangular prism. You might display Activity Master figures O and E for all to see as students answer these questions.

In answering Problem 2, some students may simply identify the figure as a triangle, while others may measure the sides, find them to be equal in length, and conclude that the face is an equilateral triangle.

Teaching Notes for LAB page 218

Students are asked to think about the attributes that are necessary in order for a shape to be a particular geometric figure. Students will likely be eager to share everything they know about these figures, so encourage them first to think of features the figures *must* have before identifying other features they *may* have.

Challenge Problem The Challenge Problem continues the search for necessary attributes, asking students to name features that describe a trapezoid.

Reflect and Summarize the Lesson

Write Math

Describe the shaded face of the polyhedron at the right. Name at least three things you notice about the face. Possible answers: The face has 5 equal sides and 5 angles. The angles are obtuse. There are no pairs of parallel or perpendicular sides.

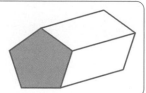

3 | Differentiated Instruction

Leveled Problem Solving

Martina is building a model of a cube using a net.

❶ Basic Level

How many squares are part of the net? Explain. 6 squares; A cube has 6 faces that are all squares.

❷ On Level

How many pairs of parallel faces does the figure have? Explain. 3 pairs; A cube has 6 faces, and each face has an opposite face that is parallel to it.

❸ Above Level

How many right angles do the faces of the cube have in all? Explain. 24 right angles; A cube has 6 square faces, and each face has 4 right angles; $6 \times 4 = 24$.

Intervention	Practice	Extension

Intervention

Activity Predicting Nets

Help students see the relationship between everyday objects and nets. Work backward from several well-known figures to their nets. Display a cereal box (or other rectangular prism), and ask students to tell how many faces will be on the net of the figure. Proceed to cut the box along its edges, describing what you are doing, to check students' predictions. Work backward with other objects, such as tissue box cubes, juice boxes, and shoeboxes.

Practice

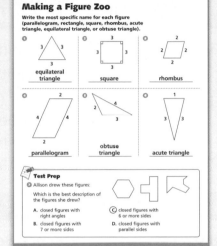

Practice P89

Extension

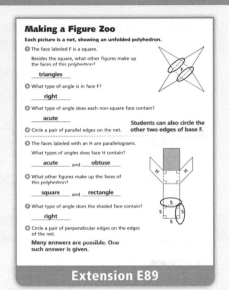

Extension E89

Spiral Review

Spiral Review Book page SR89 provides review of the following previously learned skills and concepts:

• subtracting decimals
• converting between inches, feet, and yards

You may wish to have students work with a partner to complete the page.

Number and Operations
Find the difference.

❶ 9.4 − 6.7 = 2.7	❷ 5.2 − 1.9 = 3.3	❸ 1.70 − 0.18 = 1.52	❹ 27.2 − 8.6 = 18.6	❺ 12.5 − 10.9 = 1.6
❻ 4.02 − 2.70 = 1.32	❼ 56.33 − 41.14 = 15.19	❽ 6.3 − 0.9 = 5.4	❾ 26.07 − 22.7 = 3.37	❿ 91.82 − 56.71 = 35.11

⓫ 10.11 − 8.9 = 1.21 ⓬ 0.31 − 0.22 = 0.09
⓭ 15 − 4.2 = 10.8 ⓮ 1.43 − 0.97 = 0.46
⓯ 103.4 − 74.6 = 28.8 ⓰ 10.2 − 1.8 = 8.4
⓱ 20 − 9.98 = 10.02 ⓲ 122.6 − 99.1 = 23.5
⓳ 15.05 − 8.7 = 6.35 ⓴ 159.1 − 109.1 = 50

Measurement
Write the equivalent measure.

㉑ 18 inches = $1\frac{1}{2}$ feet ㉒ 1 yard = 36 inches
㉓ 5 feet = 60 inches ㉔ 36 inches = 3 feet
㉕ 48 inches = 4 feet ㉖ $1\frac{1}{4}$ feet = 15 inches
㉗ $3\frac{1}{2}$ yards = 126 inches ㉘ $1\frac{1}{2}$ yards = $4\frac{1}{2}$ feet
㉙ 42 inches = $1\frac{1}{6}$ yards ㉚ 60 inches = $1\frac{2}{3}$ yards
㉛ $1\frac{1}{2}$ yards = 54 inches ㉜ 24 inches = $\frac{2}{3}$ yard
㉝ 20 inches = 1 foot 8 inches ㉞ 72 inches = 2 yards

Spiral Review SR89

Extension Activity
Losing Face

Have small groups of students create a variety of figures. Then have them experiment to see what happens to the number of faces when they combine figures by matching faces. For example, students can match congruent faces of a cube and a square pyramid or a triangular prism and a rectangular prism in which all seven rectangles are congruent and then describe the new figure. 9 faces; 7 faces

---

Lesson 2 Describing Three-Dimensional Figures

NCTM Standards 3, 6, 7, 8, 9, 10

Lesson Planner

STUDENT OBJECTIVES
- To sort 3-D figures into prisms and pyramids
- To describe the attributes of prisms and pyramids

1 | Daily Activities (TG p. 887)

Open-Ended Problem Solving/Headline Story	Skills Practice and Review—Identifying and Describing Parallel and Perpendicular Lines

2 | Teach and Practice (TG pp. 888–891)

	MATERIALS
(A) **Sorting Three-Dimensional Figures by Their Faces** (TG pp. 888–889)	• three-dimensional figures from Lesson 11.1
(B) **Sorting Three-Dimensional Figures by Their Angles** (TG p. 890)	• small nets of shapes from Lesson 11.1
(C) **Describing Three-Dimensional Figures** (TG p. 891)	• cylinder (e.g., paper towel roll, straw, unsharpened pencil); cone (e.g., party hat, ice cream cone)
	• ⬚ LAB pp. 219–220

3 | Differentiated Instruction (TG p. 892)

Leveled Problem Solving (TG p. 892)	Practice Book P90
Intervention Activity (TG p. 892)	Extension Book E90
Extension Activity (TG p. 892)	Spiral Review Book SR90
Science Connection (TG p. 876)	

Lesson Notes

About the Lesson

Students sort three-dimensional figures by examining attributes of faces and angles, honing their observation skills and sharpening their understanding of defining features of prisms and pyramids.

About the Mathematics

Mathematicians use *definitions* to specify items that do and do not fit into categories like *prism* and *pyramid*. They also construct *examples* that fit the definitions but vary from one another significantly, and *non-examples*—"near misses" that almost fit.

Learners depend on these contrasting examples and non-examples to make sense of definitions. This lesson goes beyond the examples given in many texts by including prisms and pyramids that slant as well as ones that stand upright. Polyhedra that fit neither category are also included as counter-examples that provide opportunities for students to distinguish between critical and non-critical attributes.

Use with Lesson Activity Book pp. 219–220.

Developing Mathematical Language

Vocabulary: prisms, pyramid

Children need formal definitions like *"extinguish* means *to put out"* to grasp the basic meanings of new words. Without instructive examples and counter-examples to clarify their meanings, however, such definitions can be useless, and may even lead to *mis*understandings ("Daddy extinguished the garbage last night"). To teach new words most effectively, back up formal definitions with sentences illustrating uses of the words in context, along with carefully chosen examples and counter-examples. See *About The Math* and Activity A for ways to help students understand this lesson's vocabulary.

Familiarize students with the terms *prisms* and *pyramid.*

Beginning Tell students that a *prism* has a flat top that matches its bottom part and a *pyramid* has a point at the top. Display several *prisms* and *pyramids.* Have students take turns identifying each figure.

Intermediate Display and name a triangular *prism* and a square *pyramid.* Then display a cube and a triangular *pyramid.* Have students identify the *prism* and the *pyramid* and tell why.

Advanced Display a triangular *prism* and a square *pyramid.* Invite students to explain which figure is a *prism* and which is a *pyramid.*

Open-Ended Problem Solving

Read the Headline Story to the students. Encourage them to look for common attributes among the items on Maria's list.

 Headline Story

> **Maria made a list of items in her house with similar shapes. The list included refrigerator, book, cereal box, crayon box, and stereo speaker.**

Possible responses: All the objects on the list are 3-dimensional and rectangular. All are prisms. Maria might have included VCR tape, DVD player, shoebox, dresser, and photo album on her list. All these objects have flat tops and 6 faces. All the faces are rectangular.

Skills Practice and Review

Identifying and Describing Perpendicular Lines

Draw several lines on the board. Tell students that some of the lines are parallel, some are perpendicular, and some are non-perpendicular intersecting lines. Ask students to identify two lines that are parallel, two lines that are perpendicular, and two lines that are neither. If you drew more than one pair of each type, encourage students to look for more such lines even after a student has identified one pair. Once students are comfortable identifying such lines, invite them to find parallel lines or edges of objects in the classroom. For example, students might notice that two edges of a door or window appear to be parallel. Finally, ask students to look around the room for perpendicular lines or edges of objects that look perpendicular. For example, two adjacent edges of a desk might be perpendicular.

whole class   10 MIN

Materials
- For the teacher: Figure Zoo figures from Lesson 11.1

NCTM Standards 3, 6, 7, 8, 9, 10

Teacher Story

"During the first sorting activity in this lesson, I had students sit in a circle. I used string to make two circles inside our own, and explained that one of the circles was for figures that are prisms and one was for figures that are pyramids. Then I placed all the zoo shapes outside the two string circles but within the circle formed by the students. I went around the circle and let each student choose one figure from the zoo and put it into either the pyramid or the prism group. If other students disagreed with where the student placed the figure, they raised their hands and, before telling which group the figure belonged to, I asked students to explain their disagreement. I warned students ahead of time that there would be figures that didn't belong in either group. Therefore, some students chose a figure and decided it belonged outside the two circles. "

Purpose To help students refine their understanding of pyramids and prisms

Introduce Gather the zoo figures from **Lesson 11.1.** Hold up a prism or pyramid and ask students if they can name the figure.

Task Direct students to help you sort the zoo figures from Lesson 11.1 into three sets, pyramids, prisms, and others. If students are uncertain about the categories, you might begin by placing one example in each category yourself.

- If a three-dimensional figure can be placed on a table so that the top face is both *level* (parallel to the table and therefore parallel to the bottom face) and *congruent to the bottom* (the same size and shape), and all other faces are parallelograms (rectangles or slanted parallelograms), the figure is a **prism.**

- If a three-dimensional figure cannot have a level top no matter how it is placed on a table, but can be placed so that all the faces that are not flat on the table are triangles meeting at a single point on top, the figure is a **pyramid.**

You may wish to conduct the activity silently, motioning students one by one to place a three-dimensional figure in one of the categories. To correct errors, make a show of setting the polyhedron on each face to see if there is any way for it to have a level top, or if it can be set so that all the visible faces (those not hidden against the table) are triangles, meeting at one top vertex. Use "other" for figures that are neither pyramids nor prisms.

After all polyhedra are sorted, ask students to describe similarities and differences among the figures in each group. Figures A, F, J, S, V, and W are pyramids. Figures B, E, G, H, I, K, L, M, O, P, Q, R, U, and X are prisms. Figures C, D, N, and T are neither. (See Teacher Story for another idea for this activity.)

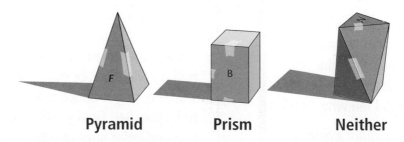

Pyramid   Prism   Neither

Use with Lesson Activity Book pp. 219–220.

Finally, help students refine the categories by asking them to classify the cylinder and the cone. Students don't yet have reasons to know that these three-dimensional figures are "neither." Cylinders *seem* like prisms; they have two congruent, parallel surfaces. But the surfaces are circles, not polygons, and the remaining surface is curved, not flat. Just as polygons must be flat and have straight-line sides, prisms and pyramids (and all polyhedra) must have polygons and only polygons as surfaces. So, a cylinder is not a prism. With its flat base and pointy top, a cone is like a pyramid. But its base is not a polygon, its remaining surface is curved, and it has no triangular surfaces. So, it is not a pyramid.

Talk Math A pyramid made of wood was cut in two, creating two polyhedra, as shown below.

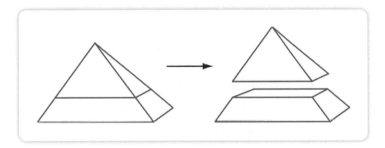

❓ Was the top polyhedron a pyramid? Explain your reasoning. yes; Possible explanation: The top cannot be level no matter how the polyhedron is placed on a table. But the polyhedron can be placed so that all its faces that are not flat on the table are triangles meeting at a single point on top.

❓ Was the bottom figure a prism? Explain your reasoning. no; Possible explanation: The polyhedron can be placed on a table so that the top face is level. However, the top face is not congruent to the bottom face, so the polyhedron is not a prism.

Differentiated Instruction

On Level Students who have a vague sense of what a pyramid and a prism are may incorrectly classify a few polyhedra that have some, but not all, of the necessary features of a pyramid or prism. For example, Figure C is like a prism in one way because it can be placed on a table such that the bottom and top faces are parallel and congruent. But it is not a prism, because all of its other faces are triangles, not parallelograms. Similarly, Figure D can be placed on a table so that the top face is parallel to the bottom face, but the two faces are different sizes and therefore not congruent; so, Figure D is also not a prism. Watch for students who classify these figures as prisms because it can help you to determine which features of a prism they understand and which they do not.

B # Sorting Three-Dimensional Figures by their Angles

Materials
- For the teacher: Figure Zoo figures from Lesson 11.1

NCTM Standards 3, 6, 7, 8, 9, 10

Purpose To sort polyhedra according to their angles

Introduce Put all the figures back into a large group.

Task **Direct students to help you sort the zoo figures by the angles on their faces.** Figures whose faces appear to have all right angles should be placed in one group, while all other figures should be placed in a second group. Again, you might carry out the sorting as a silent activity. You will likely need to put a few figures into each category first before students catch on to the sorting rule.

Share When the sorting is complete, break the silence and ask students to describe any patterns they see among the polyhedra. Some students may notice that figures in the group with all right angles on their faces (B, G, K, L, O, and P) have faces that are all both parallel and perpendicular to other faces. The same is true for the edges. Sorting the shapes in this way helps students become more familiar with the rectangular (right) prisms in the collection of three-dimensional figures. These figures will become more important later on in the chapter when students find the volumes and the areas of the faces of right rectangular prisms.

Talk Math Shannon used six different colors to paint the faces of a polyhedron. She painted the top light blue, the bottom dark blue, the front dark red, the back light red, the left side light green, and the right side dark green.

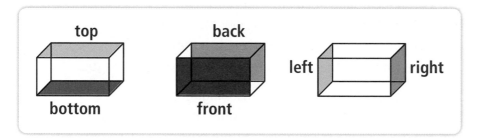

? Name the color of a face that is parallel to the dark-red face. light red

? Name the colors of all the faces that are perpendicular to the light-green face. dark red, light red, dark blue, light blue

individuals or pairs

20 MIN

Purpose To practice ideas explored during the sorting activities

NCTM Standards 3, 6, 7, 8, 9, 10

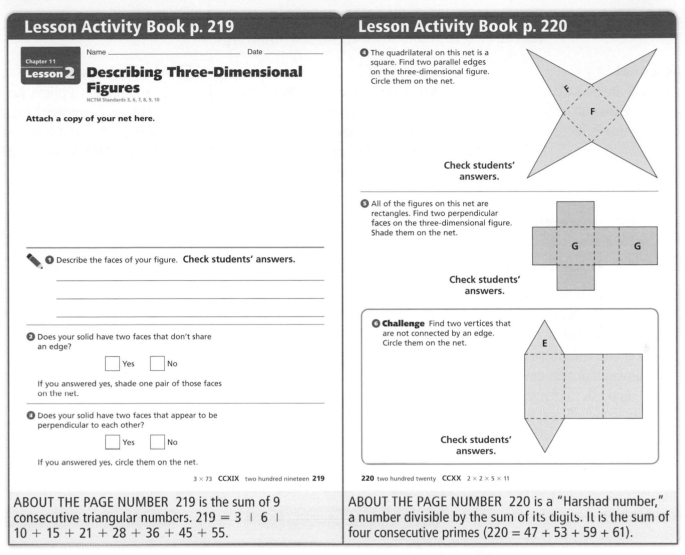

Lesson Activity Book p. 219

Chapter 11
Lesson 2 **Describing Three-Dimensional Figures**
NCTM Standards 3, 6, 7, 8, 9, 10

Name _____ Date _____

Attach a copy of your net here.

1 Describe the faces of your figure. **Check students' answers.**

2 Does your solid have two faces that don't share an edge?

☐ Yes ☐ No

If you answered yes, shade one pair of those faces on the net.

3 Does your solid have two faces that appear to be perpendicular to each other?

☐ Yes ☐ No

If you answered yes, circle them on the net.

3 × 73 **CCXIX** two hundred nineteen **219**

ABOUT THE PAGE NUMBER 219 is the sum of 9 consecutive triangular numbers. 219 = 3 + 6 + 10 + 15 + 21 + 28 + 36 + 45 + 55.

Lesson Activity Book p. 220

4 The quadrilateral on this net is a square. Find two parallel edges on the three-dimensional figure. Circle them on the net.

Check students' answers.

5 All of the figures on this net are rectangles. Find two perpendicular faces on the three-dimensional figure. Shade them on the net.

Check students' answers.

6 **Challenge** Find two vertices that are not connected by an edge. Circle them on the net.

Check students' answers.

220 two hundred twenty **CCXX** 2 × 2 × 5 × 11

ABOUT THE PAGE NUMBER 220 is a "Harshad number," a number divisible by the sum of its digits. It is the sum of four consecutive primes (220 = 47 + 53 + 59 + 61).

Teaching Notes for LAB page 219

Students will need the small nets they cut out in **Lesson 11.1** when they constructed their three-dimensional figures. They should glue or tape the nets to the LAB pages in the spaces provided. Students name faces of their three-dimensional figures and examine the relationship between the edges and faces. You may need to point out the faces, edges, and vertices on one of the figures to help students understand the terms in context. (Edges are where faces touch; vertices are where edges touch.)

Teaching Notes for LAB page 220

Students complete problems similar to those of the first LAB page but now using shapes they didn't construct. Again, encourage students to look at the corresponding figures in the zoo to help them answer the questions.

To give students further practice identifying pyramids and prisms, you might ask them to label each figure made from the nets as a prism or a pyramid.

Challenge Problem The Challenge Problem asks students to find vertices, the points where edges of polyhedra touch.

Reflect and Summarize the Lesson

Write Math

Choose a three-dimensional figure from the zoo and describe it for someone who can't see it. **You might describe the shape of the faces; the numbers of faces, edges, and vertices; or the parallel and perpendicular faces and edges.** Possible answers: If students chose Figure A, they might say that it is a pyramid, that one of its faces is a square and the other four are right triangles. There are 8 edges and 5 vertices. None of the faces is parallel or perpendicular to another face.

Leveled Problem Solving

Sara is using 2 cardboard trapezoids and 4 cardboard rectangles to make a three-dimensional figure.

❶ Basic Level

Can Sara's figure be a pyramid? Explain. No; Either all or all but one of a pyramid's faces must be triangles.

❷ On Level

Sara's shape is a prism. What do you know about the two trapezoids? They have to be congruent because a prism has 2 bases that are congruent.

❸ Above Level

Sara's shape is a prism. Are all the rectangles congruent? Explain. No; The sides of the trapezoid are not all the same length.

| Intervention | Practice | Extension |

Activity Upside-Down or Not?

Display several prisms and pyramids. For pyramids, you might use a picture in a social studies book. Put an object behind your back, and tell the class you might be turning it upside-down. Display it again, and ask students whether they can tell whether it has been turned upside-down. Lead to the conclusion that if an object looks different upside-down, it cannot be a prism because prisms have two congruent bases.

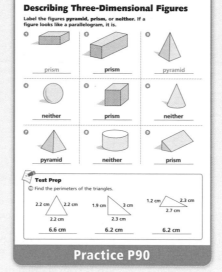

Practice P90

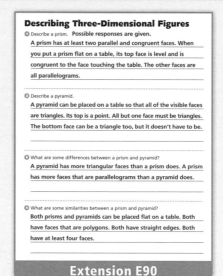

Extension E90

Spiral Review

Spiral Review Book page SR90 provides review of the following previously learned skills and concepts:

- drawing, measuring, and comparing shapes in square inches and square centimeters

- comparing the likelihood of events

You may wish to have students work with a partner to complete the page.

Spiral Review SR90

Extension Activity
Human Attributes

Have small groups of students discuss this statement: "Faces, edges, and vertices of a figure can be compared to a human being because faces are like the skin of a figure, edges are like the bones, and vertices are like the joints." Then have students write a short paragraph about whether they think the statement makes sense, giving examples and/or drawing diagrams to support their ideas.

Use with Lesson Activity Book pp. 219–220.

Teacher's Notes 🍎

Daily Notes . . .

Quick Notes

More Ideas

Lesson 3 Going On a Figure Safari

NCTM Standards 3, 6, 7, 8, 9, 10

Lesson Planner

STUDENT OBJECTIVE
- To identify three-dimensional figures according to their attributes

1 Daily Activities (TG p. 895)

Open-Ended Problem Solving/Headline Story	Skills Practice and Review—Classifying Polygons

2 Teach and Practice (TG pp. 896–899)

	MATERIALS
(A) **Playing a Game: *Figure Sit Down*** (TG p. 896)	• three-dimensional figures from Lesson 11.1
(B) **Going On a Figure Safari** (TG p. 897)	• 📖 LAB pp. 221–222
(C) **Identifying Classes of Three-Dimensional Figures** (TG p. 898)	• 📖 SH pp. 178, 188

3 Differentiated Instruction (TG p. 900)

Leveled Problem Solving (TG p. 900)	Practice Book P91
Intervention Activity (TG p. 900)	Extension Book E91
Extension Activity (TG p. 900)	Spiral Review Book SR91
Social Studies Connection (TG p. 876)	

Lesson Notes

About the Lesson

Students continue to develop ways to classify three-dimensional figures as they describe polyhedra according to their attributes. They also systematically explore figures to find all figures in the zoo with certain characteristics. This gives students an opportunity to relate the attributes of different three-dimensional figures.

About the Mathematics

Students match three-dimensional figures with sets of clues in this lesson. This activity provides practice in interpreting verbal descriptions of three-dimensional figures, as well as opportunities to classify figures based on attributes. Classifying figures by attributes is a fundamental geometric skill that lays the groundwork for reasoning geometrically.

Developing Mathematical Language

Vocabulary: edge, face, side, vertex, vertices

Although casually we might say that a cube has six *sides,* the fact that each such *side* is a square with four *sides* of its own can easily lead to confusion. For that reason, we say that prisms and pyramids have *faces,* not *sides.* The line segments that form the boundaries of a *face* are called *edges.* The places where edges intersect are called *vertices* (singular: *vertex*).

Familiarize students with the terms *edges, faces,* and *vertices.*

Beginning *Face* and *edge* are words that students might know in other contexts. Point to the *edge* of a desk, and relate it to the *edge* of prism. Relate what you see in a mirror—your *face*—with the *face* of a prism.

Intermediate Display a prism, and identify its *faces, edges,* and *vertices.* Then point to various *faces, edges,* and *vertices,* and have students name each one as you point to it.

Advanced Hold up a three-dimensional figure. Point to a *face,* an *edge,* or a *vertex,* and ask students to identify each as you do so and to explain why they chose that term.

Open-Ended Problem Solving

Read the Headline Story to the students. Encourage them to use logical reasoning to think of attributes that Figures A and B have that Figures C and D do not.

NEWS Headline Story

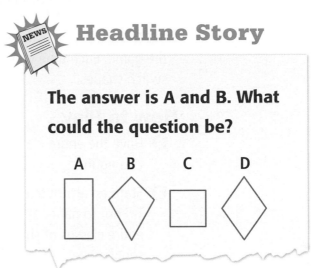

The answer is A and B. What could the question be?

A   B   C   D

Possible responses: Which shapes are quadrilaterals with sides of two different lengths? Which of the shapes aren't rhombuses? Which of the shapes don't have four equal sides?

Skills Practice and Review

Classifying Polygons

Repeat this activity from **Lesson 11.1.** Draw shapes on the board and ask your students whether each shape is a polygon. Circle the polygons. (Polygons are closed shapes with straight sides, no extra lines, and only one interior.) Here are some shapes you could draw:

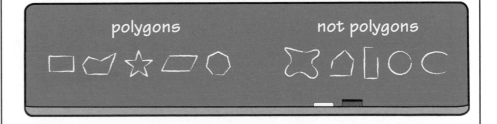

polygons   not polygons

When the shapes have been sorted, ask students if they can use other words to more specifically describe each polygon. Students might use such words as quadrilateral, triangle, parallelogram, or trapezoid.

pairs or
whole class

  10 MIN

Materials

• For each student:
Figure Zoo figure from
Lesson 11.1

NCTM Standards 3, 6, 7, 8, 9, 10

A Playing a Game: *Figure Sit Down*

Purpose To practice identifying attributes of three-dimensional figures.

Goal The object of the game is to be the last student standing after surviving a round of eliminations based on common attributes of polyhedra.

Introduce Each student will need one Figure Zoo polyhedron to play the game. Each time you begin a new round of the game, have students switch shapes.

How to Play

❶ Have the entire class stand up holding their Figure Zoo figures.

❷ State an attribute of a three-dimensional figure. Try not to name attributes that might eliminate entire classes of shapes. Possible statements you could make:

  • "It has 6 faces."

  • "It has more than 5 vertices."

  • "It has at least 2 pairs of parallel faces."

  • "It has fewer than 8 right angles."

  • "Some faces are triangles."

❸ Each student should decide whether his or her figure matches the attribute. If it does not, the student should sit down.

❹ Repeat Steps 2 and 3 until there is only one figure left. You may wish to ask students to hold up their shapes after each clue, to confirm that students who should have sat down are not still standing. Or you might ask neighboring students to verify that students still standing have correctly judged the attributes of their figures.

❺ The last student standing is the winner.

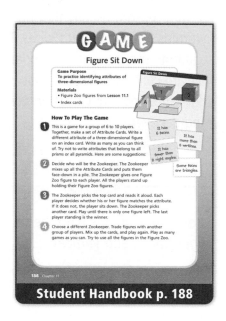

Student Handbook p. 188

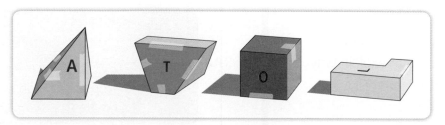

Purpose To match polyhedra with their descriptions

NCTM Standards 1, 3, 6, 7, 8, 9, 10

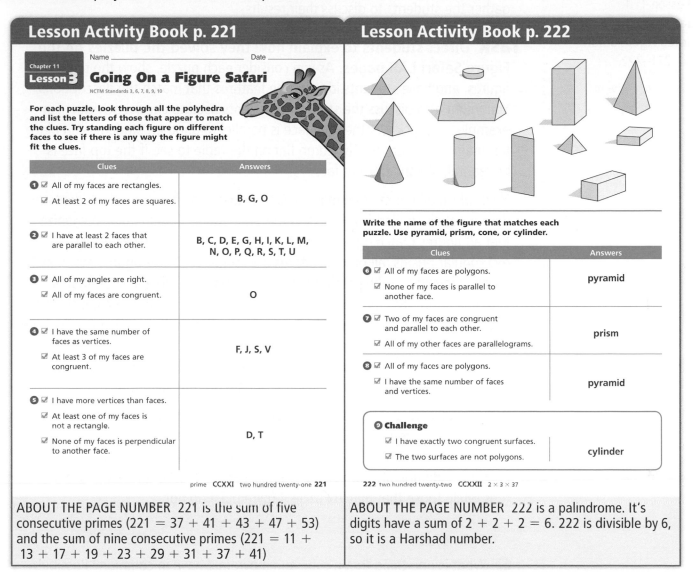

Lesson Activity Book p. 221

Chapter 11
Lesson 3 **Going On a Figure Safari**
NCTM Standards 3, 6, 7, 8, 9, 10

For each puzzle, look through all the polyhedra and list the letters of those that appear to match the clues. Try standing each figure on different faces to see if there is any way the figure might fit the clues.

Clues	Answers
❶ ☑ All of my faces are rectangles. ☑ At least 2 of my faces are squares.	B, G, O
❷ ☑ I have at least 2 faces that are parallel to each other.	B, C, D, E, G, H, I, K, L, M, N, O, P, Q, R, S, T, U
❸ ☑ All of my angles are right. ☑ All of my faces are congruent.	O
❹ ☑ I have the same number of faces as vertices. ☑ At least 3 of my faces are congruent.	F, J, S, V
❺ ☑ I have more vertices than faces. ☑ At least one of my faces is not a rectangle. ☑ None of my faces is perpendicular to another face.	D, T

prime CCXXI two hundred twenty-one **221**

Lesson Activity Book p. 222

Write the name of the figure that matches each puzzle. Use pyramid, prism, cone, or cylinder.

Clues	Answers
❻ ☑ All of my faces are polygons. ☑ None of my faces is parallel to another face.	pyramid
❼ ☑ Two of my faces are congruent and parallel to each other. ☑ All of my other faces are parallelograms.	prism
❽ ☑ All of my faces are polygons. ☑ I have the same number of faces and vertices.	pyramid
❾ **Challenge** ☑ I have exactly two congruent surfaces. ☑ The two surfaces are not polygons.	cylinder

222 two hundred twenty-two CCXXII 2 × 3 × 37

ABOUT THE PAGE NUMBER 221 is the sum of five consecutive primes (221 = 37 + 41 + 43 + 47 + 53) and the sum of nine consecutive primes (221 = 11 + 13 + 17 + 19 + 23 + 29 + 31 + 37 + 41)

ABOUT THE PAGE NUMBER 222 is a palindrome. It's digits have a sum of 2 + 2 + 2 = 6. 222 is divisible by 6, so it is a Harshad number.

Teaching Notes for LAB page 221

Students look for three-dimensional figures that match the clues in each puzzle. Students will need access to the entire figure zoo.

Differentiated Instruction **Basic Level** If students struggle with the puzzles, you might reason through one set of clues with them. For example, you might read the first clue, pick up a figure, and ask whether the figure matches the clue. Students can then explain why they think that it does or does not. If it does not, choose another shape and again ask if it matches the clue. When students agree that they have found a figure which matches the first clue, have them check to see if it matches the second clue. Be sure students understand that even though they have found a figure that matches the clues, other shapes may remain that also match these clues.

Teaching Notes for LAB page 222

Students solve puzzles involving categories of shapes, such as pyramids, prisms, and cylinders, rather than specific zoo figures. Students may use the pictures at the top of the page to help them reason about the clues and the categories of shapes.

Challenge Problem The Challenge Problem involves identifying a cylinder from a set of clues.

✔ Ongoing Assessment As students complete the LAB pages, watch to see which clues give them the most trouble and which ones they consistently match incorrectly with three-dimensional figures. Try to help students see why certain clues don't match certain figures by pointing out the relevant features on the actual figure. You might also rephrase some of the clues to help students further develop their understanding of attributes of three-dimensional figures.

C Identifying Classes of Three-Dimensional Figures

Materials

- For the teacher:
  Figure Zoo figures
  from Lesson 11.1
- For each student
  completed Figure Safari
  LAB pp. 221–222

NCTM Standards 3, 6, 7, 8, 9, 10

Purpose To identify attributes of polyhedra

Introduce After students have completed the Figure Safari LAB pages, gather the students to discuss their results.

Task Direct students to explain how they solved the puzzles on the Figure Safari LAB pages. As you consider each puzzle, show the relevant figures, and have students identify the features that match the descriptions. You might also discuss the strategies students used to check each clue. For example, to check whether one face is parallel to another, students can place (or imagine placing) a polyhedron flat on the table to see if the top face is horizontal, like the bottom face.

Next, place all figures that match a set of clues together and ask students to describe their similarities. By listing the similarities, students may recognize that all figures matching the clues for Puzzle 1 are prisms (specifically rectangular prisms, all of whose faces are rectangles). The figures that match Puzzle 2 include all the prisms in the zoo, along with other similar figures. The only figure that matches Puzzle 3 is a cube, because only a cube consists entirely of congruent rectangular faces. All the figures that match Puzzle 4 are pyramids. The figure that matches Puzzle 5 is neither a pyramid nor a prism. (While it's true that the figure has two parallel faces, those faces are not congruent; moreover, the remaining faces are not parallelograms).

Besides solidifying students' understanding of attributes of individual polyhedra, this activity will help students contrast groups of figures. For example, students may notice that all figures that match Puzzle 1 also match Puzzle 2. Additionally, figures that match Puzzles 1, 2, 3, and 5 all have flat tops while those that match Puzzle 4 (pyramids) do not.

💬 Talk Math

❷ What is one thing that a cube and a pyramid have in common? Possible answer: Both have a flat base and faces that are polygons.

❷ What is one thing that a pyramid and a cone have in common? Possible answer: Both have a flat base and a point at the top.

Reflect and Summarize the Lesson

Write Math | **All the faces of a particular polyhedron are congruent. Must it be a cube? If not, what else could it be? Explain.** no; Possible explanation: It could be a pyramid with three faces and a base that are all congruent equilateral triangles. Or, it could be made entirely of triangles, like Figure N if all its triangles were equilateral.

Review Model

Refer students to Review Model: Recognizing 3-Dimensional Figures in the *Student Handbook* p. 178, to see how they can use the faces of a three-dimensional figure to find the name of the figure.

✔ Check for Understanding

❶ prism

❷ cylinder

❸ pyramid

❹ cone

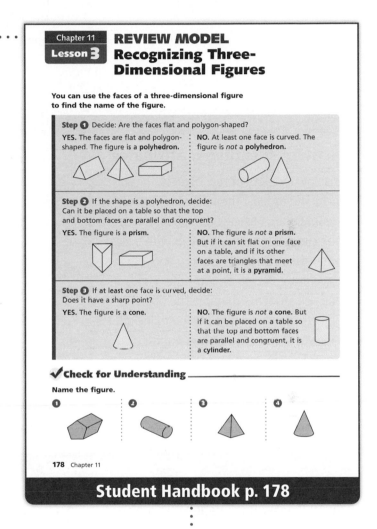

Student Handbook p. 178

Leveled Problem Solving

Jai is making a figure from a net.

❶ Basic Level
The figure has only rectangles. What figure is it? a prism

❷ On Level
The figure has more than one rectangular face. Could Jai be making a pyramid? Explain. No; A pyramid can have at most one face that is not a triangle.

❸ Above Level
All the shapes have the same number of sides. Can you tell what it is? Explain. no; It could be many things, such as a prism with all rectangular sides or a pyramid with all triangular sides.

Intervention	Practice	Extension

Activity Identifying Attributes

Display a variety of real objects, including at least the following: an ice-cream cone, a tissue box, a ball, a tissue box cube, a pyramid, a prism with bases other than rectangles, and a paper towel tube. Name an attribute aloud, and ask students to name the object or objects that have that attribute. Include types of surfaces (e.g., rectangles, circles), edges or no edges, parallel edges, number of faces, number of rectangles, triangles, circles, and so on.

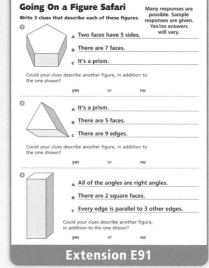

Practice P91

Extension E91

Spiral Review

Spiral Review Book page SR91 provides review of the following previously learned skills and concepts:

• modeling fractions with Cuisenaire Rods®

• solving problems using the strategy *look for a pattern*

You may wish to have students work with a partner to complete the page.

Spiral Review SR91

Extension Activity
Look for a Pattern

Have small groups of students use several of the figures in the Figure Zoo. For each figure, ask them to write the number of faces, vertices, and edges. Then have them look for any patterns they see that relate the features, either just for prisms, just for pyramids, or for all figures. The relationship Faces + Vertices − Edges = 2 is perhaps the most well-known. You may wish to have students research its history by learning about the 18th-century mathematician Leonhard Euler.

Teacher's Notes 🍎

Daily Notes . . .

Quick Notes

More Ideas

_____

_____

_____

_____

_____

_____

_____

_____

_____

_____

_____

_____

_____

_____

_____

_____

_____

_____

_____

_____

Lesson 4
Finding the Areas of Faces on Three-Dimensional Figures

NCTM Standards 1, 3, 4, 6, 7, 8, 9, 10

Lesson Planner

STUDENT OBJECTIVE ···
- To estimate and find the areas of the faces of prisms with rectangular faces

1 Daily Activities (TG p. 903)

Open-Ended Problem Solving/Headline Story	Skills Practice and Review— Estimating Rectangular Areas

2 Teach and Practice (TG pp. 904–908)

	MATERIALS
(A) **Estimating and Finding Area** (TG pp. 904–905)	• TR: Activity Masters, AM123–AM129
(B) **Finding the Areas of Faces on Three-Dimensional Figures** (TG p. 906)	• transparency of AM123 (optional) • three-dimensional figures from Lesson 11.1
(C) **Discussing Strategies for Finding the Areas of Faces** (TG p. 907)	• inch ruler • 📖 LAB pp. 223–224 • 📖 SH pp. 179–180

3 Differentiated Instruction (TG p. 909)

Leveled Problem Solving (TG p. 909)	Practice Book P92
Intervention Activity (TG p. 909)	Extension Book E92
Extension Activity (TG p. 909)	Spiral Review Book SR92

Lesson Notes

About the Lesson

Students continue to explore three-dimensional figures as they estimate and find the areas of the faces on rectangular prisms. They use copies of the nets to keep track of their measurements and to record their reasoning. This helps students recognize a good strategy for computing the total area of the faces of a polyhedron: find the area of its corresponding net.

About the Mathematics

Figure X (Activity Master 122), which looks like a "squared doughnut," has not been included in previous lessons because it is not a polyhedron. Two of its surfaces are not polygons. Polyhedra must have only polygonal surfaces.

Use with Lesson Activity Book pp. 223–224.

Developing Mathematical Language

Vocabulary: net, total area

In mathematics, a *net* is a model of a three-dimensional figure. It shows a two-dimensional view of the surface of the figure. To find the *total area* of a *net,* add the areas of each shape in the net.

Familiarize students with the terms *net* and *total area.*

Beginning Demonstrate how to deconstruct a prism made from a *net.* Explain that the *net* is a model of the surfaces of the prism. Ask: What figure does the net make if we put it back together? prism

Intermediate Demonstrate how to deconstruct a prism made from a *net.* As you hold up the *net,* have students name the shapes as you point to different faces. Elicit that to find the *total area* of the *net,* add the areas of each shape in the net.

Advanced Invite students to explain how to use a *net* to find the *total area* of the surface of a rectangular prism.

Open-Ended Problem Solving

Read the Headline Story to the students. Encourage them to make interesting statements using information from the story.

 Headline Story

> **Diana made a shape out of 6 square-inch tiles with no overlap, and then found the perimeter.**

Possible responses: If she made a long and thin 1-by-6 rectangle, then the perimeter was 14 inches. If she made a 2-by-3 rectangle, then the perimeter was 10 inches. She could have made a shape that looks like steps with 3 squares in the bottom row, 2 in the middle row, and 1 in the top row, in which case the perimeter would have been 12 inches.

Skills Practice and Review

Estimating Rectangular Areas

Hold up a piece of paper and ask students to estimate its length and width in centimeters. (A standard piece of paper measures about 21.5 cm × 28 cm.) After students have offered estimates, ask them to estimate both the perimeter and the area of the paper. Ask students to make estimates, in metric units, of the areas of other rectangular objects in the room, for example, a book, a desk, a window, or a wall. Students will have to decide the appropriate units (square centimeters or square meters) for their estimates.

individuals or pairs · 20 MIN

(A) Estimating and Finding Area

Materials

- For the teacher: transparency of AM123 (optional)
- For each student: inch ruler, Rectangular Prism B from AM123

NCTM Standards 1, 3, 4, 6, 7, 8, 9, 10

Possible Discussion

Units must match the attributes they are intended to measure. We use pounds to measure the weight of a computer but not the length of a desk. Length must be measured in units of length—inches, meters, pieces of string. In order to measure area, they must use units of area, like 1-inch squares. If you feel your students are unclear about this, say that we measure area by units of area (squares, for convenience), figuring out how many of a given unit it takes to cover the figure. Similarly, as students will see in the next lesson, we measure volume with units of volume—cubes, for instance. Area is two-dimensional and so is measured in square units—square inches or square centimeters, for example. Volume is three-dimensional and so is measured in cubic units—cubic inches or cubic centimeters, for example.

Purpose To practice estimating and finding length and area

Introduce Give each student a copy of Explore: Finding Areas and the net of rectangular prism B from Activity Master: Net of Figure B.

Task Direct students to the questions on Explore: Finding Areas. Have students answer the questions individually or with partners. Because students are first asked to estimate the lengths of the edges of Face B and then the area of Face B, delay giving them rulers until after they have made their estimates. If students are confused about how to estimate these values, you might point out that the width of two fingers is about an inch.

❶ Estimate the length of the green edge of Face B in inches. Possible estimate: 2 inches

❷ Estimate the length of the blue edge of Face B in inches. Possible estimate: 3 inches

❸ Estimate the area of Face B in square inches. Possible estimate: 6 square inches

❹ Estimate the perimeter of the net of Figure B. Possible estimate: 32 inches

❺ Using your measurements, find the perimeter of the net of Figure B. 32 inches

❻ Using your measurements, find the area of Face B in square inches. 6 square inches

❼ Using your measurements, find the area of the shaded face in square inches. 4 square inches.

❽ Find the total area of all the faces of this polyhedron in square inches. 32 square inches

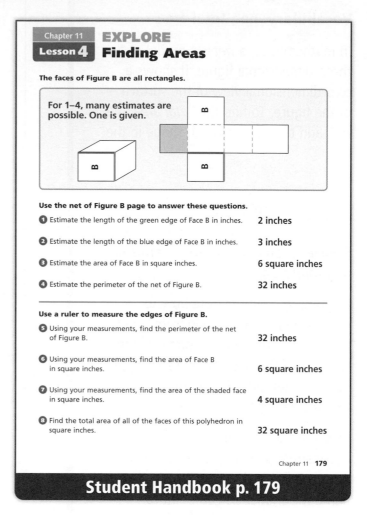

Chapter 11 · EXPLORE
Lesson 4 · Finding Areas

The faces of Figure B are all rectangles.

For 1–4, many estimates are possible. One is given.

Use the net of Figure B page to answer these questions.

❶ Estimate the length of the green edge of Face B in inches. — 2 inches

❷ Estimate the length of the blue edge of Face B in inches. — 3 inches

❸ Estimate the area of Face B in square inches. — 6 square inches

❹ Estimate the perimeter of the net of Figure B. — 32 inches

Use a ruler to measure the edges of Figure B.

❺ Using your measurements, find the perimeter of the net of Figure B. — 32 inches

❻ Using your measurements, find the area of Face B in square inches. — 6 square inches

❼ Using your measurements, find the area of the shaded face in square inches. — 4 square inches

❽ Find the total area of all of the faces of this polyhedron in square inches. — 32 square inches

Chapter 11 **179**

Student Handbook p. 179

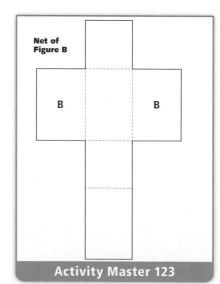

Net of Figure B

B   B

Activity Master 123

Share Once most students have completed the page, ask them to share their answers, along with their strategies for estimating and measuring the areas in square inches.

Most students should remember that they can find the area of Face B by multiplying the lengths of the two edges. Some students may realize that they don't need to find the area of each face in order to find the total area of the faces in Problem 8. If no one mentions this, ask whether it would be possible to find the total area of the faces by finding the areas of only two faces. Help students see that the two smallest faces, which are squares, are congruent, and that the four remaining faces, which share common lengths and have equal widths, are congruent to Face B. Therefore, by finding the area of the shaded square face, students also know the area of the other square face. Similarly, by finding the area of Face B, students know the areas of four of the faces. So, to find the total area of the polyhedron's faces, add four times the area of Face B to two times the area of the shaded square.

Talk Math Each edge of a cube measures 4 inches.

❷ What is the area of each face of the cube? How did you get your answer? 16 square inches; 4 inches × 4 inches = 16 square inches

❷ What is the total area of all the faces of the cubes? Explain your reasoning. 96 square inches; Possible explanation: There are six faces and they all have the same measurements, so they have the same area. That means I can multiply the area of one face by 6 to get the total area; 6 × 16 square inches = 96 square inches

B Finding the Areas of Faces on Three-Dimensional Figures LAB pp. 223–224

individuals or pairs

20 MIN

Purpose To practice finding the areas of faces of polyhedra

NCTM Standards 1, 3, 4, 6, 7, 8, 9, 10

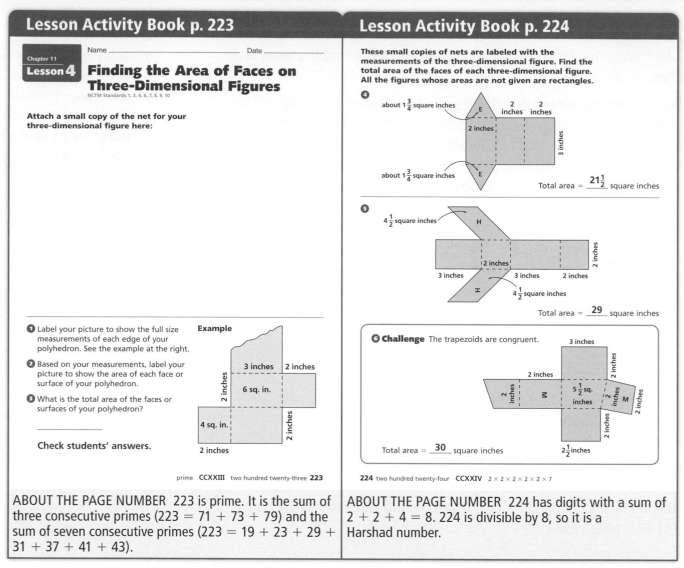

Lesson Activity Book p. 223

Name _____ Date _____

Chapter 11
Lesson 4 **Finding the Area of Faces on Three-Dimensional Figures**
NCTM Standards 1, 3, 4, 6, 7, 8, 9, 10

Attach a small copy of the net for your three-dimensional figure here:

❶ Label your picture to show the full size measurements of each edge of your polyhedron. See the example at the right.

❷ Based on your measurements, label your picture to show the area of each face or surface of your polyhedron.

❸ What is the total area of the faces or surfaces of your polyhedron?

_____

Check students' answers.

Example

3 inches | 2 inches
2 inches
6 sq. in.
4 sq. in.
2 inches
2 inches

prime **CCXXIII** two hundred twenty-three **223**

Lesson Activity Book p. 224

These small copies of nets are labeled with the measurements of the three-dimensional figure. Find the total area of the faces of each three-dimensional figure. All the figures whose areas are not given are rectangles.

❹ about 1¾ square inches E | 2 inches | 2 inches
2 inches
3 inches
about 1¾ square inches E
Total area = __21½__ square inches

❺ 4½ square inches H
2 inches
3 inches | 3 inches | 2 inches | 2 inches
H
4½ square inches
Total area = __29__ square inches

❻ **Challenge** The trapezoids are congruent.
3 inches
2 inches
2 inches | M | 5½ sq. inches | 2 inches | M | 2 inches
2 inches | 2 inches
Total area = __30__ square inches
2½ inches

224 two hundred twenty-four **CCXXIV** 2 × 2 × 2 × 2 × 2 × 7

ABOUT THE PAGE NUMBER 223 is prime. It is the sum of three consecutive primes (223 = 71 + 73 + 79) and the sum of seven consecutive primes (223 = 19 + 23 + 29 + 31 + 37 + 41 + 43).

ABOUT THE PAGE NUMBER 224 has digits with a sum of 2 + 2 + 4 = 8. 224 is divisible by 8, so it is a Harshad number.

Teaching Notes for LAB page 223

Have students complete the page individually or with partners. Each student will need a copy of a reduced net for figure G, K, L, O, X, or P (AM124–AM129) to attach to the top of the front of the page. Try to give at least one student a net for each of these figures so that the class finds the total area of the faces or surfaces on as many different three-dimensional figures as possible. Some of the figures, P and X for example, are more challenging than others.

Students will also need three-dimensional versions of their figures, from **Lesson 11.1,** or a three-dimensional version of figure X that you create, in order to measure the dimensions on the larger version of the shapes. So, you might have students with the same net work together or in the same part of the room, to allow them to share the three dimensional figures. Watch for students who measure the dimensions on the reduced copy of the net, as these dimensions are obviously smaller than the measurements of the three-dimensional figures.

Teaching Notes for LAB page 224

The nets on this page are small copies of actual nets, but they are labeled with the true dimensions of the nets. For faces that are not rectangles, the areas of the faces are given. Students should use this information to find the total areas of the faces of the three-dimensional figures that each net represents.

Challenge Problem To complete the Challenge Problem, students must recognize that, because the trapezoids are congruent, they have the same area.

Discussing Strategies for Finding the Areas of Faces

 individuals or small groups **10 MIN**

Purpose To discuss methods students can use to find areas of faces or surfaces

Introduce See that students have their Figure Zoo figures from LAB p. 223.

Materials
• Figure Zoo figure from LAB p. 223

NCTM Standards 1, 3, 4, 6, 7, 8, 9, 10

Task Ask individuals or groups of students to explain how they found the total areas of the faces on their three-dimensional figures. As they may have done in the Activity A Explore, some students may have found the area of each face, then added. Others may have recognized that, because some of the faces were congruent, they didn't need to find the area of each face. For example, the sketch at the right of the figure from Activity A shows that the blue faces are congruent and the yellow faces are congruent. By calculating the areas of one blue face and one yellow face, students learn the areas of all six faces.

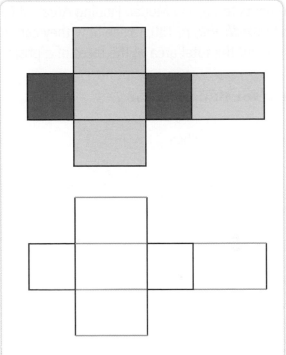

Similarly, some students may have noticed that they didn't need to re-measure common edges on their polyhedra. On the figure below, all red lines have the same length, and all green lines have the same length. By measuring the length of one red line and one green line, students learn the lengths of all the lines in the figure.

During the discussion, ask students to point to the faces on their polyhedra that correspond to the areas they are talking about, and to show how they made sure that they found the areas of all of the faces.

For the non-polyhedron, shape X, students will need an additional strategy to find the areas of the non-polygonal surfaces. These surfaces are squares but with square holes cut out. The area of the hole (4 square inches) must be subtracted from the area of what would be a large square if there were no hole (16 square inches). Another method is for students to use square tiles to cover the surface and see that the area is 12 square inches.

💬 **Talk Math**

❷ The six faces of a polyhedron have areas, in square inches, of 10, 25, 25, 10, 25, and 25. To find the total area of the faces, Joel added 10 + 25 + 25 + 10 + 25 + 25. Julie found a shortcut. What was it? Possible answer: She noticed that four of the areas were each 25 square inches and 2 of the areas were each 10 square inches. So she multiplied twice, then added: 4 × 25 = 100; 2 × 10 = 20; area = 100 + 20 = 120 square inches.

❷ The faces of a cube each measure 6 inches by 6 inches. What is the total area of the faces? Explain your method. 216 square inches; Possible explanation: The area of each face is 6 × 6 = 36 square inches. There are six faces, so the total area is 6 × 36 = 216 square inches.

Use with Lesson Activity Book pp. 223–224.

Chapter 11 • Lesson 4 **907**

Reflect and Summarize the Lesson

Write Math

How can you use the net of a polyhedron to find the total area of the faces of the polyhedron? Explain. Possible answer: Find the sum of the areas of the individual sections of the net; possible explanation: The net is a picture of the faces of the polyhedron. Therefore, the total area of the faces of the polyhedron equals the sum of the areas of the sections of the net.

Review Model

Refer students to Review Model: Finding Areas of Faces in the *Student Handbook,* p. 180, to see how they can use the net of a prism to find the total area of the faces of a prism.

✔ Check for Understanding

❶ 158 square inches

❷ 150 square inches

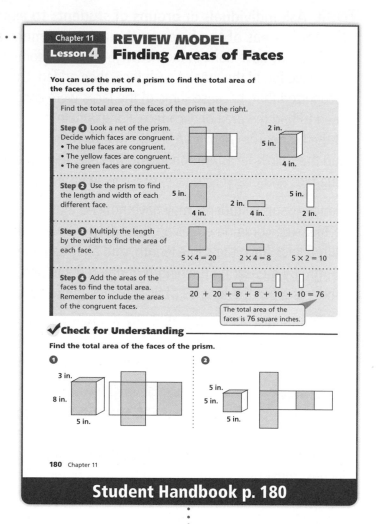

Use with Lesson Activity Book pp. 223–224.

Leveled Problem Solving

**Emily is drawing a net for a prism.
All the faces are rectangles.**

❶ Basic Level

The 6 faces are all congruent. The length of one edge is 3 inches. What is the total area of the faces? Explain. 54 sq in.; Each face is a square with area $3 \times 3 = 9$, and $6 \times 9 = 54$.

❷ On Level

Four of the faces are rectangles whose dimensions are 7 inches by 3 inches. Two are squares whose edges are 3 inches. What is the total area of the faces? Explain. 102 sq in.; $4 \times (7 \times 3) + 2 \times (3 \times 3) = 102$.

❸ Above Level

Four of the faces are rectangles whose dimensions are 6 inches by 4 inches. Two are squares. What is the greatest possible total area of the faces? Explain. 168 sq in.; $4 \times (6 \times 4) + 2 \times (6 \times 6) = 168$.

Intervention	Practice	Extension

Activity Simplifying Finding Total Area

Display real objects shaped like rectangular prisms or models of rectangular prisms. For each object or figure, ask students to tell how many *different* areas they will need to find when they find the total area of the faces. Students should see that for a shoe box or that type of rectangular prism, they will probably need to find three different areas, but for a tissue box cube, they will need to find only one area.

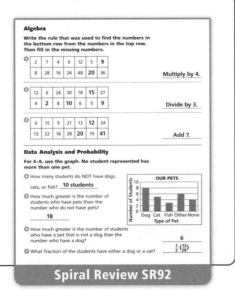

Practice P92

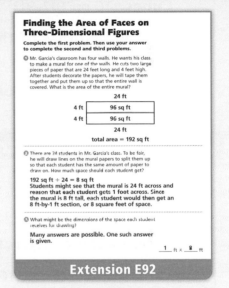

Extension E92

Extension Activity
Creating Rectangular Prisms

Give each pair of students a sheet of centimeter grid paper and a total area in square centimeters. Challenge them to work backward from the total area to find the dimensions of a rectangular prism. If they can find dimensions that work, ask them to draw a net with that total area for the rectangular prism. If they cannot find dimensions that work, ask them to change the total area as little as possible until they can find dimensions for a net.

Spiral Review

Spiral Review Book page SR92 provides review of the following previously learned skills and concepts:

• finding rules relating numbers to each other

• interpreting bar graphs

You may wish to have students work with a partner to complete the page.

Spiral Review SR92

Lesson 5 Finding Volumes of Three-Dimensional Figures

NCTM Standards 1, 3, 4, 6, 7, 8, 9, 10

Lesson Planner

STUDENT OBJECTIVES
- To find the volumes of three-dimensional figures by building them with inch cubes
- To explore using the dimensions of three-dimensional figures to compute their volumes

1 | Daily Activities (TG p. 911)

Open-Ended Problem Solving/Headline Story	Skills Practice and Review— Finding Products of Three Numbers

2 | Teach and Practice (TG pp. 912–916)

	MATERIALS
(A) **Modeling Three-Dimensional Figures with Cubes** (TG pp. 912–913)	• TR: Activity Masters, AM99–AM122
(B) **Finding Volumes of Three-Dimensional Figures** (TG p. 914)	• inch cubes • inch ruler (optional)
(C) **Finding the Volume of a More Complex Figure** (TG p. 915)	• three copies of AM99 • 📖 LAB pp. 225–226 • 📖 SH pp. 181–182

3 | Differentiated Instruction (TG p. 917)

Leveled Problem Solving (TG p. 917)	Practice Book P93
Intervention Activity (TG p. 917)	Extension Book E93
Extension Activity (TG p. 917)	Spiral Review Book SR93
Literature Connection (TG p. 876)	

Lesson Notes

About the Lesson

In the previous lesson, students measured the areas of the faces of rectangular-like prisms. Now students measure the space inside these same prisms—the volume. Volume is a three-dimensional measurement that requires measuring in three dimensions. Therefore, students begin to explore volume by building three-dimensional figures out of inch cubes. Students see that multiplying the number of cubes in each layer of a prism by the number of layers is a method for computing volume. In the next lesson, they will more explicitly relate this to the product of the three dimensions.

About the Mathematics

The size of a three-dimensional figure can be expressed as a volume or a capacity. Students explored capacity in Chapter 9, using cups, pints, quarts, gallons, milliliters, and liters. The distinction between capacity and volume is more functional than theoretical: capacity is the amount of an external substance an object can hold; volume is the amount of space the object takes up.

Developing Mathematical Language

Vocabulary: area, cubic, volume

In the previous lesson, students measured *area* in square inches; in this lesson, they measure *volume* in *cubic* inches. Students may not understand the meaning of these terms, so you might point out that squares are used to measure flat objects. So, *areas* are measured in square units. Similarly, cubes are used to measure the space occupied by a three-dimensional figure. Since *volume* units must have the same three dimensions as a cube—length, width, and height—*volume* is measured in *cubic* units.

Familiarize students with the terms *volume* and *cubic.*

Beginning Show the students a small box. Demonstrate filling the box with 1-centimeter cubes. Explain that the *volume* of the box is measured in *cubic* units and measures the amount of space the box takes up. Draw the connection between the cube-shape of the centimeter cube and a *cubic* unit.

Intermediate Ask students to build a prism with a *volume* of 10 *cubic* units. Ask them to explain what the *volume* measures. Elicit that *cubic* units tell how many cubes fit inside the prism.

Advanced Invite students to discuss what *volume* measures and why they think it is measured in *cubic* units.

---

1 | Daily Activities

Open-Ended Problem Solving

Read the Headline Story to the students. Encourage them to use logical reasoning to draw conclusions about the length of the fence and the area of the garden.

 Headline Story

> **A fence that is 24 feet long surrounds a garden.**

Possible responses: If the garden is a square, it would measure 6 feet on each side, so its area would be 36 square feet. The garden might be an 8-by-4 rectangle with an area of 32 square feet. It could be a 10-by-2 rectangle, in which case the area would be 20 square feet. The garden doesn't have to have straight sides; it could be a circle!

Skills Practice and Review

Finding Products of Three Numbers

In this quick drill, give students problems in which they must find the product of three numbers. Some suggested problems are:

5 x 7 x 2 70	2 x 9 x 5 90	2 x 7 x 3 42
2 x 8 x 5 80	3 x 6 x 2 36	2 x 7 x 5 70
5 x 9 x 2 90	4 x 9 x 5 180	2 x 6 x 5 60
5 x 7 x 4 140	3 x 7 x 2 42	5 x 9 x 4 180
6 x 4 x 5 120	5 x 6 x 4 120	7 x 4 x 5 140

The problems you choose may provide especially good practice if students can find an order that simplifies the multiplication. For example, if the problem is $5 \times 7 \times 2$, students might recognize that they can first multiply 5 and 2 to get 10, then 10 by 7 to make 70, rather than simply multiplying from left to right. Instead of explaining this strategy to students, choose problems that allow students to discover it on their own.

small groups or
whole class

20 MIN

Materials

- For each group:
  inch cubes

NCTM Standards 1, 3, 4, 6, 7, 8, 9, 10

A Modeling Three-Dimensional Figures with Cubes

Purpose To explore the meaning of volume

Introduce Give each student a copy of Explore: Exploring Volume and a supply of inch cubes. (Each group of students will need 44 cubes to construct the polyhedron.) Remind the class that in the last lesson, they measured the areas of the flat faces of polyhedra. In this lesson they will explore a way to measure the *insides* of polyhedra.

Task Direct students to read and answer the questions on the Explore page. Call attention to the dimensions of the polyhedra, especially the narrow vertical faces measuring 1 inch in width.

❶ How many cubes do you think you will need to build the shape? Many estimates are possible. A good estimate would be about 40 cubes.

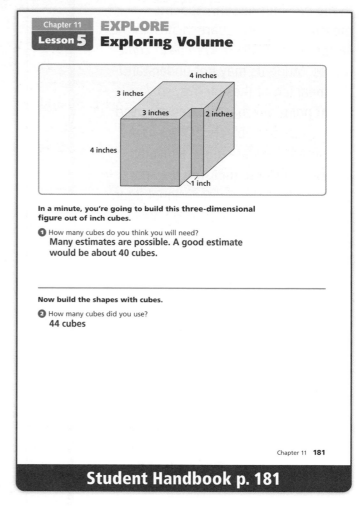

Chapter 11
Lesson 5

EXPLORE
Exploring Volume

In a minute, you're going to build this three-dimensional figure out of inch cubes.

❶ How many cubes do you think you will need?
Many estimates are possible. A good estimate would be about 40 cubes.

Now build the shapes with cubes.

❷ How many cubes did you use?
44 cubes

Chapter 11 **181**

Student Handbook p. 181

If students need guidance on how to make their estimates, you might hold up one such cube, to help students get a sense of the size of a cubic inch.

❷ How many cubes did you use? 44 cubes

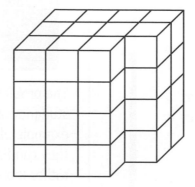

Share Go over the page together, asking students to share their strategies for finding the total number of cubes in the figure. For example, some students may have counted the cubes in one layer of the figure and then multiplied that number by the number of layers. If no students suggest this strategy, you might prompt students with the following questions:

- How many cubes are in the bottom layer of cubes? 11
- How many cubes are in each layer? 11
- How many layers are there in the shape? 4
- How many total cubes are there in the three-dimensional figure?
  $4 \times 11 = 44$

Next, connect the number of cubes in the object to the measurement of volume. Explain that volume is a measure of the amount of space an object takes up, and that to measure volume you need a unit with three dimensions, like a cube. Note that a cube has length, width, and height. Point to the length, width, and height on a cube to help students distinguish among the three dimensions. Since each cube in this activity is 1 inch long, 1 inch wide, and 1 inch tall, students have measured volume in cubic inches. Conclude the discussion by asking students to use the number of cubes in the three-dimensional figure to tell the volume of the figure. 44 cubic inches (See About the Mathematics and Developing Mathematical Language.)

Talk Math

? Suppose the figure had been only 3 inches tall, rather than 4 inches. What would its volume have been? Explain your reasoning. 33 cubic inches; Possible explanation: There would have been 3 layers, each containing 11 cubes; $3 \times 11 = 33$.

? Taylor found the volume of the figure by imagining that it started off as a prism measuring 4 inches by 4 inches by 3 inches, then had a column of four 1-inch cubes removed where the front right corner had been. How did she calculate the volume? Possible response: She subtracted the volume of the four 1-inch cubes (4 cubic inches) from the volume of the $4 \times 4 \times 3$ prism ($4 \times 4 \times 3 = 48$ cubic inches); $48 - 4 = 44$ cubic inches.

Finding Volumes of Three-Dimensional Figures LAB pp. 225–226

  individuals • 20 MIN

Purpose To practice finding the volumes of polyhedra

NCTM Standards 1, 3, 6, 7, 8, 9, 10

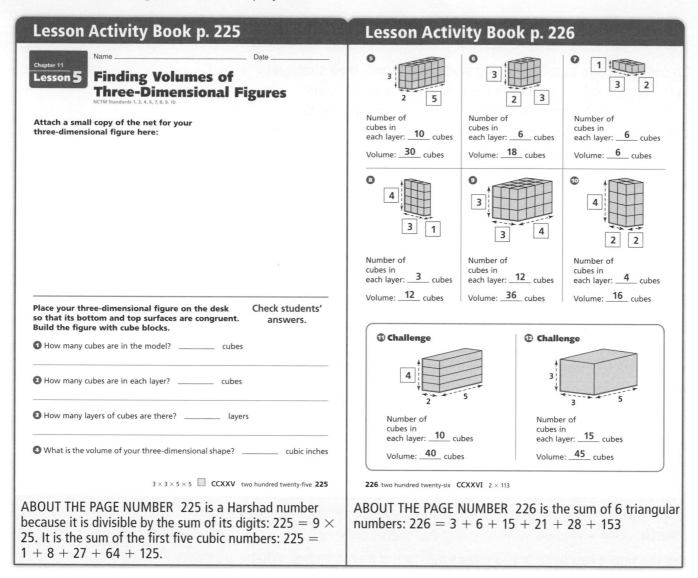

Teaching Notes for LAB page 225

Have students complete the page individually or with partners.

Each student will need a net from the Reduced Net Activity Master pages (AM98–AM122) to tape or glue to the top of the LAB page. Students will also need inch cubes and possibly inch rulers. Place all of the students with the same net in the same area of the room so that they can share the three-dimensional versions of their nets. See that every net is assigned to at least one student, so that students find the volumes of as many shapes as possible. Students should model the three-dimensional figures with 1-inch cubes.

Differentiated Instruction *Above Level* As in the previous lesson, shapes P and X are more challenging to model than others. You might want to be selective about assigning specific students to certain figures.

Teaching Notes for LAB page 226

The page displays pictures of rectangular prisms built with cubes. Students should count the number of cubes in each dimension (length, width, and height) to compute the volume of each shape.

The format of the problems encourages students to use the number of cubes in one layer multiplied by the number of layers to find the volume. In the next lesson, students will use the dimensions of one layer to figure out the number of cubes in one layer. Then, they'll find the volume by multiplying together the three dimensions.

Challenge Problem In the Challenge Problem, the cubes no longer appear. This encourages students to think about a way to compute the volume of a rectangular solid without counting cubes. Students will be led the idea that they can calculate the volume by finding the product of the length, the width, and the height.

914 Chapter 11 • Lesson 5

Use with Lesson Activity Book pp. 225–226.

C Finding the Volume of a More Complex Figure

Purpose To explore methods for finding the volumes of non-rectangular prisms

Introduce Show students three copies of Figure A, constructed from Activity Master: Net A. Then present the following puzzle.

Problem **Ask students if they can figure out the volume of the figure.** Because the figure is a pyramid, most of its faces are not rectangular. Therefore, using inch cubes to model the figure and calculate its volume is impossible.

After outlining the problem in general, give each student three copies of Activity Master: Net A. Ask students to think about ways they could find the volume of the figure. Students do not need to solve the puzzle exactly. Playing with the figures, however, will help them appreciate the challenge of finding the volumes of non-rectangular prisms, and thereby deepen their understanding of volume.

> **Net A**
>
> Cut along the solid lines. Fold along the dashed lines.
>
> A A
>
> **Activity Master 99**

Materials
- For the teacher: 3 copies of AM99
- For each student; 3 copies of AM99

NCTM Standards 1, 3, 4, 6, 7, 8, 9, 10

Share Encourage students to share their observations on finding the volume. Some students may recognize that the three copies can be fit together to form a rectangular prism. If no one notices this, show how it can be done. Then ask students how they can use this observation to find the volume of the figure. Just as students found the area of a triangle in Chapter 5 by using known areas, so they can find the volume of Figure A here by using known volumes. First, they can find the volume of the rectangular prism. Then, because the prism can be divided into three Figure As, they can divide the volume by 3 to find the volume of Figure A.

Talk Math

❷ Three congruent pyramids can be fit together to form a cube measuring 6 inches on a side. What is the volume of each pyramid? Explain your reasoning. 72 cubic inches; Possible explanation: The volume of the cube is $6 \times 6 \times 6 = 216$ cubic inches. The volume of each pyramid is one-third the volume of the cube: $216 \div 3 = 72$.

❷ Three congruent pyramids with square bases each have a volume of 9 cubic inches. The pyramids are fit together to form a cube. What is the length of each side of the cube? Explain how you found the answer. 3 inches; Possible explanation: The volume of the cube is $3 \times 9 = 27$ cubic inches. To find the length of each side of the cube, I needed to find a number which, when I multiplied it by itself three times, gave the product 27. I tried numbers until I found the one, 3, that worked.

Reflect and Summarize the Lesson

Write Math A rectangular prism measures 5 inches by 4 inches by 3 inches. How many inch cubes would you need to model the prism? What is the volume of the prism? Explain your reasoning. 60 inch cubes; 60 cubic inches; Possible explanation: Each layer has $5 \times 4 = 20$ cubes. There are 3 layers, so there are $20 \times 3 = 60$ cubes in the prism. Each cube has a volume of 1 cubic inch, so the volume of the prism is 60 cubic inches.

Review Model

Refer students to Review Model: Finding the Volume of a Three-Dimensional Figure in the *Student Handbook*, p. 182, to see how to find the volume of rectangular prisms.

✔ Check for Understanding

❶ 30 cubic units

❷ 36 cubic units

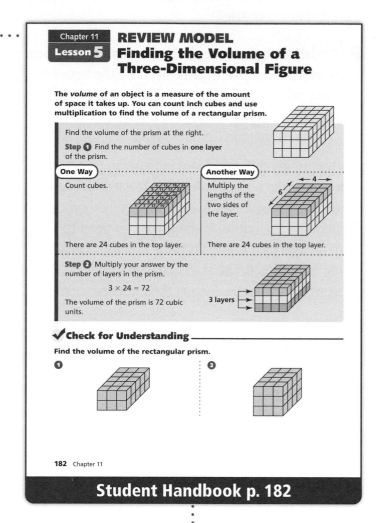

Use with Lesson Activity Book pp. 225–226.

Leveled Problem Solving

Reggie has twenty 1-inch cubes. He builds a rectangular prism and has more than 1 cube left over.

❶ Basic Level

If he builds a bigger cube, what is the greatest number of small cubes he could have used? Explain. 8 cubes; 2 × 2 cubes in the bottom layer and 2 layers; The next larger cube would need 27 cubes.

❷ On Level

He uses as many cubes as he can with 6 in the bottom layer. How many layers does he make? Explain. 3 layers; The greatest number of cubes he could have used is 18; 3 layers of 6 cubes make 18 in all.

❸ Above Level

If he uses 16 cubes, how many could be in the bottom layer? Explain. 1, 2, 4, 8, or 16; If 1, then he needs 16 layers; 2, he needs 8 layers; 4, 4 layers; 8, 2 layers; and, 16, 1 layer.

Intervention	Practice	Extension

Activity Area and Volume

Have students create a rectangular prism from twelve 1-inch cubes. Ask them to find the total area of the faces. Then ask them to find the volume. Have them make a new prism with the 12 cubes and check its area and volume. Repeat until all possible prisms are made. Ask students what they notice (the total area of the faces changed but the volume didn't).

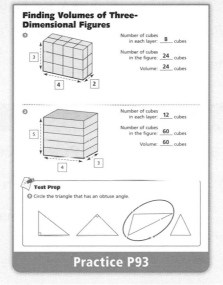

Practice P93

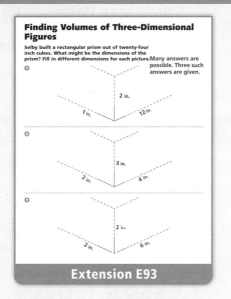

Extension E93

Spiral Review

Spiral Review Book page SR93 provides review of the following previously learned skills and concepts:

- using simpler computations to solve multi-digit multiplication problems
- converting between cups, pints, quarts, and gallons

You may wish to have students work with a partner to complete the page.

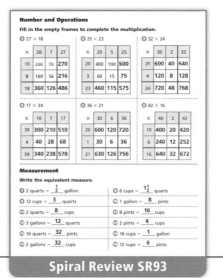

Spiral Review SR93

Extension Activity
How Many Prisms?

Provide small groups with 24, 36, or 48 cubes. Challenge them to make all the possible rectangular prisms that use all the cubes. Have them record all three dimensions (length, width, and height) in a table. Ask what they notice. (Groups of three different numbers appear six times—three if they consider length and width interchangeable, or when two of the dimensions are equal.)

Lesson 6 More Volumes of Three-Dimensional Figures

NCTM Standards 1, 3, 4, 6, 7, 8, 9, 10

Lesson Planner

STUDENT OBJECTIVES . . . .
- To find the volume of a rectangular prism by multiplying its three dimensions
- To describe a rectangular prism using its dimensions in $l \times w \times h$ format

1 │ Daily Activities (TG p. 919)

Open-Ended Problem Solving/Headline Story	Skills Practice and Review— Finding Products of Three Numbers

2 │ Teach and Practice (TG pp. 920–923)

MATERIALS

(A) **Exploring Three-Dimensional Figures with the Same Volume** (TG pp. 920–921)

(B) **Playing a Game: _Volume Builder_** (TG p. 922)

(C) **More Volumes of Three-Dimensional Figures** (TG p. 923)

- inch cubes, coins, scrap paper
- LAB pp. 227–228
- SH pp. 183, 189

3 │ Differentiated Instruction (TG p. 924)

Leveled Problem Solving (TG p. 924)	Practice Book P94
Intervention Activity (TG p. 924)	Extension Book E94
Extension Activity (TG p. 924)	Spiral Review Book SR94

Lesson Notes

About the Lesson

In this lesson, students continue to explore volume as a measure of the amount of space an object occupies. They deepen their understanding of volume by seeing that different shapes can have the same volume. They also practice estimating and finding volume by playing a game. Finally, they begin to develop and use a formula for computing volumes: the volume of a rectangular prism is the product of the length, the width, and the height.

Use with Lesson Activity Book pp. 227–228.

Developing Mathematical Language

Vocabulary: length, width, height

In this lesson, the three dimensions of space are referred to as *length, width,* and *height.* Those terms are inexact, and students might well use different names—depth for *height,* for example. Because up, down, right, and left are not absolute terms, students can refer to any dimension as *length, width,* and *height.* By rotating a solid, you can show that a given dimension can logically be seen as a *width* in one orientation and a *height* in another. To clarify your meaning as you use these terms, try to point to the dimension you are referring to on the polyhedron in question.

Familiarize students with the terms *height, length,* and *width.*

Beginning Set a box on the table. Identify the *height, length,* and *width* of the box. Then rotate the box, and again identify the *height, length,* and *width.* Rotate the box again, and have students identify the *height, length,* and *width.*

Intermediate Have pairs identify the *height, length,* and *width* of a box as their partner points to each dimension. Rotate the box, and repeat.

Advanced Discuss with students how the terms *height, length,* and *width* depend on the orientation of a figure. Invite students to explain how they are able to recognize the *height, length,* and *width* of a box.

Open-Ended Problem Solving

Read the Headline Story to the students. Encourage them to make inventive statements using information from the story.

 **Headline Story**

Kelly is packing books into a box that has a volume of 4 cubic feet.

Possible responses: The box could be $1 \times 2 \times 2$ feet. The box could also be 6 inches $\times$ 1 foot $\times$ 4 feet. Any three numbers that, when converted to feet, multiply to make a product of 4 could be the dimensions of the box.

Skills Practice and Review

Finding Products of Three Numbers

Repeat this quick drill from the previous lesson. Give students problems in which they must find the product of three numbers, to prepare them for finding the volume of a rectangular solid by multiplying its three dimensions. You might say the problem out loud or write it on the board. Some suggested problems are:

$15 \times 6 \times 2$ 180	$2 \times 9 \times 5$ 90	$4 \times 5 \times 8$ 160
$20 \times 8 \times 5$ 800	$3 \times 25 \times 2$ 150	$4 \times 7 \times 5$ 140
$5 \times 12 \times 2$ 120	$4 \times 5 \times 5$ 100	$7 \times 6 \times 5$ 210
$5 \times 7 \times 3$ 105	$11 \times 7 \times 2$ 154	$5 \times 8 \times 5$ 200
$6 \times 9 \times 5$ 270	$15 \times 6 \times 4$ 360	$9 \times 4 \times 5$ 180

The problems you choose may provide especially good practice if students can find a special order for simplifying the multiplication. For example, if the problem is $15 \times 6 \times 2$, students might recognize that they can first multiply 15 and 2 to get 30, then multiply 30 by 6 to make 180, rather than simply multiplying from left to right.

2 | **Teach and Practice**

A Exploring Three-Dimensional Figures with the Same Volume

Materials

• For each group: inch cubes

NCTM Standards 1, 3, 4, 6, 7, 8, 9, 10

✓ Ongoing Assessment

• Do students find the product of three one-digit whole numbers mentally?

• Do students know what a rectangular prism is, and do they know that it has three dimensions conventionally designated as length, width, and height?

Purpose To introduce a new notation for describing rectangular prisms, and to connect the dimensions of a prism to its volume

Introduce Give each student a copy of Explore: Prisms with the Same Volume. Give each group a supply of inch cubes for constructing prisms.

Task Direct students to read the Explore page and to answer the questions on the page.

❶ Build and then draw a sketch of a different rectangular prism with the same volume as Shelby's prism. volume of Shelby's prism = 3 × 2 × 6 = 36 cubic inches

Write an expression like the following to describe your prism: 3 in. × 2 in. × 6 in. Any set of three numbers with a product of 36 will work. One such answer is: 2 in. × 9 in. × 2 in.

Many sketches are possible. Here is one:

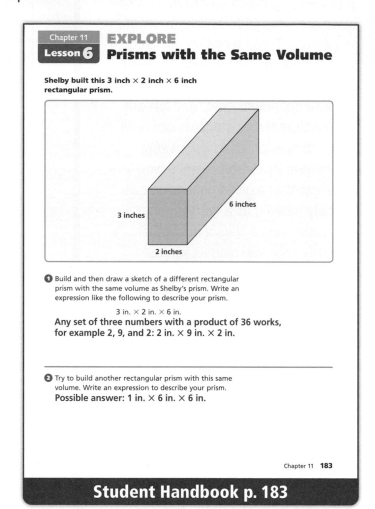

Chapter 11   **EXPLORE**

Lesson 6   **Prisms with the Same Volume**

Shelby built this 3 inch × 2 inch × 6 inch rectangular prism.

3 inches   6 inches   2 inches

❶ Build and then draw a sketch of a different rectangular prism with the same volume as Shelby's prism. Write an expression like the following to describe your prism.

3 in. × 2 in. × 6 in.
Any set of three numbers with a product of 36 works, for example 2, 9, and 2: 2 in. × 9 in. × 2 in.

❷ Try to build another rectangular prism with this same volume. Write an expression to describe your prism.
Possible answer: 1 in. × 6 in. × 6 in.

Chapter 11   **183**

Student Handbook p. 183

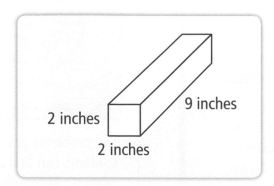

2 inches   9 inches   2 inches

❷ Try to build another rectangular prism with this same volume. Write an expression to describe your prism. Many answers are possible. One such answer is 1 in. × 6 in. × 6 in.

Use with Lesson Activity Book pp. 227–228.

Share Once students have completed the page, have them share their strategies for finding the dimensions of prisms with volumes of 36 cubic inches. Some students might use the *guess and check* strategy, guessing at the dimensions of a prism, checking the resulting volume to see if it is 36 cubic inches, and adjusting their guesses if it is not. Other students might point out that since 36 cubes represented the volume of the prism, they thought it made sense to look for different ways to stack 36 cubes in a rectangular-prism shape.

As students explain their methods and the resulting dimensions, record the dimensions using the format presented on the Explore page. So, for example, for a 2-inch by 9-inch by 2-inch prism, write 2 × 9 × 2 on the board. Some other possibilities are 1 × 6 × 6, 3 × 3 × 4, and 1 × 4 × 9.

If students suggest dimensions for prisms with the same dimensions as ones already suggested but in a different order, point out that the three-dimensional figure with the dimensions they are giving is the same as the earlier one, but oriented in a different direction.

Conclude the discussion by asking students how the new notation represents the prisms they made, and pointing out the corresponding dimensions on their own constructed polyhedra. Help students see that the product of the dimensions of each prism is 36, which is the volume of the prisms.

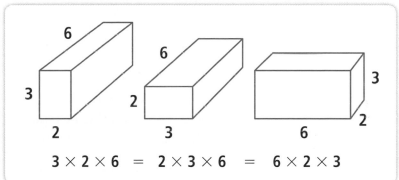

$$3 \times 2 \times 6 \ = \ 2 \times 3 \times 6 \ = \ 6 \times 2 \times 3$$

🗨 Talk Math

❷ A rectangular prism has a volume of 60 cubic inches. Its length is 5 inches and its width is 4 inches. What is its height? Explain your reasoning. 3 inches; Possible explanation: 5 × 4 × height = 60. Since 5 × 4 = 20, the height must be the number which, when I multiply it by 20, gives 60. That number is 3: 3 × 20 = 60.

❷ A rectangular prism measures 4 inches × 6 inches × 2 inches. Another rectangular prism with the same volume has a length of 8 inches and a height of 2 inches. What is its width? Explain your reasoning. 3 inches; Possible explanation: The volume of the first prism is 4 × 6 × 2 = 48 cubic inches. Since 8 × 2 = 16, the width must be the number which, when I multiply it by 16, gives 48. That number is 3: 3 × 16 = 48.

B Playing *Volume Builder*

Materials

• For each pair of students: inch cubes, coin, piece of scratch paper

NCTM Standards 1, 3, 4, 6, 7, 8, 9, 10

Purpose To practice estimating and finding volume

Goal The object of the game is to collect points by building prisms with the greatest possible volumes. The first player to score 200 points wins.

Introduce *Volume Builder* is a game for two players. Each pair of players will need a supply of inch cubes, a coin, and a piece of scratch paper. Tell students that, for this game, heads means 1 and tails means 2. You might write this on the board so that students don't have to remember it as they play.

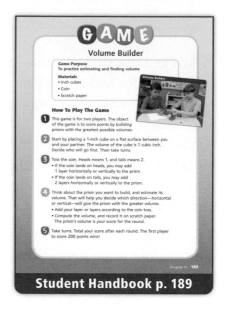

Student Handbook p. 189

✔ Ongoing Assessment

• As students play the *Volume Builder* game, do they use estimation skills to decide the direction they should build in, horizontal or vertical, in order to produce the maximum possible volume, and thus score the most possible points?

• As students play, do they randomly decide whether to add a horizontal or vertical layer or are they systematic in their play?

How to Play

❶ To start play, players place a 1-inch cube on a flat surface between them. The volume of this prism is 1 cubic inch.

❷ The first player tosses a coin. If the player gets heads, he or she can add 1 layer horizontally or vertically to the prism. If the player gets tails, he or she can add 2 layers horizontally or vertically to the prism. Encourage players to visualize the prisms they are about to build and to estimate their volumes, in order to decide which direction, horizontal or vertical, will produce the prism with the greater volume.

❸ The first player adds one or two layers of cubes, as indicated by the coin toss, creating a new prism. The player computes the volume of the prism and records it on scratch paper. The prism's volume is that player's score for the round.

Differentiated Instruction

On Level If students don't seem to be making prisms with the greatest possible volumes, suggest that players estimate volumes before deciding on their moves.

❹ The second player now tosses the coin and proceeds as the first player did, creating a new prism and recording a score.

❺ Players total their scores after each round. Play continues, with players alternating turns, until one player reaches 200 points or more. That player is declared the winner.

Use with Lesson Activity Book pp. 227–228.

Purpose To practice finding volumes of polyhedra

NCTM Standards 1, 3, 4, 6, 7, 8, 9, 10

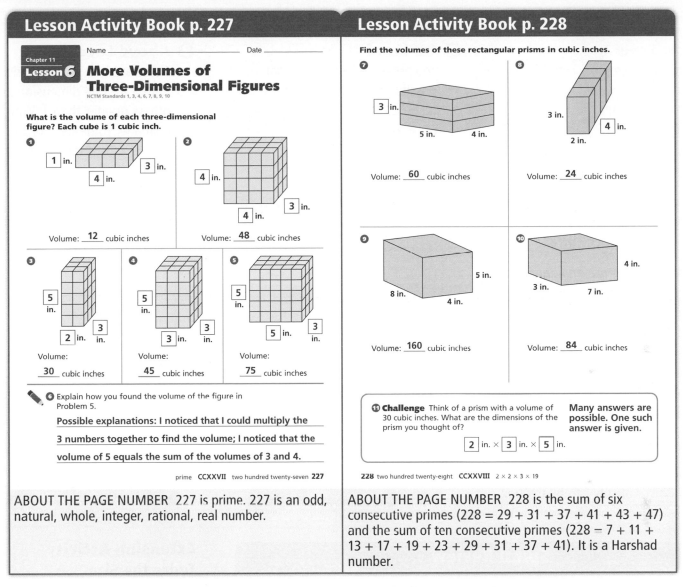

Lesson Activity Book p. 227

Name _____ Date _____

Chapter 11
Lesson 6 **More Volumes of Three-Dimensional Figures**
NCTM Standards 1, 3, 4, 6, 7, 8, 9, 10

What is the volume of each three-dimensional figure? Each cube is 1 cubic inch.

❶ 1 in. / 4 in. / 3 in.
Volume: __12__ cubic inches

❷ 4 in. / 4 in. / 4 in. / 3 in.
Volume: __48__ cubic inches

❸ 5 in. / 2 in. / 3 in.
Volume: __30__ cubic inches

❹ 5 in. / 3 in. / 3 in.
Volume: __45__ cubic inches

❺ 5 in. / 5 in. / 3 in.
Volume: __75__ cubic inches

❻ Explain how you found the volume of the figure in Problem 5.

Possible explanations: I noticed that I could multiply the 3 numbers together to find the volume; I noticed that the volume of 5 equals the sum of the volumes of 3 and 4.

prime CCXXVII two hundred twenty-seven **227**

Lesson Activity Book p. 228

Find the volumes of these rectangular prisms in cubic inches.

❼ 3 in. / 5 in. / 4 in.
Volume: __60__ cubic inches

❽ 3 in. / 4 in. / 2 in.
Volume: __24__ cubic inches

❾ 5 in. / 8 in. / 4 in.
Volume: __160__ cubic inches

❿ 4 in. / 3 in. / 7 in.
Volume: __84__ cubic inches

⓫ **Challenge** Think of a prism with a volume of 30 cubic inches. What are the dimensions of the prism you thought of? **Many answers are possible. One such answer is given.**
2 in. × 3 in. × 5 in.

228 two hundred twenty-eight CCXXVIII 2 × 2 × 3 × 19

ABOUT THE PAGE NUMBER 227 is prime. 227 is an odd, natural, whole, integer, rational, real number.

ABOUT THE PAGE NUMBER 228 is the sum of six consecutive primes (228 = 29 + 31 + 37 + 41 + 43 + 47) and the sum of ten consecutive primes (228 = 7 + 11 + 13 + 17 + 19 + 23 + 29 + 31 + 37 + 41). It is a Harshad number.

Teaching Notes for LAB page 227

For Problems 1–5, have students look for relationships among the volumes. They may recognize that the volume in Problem 5 is the sum of the volumes in Problems 3 and 4, and that the prism in Problem 2 consists of four layers of the prism in Problem 1.

Differentiated Instruction Basic Level If students have difficulty with the LAB problems, provide them with inch cubes to model the three-dimensional figures. Encourage students to count the cubes in each shape to find its volume.

Teaching Notes for LAB page 228

Lines showing the inch-cube structures of the prisms on this page have been removed, and students must rely on only the dimensions of the prisms to compute their volumes. Make inch cubes available for students who wish to use them to the prisms and compute their volumes.

Challenge Problem The Challenge Problem asks students to find possible dimensions for a prism with a volume of 30 cubic inches. Any three numbers whose product is 30 are correct solutions.

Reflect and Summarize the Lesson

 Write Math A rectangular prism-shaped box has a volume of 12 cubic feet. What might its dimensions be? Possible answers: any three dimensions whose product is 12 cubic feet. Possible dimensions include 1 × 2 × 6 feet, 1 × 3 × 4 feet, 2 × 2 × 3 feet, and 1 × 1 × 12 feet.

Leveled Problem Solving

Han is using sixty 1-inch cubes to build a rectangular prism.

❶ Basic Level

Could the prism be 1 inch high? Explain. Yes; it would have to have a rectangular base that uses all 60 cubes.

❷ On Level

The prism has 6 layers. What possible areas could the base have? Explain. 10 sq in.; $60 \div 6 = 10$.

❸ Above Level

There are two possible prisms with 3 for one dimension and the others greater than 1. Which has a smaller total area for the faces? $3 \times 4 \times 5$ (total area is 94 sq in.)

Intervention

Activity Packing Solids

Discuss how volume can be a measure of packing. Display a shoe box and at least 15 or 20 1-inch cubes (but not enough to cover the bottom). Ask students to consider how they could use the small cubes to find the total that would pack the box. Possible answer: Measure the length and width of the base using the cubes, multiply to find the area of the base, measure the height, and multiply the base area to find the number of cubes to fill the box.

Practice

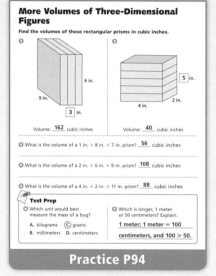

More Volumes of Three-Dimensional Figures

Find the volumes of these rectangular prisms in cubic inches.

Volume: **162** cubic inches   Volume: **40** cubic inches

❸ What is the volume of a 1 in. × 8 in. × 7 in. prism? **56** cubic inches

❹ What is the volume of a 2 in. × 6 in. × 9 in. prism? **108** cubic inches

❺ What is the volume of a 4 in. × 2 in. × 11 in. prism? **88** cubic inches

Test Prep

❻ Which unit would best measure the mass of a bug?
A. kilograms C. grams
B. millimeters D. centimeters

❼ Which is longer, 1 meter or 50 centimeters? Explain.
1 meter; 1 meter = 100 centimeters, and 100 > 50.

Practice P94

Extension

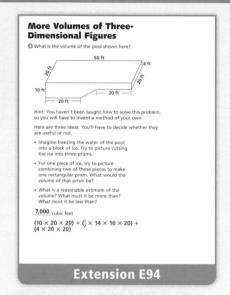

More Volumes of Three-Dimensional Figures

❶ What is the volume of the pool shown here?

Hint: You haven't been taught how to solve this problem, so you will have to invent a method of your own.

Here are three ideas. You'll have to decide whether they are useful or not.

• Imagine freezing the water of the pool into a block of ice. Try to picture cutting the ice into three prisms.

• For one piece of ice, try to picture combining two of those pieces to make one rectangular prism. What would the volume of that prism be?

• What is a reasonable estimate of the volume? What must it be more than? What must it be less than?

7,000 cubic feet

$(10 \times 20 \times 20) + (\frac{1}{2} \times 14 \times 10 \times 20) + (4 \times 20 \times 20)$

Extension E94

Spiral Review

Spiral Review Book page SR94 provides review of the following previously learned skills and concepts:

• learning the terms *acute, right,* and *obtuse* for classifying angles

• solving problems using the strategy *make a graph*

You may wish to have students work with a partner to complete the page.

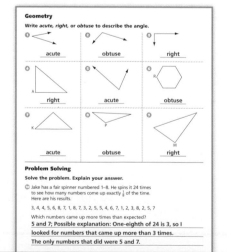

Geometry

Write *acute, right,* or *obtuse* to describe the angle.

❶ acute   ❷ obtuse   ❸ right

❹ right   ❺ acute   ❻ obtuse

❼ acute   ❽ obtuse   ❾ right

Problem Solving

Solve the problem. Explain your answer.

❿ Jake has a fair spinner numbered 1–8. He spins it 24 times to see how many numbers come up exactly ⅛ of the time. Here are his results.

3, 4, 4, 5, 6, 8, 7, 1, 8, 7, 3, 2, 5, 5, 4, 6, 7, 1, 2, 3, 8, 2, 5, 7

Which numbers came up more times than expected?
5 and 7; Possible explanation: One-eighth of 24 is 3, so I looked for numbers that came up more than 3 times. The only numbers that did were 5 and 7.

Spiral Review SR94

Extension Activity
Twice the Size

Ask students to consider how the volume of a rectangular prism changes when one of the dimensions is doubled. Direct them to test some specific example and then make a generalization. When one dimension is doubled, the volume doubles. Then ask students to predict how the volume of a rectangular prism would change if all three dimensions were doubled. Have them check their predictions using a specific example. When every dimension is doubled, the volume is 8 times as great.

Teacher's Notes 🍎

Daily Notes . . .

Quick Notes

Lesson 7 Problem Solving Strategy and Test Prep

NCTM Standards 1, 3, 4, 6, 7, 8, 9, 10

Lesson Planner

- To practice the problem solving strategy *act it out.*
- To articulate the steps and strategies used to solve problems
- To prepare for standardized tests

Problem Solving Strategy:
Act It Out (TG pp. 927–929, 930–931)

MATERIALS

Ⓐ **Discussing the Problem Solving Strategy:**
Act It Out (TG p. 927)

Ⓑ **Solving Problems by Applying the Strategy** (TG p. 928)

- transparency of LAB p. 229 (optional)
- 📖 LAB p. 229
- 📖 SH pp. 184–185

Problem Solving Test Prep (TG p. 927)

Ⓒ **Getting Ready for Standardized Tests** (TG p. 929)

- 📖 LAB p. 230

Lesson Notes

About Problem Solving

Problem Solving Strategy: Act it Out

This lesson focuses on the problem solving strategy *act it out.* Students make a model to draw connections between the work in this chapter, which has made extensive use of polyhedral models, and other mathematical problems. Although the strategy is particularly helpful when working with three-dimensional objects, this lesson encourages students to see that the strategy may be used for any situation that is difficult to picture in one's mind.

Skills Practice and Review

Finding Products of 3 Numbers

As in the previous two lessons, give students problems which require them to find products of three numbers. You might say the problems out loud or write them on the board for students to answer. Some suggested problems are:

3 × 5 × 8 120	12 × 5 × 5 300	12 × 12 × 5 720
6 × 5 × 7 210	5 × 4 × 12 240	5 × 5 × 7 175
8 × 5 × 6 240	11 × 8 × 5 440	11 × 12 × 5 660
9 × 3 × 3 81	3 × 5 × 9 135	15 × 2 × 8 240
7 × 8 × 5 280	12 × 6 × 5 60	25 × 9 × 4 900

Problem Solving Strategy

A Discussing the Problem Solving Strategy: *Act It Out*

Purpose To share strategies for solving problems and focus on the problem solving strategy, *act it out*

NCTM Standards 1, 3, 4, 6, 7, 8, 9, 10

Introduce Mention that students have been using the strategy *act it out* throughout this chapter. Each time they made and measured a model, they were acting out the process of investigating the properties of a polyhedron.

Introduce the following problem.

Problem Anthony used inch cubes to build a figure measuring 1 inch × 2 inches × 3 inches. He removed one cube to form a block letter C, as shown at the right. By removing the cube, did he increase, decrease, or leave unchanged the total area of the faces of the figure?

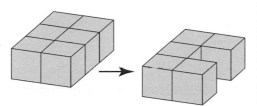

Share Ask students to share their strategies for solving the problem. If students find it hard to visualize the invisible faces in the drawing, a good strategy would be to *act out* what Anthony did, by building both figures, counting the inch-cube faces, and multiplying by the area of each face, 1 sq in.

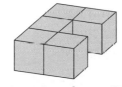

22 faces × 1 sq in. = 22 sq in.   **22 faces × 1 sq in. = 22 sq in.**

The surprising result is that the total area of the faces remains unchanged when one cube is removed.

💬 Talk Math

❓ Why was the total area unchanged when a block was removed? In the original figure, 3 faces of the cube were visible. When the cube was removed, 3 formerly invisible faces were revealed, replacing the 3 that were removed.

❓ If Anthony removed a corner cube from his original figure, would he increase, decrease, or leave unchanged the total area of the faces of the figure? He would decrease the total area by 2 sq. in.

B Solving Problems by Applying the Strategy LAB p. 229

 whole class

 15 MIN

Purpose To share strategies for solving problems and focus on the problem solving strategy *act it out*

Teaching Notes for LAB page 229

Students practice the problem solving strategy *act it out* by solving the problems independently or in pairs. Help students get started by asking questions such as the following:

 Read to Understand

What do you know? The volume of a box is 48 cubic feet.

What do you need to find out? possible dimensions of the box

 Plan

How can you solve this problem? *Act it out* and *guess and check* are the most likely strategies to use.

 Solve

How could you use the strategy *act it out* to solve the problem? Use an inch cube to represent a volume of 1 cubic foot, and build a rectangular box using 48 cubes.

What computations might you use to solve the problem? The three dimensions must multiply together to make 48, so you can choose one factor of 48 (such as 6 or 1 or 48), and figure out two other numbers to multiply it by. Those two numbers and the factor of 48 that you began with would be one solution of the problem.

 Check

Look back at the original problem. Did you answer the question that was asked? Does your answer make sense? How do you know?

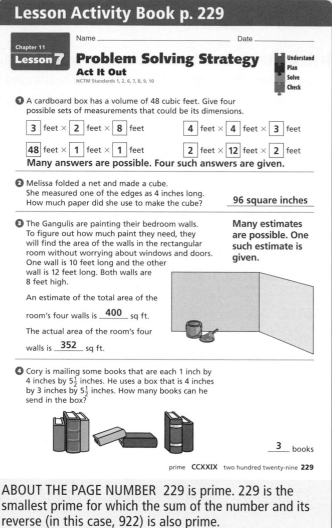

Lesson Activity Book p. 229

Name _____ Date _____

Chapter 11
Lesson 7 **Problem Solving Strategy**
Act It Out
NCTM Standards 1, 2, 6, 7, 8, 9, 10

Understand
Plan
Solve
Check

❶ A cardboard box has a volume of 48 cubic feet. Give four possible sets of measurements that could be its dimensions.

[3] feet × [2] feet × [8] feet   [4] feet × [4] feet × [3] feet

[48] feet × [1] feet × [1] feet   [2] feet × [12] feet × [2] feet
Many answers are possible. Four such answers are given.

❷ Melissa folded a net and made a cube. She measured one of the edges as 4 inches long. How much paper did she use to make the cube?   **96 square inches**

❸ The Gangulis are painting their bedroom walls. To figure out how much paint they need, they will find the area of the walls in the rectangular room without worrying about windows and doors. One wall is 10 feet long and the other wall is 12 feet long. Both walls are 8 feet high.

Many estimates are possible. One such estimate is given.

An estimate of the total area of the room's four walls is __400__ sq ft.

The actual area of the room's four walls is __352__ sq ft.

❹ Cory is mailing some books that are each 1 inch by 4 inches by 5½ inches. He uses a box that is 4 inches by 3 inches by 5½ inches. How many books can he send in the box?

__3__ books

prime **CCXXIX** two hundred twenty-nine **229**

ABOUT THE PAGE NUMBER 229 is prime. 229 is the smallest prime for which the sum of the number and its reverse (in this case, 922) is also prime.

Reflect and Summarize the Lesson

 Write Math

When might the strategy *act it out* be a good one to try to solve a problem? Possible response: when you can use a model or activities with classmates to duplicate the situation in the problem. Act out the situation and see if that helps you see how to solve the problem.

928   Chapter 11 • Lesson 7   Use with Lesson Activity Book pp. 229–230.

Problem Solving Test Prep

C Getting Ready for Standardized Tests LAB p. 230

individuals

 20 MIN

Purpose To prepare students for standardized tests

NCTM Standards 1, 3, 4, 6, 7, 8, 9, 10

Lesson Activity Book p. 230

Problem Solving Test Prep

Choose the correct answer.

1 What are the length and width of a rectangle that has the same perimeter as the figure?

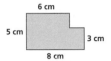

6 cm

5 cm   3 cm

8 cm

A. 3 cm by 6 cm   **C.** 8 cm by 5 cm
B. 3 cm by 8 cm   D. 8 cm by 6 cm

2 Which is the best estimate of 391 × 42?

A. 1,200   C. 12,000
B. 1,600   **D.** 16,000

3 Which pair of equivalent fractions matches the shaded area of the figure below?

A. $\frac{3}{4} = \frac{8}{12}$ C. $\frac{1}{4} = \frac{3}{12}$
B. $\frac{3}{4} = \frac{9}{12}$ D. $\frac{2}{3} = \frac{8}{12}$

4 Which is the only number that is NOT between 21.8 and 21.9?

A. 21.81   C. 21.89
B. 21.88   **D.** 21.91

Show What You Know

Solve each problem. Explain your answer.

5 Serena has 43 small cubes. Can she make a rectangular prism using all the cubes? If not, what is the greatest number of cubes she can use? Explain how you decided.

Yes; she can make a rectangular prism with any number of cubes, but since 43 is a prime number, the only possible shape is 1 × 1 × 43.

6 Alex has 35 small cubes. He begins building a staircase in which the first step has 1 cube, the next has 2 cubes, and so on. Can he use all 35 cubes? If not, how many will he have left? Explain.

No, he can use 28 of the cubes and have 7 left; 1 + 2 + 3 + 4 + 5 + 6 + 7 = 28. He would need 8 more for the next step, but he has only 7 more.

230 two hundred thirty **CCXXX** 2 × 5 × 23

ABOUT THE PAGE NUMBER 230 is a Harshad number. It is the sum of 5 consecutive triangular numbers:
230 = 28 + 36 + 45 + 55 + 66

Teaching Notes for LAB page 230

The test items on this page are written in the same style and arranged in the same format as those on many state assessments. The page is cumulative and is designed for students to apply a variety of problem solving strategies, including *act it out.* Students might share the strategies they use.

The Item Analysis Chart below highlights one of the possible strategies that may be used for each item.

Show What You Know

Short Response

Direct students' attention to Problems 5 and 6. For Problem 5, point out that 43 is a prime number. For Problem 6, explain that they can use the strategies *act it out* or *find a pattern* to solve the problems.

To provide more space for students to communicate their thinking about these problems, you may wish to have them write their responses and explanations on a separate sheet of paper. Use the Scoring Rubric below to evaluate their understanding.

Item Analysis Chart

Item	Strategy
1	Draw a picture
2	Solve a simpler problem
3	Make a model
4	Draw a picture
5	Act it out
6	Act it out

Scoring Rubric

2	• Demonstrates complete understanding of the problem and chooses an appropriate strategy to determine the solution
1	• Demonstrates a partial understanding of the problem and chooses a strategy that does not lead to a complete and accurate solution
0	• Demonstrates little understanding of the problem and shows little evidence of using any strategy to determine a solution

Review Model

Refer students to the Problem Solving Review Model: *Act It Out* to review a model of the four steps they can use with the problem solving strategy *act it out.*

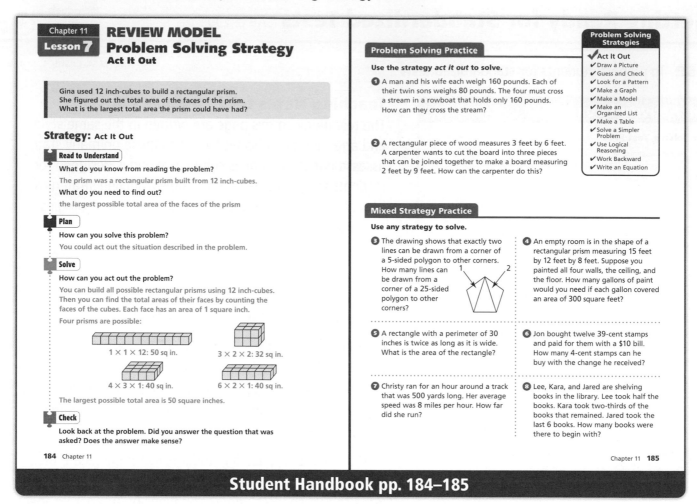

Student Handbook pp. 184–185

Task Have students read the problem at the top of the Review Model page.

💬 Talk Math

❓ What do you know? A rectangular prism is built from 12 inch-cubes.

❓ What do you need to find out? the largest possible total area of the faces of the prism

❓ How can you find the dimensions of all the possible prisms? Look for groups of three whole numbers with products of 12.

❓ What groups of three numbers have products of 12? $1 \times 1 \times 12$, $1 \times 2 \times 6$, $1 \times 3 \times 4$, and $2 \times 2 \times 3$

❓ How can you find the total areas of the faces of the prisms? Build each prism with inch cubes. Count to find the total area of its face, using the fact that each inch-cube face has an area of 1 square inch.

❓ What is the largest possible total area? 50 square inches

❓ What other strategy could you use to solve the problem? Possible answer: *Draw a picture.*

Use with Lesson Activity Book pp. 229–230.

❶ (1) sons A and B cross; (2) A returns; (3) wife; (4) B; (5) AB; (6) A; (7) husband; (8) B; (9) AB; Possible explanation: You can *act it out* to solve the problem. Four students can take the parts of the four people in the problem. They can walk back and forth across the "stream," a designated part of the room, until they find the solution.

❷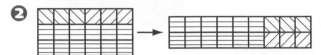

Possible explanation: You can *act it out* to solve the problem. Use 18 blocks or square tiles arranged in a 3-by-6 array. Then find a way to separate them into three pieces that can be rearranged into a 2-by-9 array.

❸ 22 lines; Possible explanation: You can *solve a simpler problem* to solve the problem. By drawing lines on 4-sided and 6-sided polygons, you can discover that the number of lines is always 3 less than the number of sides of the polygon.

❹ 3 gallons; Possible explanation: You can *use logical reasoning.* The total area of the *inside* walls, ceiling, and floor is the same as the total area of the *outside* faces of a 15-by-12-by-8 ft rectangular prism. You could find the total area, then divide by 300.

❺ 50 square inches; Possible explanation: Use *guess and check* to solve the problem. The sum of the length and width is $30 \div 2 = 15$ inches. Try numbers until you find two, one of which is twice the other, and whose sum is 15.

❻ 133 4-cent stamps; Possible explanation: Two students using play money can *act it out* to solve the problem.

❼ 8 miles; Possible explanation: You can *use logical reasoning.* It doesn't matter how long the track was. Christy ran for an hour at a speed of 8 miles per hour, so she must have run 8 miles.

❽ 36 books; Possible explanation: *Work backward* to solve. Kara took two-thirds of what remained, so Jared's portion, 6, must have been one-third. So, what remained was $6 \times 3 = 18$. That was half of the original group of books, so there were $2 \times 18 = 36$ books.

Three-Dimensional Geometry

NCTM Standards 1, 3, 4, 6, 7, 8, 9, 10

Purpose To provide students with an opportunity to demonstrate understanding of Chapter 11 concepts and skills

> **MATERIALS**
> • LAB pp. 231–232
> • Chapter 11 Test
>   (Assessment Guide
>   pp. AG89–AG90)

Chapter 11 Learning Goals and Assessment Options

These learning goals are assessed in many ways throughout the chapter. The chart below correlates each learning goal to specific formal and informal assessment options.

Learning Goals		Lesson Number	Snapshot Assessment	Chapter Review Item Numbers	Chapter Test Item Numbers
				LAB pp. 231–232	Assessment Guide pp. AG89–AG90
11-A	Identify, sort, and describe three-dimensional figures by their attributes	11.1–11.3	1, 5, 7, 8	1–7	1–8
11-B	Find the areas of faces on three-dimensional figures	11.4	2, 6	8	9
11-C	Find volumes of three-dimensional figures	11.5, 11.6	3, 4, 9	9	10
11-D	Apply problem solving strategies such as *act it out* to solve problems	11.7	10	10	11–12

Snapshot Assessment

The following Mental Math and Quick Write questions and tasks provide a quick, informal assessment of students' understanding of Chapter 11 concepts, skills, and problem solving strategies.

whole class **10 MIN**

Mental Math This oral assessment uses mental math strategies and can be used with the whole class.

❶ What do all polygons have in common? They must be closed shapes whose sides are all straight, with no extra lines and only one inside region.
  • Is a circle a polygon? No. Why not? There are no straight sides.
  • 2-dimensional figures have length and width; 3-dimensional figures have length, width, and _____ height or depth.
  What do we call a flat surface of a solid figure? face
  (Learning Goal 11-A)

❷ Explain a shortcut you could use to find the total area of the 6 faces of a rectangular prism. Possible explanation: Since I know the top and bottom of the prism are congruent, I could find just the area of the top and multiply it by 2 to get the top and bottom areas. The front and back faces are congruent, so I could find just the area of the front and multiply it by 2. The side faces are congruent so I could find the area of one and multiply it by 2. I would then add the sums to find the total area.
  (Learning Goal 11-B)

❸ How can you find the volume of a three-dimensional figure? Possible answers: Count the cubes in one layer, then multiply by the number of layers; or find the product of the length, the width, and the height.
(Learning Goal 11-C)

❹ A rectangular prism measures 3 inches, by 4 inches, by 2 inches. How many inch-cubes would you need to model the prism? What is the volume? Explain.
24 inch cubes; The volume is 24 cubic inches; Each layer would need 12 cubes since $3 \times 4 = 12$. Since there are 2 layers, I would need 2×12 or 24 cubes.
(Learning Goal 11-C)

Quick Write This informal written assessment can be administered to small groups or the whole class. Read each question and have the students record responses on their write-on boards. Encourage students to listen and think about the questions before responding.

❺ What am I?
- 1 circular base, 1 point cone
- 6 square faces cube
- 2 congruent circular bases cylinder
- all faces are triangles, 1 base pyramid
- 6 rectangular faces rectangular prism
  (Learning Goal 11-A)

❻ A cube has an edge of 2 inches. What is the total area of all 6 faces? Show your work or explain how you got your answer. One face area: $2 \times 2 = 4$ square inches; 6 faces: $6 \times 4 = 24$ square inches total
(Learning Goal 11-B)

❼ What solid figure could be made with:
- 4 rectangles and 2 squares? rectangular prism
- 3 rectangles and 2 triangles? triangular prism
- 6 squares? cube
- 1 rectangle and 4 triangles? (rectangular) pyramid
- 2 congruent circles and a rectangle? cylinder
  (Learning Goal 11-A)

❽ Explain the difference between a triangular prism and a triangular pyramid. Possible explanation: Pyramids have only 1 base; prisms have 2 parallel congruent bases.
(Learning Goal 11-A)

❾ You have a rectangular prism gift box which measures 4 inches by 3 inches, by 5 inches. What is its volume? Explain. $4 \times 3 \times 5 = 60$ cubic inches; multiply length times width times height to find volume.
- Find the dimensions of a different sized gift box, but be sure the volume is exactly the same. Answers will vary and may include: $12 \times 5 \times 1$, $5 \times 6 \times 2$, $10 \times 2 \times 3$
- A rectangular prism has a volume of 120 cubic inches. The length is 6 inches; the width is 5 inches. What is the height? Explain. The height is 4 inches. Volume is found by multiplying length times width, times height. I know $6 \times 5 = 30$. If I multiply 30 times 4, I would get a volume of 120 cubic inches. So I know the height is 4 inches.
  (Learning Goal 11-C)

❿

chair 1   chair 2   chair 3   chair 4

———   ———   ———   ———

Write a name on each chair to show where each person is seated, based on the clues below.

Scott will sit next to Amy.

Cindy won't sit on the end.

Jeff will sit in chair 1.

2 possible solutions: Jeff, Cindy, Scott, Amy; Jeff, Cindy, Amy, Scott
(Learning Goal 11-D)

Formal Assessment

Chapter Review/Assessment The Chapter 11 Review/Assessment on *Lesson Activity Book* pages 231–232 assesses students' understanding of three-dimensional geometry. Students should be able to complete these pages independently.

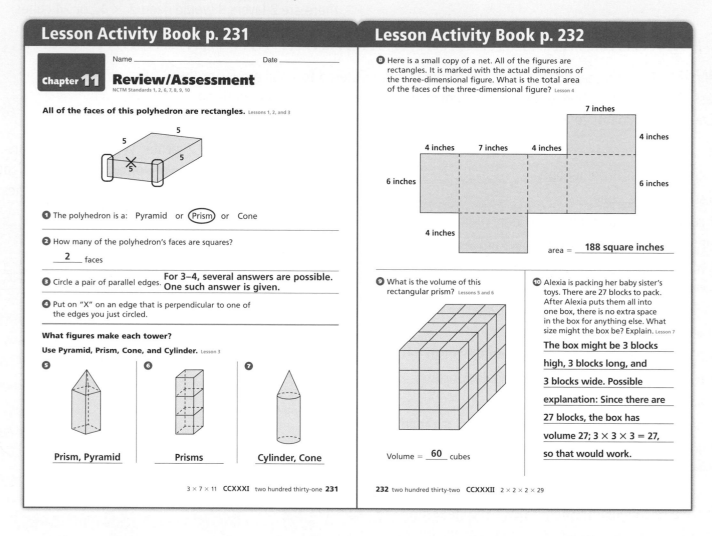

Lesson Activity Book p. 231

Name _____ Date _____

Chapter **11** **Review/Assessment**
NCTM Standards 1, 2, 6, 7, 8, 9, 10

All of the faces of this polyhedron are rectangles. Lessons 1, 2, and 3

❶ The polyhedron is a: Pyramid or (Prism) or Cone

❷ How many of the polyhedron's faces are squares?
__2__ faces

❸ Circle a pair of parallel edges. **For 3–4, several answers are possible. One such answer is given.**

❹ Put on "X" on an edge that is perpendicular to one of the edges you just circled.

What figures make each tower?
Use Pyramid, Prism, Cone, and Cylinder. Lesson 3

❺ Prism, Pyramid

❻ Prisms

❼ Cylinder, Cone

3 × 7 × 11 CCXXXI two hundred thirty-one **231**

Lesson Activity Book p. 232

❽ Here is a small copy of a net. All of the figures are rectangles. It is marked with the actual dimensions of the three-dimensional figure. What is the total area of the faces of the three-dimensional figure? Lesson 4

7 inches
4 inches
4 inches 7 inches 4 inches
6 inches 6 inches
4 inches

area = __188 square inches__

❾ What is the volume of this rectangular prism? Lessons 5 and 6

Volume = __60__ cubes

❿ Alexia is packing her baby sister's toys. There are 27 blocks to pack. After Alexia puts them all into one box, there is no extra space in the box for anything else. What size might the box be? Explain. Lesson 7

The box might be 3 blocks high, 3 blocks long, and 3 blocks wide. Possible explanation: Since there are 27 blocks, the box has volume 27; 3 × 3 × 3 = 27, so that would work.

232 two hundred thirty-two CCXXXII 2 × 2 × 2 × 29

Extra Support Students who have difficulty with items on the Chapter 11 Review/Assessment may need review of the lesson where development of the concept was provided. You can use the Intervention Activity to increase students' understanding before the Chapter Test is given.

Chapter Test Use the Chapter 11 Test in the *Assessment Guide* to assess concept, skills and problem solving from the chapter and to prepare students for standardized tests. The Chapter Test and other test items are also available online.

Chapter Notes

Quick Notes

More Ideas

Big Idea Apply negative numbers and graph number pairs on coordinate grids

Extending the Number Line

About the Chapter

This chapter uses the number line to represent numbers and space, introducing students to ideas that they will extend in fifth grade. In Chapter 8, students "zoomed" in on segments of the number line to explore decimals and fractions. In this chapter, students extend the number line to include negative numbers and then use two number lines to name and locate points in 2-dimensions.

Less than Zero While the idea of "less than nothing" can be a challenging one in the abstract, students can call on experiences from daily life, such as temperatures below zero or owing money, to help them understand negative numbers. In this chapter, students use contexts like temperature and scorekeeping for games to work with and think about numbers less than zero.

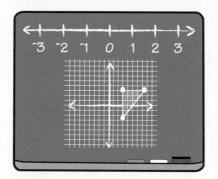

Describing Locations on a Plane

A single number is adequate for naming and locating numbers on a line, but if you want to identify a location on a flat surface (plane), you need two numbers and two number lines (axes), one for describing vertical position and one for describing horizontal position. Students begin by working with maps, using the cardinal directions (North, South, East, West) to help determine and describe locations. At the end of the chapter, students use ordered pairs of numbers to map lines and geometric figures. The ability to use numbers to describe location is an important mathematical skill, which makes it possible to make multiple connections between numbers and pictures, algebra and geometry.

Developing Concepts Across the Grades

Topic	Prior Learning	Learning in Chapter 12	Later Learning
Integers	• Label points on a number line **Grade 3, Chapter 1**	• Label number lines with positive and negative numbers **Lessons 12.1, 12.2**	• Explore negative numbers on a number line **Grade 5, Chapter 1**
Coordinate Grids	• Locate objects on a map using letter and number pairs • Locate and name intersections on a map **Grade 3, Chapter 8**	• Identify points on a coordinate grid using ordered pairs of numbers • Follow directions to draw pictures on coordinate grids • Graph ordered pairs of numbers that are related to a rule **Lessons 12.3–12.7**	• Name and locate points in all four quadrants of a coordinate grid • Add and subtract coordinates to move from one point to another **Grade 5, Chapter 6**
Two-Dimensional Geometry	• Identify congruent figures using slides, flips, and turns **Grade 3, Chapter 11**	• Investigate translations (slides) and reflections (flips) using a coordinate grid • Transform a figure by changing the coordinates according to a rule **Lessons 12.5, 12.6**	• Translate, reflect and rotate figures on a coordinate grid **Grade 5, Chapter 6**

Chapter Planner

Lesson	Objectives	NCTM Standards	Vocabulary	Materials/Resources
CHAPTER 12 World Almanac For Kids • Vocabulary • Games • Challenge Teacher Guide pp. 943A–943F, Student Handbook pp. 192–193, 202–206				
1 **Introducing Negative Numbers** PACING 1 DAY **Teacher Guide** pp. 944–951 **Lesson Activity Book** pp. 233–234 **Student Handbook** Student Letter p. 191 Game p. 204	• To investigate negative numbers in the context of Celsius temperature • To compute changes in Celsius temperature	1, 4, 6, 7, 8, 9, 10	minus negative	**For the teacher:** ■ transparency of AM130–AM131 (optional) **For the students:** ■ School-Home Connection, SHC45–SHC48 ■ TR: AM130–AM131 ■ outdoor thermometer; opaque bag or container, 2 number cubes of one color and 2 number cubes of a different color ■ P95, E95, SR95
2 **Negative Numbers on the Number Line** PACING 1 DAY **Teacher Guide** pp. 952–959 **Lesson Activity Book** pp. 235–236 **Student Handbook** Review Model p. 194	• To label number lines with positive and negative numbers • To make forward and backward jumps on the number line	1, 4, 6, 7, 8, 9, 10	negative number positive number	**For the students:** ■ P96, E96, SR96 **Social Studies Connection:** **Above and Below Sea Level** Teacher Guide p. 942
3 **Navigating on a Coordinate Grid** PACING 1 DAY **Teacher Guide** pp. 960–967 **Lesson Activity Book** pp. 237–238	• To describe paths connecting two points on a coordinate grid and to find the shortest path among them • To identify points on the coordinate grid using ordered pairs of numbers	1, 3, 6, 7, 8, 9, 10	axis (plural: axes) coordinates ordered pair origin	**For the teacher:** ■ transparency of AM132 (optional) **For the students:** ■ TR: AM132 ■ P97, E97, SR97 **Literature Connection:** **The Fly on the Ceiling** Teacher Guide p. 942
4 **Points and Lines on a Grid** PACING 1 DAY **Teacher Guide** pp. 968–975 **Lesson Activity Book** pp. 239–240 **Student Handbook** Review Model p. 195	• To use coordinates to locate points on coordinate grids • To follow directions to draw pictures on coordinate grids	1, 3, 6, 7, 8, 9, 10	endpoint line line segment	**For the teacher:** ■ transparencies of AM133 (optional) **For the students:** ■ straight edge ■ stickers ■ TR: AM133 ■ P98, E98, SR98

NCTM Standards 2000

1. Number and Operations
2. Algebra
3. Geometry
4. Measurement
5. Data Analysis and Probability
6. Problem Solving
7. Reasoning and Proof
8. Communication
9. Connections
10. Representation

Key

AG: Assessment Guide
E: Extension Book
LAB: Lesson Activity Book
P: Practice Book
SH: Student Handbook
SR: Spiral Review Book
TG: Teacher Guide
TR: Teacher Resource Book

 MATH GLOSSARY in **Student Handbook** p. 259

Planner (continued) ➡

Chapter Planner (continued)

Lesson	Objectives	NCTM Standards	Vocabulary	Materials/Resources
5 Drawing Figures on a Coordinate Grid PACING 1 DAY **Teacher Guide** pp. 976–983 **Lesson Activity Book** pp. 241–242 **Student Handbook** Explore p. 196 Game p. 205	• To label points on the coordinate grid using coordinates • To give and follow directions using the coordinate grid	1, 3, 6, 7, 8, 9, 10	**coordinate plane** **grid**	**For the teacher:** ■ transparency of Explore p. 196 (optional) ■ transparencies of LAB pp. 241–242 (optional) ■ transparency of AM134 (optional) **For the students:** ■ straight edge ■ small game token ■ P99, E99, SR99
6 Moving Figures on a Coordinate Grid PACING 1 DAY **Teacher Guide** pp. 984–993 **Lesson Activity Book** pp. 243–244 **Student Handbook** Explore p. 197 Review Model p. 198	• To investigate translations (slides) and reflections (flips) of figures using a coordinate grid • To transform a figure by changing the coordinates of all of its points according to a rule	1, 2, 3, 6, 7, 8, 9, 10	**coordinate**	**For the teacher:** ■ transparencies of AM135–136 **For the students:** ■ TR: AM135–AM136 ■ P100, E100, SR100
7 Number Sentences and Straight Lines PACING 1 DAY **Teacher Guide** pp. 994–1001 **Lesson Activity Book** pp. 245–246 **Student Handbook** Explore p. 199	• To graph ordered pairs of numbers that are related by a rule, and to represent these rules with number sentences • To explore rules that when graphed are straight lines	1, 2, 3, 6, 7, 8, 9, 10	**function**	**For the teacher:** ■ transparencies of AM137–AM138 **For the students:** ■ TR: AM137–AM138 ■ P101, E101, SR101 **Science Connection:** **Wind Chill** **Teacher Guide** p. 942
8 Problem Solving Strategy and Test Prep PACING 1 DAY **Teacher Guide** pp. 1002–1007 **Lesson Activity Book** pp. 247–248 **Student Handbook** Review Models pp. 200–201	• To practice the problem solving strategy *draw a picture.* • To articulate the steps and strategies used to solve problems • To prepare for standardized tests	1, 2, 6, 7, 8, 9, 10		

CHAPTER 12 Assessment
TG pp. 1008–1011, **LAB** pp. 248–250, **AG** pp. AG109–AG112

For the students:
■ Chapter 12 Test pp. AG109–AG110

Games

Use the following games for skills practice
and reinforcement of concepts.

Lesson 12.1 ▶

Freeze or Fry provides an opportunity
for students to practice computing with
negative numbers as the temperature
changes on a thermometer according to
the toss of their number cubes.

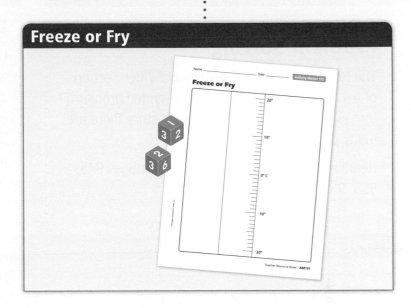

Freeze or Fry

Coordinate Hide and Seek

◀ **Lesson 12.5** *Coordinate Hide
and Seek* provides an opportunity for
students to practice working with
ordered pairs on a coordinate grid and
moving along both the vertical and
horizontal axes.

Planning Ahead

In **Lesson 12.1,** students will use a pair of number cubes to play
Freeze or Fry. Each pair of students will need a copy of AM131
to visualize the temperature changing on a thermometer as they
work with negative and positive changes in temperature.

In **Lesson 12.5,** students will play the *Coordinate Hide and Seek*
game. Each student will need a copy of AM134 and a small game
token. You will need to put a barrier between them so that they
cannot view each others' grids. A large manila folder works well.

Developing Problem Solvers

Open-Ended Problem Solving

The Headline Story in the Daily Activities section of every lesson provides an open-ended problem for students to complete. For each story there are many possible responses.

Headline Stories can be found on TG pages 945, 953, 961, 969, 977, 985, and 995.

Leveled Problem Solving

Leveled Problem Solving provides an opportunity for students to apply learning from the lesson to a real-life situation. Problems are leveled by ability to allow students of all ability levels to become successful problem solvers. Each Leveled Problem Solving begins with a real-life scenario upon which three problems are built.

The levels of problems are:

❶ Basic Level	❷ On Level	❸ Above Level
students needing extra support	students working at grade level	students who are ready for more challenging problems

Leveled Problem Solving can be found on TG pages 951, 959, 967, 975, 982, 992, and 1001.

The World Almanac for Kids feature is designed to stimulate student interest for the math concepts they are about to learn. Students use data to solve problems and explain solutions. The Chapter 12 Project can be found on SH pages 192–193.

Write Math **Reflect and Summarize the Lesson** poses a problem or question for students to think and write about. This feature can be found on TG pages 950, 958, 966, 974, 981, 991, 1000, and 1004.

Other opportunities to write about math can be found on LAB pages 242, 244, and 246.

Problem Solving Strategies

The focus of **Lesson 12.8** is the strategy *Draw a Picture.* However, students will use a variety of problem solving strategies as they work through the chapter. The chart below shows strategies that may be useful in completing each lesson.

Strategy	Lesson(s)	Description
Act It Out	12.2, 12.3	Act it out to find the results of making two moves on a number line.
✓ Draw a Picture	12.1, 12.2, 12.3, 12.4, 12.5, 12.6, 12.7	Draw a picture to see the relationship between positive and negative numbers.
Look for a Pattern	12.5	Look for a pattern to discover similarities in the coordinates of vertical and horizontal line segments.
Make a Graph	12.1, 12.2, 12.3, 12.4, 12.5, 12.6, 12.7	Make a coordinate grid to find the shortest distance between two points.
Work Backward	12.1, 12.2	Work backward to find the temperature change from one day to the next.
Write an Equation	12.7	Write and graph an equation to explore the relationship between the numbers in a set of ordered pairs.

Meeting the Needs of All Learners

Differentiated Instruction

Extra Support	On Level	Enrichment
Intervention Activities TG pp. 951, 959, 967, 975, 982, 992, 1001	**Practice Book** pp. P95–P101	**Extension Activities** TG pp. 951, 959, 967, 975, 982, 992, 1001
	Spiral Review Book pp. SR95–SR101	**Extension Book** pp. E95–E101
	LAB Challenge LAB pp. 234, 236, 240, 242, 244, 246	**LAB Challenge** LAB pp. 234, 236, 240, 242, 244, 246
Lesson Notes Basic Level TG pp. 949, 957, 978	**Lesson Notes** On Level TG p. 949	**Lesson Notes** Above Level TG pp. 950, 966
Leveled Problem Solving Basic Level TG pp. 951, 959, 967, 975, 982, 992, 1001	**Leveled Problem Solving** On Level TG pp. 951, 959, 967, 975, 982, 992, 1001	**Leveled Problem Solving** Above Level TG pp. 951, 959, 967, 975, 982, 992, 1001

English Language Learners

Suggestions for addressing the needs of students learning English as a second language are included in the Developing Mathematical Language section at the beginning of most lessons.

ELL activities for this chapter can be found on TG pages 945, 953, 961, 969, 977, 985, and 995.

The Multi-Age Classroom

Grade 3	• Students on this level should be able to complete the lessons in Chapter 12 but might need some additional practice with key concepts and skills. • Give students more practice using a coordinate grid and reading locations on a map.	See Grade 4, Intervention Activities, Lessons 12.1–12.7. See Grade 3, Lessons 8.7–8.8.
Grade 4	• Students on this level should be able to complete the lessons in Chapter 12 with minimal adjustments.	See Grade 4, Practice pages P95–P101.
Grade 5	• Students on this level should be able to complete the lessons in Chapter 12 and to extend coordinate grid concepts and skills. • Give students extended work with shapes and negative numbers on a coordinate grid.	See Grade 4, Extension pages E95–E101. See Grade 5, Lessons 6.1–6.7.

Cross Curricular Connections

Science Connection

Math Concept: negative numbers

Wind Chill

- Discuss with students the fact that when the temperature is 40°F or below, wind makes the temperature feel colder than it actually is. This phenomenon is called the "wind chill."

- Display this chart showing how wind chill effects a temperature of 5°F.

Wind Speed (in mi/hr)	0	5	10	15	20	25
Wind Chill (in °F)	5	⁻5	⁻10	⁻13	⁻15	⁻17

- Ask students to describe the numbers in the last column of the table as an ordered pair and explain what they think it means. (25, ⁻17); If the temperature was 5°F and the wind speed 25 mi/hr, the wind chill would make it feel as though it were ⁻17°F.

- Challenge students to draw a graph showing the ordered pairs and to decide whether they form a straight line. Although some points on the graph would align, they would not form a straight line.

Lesson 12.7

Social Studies Connection

Math Concept: graphs of straight lines

Above and Below Sea Level

- Share with students how negative numbers are used to identify the elevations of locations below sea level.

- Ask students to locate the Dead Sea in the Middle East (on the boundary between Israel and Jordan) and Death Valley, California on a map or globe. These two places have the lowest elevations in the world.

- Pose the following problems:

  1. On a horizontal number line representing elevations of places below sea level, how would you decide the order of the places on the line? Places would run from left to right from lowest to highest elevation.

  2. Would the answers to these questions be different if you were representing only places above sea level? No, the answers would all be the same.

Lesson 12.2

Literature Connection

Math Concept: coordinate system

The Fly on the Ceiling
By Dr. Julie Glass
Illustrated by Richard Walz

A fly on the ceiling inspires French philosopher René Descartes to invent a way to organize and keep track of his belongings using the Cartesian Coordinate System.

Lesson 12.3

School-Home Connection

Encourage students to play *Complete Rectangles,* found in the *Teacher Resource Book* on page SHC46, with a family member. Students will work with locating ordered pairs in **Lessons 12.3, 12.4** and **12.5.**

A reproducible copy of the School-Home Connection letter in English and in Spanish can be found in the *Teacher Resource Book,* pages SHC45–SHC48.

Assessment Options

There are many opportunities in *Think Math!* to assess students' understanding of concepts, skills and problem solving. Learning Goals for Chapter 12 are provided below. The assessment options provide opportunities to evaluate whether or not students have retained learning from prior experiences. Choose the forms of assessment that best meet the needs of your students.

Chapter 12 Learning Goals

	Learning Goals	Lesson Number
12-A	Measure and calculate Celsius temperature changes	12.1
12-B	Add and subtract to locate positive and negative numbers on a number line	12.2
12-C	Plot and identify points and lines on a coordinate grid	12.3–12.7
12-D	Apply problem solving strategies such as *draw a picture* to solve problems	12.8

✔ Informal Assessment

Ongoing Assessment
Provides insight into students' thinking to guide instruction (TG pp. 954, 962, 970, 979, 986, 996)

Reflect and Summarize the Lesson
Checks understanding of lesson concepts (TG pp. 950, 958, 966, 974, 981, 991, 1000, 1004)

Snapshot Assessment
Mental Math and **Quick Write**
Offers a quick observation of students' progress on chapter concepts and skills (TG pp. 1008–1009)

Performance Assessment
Provides quarterly assessment of Chapters 12–15 concepts using real-life situations
Assessment Guide
pp. AG225–AG230

✔ Formal Assessment

Standardized Test Prep
Problem Solving Test Prep
Prepares students for standardized tests
Lesson Activity Book p. 248 (TG p. 1005)

Chapter 12 Review/Assessment
Reviews and assesses students' understanding of the chapter
Lesson Activity Book pp. 249–250 (TG p. 1010)

Chapter 12 Test
Assesses the chapter concepts and skills
Assessment Guide
Form A pp. AG109–AG110
Form B pp. AG111–AG112

Benchmark 4 Assessment
Provides quarterly assessment of Chapters 12–15 concepts and skills
Assessment Guide
Benchmark 4A pp. AG125–AG132
Benchmark 4B pp. AG133–AG140

World Almanac for Kids

Use the World Almanac for Kids feature, *Fun with Golf,* found on pp. 192–193 of the ***Student Handbook,*** to provide students with an opportunity to practice using their problem solving skills by solving real world problems.

FACT·ACTIVITY 1

❶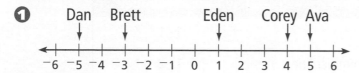

❷ Ava, Corey, Eden

❸ Dan

❹ Dan

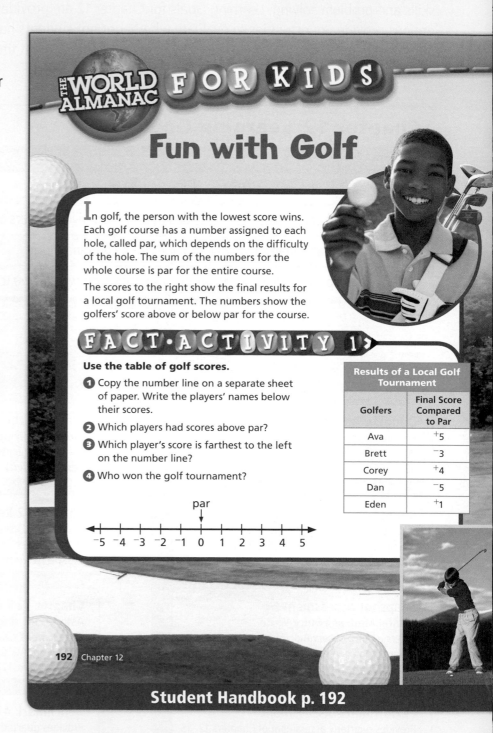

Student Handbook p. 192

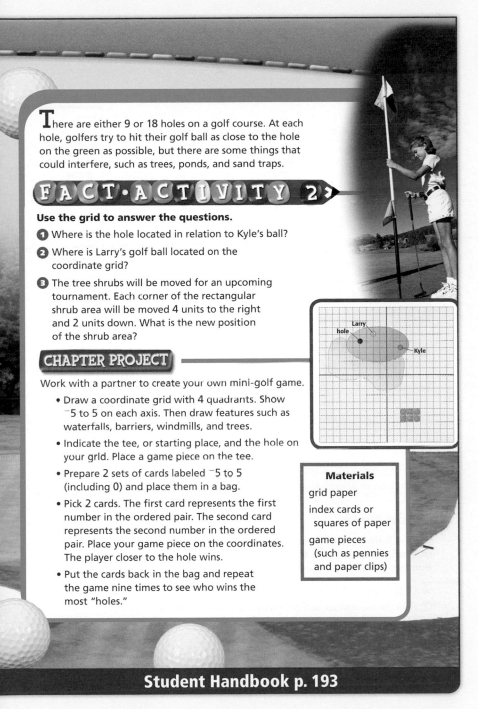

There are either 9 or 18 holes on a golf course. At each hole, golfers try to hit their golf ball as close to the hole on the green as possible, but there are some things that could interfere, such as trees, ponds, and sand traps.

FACT·ACTIVITY 2

Use the grid to answer the questions.

❶ Where is the hole located in relation to Kyle's ball?

❷ Where is Larry's golf ball located on the coordinate grid?

❸ The tree shrubs will be moved for an upcoming tournament. Each corner of the rectangular shrub area will be moved 4 units to the right and 2 units down. What is the new position of the shrub area?

CHAPTER PROJECT

Work with a partner to create your own mini-golf game.

• Draw a coordinate grid with 4 quadrants. Show ⁻5 to 5 on each axis. Then draw features such as waterfalls, barriers, windmills, and trees.

• Indicate the tee, or starting place, and the hole on your grid. Place a game piece on the tee.

• Prepare 2 sets of cards labeled ⁻5 to 5 (including 0) and place them in a bag.

• Pick 2 cards. The first card represents the first number in the ordered pair. The second card represents the second number in the ordered pair. Place your game piece on the coordinates. The player closer to the hole wins.

• Put the cards back in the bag and repeat the game nine times to see who wins the most "holes."

Materials

grid paper

index cards or squares of paper

game pieces (such as pennies and paper clips)

Student Handbook p. 193

FACT·ACTIVITY 2

❶ 6 units left and 1 unit up

❷ (⁻2,6)

❸ (6,⁻7), (6,⁻9), (9,⁻7), (9,⁻9)

CHAPTER PROJECT

Possible miniature golf course: similar to the one used in Fact Activity 2 but within the range of ⁻5 to 5 on both axes. Students should label the tee and the hole.

Vocabulary

To reinforce vocabulary concepts, invite students to complete the vocabulary activities on pp. 202–203 of the *Student Handbook.* Encourage students to record their answers in their math journals.

Many answers are possible.

12 Possible answer: The axes on a coordinate plane are number lines. The place where they intersect is called the *origin.* On the horizontal axis, the numbers to the right of the origin are *positive numbers.* The numbers to the left of the *origin* are *negative numbers.* On the vertical axis, the numbers above the *origin* are *positive numbers.* The numbers below the *origin* are *negative numbers.* Label the *origin* 0. Then label to the left and right and above and below starting with 1 for *positive numbers* and ⁻1 for *negative numbers.*

13 Possible answer: Start at the *origin.* Move right if the first coordinate is a *positive number* or left if it is a *negative number.* From there, move up if the second coordinate is a *positive number* or down if it is a *negative number.*

Chapter **12** Vocabulary

Choose the best vocabulary term from Word List A for each sentence.

Word List A
- axes
- axis
- coordinate
- coordinate plane
- coordinates
- endpoint
- function
- grid
- line
- line segment
- minus
- negative
- negative number
- ordered pair
- origin
- positive number

1 The symbol that means subtraction is the __?__ sign. **minus**

2 A(n) __?__ sign in front of a number means the opposite of that number. **negative**

3 A number to the right of zero on the number line is called a(n) __?__. **positive number**

4 A pair of numbers used to locate a point on a coordinate plane is a(n) __?__. **ordered pair**

5 The __?__ of a coordinate plane is where the two axes meet. **origin**

6 A straight path that extends in both directions is a(n) __?__. **line**

7 A(n) __?__ is the very last point on one side of a line segment. **endpoint**

8 A(n) __?__ is a part of a line that includes two endpoints and all the points between them. **line segment**

9 A grid with a horizontal axis and a vertical axis is a(n) __?__. **coordinate plane**

Complete each analogy using the best term from Word List B.

Word List B
- axis
- function
- grid
- line segment
- ordered pair

10 A house number is to an address as a coordinate is to a(n) __?__. **ordered pair**

11 A bead is to a necklace as a(n) __?__ is to a line. **line segment**

🗨 Talk Math

Discuss with a partner what you have learned about graphing numbers. Use the vocabulary terms *negative number, positive number,* and *origin.*

12 How do you label the axes on a coordinate plane?

13 How do you plot an ordered pair on a coordinate plane?

202 Chapter 12

Student Handbook p. 202

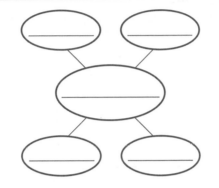
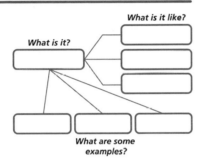

14 Many answers are possible. One example is provided.

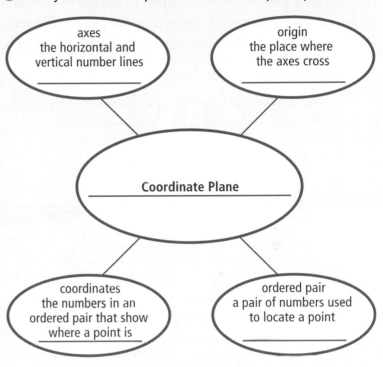

axes
the horizontal and vertical number lines

origin
the place where the axes cross

Coordinate Plane

coordinates
the numbers in an ordered pair that show where a point is

ordered pair
a pair of numbers used to locate a point

15 Many answers are possible. One example is provided.

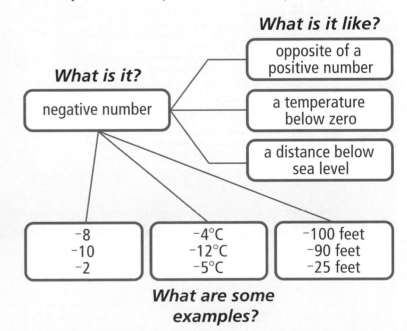

What is it like?

opposite of a positive number

a temperature below zero

a distance below sea level

What is it?

negative number

What are some examples?

−8
−10
−2

−4°C
−12°C
−5°C

−100 feet
−90 feet
−25 feet

Games

Encourage early finishers and students ready to go beyond the lesson objectives to play the games on pp. 204–205 of the *Student Handbook.* **Lesson 12.1** *Freeze or Fry* provides an opportunity for students to practice computing with negative numbers as the temperature changes on a thermometer according to the roll of their number cube. **Lesson 12.5** *Coordinate Hide and Seek* provides an opportunity for students to practice working with ordered pairs on a coordinate grid and moving along both the vertical and horizontal axes.

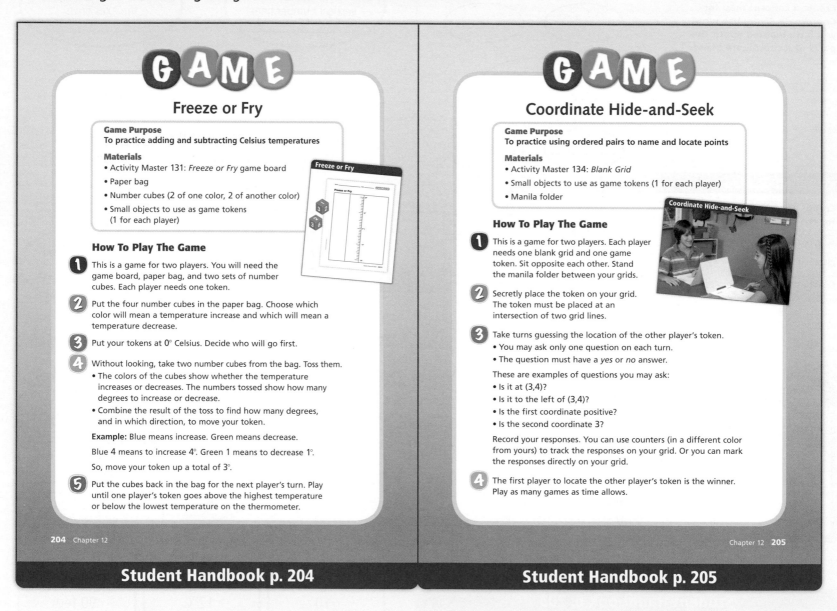

GAME

Freeze or Fry

Game Purpose
To practice adding and subtracting Celsius temperatures

Materials
• Activity Master 131: *Freeze or Fry* game board
• Paper bag
• Number cubes (2 of one color, 2 of another color)
• Small objects to use as game tokens (1 for each player)

How To Play The Game

1 This is a game for two players. You will need the game board, paper bag, and two sets of number cubes. Each player needs one token.

2 Put the four number cubes in the paper bag. Choose which color will mean a temperature increase and which will mean a temperature decrease.

3 Put your tokens at 0° Celsius. Decide who will go first.

4 Without looking, take two number cubes from the bag. Toss them.
• The colors of the cubes show whether the temperature increases or decreases. The numbers tossed show how many degrees to increase or decrease.
• Combine the result of the toss to find how many degrees, and in which direction, to move your token.

Example: Blue means increase. Green means decrease.

Blue 4 means to increase 4°. Green 1 means to decrease 1°.

So, move your token up a total of 3°.

5 Put the cubes back in the bag for the next player's turn. Play until one player's token goes above the highest temperature or below the lowest temperature on the thermometer.

204   Chapter 12

Student Handbook p. 204

GAME

Coordinate Hide-and-Seek

Game Purpose
To practice using ordered pairs to name and locate points

Materials
• Activity Master 134: *Blank Grid*
• Small objects to use as game tokens (1 for each player)
• Manila folder

How To Play The Game

1 This is a game for two players. Each player needs one blank grid and one game token. Sit opposite each other. Stand the manila folder between your grids.

2 Secretly place the token on your grid. The token must be placed at an intersection of two grid lines.

3 Take turns guessing the location of the other player's token.
• You may ask only one question on each turn.
• The question must have a *yes* or *no* answer.

These are examples of questions you may ask:
• Is it at (3,4)?
• Is it to the left of (3,4)?
• Is the first coordinate positive?
• Is the second coordinate 3?

Record your responses. You can use counters (in a different color from yours) to track the responses on your grid. Or you can mark the responses directly on your grid.

4 The first player to locate the other player's token is the winner. Play as many games as time allows.

Chapter 12   205

Student Handbook p. 205

Challenge

This activity challenges students to find missing points that would form a certain figure in a coordinate plane and write the points as ordered pairs. This activity can be found on p. 206 of the *Student Handbook.*

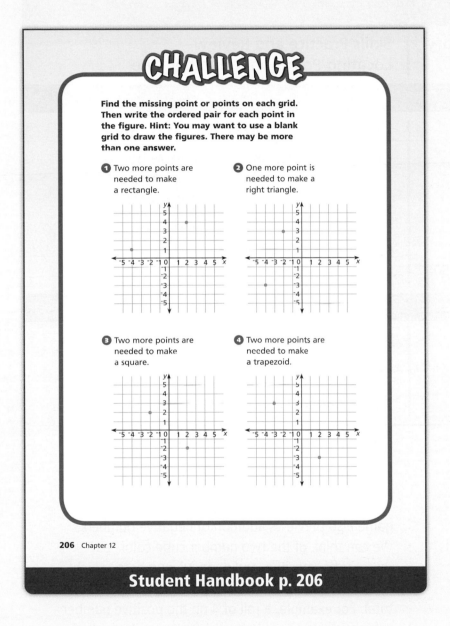

❶ (⁻4,4) and (2,1); all vertices: (⁻4,4), (2,1), (2,4), (⁻4,1)

❷ Possible answers: (⁻4,3) or (⁻2,⁻3); all vertices: (⁻4,3), (⁻2,3), (⁻4,⁻3) or (⁻2,⁻3), (⁻4,⁻3), (⁻2,3).

❸ (2,2) and (⁻2,⁻2); all vertices: (2,2), (2,⁻2), (⁻2,⁻2), (⁻2,2)

❹ Possible answer: (4,3) and (⁻3,⁻3); all vertices (4,3), (⁻3,⁻3), (⁻3,3), (2,⁻3).

Lesson 1 Introducing Negative Numbers

NCTM Standards 1, 4, 6, 7, 8, 9, 10

Lesson Planner

STUDENT OBJECTIVES
- To investigate negative numbers in the context of Celsius temperature
- To compute changes in Celsius temperature

1 | Daily Activities (TG p. 945)

Open-Ended Problem Solving/Headline Story	Skills Practice and Review—Locating Points on a Number Line

2 | Teach and Practice (TG pp. 946–950)

MATERIALS

Ⓐ **Reading the Student Letter** (TG p. 946)

Ⓑ **Computing Change in Celsius Temperature** (TG pp. 947–948)

Ⓒ **Playing a Game: Freeze or Fry** (TG p. 949)

Ⓓ **Introducing Negative Numbers** (TG p. 950)

- transparency of AM130–AM131 (optional)
- outdoor thermometer; opaque bag or container, 2 number cubes of one color and 2 number cubes of a different color
- TR: AM130–AM131 (optional)
- 📖 LAB pp. 233–234
- 📖 SH pp. 191, 204

3 | Differentiated Instruction (TG p. 951)

Leveled Problem Solving (TG p. 951)	Practice Book P95
Intervention Activity (TG p. 951)	Extension Book E95
Extension Activity (TG p. 951)	Spiral Review Book SR95

Lesson Notes

About the Lesson

Students encounter negative numbers in the context of temperatures below zero in the Celsius system. This gives students an easy way to think about negative numbers and provides practice with the metric temperature system.

About the Mathematics

The game *Freeze or Fry* encourages students to combine the effects of addition and subtraction before making a jump on the number line. They see that if you add more than you subtract, the end result is an increase in temperature, and if you subtract more than you add, the end result is a decrease. The game also previews addition of negative numbers. We can think of the two number cube colors as representing positive and negative numbers, which must be combined with a given total to get a new total. For example, a roll of 4 on the positive number cube would be recorded as ⁺4 (or 4), while a roll of a 3 would be recorded as ⁻3. To figure out how far to move on the number line, we add ⁺4 to ⁻3; in other words, we combine a jump of 4 to the right with a jump of 3 to the left. The result is ⁻1, a jump of 1 to the left.

Use with Lesson Activity Book pp. 233–234.

Developing Mathematical Language

Vocabulary: minus, negative

The *minus* sign has two uses: between two quantities it indicates that the second is to be subtracted from the first; in front of a quantity it indicates the opposite of that quantity. Some authorities distinguish between the two uses verbally, saying "*negative* two" for ⁻2 and "three *minus* two" for 3 − 2.

On thermometers and vertical number lines, *negative* temperatures are literally *below* the zero. In the context of temperature, we pronounce ⁻2° as "two below" or "*minus* two; rarely as "*negative* two."

Familiarize students with the terms *minus* and *negative.*

Beginning Show a vertical number line, including *negative* and positive numbers. Have volunteers point to numbers as you call them out; for example, *negative* 5.

Intermediate Write several subtraction expressions and *negative* numbers on the board. Have students read each aloud, emphasizing the word *minus* or *negative* in each.

Advanced Write on the board: 10 feet below sea level; 7 degrees below 0; the difference between 12 and 9. Call on students to rewrite each phrase using either the term *minus* or the term *negative* in each situation. negative 10 feet; negative 7 degrees; 12 minus 9

Open-Ended Problem Solving

Read the Headline Story to the students. Encourage them to use logical reasoning to draw conclusions about the coins.

 Headline Story

> **Kyra, Martin, and Joel each have some coins. Kyra's coins have a value that is a multiple of 6¢. Martin has a multiple of 7¢. Together, the three have 34¢. How much might they each have?**

Possible responses: All of the children have at least one coin; Kyra might have 6¢, 12¢, 18¢, 24¢, or 30¢; Martin might have 7¢, 14¢, 21¢, or 28¢; If Kyra has 30¢, then Martin would not have any coins, so Kyra must not have 30¢; If Martin has 28¢, then Kyra would have 6¢ and Joel would not have any coins, so Martin must not have 28¢; If Kyra has 18¢ and Martin has 7¢, then Joel would have 9¢.

Skills Practice and Review

Locating Points on a Number Line

Draw and label a number line like the following on the board:

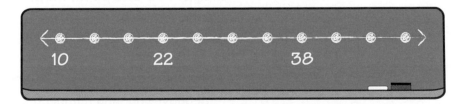

Begin by having students label the marked points on the line. Then say numbers not marked on the number line and ask students to point to their approximate locations on this line. You might start with numbers that are halfway between labeled points. To vary the activity, point to a location on the line and ask students to name and label the point. Include numbers with fractions and decimals.

NCTM Standards 1, 4, 6, 7, 8, 9, 10

whole class
5 MIN

Ⓐ Reading the Student Letter

Purpose To introduce negative numbers

Introduce Have students read the Student Letter individually or as a class.

Task Challenge students to answer the question posed at the end of the letter (Can you think of other situations in which something might go below zero?)

Among situations students might think of are the following:

- A game in which you can both win and lose points. If you have zero points and then lose some points, your score will be a negative number. If you're at ⁻5 points and you gain 5 points, your score will go up to zero. If you get a sixth point, your score will go up to positive 1.

- Owing money. If you buy something for $5 using a credit card, you must give the credit card company $5 later. If you have no money and you owe someone $5, the next $5 you get will go to pay off the debt. Another way to think about this is that you have $5 *less* than nothing right now.

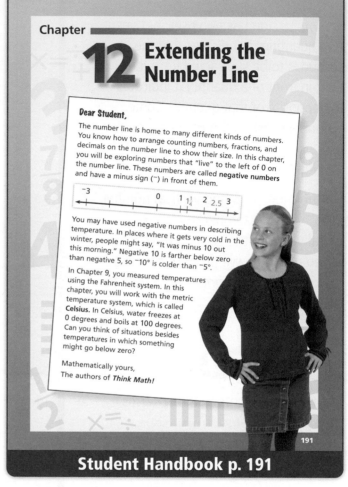

Student Handbook p. 191

Students who used *Think Math!* in Grade 3 may remember working with negative numbers.

💬 Talk Math

❓ Are there negative fractions and decimals on the number line, or only negative counting numbers? Explain your reasoning. yes; Possible explanation: Negative fractions and decimals lie between the negative counting numbers. Sometime between the time the temperature is ⁻5° to the time it falls to ⁻6°, it will be ⁻5.5° or ⁻5½°.

❓ Mr. Ting parked his car four stories below the ground floor of a skyscraper. He took the elevator to the fifth floor. How many stories did he ride up in the elevator? Explain. 9 stories; Possible explanation: He rode up 4 stories to the ground floor, then 5 more stories; $4 + 5 = 9$.

B Computing Changes in Celsius Temperature

Purpose To introduce the Celsius temperature system, and to calculate changes in Celsius temperatures

Introduce Students are familiar with reading thermometers and calculating changes in temperature using the Fahrenheit scale. Briefly introduce the Celsius temperature system. Just as there are two different sets of units for length, volume, and weight, there are also two systems for measuring temperature. Both use units called "degrees," but a change of 1 degree Celsius is almost twice as big as a change of 1 degree Fahrenheit. (10 degrees of change Celsius is 18 degrees of change Fahrenheit.) Water freezes at 0° Celsius and at 32° Fahrenheit.

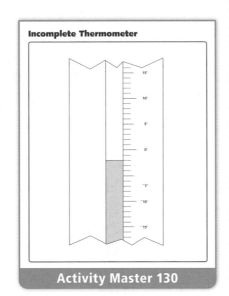

Incomplete Thermometer

Activity Master 130

Problem **Give students a starting temperature and a series of temperature changes, and ask them to find the new temperatures.** For example, you might say, "It was 24°C and the temperature increased 10°. What is the new temperature?" 34°C "Then it became much colder, and the temperature dropped 18°. What is the new temperature?" 16°C

Continue in this manner, giving other changes in temperature. Make a table on the board like the one below, to keep track of the temperatures and the changes.

Starting Temperature	Temperature Change	Ending Temperature
24°C	Up 10°C	34°C
34°C	Down 18°C	16°C

Choose changes so that all of the temperatures remain at or above 0°C. Adjust the difficulty of the numbers as appropriate for your class. Ask students which operation they used each time they found an ending temperature. For example, in the first problem above, students use addition, adding 10° to find the ending temperature.

You might also give students two temperatures and ask them to determine how much the temperature changed: "It was 37°C one day, and 32°C the next day. What was the temperature change?" It went down 5°C.

Materials
• For the teacher: transparency of AM130 (optional); outdoor thermometer

NCTM Standards: 1, 2, 4, 6, 7, 8, 9, 10

Possible Discussion

You may want to take a few minutes to talk with your class about the history and use of the two systems for measuring temperature. Both the Celsius and Fahrenheit systems are used in the United States. Fahrenheit is more commonly used in daily life, in contexts such as weather reports and recipes. Celsius is used for science and in contexts where it is important to be able to share information with other countries (most countries use Celsius exclusively). In the Fahrenheit system, water freezes at 32° and boils at 212°. In the Celsius system, water freezes at 0° and boils at 100°.

Once most students have had a chance to respond, choose a temperature change that causes the temperature to drop slightly below 0°C. If students don't suggest it, explain that negative numbers can be used to show how far below 0° the ending temperature is. Show the transparency of Activity Master: Incomplete Thermometer or draw it on the board. Ask where 4° below zero would be marked on the thermometer. Have students fill in the missing labels as part of a silent activity, or in groups where each group has a copy of the page. If there is time, ask students to name the temperature indicated on the thermometer. ⁻2° Students may refer to the labeled thermometer to help them complete the LAB pages.

As an ongoing activity, hang a thermometer outside your classroom window and, each day, have students in small groups read the temperature in degrees Celsius. To get started, record today's temperature. At the end of the day, record the temperature again. Leave the readings in an accessible place for tomorrow's math class. For the next two days, the class will read the temperature at the beginning and end of the school day and calculate the change in temperature.

Talk Math

❷ If you know the starting temperature and the fact that the temperature decreased by 10 degrees, how can you find the ending temperature? Subtract 10 degrees from the starting temperature.

❷ If the starting temperature is a negative number and the ending temperature is a positive number, has the temperature increased or decreased? It has increased.

Use with Lesson Activity Book pp. 233–234.

Playing *Freeze or Fry*

 pairs

15 MIN

Purpose To practice adding and subtracting Celsius temperatures

Goal The goal is to add or subtract temperatures by a sufficient amount to be the first to move your token off the game board.

Introduce Give each pair of students a copy of the Activity Master: *Freeze or Fry* game board, an opaque bag or container, two number cubes of one color, and two number cubes of a different color.

How to Play

❶ Each pair puts the four number cubes in the opaque bag or container. The pair should choose one color to indicate a temperature increase (addition), the other to indicate a temperature decrease (subtraction). If all groups are using the same two colors, you might want to have the class decide on the meaning of the colors and write it on the board for reference.

❷ Each player places a token at 0°C on the game board.

❸ Without looking, the first player removes two number cubes from the container and tosses them. The color of the cubes indicates whether the temperature increases or decreases; the number indicates the amount of increase or decrease, in degrees. (A player may toss two increases in temperature, two decreases in temperature, or one increase and one decrease.) The player combines the results of the two number cubes to determine how many degrees, and in which direction, to move his or her token on the thermometer. For example, if the player rolls an increase of 3 and a decrease of 5, the net result is a decrease of 2. The player should move 2 degrees down.

❹ The player returns the cubes to the bag and the second player repeats the process. The game is over when one player is able to move his or her token above the highest temperature or below the lowest temperature on the thermometer.

Student Handbook p. 204

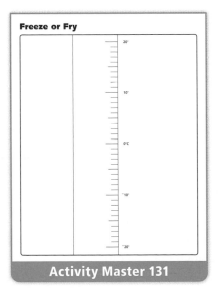

Activity Master 131

Materials
- For each pair: AM131; opaque bag or container, 2 number cubes of one color and 2 number cubes of a different color

NCTM Standards 1, 4, 6, 7, 8, 9, 10

Differentiated Instruction

Basic Level Players use only one game piece. As before, they alternate turns, rolling the number cubes and moving the game piece. Whoever moves beyond the highest or lowest temperature on the thermometer first wins.

Differentiated Instruction

On Level After tossing the number cubes, a player decides whether to keep that toss or toss again in hopes of a better outcome. This variation adds strategy to the game and encourages students to compare magnitudes of positive and negative numbers.

Purpose To read thermometers and compute changes in temperature

NCTM Standards 1, 4, 6, 7, 8, 9, 10

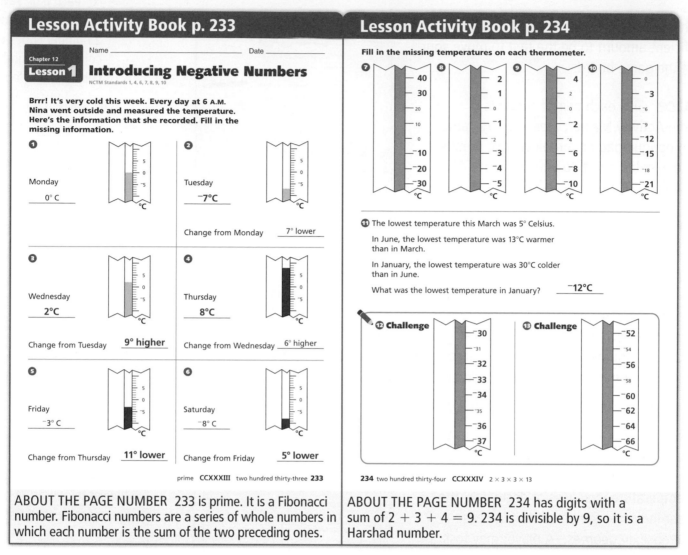

Teaching Notes for LAB page 233

Have students work on the page individually or in pairs. Students calculate changes in temperature and practice reading thermometers.

Students from colder climates may be have an easier time calculating temperature changes with negative numbers than other students, who may need additional practice in order to complete the page.

Differentiated Instruction Above Level Students who finish before the rest of the class may practice measuring the outdoor air temperature with a thermometer. They may then search the Internet to compare their measurements to the predicted temperature for the day or month.

Teaching Notes for LAB page 234

Students label thermometers with positive and negative numbers. Some of the thermometers are labeled for every degree, while others require students to skip count.

Challenge Problem The Challenge problems do not show 0°C, so students must use their understanding of negative numbers to order the labels correctly.

Reflect and Summarize the Lesson

 Write Math **When you're measuring temperature in Celsius degrees, what does a negative number on the thermometer mean?** Possible responses: a temperature below zero; a temperature colder than the temperature at which water freezes.

3 | Differentiated Instruction

On Monday, the temperature was 4° Celsius. On Tuesday, the temperature was 0° Celsius.

❶ Basic Level
On Wednesday, the temperature was 9 degrees colder than on Tuesday. What was the temperature on Wednesday? Explain. ⁻9°C; 9 degrees colder means down 9 degrees.

❷ On Level
On Wednesday, the temperature was ⁻9° Celsius. Which of the three days was the coldest? Explain. Wednesday; ⁻9° is colder than 0° and 4°.

❸ Above Level
On Wednesday, the temperature was ⁻9°, and on Thursday, it was ⁻3°. Which of the four days was the coldest? Explain. Wednesday; ⁻9° is colder than 0°, 4°, and ⁻3°.

Intervention

Activity Making Number Lines

Provide strips of adding machine-type paper. Have students fold the paper in half, in half again, in half again, and then flatten the paper. Holding the strip vertically, let students pick any crease and label it 0. Direct them to complete the vertical number line using negative numbers as needed. Display different number lines so that students can see the methods that others used. Discuss how zero helps students complete the number line.

Practice

Practice P95

Extension

Extension E95

Spiral Review

Spiral Review Book page SR95 provides review of the following previously learned skills and concepts:

- reading and writing numbers through millions
- sorting three-dimensional figures into prisms and pyramids

You may wish to have students work with a partner to complete the page.

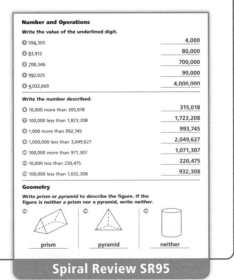

Spiral Review SR95

Extension Activity
Comparing Temperatures

Have each student write eight different random numbers on paper. Then tell them to place a negative sign in front of any four of the numbers. Tell students that their numbers represent temperatures. Have pairs of students switch papers and then list the temperatures in order from hottest to coldest. Next, have them list the temperatures in order from coldest to hottest. Finally, have the pairs of students combine their lists and list all 16 temperatures from hottest to coldest.

Lesson 2 | Negative Numbers on the Number Line

NCTM Standards 1, 4, 6, 7, 8, 9, 10

Lesson Planner

STUDENT OBJECTIVES
- To label number lines with positive and negative numbers
- To make forward and backward jumps on the number line

1 Daily Activities (TG p. 953)

Open-Ended Problem Solving/Headline Story	Skills Practice and Review—Reading a Thermometer

2 Teach and Practice (TG pp. 954–958)

	MATERIALS
(A) Locating Negative Numbers on the Number Line (TG p. 954)	• 📖 LAB pp. 235–236
(B) Jumping Across Zero (TG pp. 955–956)	• 📖 SH p. 194
(C) Negative Numbers on the Number Line (TG p. 957)	

3 Differentiated Instruction (TG p. 959)

Leveled Problem Solving (TG p. 959)	Practice Book P96
Intervention Activity (TG p. 959)	Extension Book E96
Extension Activity (TG p. 959)	Spiral Review Book SR96
Social Studies Connection (TG p. 942)	

Lesson Notes

About the Lesson

This lesson gives students an opportunity to solidify their understanding of negative numbers on the number line. It also prepares them for upcoming work on a coordinate grid.

Think Math! students are familiar with horizontal number lines because they are routinely drawn this way in class. The previous lesson used thermometer scales to introduce negative numbers on vertical number lines. The next lessons will use both orientations in coordinate grids. The sections of number lines on the LAB pages in this lesson are oriented in various directions to prepare students for using both vertical and horizontal number lines in their work with coordinate grids.

Use with Lesson Activity Book pp. 235–236.

Developing Mathematical Language

Vocabulary: negative number, positive number

If a number is left of another number on the number line, then it is less than that number. If a number is right of another number, then it is greater than that number. Numbers to the left of zero are called *negative numbers;* numbers to the right of zero are called *positive numbers.* Zero is neither positive nor negative.

When we write a *negative number,* the minus sign shows that the number is negative. If there is no minus sign, the number is positive. The number without reference to its sign tells its distance from zero. Both 4 and ⁻4 are four units from zero, but in opposite directions.

Familiarize students with the terms *negative number* and *positive number.*

Beginning Draw a horizontal number line from ⁻5 to 5 on the board. Label numbers from 1 to 5 "Positive." Label numbers ⁻5 to ⁻1 "Negative." Have students take turns naming a *positive number.* Then have students take turns naming a *negative number.*

Intermediate Draw a horizontal number line from ⁻10 to 10 on the board. Ask students to point to and name a *number* between ⁻10 and 10, saying, for example, "A *negative number* is ⁻4."

Advanced Ask students to explain where *positive numbers* and *negative numbers* are located on a number line.

Open-Ended Problem Solving

Read the Headline Story to the students. Encourage them to use logical reasoning to draw conclusions about the coins.

 Headline Story

Kyra, Martin, and Joel each have some coins. Kyra's coins have a value that is a multiple of 9¢. Martin has a multiple of 8¢. Together, the three children have 35¢. How much might they each have?

Possible responses: All of the children have at least 1 coin; Kyra might have 9¢, 18¢, or 27¢; Martin might have 8¢, 16¢, 24¢, or 32¢; If Kyra has 27¢, then Martin could have 8¢ and Joel would have no coins, so Kyra must not have 27¢;. We could make a table showing what Joel might have:

	What Martin has		
	9¢	18¢	27¢
8¢	18¢	9¢	**
16¢	10¢	1¢	**
24¢	2¢	**	**
32¢	**	**	**

(left label: What Kyra has)

Joel must have at least 1¢ and no more than 18¢.

Skills Practice and Review

Reading a Thermometer

Materials
• outdoor thermometer

Collect temperature data for today, having the class read and record Celsius temperatures from the outside thermometer at the beginning and end of school. Using the temperature measures from **Lesson 12.1,** have students calculate the change in temperature from one day to the next.

whole class **15 MIN**

NCTM Standards 1, 2, 6, 7, 8, 9, 10

A Locating Negative Numbers on the Number Line

Purpose To place negative numbers of the number line

Introduce An incompletely labeled vertical number line is shown at the right. Draw it on the board.

Problem Ask students to help you fill in the missing numbers. Then ask the following questions:

 Talk Math

❓ What happens if the temperature is 0° and then it becomes colder? The temperature will become a negative number.

Point to ⁻5 on the number line and ask:

❓ If the temperature is ⁻5°, is it warmer or colder than 0°? colder

❓ How much colder is it than 0°? 5 degrees

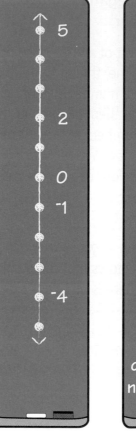

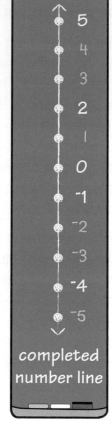

completed number line

Practice Choose a different starting temperature than ⁻5° and ask questions like those above. Continue asking questions, beginning with other starting numbers, both positive and negative. Have students place fractions and decimals (positive and negative) on the number line also.

Leave the number line visible so students can use it when completing the LAB page.

 Talk Math

❓ How can you tell, simply by looking at a Celsius temperature, that the temperature is below freezing? It will be a negative number.

❓ On a vertical number line, where are the negative numbers placed in relation to zero and the positive numbers? The negative numbers are placed below the zero. The positive numbers are placed above the zero.

✓ **Ongoing Assessment**

When students place fractions and decimals on the number line, you have an opportunity to assess how well they understand that the number line is "home" to all the numbers they know about, such as fractions and decimals. For example, you may see some students incorrectly placing fractions such as $\frac{1}{2}$ to the left of 0 on the number line, rather than between 0 and 1. Showing positive and negative fractions (and decimals) on the same number line with positive and negative whole numbers can help students clarify their ideas of the relative sizes of numbers.

Use with Lesson Activity Book pp. 235–236.

Jumping Across Zero

NCTM Standards 1, 4, 6, 7, 8, 9, 10

Purpose To predict the result of making two moves on a number line

Introduce Draw a horizontal number line labeled with positive numbers, negative numbers, and zero on the board.

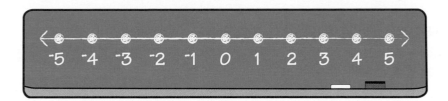

Task Ask a volunteer to place a finger on one of the points. Say that you will be giving directions for making two consecutive jumps. Before moving a finger, the student must predict whether he or she will land to the right or the left of the starting point. For example, you might say, "Jump 5 spaces forward and then 2 spaces backward." You will land to the right of where you started. Have the student check the answer by making the jumps.

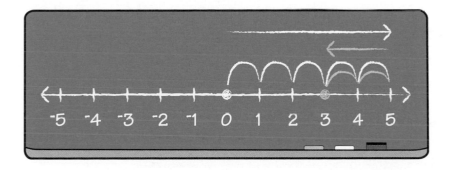

Repeat this activity with several volunteers and sequences of jumps.

Share After many students have participated in the activity, ask students to explain how they can predict the landing point if they know the starting point and the jump sizes. Students may point out ideas such as:

- If both jumps are to the right (forward), you will land to the right of the starting point. Similarly, if both jumps are to the left (backward), you will land to the left of the starting point.

- If the two jumps are in opposite directions, you will land in the direction of the larger jump. So, if the forward jump is larger than the backward jump, you will end up to the right of your starting position. If the backward jump is larger than the forward jump, you will end up to the left of your starting position.

- A special case is when the jumps are the same size but in opposite directions. In this case, you will end up at the starting point.

Concept Alert

Because 4 is greater than 2, some students may be puzzled to learn that ⁻4 is less than ⁻2. Using the number line to introduce negative numbers shows that the size of a negative number represents how far away the number is from zero, just as the size of a positive number does. Four is larger than 2 because you have to add something to 2 (jump to the right) in order to get to 4. Similarly, ⁻2 is greater than ⁻4 because you have to add something to ⁻4 (jump to the right) to reach ⁻2. Though it's hard to imagine having a negative quantity of something, intuition tells us that owing $4 is worse than owing $2: in some sense, it means you have less money.

If your students seem comfortable with these ideas, you may want to challenge them to articulate the logic behind them. They are likely to be comfortable saying that jumping forward and backward are "opposite" actions, and that whatever is left over of the larger jump is how far you end up from your starting point. They may also say that jumping forward on the number line represents adding and jumping backward represents subtracting. If you add more than you subtract, you'll end up with a greater number than you started with; if you subtract more than you add, the final number will be less than the starting number.

This line of reasoning gets a little tricky when it comes to thinking about negative numbers, since it's hard to imagine having less than nothing. However, the number line makes it visually clear that the number ⁻1 must be "less than zero."

Talk Math

❓ Casey started at 2, jumped 4 spaces forward, then jumped again, ending at zero. Describe Casey's second jump. Explain your reasoning. 6 spaces backward; Possible explanation: The first jump took Casey to 2 + 4 = 6. In order for the second jump to have ended at zero, it must have moved from 6 to zero, a 6-space-backward move.

❓ Describe two ways you can start at 3 and, in two jumps, one forward and one backward, end at ⁻3. Possible answer: Jump 2 steps forward and 8 steps backward; jump 7 steps backward and 1 step forward.

Use with Lesson Activity Book pp. 235–236.

Purpose To label number lines with positive and negative numbers

NCTM Standards 1, 2, 6, 7, 8, 9, 10

Lesson Activity Book p. 235

Name _____ Date _____

Chapter 12
Lesson 2 **Negative Numbers on the Number Line**
NCTM Standards 1, 4, 6, 7, 8, 9, 10

Fill in the missing numbers on each number line.

1 3, 2, 1, 0, ⁻1, ⁻2, ⁻3, ⁻4

2 15, 10, 5, 0, ⁻5, ⁻10, ⁻15, ⁻20

3 12, 6, 0, ⁻6, ⁻12, ⁻18, ⁻24, ⁻30

4 8, 4, 0, ⁻4, ⁻8, ⁻12, ⁻16, ⁻20

5 2.0, 1.5, 1.0, 0.5, 0, ⁻0.5, ⁻1.0, ⁻1.5

6 ⁻10 ⁻9 ⁻8 ⁻7 ⁻6 ⁻5 ⁻4 ⁻3

7 ⁻24 ⁻23 ⁻22 ⁻21 ⁻20 ⁻19 ⁻18 ⁻17

8 ⁻3.7 ⁻3.6 ⁻3.5 ⁻3.4 ⁻3.3 ⁻3.2 ⁻3.1 ⁻3.0

9 ⁻24 ⁻21 ⁻18 ⁻15 ⁻12 ⁻9 ⁻6 ⁻3

10 ⁻40 ⁻38 ⁻36 ⁻34 ⁻32 ⁻30 ⁻28 ⁻26

5 × 47 CCXXXV two hundred thirty-five **235**

ABOUT THE PAGE NUMBER 235 is the sum of three consecutive primes (235 = 73 + 79 + 83) and the sum of 3 consecutive triangular numbers: (235 = 66 + 78 + 91).

Lesson Activity Book p. 236

⁻12 ⁻11 ⁻10 ⁻9 ⁻8 ⁻7 ⁻6 ⁻5 ⁻4 ⁻3 ⁻2 ⁻1 0 1 2 3 4 5 6 7 8 9 10 11 12 13

Use this number line to help answer the questions.

11 Start at 2. Jump backward 4 spaces.
Where are you? **⁻2**

12 Start at ⁻7. Jump forward 3 spaces.
Where are you? **⁻4**

13 Start at ⁻5. Jump forward 6 spaces.
Where are you? **1**

14 Start at 4. Jump backward 4 spaces. Then jump backward 3 spaces.
Where are you? **⁻3**

15 Start at ⁻11. Jump forward 5 spaces. Then jump forward 1 space.
Where are you? **⁻5**

16 Start at ⁻4. Jump forward 2 spaces. Then jump forward 3 spaces. Then jump backward 4 spaces.
Where are you? **⁻3**

17 Yesterday's highest temperature was 10° Celsius. Today's high temperature was 15° colder than yesterday's. The forecast says tomorrow's high will be 3° warmer than today's.

What is the predicted high temperature for tomorrow? **⁻2° Celsius**

18 Challenge
Start at 2½. Jump forward 3 spaces. Then jump backward 10 spaces.
Where are you? **⁻4½**

19 Challenge
Start at 1. Jump forward 1 half space. Then jump backward 4 half spaces.
Where are you? **⁻½**

236 two hundred thirty-six CCXXXVI 2 × 2 × 59

ABOUT THE PAGE NUMBER The product of the digits (2 × 3 × 6 = 36) of 236 is the reverse of the sum of its prime factors (2 + 2 + 59 = 63).

Teaching Notes for LAB page 235

Have students work on the page individually or with partners. Students label sections of number lines with positive and negative numbers. Some of the number lines are labeled in intervals of 1, while others require skip counting or decimals.

See About the Lesson for an explanation of why the number line sections are oriented in various ways.

Differentiated Instruction **Basic Level** Students who used *Think Math!* in previous years should already be experienced with labeling number lines, but students who have difficulty with the LAB pages may find it helpful to refer to the number line on the board in Activity B. Because they are just beginning to work with negative numbers, they may still need to keep using numbers close to zero.

Teaching Notes for LAB page 236

Students apply negative numbers to the process of "jumping" on the number line. Jumping with both positive and negative numbers prepares students for work with coordinate grids. See About the Lesson for more about number lines and the LAB pages.

Challenge Problem In the Challenge problems, students must apply what they know about jumping on the number line to a fractional starting point and fractional jumps.

Write Math

Jessica chose a point on the number line. From there she moved 4 spaces right and 5 spaces left. Did she end up right of, left of, or in the same place where she started? **Explain your reasoning.** left of; Possible explanation: Jessica's backward jump of 5 was larger than her forward jump of 4. If the backward jump is larger than the forward jump, the ending position is to the left of the starting position.

Review Model

Refer students to Review Model: Understanding Negative Numbers in the *Student Handbook,* p. 194 to become more proficient at working with negative numbers.

✔ **Check for Understanding**

❶ 0

❷ 2

❸ ⁻1

❹ 4

❺ ⁻4° Celsius

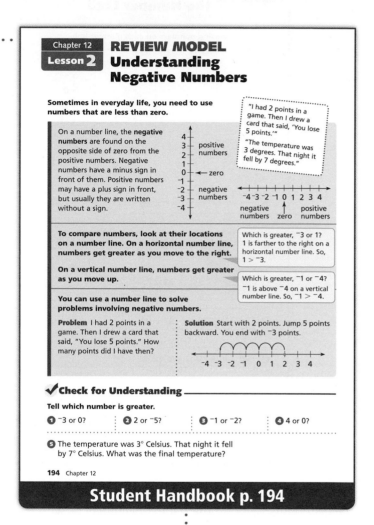

Use with Lesson Activity Book pp. 235–236.

3 | Differentiated Instruction

Gretchen is walking on a number line. She starts at 6 and jumps back 9 spaces.

❶ Basic Level

Where is she now? Explain. ⁻3; Starting at 6 on the number line, I can jump back 9 spaces and land on ⁻3.

❷ On Level

Then she jumps back another 2 spaces. Where is she now? Explain. ⁻5; If I start at 6 on the number line and jump back 9 spaces, I will land on ⁻3. Then I can jump back another 2 spaces and land on ⁻5.

❸ Above Level

Then she jumps back another 2 spaces and forward 12 spaces. Where is she now? Explain. 7; If I start at 6 on the number line and jump back 9 spaces, then back 2 more spaces, I will land on ⁻5. Then I can jump forward 12 spaces to finally land on 7.

Intervention

Activity Reading *Negative*

Help students develop the habit of reading a negative number as *negative two* rather than as *minus two*. Doing so will avoid confusion as students begin to perform operations on negative numbers. Show the class several cards, some with negative numbers on them, some with subtraction expressions. Have students read each card aloud, being sure to use the correct terminology for the negative symbol and minus sign.

Practice

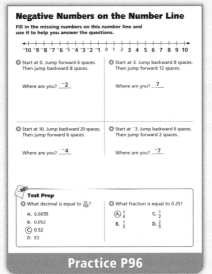

Practice P96

Extension

Extension E96

Extension Activity
Different Ways to Go

Write ⁻4 and 8 on the board. Have pairs of students find three different ways they can move from ⁻4 to 8 on a number line in two steps. Then have them find three different ways they can move from 8 to ⁻4 on a number line in two steps. Encourage students to share their strategies.

Spiral Review

Spiral Review Book page SR96 provides review of the following previously learned skills and concepts:

• predicting the results of an experiment

• using logical reasoning to complete magic squares

You may wish to have students work with a partner to complete the page.

Spiral Review SR96

Lesson 3 Navigating on a Coordinate Grid

NCTM Standards 1, 4, 6, 7, 8, 9, 10

Lesson Planner

STUDENT OBJECTIVES
- To describe paths connecting two points on a coordinate grid and to find the shortest path among them
- To identify points on the coordinate grid using ordered pairs of numbers

1 | Daily Activities (TG p. 961)

| Open-Ended Problem Solving/Headline Story | Skills Practice and Review—Changes in Temperature |

2 | Teach and Practice (TG pp. 962–966)

MATERIALS

Ⓐ **Exploring a Map** (TG pp. 962–963)

Ⓑ **Naming Locations on a Coordinate Grid** (TG pp. 964–965)

Ⓒ **Navigating on a Coordinate Grid** (TG p. 966)

- TR: Activity Master, AM132
- transparency of AM132 (optional)
- 📖 LAB pp. 237–238

3 | Differentiated Instruction (TG p. 967)

Leveled Problem Solving (TG p. 967)

Intervention Activity (TG p. 967)

Extension Activity (TG p. 967)

Literature Connection (TG p. 942)

Practice Book P97

Extension Book E97

Spiral Review Book SR97

Lesson Notes

About the Lesson

This lesson introduces the coordinate grid in the context of a map of city blocks. Students learn to use the mathematical notation of ordered pairs of numbers to identify points on a grid.

About the Mathematics

One number is sufficient to describe the location of a point on a number line and the point's location in relation to zero; the presence or absence of a minus sign indicates which side of zero the point is on; the numeral tells the point's distance from zero. On a plane (a flat surface), because it is two-dimensional, two numbers are needed to locate a point. One gives the point's distance left or right (west or east) of a vertical reference line; the other gives its distance above or below (north or south) of a horizontal reference line perpendicular to the first. So, instead of one number, we use a pair of numbers to describe the position of a point on a plane.

In three-dimensional space, three numbers are needed to locate a point in relation to three mutually perpendicular planes.

Use with Lesson Activity Book pp. 237–238.

Developing Mathematical Language

Vocabulary: axis (plural: axes), coordinates, ordered pair, origin

A point's position on a coordinate plane is specified by an *ordered pair* of numbers, such as (4,6), called the *coordinates* of the point. The first number (4 in this example) indicates the point's distance right or left from a vertical *axis*, often called the *y-axis*. The second number (6) indicates the point's distance up or down from a horizontal *axis*, often called the *x-axis*. The point where the *axes* meet, (0,0), is called the *origin.* Introduce these terms to students as you see fit. At this level, however, there is no reason for you to insist on their correct usage.

Familiarize students with the terms *axis (plural: axes), coordinates, ordered pair,* and *origin.*

Beginning Draw a coordinate plane on the board, and plot and label a point, such as (3,7). Say *axis, coordinates, ordered pair,* and *origin* as you point to each part of the graph, and have students repeat each term with you.

Intermediate Have pairs of students draw a coordinate plane. Help them name and label the *origin* and each *axis* as either *x-axis* or *y-axis.*

Advanced Have students explain how to write the *ordered pair* of a point on a coordinate plane.

Open-Ended Problem Solving

Read the Headline Story to the students. Encourage them to use logical reasoning to investigate street-avenue products.

 Headline Story

> In Karl's town, 1st, 2nd, 3rd, and 4th streets run north-south, and 1st, 2nd, 3rd, and 4th avenues run east-west. What can you say about the products of the street and avenue numbers at the intersections in the town?

Possible responses: There are 16 intersections in the town. The street-avenue products must include all the products that can occur when 1, 2, 3, and 4 are multiplied by 1, 2, 3, and 4. There are nine such products: 1, 2, 3, 4, 6, 8, 9, 12, and 16.

Skills Practice and Review

Changes in Temperature

As you did yesterday, collect Celsius temperature data for today, having the class read and record the temperature at the beginning and end of school. Using your temperature measures from yesterday, have students calculate the day's change in temperature.

Next, sketch a vertical number line on the board to help students visualize increases and decreases in temperature when negative numbers are used. Give a starting temperature, such as 10° Celsius. Say how much the temperature changed (for example, "3 degrees warmer") and ask a student to give the new temperature (13° Celsius). Use numbers that cause the temperature to switch between positive and negative numbers several times. To get students more involved, you could ask one student to give the change in temperature and another to say what the new temperature is.

pairs · 15 MIN

A Exploring a Map

Materials
- For each pair: AM132

NCTM Standards 1, 4, 6, 7, 8, 9, 10

✔ **Ongoing Assessment**

- Do students understand that they cannot move diagonally from one point to another on the map, but must move left, right, up, or down along street lines?

- Do students understand the correspondence between up and north, down and south, right and east, and left and west?

Purpose To practice finding paths between points on a coordinate grid

Introduce Students should work with partners on this activity. Provide a copy of Activity Master: Help Aaron Get to School for each pair. Explain that students will be searching for routes between Aaron's house and the school. Be sure students see that Aaron's house is in the center of the map and that the school is in the upper right corner.

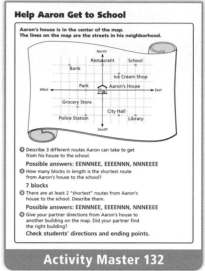

Activity Master 132

Task Direct students to familiarize themselves with the map on the Activity Master, and then to answer the questions on the page. Answers to the questions are given below.

Share Once students have completed the page, have them share the routes they found between Aaron's house and the school. Agree on a way to record the routes on the board. One way would be to abbreviate a walk of one block in a specific direction with the letter for the direction. For example, a walk of 2 blocks east, 3 blocks north, and 2 blocks east would be recorded as EENNNEE.

❶ Describe 3 different routes Aaron can take to get from his house to the school. Possible answers: EENNNEE, EEEENNN, NNNEEEE

❷ How many blocks in length is the shortest route from Aaron's house to the school? 7

❸ There are at least 2 shortest routes. Describe them. Possible answers: EENNNEE, EEEENNN, NNNEEEE

❹ Give your partner directions from Aaron's house to another building on the map. Did your partner find the right building? Check students' directions and ending points.

After discussing the questions on the Activity Master, ask students to describe various routes Aaron might take to walk from his home to the school in exactly 7 blocks. There are many possibilities, but all consist of walking a total of 4 blocks east, not necessarily along a straight line, and 3 blocks north, not necessarily along a straight line. Record these routes, using the same notation as before. You might also sketch each as a series of linked lines. For example, you could sketch the routes NEENNEE and ENENEEN as shown below. Each horizontal line shows a walk of one block east; each vertical line shows a walk of one block north. Students can confirm that no matter how each route zigs and zags, it will always have a total of four horizontal lines (4 blocks east) and three vertical lines (three blocks north).

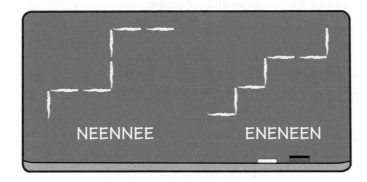

NEENNEE   ENENEEN

Talk Math

❷ Another building on the map is the same distance from Aaron's house as the school is. Which building is it? the bank or library

❷ If Aaron walks 3 blocks west, then 2 blocks south, where will he be? If he had walked 2 blocks west, then 3 blocks south, would he have arrived at the same place? Explain. the grocery store; no; He would have arrived at the police station.

B Naming Locations on the Coordinate Grid

NCTM Standards 1, 4, 6, 7, 8, 9, 10

Purpose To explore ordered pairs

Introduce Draw attention to the list of shortest routes from Aaron's house to the school that the class generated in Activity A.

Problem Ask students to describe what the routes have in common. Use the following questions to facilitate discussion.

 Talk Math

❓ How many total blocks does Aaron walk in each route? 7 blocks

❓ How many blocks does he walk east? He walks 4 blocks east.

❓ How many blocks does he walk north? He walks 3 blocks north.

❓ Does he ever walk west or south? Why not? No. Any route with a move west or south will turn out to be longer than 7 blocks.

To go to school, Aaron needs to go 4 blocks east and 3 blocks north, in any order. Because the order is not important, we could give directions in a more general way, simply specifying the number of blocks in each direction. Once the class has reached this conclusion, tell them that mathematicians write the directions this way: (4,3). This order (rather than (3,4)) is a convention that people have agreed to follow, in much the same way that everyone in the United States agrees to drive on the right side of the road rather than the left. There's no particular reason to do it one way or the other, but it's important that everyone does it the same way. In the case of the coordinate grid, mathematicians have agreed that the horizontal coordinate is written first, the vertical coordinate second. Together, the two numbers are called an ordered pair.

To help students become accustomed to this convention, repeat the process for another location, the bank. The shortest routes from Aaron's house to the bank all take him 4 blocks west and 3 blocks north. Ask students to predict how they think mathematicians would write those directions. If students suggest writing (4,3), point out that those are the directions to the school. To get to the bank, Aaron must walk west instead of east, so the first number of the ordered pair that locates the bank must be ⁻4. The second number, indicating 3 blocks north, must be 3. The ordered pair (⁻4,3) correctly locates the bank. Remind students that the order of the numbers is very important: the first number in the pair always tells how many units to move horizontally. The second number tells how many units to move vertically.

Concept Alert

Students sometimes count incorrectly on a number line or coordinate axis by pointing at their starting place, saying 1, and then counting as they jump over spaces. For example:

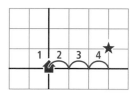

To correct this, suggest that students pretend to be an ant walking along the line. When the ant is at the starting point, how far has it walked? (0 spaces) Not until the ant has walked completely across a space is the distance 1.

Students may also be unclear about the meaning of "the distance between two points." The shortest distance from Aaron's house to the school is 7 as long as only "taxi-cab distances" are allowed—horizontal and vertical travel along streets. In this chapter, all distances between points will be calculated that way. If one allows diagonal "as the crow flies" travel, however, distances will be diminished—to just 5 units in the case of Aaron's house and the school.

Use with Lesson Activity Book pp. 237–238.

Ask students to help you write ordered pairs for other spots on the map, such as the library (3,⁻3) and the grocery store (⁻3,⁻2). Then, have the class describe rules for labeling points on the map using ordered pair notation. Some possible rules include:

- The first number locates the point in relation to east and west. If the number is positive, go east. If it's negative, go west.
- The second number locates the point in relation to north and south. If the number is positive, go north. If it's negative, go south.
- Count the blocks you travel (spaces), not the streets you cross (lines).

Some students may wonder how to specify the directions to Aaron's house. You might remind students that all directions start at Aaron's house on this map. Because Aaron doesn't have to walk in any direction to reach his house, his house is at (0,0).

Talk Math

❓ How would you find the point (⁻2,4)? Possible response: Start at the origin. Move two spaces left and then 4 spaces up.

❓ If you started at (3,3), moved left 5 units and down 4 units, what point would you arrive at? (⁻2,⁻1)

(C) Navigating on a Coordinate Grid LAB pp. 237–238

individuals **20** MIN

Purpose To use ordered pairs to identify location on a map

NCTM Standards 1, 4, 6, 7, 8, 9, 10

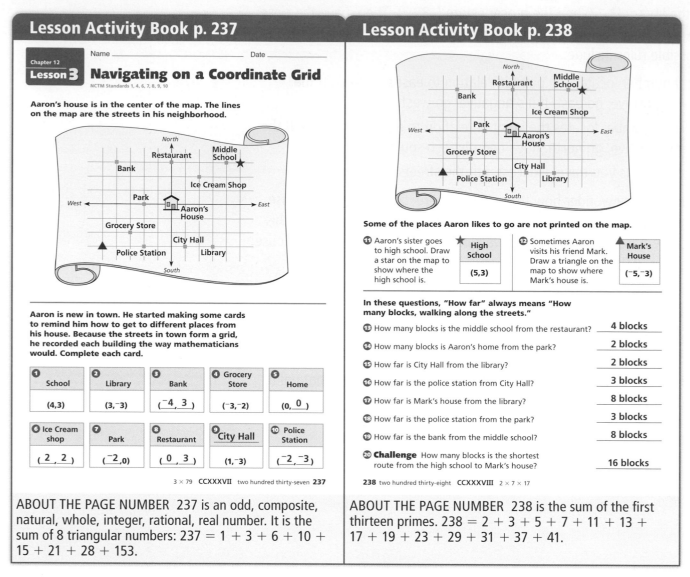

Lesson Activity Book p. 237

Name _____ Date _____

Chapter 12
Lesson 3 **Navigating on a Coordinate Grid**
NCTM Standards 1, 4, 6, 7, 8, 9, 10

Aaron's house is in the center of the map. The lines on the map are the streets in his neighborhood.

Aaron is new in town. He started making some cards to remind him how to get to different places from his house. Because the streets in town form a grid, he recorded each building the way mathematicians would. Complete each card.

❶ School	❷ Library	❸ Bank	❹ Grocery Store	❺ Home
(4,3)	(3,⁻3)	(⁻4, 3)	(⁻3,⁻2)	(0, 0)

❻ Ice Cream shop	❼ Park	❽ Restaurant	❾ City Hall	❿ Police Station
(2 , 2)	(⁻2,0)	(0 , 3)	(1,⁻3)	(⁻2, ⁻3)

3 × 79   CCXXXVII   two hundred thirty-seven **237**

ABOUT THE PAGE NUMBER 237 is an odd, composite, natural, whole, integer, rational, real number. It is the sum of 8 triangular numbers: 237 = 1 + 3 + 6 + 10 + 15 + 21 + 28 + 153.

Lesson Activity Book p. 238

Some of the places Aaron likes to go are not printed on the map.

⓫ Aaron's sister goes to high school. Draw a star on the map to show where the high school is. **High School (5,3)**

⓬ Sometimes Aaron visits his friend Mark. Draw a triangle on the map to show where Mark's house is. **Mark's House (⁻5,⁻3)**

In these questions, "How far" always means "How many blocks, walking along the streets."

⓭ How many blocks is the middle school from the restaurant? **4 blocks**

⓮ How many blocks is Aaron's home from the park? **2 blocks**

⓯ How far is City Hall from the library? **2 blocks**

⓰ How far is the police station from City Hall? **3 blocks**

⓱ How far is Mark's house from the library? **8 blocks**

⓲ How far is the police station from the park? **3 blocks**

⓳ How far is the bank from the middle school? **8 blocks**

⓴ **Challenge** How many blocks is the shortest route from the high school to Mark's house? **16 blocks**

238 two hundred thirty-eight   CCXXXVIII   2 × 7 × 17

ABOUT THE PAGE NUMBER 238 is the sum of the first thirteen primes. 238 = 2 + 3 + 5 + 7 + 11 + 13 + 17 + 19 + 23 + 29 + 31 + 37 + 41.

Teaching Notes for LAB page 237

Have students work on the pages individually or in pairs. Students use ordered pairs to identify locations on the map. For one card, students need to fill in the name of the location, City Hall, instead of the coordinates.

Differentiated Instruction *Above Level* Students who finish early can make worksheets for their classmates. Using Blank Grid pages, they can draw objects at various grid points and write questions asking for directions relative to the house in the center. Some examples of prompts they could write include: What shape is at (⁻3,6)? or, Draw a dog at (5,⁻2).

Teaching Notes for LAB page 238

Students read ordered pairs, mark the corresponding locations, and calculate "taxi-cab distances" between locations on the grid. For all questions but the Challenge, both locations are on the same street.

Challenge Problem In the Challenge problem, the two locations are not on the same street. Students can reason that the distance between the locations is the same as the distance Aaron would travel if he walked from one location to the other.

Reflect and Summarize the Lesson

 Write Math

Is the point (2,5) the same as the point (5,2)? Explain. No; Possible explanation: To reach (2,5), start at the origin, move right 2 units and up 5 units. To reach (5,2), start at the origin, move right 5 units and up 2 units. The location you reach will be different from the point (2,5).

Use with Lesson Activity Book pp. 237–238.

3 | Differentiated Instruction

Leveled Problem Solving

Leo's map shows his home at (0,0), a school at (⁻4,7), and a bank at (3,6). Each number represents the number of blocks.

❶ Basic Level
How many blocks is it from Leo's home to the bank? Explain.
9 blocks; 3 blocks east + 6 blocks north = 9 blocks

❷ On Level
How many blocks is it from Leo's home to the school? Explain.
11 blocks; 4 blocks west + 7 blocks north = 11 blocks

❸ Above Level
How many blocks is it from the school to the bank? Explain.
8 blocks; the bank is 1 block south and 7 blocks east of the school; 1 + 7 = 8.

Intervention	Practice	Extension

Activity Counting Segments

Help students discriminate between counting intersections and counting segments between intersections on a coordinate grid. Show students two points on a grid. Model for them, counting the segments. Stress that you do not count 1 until you reach the end of the first segment past the beginning point. Highlight that move with a marker. Continue moving one segment at a time, highlighting each move. Then count the segments to reinforce the idea.

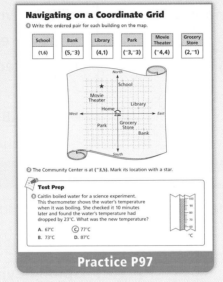

Practice P97

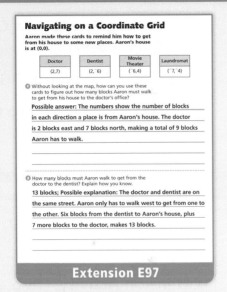

Extension E97

Spiral Review

Spiral Review Book page SR97 provides review of the following previously learned skills and concepts:

- estimating, measuring, and comparing weights in grams and kilograms
- solving problems using the strategy *act it out*

You may wish to have students work with a partner to complete the page.

Spiral Review SR97

Extension Activity How Far?

Have each student write an ordered pair using numbers between ⁻10 and 10. Then have pairs of students determine the number of "blocks" from one point to another. Challenge students to do this without a coordinate grid. Then they can check their work by using a coordinate grid.

Use with Lesson Activity Book pp. 237–238.

Lesson 4 Points and Lines on a Grid

NCTM Standards 1, 4, 6, 7, 8, 9, 10

Lesson Planner

STUDENT OBJECTIVES ·
- To use coordinates to locate points on coordinate grids
- To follow directions to draw pictures on coordinate grids

1 | Daily Activities (TG p. 969)

Open-Ended Problem Solving/Headline Story	**Skills Practice and Review—** Changes in Temperature to Tenths and Hundredths

2 | Teach and Practice (TG pp. 970–974)

Ⓐ **Labeling Points on a Coordinate Grid** (TG pp. 970–971)	**MATERIALS**
Ⓑ **Connecting Points** (TG p. 972)	• TR: Activity Master, AM133
Ⓒ **Points and Lines on a Grid** (TG p. 973)	• transparency of AM133 (optional)
	• straightedge
	• stickers
	• 📖 LAB pp. 239–240
	• 📖 SH p. 195

3 | Differentiated Instruction (TG p. 975)

Leveled Problem Solving (TG p. 975)	**Practice Book P98**
Intervention Activity (TG p. 975)	**Extension Book E98**
Extension Activity (TG p. 975)	**Spiral Review Book SR98**

Lesson Notes

About the Lesson

Students gain more experience with ordered pairs on the coordinate grid by following and giving directions to locate points and to draw pictures. In this and the next lesson, giving and following directions to draw pictures are the context in which students practice working with coordinates, but they are also important organizational skills in themselves.

Use with Lesson Activity Book pp. 239–240.

Developing Mathematical Language

Vocabulary: **endpoint, line, line segment**

A *line* goes on forever. A *line segment* is a part of a *line* with two *endpoints.* If we call the endpoints *A* and *B,* then we refer to the *line segment* in shorthand as $\overline{AB}.$ Outside of mathematics, most people use the word *line* to refer to both a *line* and a *line segment.* Your students will see the term *line segment* on these pages, but unless they find the term confusing, there is no need to call attention to it. Introduce the terms *line segment* and *endpoint* if you find they make class discussions easier.

Familiarize students with the terms *endpoint, line,* and *line segment.*

Beginning Tell students that the word *segment* means "a piece of something". Draw a *line segment* on the board. Discuss with students that a *line segment* is a piece of a *line.*

Intermediate Draw several *line segments* on the board, labeling the *endpoints* of each with different letters. As you point to a *line segment,* ask students to name each *endpoint* of that segment.

Advanced Discuss with students the fact that a *line segment* is a piece of a *line.* Have students draw a *line segment* such that one *endpoint* is *P* and the other *endpoint* is *Q.* Encourage students to make the distinction between a *line* and a *line segment.*

Open-Ended Problem Solving

Read the Headline Story to the students. Encourage them to make interesting statements using information from the story.

 Headline Story

The streets in June's town form a grid. Some of the streets run north-south and the rest run east-west. The shortest route from June's house to school is 6 blocks. What are some of the routes she might follow?

Possible responses: She might walk 3 blocks east and then 3 blocks north. She could walk 1 block west and 5 blocks north. Some possible routes are ENENEN, SSWWWS, EEEESS, and NNWWWW. Her school could be 4 blocks south and 2 blocks east of her house.

Skills Practice and Review

Changes in Temperature to Tenths and Hundredths

Give students practice finding changes in temperature to the nearest tenth of a degree by tracking the (imaginary) course of Jason's cold. The day before he gets sick, his temperature is normal: 37°C. The next day, his temperature is 37.8°C. Write the subtraction problem $37.8 - 37$ on the board and draw a grid representing tenths, to help students figure out the difference between the two temperatures (0.8). The next day, his temperature is 38.2°C. His temperature has risen 0.4 of a degree ($38.2 - 37.8 = 0.4$).

Continue with other temperature changes. Try finding some differences to the hundredths place as well. Students can use graph paper sketches to represent the decimal portions of the numbers. For example:

$25.20 - 25.15 \ 0.05$ $37.37 - 25.15 \ 12.22$
$12.07 - 11.04 \ 1.03$ $13.70 - 12.40 \ 1.30$

whole class

⏱ **10 MIN**

Ⓐ Labeling Points on the Coordinate Grid

Materials

- For the teacher: transparency of AM133 (optional), or graph paper; stickers

NCTM Standards 1, 4, 6, 7, 8, 9, 10

Purpose To use ordered pairs to locate points on a coordinate grid

Introduce Draw a pair of coordinate axes on a large piece of graph paper. Alternatively, draw a grid on the board or use Activity Master: Blank Grid.

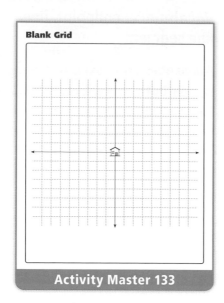

Blank Grid

Activity Master 133

Remind students that the center of the graph, where the two number lines (axes) meet, is where all directions start. If you like, you can call it Aaron's house, as it was labeled in **Lesson 12.3,** or you may choose to use the mathematical name, the *origin.* Write the directions N, S, E, and W on your map. If you prefer, you can introduce the convention of labeling the axes with *x* and *y.* This convention will not be used until **Lesson 12.6.**

The graph should look something like this:

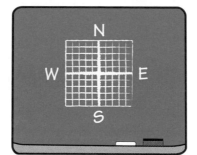

✔ Ongoing Assessment

- Do students use coordinates to locate points? Some students make occasional errors, but others may be consistently counting incorrectly. Have these students explain carefully what they are doing, so you can help them recognize and correct their errors.

Task Place a sticker on the map. Ask students to name the ordered pair of numbers that gives the directions from the center of the graph to the sticker.

Repeat several times, placing the sticker at various locations. Some points you might use include (2,6), (6,2), (⁻4,1), (1,⁻4), (⁻5,⁻3), (0,6), and (⁻6,0). Be sure to choose several pairs like (2,6) and (6,2) which use the same coordinates but in reverse order. This will allow you to call attention to the fact that the order of the numbers in an ordered pair is important; reverse the order and you have directions to an entirely different point.

After students have identified several sticker locations correctly, name an ordered pair and let a volunteer place the sticker at the appropriate grid point. Repeat with several other students. You might need to remind students that the first number tells whether to travel east or west and how many spaces; the second number tells whether to travel north or south and how many spaces. Make sure students are counting the *spaces* they are traveling, not the intersections.

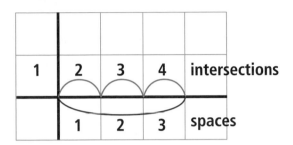

Talk Math

❷ What directions could you give to tell another student how to find the point (⁻2,5)? Possible response: Start at the origin. Go 2 spaces left, then 5 spaces up.

❷ Jodie started at the origin. She moved 4 spaces right and 3 spaces down. She placed a sticker where she stopped. What ordered pair gives the location of the sticker? (4,⁻3)

B Connecting Points

Materials

- For the teacher: grid with stickers from Activity A; straightedge

NCTM Standards 1, 4, 6, 7, 8, 9, 10

Purpose To introduce notation and to practice connecting points on the coordinate grid

Introduce Remove enough stickers from the coordinate grid used in Activity A so that there is room to draw on the grid. Leave at least 10 stickers. Label the stickers alphabetically. Explain that this activity will be conducted silently. Students will have to figure out what to do without receiving directions from you.

Task Write $\overline{AB}$ on the board. **Allow students to determine what they should do.** If they need prompting, silently connect points A and B on the coordinate grid. Give students a moment to see what you drew. Then write the symbol for connecting two other points, such as $\overline{BD}$. Invite a volunteer to come to the board. The volunteer should draw a line connecting points B and D. Continue writing symbols representing lines and asking students to draw the lines.

 Talk Math

- ❷ Tomas drew a line connecting points K and P on a coordinate grid. What symbol could he write to represent the line? $\overline{KP}$ or $\overline{PK}$

- ❷ Briana drew the line segment $\overline{GR}$ on a coordinate grid, then erased it. Kyel then drew the line segment $\overline{RG}$. What can you say about the two line segments? They were the same.

Purpose To practice placing and connecting points on a coordinate grid

NCTM Standards 1, 4, 6, 7, 8, 9, 10

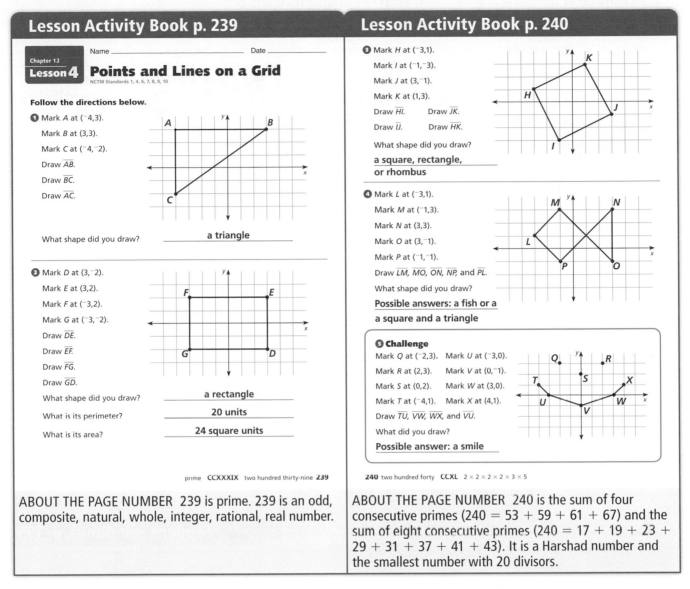

Lesson Activity Book p. 239

Name _____ Date _____

Chapter 12
Lesson 4 **Points and Lines on a Grid**
NCTM Standards 1, 4, 6, 7, 8, 9, 10

Follow the directions below.

❶ Mark A at (⁻4,3).
Mark B at (3,3).
Mark C at (⁻4,⁻2).
Draw $\overline{AB}$.
Draw $\overline{BC}$.
Draw $\overline{AC}$.

What shape did you draw? ___ **a triangle** ___

❷ Mark D at (3,⁻2).
Mark E at (3,2).
Mark F at (⁻3,2).
Mark G at (⁻3,⁻2).
Draw $\overline{DE}$.
Draw $\overline{EF}$.
Draw $\overline{FG}$.
Draw $\overline{GD}$.

What shape did you draw? ___ **a rectangle** ___
What is its perimeter? ___ **20 units** ___
What is its area? ___ **24 square units** ___

prime CCXXXIX two hundred thirty-nine **239**

Lesson Activity Book p. 240

❸ Mark H at (⁻3,1).
Mark I at (⁻1,⁻3).
Mark J at (3,⁻1).
Mark K at (1,3).
Draw $\overline{HI}$.   Draw $\overline{JK}$.
Draw $\overline{IJ}$.   Draw $\overline{HK}$.

What shape did you draw?
a square, rectangle,
or rhombus

❹ Mark L at (⁻3,1).
Mark M at (⁻1,3).
Mark N at (3,3).
Mark O at (3,⁻1).
Mark P at (⁻1,⁻1).
Draw $\overline{LM}$, $\overline{MO}$, $\overline{ON}$, $\overline{NP}$, and $\overline{PL}$.

What shape did you draw?
Possible answers: a fish or a
a square and a triangle

❺ **Challenge**
Mark Q at (⁻2,3).   Mark U at (⁻3,0).
Mark R at (2,3).   Mark V at (0,⁻1).
Mark S at (0,2).   Mark W at (3,0).
Mark T at (⁻4,1).   Mark X at (4,1).
Draw $\overline{TU}$, $\overline{VW}$, $\overline{WX}$, and $\overline{VU}$.

What did you draw?
Possible answer: a smile

240 two hundred forty CCXL $2 \times 2 \times 2 \times 2 \times 3 \times 5$

ABOUT THE PAGE NUMBER 239 is prime. 239 is an odd, composite, natural, whole, integer, rational, real number.

ABOUT THE PAGE NUMBER 240 is the sum of four consecutive primes ($240 = 53 + 59 + 61 + 67$) and the sum of eight consecutive primes ($240 = 17 + 19 + 23 + 29 + 31 + 37 + 41 + 43$). It is a Harshad number and the smallest number with 20 divisors.

Teaching Notes for LAB page 239

Have students work on the page individually or in pairs. Students will need straightedges to complete the problems, which give instructions for placing and connecting points on a coordinate grid. The shapes formed are common polygons.

See Developing Mathematical Language on TG p. 969 for information about the symbols on this page.

Teaching Notes for LAB page 240

The points in Problem 3 are chosen to help you determine if students are moving in the right direction for each number in the ordered pairs. You will also be able to determine if students correctly interpreted the meaning of the negative sign.

Challenge Problem The Challenge Problem gives students practice in finding points that are on the coordinate axes. Moving "zero spaces" is often confusing to students.

Write Math
Tymah drew line segment $\overline{CS}$ on a grid. Then Stefan drew line segment $\overline{SC}$ on the same grid. What can you say about the line segments the students drew? Possible answer: The students drew the same line segment. Each has endpoints C and S.

Review Model . . . .

Refer students to Review Model: Finding and Identifying Points on a Grid in the *Student Handbook,* p. 195 to see how to count spaces on a grid and find a point's distance from an axis.

✔ Check for Understanding

❶ 2 spaces left of the vertical axis, 6 spaces above the horizontal axis

❷ (3,7)

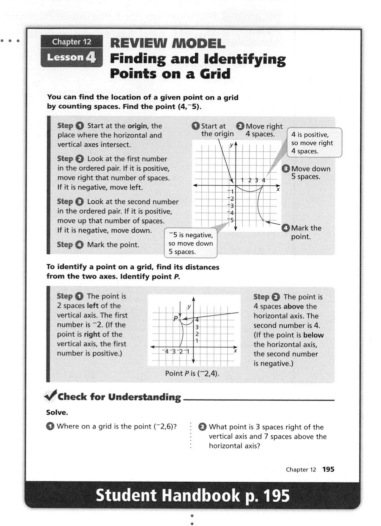

Student Handbook p. 195

Leveled Problem Solving

Celine marks point *A* at (⁻4,1), point *B* at (6,1), and point *C* at (6,⁻4). Then she draws $\overline{AB}$, $\overline{BC}$, and $\overline{AC}$.

❶ Basic Level

What figure does she draw? Explain. triangle; She drew 3 line segments, which are the three sides of a triangle.

❷ On Level

She wants to change the length of $\overline{AB}$ so that it is the same length as $\overline{BC}$. Will she shorten or lengthen $\overline{AB}$? Explain. shorten it; Point *A* is 5 units farther from point *B* than point *C* is.

❸ Above Level

Of points (0,0), (1,1), and (1,⁻6), which is on a side of the triangle? Explain. (1,1); All points one unit above the horizontal axis and from ⁻4 to 6 on the vertical axis are on the triangle.

Intervention

Activity Ordered Pairs

Help students relate the importance of order to everyday activities. Describe several two-part activities in which order is important; for example, cooking dinner and eating it, or putting on socks and shoes. Ask students to tell how they think these examples relate to locating points on the coordinate grid. Summarize by reminding students that the points are called *ordered pairs*. If you change the order, the outcome on the grid changes.

Practice

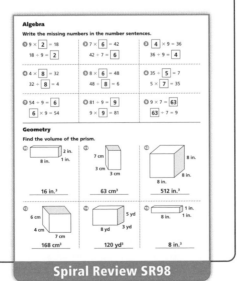

Practice P98

Extension

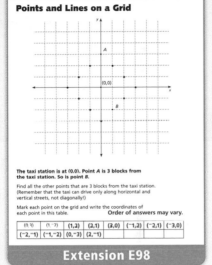

Extension E98

Spiral Review

Spiral Review Book page SR98 provides review of the following previously learned skills and concepts:

- finding missing numbers in related multiplication and division sentences
- finding the volume of rectangular prisms by multiplying the three dimensions together

You may wish to have students work with a partner to complete the page.

Spiral Review SR98

Extension Activity
Aligning Points

Have students work in pairs, and give each student a copy of Activity Master: Blank Grid and a straightedge. Have each partner name an ordered pair and plot both points on the grid. Direct students to use the straightedge to draw a line through the two points. Challenge students to each find a different third point that could be used to create a right triangle with the other two points.

Lesson 5 Drawing Figures on a Coordinate Grid

NCTM Standards 1, 4, 6, 7, 8, 9, 10

Lesson Planner

STUDENT OBJECTIVES ⋯⋯⋯⋯⋯⋯⋯⋯⋯⋯⋯
- To label points on the coordinate grid using coordinates
- To give and follow directions using the coordinate grid

1 Daily Activities (TG p. 977)

Open-Ended Problem Solving/Headline Story	Skills Practice and Review—Adding and Subtracting in Chains

2 Teach and Practice (TG pp. 978–981)

MATERIALS

Ⓐ **Giving Directions** (TG pp. 978–979)

Ⓑ **Playing a Game: *Coordinate Hide-and-Seek*** (TG p. 980)

Ⓒ **Drawing Figures on a Coordinate Grid** (TG p. 981)

- TR: Activity Master, AM134
- straightedge
- small game token
- LAB pp. 241–242
- SH pp. 196, 205

3 Differentiated Instruction (TG p. 982)

Leveled Problem Solving (TG p. 982)	Practice Book P99
Intervention Activity (TG p. 982)	Extension Book E99
Extension Activity (TG p. 982)	Spiral Review Book SR99

Lesson Notes

About the Lesson

Students gain further experience using coordinates to identify points as they draw and connect points on a grid. Having practiced using coordinates to locate points on the grid in Lesson 4, students now focus on recording coordinates of points.

Developing Mathematical Language

Vocabulary: coordinate plane, grid

A *coordinate plane* is made of two number lines, each intersecting the other at zero (the origin). Each number line extends infinitely in both directions. These number lines lie in a plane, which is a flat surface extending in all directions. The *grid* of a *coordinate plane* serves as a guide for locating points or reading a graph.

There are many different ways to refer to a *coordinate plane,* such as coordinate *grid,* quadrant plane, graph, graphing *grid,* and so on. Technically, *graph* usually refers to the representative figure on the grid. *Think Math!* uses the terms *coordinate plane* and coordinate *grid* interchangeably.

Familiarize students with the terms *coordinate plane* and *grid.*

Beginning Draw a *coordinate plane* with a *grid* on the board. Have students point to the *coordinate plane.* Then have them show you where the *grid* is.

Intermediate Have students direct you in drawing on the board a *coordinate plane,* including the axes, origin, and *grid.*

Advanced Have students write one or two sentences explaining how the *grid* of the *coordinate plane* allows you to locate points.

---

1 | Daily Activities

Open-Ended Problem Solving

Read the Headline Story to the students. Encourage them to use logical reasoning to draw conclusions about the line.

 Headline Story

> John drew the points (3,0), (5,0), and (⁻1,0) on a coordinate grid. All the points lay on a line. What line was it? Can you name more points on the line?

Possible responses: The line was the horizontal axis (or the *x*-axis). All points on the line are represented by ordered pairs with zero as the second number. Some other points on the line are (⁻5,0), (0,0), and (2,0).

Skills Practice and Review

Adding and Subtracting in Chains

To help students review addition and subtraction in the context of moving along the number line, do this fast-paced activity with your class when you have ten minutes during the day. Give a starting number. Ask a student to add or subtract some number to or from it. Then ask another student to add or subtract something else to or from the resulting number. For example, you might say, "Start at 5. Add 4. Where are you? 9 Now subtract 8. Where are you? 1 Now add 23. Where are you? 24 Add 6. Where are you? 30" Adjust the additions and subtractions as needed for each student. Use larger numbers and numbers with fractions and decimals as appropriate. You might draw a number line on the board for students to use as a reference.

2 | Teach and Practice

A Giving Directions

Materials

- For each student:
  AM134 (2 copies);
  straightedge

NCTM Standards 1, 4, 6, 7, 8, 9, 10

Differentiated Instruction

Basic Level If some students are challenged by the task of creating a design in Activity A, you might tell them to mark eight points on the grid and then to connect them to form a design. That way, students don't spend a lot of time carefully choosing their points in an effort to make an intricate design. If you feel that certain students could use more guidance than is suggested in the lesson, you might name a few starting points and line segments, and have students add them to their designs.

Purpose To create a grid design and write directions for copying the design

Introduce Each student should have Explore: Can You Copy My Picture? and two copies of Activity Master: Blank Grid. Remind students that they can use an ordered pair to specify a point on a coordinate grid. The first number in the ordered pair gives the point's distance from the vertical axis. The second number gives its distance from the horizontal axis. Remind students, too, that they can use the two endpoints of a line segment to name the segment.

- $(2, ^-3)$ is located 2 spaces to the right of the vertical axis and 3 spaces below the horizontal axis.

- $\overline{MN}$ is a line segment connecting points M and N.

Task Direct students' **attention to the following challenges, which appear on Explore: Can You Copy My Picture?. Students are asked make a design on a blank grid, then to write a set of directions explaining how to copy the design.** Students' directions should list the coordinates and alphabetical labels of all the points to be copied. They should also give directions on how to draw the line segments in the design. For example, students might write something like the following:

- Mark A at (3, 3).
- Mark B at ($^-1$, 2).
- Draw $\overline{AB}$.

For the final step, have each student switch directions with a partner and follow the partner's directions to draw a design on a second blank grid. Students should then compare their designs to the originals, to see if the directions they were given enabled them to reproduce their partners' designs correctly.

Chapter 12 **EXPLORE**
Lesson 5 **Can You Copy My Picture?**

❶ On a blank grid page, make a design with points and line segments, following these rules:

- Points must go on intersections of the grid.
- A line segment must begin at one point and end at another.

- You must use at least 3 points and not more than 8 points in your design.
- You must use at least 3 line segments and not more than 8 line segments in your design.
- Label each point with a different letter.

❷ Write directions explaining how to copy your design onto a blank grid.

- Use ordered pairs such as (2,3) to describe where to draw points.
- Use the letter labels of the points to describe which points to connect.
  $\overline{AB}$

❸ Exchange sets of directions with a partner. Follow your partner's directions to draw a design on a blank grid, while your partner follows yours.

❹ Did you copy your partner's design accurately?
Check student's drawing against their partner's drawing for accuracy.

196   Chapter 12

Student Handbook p. 196

Blank Grid

Activity Master 134

Share Ask one or two students to share their designs with the class by giving you directions while you (or a different student) draw the designs on the board. Choose examples so that at least one of the designs contains some vertical line segments and at least one contains some horizontal line segments.

Once you have a couple of examples, point out some of the horizontal and vertical line segments within the designs. Ask the class if they noticed any patterns in the coordinates of these lines. How could they recognize a horizontal or vertical line segment just from the instructions for drawing it, without seeing the picture? Could they tell how long a horizontal or vertical line segment is if they just had the instructions for drawing it and not the picture?

Some ideas that may come up include:

- Points that are on the same horizontal segment have the same second coordinate.
- The length of a horizontal line segment is the difference between the first coordinates of its two endpoints.
- Points that are on the same vertical segment have the same first coordinates.
- The length of a vertical line segment is the difference between the second coordinates of its two endpoints.

Talk Math

❷ Maggie drew a line segment connecting the two points (3,5) and (9,5) on a coordinate grid. How long was the segment? Explain your reasoning. 6 units or spaces; Possible answer: The second coordinates of the points are the same, so the segment is horizontal. Its length is the difference of its first coordinates: $9 - 3 = 6$.

❷ A vertical line segment 5 units (spaces) in length has as one of its endpoints the point ($^-3$,4). What two points could be its other endpoint? Explain your reasoning. ($^-3$,9) and ($^-3$,$^-1$); Possible explanation: The segment is vertical, so the first coordinates of its endpoints are equal. The point 5 units above ($^-3$,4) is ($^-3$,9). The point 5 units below ($^-3$,4) is ($^-3$,$^-1$).

Ongoing Assessment

- Given an ordered pair of numbers, can students find the point on a coordinate plane that is specified by the ordered pair?
- Given a point on a coordinate plane, can students name the ordered pair that gives the point's location.

B Playing a Game: *Coordinate Hide-and-Seek*

Materials
- For each student:
  AM134; small
  game token

NCTM Standards 1, 4, 6, 7, 8, 9, 10

Teacher Story

"When my students played *Coordinate Hide-and-Seek*, some of them were worried about the possibility of cheating. They suggested that instead of using a token to mark their secret points, they should use stickers, as we did to mark points on the map in **Lesson 12.4.** One student said that if you played the game a lot, or didn't want to use up your stickers, you could simply mark the points on the grid with a pen, and label them *A, B,* and so on. In this way, you could play multiple rounds and not get confused about which point you were using each time."

Purpose To practice using ordered pairs to name and locate points

Goal The goal of the game is, through the use of yes-no questions, to be the first to locate a hidden point on a grid.

Introduce Pair each student with a partner to play the game. Each player should have a copy of Activity Master: Blank Grid and a small game token.

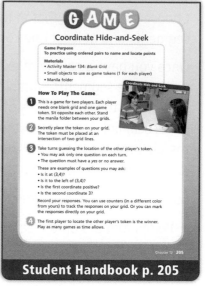

Student Handbook p. 205

How to Play

① Players sit opposite each other, with their copies of the blank grid before them. To prevent each player from seeing the other player's grid, players should place a screen, such as an opened manila folder, between themselves.

② Each player secretly places a token on his or her grid. The token must be placed at an intersection of two grid lines.

③ Players take turns guessing the location of each other's tokens. On each turn, a player may ask only one question, which the other player must answer saying "Yes" or "No." Possible strategies include asking whether a token is at a particular location. For example, "Is it at (3,4)?"; where the token is in relation to other points, "Is it to the right of (3,4)?"; and what are the characteristics of its coordinates, "Is the second coordinate smaller than 2?" or "Is the first coordinate positive?"; "Is the second coordinate 3?".

④ Students may use different colored tokens to mark responses to their questions, or they may write the responses on their grids. If you allow students to write on their grids, they will need new blank grids for each game.

⑤ The first player to locate the other player's token is the winner. Pairs should play the game again as time allows.

Purpose To practice giving directions for drawing given pictures

NCTM Standards 1, 6, 7, 8, 9, 10

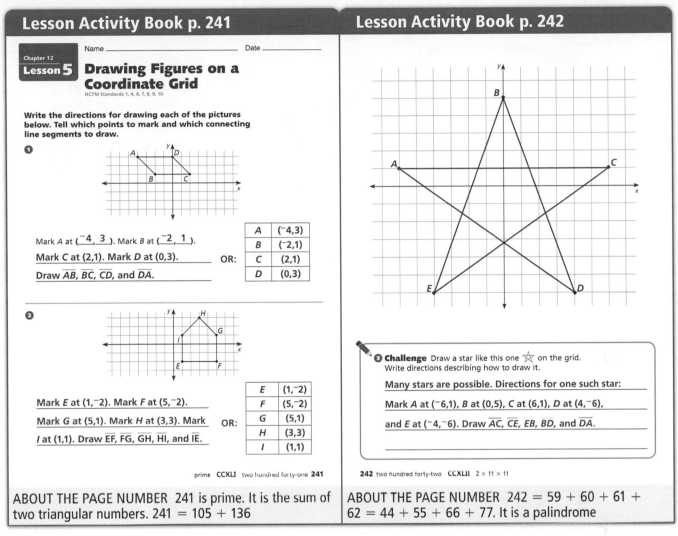

Lesson Activity Book p. 241

Name _____ Date _____

Chapter 12
Lesson 5 **Drawing Figures on a Coordinate Grid**
NCTM Standards 1, 4, 6, 7, 8, 9, 10

Write the directions for drawing each of the pictures below. Tell which points to mark and which connecting line segments to draw.

① Mark A at (⁻4, 3). Mark B at (⁻2, 1).
Mark C at (2,1). Mark D at (0,3).
Draw $\overline{AB}$, $\overline{BC}$, $\overline{CD}$, and $\overline{DA}$.

OR:

A	(⁻4,3)
B	(⁻2,1)
C	(2,1)
D	(0,3)

② Mark E at (1,⁻2). Mark F at (5,⁻2).
Mark G at (5,1). Mark H at (3,3). Mark I at (1,1). Draw $\overline{EF}$, $\overline{FG}$, $\overline{GH}$, $\overline{HI}$, and $\overline{IE}$.

OR:

E	(1,⁻2)
F	(5,⁻2)
G	(5,1)
H	(3,3)
I	(1,1)

prime CCXLI two hundred forty-one **241**

Lesson Activity Book p. 242

❸ **Challenge** Draw a star like this one ☆ on the grid. Write directions describing how to draw it.

Many stars are possible. Directions for one such star:

Mark A at (⁻6,1), B at (0,5), C at (6,1), D at (4,⁻6), and E at (⁻4,⁻6). Draw $\overline{AC}$, $\overline{CE}$, $\overline{EB}$, $\overline{BD}$, and $\overline{DA}$.

242 two hundred forty-two CCXLII 2 × 11 × 11

ABOUT THE PAGE NUMBER 241 is prime. It is the sum of two triangular numbers. 241 = 105 + 136

ABOUT THE PAGE NUMBER 242 = 59 + 60 + 61 + 62 = 44 + 55 + 66 + 77. It is a palindrome

Teaching Notes for LAB page 241

Have students work on the page individually or in pairs. Students write directions to draw given pictures. They should write ordered pairs such as (3,4) to identify points. If they aren't comfortable with the notation for line segments, they may simply write "Connect A and B" instead of "Draw $\overline{AB}$." If they choose the line segment notation, they may vary the order of the points, since $\overline{AB}$ is the same as $\overline{BA}$.

Teaching Notes for LAB page 242

Challenge Problem Students draw a 5-pointed star on the grid. Then they describe how they drew it. Students may draw their versions of the star in different sizes, or orient them differently on the grid. In a symmetrical star, the x-coordinate of the topmost point will be halfway between the x-coordinates of the right and left points, and of the two lower points. The y-coordinates of the right and left points will be the same, and will be halfway between the y-coordinates of the top point and the two lower points. The two lower points will also have the same y-coordinates.

Reflect and Summarize the Lesson

Write Math

Lizmary drew a point at (2,6) and a point at (7,6). She says the points are located on the same horizontal line segment. Is she correct? How do you know? Yes; Possible answer: Two points are on the same horizontal line segment if they have the same second coordinate.

Leveled Problem Solving

Paulo marks point Q at ($^-$4,3), point R at ($^-$4,$^-$5), and point S at (7,$^-$5).

❶ Basic Level

He moves point S left to make Q and S the same distance from R. Where is S now? Explain. (4,$^-$5); Q is 8 units from R, and (4,$^-$5) is also 8 units from R.

❷ On Level

He moves point Q up to make Q and S the same distance from R. Where is Q now? Explain. ($^-$4,6); S is 11 units from R, and ($^-$4,6) is also 11 units from R.

❸ Above Level

Where does Gil place point T to complete a rectangle? Explain. (7,3); S and T should both be 7 units right of (0,0), and Q and T should both be 3 units up from (0,0).

Intervention

Activity Coordinate Lines

In previous lessons, students have moved only horizontally or vertically on a coordinate grid. Reinforce the idea that when drawing lines between ordered pairs, they will only sometimes be horizontal or vertical. Using the strategy of finding a pattern, lead students to see how they can tell when a line between two points will be horizontal (the second coordinates will be the same) or vertical (the first coordinates will be the same).

Practice

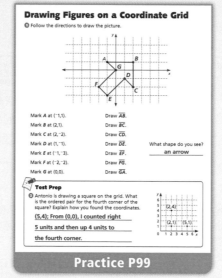

Practice P99

Extension

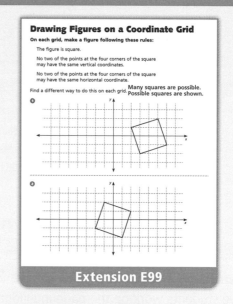

Extension E99

Spiral Review

Spiral Review Book page SR99 provides review of the following previously learned skills and concepts:

- using multiplication to solve word problems
- investigating the possible types of angles in a triangle

You may wish to have students work with a partner to complete the page.

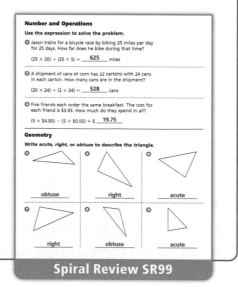

Spiral Review SR99

Extension Activity
Designing Students

Give pairs of students two copies of Activity Master: Blank Grid and a straightedge. Ask students to use the straightedge to draw a figure made of line segments on one grid. On a separate paper, students should list the ordered pair for each corner of the figure. Have students trade their lists of ordered pairs with another pair of students and draw that figure on the other grid. Then let students compare the completed figure with the original figure to correct any errors.

Teacher's Notes 🍎

Daily Notes . . .

Quick Notes

More Ideas

Lesson 6 Moving Shapes on a Coordinate Grid

NCTM Standards 1, 2, 3, 6, 7, 8, 9, 10

Lesson Planner

STUDENT OBJECTIVES
- To investigate translations (slides) and reflections (flips) of figures using a coordinate grid
- To transform a figure by changing the coordinates of all of its points according to a rule

1 | Daily Activities (TG p. 985)

Open-Ended Problem Solving/Headline Story	Skills Practice and Review— Adding and Subtracting in Chains

2 | Teach and Practice (TG pp. 986–991)

MATERIALS

(A) **Translating Figures on the Grid**
(TG pp. 986–987)

(B) **Introducing Reflection on the Grid**
(TG pp. 988–989)

(C) **Moving Figures on a Coordinate Grid**
(TG p. 990)

- TR: Activity Masters, AM135–AM136
- transparency of AM136 (optional)
- 📖 LAB pp. 243–244
- 📖 SH pp. 197–198

3 | Differentiated Instruction (TG p. 992)

Leveled Problem Solving (TG p. 992)	Practice Book P100
Intervention Activity (TG p. 992)	Extension Book E100
Extension Activity (TG p. 992)	Spiral Review Book SR100

Lesson Notes

About the Lesson

Students investigate how the coordinates of a figure's vertices change when the figure is translated or reflected.

About the Mathematics

If a figure is translated, the coordinates of its points change by fixed amounts. A translation may cause some or all of the points in the figure to cross one axis or both, just as adding and subtracting an amount to a point on the number line can cause the point to move past zero. In the example below, adding 7 to

the y-coordinates of the original triangle moves the triangle above the y-axis.

Original	Translation
(2,⁻5)	(2,2)
(5,⁻5)	(5,2)
(5,⁻1)	(5,6)

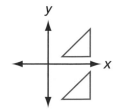

Similarly, reflection changes the coordinates of a figure's points according to a pattern or rule. An example is when the figure is reflected across the

(continued on page R5)

Use with Lesson Activity Book pp. 243–244.

Developing Mathematical Language

Vocabulary: coordinate

If your students are not already familiar with the terminology, tell them that each number in an ordered pair is called a *coordinate.* Try not to focus on this vocabulary, as it is introduced only to make the directions for the activities clearer. Students should understand the term if you use it in context.

Familiarize students with the term *coordinate.*

Beginning Write several ordered pairs on the board. Point to each one and have students identify the *coordinates.*

Intermediate Have a student write a dictated ordered pair on the board. Then have another student locate the point on a coordinate grid. Repeat with other ordered pairs.

Advanced Have each student write an ordered pair on paper. Call on students to tell you their ordered pairs by saying, for example, "The *coordinate* for *x* is 2, and the *coordinate* for *y* is 1."

Open-Ended Problem Solving

Read the Headline Story to the students. Encourage them to think of innovative ways to solve the problem.

 Headline Story

> **Destiny bought three shirts and three pairs of pants. How many different outfits can she make from them?**

Possible responses: I made up colors for each item. Then I wrote down each shirt color and matched it with each pants color. Finally, I counted each combination on my list—blue shirt, black pants; green shirt, black pants; yellow shirt, black pants; blue shirt, tan pants; and so on. There were nine outfits in all. Another way is to show each shirt in one row and each pair of pants in another row. Then connect the pairs and count the connecting lines.

Skills Practice and Review

Adding and Subtracting in Chains

Do this fast-paced activity from **Lesson 12.5** when you have ten minutes during the day. Give a starting number and ask a student to add or subtract some number to or from it. Then ask another student to add or subtract something else to or from the resulting number. For example, you might say, "Start at 5. Add 4. Where are you? 9 Now subtract 8. Where are you? 1 Now add 23. Where are you? 24 Add 6. Where are you? 30" Adjust the additions and subtractions as needed for each student. Use larger numbers and numbers with fractions and decimals as appropriate. You might draw a number line on the board for students to use as a reference.

individuals ⏱ **15 MIN**

Ⓐ Translating Figures on the Grid

Materials

• For each student: AM135

NCTM Standards 1, 2, 3, 6, 7, 8, 9, 10

Purpose To explore the effects of changing the coordinates of a figure on a coordinate grid

Introduce Each student should have a copy of Explore: Changing a Figure's Coordinates and a copy of Activity Master: Figure Changing Rules. Explain that students will start with a triangle, apply a series of rules to change the triangle's coordinates, and record the results.

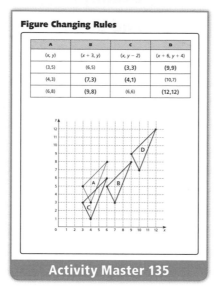

Activity Master 135

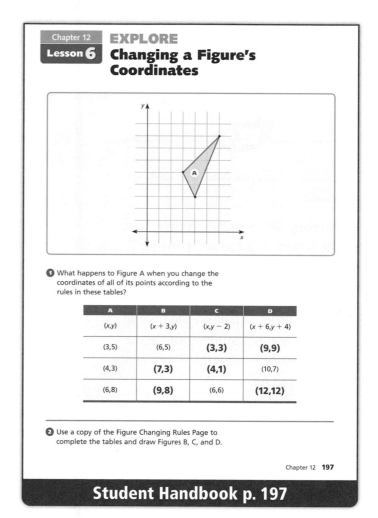

Student Handbook p. 197

✓ Ongoing Assessment

• While students work on the exploration page, take the opportunity to walk around the class and observe how comfortable they are with using coordinates to locate points on the grid.

Task Direct students to work through Explore: Changing a Figure's Coordinates independently. Point out that they will be recording their answers on Activity Master: Figure Changing Rules. Be sure students understand how the "rules" work:

• The rule $(x + 3, y)$ directs students to add 3 to the first coordinate, x, but to do nothing to the second coordinate, y. The coordinates (3,5) in Figure A are changed to (6,5) in Figure B.

• The rule $(x, y - 2)$ directs students to do nothing to the first coordinate, but to subtract 2 from the second coordinate. The coordinates (6,8) in Figure A are changed to (6,6) in Figure C.

• The rule $(x + 6, y + 4)$ directs students to add 6 to the first coordinate and 4 to the second coordinate.

Use with Lesson Activity Book pp. 243–244.

Here are the correct solutions:

Ⓐ	Ⓑ	Ⓒ	Ⓓ
(x, y)	$(x + 3, y)$	$(x, y - 2)$	$(x + 6, y + 4)$
(3,5)	(6,5)	**(3,3)**	**(9,9)**
(4,3)	**(7,3)**	**(4,1)**	(10,7)
(6,8)	**(9,8)**	(6,6)	**(12,12)**

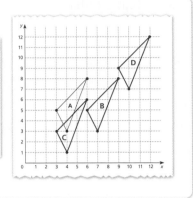

When students draw and connect the new sets of points they generate, they will find that application of each rule causes the triangle to move to a new position on the grid. Recalling their work with geometrical transformations earlier in the year, students should recognize this change as a *translation.*

Share When they have had time to draw and investigate all the shapes, discuss with the class how application of each rule affected Figure A. Students should see that Figure B was generated by sliding Figure A to the right, Figure C by sliding Figure A down, and Figure D by sliding Figure A up and to the right.

💬 Talk Math

❓ How would the point (0,0) be changed by applying the rule $(x + 3, y + 5)$? Explain your reasoning. If I add 3 to the *x*-coordinate, I get 3. If I add 5 to the *y*-coordinate, I get 5. The point would change to (3,5).

❓ After using the rule $(x - 4, y + 6)$ to change the coordinates of a point, Jamie found that the new coordinates were (3,9). What were the coordinates of the original point? Explain your reasoning. (7,3); Possible explanation: To find the first coordinate, I thought: What number minus 4 leaves 3. That number is 7. To find the second coordinate, I thought: What number plus 6 gives 9. That number is 3. So the coordinates of the starting point were (7,3).

" When we discussed the exploration activity, I was surprised at the way some of my students were able to generalize about how the figures moved. One student said that the triangle moved because we moved each of the points the same way; if we'd just changed the coordinates of one of the points, the triangle would stretch. Another student pointed out that when we added a number to the second coordinate of each point, the figure moved up, and when we subtracted a number from that coordinate, it moved down. Since adding to the first coordinate of each point moved the figure to the right, she thought that subtracting from the first coordinate would move the figure to the left. We tried subtracting 3 from the *x* coordinate of each point in the original triangle, and the class was excited to see that the prediction was correct. "

B Introducing Reflection on the Grid

Materials

- For the teacher: transparency of AM136 (optional)

NCTM Standards 1, 3, 6, 7, 8, 9, 10

Purpose To explore the effects of switching the x- and y-coordinates of a figure on a coordinate grid

Introduce Show a transparency of Activity Master: Reflecting a Figure or draw a large grid on the board with an eight-sided figure outlined as it is shown on the Activity Master.

Task Ask the class to predict what would happen to the figure if you switched the x- and y-coordinates of each point. Record the predictions on the board so that students can refer to them later.

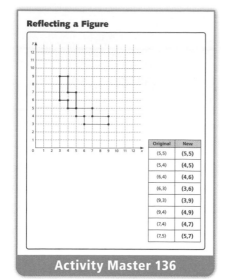

Original	New
(5,5)	(5,5)
(5,4)	(4,5)
(6,4)	(4,6)
(6,3)	(3,6)
(9,3)	(3,9)
(9,4)	(4,9)
(7,4)	(4,7)
(7,5)	(5,7)

Activity Master 136

After students have made their predictions, have volunteers help you fill out the table of new points by switching the x- and y-coordinates of each point in the figure. So, for example, the old point (5,4) becomes (4,5) in the new figure. Graph the new points on the grid and connect them to make the new figure.

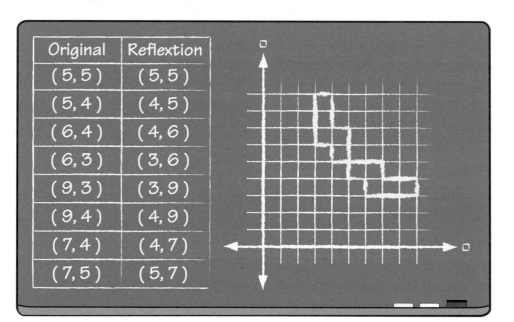

Original	Reflextion
(5,5)	(5,5)
(5,4)	(4,5)
(6,4)	(4,6)
(6,3)	(3,6)
(9,3)	(3,9)
(9,4)	(4,9)
(7,4)	(4,7)
(7,5)	(5,7)

The figure has been reflected across the diagonal line $y = x$. Students may recognize that if you were to place a mirror along the red line in the diagram, the new figure would be the reflection of the original figure.

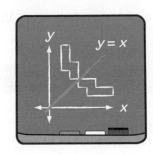

The general rule for how coordinates change in a reflection is more challenging to see and describe than the rule for transformations, and there is no need for your students to try to come up with such a rule. The goal of this activity is to provide another context for students to explore how changes in the coordinates of a point relate to changes in the position of the point on the graph, and to recall their work with transformations from earlier in the year.

 Talk Math

❷ Carlos drew a figure on a coordinate grid. He reversed the x- and y-coordinates of the points in the figure and drew a new figure. Then he reversed the x- and y-coordinates of the points in the new figure and drew a third figure. What can you say about the third figure? It was identical to the first figure.

❷ Matt marked some points on the vertical axis (the y-axis) of a coordinate grid. Then he reversed the x- and y-coordinates of the points and marked the new points on the grid. What can you say about the locations of the new points? They all were on the horizontal axis (the x-axis).

Purpose To explore how figures are changed when the coordinates of their points are changed according to given rules

NCTM Standards 1, 3, 6, 7, 8, 9, 10

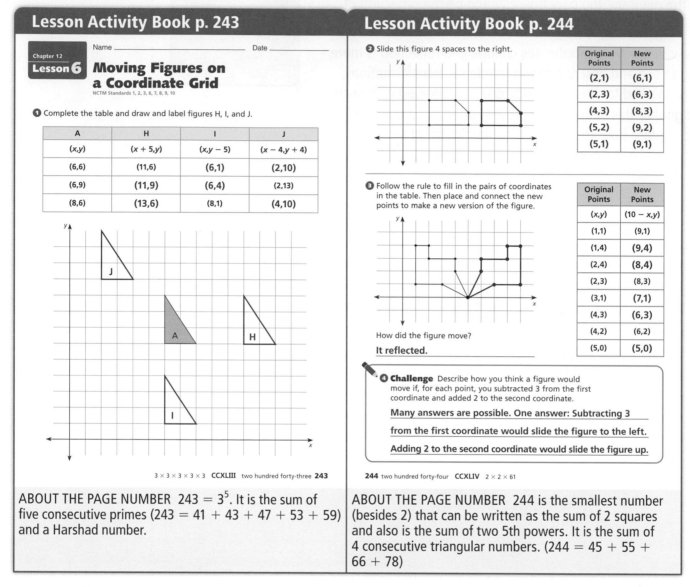

Lesson Activity Book p. 243

Name _____ Date _____

Chapter 12
Lesson 6 **Moving Figures on a Coordinate Grid**
NCTM Standards 1, 2, 3, 6, 7, 8, 9, 10

❶ Complete the table and draw and label figures H, I, and J.

A	H	I	J
(x,y)	$(x + 5,y)$	$(x,y − 5)$	$(x − 4,y + 4)$
(6,6)	(11,6)	(6,1)	(2,10)
(6,9)	(11,9)	(6,4)	(2,13)
(8,6)	(13,6)	(8,1)	(4,10)

$3 \times 3 \times 3 \times 3 \times 3$ CCXLIII two hundred forty-three **243**

Lesson Activity Book p. 244

❷ Slide this figure 4 spaces to the right.

Original Points	New Points
(2,1)	(6,1)
(2,3)	(6,3)
(4,3)	(8,3)
(5,2)	(9,2)
(5,1)	(9,1)

❸ Follow the rule to fill in the pairs of coordinates in the table. Then place and connect the new points to make a new version of the figure.

Original Points	New Points
(x,y)	$(10 − x,y)$
(1,1)	(9,1)
(1,4)	(9,4)
(2,4)	(8,4)
(2,3)	(8,3)
(3,1)	(7,1)
(4,3)	(6,3)
(4,2)	(6,2)
(5,0)	(5,0)

How did the figure move?

It reflected.

🖉 ❹ **Challenge** Describe how you think a figure would move if, for each point, you subtracted 3 from the first coordinate and added 2 to the second coordinate.

Many answers are possible. One answer: Subtracting 3
from the first coordinate would slide the figure to the left.
Adding 2 to the second coordinate would slide the figure up.

244 two hundred forty-four CCXLIV $2 \times 2 \times 61$

ABOUT THE PAGE NUMBER $243 = 3^5$. It is the sum of five consecutive primes ($243 = 41 + 43 + 47 + 53 + 59$) and a Harshad number.

ABOUT THE PAGE NUMBER 244 is the smallest number (besides 2) that can be written as the sum of 2 squares and also is the sum of two 5th powers. It is the sum of 4 consecutive triangular numbers. ($244 = 45 + 55 + 66 + 78$)

Teaching Notes for LAB page 243

Have students complete the page individually or in pairs. Students use the pattern tables and examples to determine how to change the coordinates of Figure A to create figures H, I, and J. Figure H is Figure A translated horizontally. Figure I is Figure A translated vertically. Figure J is Figure A translated both vertically and horizontally.

Teaching Notes for LAB page 244

To slide the first figure 4 spaces to the right, students should add 4 to the first coordinate of each point.

For the second figure, students can use the pattern table to determine that the x-coordinate of each new point is 10 minus the x-coordinate of the original point; or they can note that in the examples, the original x-coordinate and the new one always add up to 10. They will find that changing the coordinates according to either of these rules reflects the figure across the vertical line $x = 5$. Simply recording that the figure is reflected across a vertical line should be considered a correct response.

Challenge Problem The Challenge Problem asks students to describe, without seeing a picture of a figure, the effects of a change in the coordinates of the figure.

Reflect and Summarize the Lesson

Write Math The rule $(x + 2, y - 3)$ was used to change the coordinates of each point in a figure drawn on a coordinate grid. Describe the new figure that was formed. The new figure was congruent to the original figure but moved 2 spaces right and 3 spaces down.

Review Model . . . .

Refer students to Review Model: Translating and Reflecting Figures in the **Student Handbook,** p. 198 to see how to move and reflect figures on a grid.

✔ Check for Understanding

❶ translated

❷ reflected

❸ translated: $(2, ^-2)$; reflected: $(^-5, ^-1)$

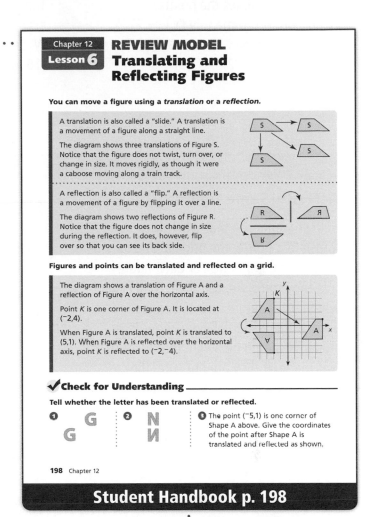

Student Handbook p. 198

Leveled Problem Solving

Helena marks two points on a coordinate grid: (3,5) and (4,1).

❶ Basic Level

Then she slides the points according to the rule $(x, y - 2)$. Where does (3,5) move? Explain. (3,3); $(3, 5 - 2) = (3,3)$

❷ On Level

Then she slides the points according to the rule $(x + 6, y)$. Where does (4,1) move? Explain. (10,1); $(4 + 6, 1) = (10,1)$

❸ Above Level

Then she moves the points according to the rule $(x + 3, y - 1)$. Where are the points? Explain. (6,4) and (7,0); $(3 + 3, 5 - 1) = (6,4)$ and $(4 + 3, 1 - 1) = (7,0)$.

Intervention	Practice	Extension

Activity Same Figures

Help students see that when they translate a figure, the original and its image are congruent. For each figure that they translate, ask them to decide whether the figure and its image look alike. If there is an obvious difference, students should be aware that an error was made. If they are not sure, they can trace the original and compare the tracing to the image. If the tracing does not exactly cover the image, the figures are not congruent.

Practice P100

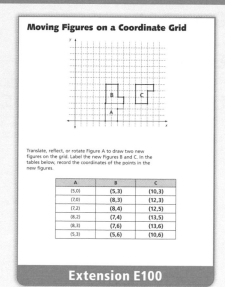

Extension E100

Spiral Review

Spiral Review Book page SR100 provides review of the previously learned skills and concepts:

- understanding that fractions and decimals are different ways of recording the same number
- using the problem solving strategy *make a model*

You may wish to have students work with a partner to complete the page.

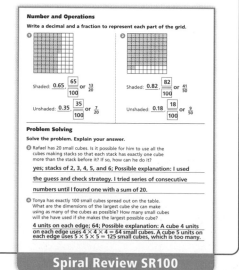

Spiral Review SR100

Extension Activity
Slide Reflections

Let students work in pairs. Give each student a copy of Activity Master: Blank Grid. Have them draw a capital letter on the grid and write an ordered pair for each endpoint of each line segment. Then have them write a rule that slides the letter and a second rule that reflects the moved letter. Students should show the position after each transformation. If time permits, have them first reflect the original letter and then slide the reflected letter.

Use with Lesson Activity Book pp. 243–244.

Teacher's Notes 🍎

Daily Notes . . .

Quick Notes

More Ideas

Lesson 7 Number Sentences and Straight Lines

NCTM Standards 1, 2, 3, 6, 7, 8, 9, 10

Lesson Planner

STUDENT OBJECTIVES
- To graph ordered pairs of numbers that are related by a rule, and to represent these rules with number sentences
- To explore rules that when graphed are straight lines

1 | Daily Activities (TG p. 995)

Open-Ended Problem Solving/Headline Story	Skills Practice and Review— How Many Fives?

2 | Teach and Practice (TG pp. 996–1000)

	MATERIALS
Ⓐ **Graphing Number Sentences** (TG pp. 996–998)	• TR: Activity Masters, AM137–138
Ⓑ **Approximating Temperature** (TG p. 999)	• transparencies of AM137 and AM138 (optional)
Ⓒ **Number Sentences and Straight Lines** (TG p. 1000)	• straightedge
	• 📖 LAB pp. 245–246
	• 📖 SH p. 199

3 | Differentiated Instruction (TG p. 1001)

Leveled Problem Solving (TG p. 1001)	Practice Book P101
Intervention Activity (TG p. 1001)	Extension Book E101
Extension Activity (TG p. 1001)	Spiral Review Book SR101
Science Connection (TG p. 942)	

Lesson Notes

About the Lesson

Students explore graphs of straight lines on a coordinate grid, and the number sentences that generate the lines. As students investigate how the patterns of an input-output rule become visual patterns on the grid, they are introduced to ideas that will be important when they study algebra in later years.

About the Mathematics

In the exploration activity of this lesson, students graph three input-output rules. All sorts of other rules can be graphed. A few are shown on the continuation page, to give you a sense of the wide variety.

(continued on page R6)

Use with Lesson Activity Book pp. 245–246.

Developing Mathematical Language

Vocabulary: function

A *function* is a rule for two values, such as x and y, so that there is just one y-value for every x-value. Any equation in the form $y = mx + b$ (where m and b are any integers, one or both of which can be 0) is a *function*. Your students will not need to identify which equations represent a *function* and which do not until they take a formal class in algebra. For now, your students need only to recognize a *function* as a rule represented in a graph, in an input-output table, in a set of ordered pairs, or in an equation.

Familiarize students with the term *function.*

Beginning Relate the idea of *function* to input-output tables. Show an input-output table for x and $x + 1$. Then write the equation $y = x + 1$, and explain that both are ways to represent the same *function.*

Intermediate Write the word *function* on the board. Invite individual students to name a representation of a *function* as you list them on the board. Possible list: table, graph, equation, set of ordered pairs

Advanced Tell students that a *function* describes a relationship between two quantities. Relate the idea of *function* to input-output tables. Have students write a sentence or short paragraph describing what they know about a *function.*

Open-Ended Problem Solving

Read the Headline Story to the students. Encourage them to make interesting statements using information from the story.

 Headline Story

> The temperature in Laura's town was below 0°C today and ten degrees colder than Capital City, where her aunt lives. Capital City's temperature was above 0°C. What can you say about the temperature in Laura's town?

Possible responses: The temperature in Laura's town has to be less than 0°C. That means it's a negative number. But it can't be lower than ⁻10°C, because that would mean that the temperature in her aunt's town wasn't above 0°C after all. If the temperature where her aunt lives is 5°C, the temperature where Laura lives is ⁻5°C.

Skills Practice and Review

How Many Fives?

Write or say a number, and ask a student to estimate how many fives there are in the number. Start with examples that are multiples of 10, then progress to multiples of 50 and multiples of 100. You might write the numbers of fives in these numbers on the board, and encourage students to use this information to estimate the numbers of fives in larger numbers. For example, to estimate the numbers of fives in 2003, students might reason that 2003 is close to 2000, which is twenty hundreds, so there should be about twenty times more fives in 2003 than in 100, which makes $20 \times 20 = 400$. Encourage students to avoid exact calculations. Optionally, have students use calculators to check the estimates.

2 | Teach and Practice

or pairs   20 MIN

A Graphing Number Sentences

Materials
- For the teacher: transparency of AM137 (optional)
- For each student: AM137

NCTM Standards 1, 2, 3, 6, 7, 8, 9, 10

Purpose To explore the relationship between number sentences and their graphs

Introduce Students should work independently or with partners. Each student should have a copy of Explore: Graphing Number Sentences and Activity Master: Graphing on a Coordinate Grid. Explain that students will be exploring three number sentences: $y = x + 4$, $y = x + 3$, and $y = x + 1$. Each sentence is a "rule." This means that the sentence $y = x + 4$ is shorthand for the rule "To find the number y, add 4 to the number x."

Task Direct students to complete the activity described on Explore: Graphing Number Sentences.

For each number sentence, many ordered pairs (x,y) are possible. Here are six such for each sentence:

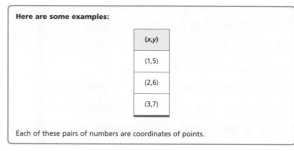

✓ Ongoing Assessment
- Do students understand that pairs of numbers which make the number sentences true are the ordered pairs they are to graph on the coordinate grid? For example, since $x = 2$ and $y = 6$ make the number sentence $y = x + 4$ true, students can graph (2,6) as one of the ordered pairs for the graph of $y = x + 4$.

Student Handbook p. 199

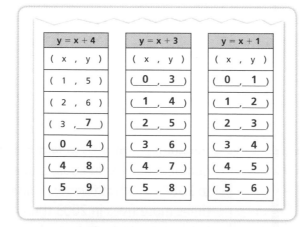

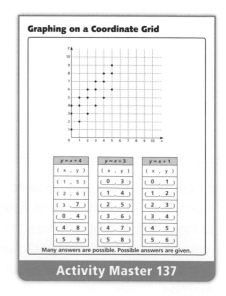

Students should find that when they graph these three sets of ordered pairs on a coordinate grid, they obtain three parallel lines.

Use with Lesson Activity Book pp. 245–246.

Share Once students have had a chance to work through the page, ask the class what they noticed about the sets of points they graphed. What patterns did they see in the tables of coordinate pairs? What patterns did they see on the grid when they graphed the points?

Students will probably notice that for each number sentence, the points seem to lie on a straight line. Use a transparency of the Blank Grid from **Lesson 12.5** or sketch a coordinate grid on the board. Plot several points from each set. Then connect the points to show that they do lie on a line.

Some other things students may notice:

- There are patterns in the coordinates, such as the fact that in each set of points, every time x increases by 1, y also increases by 1. Encourage students to think about how patterns in the numbers correspond to patterns on the graph. For example, if you start at any point on a line and move up and right the same distance, you will always end up on the line.

- The three lines are parallel. You might ask students whether the same point might ever be on two of the lines, and to explain their reasoning. No; if a point were on two lines, the lines would cross at that point. But that would be impossible, because the lines are parallel. Furthermore, no x and y pair can make two different sentences true. Reason: How could there be a number such that you can add 1 or 4 to it and get the same total?

- There are many points that lie on each line. In fact, you can come up with as many examples as you like and will never run out. Encourage students to think about why that is true. You can always think of a bigger number for x or y than the ones you have already used. You can also use fractions or decimals to name points between ones already on the graph.

- The three number sentences look similar; the only difference is the number added to x. Encourage students to think about how the line changes as the number added to x changes. The line looks "higher" as the number added to x gets larger.

During the exploration, students graphed points both of whose coordinates were positive. As a result, the line segments they drew were above the *x*-axis and to the right of the *y*-axis. On the overhead, use a straightedge to extend one of these lines downward and to the left.

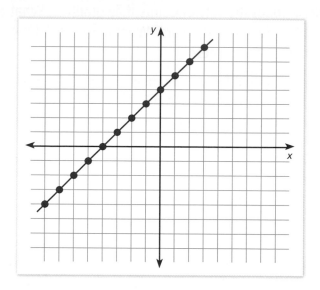

Ask students to name some of the points on this part of the line. For example, the line $y = x + 4$ shown above will pass through, among others, (⁻1,3), (⁻2,2), (⁻3,1), (⁻4,0), and (⁻5,⁻1). Students may try to use the number sentence to generate new points, but, more likely, they will find them visually, either by looking at the line or by counting over and down, following the pattern of the points that have already been identified. It is not important for students to relate these new points back to the number sentence, but they can see that the line can be extended in both directions, following the rule for generating the coordinates of points on the line.

Talk Math

❷ On the line $y = x + 4$, list two points that fall between (1,5) and (2,6). Many answers are possible. Two such answers are: (1.5,5.5) and ($1\frac{3}{4}$,$5\frac{3}{4}$).

❷ What are two points on the graph of the number sentence $y = x + 6$? Many answers are possible. Two such answers are (1,7) and (2,8).

❷ The point (4,6) is on the graph of a certain number sentence. What might the sentence be? Many answers are possible. One answer is $y = x + 2$.

Use with Lesson Activity Book pp. 245–246.

Purpose To use a graph to estimate Fahrenheit and Celsius temperature conversions

Introduce Ask the class to name some of the rules they know for converting between measurement units (for example, 12 inches = 1 foot or 16 ounces = 1 pound). Remind them that they know about two different systems of measurement, metric and U.S. customary. There are rules for converting between the systems—for example, translating inches into centimeters—but these usually involve less convenient numbers than those used for conversions *within* a system. One example is temperature: to convert between Fahrenheit and Celsius is complicated. But we can estimate the conversion easily, using a graph.

Task Ask volunteers to remind the class of the temperature at which water freezes, on the Celsius and Fahrenheit scales (0°C and 32°F); and the temperature at which it boils on both scales (100°C and 212°F).

Hand out copies of Activity Master: Graphing Celsius and Fahrenheit Temperatures. Have students plot the points (0,32), and (100,212). Also, use normal room temperature of 20°C and 68°F to plot a third pair of temperatures, (20,68). Since the axes are marked in jumps of 10, students will have to approximate some of the positions.

Use a straightedge to connect the points with a straight line. Extend the line to the edges of the graph. Point out that the conversion rule for temperature, like the rules students worked with in Activity A, produces a straight line when the equivalent temperatures are graphed.

Pick a temperature in Celsius and ask a student to use the graph to estimate the corresponding Fahrenheit temperature. (Most likely, the Fahrenheit temperature will not be a multiple of 10, so students will need to pick an approximate value, based on how close the point is to the nearest label on the vertical axis.) Record the two temperatures in the table. Repeat for several more examples, sometimes giving the Celsius temperature and sometimes giving the Fahrenheit temperature. Make sure the class realizes that the values they are generating are approximations: when a point falls between axis labels, it's hard to see exactly what number it's on. To calculate the exact number, you must apply the precise conversion rule.

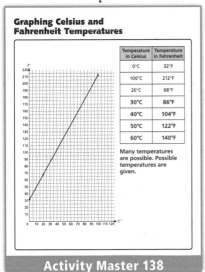

Graphing Celsius and Fahrenheit Temperatures

Temperature in Celsius	Temperature in Fahrenheit
0°C	32°F
100°C	212°F
20°C	68°F
30°C	86°F
40°C	104°F
50°C	122°F
60°C	140°F

Many temperatures are possible. Possible temperatures are given.

Activity Master 138

Materials
- For the teacher: transparency of AM138 (optional)
- For the students: AM138

NCTM Standards 1, 2, 3, 6, 7, 8, 9, 10

Talk Math

❷ How you would use the temperature graph to find the Celsius temperature equivalent to 45°F? Possible description: I would find 45 on the vertical axis. I would move right from that point until I came to the graph. From the point where I intersected the graph, I would move straight down to the horizontal axis. The number where I intersected the horizontal axis would be the Celsius temperature.

❷ Stacey said that the Fahrenheit temperature is always 32° more than the Celsius temperature. Was she right? Explain. No; Possible explanation: Stacey's rule works for 0°C (32°F = 0°C + 32°) but not for other temperatures (212°F ≠ 100°C + 32°).

C Number Sentences and Straight Lines LAB pp. 245–246

individuals or pairs **20 MIN**

Purpose To practice finding and graphing number pairs that make number sentences true

NCTM Standards 1, 2, 3, 6, 7, 8, 9, 10

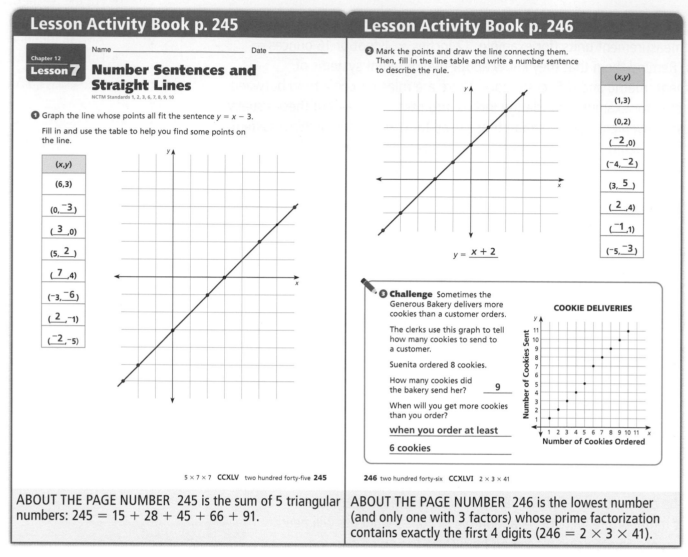

Lesson Activity Book p. 245

Name _____ Date _____

Chapter 12
Lesson 7 **Number Sentences and Straight Lines**

NCTM Standards 1, 2, 3, 6, 7, 8, 9, 10

❶ Graph the line whose points all fit the sentence $y = x - 3$.

Fill in and use the table to help you find some points on the line.

(x,y)
(6,3)
(0,⁻3)
(3,0)
(5,2)
(7,4)
(⁻3,⁻6)
(2,⁻1)
(⁻2,⁻5)

5 × 7 × 7 **CCXLV** two hundred forty-five **245**

Lesson Activity Book p. 246

❷ Mark the points and draw the line connecting them. Then, fill in the line table and write a number sentence to describe the rule.

(x,y)
(1,3)
(0,2)
(⁻2,0)
(⁻4,⁻2)
(3,5)
(2,4)
(⁻1,1)
(⁻5,⁻3)

$y = x + 2$

❸ **Challenge** Sometimes the Generous Bakery delivers more cookies than a customer orders.

The clerks use this graph to tell how many cookies to send to a customer.

Suenita ordered 8 cookies.

How many cookies did the bakery send her? **9**

When will you get more cookies than you order?

when you order at least 6 cookies

COOKIE DELIVERIES

246 two hundred forty-six **CCXLVI** 2 × 3 × 41

ABOUT THE PAGE NUMBER 245 is the sum of 5 triangular numbers: 245 = 15 + 28 + 45 + 66 + 91.

ABOUT THE PAGE NUMBER 246 is the lowest number (and only one with 3 factors) whose prime factorization contains exactly the first 4 digits (246 = 2 × 3 × 41).

Teaching Notes for LAB page 245

Have students work on the page individually or with partners. Students find pairs of numbers that make the sentence $y = x - 3$ true. Then they graph the corresponding points, forming a line.

This number sentence involves subtraction of a constant, rather than addition. Nevertheless, students will find that, like the earlier example, $y = x - 3$ produces a line when they graph coordinate pairs.

Teaching Notes for LAB page 246

Challenge Problem Students read a graph to answer questions. Two different rules are graphed. When a customer orders one to five cookies, the rule is $y = x$. When a customer orders six or more cookies, the rule is $y = x + 1$. Students can solve the problem without thinking about the rules. The sets of points they describe do lie on a line. However, since the problem is about buying cookies, it doesn't make sense to talk about non-whole numbers. Similarly, it doesn't make sense to talk about buying zero cookies or a negative number of cookies.

Students can answer the first question by figuring out the rule, or by reading the graph to determine the vertical coordinate of the point whose horizontal coordinate is 8.

Reflect and Summarize the Lesson

Write Math **Does the ordered pair (5,1) make the number sentence $y = x - 5$ true? Explain.** No; Possible explanation: When I use the ordered pairs in the number sentence, I get 1 = 5 − 5, which is 1 = 0. This is not true.

3 | Differentiated Instruction

Leveled Problem Solving

Marci is graphing the number sentence $y = x + 5$.

❶ Basic Level

What is the value of y when $x = 0$? Explain. 5; for $y = x + 5$, $5 = (0) + 5 = 5$.

❷ On Level

What is the value of y when $x = 4$? Explain. 9; for $y = x + 5$, $9 = (4) + 5 = 9$.

❸ Above Level

What is the value of y when $x = {}^-8$? Explain. $^-3$; for $y = x + 5$, $^-3 = (^-8) + 5 = {}^-3$.

Intervention	Practice	Extension

Intervention

Activity Finding a Pattern

Display a coordinate grid. Ask students to name a point where the x-coordinate is one less than the y-coordinate, such as (1,2) or (5,6). Have students name several similar points and then describe what they see. The points form a line. Draw a line through the points, and help students develop the equation $y = x + 1$ for the line. Then have them look for other points on the line to verify that they fit the pattern.

Practice

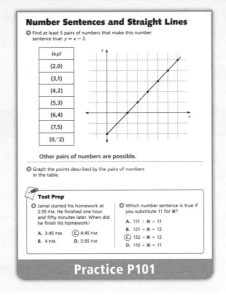

Practice P101

Extension

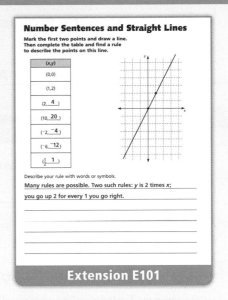

Extension E101

Spiral Review

Spiral Review Book page SR101 provides review of the following previously learned skills and concepts:

- using minutes or days as the common unit of measurement for computations involving various units of time
- graphing and analyzing survey data

You may wish to have students work with a partner to complete the page.

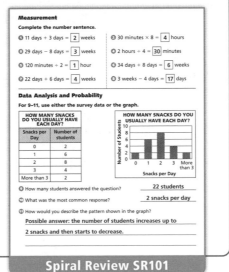

Spiral Review SR101

Extension Activity
Intersections

Give each student a copy of Activity Master: Blank Grid. Have students write and graph a number sentence in the form $y = x \pm b$. They should write values for y when $x = 0, 1, 2, 3, 4$, and 5, and write the number sentence near the graph. Then have students work in pairs, and have each partner graph the other's number sentence to find whether the graphs intersect. Suggest that students extend their lines until they are certain. Display the graphs so students can compare.

Lesson 8 Problem Solving Strategy and Test Prep

NCTM Standards 1, 2, 6, 7, 8, 9, 10

Lesson Planner

STUDENT OBJECTIVES
- To practice the problem solving strategy *draw a picture*
- To articulate the steps and strategies used to solve problems
- To prepare for standardized tests

Problem Solving Strategy:
Draw a Picture (TG pp. 1003–1007)

MATERIALS

Ⓐ **Discussing the Problem Solving Strategy: Draw a Picture** (TG p. 1003)

Ⓑ **Solving Problems by Applying the Strategy** (TG p. 1004)

- transparency of LAB p. 247 (optional)
- 📖 LAB pp. 247–248
- 📖 SH pp. 200–201

Problem Solving Test Prep (TG p. 1005)

Ⓒ **Getting Ready for Standardized Tests** (TG p. 1005)

- 📖 LAB p. 248

Lesson Notes

About Problem Solving

Problem Solving Strategy: Draw a Picture

This lesson gives you an opportunity to assess your students' understanding of negative numbers and of locating points on a coordinate grid, which they have been working on throughout this chapter. The problem solving page encourages students to use the strategy *draw a picture* to help them model addition and subtraction when the answers can be either positive or negative.

Skills Practice and Review

How Many Fives?

Repeat this Skills Practice activity from **Lesson 12.7**. Write or say a number, and ask a student to estimate how many fives there are in the number. Start with examples that are multiples of 10, then progress to multiples of 50 and 100. You might write the numbers of fives in these numbers on the board, and encourage students to use this information to estimate the numbers of fives in larger numbers. Encourage students to avoid exact calculations. Optionally, have students use calculators to check their estimations.

Use with Lesson Activity Book pp. 247–248.

Problem Solving Strategy

(A) **Discussing the Problem Solving Strategy: Draw a Picture**

   🕐 **15 MIN**

NCTM Standards 1, 2, 6, 7, 8, 9, 10

Purpose To share strategies for solving problems and focus on the problem solving strategy *draw a picture.*

Introduce Remind students that throughout this chapter they have been using the strategy *draw a picture* to solve problems. They have drawn maps to find how far it was from one location to another, translated shapes on a coordinate grid, found the relationship between a number sentence and its graph, identified negative numbers on a number line, and explored changes in temperature on thermometers.

Introduce the following problem:

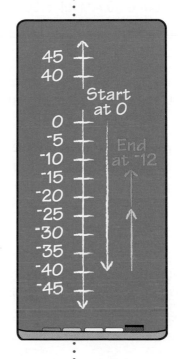

Problem **A scuba diver descended 39 feet below sea level. He then swam ahead 16 feet and ascended 15 feet. After swimming ahead another 20 feet he ascended 12 feet. At what depth is he now?** 12 feet below sea level

Share Ask students to share their strategies for solving the problem. *Draw a picture* is a good strategy to try, because it allows you to "see" the scuba diver and his different depths. Send several students to the chalkboard to show how they would solve the problem.

 Talk Math

❓ What information do we have? We know how far the scuba diver descended and ascended and how far the diver moved forward.

❓ What do we need to find? We need to know what depth the diver is at now.

❓ Is there any information you will not use in order to solve the problem? Yes. Explain. Possible explanation: In order to find the depth of the scuba diver, we will not need to know the distance the diver swam ahead. We need to use only the ascending and descending distances.

❓ How is the scuba diver's motion of descending and ascending similar to movement on a number line? Possible answer: When the scuba diver descends, it is like moving backward or down on a number line. When the scuba diver ascends, it is like moving forward or up on a number line.

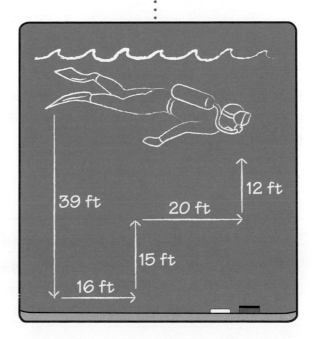

Use with Lesson Activity Book pp. 247–248.

Chapter 12 • Lesson 8 **1003**

Solving Problems by Applying the Strategy LAB p. 247

Purpose To share strategies for solving problems and focus on the problem solving strategy *draw a picture*

Teaching Notes for LAB page 247

Students practice the problem solving strategy *draw a picture* by solving the problems independently or in pairs. Help students get started by asking questions such as the following:

Read to Understand

What do you know? information about the temperature every three hours from 6:00 A.M. till 6:00 P.M.

What do you need to find out? the temperature at 6:00 P.M.

Plan

How can you solve this problem? Think about the strategies you might use.

How might you use a picture to solve the problem? You could draw a thermometer. This would allow you to track temperature changes throughout the day, jumping upward or downward with each change, landing on the new temperature.

Solve

How can you figure out the temperature after each change? If the temperature gets warmer, that's addition; move upward on the thermometer. If the temperature gets colder, that's subtraction; move downward.

Check

Look back at the original problem. Did you answer the question that was asked? Does your answer make sense? How do you know?

Students can use this method to solve other problems on the page. Supplement these questions with ones that are specifically tailored to the individual problems.

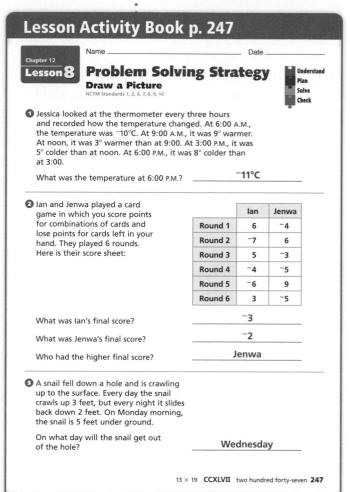

Lesson Activity Book p. 247

Name _____ Date _____

Chapter 12
Lesson 8 **Problem Solving Strategy**
Draw a Picture
NCTM Standards 1, 2, 6, 7, 8, 9, 10

Understand
Plan
Solve
Check

❶ Jessica looked at the thermometer every three hours and recorded how the temperature changed. At 6:00 A.M., the temperature was ⁻10°C. At 9:00 A.M., it was 9° warmer. At noon, it was 3° warmer than at 9:00. At 3:00 P.M., it was 5° colder than at noon. At 6:00 P.M., it was 8° colder than at 3:00.

What was the temperature at 6:00 P.M.? ___ ⁻11°C ___

❷ Ian and Jenwa played a card game in which you score points for combinations of cards and lose points for cards left in your hand. They played 6 rounds. Here is their score sheet:

	Ian	Jenwa
Round 1	6	⁻4
Round 2	⁻7	6
Round 3	5	⁻3
Round 4	⁻4	⁻5
Round 5	⁻6	9
Round 6	3	⁻5

What was Ian's final score? ___ ⁻3 ___

What was Jenwa's final score? ___ ⁻2 ___

Who had the higher final score? ___ Jenwa ___

❸ A snail fell down a hole and is crawling up to the surface. Every day the snail crawls up 3 feet, but every night it slides back down 2 feet. On Monday morning, the snail is 5 feet under ground.

On what day will the snail get out of the hole? ___ Wednesday ___

13 × 19 **CCXLVII** two hundred forty-seven **247**

ABOUT THE PAGE NUMBER 247 has digits that add to its smallest prime factor ($247 = 13 \times 19$ and $2 + 4 + 7 = 13$).

Reflect and Summarize the Lesson

Write Math **When might the strategy *draw a picture* be a good one to try to solve a problem?** Possible answer: when *thinking* about how to solve the problem isn't enough, and you'd like to *see* what's going on

Use with Lesson Activity Book pp. 247–248.

Problem Solving Test Prep

(C) Getting Ready for Standardized Tests LAB p. 248

individuals **20 MIN**

Purpose To prepare students for standardized tests

NCTM Standards 1, 2, 6, 7, 8, 9, 10

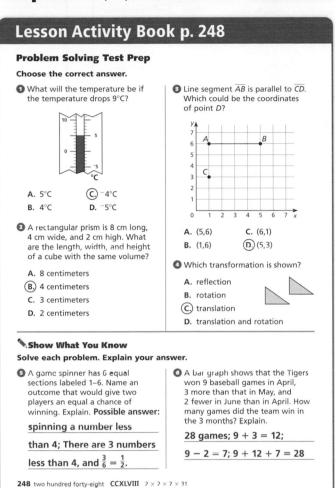

Lesson Activity Book p. 248

Problem Solving Test Prep

Choose the correct answer.

❶ What will the temperature be if the temperature drops 9°C?

A. 5°C   (C.) −4°C
B. 4°C   D. −5°C

❷ A rectangular prism is 8 cm long, 4 cm wide, and 2 cm high. What are the length, width, and height of a cube with the same volume?

A. 8 centimeters
(B.) 4 centimeters
C. 3 centimeters
D. 2 centimeters

❸ Line segment $\overline{AB}$ is parallel to $\overline{CD}$. Which could be the coordinates of point D?

A. (5,6)   C. (6,1)
B. (1,6)   (D.) (5,3)

❹ Which transformation is shown?

A. reflection
B. rotation
(C.) translation
D. translation and rotation

Show What You Know

Solve each problem. Explain your answer.

❺ A game spinner has 6 equal sections labeled 1–6. Name an outcome that would give two players an equal chance of winning. Explain. **Possible answer:** spinning a number less than 4; There are 3 numbers less than 4, and $\frac{3}{6} = \frac{1}{2}$.

❻ A bar graph shows that the Tigers won 9 baseball games in April, 3 more than that in May, and 2 fewer in June than in April. How many games did the team win in the 3 months? Explain.

28 games; 9 + 3 = 12;
9 − 2 = 7; 9 + 12 + 7 = 28

248 two hundred forty-eight CCXLVIII 2 × 2 × 2 × 31

ABOUT THE PAGE NUMBER 248 is the sum of 6 triangular numbers: 248 = 3 + 15 + 28 + 45 + 66 + 91

Teaching Notes for LAB page 248

The test items on this page are written in the same style and arranged in the same format as those on many state assessments. The page is cumulative and is designed for students to apply a variety of problem solving strategies, including *draw a picture.* Students might share the strategies they use.

The Item Analysis Chart below highlights one of the possible strategies that may be used for each item.

Show What You Know

Direct students' attention to Problems 5 and 6. For Problem 5, remind students that players have equal chances of winning when the probabilities that they will achieve the outcomes they want are equal. For Problem 6, explain that students will need to find the number of wins in May and June. Then have them write explanations of how they know their answers are correct. To provide more space for students to communicate their thinking about these problems, you may wish to have them write their responses and explanations on a separate sheet of paper. Use the Scoring Rubric below to evaluate their understanding.

Item Analysis Chart

Item	Strategy
1	Draw a picture
2	Make a model, act it out
3	Draw a picture
4	Draw a picture
5	Draw a picture, act it out
6	Make a graph, guess and check

Scoring Rubric

2	• Demonstrates complete understanding of the problem and chooses an appropriate strategy to determine the solution
1	• Demonstrates a partial understanding of the problem and chooses a strategy that does not lead to a complete and accurate solution
0	• Demonstrates little understanding of the problem and shows little evidence of using any strategy to determine a solution

Review Model

Refer students to Review Model: Problem Solving Strategy: Draw a Picture to review a model of the four steps they can use with the problem solving strategy *draw a picture.*

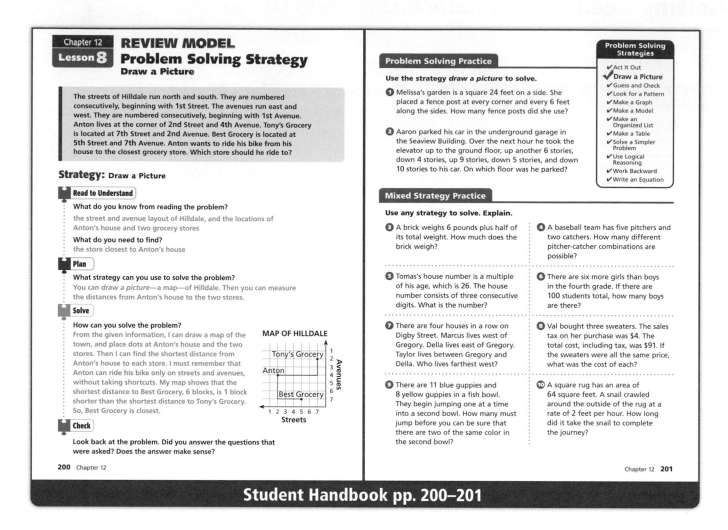

Student Handbook pp. 200–201

Task Have students read the problem at the top of the Review Model page.

Talk Math

❷ What do you know from reading the problem? Hilldale's streets run north-and-south. Its avenues run east-and-west. Both are numbered consecutively, beginning with 1. I also know the locations of Anton's house and two grocery stores.

❷ What do you need to find out? the store closest to Anton's house

❷ What strategy can you use to solve the problem? You can *draw a picture*–a map of Hilldale.

❷ How can a map of Hilldale help you to solve the problem? Possible answer: It allows you to see the locations of Anton's house and the stores, and to measure the distances between them.

❷ Why can you draw straight lines between Anton's house and each store? Anton can ride his bike only on streets and avenues.

❷ How far is the shortest distance from Anton's house to Tony's Grocery? to Best Grocery? 7 blocks; 6 blocks

❷ Which store is closest to Anton's house? Best Grocery, by 7 − 6 = 1 block.

1 16 posts; Possible explanation: You can *draw a picture* of the garden and then count the posts.

2 ⁻4, or 4 stories below the ground floor; Possible explanation: You can *draw a picture* showing the floors of the skyscraper above and below ground, and then trace Aaron's elevator rides up and down.

3 12 pounds; Possible explanation: You can *guess and check* to solve the problem. When you guess 12 pounds, you will find that the guess checks: a 12-pound brick weighs 6 pounds plus 6 pounds (half of the total weight of 12 pounds).

4 10; Possible explanation: You can *make an organized list.* If the pitchers are P1, P2, P3, P4, and P5, and the catchers are C1 and C2, the possible combinations are P1C1, P1C2, P2C1, P2C2, P3C1, P3C2, P4C1, P4C2, P5C1, and P5C2.

5 234; Possible explanation: You can *make a table* to solve the problem. In your table, list multiples of 26 (26,52,78,…) until you find one that consists of three consecutive numbers.

6 47 boys; Possible explanation: You can *guess and check* to solve the problem. Try pairs of numbers that have a sum of 100 and that differ by 6.

7 Marcus; Possible explanation: You can *draw a picture* to solve the problem. Using M, G, D, and T to represent Marcus, Gregory, Della, and Taylor, only the arrangement below, with Marcus farthest west, works:

M G T D

8 $29; Possible explanation: *Work backward* to solve: cost of one sweater = total price minus sales tax divided by 3 = ($91 − $4) ÷ 3 = $87 ÷ 3 = $29.

9 three; Possible explanation: *Use logical reasoning* to solve. If the first two jumpers have different colors, then one will be blue and one will be yellow. The third jumper must be blue or yellow, so it will match one of the first two.

10 16 hours; Possible explanation: *Use logical reasoning* to solve. The rug must measure 8 feet-by-8 feet. Its perimeter is 4 × 8 feet = 32 feet. At 2 feet per hour, the snail will need 32 ÷ 2 = 16 hours to make the journey.

Extending the Number Line

NCTM Standards 1, 2, 3, 4, 6, 7, 8, 9, 10

Purpose To provide students with an opportunity to demonstrate understanding of Chapter 12 concepts and skills

Chapter 12 Learning Goals and Assessment Options

These learning goals are assessed in many ways throughout the chapter. The chart below correlates each learning goal to specific formal and informal assessment options.

	Learning Goals	Lesson Number	Snapshot Assessment	Chapter Review Item Numbers	Chapter Test Item Numbers
				LAB pp. 249–250	Assessment Guide pp. AG109–AG110
12-A	Measure and calculate Celsius temperature changes	12.1	1, 5, 7	1–4	1–4
12-B	Add and subtract to locate positive and negative numbers on a number line	12.2	2, 6, 8	5–8	5–8
12-C	Plot and identify points and lines on a coordinate grid	12.3–12.7	3, 4, 9	9–13	9–14
12-D	Apply problem solving strategies such as *draw a picture* to solve problems	12.8	10	14	15

📷 Snapshot Assessment

whole class 10 MIN

The following Mental Math and Quick Write questions and tasks provide a quick, informal assessment of students' understanding of Chapter 12 concepts, skills, and problem solving strategies.

Mental Math This oral assessment uses mental math strategies and can be used with the whole class.

❶ The temperature is 13° Celsius at noon. Tell the temperature change (increase or decrease) when it is reported freezing at 5 P.M. Decreases (down) 13°
  - At midnight, the temperature is ⁻8° Celsius. What has happened to the temperature since noon? Dropped (decreases, goes down) 21°
  - The thermometer said 4° Celsius the next day at noon. What happened to the temperature since midnight? It increased (went up, rises) 12°.
  (Learning Goal 12-A)

❷ You are located at 5 on a number line. You make a forward move of 6. Where are you? 11
  - You are at 3 on a number line. You make a backward move of 6. Where are you? ⁻3
  - You are at ⁻5 on a number line. You move backward 4. Where are you? ⁻9
  - You are at ⁻5 on the number line. You move forward 6. Where are you? 1
  (Learning Goal 12-B)

❸ You have a coordinate grid, and start at the point of origin, or (0,0). Which direction will you travel:

- if the first coordinate is positive? Right
- if the second coordinate is negative? Down
- if the first coordinate is negative? Left

(Learning Goal 12-C)

❹ You have a coordinate grid, and start at the point of origin, or (0,0). Which direction will you travel:

- if both coordinates are negative? Left, then down
- if both coordinates are zero? You don't travel

(Learning Goal 12-C)

Quick Write This informal written assessment can be administered to small groups or the whole class. Read each question and have the students record responses on their write-on boards. Encourage students to listen and think about the questions before responding.

❺ It was 23°C one day, and the next day the temperature was 18°C. What was the temperature change? 5°; Temperature fell (went down, decreased)

- It was 5°C and the temperature fell 8°. What is the temperature now? ⁻3°C
- The thermometer said ⁻4°C, and the temperature rose 10°. What is the temperature now? 6°C
- The temperature is 17°C, and went up 9° in four hours. What is the temperature now? 26°C
- At midnight the thermometer said ⁻5° Celsius. At noon the thermometer said 4° Celsius. What happened to the temperature since midnight? It increased (went up) 9°.

(Learning Goal 12-A)

❻ Sonya starts at 2 on a number line and move 4 spaces forward, then 6 spaces backward. Where does she end? 0

- Sam starts at 7 on a number line, moves 3 spaces forward, and moves again ending at 1. Describe his last move. He moved backward 9.
- Tony starts at ⁻6 on the number line and moves forward 3 times. Each move forward is 3. Where does he end up? 3
- Sally starts at ⁻2 on the number line. She jumps forward 5 spaces, then jumps backward 6 spaces. Where does she end up? ⁻3

(Learning Goal 12-B)

❼ What is the difference between the temperatures?

- 29°C and 18°C 11°C
- ⁻8°C and 4°C 12°C
- ⁻20°C and ⁻5°C 15°C

(Learning Goal 12-A)

❽ What is the ending number?

- Start at ⁻7 on a number line. Move forward 14 numbers, then back 3 numbers. What is the ending number? 4
- Start at 5 on a number line. Move backwards 6 numbers. What is the ending number? ⁻1

(Learning Goal 12-B)

❾ On a coordinate grid:

- How do you find the point (⁻3,4)? Start at the point of origin, move 3 spaces left, then 4 spaces up.
- If you are located at (2,⁻5) and move 3 units right and 2 units up, where are you? (5,⁻3)
- If you start at (4,0) and move 5 units left and 3 units up, where are you? (⁻1,3)
- You begin at the (0,0) point of origin. You move 5 units left, and 6 units up. Name the ordered pair where you are now located. (⁻5,6)

(Learning Goal 12-C)

❿ Natalie really wants to go ice skating on the pond in her backyard. She knows water freezes at 0°C, so she keeps track of the thermometer readings as the temperature drops. At 10 A.M., the temperature is 5°C, and drops 10° by 8 P.M. What is the temperature 12 hours later when the temperature rises 2°? Use pictures, numbers, or words to explain your answer. ⁻3° Possible explanation: at 8 PM, the temperature falls to ⁻5°C, and 12 hours later the temperature rises to ⁻3°C.

(Learning Goal 12-D)

Chapter 12 ASSESSMENT

Formal Assessment

Chapter Review/Assessment The Chapter 12 Review/Assessment on *Lesson Activity Book* pages 249–250 assesses students' understanding of computation in puzzles, tables and problem solving. Students should be able to complete these pages independently.

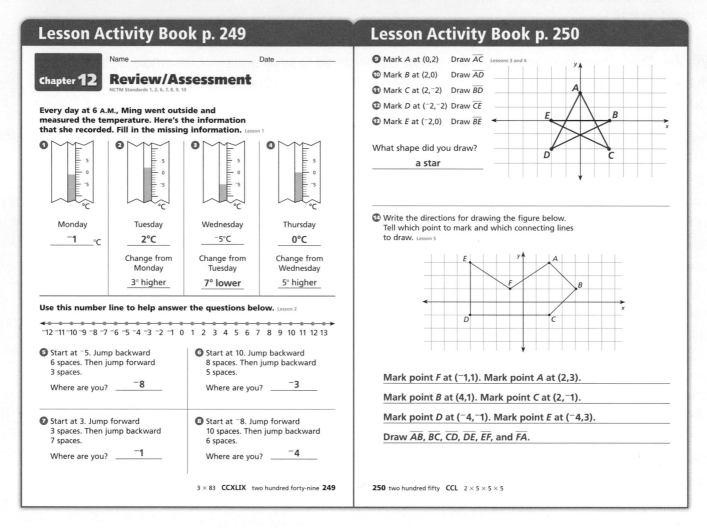

Extra Support Students who have difficulty with items on the Chapter 12 Review/Assessment may need review of the lesson where development of the concept was provided. You can use the Intervention Activity to increase students' understanding before the Chapter Test is given.

Chapter Test Use the Chapter 12 Test in the *Assessment Guide* to assess concepts, skills, and problem solving from the chapter and to prepare students for standardized tests. The Chapter Test and other test items are also available online.

Chapter Notes

Quick Notes

More Ideas

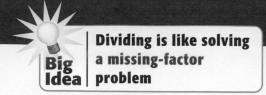

Big Idea Dividing is like solving a missing-factor problem

Division

About the Chapter

In this chapter, students return to work with multiplication and division concepts. They use their knowledge of multiplication to reason about division, solidifying their understanding of the inverse relationship between multiplication and division.

Multiplication and Division "Undo" Each Other Students continue to explore this inverse relationship by working with missing factor problems. When they rewrite missing factor problems as division problems, they see that they have actually been dividing all along.

Building Up to a Missing Factor At the beginning of the year, students explored the fact that they could decompose and recompose *groups* in order to make multiplication easier, partitioning arrays into smaller, more manageable problems, and then putting them back together. This chapter returns to this idea as students begin to solve division problems using an area model. For example, to divide 153 by 9, students break 153 into the sum of 90 and 63 and divide each part by 9.

	10	7
9	90	63

They use this same idea when building up to a missing factor using a vertical division record which mirrors many of the steps of a standard division algorithm.

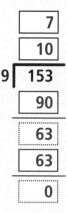

In Grade 5, students will review this work and build on it to formally develop a standard division algorithm.

Developing Concepts Across the Grades

Topic	Prior Learning	Learning in Chapter 13	Later Learning
Multiplication	• Multiply 2-digit by 1-digit numbers **Grade 3, Chapter 12**	• Find missing factors in multiplication sentences • Practice multiplication **Lessons 13.1–13.5**	• Use multiplication to check division **Grade 5, Chapter 8**
Division	• Model division problems using an area model • Connect division to multiplication **Grade 3, Chapter 12**	• Review the relationship between multiplication and division by writing fact families • Translate between division problems and missing-factor multiplication • Solve division problems **Lessons 13.1–13.6**	• Use division to solve problems • Given a context, decide whether to ignore remainders, add remainders to the quotient as fractions or decimals, or round the quotient up **Grade 5, Chapter 8**
Estimation	• Estimate to approximate quotients **Grade 3, Chapter 12**	• Use rounding and compatible numbers to estimate missing factors and quotients **Lessons 13.4–13.5**	• Use rounding and compatible numbers to estimate solutions to multiplication and division problems **Grade 5, Chapter 8**

Chapter Planner

Lesson	Objectives	NCTM Standards	Vocabulary	Materials/Resources
CHAPTER 13 World Almanac For Kids • Vocabulary • Games • Challenge Teacher Guide pp. 1019A–1019F, **Student Handbook** pp. 208–209, 218–222				
1 **Finding Missing Dimensions** PACING 1 DAY **Teacher Guide** pp. 1020–1027 **Lesson Activity Book** pp. 251–252 **Student Handbook** Student Letter p. 207 Explore p. 210	• To find missing factors in multiplication sentences in the context of area • To review the relationship between multiplication and division by writing fact families	1, 2, 4, 6, 7, 8, 9, 10	fact family	**For the students:** ■ School-Home Connection, pp. SHC49–SHC52 ■ square tiles ■ graph paper ■ P102, E102, SR102
2 **Finding Missing Factors** PACING 1 DAY **Teacher Guide** pp. 1028–1035 **Lesson Activity Book** pp. 253–254 **Student Handbook** Explore p. 211	• To practice multiplication and division • To find missing factors in multiplication sentences	1, 2, 4, 6, 7, 8, 9, 10	factor multiplication	**For the teacher:** ■ transparency of LAB pp. 253–254 (optional) **For the students:** ■ P103, E103, SR103 **Literature Connection:** **Arithmetricks: 50 Easy Ways to Add, Subtract, Multiply, and Divide Without a Calculator** Teacher Guide p. 1018
3 **Finding Missing Factors More Efficiently** PACING 1 DAY **Teacher Guide** pp. 1036–1043 **Lesson Activity Book** pp. 255–256 **Student Handbook** Game p. 220	• To practice finding missing factors in multiplication sentences • To use estimation and compatible numbers to find the greatest number that can be multiplied by a given factor to approximate a product	1, 2, 6, 7, 8, 9, 10	estimate	**For the teacher:** ■ transparencies of AM139–AM142 (optional) **For the students:** ■ TR: AM139–AM142 ■ P104, E104, SR104
4 **Estimating Missing Factors and Quotients** PACING 1 DAY **Teacher Guide** pp. 1044–1051 **Lesson Activity Book** pp. 257–258 **Student Handbook** Review Model p. 212	• To relate multiplication and division number families by rewriting them as missing-number sentences • To use rounding and compatible numbers to estimate missing factors and quotients • To build up missing factors using multiples of 10 and 1	1, 2, 6, 7, 8, 9, 10	compatible numbers round	**For the students:** ■ P105, E105, SR105

NCTM Standards 2000
1. Number and Operations
2. Algebra
3. Geometry
4. Measurement
5. Data Analysis and Probability
6. Problem Solving
7. Reasoning and Proof
8. Communication
9. Connections
10. Representation

Key
AG: Assessment Guide
E: Extension Book
LAB: Lesson Activity Book
P: Practice Book
SH: Student Handbook
SR: Spiral Review Book
TG: Teacher Guide
TR: Teacher Resource Book

MATH GLOSSARY in **Student Handbook** p. 259

Planner (continued) ➤

Chapter Planner *(continued)*

Lesson	Objectives	NCTM Standards	Vocabulary	Materials/ Resources
5 **Dividing Using Multiplication Puzzles** PACING **1** DAY **Teacher Guide** pp. 1052–1059 **Lesson Activity Book** pp. 259–260 **Student Handbook** Explore p. 213 Review Model p. 214	• To translate between division problems and missing-factor multiplication • To solve division problems using multiplication strategies	1, 2, 6, 7, 8, 9, 10	**dividend** **divisor** **factor** **product** **quotient**	**For the teacher:** ■ transparency of AM143 (optional) **For the students:** ■ square tiles (optional) ■ P106, E106, SR106 **Art Connection:** **The Golden Rectangle** **Teacher Guide** p. 1018
6 **Completing Division Sentences** PACING **1** DAY **Teacher Guide** pp. 1060–1065 **Lesson Activity Book** pp. 261–262 **Student Handbook** Explore p. 215 Game p. 221	• To practice solving division problems • To use rounding and compatible numbers to estimate quotients	1, 2, 6, 7, 8, 9, 10	**multiple**	**For the teacher:** ■ transparency of AM144–AM145 (optional) **For the students:** ■ TR: AM144–AM145 ■ P107, E107, SR107 **Science Connection:** **Half-Life** **Teacher Guide** p. 1018
7 **Problem Solving Strategy and Test Prep** PACING **1** DAY **Teacher Guide** pp. 1066–1071 **Lesson Activity Book** pp. 263–264 **Student Handbook** Review Model pp. 216–217	• To practice the problem solving strategy *work backward* • To articulate the steps and strategies used to solve problems • To prepare for standardized tests	1, 2, 4, 6, 7, 8, 9, 10		

CHAPTER 13 Assessment
TG pp. 1072–1075, **LAB** pp. 265–266, **AG** pp. AG113–AG116

For the students:
■ Chapter 13 Test pp. AG113–AG114

Games

Use the following games for skills practice and reinforcement of concepts.

Lesson 13.3 ▶

Greatest Factors provides an opportunity for students to practice strategies for finding missing factors in number sentences.

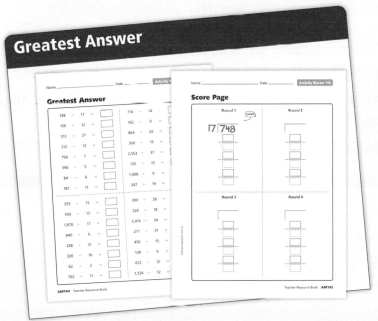

◀ **Lesson 13.6** *Greatest Answer* provides an opportunity for students to practice estimating quotients.

Planning Ahead

In **Lesson 13.3**, students will use scratch paper and pencils to play *Greatest Factors*. Be sure each pair of students have the three Activity Masters 139–142 (Missing Factors).

In **Lesson 13.6**, students will play the *Greatest Answer*. Each student pair will need a copy of the Activity Master 144 (Greatest Answer) and Activity Master 145 (Score Page).

Developing Problem Solvers

Open-Ended Problem Solving

The Headline Story in the Daily Activities section of every lesson provides an open-ended problem for students to complete. For each story, there are many possible responses.

Headline Stories can be found on TG pages 1021, 1029, 1037, 1045, 1053, and 1061.

Leveled Problem Solving

Leveled Problem Solving provides an opportunity for students to apply learning from the lesson to a real-life situation. Problems are leveled by ability to allow students of all ability levels to become successful problem solvers. Each Leveled Problem Solving begins with a real-life scenario upon which three problems are built.

The levels of problems are:

1 Basic Level	**2 On Level**	**3 Above Level**
students needing extra support	students working at grade level	students who are ready for more challenging problems

Leveled Problem Solving can be found on TG pages 1026, 1034, 1042, 1050, 1059, and 1065.

 **FOR KIDS**

The World Almanac for Kids feature is designed to stimulate student interest in the math concepts they are about to learn. Students use data to solve problems and explain solutions. The Chapter 13 Project can be found on SH pages 208–209.

Write Math **Reflect and Summarize the Lesson** poses a problem or question for students to think and write about. This feature can be found on TG pages 1026, 1033, 1041, 1049, 1058, 1064, and 1068.

Other opportunities to write about math can be found on LAB pages 258, 260, and 262.

Problem Solving Strategies

The focus of **Lesson 13.7** is the strategy *work backward*. However, students will use a variety of problem solving strategies as they work through the chapter. The chart below shows strategies that may be useful in completing each lesson.

Strategy	Lesson(s)	Description
Draw a Picture	13.1, 13.5	Draw a picture to find the combined length of two rectangles or two rectangular items, such as quilts.
Guess and Check	13.2, 13.3, 13.4, 13.5, 13.6	Guess and check to find missing factors in missing-factor puzzles.
Look for a Pattern	13.6	Look for a pattern to estimate which of several division problems has the largest quotient.
Solve a Simpler Problem	13.5, 13.6	Solve a simpler problem to build up a quotient in small, efficient steps.
Use Logical Reasoning	13.3, 13.4, 13.5, 13.6	Use logical reasoning to choose the greatest possible factor from a list of possible factors.
✓ Work Backward	13.1, 13.5	Work backward to find missing numbers in fact families.

Meeting the Needs of All Learners

Differentiated Instruction

Extra Support	Activities for All	Enrichment
Intervention Activities TG pp. 1027, 1034, 1042, 1050, 1059, 1065	**Practice Book** pp. 102–107	**Extension Activities** TG pp. 1027, 1034, 1042, 1050, 1059, 1065
	Spiral Review Book pp. 102–107	**Extension Book** pp. E102–E107
	LAB Challenge LAB pp. 252, 254, 256, 258, 260, 262	**LAB Challenge** LAB pp. 252, 254, 256, 258, 260, 262
Lesson Notes **Basic Level** TG p. 1026	**Lesson Notes** **On Level** TG p. 1054	**Lesson Notes** **Above Level** TG p. 1039
Leveled Problem Solving **Basic Level** TG pp. 1027, 1034, 1042, 1050, 1059, 1065	**Leveled Problem Solving** **On Level** TG pp. 1027, 1034, 1042, 1050, 1059, 1065	**Leveled Problem Solving** **Above Level** TG pp. 1027, 1034, 1042, 1050, 1059, 1065

English Language Learners

Suggestions for addressing the needs of students learning English as a second language are included in the Developing Mathematical Language section at the beginning of most lessons.

ELL activities for this chapter can be found on TG pages 1021, 1029, 1037, 1045, 1053, and 1061.

The Multi-Age Classroom

Grade 3	• Students on this level should be able to complete the lessons in Chapter 13 but might need some additional practice with key concepts and skills. • Give students more practice with multiplication.	See Grade 4, Intervention Activities, Lessons 13.1–13.6. See Grade 3, Lessons 9.1–9.6, 12.4–12.6.
Grade 4	• Students on this level should be able to complete the lessons in Chapter 13 with minimal adjustments.	See Grade 4, Practice pages P102–P107.
Grade 5	• Students on this level should be able to complete the lessons in Chapter 13 and to extend division concepts and skills. • Give students extended division work.	See Grade 4, Extension pages E102–E107. See Grade 5, Lessons 8.1–8.7.

Chapter 13 Division

Cross Curricular Connections

Science Connection

Math Concept: division

Half-Life

- Ask the students how they think the age of a fossil is determined and discuss the idea of a half-life. Half-life is the time it takes half of the radioactive atoms in a fossil to break down into something else. For example, carbon-14 has a half-life of 5,730 years.

- Share this example with students: There were originally 40 grams of carbon in a fossil. After 5,730 years there would be 20 grams. How many grams of carbon would remain after another 5,730 years? 10 grams When scientists knows how much carbon-14 is in a fossil, they can work backward to determine the age of the fossil.

- Ask students to determine the number of grams left over in each situation:

  ❶ There are 128 grams of carbon-10. The half-life is about 20 seconds. How many grams are left after 1 minute? about 16 grams

  ❷ There are 128 grams of nitrogen-17. The half-life is about 4 seconds. How many grams are left after 24 seconds? about 2 grams

Lesson 13.6

Art Connection

Math Concept: relate multiplication and division

The Golden Rectangle

- Explain that some artists believe that a "golden rectangle"—a rectangle with a length a little more than 1.6 times its width—has the most beautiful shape for a rectangle.

- Have students measure and cut out rectangles measuring 16 inches by 10 inches. Ask if the figures are golden rectangles. They are, approximately. Ask students to write the multiplication and division fact family for the length, width, and area of each rectangle. $16 \times 10 = 160$, $10 \times 16 = 160$, $160 \div 10 = 16$, $160 \div 16 = 10$

- Have students cut 10-inch squares from the ends of their rectangles. Ask if the figures that remain are golden rectangles. They are, approximately. Students can continue to cut squares from the ends of their rectangles to find that the figures that remain are approximately golden rectangles.

Lesson 13.5

Literature Connection

Math Concept: division

Arithmetricks: 50 Easy Ways to Add, Subtract, Multiply, and Divide Without a Calculator
By Edward H. Julius

Students will learn mental math tips to help them perform calculations quickly and easily. There are 10 math "tricks" dedicated to understanding division.

Lesson 13.2

School-Home Connection

A reproducible copy of the School-Home Connection letter in English and Spanish can be found in the *Teacher Resource Book* page SHC49–SHC52.

Encourage students to play *Missing Factor Game,* found in the *Teacher Resource Book* on page SHC50, with family members. Students will use missing factors in **Lessons 13.1, 13.2,** and **13.3.**

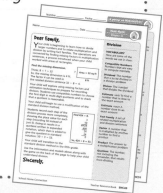

Assessment Options

There are many opportunities in *Think Math!* to assess students' understanding of concepts, skills and problem solving. Learning Goals for Chapter 13 are provided below. The assessment options provide opportunities to evaluate whether or not students have retained learning from prior experiences. Choose the forms of assessment that best meet the needs of your students.

Chapter 13 Learning Goals

	Learning Goals	Lesson Number
13-A	Determine missing factors and products within multiplication sentences	13.1–13.3
13-B	Estimate missing factors and quotients to complete number sentences	13.4–13.6
13-C	Apply problem solving strategies such as *work backward* to solve problems	13.7

✔ Informal Assessment

Ongoing Assessment
Provides insight into students' thinking to guide instruction (TG pp. 1023, 1025, 1030, 1033, 1040, 1046)

Reflect and Summarize the Lesson
Checks understanding of lesson concepts (TG pp. 1026, 1033, 1041, 1049, 1058, 1064, 1068)

Snapshot Assessment
Mental Math and Quick Write
Offers a quick observation of students' progress on chapter concepts and skills (TG pp. 1072–1073)

Performance Assessment
Provides quarterly assessment of Chapters 12–15 concepts using real-life situations
Assessment Guide
pp. AG225–AG230

✔ Formal Assessment

Standardized Test Prep
Problem Solving Test Prep
Prepares students for standardized tests
Lesson Activity Book p. 264 (TG p. 1069)

Chapter 13 Review/Assessment
Reviews and assesses students' understanding of the chapter
Lesson Activity Book pp. 265–266 (TG p. 1074)

Chapter 13 Test
Assesses the chapter concepts and skills
Assessment Guide
Form A pp. AG113–AG114
Form B pp. AG115–AG116

Benchmark 4 Assessment
Provides quarterly assessment of Chapters 12–15 concepts and skills
Assessment Guide
Benchmark 4A pp. AG125–AG132
Benchmark 4B pp. AG133–AG140

World Almanac for Kids

Use the World Almanac for Kids feature, *Denim Data,* found on pp. 208–209 of the **Student Handbook,** to provide students with an opportunity to practice using their problem solving skills by solving real world problems.

FACT • ACTIVITY 1

1 $5 \times \blacksquare = 60$ rivets; $5 \times 12 = 60$;
12 pairs of jeans can be made

2 about 70 pairs; 135 is about 140;
$1\frac{3}{4}$ is about 2; $140 \div 2 = 70$

3 $342 \div 9 = 38$. I can make 38 pairs of jeans.

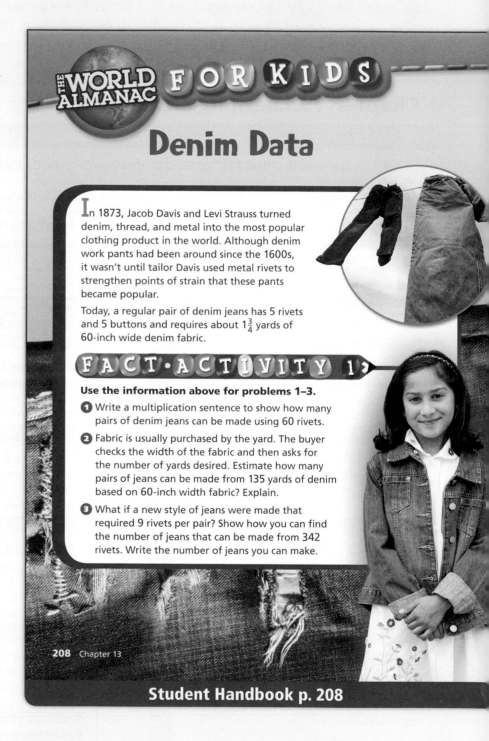

THE WORLD ALMANAC FOR KIDS

Denim Data

In 1873, Jacob Davis and Levi Strauss turned denim, thread, and metal into the most popular clothing product in the world. Although denim work pants had been around since the 1600s, it wasn't until tailor Davis used metal rivets to strengthen points of strain that these pants became popular.

Today, a regular pair of denim jeans has 5 rivets and 5 buttons and requires about $1\frac{3}{4}$ yards of 60-inch wide denim fabric.

FACT • ACTIVITY 1

Use the information above for problems 1–3.

1 Write a multiplication sentence to show how many pairs of denim jeans can be made using 60 rivets.

2 Fabric is usually purchased by the yard. The buyer checks the width of the fabric and then asks for the number of yards desired. Estimate how many pairs of jeans can be made from 135 yards of denim based on 60-inch width fabric? Explain.

3 What if a new style of jeans were made that required 9 rivets per pair? Show how you can find the number of jeans that can be made from 342 rivets. Write the number of jeans you can make.

208 Chapter 13

Student Handbook p. 208

FACT·ACTIVITY 2

One bale of cotton weighs about 500 pounds and can make more than 225 pairs of denim jeans.

Answer the questions.

A tailor, Mrs. Elliott, has purchased some yards of 60-inch wide denim to make denim jeans.

1 Mrs. Elliott has 360 inches of denim to make regular denim jeans. If it takes exactly 63 inches of denim to make a pair of men's jeans, will she be able to make 6 pairs of jeans? Use estimation to explain.

2 Mrs. Elliot uses 324 inches of denim to make 6 different styles of women's jeans. If each style requires the same number of inches of denim, how many inches of denim per pair of jeans does she use?

3 About how many bales of cotton are needed to manufacture 925 pairs of jeans?

CHAPTER PROJECT

Some people make quilts from discarded denim jeans. A patchwork quilt can be made from equal-sized square patches of denim sewn together.

- Decide on and draw a design for a rectangular quilt up to 4 feet by 6 feet in size.
- How many inches long will it be? How many inches wide will it be?
- How many equal-sized patches will fit across and down? Try several variations before you decide on one.
- Use division to show the size of each patch in the width and length of your quilt.
- Draw a picture of your final design. You may want to decorate the patches with symbols, letters, or words.

ALMANAC Fact

Levi Strauss always disliked the term "jeans." The denim work pants were called "waist-high overalls." Not until the mid-1930s did the company ever refer to them as jeans.

Student Handbook p. 209

FACT·ACTIVITY 2

1 No; Possible explanation: 63 is about 60 and $6 \times 60 = 360$. Since the tailor needs more than 60 inches per pair, she will not be able to make 6 pairs.

2 $324 \div 6 = 54$ inches

3 about 4 bales

CHAPTER PROJECT

- Total area: 4 feet by 5 feet, or 48 in. $\times$ 60 in.
- If patches are 4-inch squares, 12 will fit across the quilt width and 15 will fit down its length.
- $48 \div 4 = 12$; $60 \div 4 = 15$

Vocabulary

To reinforce vocabulary concepts, invite students to complete the vocabulary activities on pp. 218–219 of the *Student Handbook.* Encourage students to record their answers in their math journals.

Many responses are possible.

⑩ Possible answer: A missing factor problem is a multiplication fact for which you know the product and one factor. In order to solve, find the fact family it belongs to. For example, the missing factor problem $3 \times \blacksquare = 12$ belongs to the fact family $3 \times 4 = 12$, so the missing factor is 4.

⑪ Possible answer: First, write the given product. Then write the ÷ symbol. Then write the given factor. Then write the equal sign. Finally, write the other factor when you know what it is. For example, $3 \times \blacksquare = 12$ becomes $12 \div 3 = 4$ because $3 \times 4 = 12$.

⑫ Possible answer: Find which two multiples of 10 the product is between by multiplying the known factor by 10, 20, 30, and so on. For example, for $12 \times \blacksquare = 324$, $12 \times 20 = 240$ and $12 \times 30 = 360$, and 324 is between 240 and 360. The product is closer to 360 than 240, so the missing factor is greater than 25 and less than 30. Since 324 has a 4 in the units place and 2×7 also has a 4 in the units place, you can guess that $12 \times 27 = 324$.

Chapter **13** Vocabulary

Choose the best vocabulary term from Word List A for each sentence.

Word List A

compatible numbers
dividend
divisor
fact family
factor
multiple
multiplication
product
quotient
round

❶ The number that is to be divided in a division problem is the __?__. **dividend**

❷ The number that divides the dividend is the __?__. **divisor**

❸ The __?__ is the result of multiplication. **product**

❹ To replace a number with another number that tells about how many or how much is to __?__ a number. **round**

❺ A set of related multiplication and division equations is a(n) __?__. **fact family**

❻ The process of finding the total number of items in equal-sized groups is called __?__. **multiplication**

❼ Numbers that are easy to compute mentally are called __?__. **compatible numbers**

Complete each analogy using the best term from Word List B.

Word List B

divisor
estimate
factor
quotient

❽ Addend is to addition as __?__ is to multiplication. **factor**

❾ Product is to multiplication as __?__ is to division. **quotient**

💬 Talk Math

Discuss with a partner what you have learned about multiplication and division. Use the vocabulary terms *factor* and *product*.

⑩ How can you solve a missing-factor problem?

⑪ How can you write a missing-factor problem as a division problem?

⑫ Suppose you have a missing-factor problem and you know that the missing factor is greater than 10. How can you estimate the missing factor?

218 Chapter 13

Student Handbook p. 218

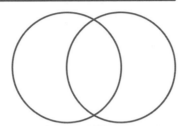
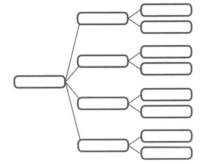

⓫

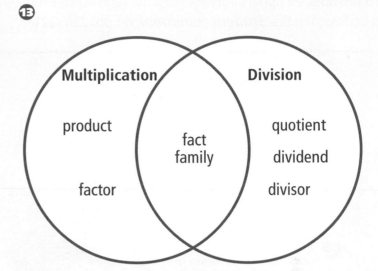

⓮ Many answers are possible. One example is provided.

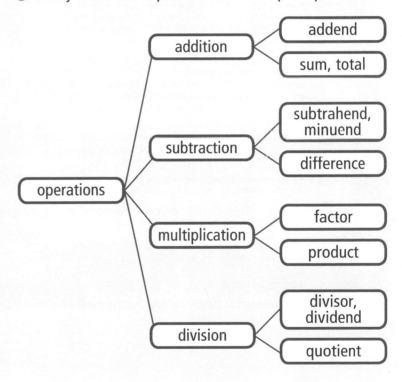

Games

Greatest Factors in **Lesson 13.3** provides an opportunity for students to practice strategies for finding missing factors in number sentences. *Greatest Answer* in **Lesson 13.6** provides an opportunity for students to practice estimating quotients. These games can be found in the *Student Handbook* on pp. 220–221.

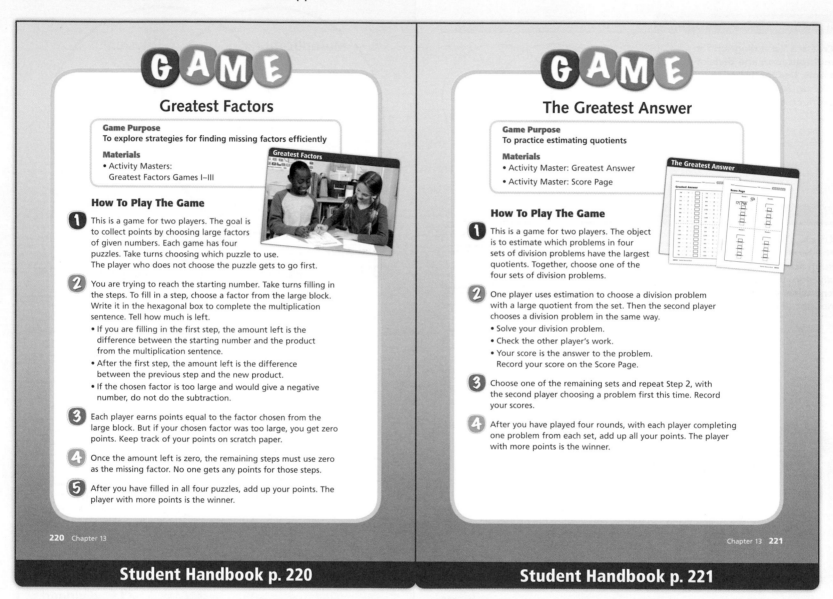

GAME

Greatest Factors

Game Purpose
To explore strategies for finding missing factors efficiently

Materials
• Activity Masters:
  Greatest Factors Games I–III

How To Play The Game

1 This is a game for two players. The goal is to collect points by choosing large factors of given numbers. Each game has four puzzles. Take turns choosing which puzzle to use. The player who does not choose the puzzle gets to go first.

2 You are trying to reach the starting number. Take turns filling in the steps. To fill in a step, choose a factor from the large block. Write it in the hexagonal box to complete the multiplication sentence. Tell how much is left.

• If you are filling in the first step, the amount left is the difference between the starting number and the product from the multiplication sentence.

• After the first step, the amount left is the difference between the previous step and the new product.

• If the chosen factor is too large and would give a negative number, do not do the subtraction.

3 Each player earns points equal to the factor chosen from the large block. But if your chosen factor was too large, you get zero points. Keep track of your points on scratch paper.

4 Once the amount left is zero, the remaining steps must use zero as the missing factor. No one gets any points for those steps.

5 After you have filled in all four puzzles, add up your points. The player with more points is the winner.

220 Chapter 13

Student Handbook p. 220

GAME

The Greatest Answer

Game Purpose
To practice estimating quotients

Materials
• Activity Master: Greatest Answer
• Activity Master: Score Page

How To Play The Game

1 This is a game for two players. The object is to estimate which problems in four sets of division problems have the largest quotients. Together, choose one of the four sets of division problems.

2 One player uses estimation to choose a division problem with a large quotient from the set. Then the second player chooses a division problem in the same way.

• Solve your division problem.
• Check the other player's work.
• Your score is the answer to the problem. Record your score on the Score Page.

3 Choose one of the remaining sets and repeat Step 2, with the second player choosing a problem first this time. Record your scores.

4 After you have played four rounds, with each player completing one problem from each set, add up all your points. The player with more points is the winner.

Chapter 13 221

Student Handbook p. 221

Challenge

This activity challenges students to estimate quotients so that they can be ordered from least to greatest to help solve a puzzle. This activity can be found on p. 222 of the *Student Handbook.*

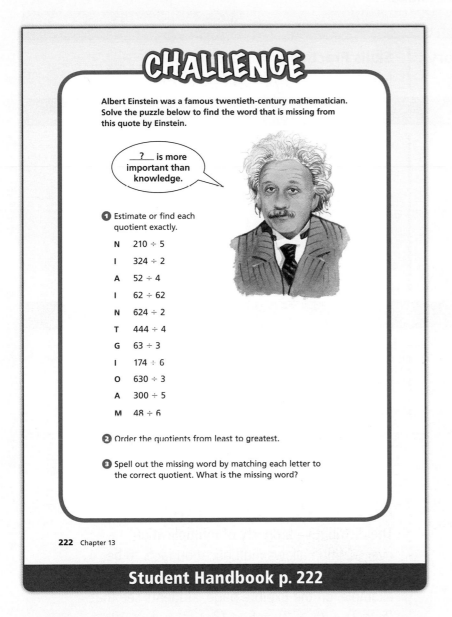

Methods for finding quotients or estimates may vary. Actual quotients are shown.

1 42; 162; 13; 1; 312; 111; 21; 29; 210; 60; 8

2 1, 8, 13, 21, 29, 42, 60, 111, 162, 210, 312

3 IMAGINATION

Lesson 1 Finding Missing Dimensions

NCTM Standards 1, 2, 4, 6, 7, 8, 9, 10

Lesson Planner

STUDENT OBJECTIVES
- To find missing factors in multiplication sentences in the context of area
- To review the relationship between multiplication and division by writing fact families

1 Daily Activities (TG p. 1021)

Open-Ended Problem Solving/Headline Story	Skills Practice and Review—Multiplying by Multiples of 10

2 Teach and Practice (TG pp. 1022–1026)

MATERIALS

- **A** **Reading the Student Letter** (TG p. 1022)
- **B** **Finding a Missing Dimension** (TG pp. 1023–1024)
- **C** **Relating Multiplication and Division** (TG p. 1025)
- **D** **Finding Missing Dimensions** (TG p. 1026)

- square tiles, graph paper (optional)
- LAB pp. 251–252
- SH pp. 207, 210

3 Differentiated Instruction (TG p. 1027)

Leveled Problem Solving (TG p. 1027)	Practice Book P102
Intervention Activity (TG p. 1027)	Extension Book E102
Extension Activity (TG p. 1027)	Spiral Review Book SR102

Lesson Notes

About the Lesson

In this chapter, students use their understanding of multiplication to solve division problems. To lay the groundwork, this lesson gives students practice with multiplication facts by asking them to find missing factors in multiplication sentences. Students use the context of area and the strategy of drawing a picture to solve the problems, revisiting the distributive property of multiplication over addition as they do so. (See About the Mathematics.) To find larger missing factors in multiplication statements, students combine basic multiplication facts and see that the missing factor is the sum of the smaller factors. This prepares them to understand long division in upcoming lessons.

About the Mathematics

The distributive property of multiplication over addition allows multiplication facts to be combined to find a larger missing factor. For example, on the Explore page, students see that $(5 \times 3) + (5 \times 7) = 5 \times (3 + 7) = 5 \times 10$. Based on their understanding of multiplication, students should reason that this number sentence says that "3 groups of 5" plus "7 groups of 5" makes "10 groups of 5." Drawing a picture clarifies the meaning of this property because it allows students to see the result of combining the two rectangles.

(continued on page R7)

Use with Lesson Activity Book pp. 251–252.

Developing Mathematical Language

Vocabulary: fact family

Students are already familiar with the term *fact family* from work with addition and subtraction. At this point, students are beginning to understand how all four operations relate to one another: multiplication as repeated addition, division as repeated subtraction, addition and subtraction in one *fact family*, and multiplication and division in another *fact family*. It is important that students recognize these relationships and, just as important, that they understand which relationships constitute a *fact family*.

Familiarize students with the term *fact family*.

Beginning Remind students that just as family members often resemble one another, *fact families* resemble one another because the same numbers are involved in each *fact family* number sentence. Write an addition or subtraction sentence, such as $4 + 5 = 9$, on the board. Ask students to write other members of that *fact family*.

Intermediate Name an operation used in a *fact family*, such as addition, and have students say in unison the other operation that is part of that *fact family*. Repeat with the other operations.

Advanced Ask students to explain why multiplication and division make a *fact family* but multiplication and addition do not.

Open-Ended Problem Solving

Read the Headline Story to the students. If students have trouble coming up with responses, you might prompt them by giving an example of how $5 in change could result from a purchase.

 Headline Story

Pete sells birthday cards for $3. One day he notices that he keeps running out of $5 bills because most of his customers are receiving exactly $5 in change for their purchases. No customer bought more than 10 cards.

Possible responses: A customer who bought one card would have to pay $8 to receive $5 in change. That wouldn't make sense because the customer could have paid $3 exactly. Two cards would cost $6. To receive $5 in change, the customer would have to pay $11. This is a reasonable amount to give a cashier because it would provide the convenience of a $5 bill in change instead of four $1 bills. Customers who bought three or four birthday cards would have to give Pete $14 or $17 to receive $5 in change, but those amounts don't make sense for the same reason that paying with $8 doesn't make sense.

Skills Practice and Review

Multiplying by Multiples of 10

Students will need to perform many mental computations in this chapter. To review mental multiplication, have students multiply one-digit numbers by various multiples of 10 (20, 50, 80, and so on). Keep the pace quick so that all students have a chance to respond to at least one problem. Record the questions and answers on the board. Some examples:

$9 \times 30 = 270$ $60 \times 8 = 480$ $40 \times 6 = 240$ $8 \times 70 = 560$

pairs or whole class · **15 MIN**

NCTM Standards 1, 2, 4, 6, 7, 8, 9, 10

A Reading the Student Letter

Purpose To review multiplication fact family relationships

Introduce Have students read the Student Letter with a partner or as a class.

Problem Ask students to answer the question posed in the letter:

How can this picture help you solve the problem 72 ÷ 6?

6 feet | Area = 72 sq ft

Help students to recall patterns and relationships in multiplication fact families. In this example, $12 \times 6 = 72$, so $72 \div 6 = 12$. Relate the same patterns and relationships to areas of rectangles. Since, for a rectangle, length × width = area, length = area ÷ width. So, $72 \div 6$ is the length of a rectangle with an area of 72 square feet and a width of 6 feet.

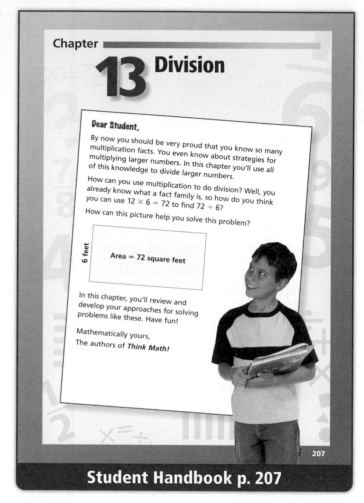

Student Handbook p. 207

To summarize the activity, you might ask students to provide some multiplication facts, some strategies for solving multi-digit multiplication problems, and any division facts they might know. If students don't mention it, you might tell them that they will be using an area model and combining multiplication facts to complete more challenging problems in this lesson.

💬 Talk Math

❷ Janis knows the area of a rectangle and the length of the rectangle. How can she find the rectangle's width? **by dividing the area by the length**

❷ What facts related to the product $9 \times 12 = 108$ can you write? **$12 \times 9 = 108$, $108 \div 9 = 12$, and $108 \div 12 = 9$**

Use with Lesson Activity Book pp. 251–252.

B Finding a Missing Dimension

Purpose To combine multiplication facts to solve a problem involving the dimensions and areas of two quilts.

Introduce Have students work in pairs. Make square tiles available to each pair.

Task Challenge students to solve the problems on Explore: Making Quilts.

❶ What length of fabric should they buy to make both of their quilts? Andrea needs 15 ÷ 5 = 3 feet. Lynn needs 35 ÷ 5 = 7 feet. Total: 3 feet + 7 feet = 10 feet.

❷ Draw a picture of this quilt to find the new length. Possible picture:

3 ft + 7 ft = 10 ft

5 ft ▯▯

❸ Write a number sentence to describe the area of the two joined quilts. Possible number sentences: (5 × 3) + (5 × 7) = 50; 5 × 10 = 50; 5 × (3 × 7) = 50.

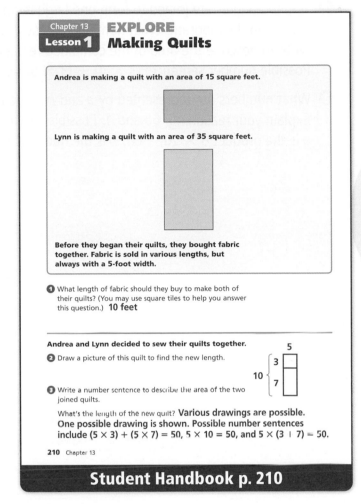

Chapter 13 **EXPLORE**
Lesson 1 **Making Quilts**

Andrea is making a quilt with an area of 15 square feet.

Lynn is making a quilt with an area of 35 square feet.

Before they began their quilts, they bought fabric together. Fabric is sold in various lengths, but always with a 5-foot width.

❶ What length of fabric should they buy to make both of their quilts? (You may use square tiles to help you answer this question.) **10 feet**

Andrea and Lynn decided to sew their quilts together.

❷ Draw a picture of this quilt to find the new length.

❸ Write a number sentence to describe the area of the two joined quilts.

What's the length of the new quilt? **Various drawings are possible. One possible drawing is shown. Possible number sentences include (5 × 3) + (5 × 7) = 50, 5 × 10 = 50, and 5 × (3 + 7) = 50.**

210 Chapter 13

Student Handbook p. 210

Materials

- For each student: square tiles; graph paper (optional)

NCTM Standards 1, 2, 4, 6, 7, 8, 9, 10

✓ **Ongoing Assessment**

- Do students show mastery of multiplication facts? Students should be able to complete sentences like 4 × ■ = 28 without much thought.

- Do students have strategies for solving difficult multiplication facts? Sentences like 4 × ■ = 56 are likely to be challenging and to require solution strategies other than remembering multiplication facts. For example, students might use *guess and check* or *solve a simpler problem* to find a missing factor.

Share Once students have answered the questions, go over the answers as a class and have students explain their strategies. Some students may have guessed possible lengths and then checked their guesses by multiplying the lengths and widths to find the area.

Others may have drawn a picture to represent the two smaller quilts. Others still may have used square tiles to model the quilts. Ask students to help you draw a picture to represent the situation. This will ensure that all of your students can use the area models of multiplication on the LAB pages.

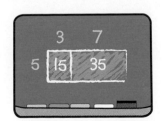

No matter what strategy students use, all should have written a number sentence that represents the process of combining two quilts with a width of 5 feet to produce a new length of 3 feet + 7 feet and a total area of 50 square feet.

Talk Math

❷ Two rectangles are joined to form one large rectangle, as shown in the diagram. What number sentence can you write to describe the area of the combined rectangles? Possible number sentence: $(3 \times 4) + (3 \times 5) = 27$

	4	5
3	12	15

❷ What numbers are represented by *a* and *b* in the diagram? Explain your reasoning. 60 and 4; Possible explanation: *a* is the product $6 \times 10 = 60$; *b* is the quotient $24 \div 6 = 4$.

	10	*b*
6	*a*	24

Purpose To review the relationship between multiplication and division by writing fact families

NCTM Standards 1, 2, 4, 6, 7, 8, 9, 10

Introduce Tell students a multiplication (and, consequently, division) story. Ask them for a number sentence that represents the situation. For example, you might tell them that 7 swim teams are going to a swim meet. The organizers of the swim meet want to give each participant a T-shirt, so they ordered 91 shirts. Students might represent this situation with any of these sentences:

$$7 \times \blacksquare = 91$$
$$\blacksquare \times 7 = 91$$
$$91 \div 7 = \blacksquare$$
$$91 \div \blacksquare = 7$$

Help your students list all the sentences in the fact family.

✓ Ongoing Assessment

• Do students understand multiplication and division fact families?

Problem Call attention to the fact that one number is missing from the four sentences in the fact family (13 in the swim-team example). Challenge your students to change the story so that a different number is missing.

For example, students might suggest a story about 7 teams of 13 swimmers that omits the total number of swimmers (91). Or they might say that 13 shirts were ordered for each team and that a total of 91 shirts were ordered, omitting the number of teams (7). For each missing number, ask students which number sentence in the fact family they would use to solve the problem. For example, when 91 is the missing number, multiplication is likely easier for most students than solving a division sentence with a missing dividend. Still, make sure students see that both operations can be used to describe any of the situations, and that they should use whichever operation they find easier.

If you have time, you might have students write problems of their own, and then rewrite them so that different numbers in the fact family are left out. You might have students exchange problems and solve them.

 Talk Math Casey bought 6 CDs costing $12 apiece.

❷ Write a fact family to describe the situation.

$$6 \times 12 = 72 \qquad 72 \div 6 = 12$$
$$12 \times 6 = 72 \qquad 72 \div 12 = 6$$

❷ Change the story so that a number other than 72 is missing. Possible story: Casey spent $72 on 6 CDs.

individuals
or pairs

20 MIN

Purpose To use the areas of rectangles to find their dimensions

NCTM Standards 1, 2, 4, 6, 7, 8, 9, 10

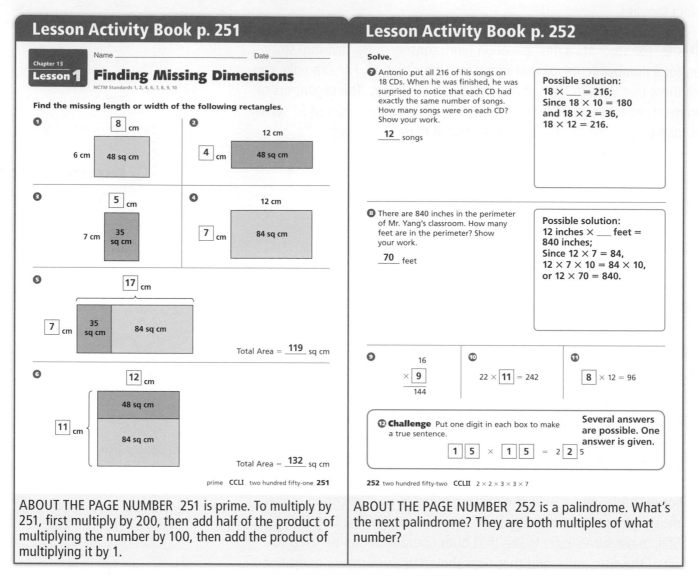

Lesson Activity Book p. 251

Name _____ Date _____

Chapter 13
Lesson 1 **Finding Missing Dimensions**
NCTM Standards 1, 2, 4, 6, 7, 8, 9, 10

Find the missing length or width of the following rectangles.

① 8 cm, 6 cm, 48 sq cm

② 12 cm, 4 cm, 48 sq cm

③ 5 cm, 7 cm, 35 sq cm

④ 12 cm, 7 cm, 84 sq cm

⑤ 17 cm, 7 cm, 35 sq cm, 84 sq cm, Total Area = 119 sq cm

⑥ 12 cm, 11 cm, 48 sq cm, 84 sq cm, Total Area = 132 sq cm

prime CCLI two hundred fifty-one **251**

Lesson Activity Book p. 252

Solve.

⑦ Antonio put all 216 of his songs on 18 CDs. When he was finished, he was surprised to notice that each CD had exactly the same number of songs. How many songs were on each CD? Show your work.

___12___ songs

Possible solution:
18 × ___ = 216;
Since 18 × 10 = 180
and 18 × 2 = 36,
18 × 12 = 216.

⑧ There are 840 inches in the perimeter of Mr. Yang's classroom. How many feet are in the perimeter? Show your work.

___70___ feet

Possible solution:
12 inches × ___ feet = 840 inches;
Since 12 × 7 = 84,
12 × 7 × 10 = 84 × 10,
or 12 × 70 = 840.

⑨ 16 × 9 = 144

⑩ 22 × 11 = 242

⑪ 8 × 12 = 96

⑫ **Challenge** Put one digit in each box to make a true sentence.

1 5 × 1 5 = 2 2 5

Several answers are possible. One answer is given.

252 two hundred fifty-two CCLII 2 × 2 × 2 × 3 × 3 × 7

ABOUT THE PAGE NUMBER 251 is prime. To multiply by 251, first multiply by 200, then add half of the product of multiplying the number by 100, then add the product of multiplying it by 1.

ABOUT THE PAGE NUMBER 252 is a palindrome. What's the next palindrome? They are both multiples of what number?

Teaching Notes for LAB page 251

Students find missing dimensions of rectangles with given areas. Encourage students to look for clues at the top of the page that can help them solve Problems 5 and 6 at the bottom of the page. (Rectangles 5 and 6 are combinations of rectangles from the top part of the page, so their missing dimensions are combinations of the dimensions of the smaller rectangles.)

Differentiated Instruction Basic Level Provide square tiles or graph paper to students who need additional support to complete the LAB pages. Students can use tiles to model the given areas or graph paper to outline the areas.

Teaching Notes for LAB page 252

This page presents situations similar to the ones encountered in Activity C. Students can use multiplication or division to solve the problems.

Challenge Problem The Challenge Problem asks students to find two 2-digit numbers that have a 3-digit product with a 2 in the hundreds place and a 5 in the ones place. There are many possible answers, so you might encourage students who finish quickly to search for additional solutions. Possible solutions include 15 × 15 = 225, 15 × 17 = 255, 15 × 19 = 285, and 11 × 25 = 275.

Reflect and Summarize the Lesson

Write Math
Complete this number sentence: 7 × (■ + ■) = 56. Explain your reasoning. Possible answers: Since 7 × 8 = 56, any pair of numbers that add to 8 is correct, for example 1 and 7, 2 and 6, or 3 and 5.

3 | Differentiated Instruction

Leveled Problem Solving

The packers are putting 408 books in cartons.
There are 24 books in each carton.

❶ Basic Level

How many cartons do they use? Explain. 17; 17 × 24 = 408.

❷ On Level

After packing 10 cartons, how many more cartons do they need? Explain. 7 more; 10 × 24 = 240; 408 − 240 = 168 and 7 × 24 = 168.

❸ Above Level

Can the packers take a break after exactly half the cartons are full? Explain. No; 17 cartons are needed, and 17 is not divisible by 2.

Intervention	Practice	Extension

Activity Reorder and Change Operations

Give students a multiplication or division number sentence such as 5 × 9 = 45. Have students number vertically from 1 to 4 on four lines of notebook paper and write the given number sentence next to 1. Next to 2, have them write the related number sentence using the same operation. Beside 3 and 4, have them change the operation using the same numbers they used in 1 and 2.

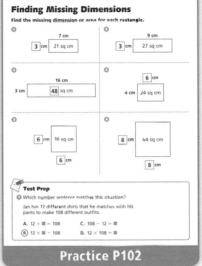

Practice P102

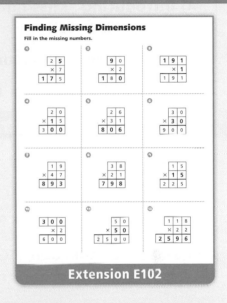

Extension E102

Spiral Review

Spiral Review Book page SR102 provides review of the following previously learned skills and concepts:

- estimating and finding areas of the faces of prisms with rectangular faces
- measuring lengths in centimeters using Cuisenaire® Rods

You may wish to have students work with a partner to complete the page.

Spiral Review SR102

Extension Activity
Garden Math

Give pairs of students a sheet of centimeter grid paper. Have them draw a large rectangle to represent a garden. Then have them divide the garden into two sections using a line segment. Have them write the following under their picture:

- One multiplication sentence that can be used to find the total area.
- One fact family for the area of the entire garden.
- One fact family for the area of each section.

Lesson 2 Finding Missing Factors

NCTM Standards 1, 2, 4, 6, 7, 8, 9, 10

Lesson Planner

STUDENT OBJECTIVES
- To practice multiplication and division
- To find missing factors in multiplication sentences

1 Daily Activities (TG p. 1029)

Open-Ended Problem Solving/Headline Story	Skills Practice and Review—Multiplying by Multiples of 100

2 Teach and Practice (TG pp. 1030–1033)

MATERIALS

- Ⓐ **Introducing "Missing-Factor" Puzzles** (TG pp. 1030–1031)
- Ⓑ **Finding Missing Factors** (TG p. 1032)
- Ⓒ **Writing Fact Families** (TG p. 1033)

- transparency of LAB p. 253 (optional)
- LAB pp. 253–254
- SH p. 211

3 Differentiated Instruction (TG p. 1034)

Leveled Problem Solving (TG p. 1034)	Practice Book P103
Intervention Activity (TG p. 1034)	Extension Book E103
Extension Activity (TG p. 1034)	Spiral Review Book SR103
Literature Connection (TG p. 1018)	

Lesson Notes

About the Lesson

Students continue to work with missing factors as they review breaking multiplication problems into simpler ones and adding the results to find the total product. Repeated use of this process will enable students to begin to see connections between multiplication and division, and to develop a strategy for solving division problems.

About the Mathematics

Students continue to apply the fact that multiplication distributes over addition to solve challenging "missing-factor" problems in this lesson. A multiplication problem can be thought of as a sum of several simpler multiplication problems. Recognition that repeated addition is a way to think about multiplication and that multiplication problems can be broken apart will help students understand division and standard division algorithms, which rely on repeated subtraction.

Use with Lesson Activity Book pp. 253–254.

Developing Mathematical Language

Vocabulary: factor, multiplication

Because *multiplication* fact and *multiplication factor* sound so similar, students might confuse the two as you discuss *multiplication* in the classroom. Students reviewed *multiplication* facts in the previous lesson and repositioned *factors* to write the facts. Students will especially benefit if they can identify each *factor* in the *multiplication* fact family as well as where each *factor* appears in the two related division facts.

Familiarize students with the terms *factor* and *multiplication*.

Beginning Write a *multiplication* fact family on the board. Have volunteers circle each *factor*.

Intermediate Ask students to write a *multiplication* fact using the number 6 as one *factor*. Compare and discuss the second *factor* that students choose.

Advanced Show students a division fact. Ask students to identify each *factor* for the two related *multiplication* facts.

Open-Ended Problem Solving

Read the Headline Story to the students. This problem involves comparing fractions and also approximation, as we are not told exactly how much Wendy's parents and brothers shared.

 Headline Story

Wendy, Julie, and Carla were having a sleepover. For dinner, they shared two small pizzas equally. Wendy's parents and brother shared more than two small pizzas equally.

Possible responses: To share one pizza three ways, the girls might cut it into 3 pieces and each have 1 piece ($\frac{1}{3}$ of a pizza). Sharing two pizzas, each girl would get *two* thirds of a pizza: $\frac{2}{3}$. (If they cut a pizza into six parts, each girl would get two parts, or $\frac{2}{6}$ of that pizza, and so four sixths-of-a-pizza altogether: $\frac{4}{6}$.) Wendy's parents and brother shared *more* than two pizzas, so they must have eaten more than two thirds of a pizza (more than $\frac{4}{6}$). Sharing three pizzas, they'd each get 1. Sharing 4 pizzas (and cutting each into thirds), they'd each get 1 piece of each pizza, or four thirds.

Skills Practice and Review

Multiplying by Multiples of 100

As in the previous lesson, have students practice mental computation by multiplying by various multiples of 100 (200, 400, 900, and so on). Keep the pace quick so that all students can respond to at least one problem. Record the questions and answers on the board. Some examples:

$$8 \times 200 = 1,600 \qquad 90 \times 600 = 54,000$$
$$300 \times 3 = 900 \qquad 400 \times 400 = 160,000$$
$$70 \times 500 = 35,000 \qquad 700 \times 400 = 280,000$$

pairs

20 MIN

(A) Introducing "Missing-Factor" Puzzles

NCTM Standards 1, 2, 4, 6, 7, 8, 9, 10

Purpose To introduce the idea that a missing factor can be the sum of two numbers

Introduce Students should work with partners on this activity. Provide each student with a copy of Explore: "Missing-Factor" Puzzles.

✔ **Ongoing Assessment**

• Do students know multiplication and division facts for whole numbers 1–10?

• Do students understand the distributive property of multiplication over addition? Example: $(4 \times 2) + (4 \times 3) = 4 \times 5$

Task Direct students to answer the questions on Explore: "Missing-Factor Puzzle."

❶ $5 \times 4 = 20$

❷ $9 \times 2 = 18$

❸ $3 \times 8 = 24$

❹ $6 \times 1 = 6$

❺ $5 \times 3 = 15$

❻ $4 \times 7 = 28$

❼ How can you complete number sentences 5 and 6 using a sum of numbers from the green block? Possible response:
$5 \times 3 = (5 \times 1) + (5 \times 2)$;
$4 \times 7 = (4 \times 1) + (4 \times 2) + (4 \times 4)$

Chapter 13

EXPLORE

Lesson 2 **"Missing-Factor" Puzzles**

0	1	2	4	8	16

Some of these number sentences can be completed using the numbers from the green block above. Copy and complete those sentences.

❶ $5 \times \blacksquare = 20$ **4**

❷ $9 \times \blacksquare = 18$ **2**

❸ $3 \times \blacksquare = 24$ **8**

❹ $6 \times \blacksquare = 6$ **1**

❺ $5 \times \blacksquare = 15$

❻ $4 \times \blacksquare = 28$

Problems 5 and 6 can't be completed using only one number from the green block

❼ How can you complete the other number sentences using a *sum* of numbers from the green block?
Problem 5 can be solved by multiplying 5 by 2 + 1.
Problem 6 can be solved by multiplying 4 by 1 + 2 + 4.

Chapter 13 **211**

Student Handbook p. 211

Share After a few minutes, bring the class together to discuss their answers. Students should have easily filled in the missing factors in Problems 1–4, based on their knowledge of multiplication facts. Problems 5 and 6 cannot be solved by putting in a number from the green block at the top of the page. Students should have found, however, that they could solve those problems once they were able to add numbers.

Use with Lesson Activity Book pp. 253–254.

Task Show students a new format for displaying the addition used to complete number sentences 5 and 6.

First ask students to name the numbers in the green block that they added together to fill in the missing factor for Problem 5. Write number sentences for 5 times each of these numbers, as shown below. Then draw a black line and write the total multiplication sentence below the line.

$$5 \times \langle 2 \rangle = \boxed{10}$$
$$5 \times \langle 1 \rangle = \boxed{5}$$
$$5 \times \langle 3 \rangle = \boxed{15}$$

$$4 \times \langle 4 \rangle = \boxed{16}$$
$$4 \times \langle 2 \rangle = \boxed{8}$$
$$4 \times \langle 1 \rangle = \boxed{4}$$
$$4 \times \langle 7 \rangle = \boxed{28}$$

Go over the new format with your students to make sure they understand what it means. Putting the discussion in the context of area, which is familiar to students from the previous lesson, may be helpful. For example (for Problem 5), students might think of two rectangles that each have a width of 5. When the rectangles are placed side-by-side, the width of the large rectangle that is formed is still 5, but the length is now the sum of the lengths of the smaller rectangles. The area is the sum of the areas of the smaller rectangles. Draw a picture to help students visualize this.

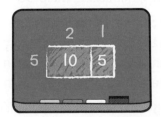

🗨 Talk Math

❷ How do you know that 5×2 plus 5×1 means the same thing as 5×3? Possible response: 2 groups of 5 plus 1 group of 5 must equal 3 groups of 5.

❷ How can you use the facts that $6 \times 4 = 24$ and $6 \times 3 = 18$ to find the product 6×7? Explain your reasoning. Possible explanation: $7 = 4 + 3$, so 6×7 must equal $(6 \times 4) + (6 \times 3)$; $6 \times 7 = 24 + 18 = 42$.

individuals
or pairs

20 MIN

Purpose To practice finding missing factors in multiplication sentences

NCTM Standards 1, 2, 4, 6, 7, 8, 9, 10

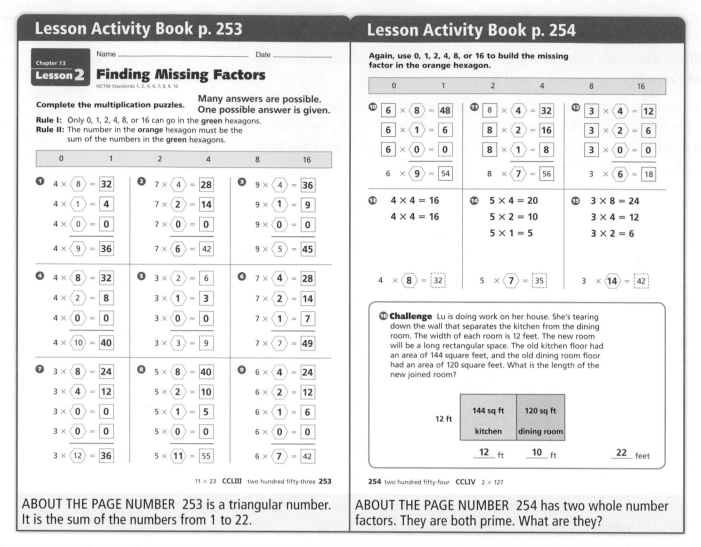

Lesson Activity Book p. 253

Chapter 13
Lesson 2 **Finding Missing Factors**
NCTM Standards 1, 2, 4, 6, 7, 8, 9, 10

Name _____ Date _____

Complete the multiplication puzzles.

Many answers are possible.
One possible answer is given.

Rule I: Only 0, 1, 2, 4, 8, or 16 can go in the **green** hexagons.
Rule II: The number in the **orange** hexagon must be the sum of the numbers in the **green** hexagons.

| 0 | 1 | 2 | 4 | 8 | 16 |

1
$4 \times 8 = 32$
$4 \times 1 = 4$
$4 \times 0 = 0$
$4 \times 9 = 36$

2
$7 \times 4 = 28$
$7 \times 2 = 14$
$7 \times 0 = 0$
$7 \times 6 = 42$

3
$9 \times 4 = 36$
$9 \times 1 = 9$
$9 \times 0 = 0$
$9 \times 5 = 45$

4
$4 \times 8 = 32$
$4 \times 2 = 8$
$4 \times 0 = 0$
$4 \times 10 = 40$

5
$3 \times 2 = 6$
$3 \times 1 = 3$
$3 \times 0 = 0$
$3 \times 3 = 9$

6
$7 \times 4 = 28$
$7 \times 2 = 14$
$7 \times 1 = 7$
$7 \times 7 = 49$

7
$3 \times 8 = 24$
$3 \times 4 = 12$
$3 \times 0 = 0$
$3 \times 12 = 36$

8
$5 \times 8 = 40$
$5 \times 2 = 10$
$5 \times 1 = 5$
$5 \times 0 = 0$
$5 \times 11 = 55$

9
$6 \times 4 = 24$
$6 \times 2 = 12$
$6 \times 1 = 6$
$6 \times 0 = 0$
$6 \times 7 = 42$

11 × 23 **CCLIII** two hundred fifty-three **253**

ABOUT THE PAGE NUMBER 253 is a triangular number. It is the sum of the numbers from 1 to 22.

Lesson Activity Book p. 254

Again, use 0, 1, 2, 4, 8, or 16 to build the missing factor in the orange hexagon.

| 0 | 1 | 2 | 4 | 8 | 16 |

10
$6 \times 8 = 48$
$6 \times 1 = 6$
$6 \times 0 = 0$
$6 \times 9 = 54$

11
$8 \times 4 = 32$
$8 \times 2 = 16$
$8 \times 1 = 8$
$8 \times 7 = 56$

12
$3 \times 4 = 12$
$3 \times 2 = 6$
$3 \times 0 = 0$
$3 \times 6 = 18$

13
$4 \times 4 = 16$
$4 \times 4 = 16$

14
$5 \times 4 = 20$
$5 \times 2 = 10$
$5 \times 1 = 5$

15
$3 \times 8 = 24$
$3 \times 4 = 12$
$3 \times 2 = 6$

$4 \times 8 = 32$

$5 \times 7 = 35$

$3 \times 14 = 42$

16 Challenge Lu is doing work on her house. She's tearing down the wall that separates the kitchen from the dining room. The width of each room is 12 feet. The new room will be a long rectangular space. The old kitchen floor had an area of 144 square feet, and the old dining room floor had an area of 120 square feet. What is the length of the new joined room?

	144 sq ft	120 sq ft
12 ft	kitchen	dining room

__12__ ft   __10__ ft   __22__ feet

254 two hundred fifty-four **CCLIV** 2 × 127

ABOUT THE PAGE NUMBER 254 has two whole number factors. They are both prime. What are they?

Teaching Notes for LAB page 253

Have students complete the page individually or with partners. Students continue to find missing factors in multiplication sentences. The format from Activity A is used to guide students in finding the missing factor.

Students should put a zero in any green hexagon they don't need. If students have difficulty with this rule, you might encourage them to cross out sentences they don't need.

Teaching Notes for LAB page 254

Some of the structure of the format from Activity A is removed, to help students apply the strategy of building larger multiplication sentences from smaller ones on their own.

In Problems 13–15, students complete multiplication sentences on their own, mimicking the process of the division algorithm.

Teacher Story "I collected the LAB pages at the end of the lesson to check students' fluency with multiplication facts. Because finding missing factors is, in a sense, dividing, it also showed me how comfortable students were with division facts."

Challenge Problem The Challenge Problem requires students to combine smaller multiplication facts to find a larger missing factor.

C **Writing Fact Families**

Purpose To relate multiplication and division, in preparation for solving division problems

Introduce Students will need their completed LAB page 253 for this exercise.

Task Challenge students to write fact families for some of the multiplication sentences that appear beneath the solid lines on LAB page 253. You might display a transparency of the page, or simply rewrite each sentence that you choose on the board. Direct students to write entire fact families on pieces of scratch paper before you invite volunteers to write each member of chosen fact families on the board.

Some examples:

Problem 1: $4 \times 9 = 36$ Problem 7: $9 \times 5 = 45$
$9 \times 4 = 36$ $5 \times 9 = 45$
$36 \div 9 = 4$ $45 \div 5 = 9$
$36 \div 4 = 9$ $45 \div 9 = 5$

If students need reminding, point out that fact families with identical multiplication factors have only two distinctly different family members. The family for Problem 5, for example, has only $3 \times 3 = 9$ and $9 \div 3 = 3$ as members. Both multiplication members are $3 \times 3 = 9$; both division members are $9 \div 3 = 3$.

You might walk around the room to see if any students need more practice writing multiplication and division fact families outside of class; they will need this skill in the next few lessons. Also, encourage students to write their sentences both horizontally and vertically. This will prepare them for the formats they will encounter in upcoming lessons.

 Talk Math

❓ Write two fact families that use 4 and 12 as two of the numbers.
Possible answers: (1) $4 \times 3 = 12$; $3 \times 4 = 12$; $12 \div 4 = 3$; $12 \div 3 = 4$;
(2) $4 \times 12 = 48$; $12 \times 4 = 48$; $48 \div 4 = 12$; $48 \div 12 = 4$

❓ Morgan rode her bike for 3 hours at an average rate of 6 miles per hour.
Write a fact family to describe the situation. Possible answer: $3 \times 6 = 18$;
$6 \times 3 = 18$; $18 \times 3 = 6$; $18 \times 6 = 3$

Materials
- For the teacher: transparency of LAB p. 253 (optional)
- For each student: completed copy of LAB p. 253

NCTM Standards 1, 2, 4, 6, 7, 8, 9, 10

 Ongoing Assessment
- Do students know how to write fact families?

Reflect and Summarize the Lesson

 Write Math How do you know that 4×8 plus 4×2 equals 4×10? Possible answers: Eight groups of 4 buttons plus 2 groups of 4 buttons makes 10 groups of 4 buttons, which is 40 total buttons; $(4 \times 8) + (4 \times 2) = 32 + 8 = 40 = 4 \times 10$.

Leveled Problem Solving

Veggie burgers come in packages of 8. Jessie has 5 packages, Henry has 3 packages, and Ravi has 1 package.

❶ Basic Level
How many veggie burgers are in the packages Jessie has? Explain. 40; 5 packages of 8 means 5×8, and $5 \times 8 = 40$.

❷ On Level
If all the veggie burgers are eaten, how many are eaten? Explain. 72; $5 \times 8 + 3 \times 8 + 1 \times 8 = 40 + 24 + 8 = 72$ or $(5 \times 8) + (3 \times 8) + (1 \times 8) = 9 \times 8 = 72$.

❸ Above Level
Ravi's package is not used. How many veggie burgers are used? Explain. 64; $5 \times 8 = 40$, and $3 \times 8 = 24$; $40 + 24 = 64$, or $(5 \times 8) + (3 \times 8) = 8 \times 8 = 64$.

Intervention

Activity Remaining Product Column

To solve missing factors problems, have students make a column to the right of each multiplication problem to keep track of the remaining product.

Here is an example for the fact $6 \times \blacksquare = 72$.

$6 \times 4 = 24$

$6 \times 5 = 30$

$6 \times 3 = 18$

$$\begin{array}{r} 72 \\ -\ 24 \\ \hline 48 \\ -\ 30 \\ \hline 18 \\ -\ 18 \\ \hline 0 \end{array}$$

Practice

Finding Missing Factors
Write the correct number in each box.

❶
$4 \times 3 = \underline{12}$
$40 \times 3 = \underline{120}$
$4 \times 30 = \underline{120}$
$40 \times 30 = \underline{1,200}$

❷
$5 \times 7 = \underline{35}$
$5 \times 70 = \underline{350}$
$50 \times 7 = \underline{350}$
$50 \times 70 = \underline{3,500}$

❸
$3 \times 11 = \underline{33}$
$30 \times 11 = \underline{330}$
$30 \times 110 = \underline{3,300}$
$3 \times 110 = \underline{330}$

❹
$7 \times 9 = \underline{63}$
$7 \times 90 = \underline{630}$
$70 \times 90 = \underline{6,300}$
$70 \times 9 = \underline{630}$

❺
$8 \times 700 = \underline{5,600}$
$80 \times \underline{70} = 5,600$
$8 \times \underline{70} = 560$
$\underline{800} \times 70 = 56,000$

❻
$50 \times \underline{4} = 200$
$50 \times \underline{40} = 2,000$
$\underline{5} \times 400 = 2,000$
$\underline{50} \times 400 = 20,000$

Test Prep
❶ 1 dozen = 12
How many in 50 dozen?
A. 60   C. 600
B. 120   D. 1,000

❷ 1 score = 20
How many scores in 800?
A. 4   C. 1,600
B. 40   D. 16,000

Practice P103

Extension

Finding Missing Factors Many multiplication facts are possible. One possible set of facts is given.
Find the missing factor. Use any numbers you want to build it.

❶
$8 \times 10 = 80$
$8 \times 3 = 24$

❷
$9 \times 10 = 90$
$9 \times 5 = 45$

❸
$10 \times 7 = 70$
$4 \times 7 = 28$

$8 \times \underline{13} = 104$
$9 \times \underline{15} = 135$
$\underline{14} \times 7 = 98$

❹
$20 \times 10 = 200$
$20 \times 3 = 60$
$6 \times 10 = 60$
$6 \times 3 = 18$
$26 \times 13 = \underline{338}$

❺
$30 \times 15 = 450$
$2 \times 15 = 30$
$32 \times 1 = 32$
$32 \times 16 = \underline{512}$

❻
$19 \times 20 = 380$
$19 \times 1 = 19$
$19 \times \underline{21} = 399$

Solve.
Sam is making a collage using 4-inch by 6-inch photographs. He bought a rectangular frame that is big enough to hold 18 of his photographs. What might the dimensions of the frame be?

One possible answer is given. Other answers are possible.

6 6 6 6 6
4
4
4

$\underline{12}$ inches by $\underline{36}$ inches

Extension E103

Spiral Review

Spiral Review Book page SR103 provides review of the previously learned skills and concepts:

- labeling number lines with positive and negative numbers
- solving problems using the strategy *make a graph*

You may wish to have students work with a partner to complete the page.

Number and Operations
Fill in the missing numbers on the number line.

❶ –6 –5 –4 –3 –2 –1 0 1 2 3 4 5 6 7

❷ –9 –8 –7 –6 –5 –4 –3 –2 –1 0 1 2 3 4

❸ –12 –11 –10 –9 –8 –7 –6 –5 –4 –3 –2 –1 0 1

Problem Solving
Solve the problem. Explain your answer.

Antonio asked his classmates to name their favorite after-school activity. Here are the results.

play sports	play a game	play sports	watch TV	play a game
watch TV	play a game	watch TV	play sports	play a game
play a game	read	play a game	play a game	play a game
watch TV	read	play sports	play a game	do homework
play sports	play a game	read	read	play sports

watch TV and read; Possible explanation: I made a list of all the activities and counted how many times each had been chosen. "Watch TV" and "read" were both chosen 4 times.

Spiral Review SR103

Extension Activity
Our "Fact" Families

Give pairs of students a 1–6 number cube. Have them toss the cube 3 times—the first 2 tosses to produce a 2-digit number and the next toss to produce a 1-digit number. Then have students write fact families for the numbers. If the 1-digit number is a factor of the 2-digit number, have them use the 2-digit number as the product. If it is not, have them use both numbers as factors.

Teacher's Notes 🍎

Daily Notes . . .

Quick Notes

More Ideas

Lesson 3 | Finding Missing Factors More Efficiently

NCTM Standards 1, 2, 6, 7, 8, 9, 10

Lesson Planner

- To practice finding missing factors in multiplication sentences
- To use estimation and compatible numbers to find the greatest number that can be multiplied by a given factor to approximate a product

1 | Daily Activities (TG p. 1037)

Open-Ended Problem Solving/Headline Story	Skills Practice and Review— Estimating Products

2 | Teach and Practice (TG pp. 1038–1041)

MATERIALS

(A) **Playing a Game: *Greatest Factors*** (TG pp. 1038–1039)

(B) **Discussing Game Strategies** (TG p. 1040)

(C) **Finding Missing Factors More Efficiently** (TG p. 1041)

- TR: Activity Masters, AM139–AM142
- transparency of one of AM139–AM142 (optional)
- LAB pp. 255–256
- SH p. 220

3 | Differentiated Instruction (TG p. 1042)

Leveled Problem Solving (TG p. 1042)	Practice Book P104
Intervention Activity (TG p. 1042)	Extension Book E104
Extension Activity (TG p. 1042)	Spiral Review Book SR104

Lesson Notes

About the Lesson

Students now focus on efficient strategies for finding missing factors in multiplication sentences. This lesson emphasizes a strategy that relies on estimates, using the largest possible factor in each step. This method mimics the strategy for completing the division problems in **Lesson 13.5**.

Developing Mathematical Language

Vocabulary: estimate

Students have used compatible numbers and rounding to *estimate* products in previous lessons. Students should become proficient in estimation for all four operations. Discuss with students the idea that *estimate* is both a verb and a noun—to *estimate* is to take an action, often rounding or finding compatible numbers and then performing an operation. The result of the action is the noun *estimate*.

Familiarize students with the term *estimate*.

Beginning Write 29 × 22 on the board. Then write on the board the exact product, 638, and an *estimate*, 600. Have students point to the *estimate*. Invite students to explain why it is the *estimate*.

Intermediate Have students describe how they decide whether to round a number up or down when using it to make an *estimate*.

Advanced Have students explain how they might use an *estimate* when shopping.

Open-Ended Problem Solving

Read the Headline Story to the students. If students seem stuck, you might prompt them with further questions such as: What were the missing numbers? What might the grocer have been counting?

 Headline Story

> At the grocery store, Nan overheard the grocer counting to himself: 12, 24, 36, 48, ... Her mom asked her a question. The next number Nan heard was 120.

Possible responses: The grocer is counting by 12s. The missing numbers are 60, 72, 84, 96, and 108. After 120 come 132, 144, and 156. The grocer may have been counting eggs because eggs are sold by the dozen.

Skills Practice and Review

Estimating Products

To review estimating, write a product involving two 2-digit numbers on the board. Choose problems that lend themselves to rounding and using compatible numbers, for example 37 × 43 or 71 × 54. Ask students to name factors they can use to estimate each product. Possible methods: (1) round to the nearest 10 (to estimate 37 × 43, multiply 40 × 40, 40 × 45, or 40 × 43); (2) use compatible numbers (to estimate 71 × 54, multiply 7 × 5). Once students have described their methods, have them estimate the answer and say whether the actual product would be higher or lower than their estimate. For 37 × 43, students might reason that 40 is greater than 37 and 45 is greater than 43, so the actual product will be less than this estimate. For 40 × 40, students may reason that the estimate must be greater than the actual product, because three more 40s were gained at the expense of three fewer 37s.

pairs   ⏱ 20 MIN

Ⓐ Playing *Greatest Factors*

Materials

- For the teacher:
  transparency of one
  of AM139–AM142
  (optional)
- For each pair:
  AM139–AM141;
  AM142 (optional)

NCTM Standards 1, 2, 6, 7, 8, 9, 10

Purpose To explore strategies for finding missing factors efficiently

Goal The object of the game *Greatest Factors* is to accumulate points by choosing large factors of given numbers more successfully than one's opponent.

Prepare Materials Each pair of players will need one of Activity Masters: Missing Factors Game. Each page has four puzzles for students to complete. Begin by showing the class a transparency of one of the Greatest Factors Game pages and, with a volunteer, demonstrate how to play the game.

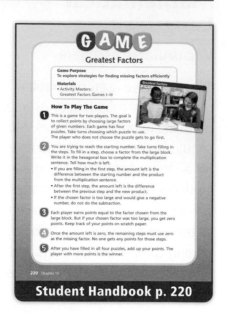

Student Handbook p. 220

Teacher Story "When pairs of students played the *Greatest Factors* game in my class, I had them take turns choosing which of the four puzzles to complete next. The student who didn't choose the puzzle got to fill in the first step. Students could use strategic thinking to find the puzzle that would give the fewest points to their partner, namely, the puzzle with the smallest first factor."

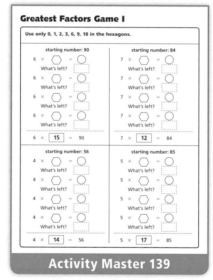

Activity Master 139

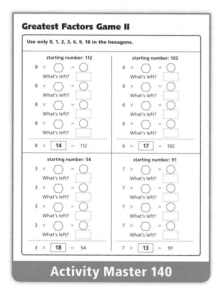

Activity Master 140

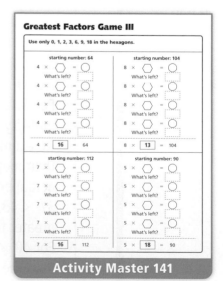

Activity Master 141

How to Play

❶ Students take turns filling in the steps in each puzzle. (See the Teacher Story for an idea about how students might decide who gets to choose the first factor.)

❷ The starting number is the product players are trying to reach. To fill in a step, the player chooses a factor from the large block, writes it in the hexagonal box to complete the multiplication sentence, and tells how much is left. (If the student is filling in the first step in a puzzle, the amount that is left is the difference between the starting number and the product from the multiplication sentence. Otherwise, it is the difference between the previous step and the new product.) If the chosen factor is too large (i.e. the subtraction would yield a negative number), the player should not perform the subtraction.

❸ The student earns points equal to the factor chosen from the large block. (If the chosen factor was too large, the student gets zero points.) Students should keep track of their points for each turn on scratch paper, so that they can total them once all four puzzles have been completed.

❹ Once the amount that is left is 0, the remaining steps in the puzzle must use 0 as the missing factor. Neither student gets points for these steps.

❺ The player with the most points (the player who, in effect, chose the greatest factors) after all four puzzles have been completed wins.

Extend Students who finish quickly can play again with a different game page. (See Differentiated Instruction to learn how to use the fourth game page.)

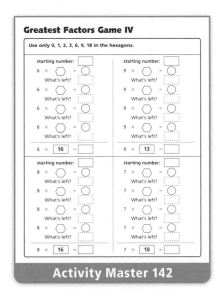

Activity Master 142

B Discussing Game Strategies

NCTM Standards 1, 2, 6, 7, 8, 9, 10

Purpose To discuss strategies for finding the greatest possible factor of a number

Introduce Give all students an opportunity to complete a round of the *Greatest Factors* game (Activity A). Then bring the class together.

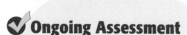
✔ Ongoing Assessment

- Do students use appropriate strategies to find the greatest possible factor of a number?

Task Ask students to explain the strategies they used to play *Greatest Factors.* Because of the way points are earned, most students likely used the greatest available factor from the block at the top of the page for each step. If students don't bring this up, mention it yourself. Help them to understand that, aside from earning them more points, this strategy yields the best estimate of the missing factor. Furthermore, it completes the puzzle in the fewest steps and so is a very efficient strategy. Students will use this strategy on the student page and in later lessons.

Instead of using this strategy, students who are uncomfortable with certain multiplication facts may have used only numbers from the block that they could easily multiply by the given factor. Encourage these students to gradually use larger missing factors, as this will better prepare them for solving division problems.

Talk Math

❷ You are going to multiply 7 times either 4 or 5, then subtract the product from 40. Which of the two possible factors, 4 or 5, will yield the smallest difference after subtraction? How do you know? 5; Possible response: Because 5 is greater than 4, the product 7 × 5 is greater than the product 7 × 4. Therefore, the difference, after subtraction from 40, will be less.

❷ You are going to multiply 9 times either 6 or 7, then subtract the product from 70. Which of the two possible factors, 6 or 7, will yield the greatest difference after subtraction? How do you know? 6; Possible response: Because 6 is less than 7, the product 6 × 9 is less than the product 7 × 9. Therefore, the difference, after subtraction from 70, will be greater.

Use with Lesson Activity Book pp. 255–256.

Finding Missing Factors More Efficiently LAB pp. 255–256

 individuals or pairs

 20 MIN

Purpose To practice solving missing-factor puzzles

NCTM Standards 1, 2, 6, 7, 8, 9, 10

Lesson Activity Book p. 255

Chapter 15
Lesson 3
Finding Missing Factors More Efficiently
NCTM Standards 1, 2, 6, 7, 8, 9, 10

Many answers are possible. One possible answer is given.

Rule I: Use only numbers from the **green** block to fill in the **green** hexagons.
Rule II: Try to use the largest number possible at each step.
Rule III: Use a zero for any green hexagon that you do not need.

| 0 | 1 | 2 | 3 | 6 | 9 | 18 |

1 starting number: 45
$9 \times \langle 3 \rangle = 27$
What's left? 18
$9 \times \langle 2 \rangle = 18$
What's left? 0
$9 \times \langle 0 \rangle = 0$
What's left? 0
$9 \times \langle 5 \rangle = 45$

2 starting number: 42
$7 \times \langle 6 \rangle = 42$
What's left? 0
$7 \times \langle 0 \rangle = 0$
What's left? 0
$7 \times \langle 0 \rangle = 0$
What's left? 0
$7 \times \langle 6 \rangle = 42$

3 starting number: 96
$8 \times \langle 9 \rangle = 72$
What's left? 24
$8 \times \langle 3 \rangle = 24$
What's left? 0
$8 \times \langle 0 \rangle = 0$
What's left? 0
$8 \times \langle 12 \rangle = 96$

4 starting number: 75
$5 \times \langle 9 \rangle = 45$
What's left? 30
$5 \times \langle 6 \rangle = 30$
What's left? 0
$5 \times \langle 0 \rangle = 0$
What's left? 0
$5 \times \langle 15 \rangle = 75$

5 starting number: 104
$8 \times \langle 9 \rangle = 72$
What's left? 32
$8 \times \langle 3 \rangle = 24$
What's left? 8
$8 \times \langle 1 \rangle = 8$
What's left? 0
$8 \times \langle 13 \rangle = 104$

6 starting number: 98
$7 \times \langle 9 \rangle = 63$
What's left? 35
$7 \times \langle 3 \rangle = 21$
What's left? 14
$7 \times \langle 2 \rangle = 14$
What's left? 0
$7 \times \langle 14 \rangle = 98$

$3 \times 5 \times 17$ CCLV two hundred fifty five **255**

ABOUT THE PAGE NUMBER 255 is the product of three prime numbers. What are they?

Lesson Activity Book p. 256

Again, use 0, 1, 2, 3, 6, 9, or 18 to build the missing factor in the orange hexagon. Various multiplication facts are possible. One set of facts is given.

| 0 | 1 | 2 | 3 | 6 | 9 | 18 |

7 starting number: 32
$2 \times 9 = 18$
$2 \times 6 = 12$
$2 \times 1 = 2$

8 starting number: 51
$3 \times 9 = 27$
$3 \times 6 = 18$
$3 \times 2 = 6$

9 starting number: 275
$25 \times 9 = 225$
$25 \times 2 = 50$

$2 \times \langle 16 \rangle = 32$

$3 \times \langle 17 \rangle = 51$

$25 \times \langle 11 \rangle = 275$

10 $15 \times 9 = 135$
$15 \times 3 = 45$
$15 \times 1 = 15$

11 $4 \times 18 = 72$
$4 \times 9 = 36$
$4 \times 6 = 24$

12 $9 \times 18 = 162$
$9 \times 6 = 54$
$9 \times 1 = 9$

$15 \times \langle 13 \rangle = 195$

$4 \times \langle 33 \rangle = 132$

$9 \times \langle 25 \rangle = 225$

13 Challenge Soo Jin wants to give 12 stickers to each of her 8 friends. She has 71 stickers. How many more stickers does Soo Jin need? Show your work.

$12 \times 8 = 96$
$96 - 71 = 25$

__25__ stickers

256 two hundred fifty-six CCLVI $2 \times 2 \times 2 \times 2 \times 2 \times 2 \times 2 \times 2$

ABOUT THE PAGE NUMBER 256 is a square number. What square number is a factor of 256? 16 pounds is 256 ounces.

Teaching Notes for LAB page 255

Have students work on the page independently or in pairs. The page presents missing-factor puzzles in the format of the *Greatest Factors* game. For each puzzle, encourage students to look for the greatest missing factor first. There is enough space for students to use three steps in each puzzle. They may be able to complete some of the puzzles in fewer steps.

Teaching Notes for LAB page 256

On this page, students are not given a format for finding the missing factors.

Challenge Problem The Challenge Problem is a multi-step word problem involving multiplication and subtraction.

Reflect and Summarize the Lesson

Write Math The Dairy Barn sells milk cartons in packs of 6. You need to buy enough cartons so that 75 people each get at least one carton. How many packs do you need to buy? How did you find the answer?
13 cartons are needed; Possible explanation: 10 packs will be enough for $10 \times 6 = 60$ people. That leaves $75 - 60 = 15$ people who need milk. Two more packs won't be quite enough ($2 \times 6 = 12$ people) but 3 more packs will be ($3 \times 6 = 18$ people). So, $10 + 3 = 13$ packs will provide for 75 people.

3 | Differentiated Instruction

Leveled Problem Solving

Cans of soft drinks come in cartons of 12.
Jai is selling cans at the fair. He sells 108 cans.

❶ Basic Level
How many cartons does he sell in all? Explain. 9 cartons; $9 \times 12 = 108$.

❷ On Level
After Jai sells the first 7 cartons, how many cartons are left? Explain. 2; $7 \times 12 = 84$; $108 - 84 = 24$, and $24 \div 12 = 2$.

❸ Above Level
He sells all of 3 cartons and then all of 2 more cartons. How many cartons are left? Explain. 4; $(3 \times 12) + (2 \times 12) = 5 \times 12 = 60$; $108 - 60 = 48$, and $48 \div 12 = 4$.

Intervention	Practice	Extension

Activity Even/Odd

Have students look at the product before estimating a missing factor. Tell students that if the product is even, one or both factors must be even; if the product is odd, both factors must be odd. Once students have determined whether the missing factor is even or odd, have them estimate.

If *both* the given product and factor are even, then the missing factor can be either even or odd.

Practice P104

Extension E104

Spiral Review

Spiral Review Book page SR104 provides review of the following previously learned skills and concepts:

- practicing comparing numbers expressed as decimals
- expressing the probability of an event as a fraction

You may wish to have students work with a partner to complete the page.

Spiral Review SR104

Extension Activity
Distributing the Area

Have pairs of students draw a large rectangle on grid paper. For each toss of a 1–6 number cube, have them draw a line through the rectangle, making a smaller rectangle whose width is the number tossed. They should continue until a toss cannot be used and then write a number sentence to illustrate how they used the distributive property to find the total area. 15 × 20 rectangle; tosses of 6, 4, and 5: $(6 \times 20) + (4 \times 20) + (5 \times 20) = 300$ sq units

Teacher's Notes 🍎

Daily Notes . . .

Quick Notes

More Ideas

Lesson 4 Estimating Missing Factors and Quotients

NCTM Standards 1, 2, 6, 7, 8, 9, 10

Lesson Planner

STUDENT OBJECTIVES
- To relate multiplication and division number families by rewriting them as missing-number sentences
- To use rounding and compatible numbers to estimate missing factors and quotients
- To build up missing factors using multiples of 10 and 1

1 | Daily Activities (TG p. 1045)

Open-Ended Problem Solving/Headline Story	Skills Practice and Review— Estimating Products

2 | Teach and Practice (TG pp. 1046–1049)

MATERIALS

Ⓐ **Rewriting Missing Factor Problems** (TG p. 1046)

Ⓑ **Estimating Missing Products and Quotients** (TG p. 1047)

Ⓒ **Estimating Missing Factors and Quotients** (TG p. 1048)

- 📖 LAB pp. 257–258
- 📖 SH p. 212

3 | Differentiated Instruction (TG p. 1050)

Leveled Problem Solving (TG p. 1050)	Practice Book P105
Intervention Activity (TG p. 1050)	Extension Book E105
Extension Activity (TG p. 1050)	Spiral Review Book SR105

Lesson Notes

About the Lesson

In this lesson, students apply the strategies they've been developing in this chapter directly to division. First, they rewrite missing-factor problems as division problems and notice that they have been dividing all along. On the LAB pages, they rewrite division sentences as missing-factor sentences. To prepare for completing vertical division problems in the next lesson, students continue to develop the strategy of estimating larger parts of a missing factor before smaller parts, now focusing on multiples of 10 and 1 to build up the missing factor.

About the Mathematics

The space for students to write how much is left after each step in the missing-factor puzzles on the LAB pages is similar to the standard vertical division format students will see in **Lesson 13.5**. In standard division algorithms, students use estimates and compatible numbers to figure out how many times the divisor goes into the number of hundreds, tens, or ones of the dividend. In the following problem, students begin by figuring out how many hundreds of times 3 goes into 400.

(continued on page R7)

Developing Mathematical Language

Vocabulary: compatible numbers, round

Students have used both terms, *rounding* and *compatible numbers,* in lessons involving multiplication estimates. Now they will use them as they find larger missing factors. For example, in 560 ÷ 8, the numbers 56 and 8 are *compatible numbers* because 8 × 7 = 56 so 8 × 70 = 560. The number 560 could have been *rounded* from a number between 555 to 564 or it could have been chosen as a compatible number for any number from 520 to 600 to estimate the missing factor, 70.

Familiarize students with the terms *compatible numbers* and *round.*

Beginning Remind students that *compatible* means "agreeable." Tell students that if two people are compatible, then they like each other and are friendly. Relate *compatible numbers* or friendly numbers to the idea of fact families and that numbers in the same fact family are compatible.

Intermediate Write a number on the board. Have students write on paper one or two sentences describing how to *round* it.

Advanced Have students describe how they would find *compatible numbers.*

Open-Ended Problem Solving

Read the Headline Story to the students. Encourage them to think of interesting scenarios that incorporate information from the story.

 Headline Story

> At the beginning of every math class, Mrs. Star has the class count by a particular number. Robin arrived late to class and heard someone say the number 39. Mrs. Star challenged her to give the next multiple, even though she hadn't heard the previous numbers.

Possible responses: Since 39 is a multiple of 1, 3, 13, and 39, the next number could be 40, 42, 52, or 78. If the next number is 42, then Mrs. Star started with 3 and the previous numbers named were 36, 33, 30, 27, 24, and so on. If the next number is 52, the previous numbers were 26 and 13. If the next number is 78, Mrs. Star must have started 39, and the next few numbers after 78 would be 117, 156, 195, and 234.

Skills Practice and Review

Estimating Products

As in the previous lesson, write a multiplication problem on the board involving two 2-digit numbers. Choose problems that lend themselves to using rounding or compatible numbers to make estimates. For example, you might write 36 × 92 or 24 × 38 on the board, and ask students for the factors they would use to estimate the product. Using rounding, students might multiply 40 × 90 for the first problem and 20 × 40 for the second problem. Using compatible numbers, they might multiply 36 × 100 for the first problem and 25 × 40 for the second problem. For each problem, ask students whether the resulting estimate would be more or less than the actual product.

whole class | 15 MIN

NCTM Standards 1, 2, 6, 7, 8, 9, 10

A Rewriting Missing Factor Problems

Purpose To apply strategies developed in this chapter to the solution of division problems

Introduce Write a missing-factor problem on the board, for example 5 × ■ = 55.

Task Challenge students to rewrite the problem as a division problem. Then, to illustrate how multiplication and division problems can involve identical information, have students use both the missing-factor number sentence and the division sentence to tell the same (or similar) stories.

For example, if you write 5 × ■ = 55, students might tell a story about having 5 bags of marbles and 55 total marbles, but no knowledge how many marbles are in each bag. Students can rewrite this sentence as the division sentence 55 ÷ 5 = ■. Then they might tell a similar story about putting 55 marbles into 5 bags.

In each of these stories, the missing piece of information is the number of marbles in each bag. Ask students to draw pictures to match their stories. For example, students might draw 5 bags with 11 marbles in each of them.

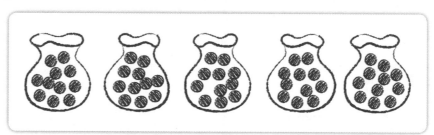

To connect these sentences to pictures from previous lessons, you might also (for the sentences 5 × ■ = 55 and 55 ÷ 5 = ■) have students draw a rectangle with an area of 55 square units and one side that measures 5 units. The missing side (11 units) is the missing number in the number sentences.

	11 units
5 units	55 square units

Repeat with another missing-factor problem, but now ask students to write the division sentence in both a horizontal and a vertical format. For example, if you wrote 8 × ■ = 136, then students should write 136 ÷ 8 = ■ and 8)136. (Some students may reverse the positions of the 8 and the blank space, which is not incorrect, but you might encourage them to write the problem so that the missing number is the answer or result of the sentence.) When the problem has been written on the board in both formats, again consider them one at a time, discussing what the problem is asking and what number goes in the blank space.

💬 Talk Math

❷ Marlie bought 4 printers for a total cost of $800. Write a multiplication sentence and a division sentence to describe the story. 4 × ■ = 800 and 800 ÷ 4 = ■

❷ What multiplication sentence and division sentence can you write to describe the drawing? 7 × ■ = 28 and 28 ÷ 7 = ■

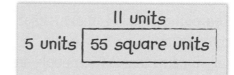

7 units
28 square units

B Estimating Missing Products and Quotients

  whole class · 15 MIN

Purpose To choose convenient missing factors and quotients

NCTM Standards 1, 2, 6, 7, 8, 9, 10

Introduce Review the strategy students practiced in the previous lesson. They estimated a missing factor by finding the greatest possible factor, both in missing-factor problems and in the corresponding division problems. Now, instead of being given factors to choose from in building a missing factor, students will choose ones that they find "convenient." You might spend a minute brainstorming with your students to identify characteristics that might make a number "convenient." Make sure students realize that they can always use multiples of 10, which are easy to multiply by.

Problem Write a missing-factor problem on the board, such as $12 \times \blacksquare = 468$. Ask students to name the closest multiple of 10 that is smaller than the missing factor.

Students should recognize that the missing factor in this sentence is close to 40, since $12 \times 4 = 48$. But $12 \times 40 = 480$, and 480 is greater than the given product. Therefore, the closest multiple of 10 that is smaller than the missing factor must be 30 ($12 \times 30 = 360$, which is less than 468).

Now ask students for the corresponding division sentence. Ask them to estimate the nearest multiple of 10 that is smaller than the missing factor. Students should realize that the same multiple of 10 that gave the closest estimate without going over the given product, will also be the answer to the corresponding division sentence. That is, $468 \div 12$ is more than 30 (and less than 40).

Practice Repeat this activity with additional missing factor problems. For each problem, have students estimate the missing factor or quotient using a multiple of 10 or some other convenient number. Some other missing factor sentences you might use are given at the right.

$6 \times \blacksquare = 78$ Possible estimate: 10

$23 \times \blacksquare = 253$ Possible estimate: 10

$11 \times \blacksquare = 233$ Possible estimate: 20

$49 \times \blacksquare = 1499$ Possible estimate: 30

$29 \times \blacksquare = 1508$ Possible estimate: 50

💬 Talk Math

❷ For the problem $15 \times \blacksquare = 400$, what is the closest multiple of 10 that is smaller than the missing factor? Explain your reasoning. 20; Possible explanation: $15 \times 20 = 300$, which is less than 400. The next larger multiple of 10 after 20 is 30, but $15 \times 30 = 450$, which is too large. So, 20 is the closest multiple of 10 that is smaller than the missing factor.

❷ For the problem $15 \times \blacksquare = 595$, what is the closest multiple of 10 that is smaller than the missing factor? Explain your reasoning. 30; Possible explanation: $15 \times 40 = 600$, which is very close to 595, but not smaller than 595. So, the next smaller multiple of 10 before 40, which is 30, must be the answer: $15 \times 30 = 450$.

Estimating Missing Factors and Quotients LAB pp. 257–258

  20 MIN

Purpose To deepen students' understanding of the connection between missing-factor problems and division problems

NCTM Standards 1, 2, 6, 7, 8, 9, 10

Lesson Activity Book p. 257

Chapter 13
Lesson 4

Name _____ Date _____

Estimating Missing Factors and Quotients

NCTM Standards 1, 2, 6, 7, 8, 9, 10

Complete the puzzles. Begin by rewriting each division sentence as a multiplication sentence.

Rule I: Use only numbers from the **green** block to fill in the **green** boxes.
Rule II: Try to use the largest number possible at each step.
Rule III: Use a zero for any **green** box that you do not need.

Various answers are possible. One possible answer is given.

0	1	2	3	4	5	6	7	8	9
0	10	20	30	40	50	60	70	80	90

Hint: Fill in the green boxes before the blue boxes.

❶ 136 ÷ 8 = **17**
8 × **17** = 136
8 × **10** = 80
What's left? **56**
8 × **7** = **56**
What's left? **0**
8 × **0** = **0**
What's left? **0**

❷ 712 ÷ 8 = **89**
8 × **89** = 712
8 × **80** = **640**
72
8 × **9** = **72**
0
8 × **0** = **0**
0

❸ 216 ÷ 9 = **24**
9 × **24** = 216
9 × **20** = **180**
36
9 × **4** = **36**
0
9 × **0** = **0**
0

prime   CCLVII   two hundred fifty-seven   **257**

ABOUT THE PAGE NUMBER 257 is a prime number. It is also the sum of two perfect squares. What are they?

Lesson Activity Book p. 258

Use numbers, words, or pictures to solve these problems.

❹ Tim and four of his friends found 185 nickels! They shared the coins so that each ended up with the same number of nickels. How many nickels does each have? Write a number sentence to explain your answer.

185 ÷ 5 = 37
or
5 × 37 = 185 ·

_____**37**_____ nickels

❺ The police department spent $357 to buy seven identical winter coats for their officers. How much did each coat cost? Write a number sentence to explain your answer.

7 × 51 = 357
or
357 ÷ 7 = 51

$ ____**51.00**____

❻ Challenge State Elementary School is having a field day. All 283 students were put onto six different teams as evenly as possible. Did all the teams have the same number of students? Explain your answer.

No; Possible explanation: 5 teams can have 47 students,

but 1 team must have 48 students.

_____

_____

258 two hundred fifty-eight   CCLVIII   2 × 3 × 43

ABOUT THE PAGE NUMBER Is 258 even or odd? What can you divide it by?

Teaching Notes for LAB page 257

Have students work on the page individually or with partners. Students continue to relate multiplication and division as they use multiples of 10 and 1 to find missing factors and quotients. You might go over the rules for this page with your students before they begin. While the problems on the page are similar to previous ones in this chapter, there are now two green blocks, and students can choose numbers from either block. They are encouraged, nevertheless, to use a multiple of 10 first, so that they can get the best estimate from the start.

Teaching Notes for LAB page 258

Students can use multiplication or division to solve each of the problems on the page. This further demonstrates the connection between missing-factor problems and division problems.

Challenge Problem The Challenge Problem presents a situation in which dividing does not result in an even answer. Students must use their understanding of the context to obtain the answer from the related division sentence.

Write Math

Estimate the missing factor in this sentence: 12 × ■ = 216. Explain your reasoning.
Possible estimate: 18; possible explanation: 12 × 20 = 240 and 12 × 10 = 120, so the missing factor must be between 10 and 20. It must be closer to 20 than it is to 10, because 240 is closer to 216 than 120 is. Guess 18 as it is closer to 20.

Review Model . . . .

Refer students to Review Model: Finding Missing Factors in the *Student Handbook,* p. 212, to review the steps that will help them solve missing-factor problems.

✔ Check for Understanding

❶ 16

❷ 24

❸ 31

❹ 15

❺ 33

❻ 21

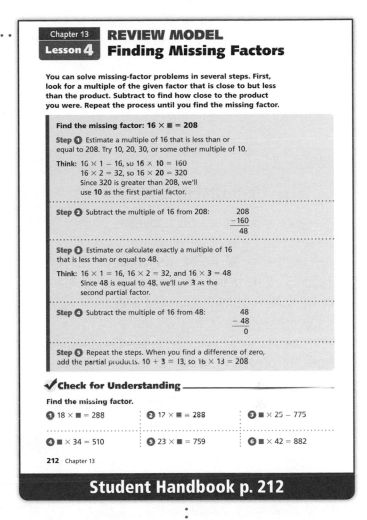

Chapter 13   **REVIEW MODEL**
Lesson **4**   **Finding Missing Factors**

You can solve missing-factor problems in several steps. First, look for a multiple of the given factor that is close to but less than the product. Subtract to find how close to the product you were. Repeat the process until you find the missing factor.

Find the missing factor: 16 × ■ = 208

Step ❶ Estimate a multiple of 16 that is less than or equal to 208. Try 10, 20, 30, or some other multiple of 10.

Think: 16 × 1 = 16, so 16 × 10 = 160
16 × 2 = 32, so 16 × 20 = 320
Since 320 is greater than 208, we'll use **10** as the first partial factor.

Step ❷ Subtract the multiple of 16 from 208:
208
−160
48

Step ❸ Estimate or calculate exactly a multiple of 16 that is less than or equal to 48.

Think: 16 × 1 = 16, 16 × 2 = 32, and 16 × 3 = 48. Since 48 is equal to 48, we'll use **3** as the second partial factor.

Step ❹ Subtract the multiple of 16 from 48:
48
− 48
0

Step ❺ Repeat the steps. When you find a difference of zero, add the partial products. 10 + 3 = 13, so 16 × 13 = 208

✔ Check for Understanding

Find the missing factor.

❶ 18 × ■ = 288   **❷** 12 × ■ = 288   **❸** ■ × 25 = 775

❹ ■ × 34 = 510   **❺** 23 × ■ = 759   **❻** ■ × 42 = 882

212 Chapter 13

Student Handbook p. 212

Leveled Problem Solving

The Sweater Shoppe is unpacking a shipment of sweaters.
Each carton holds 24 sweaters. There are 864 sweaters.

❶ Basic Level

After unpacking 10 cartons, how many sweaters are left to unpack? Explain. 624; 10 × 24 = 240, and 864 − 240 = 624.

❷ On Level

The clerks unpack 20 cartons, take a break, and then unpack 10 more cartons. How many sweaters are left to unpack? Explain. 144; 20 × 24 = 480, 10 × 24 = 240, 480 + 240 = 720, and 864 − 720 = 144.

❸ Above Level

There are 6 cartons left after 3 clerks each unpack the same number of cartons. How many does each clerk unpack? Explain. 10; 3 × 10 = 30, 30 × 24 = 720, 864 − 720 = 144, and 144 ÷ 6 = 24.

Intervention

Activity Underlining Division

To estimate, have students underline the first two digits of the dividend, such as in 14 × ■ = 294. Then have students estimate the missing factor for 14 × ■ = 29 without going over. In this problem, 14 × 2 = 28, but 14 × 3 = 42 (too high). The estimate should be greater than 20 and less than 30. Since 29 is very close to 28, the estimate will be much closer to 20 than to 30. Give students similar practice problems.

Practice

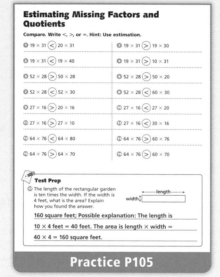

Practice P105

Extension

Estimating Missing Factors and Quotients

Extension E105

Spiral Review

Spiral Review Book page SR105 provides review of the following previously learned skills and concepts:

- exploring rules that when graphed are straight lines
- estimating area with copies of standard area units

You may wish to have students work with a partner to complete the page.

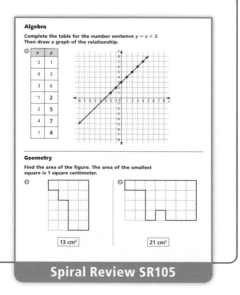

Spiral Review SR105

Extension Activity
Multiply or Divide?

Allow pairs of students to choose a 1-digit factor and a 2-digit factor. Ask them to write the numbers' fact family. Then have each pair of students write a story problem, leaving out the 2-digit factor, so that the problem can be solved by either multiplication or division.

When they have finished, have pairs exchange their work with that of another pair and solve the story problem.

Teacher's Notes 🍎

Daily Notes . . .

Quick Notes

More Ideas

Lesson 5 Dividing Using Multiplication Puzzles

NCTM Standards 1, 2, 6, 7, 8, 9, 10

Lesson Planner

- To translate between division problems and missing-factor multiplication
- To solve division problems using multiplication strategies

1 Daily Activities (TG p. 1053)

Open-Ended Problem Solving/Headline Story	Skills Practice and Review—Estimating Quotients

2 Teach and Practice (TG pp. 1054–1058)

	MATERIALS
Ⓐ **Representing Division** (TG pp. 1054–1055)	• transparency of AM143 (optional)
Ⓑ **Recording Division** (TG p. 1056)	• square tiles (optional)
Ⓒ **Dividing Using Multiplication Puzzles** (TG p. 1057)	• 📖 LAB pp. 259–260 • 📖 SH pp. 213–214

3 Differentiated Instruction (TG p. 1059)

Leveled Problem Solving (TG p. 1059)	Practice Book P106
Intervention Activity (TG p. 1059)	Extension Book E106
Extension Activity (TG p. 1059)	Spiral Review Book SR106
Art Connection (TG p. 1018)	

Lesson Notes

About the Lesson

Students continue to solve division problems, using the strategies they've developed for completing missing-factor puzzles.

Developing Mathematical Language

Vocabulary: dividend, divisor, factor, product, quotient

Because students were working entirely within the context of multiplication earlier in this chapter, it was natural for them to use the terms *factor* and *product.* Now that they are working explicitly with division, it may seem less obvious that, since the numbers are still related in the same way, they can continue to be called *factors* and *products.* The terms *quotient, divisor,* and *dividend* specify the three numbers in division sentences, but it is not necessary for students to memorize these terms; you may, without harm, encourage continued use of the terms *factor* and *product.*

Review the terms *dividend, divisor, factor, product,* and *quotient.*

Beginning Write a division sentence and the terms *dividend, divisor,* and *quotient* on the board. Ask a student to draw a line from each term to a part of the division sentence. Write the related multiplication sentence and the terms *factor* and *product,* and repeat the activity.

Intermediate Write a multiplication sentence on the board. Have a volunteer rewrite it as a division sentence and use the terms *dividend, divisor, factor, product,* or *quotient* to identify each part of the sentence.

Advanced Have students write a paragraph comparing the division terms to the multiplication terms.

---

1 | Daily Activities

Open-Ended Problem Solving

Read the Headline Story to the students. Encourage them to make imaginative statements using information from the story.

 Headline Story

> **Jake and three friends bought a packet of 24 baseball cards. They planned to treat some other friends by sharing all the cards evenly with them.**

Possible responses: If just Jake and his 3 friends shared the cards, each would get 6 cards. The more people they share with, the fewer cards each will get. The cards can be shared equally among 2, 3, 4, 6, 8, 12, or 24 people. If 12 people share the cards, each will get 2. If Jake and his 3 friends each gave away half of their cards, then 8 people would have 3 cards each.

Skills Practice and Review

Estimating Quotients

As in previous lessons, write a number sentence on the board, but this time write a division problem instead of a missing-factor problem. For example, you might write $180 \div 8 = \blacksquare$. Ask students how they can use compatible numbers to estimate this quotient. Students may reason that 8 is close to 9 and use $180 \div 9$ to estimate the answer (20). You might next challenge students to consider whether the actual quotient is more or less than their estimate. This will help you assess students' understanding of division. The greater the number of pieces that the whole is split into, the smaller the quotient. Therefore, using 9 instead of 8 to estimate the quotient results in a smaller answer than the actual quotient. Repeat this activity with other division problems. Remind students that compatible numbers don't have to be multiples of 10. For example, students can use $240 \div 24$ to estimate the quotient $248 \div 24$, obtaining an estimate of 10.

pairs · 15 MIN

A Representing Division

Materials
- For each student: square tiles (optional)

NCTM Standards 1, 2, 6, 7, 8, 9, 10

Purpose To apply strategies for solving missing-factor problems to division problems

Introduce Students should complete this activity with partners. Give each student a copy of Explore: A Division Story. The page asks students to draw a picture to represent the situation, but, as an added aid, you might also provide students with square tiles.

Differentiated Instruction

On Level As students answer the Explore questions, walk around the room and informally assess students' fluency with finding missing factors. This will help you determine students' readiness for solving division problems.

Task Direct students to read the story of Angi's lawn and then to answer the questions at the bottom of the page. The story can be translated into a number sentence in either of two equivalent ways:

$7 \times \blacksquare = 126$ OR
$126 \div 7 = \blacksquare$

Students may choose any numbers they wish to build up the missing factor (or quotient). This will help them develop their own ways of solving problems similar to this one.

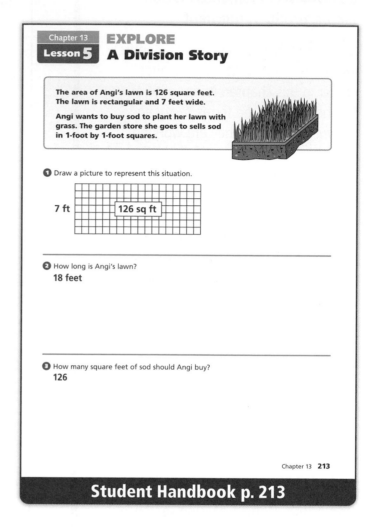

Student Handbook p. 213

Share When all students have had time to work through the page, gather the class to discuss their answers to the questions.

❶ Draw a picture to represent this situation.

Most students will have used an area model or rectangular array to represent the picture. Invite a student to draw such a picture on the board:

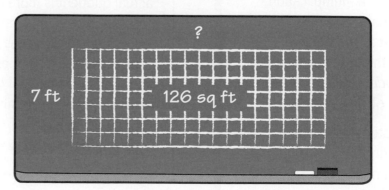

❷ How long is Angi's lawn?

Ask students to give the corresponding multiplication and division number sentences for this picture. $7 \times \blacksquare = 126$ or $126 \div 7 = \blacksquare$

Next, ask volunteers to share their strategies for completing the number sentences. Students likely used multiples of 10 to build up the missing number. They might have reasoned that a length of 10 feet would be too short and a length of 20 feet would be too long. Since a length of 10 feet results in an area of 70 square feet, the remaining length must account for another 56 square feet of area. Because $7 \times 8 = 56$, the remaining length must be 8 feet, for a total length of $10 + 8 = 18$ feet.

❸ How many square feet of sod should Angi buy? 126 square feet

💬 **Talk Math** Mark's lawn also has an area of 126 square feet, but it is 9 feet wide.

❓ What two number sentences can you write to represent the situation? $9 \times \blacksquare = 126$ or $126 \div 9 = \blacksquare$

❓ How long is Mark's lawn? 14 feet

❓ How did you find the answer? Possible response: $10 \times 9 = 90$, so I knew the length must be more than 10 feet. Since $126 - 90 = 36$, I reasoned that the length in excess of 10 feet had to account for an additional 36 square feet of area. Since $9 \times 4 = 36$, the total length must be $10 + 4 = 14$ feet.

B Recording Division

Materials

- For the teacher: transparency of AM143 (optional)

NCTM Standards 1, 2, 6, 7, 8, 9, 10

Concept Alert

Many fourth-graders have difficulty reading the vertical format for division. For example, students may read 9)153 as "9 divided by 153." To forestall such confusion, these lessons encourage students to think about the meaning behind each problem. Support struggling students by suggesting that they read a problem like the above as "9 goes into 153 how many times?" Although this approach omits the word "divide," it clearly conveys the idea that division is the requisite operation, at the same time allowing students to read the problem from left to right.

Purpose To introduce a new format for recording division problems

Introduce This activity introduces students to a format for recording division that resembles the formats they have been using in the chapter, but that mimics standard formats for multi-digit division. If possible, display a transparency of Activity Master: Blank Division Format. Alternatively, draw the blank format on the board.

Task Recall the division problem from Activity A, $126 \div 7 = \blacksquare$. Challenge students to work with you to record the steps for solving that problem using a new format.

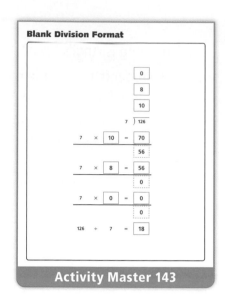

Activity Master 143

The solution shown on Activity Master: Blank Division Format begins by finding the greatest factor that is a multiple of 10. That is one approach but you should proceed by recording the steps that make the most sense to your students. One solution that is different from the one shown on the Activity Master is shown at the right.

As you have students fill in the empty boxes on the page, have them explain what they are doing in each step, and relate that step to the corresponding step in a missing-factor problem. Students should see that the only change between this new format and the missing-factor format is that the numbers they use to build the missing factor are now also recorded on top of the division bar at the top of the problem. Students will get more practice with this format and the reasoning behind it as they complete the LAB pages. If you have time, have students complete another problem as a class, using this format. For example, you might ask them to solve $153 \div 9 = \blacksquare$. 17

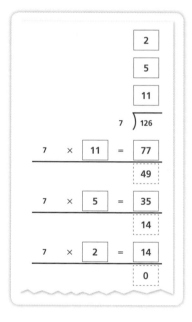

Talk Math

❷ When Jo divided 126 by 7, she tried 12 as her first missing factor and 4 as her second missing factor. What was her third and last missing factor? Explain your reasoning. 2; Possible explanation: Her first two missing factors had a sum of 16. Since the quotient is 18, her third missing factor must have been $18 - 16 = 2$.

❷ When Tomas divided 126 by 7, he tried 20 as his first missing factor. How did he find out that 20 was incorrect? Possible answer: He multiplied 20×7 and found that the product, 140, was greater than 126.

Purpose To practice solving division problems using both vertical and horizontal formats

NCTM Standards 1, 2, 6, 7, 8, 9, 10

Lesson Activity Book p. 259

Name _____ Date _____

Chapter 13
Lesson 5 **Dividing Using Multiplication Puzzles**

NCTM Standards 1, 2, 6, 7, 8, 9, 10

Complete the puzzles. Rewrite each division sentence as a multiplication sentence. Choose numbers for the green boxes from this list:
0, 1, 2, 3, 4, 5, 6, 7, 8, 9, 10, 20, 30, 40, 50, 60, 70, 80, 90

Various answers are possible. One possible answer is given.

1
```
        4
       30
   7 ) 238
```
$7 \times 30 = 210$
28
$7 \times 4 = 28$
0
$238 \div 7 = 34$

2
```
        8
       40
   9 ) 432
```
$9 \times 40 = 360$
72
$9 \times 8 = 72$
0
$432 \div 9 = 48$

3
```
        7
       60
   8 ) 536
```
$8 \times 60 = 480$
56
$8 \times 7 = 56$
0
$536 \div 8 = 67$

4
```
        7
       90
   6 ) 582
```
$6 \times 90 = 540$
42
$6 \times 7 = 42$
0
$582 \div 6 = 97$

5
```
        8
       70
   4 ) 312
```
$4 \times 70 = 280$
32
$4 \times 8 = 32$
0
$312 \div 4 = 78$

6
```
        7
       10
   9 ) 153
```
$9 \times 10 = 90$
63
$9 \times 7 = 63$
0
$153 \div 9 = 17$

7 × 37 **CCLIX** two hundred fifty-nine **259**

ABOUT THE PAGE NUMBER What two primes are factors of 259?

Lesson Activity Book p. 260

Complete the puzzles. Rewrite each division sentence as a multiplication sentence. Choose numbers for the green boxes from this list:
0, 1, 2, 3, 4, 5, 6, 7, 8, 9, 10, 20, 30, 40, 50, 60, 70, 80, 90

Various answers are possible. One possible answer is given.

7
```
        7
       90
   3 ) 291
```
$3 \times 90 = 270$
21
$3 \times 7 = 21$
0
$291 \div 3 = 97$

8
```
        4
       30
   8 ) 272
```
$8 \times 30 = 240$
32
$8 \times 4 = 32$
0
$272 \div 8 = 34$

9
```
        9
       40
   5 ) 245
```
$5 \times 40 = 200$
45
$5 \times 9 = 45$
0
$245 \div 5 = 49$

10 Challenge Write a word problem to match 138 ÷ 6 and then solve it.

Possible problem and solution: Raquel can make 138 shirt and pants outfits. She has 6 different pants. How many shirts does she have?

$138 \div 6 = 23$

So, Raquel has 23 shirts.

260 two hundred sixty **CCLX** 2 × 2 × 5 × 13

ABOUT THE PAGE NUMBER 260 cents is made up of how many quarters and dimes? Quarters and nickels?

Teaching Notes for LAB page 259

Have students work on the page individually or with partners. The problems use the vertical format introduced in Activity B. Students are prompted to use multiples of 10 and 1 to build up the missing factors. They are solving division problems in the standard format and recording the multiplication involved in each step. For each problem, the division is rewritten in horizontal format; that's where students take the final step of combining the partial factors (or quotients). Each problem gives space for only two multiplication steps, but students may use scratch paper if they need to use more steps. The goal of this chapter is for students to solve division problems, not necessarily to do so in the fewest number of steps.

Teaching Notes for LAB page 260

These problems are written in both vertical and horizontal division formats. See Concept Alert for ways to help students read division problems written in vertical format.

Challenge Problem The Challenge Problem requires students to write their own word problem to match a division problem, and then to solve it.

Reflect and Summarize the Lesson

Write Math

Write a word problem for the number sentence 144 ÷ 8 = ■. Then solve using the new division format. 18; Possible answer: There are 144 fourth grade students in 8 different classrooms. How many students are in each room?

Review Model

Refer students to Review Model: Recording Division Steps in the *Student Handbook,* p. 214, to review how they can find quotients using the new division format.

✔ Check for Understanding

1 17

2 22

3 27

4 34

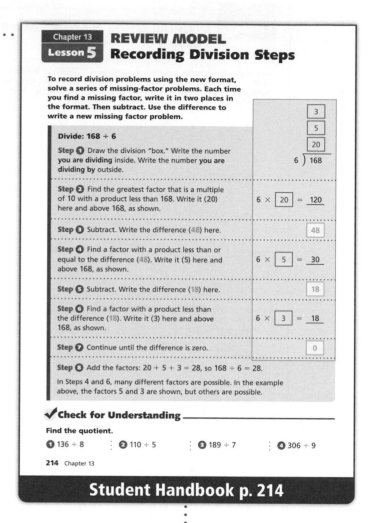

Use with Lesson Activity Book pp. 259–260.

3 | Differentiated Instruction

Leveled Problem Solving

Sierra and her friends have collected 336 tickets to use at the amusement park. They need 7 tickets for each ride.

❶ Basic Level

After they use their tickets on 10 rides, how many tickets will they have left? Explain. 266; $7 \times 10 = 70$, and $336 - 70 = 266$.

❷ On Level

They use tickets for 20 rides. Then they use what is left for another 10 rides. How many tickets are left? Explain. 126; $20 \times 7 + 10 \times 7 = 30 \times 7 = 210$, and $336 - 210 = 126$.

❸ Above Level

After they use tickets for 40 rides, how many rides can they still go on? Explain. 8; $7 \times 40 = 280$, $336 - 280 = 56$, and $56 \div 7 = 8$.

Intervention

Activity Relating Division Families

Write a vertical division problem on the board. Have students name all members of the corresponding fact family. Repeat until students are comfortable with this process. Then switch to naming a member of a fact family and having students write two related vertical division problems.

Practice

Dividing Using Multiplication Puzzles

Solve.

$7 \times 10 = $ __70__	$9 \times 20 = $ __180__	$6 \times 6 = $ __36__
$7 \times 3 = $ __21__	$9 \times 1 = $ __9__	$6 \times 40 = $ __240__
$7 \times 13 = $ __91__	$9 \times 21 = $ __189__	$6 \times 46 = $ __276__
$5 \times 30 = $ __150__	$8 \times 90 = $ __720__	$4 \times 60 = $ __240__
$5 \times 6 = $ __30__	$8 \times 4 = $ __32__	$4 \times 2 = $ __8__
$5 \times 36 = $ __180__	$8 \times 94 = $ __752__	$4 \times 62 = $ __248__
$11 \times 30 = $ __330__	$25 \times 4 = $ __100__	$30 \times 90 = $ __2,700__
$11 \times 5 = $ __55__	$25 \times 80 = $ __2,000__	$30 \times 1 = $ __30__
$11 \times 35 = $ __385__	$25 \times 84 = $ __2,100__	$30 \times 91 = $ __2,730__
$90 \times 5 = $ __450__	$50 \times 70 = $ __3,500__	$200 \times 20 = $ __4,000__
$90 \times 50 = $ __4,500__	$50 \times 5 = $ __250__	$200 \times 9 = $ __1,800__
$90 \times 55 = $ __4,950__	$50 \times 75 = $ __3,750__	$200 \times 29 = $ __5,800__

Test Prep

Markers come in boxes of 8. Mrs. Snow bought 27 boxes, but then she returned 4 boxes. How many markers did she have then? Explain how you found the answer.

184 markers; Possible explanation: I saw that the answer was the same as if she had bought $27 - 4 = 23$ boxes. $23 \times 8 = 184$.

Practice P106

Extension

Dividing Using Multiplication Puzzles

Use the largest number possible from the chart at each step.

0	1	2	3	4	5	6	7	8	9
0	10	20	30	40	50	60	70	80	90

$11 \overline{)583}$ — 50, 3; $11 \times 50 = 550$; 33; $11 \times 3 = 33$; 0; $583 \div 11 = 53$

$24 \overline{)312}$ — 10, 3; $24 \times 10 = 240$; 72; $24 \times 3 = 72$; 0; $312 \div 24 = 13$

$35 \overline{)1,155}$ — 30, 3; $35 \times 30 = 1,050$; 105; $35 \times 3 = 105$; 0; $1,155 \div 35 = 33$

$72 \overline{)2,664}$ — 30, 7; $72 \times 30 = 2,160$; 504; $72 \times 7 = 504$; 0; $2,664 \div 72 = 37$

$105 \overline{)2,625}$ — 20, 5; $105 \times 20 = 2,100$; 525; $105 \times 5 = 525$; 0; $2,625 \div 105 = 25$

$39 \overline{)1,404}$ — 30, 6; $39 \times 30 = 1,170$; 234; $39 \times 6 = 234$; 0; $1,404 \div 39 = 36$

Extension E106

Spiral Review

Spiral Review Book page SR106 provides review of the following previously learned skills and concepts:

- determining the whole from a given representation of a fractional part
- using cents as the common unit of measurement for computations involving various units of money

You may wish to have students work with a partner to complete the page.

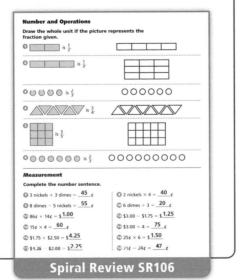

Number and Operations

Draw the whole unit if the picture represents the fraction given.

is $\frac{1}{2}$

is $\frac{1}{3}$

is $\frac{4}{5}$

is $\frac{3}{4}$

is $\frac{3}{5}$

is $\frac{2}{3}$

Measurement

Complete the number sentence.

3 nickels + 3 dimes = __45__ ¢   2 nickels × 4 = __40__ ¢

8 dimes − 5 nickels = __55__ ¢   6 dimes ÷ 3 = __20__ ¢

86¢ + 14¢ = $__1.00__ $3.00 − $1.75 = $__1.25__

15¢ × 4 = __60__ ¢ $3.00 ÷ 4 = __75__ ¢

$1.75 + $2.50 = $__4.25__   25¢ × 6 = $__1.50__

$4.25 − $2.00 = $__2.25__   71¢ − 24¢ = __47__ ¢

Spiral Review SR106

Extension Activity
Modeling Division

Have students choose a division problem that they have already solved. For the problem, have them draw a rectangle and use it to model the way in which they solved the division. For example, a student chooses $238 \div 7$. After finding the quotient 34 by estimating 20, 10, and 4, he or she would sketch a 34×7 rectangle and then divide it by estimating and marking a 20×7, 10×7, and finally a 4×7 rectangle to model the division. Encourage students to share their models in small groups.

Lesson 6 Completing Division Sentences

NCTM Standards 1, 2, 6, 7, 8, 9, 10

Lesson Planner

STUDENT OBJECTIVES ···
- To practice solving division problems
- To use rounding and compatible numbers to estimate quotients

1 Daily Activities (TG p. 1061)

| Open-Ended Problem Solving/Headline Story | Skills Practice and Review— Estimating Quotients |

2 Teach and Practice (TG pp. 1062–1064)

MATERIALS

(A) **Estimating Quotients** (TG p. 1062)

(B) **Playing *The Greatest Answer*** (TG p. 1063)

(C) **Completing Division Sentences** (TG p. 1064)

- TR: Activity Masters, AM144–AM145
- transparencies of AM144–AM145 (optional)
- 📖 LAB pp. 261–262
- 📖 SH pp. 215, 221

3 Differentiated Instruction (TG p. 1065)

Leveled Problem Solving (TG p. 1065)	Practice Book P107
Intervention Activity (TG p. 1065)	Extension Book E107
Extension Activity (TG p. 1065)	Spiral Review Book SR107
Science Connection (TG p. 1018)	

Lesson Notes

About the Lesson

Students practice solving division problems in this lesson. They play a game in which they estimate quotients, then continue to use multiples of 10 and 1 to build up missing factors in division problems.

Use with Lesson Activity Book pp. 261–262.

Developing Mathematical Language

Vocabulary: multiple

Students should think of *multiple* as a product of two whole numbers. Often when we think of *multiples,* we think of a list of *multiples* for one particular factor at a time. For example, the *multiples* of 3 are 0, 3, 6, 9, 12, 15, and so on. Each *multiple* of 3 is a product of 3 and the counting numbers or 0, in order: 3×0, 3×1, 3×2, 3×3, 3×4, 3×5, and so on.

Familiarize students with the term *multiple.*

Beginning Write the term *multiple* on the board and below it write *multiply.* Have students notice the similarity in the two words, differing only in the final letter. When students see the phrase "*multiple* of 5," they can think "multiply by 5" to help them remember how the *multiples* are created.

Intermediate Write a number, such as 54, on the board. Have students determine of what numbers it is a *multiple,* saying, "54 is a *multiple* of ■." 1, 2, 3, 6, 9, 18, 28, 54

Advanced Choose a factor from 2 to 6. Have students take turns counting off numbers starting at 1. Students in position to count off a *multiple* of the factor should, instead, say "*Multiple.*" Stop around 50. Repeat with other factors.

---

1 | Daily Activities

Open-Ended Problem Solving

Read the Headline Story to the students. No question is asked. Encourage children to find good questions themselves. Examples: How many people could be sharing the cupcakes? How many cupcakes would each get?

 Headline Story

> Jenna's mom brought 40 cupcakes to school for Jenna's birthday. She asked the teacher to give out as many cupcakes as possible. The students figured out that they could share all the cupcakes evenly, but only if they cut some of the cupcakes in half.

Possible responses: If there were 20 students in the class, each student could have 2 cupcakes, but they wouldn't need to cut any. If there were 30 students, each student could have 1 cupcake but the remaining 10, cut in half, wouldn't be enough for each to have another half.

Skills Practice and Review

Estimating Quotients

To prepare students for completing division problems, ask them to estimate the quotient in problems like those given below. Encourage students to round the given factor to the nearest multiple of 10 or to use other compatible numbers. Possible estimates are given.

$59 \times \underline{\quad} = 354$ 6	$410 \div 8 = \underline{\quad}$ 50
$330 \div 5 = \underline{\quad}$ 60	$322 \div 14 = \underline{\quad}$ 20
$63 \times \underline{\quad} = 1,827$ 30	$978 \div 51 = \underline{\quad}$ 20

pairs 15 MIN

A Estimating Quotients

NCTM Standards 1, 2, 6, 7, 8, 9, 10

Purpose To develop estimation strategies for division

Introduce Students should complete this activity with partners. Give each student a copy of Explore: Exploring Division.

Concept Alert

Students' previous work with division may have led them to conclude that dividing always makes a quantity smaller. (Similarly, many students think that multiplying always makes a quantity larger.) Associated with this idea is the assumption that one always divides the larger number by the smaller number. For students who have reached these conclusions, statements like $3 \div \frac{1}{2} = 6$ and $3 \div 6 = \frac{1}{2}$ may not make sense. Because division is so often presented in relation to sharing situations, these are legitimate misconceptions. Providing students with examples like those above will help them generalize and expand their understanding of division. (Students will see many more examples like these in fifth grade.)

Task Challenge students to determine which of the six problems on the Explore page has the smallest answer and which has the largest. Be sure students understand that this is an estimation activity. They should *not* find the exact answers to any of the problems. To ensure that students use estimation strategies, you might decide to disallow the use of pencils in this activity. 808 ÷ 8 yields the largest answer, about 100. 33 ÷ 33 yields the smallest answer, 1.

Share Once students have made their decisions, bring the class together and ask students to share their conclusions and strategies.

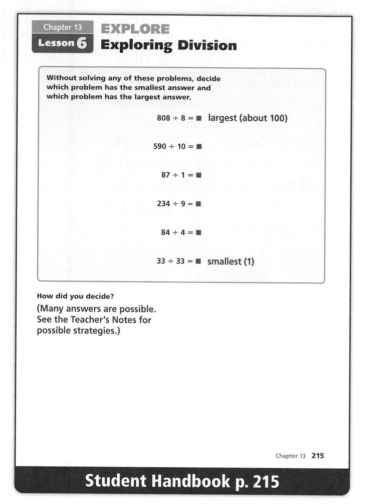

Student Handbook p. 215

During the discussion, make sure that students see how rounding to multiples of 10 and 100 helps in estimating the answers. For example, in the first problem (808 ÷ 8 = ■) students could estimate the answer by dividing 800 ÷ 8 = 100. This problem also illustrates that certain numbers are easier to work with than others, given the specific situation. In this same problem, it can be easier (and more exact) to leave the divisor as 8, rather than rounding it to 10.

Talk Math

❓ Which answer is larger, 150 ÷ 7 or 150 ÷ 8? Explain your reasoning.
150 ÷ 7; Possible explanation: The smaller the number you divide a given number by, the larger the answer. Since 7 is smaller than 8, the quotient 150 ÷ 7 must be larger than 150 ÷ 8.

❓ Which answer is larger, 120 ÷ 7 or 100 ÷ 7? Explain your reasoning.
120 ÷ 7; Possible explanation: Since 120 is 20 larger than 100, there must be more 7s in 120 than there are in 100. So, 120 ÷ 7 is larger than 100 ÷ 7.

pairs 20 MIN

Purpose To practice estimating quotients

Goal The goal of the game is to do a better job than one's opponent at estimating which problems in four sets of division problems have the largest quotients.

Introduce Students should play this game in pairs. Each student will need copies of Activity Master: Greatest Answer and Activity Master: Score Page. Because points are assigned based on answer to problems, encourage students to choose division problems that they expect will have the largest answers (i.e., the largest missing factors).

Materials
- For the teacher: transparencies of AM144–AM145 (optional)
- For each student: AM144–AM145

NCTM Standards 1, 2, 6, 7, 8, 9, 10

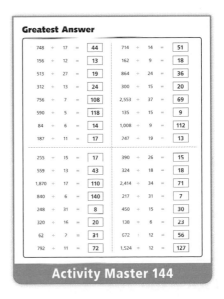

Activity Master 144

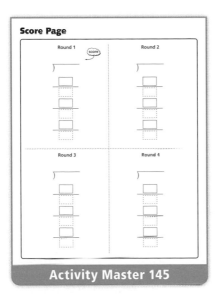

Activity Master 145

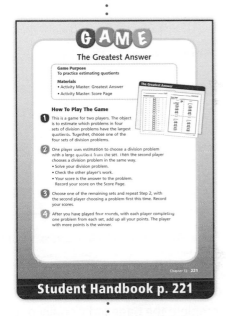

Student Handbook p. 221

How to Play

❶ Together, the two players chose one of the four sets of division problems on Activity Master: Greatest Answer.

❷ One player chooses a division problem from the set. The other player does the same. To ensure that students are estimating to make their choices and not actually solving the problems, you might ask students to set a time limit of one minute for choosing a problem.

❸ Each player solves his or her own division problem, then checks the other player's work. The answers to the problems are the players' scores for the round. Students may use the Score Page to record their scores.

❹ Students repeat Steps 1–3 for the other sets of division problems on the page. The student who picked a division problem second in the previous round now picks first.

❺ The student with the most points (the sum of the answers from all four rounds) wins the game.

Teacher Story

❝When any of my students played the Greatest Answer game more than once, I didn't give them a new copy of the Score Page. Instead, I asked them to use scratch paper to record their work. This gave them further practice creating and using the vertical division format. Even though what students wrote didn't look like the record on the Score Page, they were able to keep track of their computations to find correct answers. I was pleased that they understood the reasoning!❞

C Completing Division Sentences LAB pp. 261–262

individuals or pairs

20 MIN

Purpose To practice solving division problems in the standard vertical format

NCTM Standards 1, 2, 6, 7, 8, 9, 10

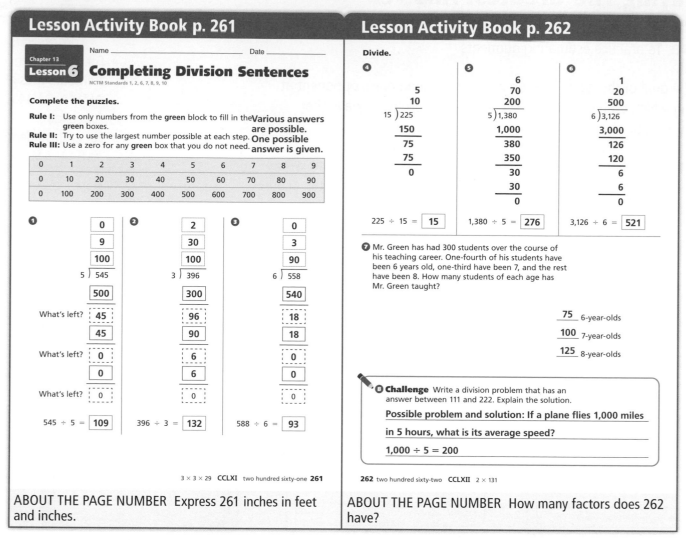

Lesson Activity Book p. 261

Name _____ Date _____

Chapter 13
Lesson 6 Completing Division Sentences
NCTM Standards 1, 2, 6, 7, 8, 9, 10

Complete the puzzles.

Rule I: Use only numbers from the **green** block to fill in the green boxes. Various answers are possible.
Rule II: Try to use the largest number possible at each step. One possible
Rule III: Use a zero for any **green** box that you do not need. answer is given.

0	1	2	3	4	5	6	7	8	9
0	10	20	30	40	50	60	70	80	90
0	100	200	300	400	500	600	700	800	900

1
5) 545
  0
  9
  100
  500
What's left? 45
  45
What's left? 0
  0
What's left? 0
545 ÷ 5 = **109**

2
3) 396
  2
  30
  100
  300
  96
  90
  6
  6
  0
396 ÷ 3 = **132**

3
6) 558
  0
  3
  90
  540
  18
  18
  0
  0
  0
588 ÷ 6 = **93**

3 × 3 × 29 CCLXI two hundred sixty-one **261**

ABOUT THE PAGE NUMBER Express 261 inches in feet and inches.

Lesson Activity Book p. 262

Divide.

4
15) 225
  150
  75
  75
  0
(5, 10)
225 ÷ 15 = **15**

5
5) 1,380
  1,000
  380
  350
  30
  30
  0
(6, 70, 200)
1,380 ÷ 5 = **276**

6
6) 3,126
  3,000
  126
  120
  6
  6
  0
(1, 20, 500)
3,126 ÷ 6 = **521**

7 Mr. Green has had 300 students over the course of his teaching career. One-fourth of his students have been 6 years old, one-third have been 7, and the rest have been 8. How many students of each age has Mr. Green taught?

75 6-year-olds
100 7-year-olds
125 8-year-olds

8 Challenge Write a division problem that has an answer between 111 and 222. Explain the solution.

Possible problem and solution: If a plane flies 1,000 miles in 5 hours, what is its average speed?

1,000 ÷ 5 = 200

262 two hundred sixty-two CCLXII 2 × 131

ABOUT THE PAGE NUMBER How many factors does 262 have?

Teaching Notes for LAB page 261

Have students complete the page individually or with partners. Go over the rules on the page, which ask students to choose numbers from three green blocks containing 1s and multiples of 10 and 100. This is to encourage students to use these numbers when they solve division problems. Because they record the parts of the missing factor separately in the vertical format, students are also asked to fill in the entire missing factor in a horizontal version of the problem.

Teaching Notes for LAB page 262

The page presents problems in an unstructured format. Students must use their experience with division problems throughout the chapter to decide what computations to perform. They then record their computations and write the missing factors in the horizontal division sentences beneath the vertical format. They also preview the connection between fractions and division when they find the numbers of students that make up one-fourth and one-third of the 300 students Mr. Green has taught.

Challenge Problem The Challenge Problem asks students to write a division problem to match a given answer (that is, a given missing factor).

Reflect and Summarize the Lesson

Write Math Which has the largest answer, 297 ÷ 9, 796 ÷ 8, or 54 ÷ 54? Explain your reasoning.
796 ÷ 8; Possible explanation: 297 ÷ 9 is about 300 ÷ 10, or 30; 796 ÷ 8 is about 800 ÷ 8, or 100; 54 ÷ 54 = 1. The largest of the three answers is 100, so 796 ÷ 8 has the largest answer.

Leveled Problem Solving

There are 3,080 beads in 8 boxes. Each box has the same number of beads.

❶ Basic Level

David's first estimate of the number beads in each box is 400. Is that a good choice? Explain. No; 8 × 400 = 3,200, and 3,200 is greater than the dividend 3,080.

❷ On Level

What is the greatest number of hundreds that makes sense as a first estimate of the number of beads in each box? Explain. 300; 8 × 300 = 2,400, which is less than 3,080; 400 gives an estimate that is greater than the dividend.

❸ Above Level

After estimating 300 as the number of beads in each box, Janette's next estimate is the greatest multiple of 10 that makes sense. What is it? Explain. 80; there are 680 left, and 8 × 80 = 640.

Intervention	Practice	Extension

Activity Calculating with Zeros

Remind students of the pattern that develops when finding the quotients of division facts with multiples of 10 and 100, such as:

$$12 \div 4 = 3$$
$$120 \div 4 = 30$$
$$1,200 \div 4 = 300$$

Have students work in pairs to develop the pattern for three other division facts.

Completing Division Sentences

Write the correct number in each box.

❶ 6 × 20 = **120**	❹ 4 × 10 = **40**	❼ 7 × 30 = **210**
6 × 3 = **18**	4 × 7 = **28**	7 × 4 = **28**
6 × 23 = **138**	4 × 17 = **68**	7 × 34 = **238**
❷ 5 × 7 = **35**	❺ 9 × 6 = **54**	❽ 8 × 90 = **720**
5 × 80 = **400**	9 × 50 = **450**	8 × 7 = **56**
5 × 87 = **435**	9 × 56 = **504**	0 × 97 = **776**

❸ 1,500 ÷ 30 = 50	❻ 1,250 ÷ 50 = 25	❾ 5,000 ÷ 5 = 1,000
400 ÷ 8 = 50	225 ÷ 9 = 25	10,000 ÷ 10 = 1,000
1,900 ÷ 38 = 50	1,475 ÷ 59 = 25	15,000 ÷ 15 = 1,000

Test Prep

⑩ 16 quarters are worth how many cents?

A 4
B. 40
C. 400
D. 4,000

⑪ How many quarters are worth $5?

A. 20
B. 40
C. 50
D. 125

Practice P107

Completing Division Sentences

Complete the problems.

(division problems shown)

872 ÷ 8 = **109**   819 ÷ 9 = **91**   1,287 ÷ 9 = **143**

The students in Miss Sterling's class were sponsored for a read-a-thon. For every book they read, they received 1 quarter. By the end of the read-a-thon, the class had read 129 books. The class decided to buy 7 new books with the money they raised.
                                    Possible answers are given.

⑫ If each book costs the same amount, what is the most each one could cost?
129 books means the class made 129 quarters, which is $32.25, or 3,225¢. 129 quarters ÷ 7 = 18 quarters with 3 left over, or $4.50 with 75¢ left over. But 75¢ can be divided among the 7 groups by giving each group 10¢ with 5¢ left over. So, each book can cost at most $4.60.

⑬ Describe how students can divide up the money in order to buy each book separately (Note: They can't just divide the quarters into 7 equal groups.)
First, divide 126 quarters into 7 equal groups of 18. The 3 leftover quarters should be traded for pennies, nickels, or dimes so that they can be shared further among the 7 groups. At the end there will still be 5¢ that cannot be shared.

Extension E107

Spiral Review

Spiral Review Book page SR107 provides review of the following previously learned skills and concepts:

- analyzing and comparing data using bar graphs
- solving problems using the strategy *draw a picture*

You may wish to have students work with a partner to complete the page.

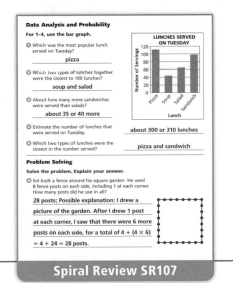

Data Analysis and Probability

For 1–4, use the bar graph.

❶ Which was the most popular lunch served on Tuesday?
pizza

❷ Which two types of lunches together were the closest to 100 lunches?
soup and salad

❸ About how many more sandwiches were served than salads?
about 35 or 40 more

❹ Estimate the number of lunches that were served on Tuesday.
about 300 or 310 lunches

❺ Which two types of lunches were the closest in the number served?
pizza and sandwich

(bar graph: LUNCHES SERVED ON TUESDAY; Number of Servings vs Lunch: Pizza, Soup, Salad, Sandwich)

Problem Solving

Solve the problem. Explain your answer.

❻ Sol built a fence around his square garden. He used 8 fence posts on each side, including 1 at each corner. How many posts did he use in all?
28 posts; Possible explanation: I drew a picture of the garden. After I drew 1 post at each corner, I saw that there were 6 more posts on each side, for a total of 4 + (4 × 6) = 4 + 24 = 28 posts.

Spiral Review SR107

Extension Activity Leftovers

Ask students to choose a division problem they have done and to change the dividend by 1, making it either 1 less or 1 greater. Ask them to predict what will be different. Then have them divide again, using the same estimates they used before. When students have finished, ask what was different. Ask them to make up a situation for the original and new problems and explain the difference in the context of the story.

Lesson 7 Problem Solving Strategy and Test Prep

NCTM Standards 1, 2, 4, 6, 7, 8, 9, 10

Lesson Planner

STUDENT OBJECTIVES ·····························
- To practice the problem solving strategy *work backward*
- To articulate the steps and strategies used to solve problems
- To prepare for standardized tests

Problem Solving Strategy:
Work Backward (TG pp. 1067–1068, 1070–1071)

MATERIALS

Ⓐ **Discussing the Problem Solving Strategy: Work Backward** (TG p. 1067)

Ⓑ **Solving Problems by Applying the Strategy** (TG p. 1068)

-  LAB p. 263
- SH pp. 216–217

Problem Solving Test Prep (TG p. 1069)

Ⓒ **Getting Ready for Standardized Tests** (TG p. 1069)

- LAB p. 264

Lesson Notes

About Problem Solving

Problem Solving Strategy: Work Backward

In this chapter, students have developed division strategies using their knowledge of multiplication—that is, by working backward. This lesson focuses on the problem solving strategy on which that idea is based, *work backward,* to help students draw connections between the content of this chapter and other mathematical problems. Although the strategy is particularly helpful with inverse operations, this lesson encourages students to see that it may be used in a variety of situations.

Skills Practice and Review

Estimating Quotients

As in **Lesson 13.6,** have students use missing factor problems to estimate answers to division problems. Adjust the difficulty of the problems as appropriate. Encourage students to use rounding or compatible numbers to find the answers. Some problems you might use, with possible estimates:

$39 \times \blacksquare = 7,683$ 200

$6,692 \div 6 = \blacksquare$ 1,000

$191 \div 2 = \blacksquare$ 100

$2,778 \div 9 = \blacksquare$ 300

$83 \times \blacksquare = 6,889$ 80

Problem Solving Strategy

(A) Discussing the Problem Solving Strategy: Work Backward

 whole class **15 MIN**

NCTM Standards 1, 2, 4, 6, 7, 8, 9, 10

Purpose To share strategies for solving problems and focus on the problem solving strategy *work backward*

Introduce To introduce the strategy *work backward,* ask students to find the missing number in this problem: $11 \times \blacksquare = 55$. 5 Ask how they solved the problem. Students should see that they can solve this multiplication problem by dividing: $55 \div 11 = 5$. Remind students that throughout this chapter, they have been solving multiplication problems by working backward from division and division problems by working backward from multiplication.

Problem Old Badger Park has an area of 20 square miles. New Badger Park has just opened next to the old park. The new park is 12 miles long and has an area of 48 square miles. What are the length and width of the old park?

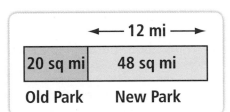

Share Ask students to share their strategies for solving the problem. *Work backward* is a good strategy to try, because the problem provides information that allows you to start at the end (the new park) and work your way back to the beginning (the old park).

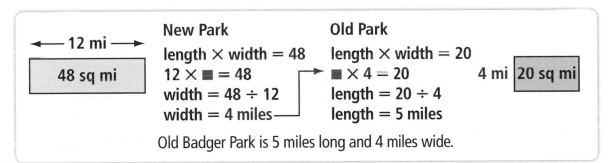

New Park
length × width = 48
$12 \times \blacksquare = 48$
width = 48 ÷ 12
width = 4 miles

Old Park
length × width = 20
$\blacksquare \times 4 = 20$
length = 20 ÷ 4
length = 5 miles

4 mi | 20 sq mi

Old Badger Park is 5 miles long and 4 miles wide.

💬 Talk Math

❷ How can you use the information in the problem to find the width of the new park? Possible answer: The product of its length and width is 48 square miles. Since the length is 12 miles, the width must be 48 ÷ 12, or 4 miles.

❷ Why does it help to know that the new park has a width of 4 miles? Possible answer: Both parks have the same width. Knowing that the new park has a width of 4 miles tells you that the old park has a width of 4 miles.

B Solving Problems by Applying the Strategy LAB p. 263

NCTM Standards 1, 2, 4, 6, 7, 8, 9, 10

Purpose
To share strategies for solving problems and focus on the problem solving strategy *work backward*

Teaching Notes for LAB page 263

Introduce Students practice the problem solving strategy *work backward* by solving the problems independently or in pairs. Help students get started by asking questions such as the following:

 Read to Understand

What do you need to find out? the width of Charles's playground

 Plan

How can you solve this problem? Think about the strategies you might use.

How could you work backward to solve the problem? Charles multiplied the length times the width to find the area. Since one of the dimensions is now missing, *work backward* from the known area to the missing dimension. To do this, find how many 24s make 432. You might use the following number sentences: $432 \div 24 = $ ■ or $24 \times $ ■ $= 432$.

 Solve

How can you solve $432 \div 24 = $ ■ or $24 \times $ ■ $= 432$? Students might choose to use multiples of 24 to build up factors of 432, keeping track of how many 24s they used. Using the vertical format, students might instead decide to subtract multiples of 24 from 432, again keeping track of the total number of 24s subtracted.

What multiples of 24 might be used to solve the problem? $10 \times 24 = 240$, and $8 \times 24 = 192$, so $18 \times 24 = 432$.

 Check

Look back at the original problem. Did you answer the question that was asked? Does your answer make sense? How do you know?

Students can use this method to solve other problems on the page. Supplement these questions with ones that are specifically tailored to the individual problems.

Lesson Activity Book p. 263

Name _____ Date _____

Chapter 13
Lesson 7 **Problem Solving Strategy**
Working Backward
NCTM Standards 1, 2, 4, 6, 7, 8, 9, 10

 Understand Plan Solve Check

❶ Charles measured his rectangular playground and found the area to be 432 square feet. He recorded the length as 24 feet but forgot to record the width. What was the width? Show your work.

$$\boxed{18} \times 24 = 432 \text{ or}$$
$$432 \div 24 = \boxed{18}$$

_18_ feet

❷ Mr. Tran made a list of some items he sells in his store. He has 10 umbrellas, 8 beach balls, 13 shovels, and 13 sunglasses. There are beach towels stacked equally on two shelves. Mr. Tran determined there are 76 items. How many towels are on each shelf?

There are 16 towels on each shelf. Possible solution: I can work
backward to find the number of beach towels on each shelf:
76 items − 10 umbrellas − 8 balls − 13 shovels − 13 glasses =
32 towels; 32 beach towels ÷ 2 shelves = 16 towels on each shelf.

❸ There are 192 people at a dinner party. An equal number of people are sitting at each of 12 tables. Fifty-seven people ordered steak and 63 people ordered salmon. The same number of people at each table ordered chicken. How many chicken dinners should be served at each table? Explain.

6 chicken dinners should be served at each table. Possible
solution: I can work backward to find the number of chicken
dinners at each table: 192 dinners − 57 steak − 63 salmon =
72 chicken dinners; 72 chicken dinners ÷ 12 tables = 6 chicken
dinners per table.

prime   **CCLXIII**   two hundred sixty-three   **263**

ABOUT THE PAGE NUMBER Can 263 be divided by 3? Can it be divided by anything?

Reflect and Summarize the Lesson

 Write Math **When might the strategy *work backward* be a good one to try to solve a problem?** Possible answer: when information is provided that allows you to work your way from the last step in a series of steps to the first step

Problem Solving Test Prep

C Getting Ready for Standardized Tests LAB p. 264

individuals

20 MIN

Purpose To prepare students for standardized tests

NCTM Standards 1, 2, 4, 6, 7, 8, 9, 10

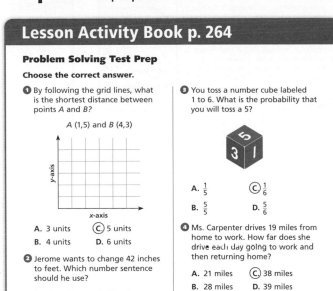

Lesson Activity Book p. 264

Problem Solving Test Prep

Choose the correct answer.

1 By following the grid lines, what is the shortest distance between points *A* and *B*?

A (1,5) and B (4,3)

y-axis

x-axis

A. 3 units   C. 5 units
B. 4 units   D. 6 units

2 Jerome wants to change 42 inches to feet. Which number sentence should he use?

A. 42×12 C. 42×3
B. $42 \div 12$ D. $42 \div 3$

3 You toss a number cube labeled 1 to 6. What is the probability that you will toss a 5?

A. $\frac{1}{5}$ C. $\frac{1}{6}$
B. $\frac{5}{5}$ D. $\frac{5}{6}$

4 Ms. Carpenter drives 19 miles from home to work. How far does she drive each day going to work and then returning home?

A. 21 miles   C. 38 miles
B. 28 miles   D. 39 miles

Show What You Know

Solve each problem. Explain your answer.

5 Jean Marie planted 9 rows of tomatoes and 9 rows of beans. Each row has the same number of plants. In all, there are 396 plants. How many plants are in each row? Explain.

22 plants; $9 + 9 = 18$;

$396 \div 18 = 22.$

6 Pablo is walking on a rectangular path. He walks 35 feet, turns right, and walks some more. He turns right and walks another 35 feet. He turns right and walks back to where he began. In all, he walks 100 feet. What is the area of the rectangle? Explain.

525 sq ft; $100 - (2 \times 35) = 30$;

$30 \div 2 = 15$; $35 \times 15 = 525.$

264 two hundred sixty-four **CCLXIV** $2 \times 2 \times 2 \times 3 \times 11$

ABOUT THE PAGE NUMBER You can make 264 cents with 10 quarters, 1 dime, and 4 pennies. What are the fewest coins and bills to make 264 cents?

Teaching Notes for LAB page 264

The test items on this page are written in the same style and arranged in the same format as those on many state assessments. The page is cumulative and is designed for students to apply a variety of problem solving strategies, including *work backward.* Students might share the strategies they use.

The Item Analysis Chart indicates one of the possible strategies that may be used for each test item.

Show What You Know

Written Response

Direct students' attention to Problems 5 and 6. For Problem 5, mention that students can begin by finding the number of rows, then *work backward* from 396 to find the number of plants in each row. For Problem 6, suggest that students *draw a picture* to find the dimensions of the rectangle. Then have them write explanations of how they know their answers are correct. To provide more space for children to communicate their thinking about these problems, you may wish to have them write their responses and explanations on a separate sheet of paper. Use the Scoring Rubric below to evaluate their understanding.

Item Analysis Chart

Item	Strategy
1	Act it out
2	Draw a picture
3	Draw a picture, act it out
4	Solve a simpler problem
5	Work backward
6	Work backward

Scoring Rubric

2	• Demonstrates complete understanding of the problem and chooses an appropriate strategy to determine the solution
1	• Demonstrates a partial understanding of the problem and chooses a strategy that does not lead to a complete and accurate solution
0	• Demonstrates little understanding of the problem and shows little evidence of using any strategy to determine a solution

Refer students to Review Model: Work Backward in the ***Student Handbook,*** pp. 216–217, to review a model of the four steps they can use with the problem solving strategy *work backward.*

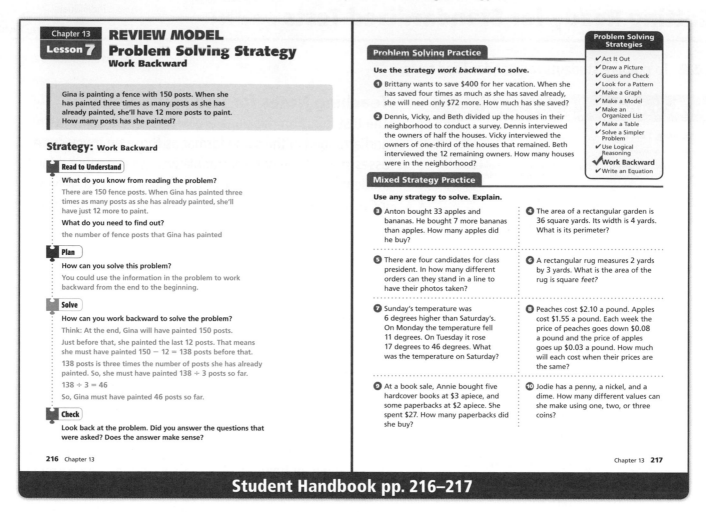

Student Handbook pp. 216–217

Task Have students read the problem at the top of the Review Model page.

💬 Talk Math

❓ What do you know about the fence? It has 150 posts.

❓ What do you know about the number of posts Gina has painted? When she has painted three times that many, 12 posts will remain to be painted.

❓ What do you need to find out? the number of posts that Gina has already painted

❓ What strategy could you use to solve the problem? You could use information about the fully painted fence and work backward from there.

❓ When Gina has painted three times as many posts as she has already painted, how many posts will she have painted? Explain your reasoning. 138; 12 posts will remain to be painted. Since there are 150 posts in all, she will have painted 150 − 12 = 138 posts.

❓ How can you find the number of posts she has painted so far? How many is it? by dividing 138 by 3; 46

❓ What other strategy could you use to solve the problem? Possible answer: *draw a picture*

1 $82; Possible explanation: You can *work backward* from $400: $400 − $72 = $328, the amount she needs to save after saving four times the amount she has already saved: $328 ÷ 4 = $82, the amount she has saved.

2 36 houses; You can *work backward* from Beth's 12 houses, which must be two-thirds of those that remained after Dennis's were chosen (since Vicky's were one-third). So, two-thirds of those that remained were 2 × 12 = 24 houses. That's half of the total, which must be 2 × 24 = 48 houses.

3 13; Possible explanation: You can *guess and check* to solve the problem. When you guess 13 apples, you will find that the guess checks: 13 apples + (13 + 7) bananas = 13 + 20, or 33 pieces of fruit.

4 26 yards; Possible explanation: You can use *logical reasoning* to solve the problem. The length of the garden must be 36 (area) ÷ 4 (width) = 9 yards. So, the perimeter is 4 + 9 + 4 + 9 = 26 yards.

5 24; Possible explanation: You can *make an organized list* to solve the problem, using A, B, C, and D to represent the candidates. With A listed first, there are 6 orders: ABCD, ABDC, ACBD, ACDB, ADBC, and ADCB. Likewise, there are 6 orders each when B, C, and D are listed first, for a total of 6 × 4 = 24 orders.

6 54 square feet; Possible explanation: You can *draw a picture* to solve the problem:

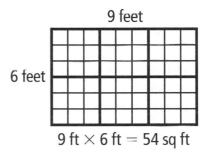

9 ft × 6 ft = 54 sq ft

7 34 degrees; Possible explanation: You can *work backward* to Saturday's temperature, beginning with Tuesday's temperature of 46 degrees.

8 $1.70; Possible explanation: You can *make a table* to solve the problem.

Week	1	2	3	4	5	6
Peaches	2.10	2.02	1.94	1.86	1.78	1.70
Apples	1.55	1.58	1.61	1.64	1.67	1.70

9 6; Possible explanation: You can *work backward* to solve. $27 (total) − $15 (5 hardcovers at $3 apiece) = $12 for paperbacks. At $2 apiece, that's $12 ÷ 2 = 6 paperbacks.

10 7; Possible explanation: You can *make an organized list* to solve. With a penny (1¢), a nickel (5¢), and a dime (10¢), the possible values are 1¢, 5¢, 6¢, 10¢, 11¢, 15¢, and 16¢.

Division

NCTM Standards 1, 2, 4, 6, 7, 8, 9, 10

Purpose To provide students with an opportunity to demonstrate understanding of Chapter 13 concepts and skills

MATERIALS
- LAB pp. 265–266
- Chapter 13 Test (Assessment Guide pp. AG113–AG114)

Chapter 13 Learning Goals and Assessment Options

These learning goals are assessed in many ways throughout the chapter. The chart below correlates each learning goal to specific formal and informal assessment options.

	Learning Goals	Lesson Number	Snapshot Assessment	Chapter Review Item Numbers	Chapter Test Item Numbers
				LAB pp. 265–266	Assessment Guide pp. AG113–AG114
13-A	Determine missing factors and products within multiplication sentences	13.1–13.3	1, 2, 5–7	1–2	1–5
13-B	Estimate missing factors and quotients to complete number sentences	13.4–13.6	3, 4, 8–10	3–8	6–10
13-C	Apply problem solving strategies such as *work backward* to solve problems	13.7	11, 12	9	11, 12

Snapshot Assessment

The following Mental Math and Quick Write questions and tasks provide a quick, informal assessment of students' understanding of Chapter 13 concepts, skills, and problem solving strategies.

whole class   10 MIN

Mental Math This oral assessment uses mental math strategies and can be used with the whole class.

❶ Complete:
- 4 groups of 6 + 5 groups of 6 = ■ groups of 6 **9** Turn the above into a multiplication equation, and solve. **(4 × 6) + (5 × 6) = 9 × 6 = 54**
- Find a division sentence in the same fact family: 15 × 4 = 60 **60 ÷ 4 = 15 or 60 ÷ 15 = 4**
- Determine two different multiplication sentences and two different division sentences using these numbers: 7, 9, 63. **7 × 9 = 63, 9 × 7 = 63, 63 ÷ 9 = 7, 63 ÷ 7 = 9**
(Learning Goal 13-A)

❷ Complete:
- 8 × (■ + ■) = 72. Explain. **Possible explanation: Since 8 × 9 = 72, any two numbers which add to 9 would work, such as 5 and 4, 6 and 3, etc.**
- Complete: 7 × ■ = 21 **3** and 7 × ■ = 56 **8** so 7 × ■ = 77 **11**
- If pencils are sold in packs of 3, how many packs are needed for 26 people, so each gets 1? **9** Explain. **3 × 8 = 24, not enough; 3 × 9 = 27, enough with 1 extra**
(Learning Goal 13-A)

3 Estimate the missing factor, using some multiple of 10:
- $7 \times \blacksquare = 84$ possible estimate: 10
- $24 \times \blacksquare = 504$ possible estimate: 20
- $39 \times \blacksquare = 1,209$ possible estimate: 30
(Learning Goal 13-B)

4 For the product $16 \times \blacksquare = 256$, what is the closest multiple of 10 that is smaller than the missing factor? 10 Explain. Possible explanation: $16 \times 10 = 160$ and $16 \times 20 = 320$, which is more than the product.
(Learning Goal 13-B)

Quick Write This informal written assessment can be administered to small groups or the whole class. Read each question and have the students record responses on their write-on boards. Encourage students to listen and think about the questions before responding.

5 Saco needs to deal 14 cards to each of his 6 friends. He now has 72 cards. How many more cards does he need? Use pictures, numbers, or words to explain your answer. 12; Possible explanation: $14 \times 6 = 84$ cards are needed in all; $84 - 72 = 12$ more cards are needed to give each friend 14 cards.
(Learning Goal 13-A)

6 If you multiply 8 times both 5 and 6, and then subtract the product from 50, which of the two factors, 5 or 6, will yield the smallest difference after subtraction? How do you know? 6; Possible answer: $8 \times 6 = 48$ and $50 - 48 = 2$; $8 \times 5 = 40$ and $50 - 40 = 10$, which is greater than 2.
(Learning Goal 13-A)

7 How could you break 13×9 into two easier multiplication problems that would allow you to find the product of 13×9? Possible answer: 13×9 is the same as 13 groups of 9, which is the same as 5 groups of 9 added to 8 groups of 9. Since $5 \times 9 = 45$ and $8 \times 9 = 72$, I can add to give $45 + 72$, or 117.
(Learning Goal 13-A)

8 Which answer is larger, $160 \div 5$ or $160 \div 6$? Explain. $160 \div 5$; Possible explanation: The fewer the number of groups into which you divide a number, the larger the groups.
Which has the largest answer, $252 \div 9$, $696 \div 8$, or $32 \div 32$? Explain. $696 \div 8$; Possible explanation: $252 \div 9$ is about $252 \div 10$, or about 25; $696 \div 8$ is about $700 \div 10$, or about 70; $32 \div 32$ equals 1. So $696 \div 8$ would have the largest answer.
(Learning Goal 13-B)

9 Mr. Darling's fourth grade class spent $24.50 to buy binders that cost $3.50 each. How many binders did they purchase? Use pictures, numbers, or words to explain your answer. 7 binders; Possible explanation: $7 \times \$3.50 = \$24.50$, so $\$24.50 \div 7 = \$3.50$.
(Learning Goal 13-B)

10 Sheila had 128 polished stones and wanted to share them equally with 3 of her friends. How many stones will each of the 4 people get? Write a number sentence to explain your answer. $128 \div 4 = 32$ stones each.
(Learning Goal 13-B)

11 Harris School has a rectangular playground. The new playground addition has an area of 147 square yards. It was built alongside the old playground, which is 21 yards wide and has an area of 210 square yards. What are the length and width of the new playground addition? Use pictures, numbers, or words to explain your answer. 21 yards × 7 yards; Possible explanation: $21 \times \blacksquare = 210$, so the old playground must be 10 yards long. The new playground must have a width of 21, and $21 \times 7 = 147$.
(Learning Goal 13-C)

12 Ken returned home after doing some grocery shopping and seeing a movie. He has $4.50 left in his pocket. He knows he spent $12.25 at the grocery store, $5.75 on movie refreshments, and $6.50 on a movie ticket. How much money did Ken start with? Use pictures, numbers, or words to explain your answer. $29.00; Possible explanation: $\$12.25 + \$5.75 + \$6.50 = \$24.50$ spent. Add the money left to find the amount he started with: $\$24.50 + \$4.50 = \$29.00$.
(Learning Goal 13-C)

Formal Assessment

Chapter Review/Assessment The Chapter 13 Review/Assessment on *Lesson Activity Book* pages 265–266 assesses students' understanding of computation in puzzles and tables and problem solving. Students should be able to complete these pages independently.

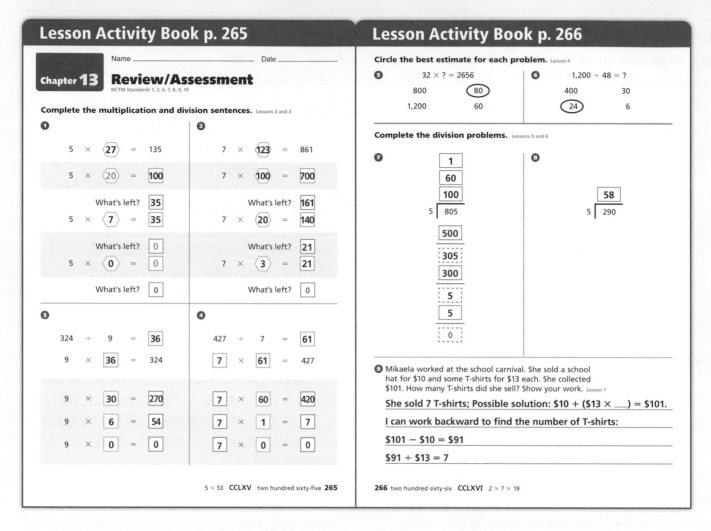

Extra Support Students who have difficulty with items on the Chapter 13 Review/Assessment may need review of the lesson where development of the concept was provided. You can use the Intervention Activity to increase students' understanding before the Chapter Test is given.

Chapter Test Use the Chapter 13 Test in the *Assessment Guide* to assess concepts, skills, and problem solving from the chapter and to prepare students for standardized tests. The Chapter Test and other test items are also available online.

Chapter Notes

 **Quick Notes**

More Ideas

Big Idea | A picture or a letter can represent any number on the number line

Algebraic Thinking

About the Chapter

In this chapter, students continue to formalize the thinking they have been using since kindergarten. Throughout the grades, students have used their understanding of arithmetic operations to solve problems. They have also learned to notice patterns, using them to make generalizations that, in turn, promote predictions. In this chapter, students apply these kinds of algebraic thinking. Much of this work is in the context of number puzzles that have some surprising solutions. This chapter includes the following central ideas:

Working Forward and Backward ("Doing" and "Undoing")
One characteristic of algebraic thinking involves being able to work backward to find a solution. While at first glance problems like $\blacksquare - 279 = 573$ or $7 \times \blacksquare = 140$ may not seem algebraic, they require just this kind of approach to solve. At the heart of working both forward and backward is an understanding of the relations among the four arithmetic operations. In particular, students rely on the fact that addition and subtraction "undo" each other, as do multiplication and division.

Using Shorthand Notation
In this chapter, students work on a variety of number puzzles. As they solve these puzzles, they develop a shorthand for describing mathematical situations. They start by representing an unknown quantity as a bag (which holds an unspecified amount), eventually replacing the bag with "x."

Think of a number.	♗	x
Add 50.	♗ + 50	$x + 50$

Making Generalizations
Identifying relations that always hold for all situations makes it possible to use observed regularities to solve new problems. Students have been making such generalizations for years. In this chapter, they generalize a multiplication pattern and think about why it works. In middle school and high school, students will further develop this kind of inquiry.

Developing Concepts Across the Grades

Topic	Prior Learning	Learning in Chapter 14	Later Learning
Patterns	• Identify, describe and extend patterns involving parts and wholes Grade 3, Chapter 6	• Explore patterns in number puzzles • Explore and apply the multiplication pattern of nearby squares Lessons 14.1, 14.5, 14.6	• Explore visual patterns and find rules to describe them Grade 5, Chapter 15
Multiplication	• Multiply 2-digit by 1-digit numbers Grade 3, Chapter 12	• Use square numbers to find related multiplication facts • Practice multiplication Lessons 14.1, 14.5, 14.6	• Use the patterns of multiplying by 10 • Use multiplication to solve problems involving whole numbers Grade 5, Chapter 2
Symbolic Notation	• Find missing operation signs and numbers in addition and subtraction sentences Grade 3, Chapter 1	• Read and write symbols that describe steps in a number puzzle • Make sense of number sentences with variables Lessons 14.2–14.5	• Represent mathematical relationships using diagrams and equations Grade 5, Chapter 15

Chapter Planner

Lesson	Objectives	NCTM Standards	Vocabulary	Materials/Resources
CHAPTER 14 World Almanac For Kids • Vocabulary • Games • Challenge Teacher Guide pp. 1083A–1083F, Student Handbook pp. 224–225, 234–238				
1 **Number Puzzles** **PACING 1 DAY** **Teacher Guide** pp. 1084–1089 **Lesson Activity Book** pp. 267–268 **Student Handbook** Student Handbook p. 223	• To explore patterns in number puzzles • To practice addition, subtraction, multiplication, and division	1, 2, 6, 7, 8, 10	algebra	**For the teacher:** ■ transparency of AM146 (optional) **For the students:** ■ School-Home Connection, pp. SHC53–SHC56 ■ calculator ■ TR: AM146 ■ P108, E108, SR108
2 **Introducing Variables** **PACING 1 DAY** **Teacher Guide** pp. 1090–1097 **Lesson Activity Book** pp. 269–270 **Student Handbook** Explore p. 226 Review Model p. 227 Game p. 236	• To use pictures of bags and counters to describe the steps in a number puzzle • To use problem solving strategies to find missing parts of number puzzles • To relate arithmetic operations by making a number puzzle	1, 2, 7, 8, 9, 10	variable	**For the students:** ■ TR: AM147–AM149 ■ counters (optional) ■ scissors ■ P109, E109, SR109
3 **Introducing a Shorthand Notation** **PACING 1 DAY** **Teacher Guide** pp. 1098–1105 **Lesson Activity Book** pp. 271–272 **Student Handbook** Review Model p. 228	• To read and write symbols that describe the steps in a number puzzle	1, 2, 7, 8, 9, 10	x, y, z	**For the students:** ■ P110, E110, SR110 **Social Studies Connection:** **Finding Dates in History** Teacher Guide p. 1082
4 **Using Shorthand Notation to Complete Number Puzzles** **PACING 1 DAY** **Teacher Guide** pp. 1106–1113 **Lesson Activity Book** pp. 273–274 **Student Handbook** Explore p. 229 Game p. 237	• To use shorthand notation to describe steps in and complete number puzzles • To make sense of number sentences with variables • To find the value of x in number sentences	1, 2, 7, 8, 9, 10	equation	**For the students:** ■ base-ten blocks or counters ■ 2 game tokens ■ TR: AM150–AM151 ■ P111, E111, SR111 **Science Connection:** **Temperature Scales** Teacher Guide p. 1082

NCTM Standards 2000
1. Number and Operations
2. Algebra
3. Geometry
4. Measurement
5. Data Analysis and Probability
6. Problem Solving
7. Reasoning and Proof
8. Communication
9. Connections
10. Representation

Key
AG: Assessment Guide
E: Extension Book
LAB: Lesson Activity Book
P: Practice Book
SH: Student Handbook
SR: Spiral Review Book
TG: Teacher Guide
TR: Teacher Resource Book

MATH GLOSSARY in Student Handbook p. 259

Planner (continued)

Chapter Planner (continued)

	Lesson	Objectives	NCTM Standards	Vocabulary	Materials/ Resources
5	**Using Square Numbers to Remember Other Multiplication Facts** **PACING 1 DAY** **Teacher Guide** pp. 1114–1121 **Lesson Activity Book** pp. 275–276 **Student Handbook** Explore p. 230 Review Model p. 231	• To use square numbers to find related multiplication facts • To generalize a multiplication pattern using variables	1, 2, 6, 7, 8, 9, 10	**dot** **parentheses**	**For the students:** ▪ P112, E112, SR112
6	**Generalizing a Multiplication Problem** **PACING 1 DAY** **Teacher Guide** pp. 1122–1127 **Lesson Activity Book** pp. 277–278	• To practice multiplication • To continue exploring and applying the multiplication pattern of nearby squares	1, 2, 6, 7, 8, 9, 10	**square**	**For the students:** ▪ square tiles or counters ▪ graph paper ▪ P113, E113, SR113 **Literature Connection:** **The Ancient Civilizations of Greece and Rome: Solving Algebraic Equations** **Teacher Guide** p. 1082
7	**Problem Solving Strategy and Test Prep** **PACING 1 DAY** **Teacher Guide** pp. 1128–1133 **Lesson Activity Book** pp. 279–280 **Student Handbook** Review Model pp. 232–233	• To practice the problem solving strategy *work backward* • To articulate the steps and strategies used to solve problems • To prepare for standardized tests	1, 2, 6, 7, 8, 9, 10		

CHAPTER 14 Assessment
TG pp. 1134–1137, **LAB** pp. 281–282, **AG** pp. AG117–AG120

For the students:
▪ Chapter 14 Test pp. AG117–AG118

Games

Use the following games for skills practice and reinforcement of concepts.

Make a Puzzle

Lesson 14.2 ▶

Make a Puzzle provides an opportunity for students to have further practice working with number puzzles and applying the strategy *work backward*.

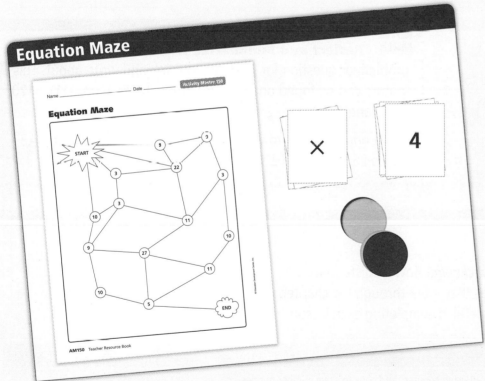

Equation Maze

◀ Lesson 14.4

Equation Maze provides an opportunity for students to practice finding the value of x in a number sentence using shorthand notation.

Planning Ahead

In **Lesson 14.2**, students will use counters and decks of cards cut from two Activity Masters to play *Make a Puzzle*. Cut out the Make a Puzzle Cards I and II from Activity Masters 148 and 149 ahead of time. Be sure each pair of students also has counters and a copy of Activity Master 147 (*Make a Puzzle*).

In **Lesson 14.4**, students will play the *Equation Maze* Game. Cut out the Equation Maze Cards from Activity Master 151 ahead of time. Each pair of students will need a copy of Activity Master 150 and each student will need a small game token.

Developing Problem Solvers

Open-Ended Problem Solving

The Headline Story in the Daily Activities section of every lesson provides an open-ended problem for students to complete. For each story, there are many possible responses.

Headline Stories can be found on TG pages 1085, 1091, 1099, 1107, 1115, and 1123.

Headline Story

Leveled Problem Solving

Leveled Problem Solving provides an opportunity for students to apply learning from the lesson to a real-life situation. Problems are leveled by ability to allow students of all ability levels to become successful problem solvers. Each Leveled Problem Solving begins with a real-life scenario upon which three problems are built.

The levels of problems are:

❶ Basic Level	❷ On Level	❸ Above Level
students needing extra support	students working at grade level	students who are ready for more challenging problems

Leveled Problem Solving can be found on TG pages 1089, 1096, 1104, 1112, 1121, and 1127.

THE WORLD ALMANAC FOR KIDS

The World Almanac for Kids feature is designed to stimulate student interest for the math concepts they are about to learn. Students use data to solve problems and explain solutions. The Chapter 14 Project can be found on SH pages 224–225.

Write Math

Reflect and Summarize the Lesson poses a problem or question for students to think and write about. This feature can be found on TG pages 1088, 1095, 1103, 1111, 1120, 1126, and 1130.

Other opportunities to write about math can be found on LAB pages 267–268, and 274.

Problem Solving Strategies

The focus of **Lesson 14.7** is the strategy *work backward*. However, students will use a variety of problem solving strategies as they work through the chapter. The chart below shows strategies that may be useful in completing each lesson.

Strategy	Lesson(s)	Description
Act It Out	14.2, 14.4	Act it out using counters and bags to solve number puzzles.
Guess and Check	14.2, 14.3, 14.4	Guess and check to use the last number in a number puzzle to find the first number.
Look for a Pattern	14.5, 14.6	Look for a pattern in square numbers to simplify multiplying large numbers.
Make a Model	14.6	Model a multiplication pattern to show why it works.
Use Logical Reasoning	14.3	Use logical reasoning to determine the number that will remain when all the steps in a number puzzle are completed.
✓ Work Backward	14.1, 14.2, 14.3, 14.4, 14.5	Work backward to create number puzzles and to explain the patterns in them.
Write an Equation	14.4	Write an equation to represent the steps in a number puzzle.

Meeting the Needs of All Learners

Differentiated Instruction

Extra Support	On Level	Enrichment
Intervention Activities TG pp. 1089, 1096, 1104, 1112, 1121, 1127	**Practice Book** pp. P108–P113	**Extension Activities** TG pp. 1089, 1096, 1104, 1112, 1121, 1127
	Spiral Review Book pp. SR108–SR113	**Extension Book** pp. E108–E113
	LAB Challenge LAB p. 268, 270, 272, 274, 276, 278	**LAB Challenge** LAB p. 268, 270, 272, 274, 276, 278
Lesson Notes **Basic Level** TG pp. 1086, 1094, 1126	**Lesson Notes** **On Level** TG pp. 1092, 1125	**Lesson Notes** **Above Level** TG p. 1094
Leveled Problem Solving **Basic Level** TG pp. 1089, 1096, 1104, 1112, 1121, 1127	**Leveled Problem Solving** **On Level** TG pp. 1089, 1096, 1104, 1112, 1121, 1127	**Leveled Problem Solving** **Above Level** TG pp. 1089, 1096, 1104, 1112, 1121, 1127

English Language Learners

Suggestions for addressing the needs of children learning English as a second language are included in the Developing Mathematical Language section at the beginning of most lessons.

ELL activities for this chapter can be found on TG pages 1085, 1091, 1099, 1107, 1115, and 1123.

The Multi-Age Classroom

Grade 3	• Students on this level should be able to complete the lessons in Chapter 14 but might need some additional practice with key concepts and skills. • Give students more practice with multiplication and finding missing factors.	See Grade 4, Intervention Activities, Lessons 14.1–14.6. See Grade 3, Lessons 9.1–9.6, 12.4–12.6.
Grade 4	• Students on this level should be able to complete the lessons in Chapter 14 with minimal adjustments.	See Grade 4, Practice pages P108–P113.
Grade 5	• Students on this level should be able to complete the lessons in Chapter 14 and to extend algebraic concepts and skills. • Give students extended work representing mathematical relationships with diagrams and symbolic notation.	See Grade 4, Extension pages E108–E113. See Grade 5, Lessons 15.1–15.9.

Cross Curricular Connections

Science Connection

Math Concept: variables

Temperature Scales

- Have students share what they know about temperature. Remind students that they used the Fahrenheit scale when measuring temperature in Chapter 9. Explain that most scientific measurements are made using the Celsius scale but that in the United States most everyday measurements use the Fahrenheit scale.

- Share the formula for converting from Fahrenheit to Celsius: $C = \dfrac{5 \cdot (F - 32)}{9}$.

  Write this formula on the board. Then write the formula again, replacing the variable F with 212. Explain the steps of converting from Fahrenheit to Celsius with the students:

  First, subtract 32 from 212. 180

  Next, multiply 180 by 5. 900

  Finally, divide 900 by 9. 100

  The result is the equivalent Celsius temperature. $212°F = 100°C$

Lesson 14.4

Social Studies Connection

Math Concept: equations

Finding Dates in History

- Share with students that in 1969, Neil Armstrong was the first astronaut to walk on the moon. Have them write an equation, using the variable x, to find how long ago Armstrong walked on the moon. Then solve the equation. If students know that the year was 1969 and if this year is 2007, they can write $2007 - x = 1969$ or $1969 + x = 2007$; $x = 38$.

- Ask students to write and solve equations using a variable to find the number of years ago each of the following events took place. Possible answers are given.

  Columbus came to the New World in 1492. $2007 - x = 1492$; $x = 515$.

  The Declaration of Independence was signed in 1776. $2007 - x = 1776$; $x = 231$.

  The compact disk was invented in 1965. $2007 - x = 1965$; $x = 42$.

Lesson 14.3

Literature Connection

Math Concept: algebraic thinking

The Ancient Civilizations of Greece and Rome: Solving Algebraic Equations
By Kerri O'Donnell

Using the backdrop of ancient Greece and Rome, students explore algebra. Facts about topics such as Greek literature, Roman architecture, and government are presented throughout this book. With these numerical facts, students are encouraged to write equations in order to solve for variables.

Lesson 14.6

School-Home Connection

A reproducible copy of the School-Home Connection letter in English and Spanish can be found in the *Teacher Resource Book,* pages SHC53–SHC56.

Encourage students to play *Equation Match,* found in the *Teacher Resource Book* on page SHC54, with a family member. Students will work with the concept of equations in **Lessons 14.3** and **14.4**.

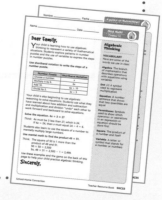

Assessment Options

There are many opportunities in *Think Math!* to assess students' understanding of concepts, skills, and problem solving. Learning Goals for Chapter 14 are provided below. The assessment options provide opportunities to evaluate whether or not students have retained learning from prior experiences. Choose the forms of assessment that best meet the needs of your students.

Chapter 14 Learning Goals

	Learning Goals	Lesson Number
14-A	Represent numbers and equations using pictures and variables	14.1–14.4
14-B	Use algebra to express and apply a generalization or pattern	14.5, 14.6
14-C	Apply problem solving strategies such as *work backward* to solve problems	14.7

✔ Informal Assessment

Ongoing Assessment
Provides insight into students' thinking to guide instruction (TG pp. 1092, 1100, 1102, 1108, 1116)

Reflect and Summarize the Lesson
Checks understanding of lesson concepts
(TG pp. 1088, 1095, 1103, 1111, 1120, 1126, 1130)

Snapshot Assessment
Mental Math and **Quick Write**
Offers a quick observation of students' progress on chapter concepts and skills
(TG pp. 1134–1135)

Performance Assessment
Provides quarterly assessment of Chapters 12–15 concepts using real-life situations
Assessment Guide
pp. AG225–AG230

✔ Formal Assessment

Standardized Test Prep
Problem Solving Test Prep
Prepares students for standardized tests
Lesson Activity Book p. 280 (TG p. 1131)

Chapter 14 Review/Assessment
Reviews and assesses students' understanding of the chapter
Lesson Activity Book pp. 281–282 (TG p. 1136)

Chapter 14 Test
Assesses the chapter concepts and skills
Assessment Guide
Form A pp. AG117–AG118
Form B pp. AG119–AG120

Benchmark 4 Assessment
Provides quarterly assessment of Chapters 12–15 concepts and skills
Assessment Guide
Benchmark 4A pp. AG125–AG132
Benchmark 4B pp. AG133–AG140

World Almanac for Kids

Use the World Almanac for Kids feature, *Model Trains: More Than Just Toys,* found on pp. 224–225 of the **Student Handbook,** to provide students with an opportunity to practice using their problem solving skills by solving real world problems.

FACT·ACTIVITY 1

Facts / Operations	A Gallons of glue used	B Height of Sears Tower (feet)	C Number of people worked on this model	D Pounds of dirt used on layout
Start with a number	47	11	37	597
Add 5.	52	16	42	602
Multiply by 2.	104	32	84	1,204
Subtract 4.	100	28	80	1,200
Divide by 2.	50	14	40	600

A 50 gallons of glue

B 14 feet

C 40 people

D 600 pounds of dirt

THE WORLD ALMANAC FOR KIDS

Model Trains: More Than Just Toys

The Great Train Story is a famous 3,500 square foot model railroad exhibit at the Museum of Science and Industry in Chicago, Illinois. It has 34 trains running along 1,425 feet of track between the miniature cities of Chicago and Seattle. At night, 80,000 windows and 1,291 streetlights light up the scene.

Copy the puzzle below on a piece of paper. If you follow the steps, the last line of the puzzle reveals some interesting facts about the Great Train Story.

Facts / Operations	A Gallons of glue used	B Height of Sears Tower (feet)	C Number of people worked on this model	D Pounds of dirt used on layout
Start with a number.	47			
Add 5.		16		
Multiply by 2.			84	
Subtract 4.				1,200
Divide by 2.				

FACT·ACTIVITY 1

Complete the puzzle and the sentences below.

A ■ gallons of glue were used.

B ■ feet is the height of the Sears Tower in the model.

C ■ people worked on the project.

D ■ pounds of dirt were used on the layout.

224 Chapter 14

Student Handbook p. 224

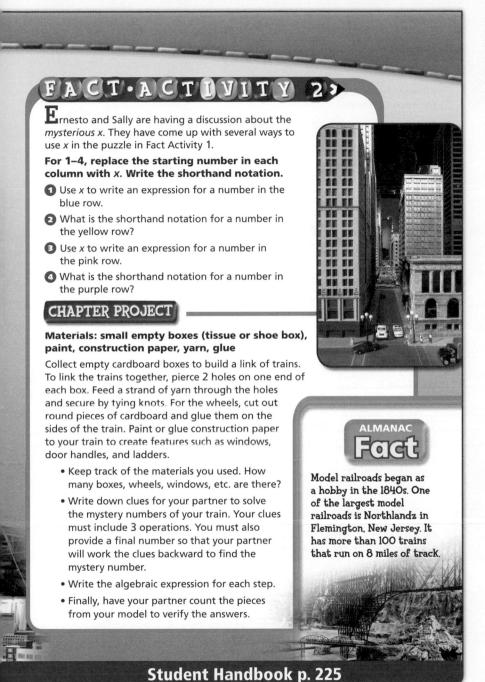

FACT·ACTIVITY 2

Ernesto and Sally are having a discussion about the *mysterious x*. They have come up with several ways to use *x* in the puzzle in Fact Activity 1.

For 1–4, replace the starting number in each column with *x*. Write the shorthand notation.

1 Use *x* to write an expression for a number in the blue row.

2 What is the shorthand notation for a number in the yellow row?

3 Use *x* to write an expression for a number in the pink row.

4 What is the shorthand notation for a number in the purple row?

CHAPTER PROJECT

Materials: small empty boxes (tissue or shoe box), paint, construction paper, yarn, glue

Collect empty cardboard boxes to build a link of trains. To link the trains together, pierce 2 holes on one end of each box. Feed a strand of yarn through the holes and secure by tying knots. For the wheels, cut out round pieces of cardboard and glue them on the sides of the train. Paint or glue construction paper to your train to create features such as windows, door handles, and ladders.

- Keep track of the materials you used. How many boxes, wheels, windows, etc. are there?
- Write down clues for your partner to solve the mystery numbers of your train. Your clues must include 3 operations. You must also provide a final number so that your partner will work the clues backward to find the mystery number.
- Write the algebraic expression for each step.
- Finally, have your partner count the pieces from your model to verify the answers.

ALMANAC Fact

Model railroads began as a hobby in the 1840s. One of the largest model railroads is Northlandz in Flemington, New Jersey. It has more than 100 trains that run on 8 miles of track.

Student Handbook p. 225

FACT·ACTIVITY 2

1 $x + 5$

2 $2x + 10$

3 $2x + 6$

4 $x + 3$

CHAPTER PROJECT

Sample response: Total number of wheels: 20

Words	Algebraic Expressions	Numbers
Mystery number	x	20
Multiply by 6.	$6x$	120
Divide by 3.	$2x$	40
Subtract 7.	$2x - 7$	33 (GIVEN FINAL NUMBER)

Vocabulary

To reinforce vocabulary concepts, invite students to complete the vocabulary activities on pp. 234–235 of the *Student Handbook.* Encourage students to record their answers in their math journals.

Many answers are possible.

11 Possible answer: Use a *variable,* such as *x,* and write the operations you want to perform on that number. For example, if the puzzle is "Add 6, subtract 4, add 3, subtract 5," you could record it this way: $x + 6 - 4 + 3 - 5$.

12 Possible answer: I can use a *variable,* such as *x,* to represent a number. Its square would be $x \cdot x$. For example, if I already know the square is 9, then I could write an *equation:* $x \cdot x = 9$.

Chapter 14 Vocabulary

Choose the best vocabulary term from Word List A for each sentence.

Word List A

algebra
dot
equation
parentheses
square
variable
x
y
z

1 A study of number patterns with symbols is called __?__. **algebra**

2 The most commonly used variable is __?__. **x**

3 A letter or symbol that stands for one or more numbers is called a(n) __?__. **variable**

4 A(n) __?__ is a number sentence that shows that two quantities are equal. **equation**

5 In algebra, a raised __?__ between two numbers means to multiply those two numbers. **dot**

6 Symbols used to show which operation or operations in a expression should be done first are called __?__. **parentheses**

7 The product of a number and itself is called the __?__ of the number. **square**

Complete each analogy using the best term from Word List B.

Word List B

algebra
dot
equation
variable
y

8 A plus sign is to addition as a(n) __?__ is to multiplication. **dot**

9 Sentence is to language as __?__ is to algebra. **equation**

10 Number is to 7 as __?__ is to *x.* **variable**

Talk Math

Discuss with a partner what you have learned about algebra. Use the vocabulary terms *equation* and *variable.*

11 How can you record a number puzzle that works for all numbers?

12 How can you use symbols to represent a square number?

234 Chapter 14

Student Handbook p. 234

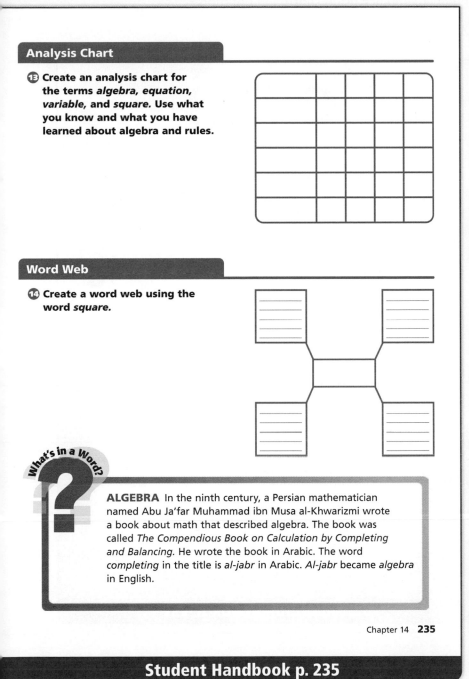

Analysis Chart

13 Create an analysis chart for the terms *algebra, equation, variable,* and *square.* Use what you know and what you have learned about algebra and rules.

Word Web

14 Create a word web using the word *square.*

What's in a Word?

ALGEBRA In the ninth century, a Persian mathematician named Abu Ja'far Muhammad ibn Musa al-Khwarizmi wrote a book about math that described algebra. The book was called *The Compendious Book on Calculation by Completing and Balancing.* He wrote the book in Arabic. The word *completing* in the title is *al-jabr* in Arabic. *Al-jabr* became *algebra* in English.

Chapter 14 **235**

Student Handbook p. 235

13 Many answers are possible. One example is provided.

	algebra	equation	variable	square
Is it a number sentence?	no	yes	no	no
Is it a symbol in a number sentence?	no	no	yes	no
Can it be written in shorthand notation?	yes	yes	yes	yes
Is it the result of multiplication?	no	no	no	yes

14 Many answers are possible. One example is provided.

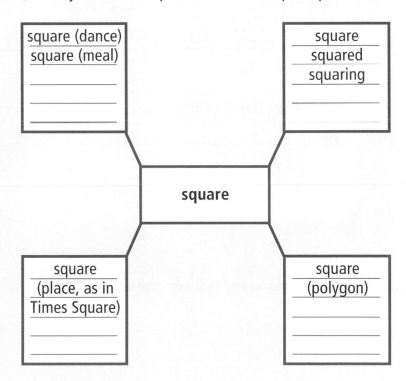

Games

Make a Puzzle in **Lesson 14.2** provides an opportunity for students to have further practice working with numbers puzzles and applying the strategy *work backward. Equation Maze* in **Lesson 14.4** provides an opportunity for students to practice finding the value of *x* in a number sentence using shorthand notation.

These games can be found in the *Student Handbook* on pp. 236–237.

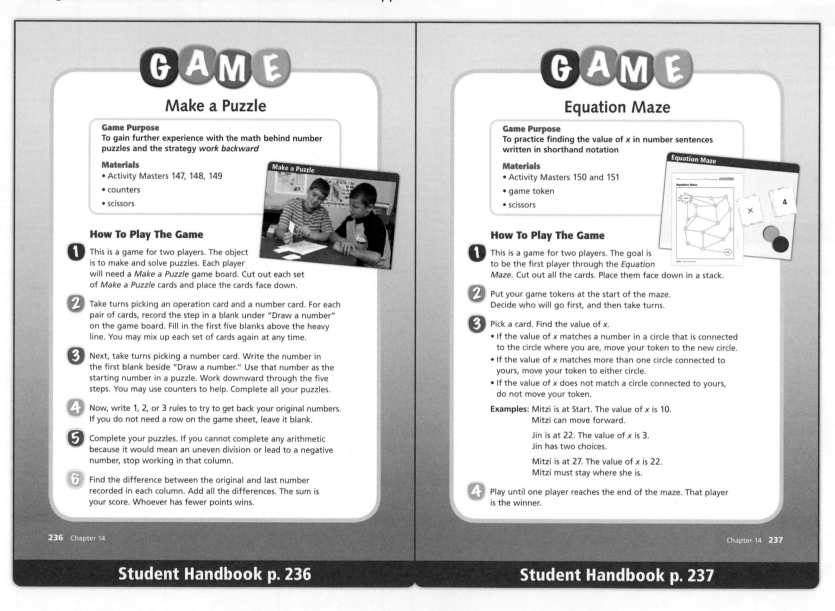

GAME

Make a Puzzle

Game Purpose
To gain further experience with the math behind number puzzles and the strategy *work backward*

Materials
• Activity Masters 147, 148, 149
• counters
• scissors

How To Play The Game

1 This is a game for two players. The object is to make and solve puzzles. Each player will need a *Make a Puzzle* game board. Cut out each set of *Make a Puzzle* cards and place the cards face down.

2 Take turns picking an operation card and a number card. For each pair of cards, record the step in a blank under "Draw a number" on the game board. Fill in the first five blanks above the heavy line. You may mix up each set of cards again at any time.

3 Next, take turns picking a number card. Write the number in the first blank beside "Draw a number." Use that number as the starting number in a puzzle. Work downward through the five steps. You may use counters to help. Complete all your puzzles.

4 Now, write 1, 2, or 3 rules to try to get back your original numbers. If you do not need a row on the game sheet, leave it blank.

5 Complete your puzzles. If you cannot complete any arithmetic because it would mean an uneven division or lead to a negative number, stop working in that column.

6 Find the difference between the original and last number recorded in each column. Add all the differences. The sum is your score. Whoever has fewer points wins.

236 Chapter 14

GAME

Equation Maze

Game Purpose
To practice finding the value of *x* in number sentences written in shorthand notation

Materials
• Activity Masters 150 and 151
• game token
• scissors

How To Play The Game

1 This is a game for two players. The goal is to be the first player through the *Equation Maze*. Cut out all the cards. Place them face down in a stack.

2 Put your game tokens at the start of the maze. Decide who will go first, and then take turns.

3 Pick a card. Find the value of *x*.
• If the value of *x* matches a number in a circle that is connected to the circle where you are, move your token to the new circle.
• If the value of *x* matches more than one circle connected to yours, move your token to either circle.
• If the value of *x* does not match a circle connected to yours, do not move your token.

Examples: Mitzi is at Start. The value of *x* is 10.
Mitzi can move forward.

Jin is at 22. The value of *x* is 3.
Jin has two choices.

Mitzi is at 27. The value of *x* is 22.
Mitzi must stay where she is.

4 Play until one player reaches the end of the maze. That player is the winner.

Chapter 14 237

Student Handbook p. 236   **Student Handbook p. 237**

Challenge

The activity challenges students to recognize a pattern in algebra tricks and to write an original algebra trick. This activity can be found on p. 238 of the *Student Handbook.*

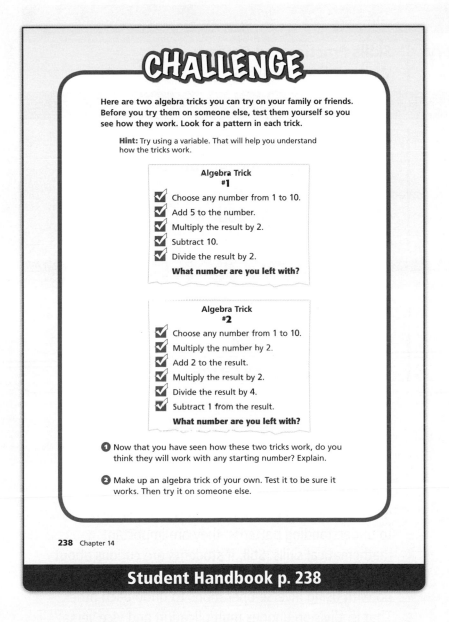

① CHALLENGE

Here are two algebra tricks you can try on your family or friends. Before you try them on someone else, test them yourself so you see how they work. Look for a pattern in each trick.

Hint: Try using a variable. That will help you understand how the tricks work.

Algebra Trick #1
- ✓ Choose any number from 1 to 10.
- ✓ Add 5 to the number.
- ✓ Multiply the result by 2.
- ✓ Subtract 10.
- ✓ Divide the result by 2.

What number are you left with?

Algebra Trick #2
- ✓ Choose any number from 1 to 10.
- ✓ Multiply the number by 2.
- ✓ Add 2 to the result.
- ✓ Multiply the result by 2.
- ✓ Divide the result by 4.
- ✓ Subtract 1 from the result.

What number are you left with?

❶ Now that you have seen how these two tricks work, do you think they will work with any starting number? Explain.

❷ Make up an algebra trick of your own. Test it to be sure it works. Then try it on someone else.

238 Chapter 14

Student Handbook p. 238

❶ Yes. Using a variable for the starting number, I got the same variable as the last number. So any starting number will work.

❷ Check students' work.

Lesson 1 | Number Puzzles

NCTM Standards 1, 2, 6, 7, 8, 9, 10

Lesson Planner

STUDENT OBJECTIVES ·
- To explore patterns in number puzzles
- To practice addition, subtraction, multiplication, and division

1 | Daily Activities (TG p. 1085)

Open-Ended Problem Solving/Headline Story	Skills Practice and Review— Writing Fact Families

2 | Teach and Practice (TG pp. 1086–1088)

	MATERIALS
Ⓐ **Reading the Student Letter** (TG p. 1086)	• TR: Activity Master, AM146
Ⓑ **Exploring a Number Puzzle** (TG p. 1087)	• transparency of AM146 (optional)
Ⓒ **Number Puzzles** (TG p. 1088)	• calculator
	• 📖 LAB pp. 267–268
	• 📖 SH p. 223

3 | Differentiated Instruction (TG p. 1089)

Leveled Problem Solving (TG p. 1089)	Practice Book P108
Intervention Activity (TG p. 1089)	Extension Book E108
Extension Activity (TG p. 1089)	Spiral Review Book SR108

Lesson Notes

About the Lesson

Throughout this chapter, students use the number puzzles introduced in this lesson to explore algebraic ideas, such as variables. In this first lesson of the chapter, students practice adding, subtracting, multiplying, and dividing, as they find that in any puzzle, all starting numbers lead to the same final number. Thinking in terms of "any" number prepares students for the idea of a variable, which they will encounter in later lessons.

About the Mathematics

Even though students are unlikely to be able to articulate the basis of the patterns they find in this lesson, they should still be able to recognize the patterns. Recognizing patterns and being able to make predictions based on them is a prerequisite to understanding patterns; they are important mathematical skills. Still, if students are curious about the basis of the patterns, you might tell them it has to do with using inverse operations to undo each other. That is, division undoes multiplication and vice versa, and subtraction undoes addition, and vice versa. Students will discover more about these techniques or "tricks" in future lessons.

For example, here is why the trick in Activity B works. The N stands for any number thought of and is therefore a variable.

(continued on page R8)

Developing Mathematical Language

Vocabulary: algebra

There is a fundamental difference between arithmetic and *algebra.* Arithmetic is simple addition, subtraction, multiplication, and division. *Algebra* deals with general numerical statements. It uses letters and symbols to analyze and interpret the way numbers interact. *Algebra* is required in the study of advanced, including high school, mathematics.

Students will enjoy *algebra* as a way to perform numerical magic tricks that can astound friends and family members. As students experiment with number tricks, they will notice patterns and hone their number sense.

Familiarize students with the term *algebra.*

Beginning Write the word *algebra* on the board. Then tell students that it is pronounced *al-juh-bruh.* Have students copy the word and say it aloud.

Intermediate Write the word *algebra* on the board. Have students look up the word in the dictionary and discuss its meaning. Then write an arithmetic statement on the board. Ask students to help you use letters and symbols to change it into an algebraic statement.

Advanced Have students write a sentence or two explaining what they know about *algebra.*

Open-Ended Problem Solving

Read the Headline Story to the students. Encourage them to think of imaginative ways to name solutions.

 Headline Story

Mary learned a math trick. She asked each of her friends to think of a number. She told them to multiply their number by ■, then divide their number by ■. Their final number was always the same as their original number.

Possible responses: If Jen picks the number 6 and Mary tells her to multiply by 3, then divide by 3, Jen will end up with 6 again. Mary should tell the person to multiply and divide by the same non-zero number.

Skills Practice and Review

Writing Fact Families

To remind students of the relationship between the operations, write an incomplete number sentence such as $3 + ■ = 17$ on the board. Invite students to fill in the missing number and to write the other members of the fact family. 14; $14 + 3 = 17$, $17 - 3 = 14$, $17 - 14 = 3$ Use both addition/subtraction and multiplication/division fact families. Vary the magnitude of the numbers to provide an appropriate challenge for your class. Here are some fact families you might use:

$8 \times 12 = 96$	$12 \times 8 = 96$	$96 \div 8 = 12$	$96 \div 12 = 8$
$95 \div 5 = 19$	$95 \div 19 = 5$	$5 \times 19 = 95$	$19 \times 5 = 95$
$76 - 25 = 51$	$76 - 51 = 25$	$25 + 51 = 76$	$51 + 25 = 76$

individuals or whole class · 10 MIN

A Reading the Student Letter

NCTM Standards 1, 2, 6, 7, 8, 9, 10

Purpose To introduce number puzzles

Introduce Read the puzzle in the Student Letter to the class. Without revealing the answer, have students try the puzzle. Then discuss their results so that everyone sees that all students got the same answer, 1.

Differentiated Instruction

Basic Level Students practice all four operations (+, −, ×, ÷) as they complete the number puzzles in this lesson. Students who find particular parts of the puzzles challenging may need additional practice with the operations.

Task Direct students to read the Student Letter independently or as a class.

Share Ask students to share any ideas they have about how the puzzle worked. Tell students that in this chapter they will complete more puzzles like this one, and figure out on their own how they work.

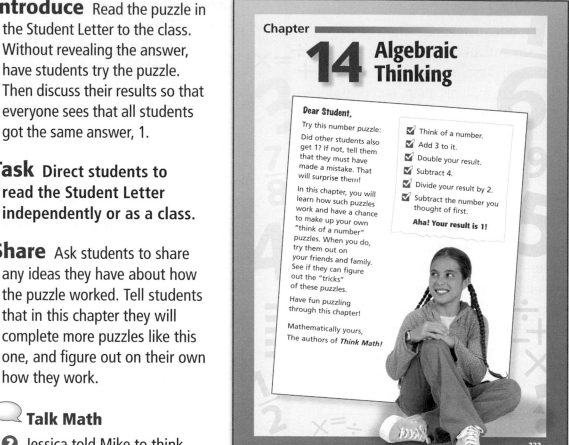

Chapter

14 Algebraic Thinking

Dear Student,

Try this number puzzle:

Did other students also get 1? If not, tell them that they must have made a mistake. That will surprise them!

In this chapter, you will learn how such puzzles work and have a chance to make up your own "think of a number" puzzles. When you do, try them out on your friends and family. See if they can figure out the "tricks" of these puzzles.

Have fun puzzling through this chapter!

Mathematically yours,
The authors of *Think Math!*

☑ Think of a number.
☑ Add 3 to it.
☑ Double your result.
☑ Subtract 4.
☑ Divide your result by 2.
☑ Subtract the number you thought of first.

Aha! Your result is 1!

223

Student Handbook p. 223

💬 **Talk Math**

❓ Jessica told Mike to think of a number, divide it by 3, and tell her the answer. Mike told her his answer was 7. Explain how Jessica can figure out the number Mike started with. Possible explanation: Since multiplication is the inverse of division, she can multiply Mike's answer by 3. So, Mike must have started with 3 × 7, or 21.

❓ If your friend thought of a number, added 6 to it, and then told you the answer, how could you figure out the number your friend started with? by subtracting 6

Purpose To explore patterns in number puzzles

Introduce If possible, display a transparency of Activity Master: A Surprising Puzzle. Explain that the class will be completing a number puzzle like the one in the Student Letter.

Task **Direct students to help you complete the puzzle.** Start by asking a student to name a number. Write it in the top row of the transparency or on the board.

Continue, reading each instruction in turn and asking students for the resulting number. Write the number in the puzzle or on the board. At the end, you should be left with the number 4.

Now give students their own copies of Activity Master: A Surprising Puzzle. Have them try several different starting numbers, including at least one decimal. Starting with a decimal will help students see that the puzzle produces the same result even when the initial numbers are non-whole numbers. It will also give them practice operating with decimals. Make sure that students have calculators when they use decimals, as they have not yet learned how to multiply and divide decimals.

Task Have students share their observations about the puzzles. Make sure you ask them why there is always a 4 in the last row of the puzzle. Encourage students to look for patterns in the puzzle.

Talk Math

❓ Think of a number. Add 3. Subtract your original number. What is the result? Why did you get that result? 3; Possible explanation: The sum is the sum of 3 and the original number. Subtracting the original number is bound to give a difference of 3, regardless of the original number.

❓ Think of a number. Multiply it by 4. Divide by your original number. What is the result? Why did you get that result? 4; Possible explanation: The product is the product of 4 and the original number. Dividing by the original number is bound to give a quotient of 4, regardless of the original number.

Activity Master 146

Materials

- For the teacher: AM146 (optional)
- For each student: AM146; calculator

NCTM Standards 1, 2, 6, 7, 8, 9, 10

Possible Discussion

Even though all of the students in your class will end up with the same number when they complete the number puzzle in this activity, some students may still think that certain initial numbers might produce different final numbers. Tell such students that, to test this theory, they should search for examples that don't fit the pattern. Later in this chapter, students will learn how to figure out whether there are numbers for which a "trick" does not work. In fact, showing that a "trick" will work for all numbers is one of the purposes of algebra.

Teacher Story

❝To prepare students to understand the 'tricks' of the number puzzles, I used counters to model the sequences of operations in the lesson activities.❞

Purpose To practice finding patterns and completing number puzzles

NCTM Standards 1, 2, 6, 7, 8, 9, 10

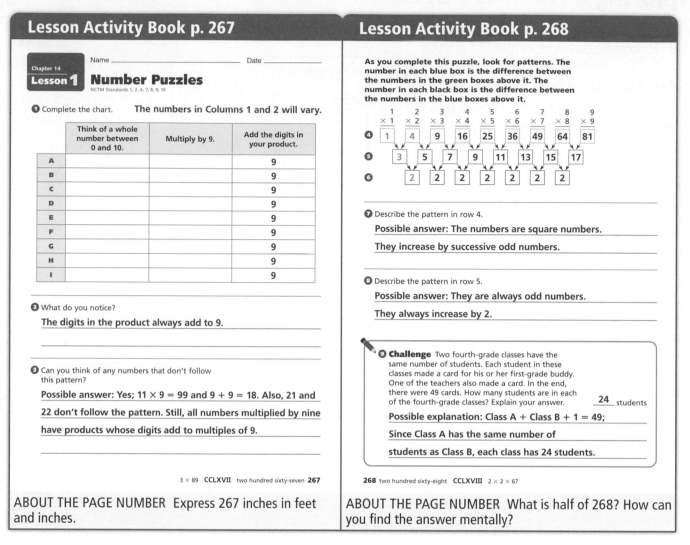

Lesson Activity Book p. 267

Chapter 14
Lesson 1 **Number Puzzles**
NCTM Standards 1, 2, 6, 7, 8, 9, 10

Name _____ Date _____

❶ Complete the chart.   **The numbers in Columns 1 and 2 will vary.**

	Think of a whole number between 0 and 10.	Multiply by 9.	Add the digits in your product.
A			9
B			9
C			9
D			9
E			9
F			9
G			9
H			9
I			9

❷ What do you notice?
The digits in the product always add to 9.

❸ Can you think of any numbers that don't follow this pattern?
Possible answer: Yes; 11 × 9 = 99 and 9 + 9 = 18. Also, 21 and
22 don't follow the pattern. Still, all numbers multiplied by nine
have products whose digits add to multiples of 9.

3 × 89 CCLXVII two hundred sixty-seven **267**

ABOUT THE PAGE NUMBER Express 267 inches in feet and inches.

Lesson Activity Book p. 268

As you complete this puzzle, look for patterns. The number in each blue box is the difference between the numbers in the green boxes above it. The number in each black box is the difference between the numbers in the blue boxes above it.

| 1 | 2 | 3 | 4 | 5 | 6 | 7 | 8 | 9 |
| × 1 | × 2 | × 3 | × 4 | × 5 | × 6 | × 7 | × 8 | × 9 |

❹ | 1 | 4 | 9 | 16 | 25 | 36 | 49 | 64 | 81 |

❺ | 3 | 5 | 7 | 9 | 11 | 13 | 15 | 17 |

❻ | 2 | 2 | 2 | 2 | 2 | 2 | 2 |

❼ Describe the pattern in row 4.
Possible answer: The numbers are square numbers.
They increase by successive odd numbers.

❽ Describe the pattern in row 5.
Possible answer: They are always odd numbers.
They always increase by 2.

❾ **Challenge** Two fourth-grade classes have the same number of students. Each student in these classes made a card for his or her first-grade buddy. One of the teachers also made a card. In the end, there were 49 cards. How many students are in each of the fourth-grade classes? Explain your answer. ___**24**___ students
Possible explanation: Class A + Class B + 1 = 49;
Since Class A has the same number of
students as Class B, each class has 24 students.

268 two hundred sixty-eight CCLXVIII 2 × 2 × 67

ABOUT THE PAGE NUMBER What is half of 268? How can you find the answer mentally?

Teaching Notes for LAB page 267

Have students complete the page individually or with partners. Students complete a number puzzle in which they multiply a one-digit number by 9, then add the digits of the product. They should notice that the sum of the digits is always 9. In Problem 3, students may find examples in which the digits sum to 18, 27, or some other multiple of 9. If they find a digit sum that is not a multiple of 9, however, they have made a mistake. Encourage them to check their work.

Teaching Notes for LAB page 268

Students find a pattern in square numbers, concluding that the differences between consecutive square numbers are consecutive odd numbers. Encourage students to look for a pattern in row 4 before they complete row 5, and in row 5 before they complete row 6. This will allow them to look for patterns before they receive clues about the patterns.

Challenge Problem The Challenge Problem requires students to work backward, reasoning that if the number of students in two classes of the same size is 1 less than 49, each class must have 24 students.

Reflect and Summarize the Lesson

Write Math

Choose a number. Multiply it by 25. Then multiply the product by 4. Finally, divide the result by the number you started with. Repeat for two other numbers. What pattern do you see in your results? Why do you think the pattern occurs? The answer is always 100; Possible explanation: Multiplying a number by 25 and then by 4 is the same as multiplying the number by 100. Dividing the result by the number, then, will leave 100.

3 | Differentiated Instruction

Leveled Problem Solving

A number in the pattern 0, 2, 2, 4, 6, ■, 16, 26, 42, 68, . . .
is found by adding the two numbers that come before it.

❶ Basic Level
What is the missing number? Explain. 10; 4 and 6 come just before 10, and $4 + 6 = 10$.

❷ On Level
What is the next number in the pattern? Explain. 110; the sum of 42 and 68 is 110.

❸ Above Level
What would be the fifteenth number in the pattern? Explain. 754; the next five numbers would be 110, 178, 288, 466, and 754.

Intervention

Activity Doing and Undoing

Write the words *add, subtract, multiply,* and *divide* on the board. Ask a student to pick one of the words, read it aloud, and include a number with it; for example, add 7. Then have another student tell how to undo the operation; for example, subtract 7. Continue the activity with other students, giving all students opportunities in both roles.

Practice

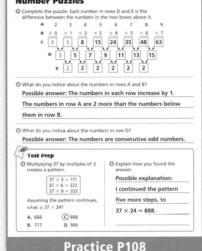

Practice P108

Extension

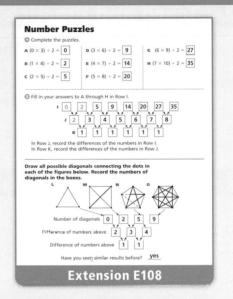

Extension E108

Extension Activity
Puzzling

Give students these directions:
- Pick a number between 1 and 9.
- Multiply the number by 2.
- Add 4 to the total.
- Divide by 2.
- Subtract your original number.
- Write what is left.

The answer will always be 2. Challenge students to multiply by a number other than 2. Ask them how to change each subsequent step so that the final result, 2, will stay the same.

Spiral Review

Spiral Review page SR108 provides review of the following previously learned skills and concepts:

- investigating translations (slides) and reflections (flips) of shapes using a coordinate grid
- solving problems using a problem solving strategy *make a model*

You may wish to have students work with a partner to complete the page.

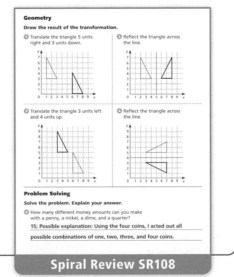

Spiral Review SR108

Lesson 2 Introducing Variables

NCTM Standards 1, 2, 6, 7, 8, 9, 10

Lesson Planner

STUDENT OBJECTIVES ·

- To use pictures of bags and counters to describe the steps in a number puzzle
- To use problem-solving strategies to find missing parts of number puzzles
- To use number puzzles to relate arithmetic operations

1 | Daily Activities (TG p. 1091)

Open-Ended Problem Solving/Headline Story	Skills Practice and Review— Estimating Multiplication and Division Using Rounding and Compatible Numbers

2 | Teach and Practice (TG pp. 1092–1095)

Ⓐ **Working Backward Through a Number Puzzle** (TG p. 1092)

Ⓑ **Playing a Game: *Make a Puzzle*** (TG p. 1093)

Ⓒ **Introducing Variables** (TG p. 1094)

MATERIALS

- TR: Activity Masters, AM147–AM149
- counters
- scissors
- 📖 LAB pp. 269–270
- 📖 SH pp. 226–227, 236

3 | Differentiated Instruction (TG p. 1096)

Leveled Problem Solving (TG p. 1096)	Practice Book P109
Intervention Activity (TG p. 1096)	Extension Book E109
Extension Activity (TG p. 1096)	Spiral Review Book SR109

Lesson Notes

About the Lesson

In the previous lesson, students completed several number puzzles. In this lesson, they study why these puzzles work. They use symbols to make sense of each step of the puzzle. Students apply their understanding of number puzzles and the relation between arithmetic operations by constructing their own number puzzles.

About the Mathematics

No matter how a number puzzle begins, it can always be constructed so that the final number is a constant. Take, for example, a puzzle beginning: (1) Think of a number (the "original number"); (2) Add 1; (3) Double it.

A possible ending for this puzzle is: (4) Divide by 2; and (5) Subtract the original number. The result

will always be 1. Reason: Dividing by 2 undoes the doubling, and subtracting the original number undoes that number, leaving the 1 that was added.

Most students are unlikely to be able to create puzzles that end with a constant final number at this point. It's even more unlikely that they will do so in such a concise manner. Students must realize several things in order to construct a puzzle that results in a constant number. First, they need to understand that the end of the puzzle is signified by the absence of any bags (variables). Second, they need to realize that the step that accomplishes removing bags involves taking away the original number (or, in a few specific cases,

(continued on page R8)

Developing Mathematical Language

Vocabulary: variable

A *variable* is represented with a symbol.

$$6 + \blacksquare = 10 \qquad \blacksquare - \blacktriangle = 5$$

The square on the left equals 4. The symbol stands for a definite number. On the right, the symbols could represent many pairs of numbers. The square could be 10, the triangle 5; the square could be 20, the triangle 15. This shows that a *variable* can stand for more than one number; it *varies*. In a given sentence, however, equivalent *variables* must stand for the same number. That is, if there are two squares, both must have the same value. In this lesson, a picture of a bag represents a *variable*. The bag unites both cases described above.

Familiarize students with the term *variable*.

Beginning Tell students that a *variable* is something that changes. Write an algebraic sentence on the board, using a geometric shape in place of a number. Have students identify the *variable* used.

Intermediate Write an arithmetic sentence on the board. Ask students to tell you how to use a *variable* in place of one of the numbers.

Advanced Have students go to the board and write two examples, one of a number sentence with no *variable* and the other of a number sentence with a *variable*.

Open-Ended Problem Solving

Read the Headline Story to the students. Encourage them to make interesting statements using information from the story.

 Headline Story

> Jose is building a tower out of popsicle sticks. He used ____ sticks for the first level. He used half as many sticks for the second level and half that number of sticks on the top level. He used fewer than 50 sticks total.

Possible responses: For the first level, Jose must have used a number of sticks that is a multiple of 4. If Jose used 20 sticks on the first level, then he used 10 on the second level and 5 on the top level, for a total of 35 sticks. There could not have been more than 7 sticks on the top level. There were $\frac{1}{4}$ as many sticks on the top level as on the bottom level.

Skills Practice and Review

Estimating Multiplication and Division Using Rounding and Compatible Numbers

Write a multiplication problem on the board, such as 27×6. Ask students how they could quickly approximate this product. Some students may suggest a rounding strategy such as 30×6, or a compatible number strategy such as 25×6. Make sure that students make estimates with both strategies. Then ask whether using the estimates will result in a product that is larger or smaller than the actual product. Repeat this with other products, such as 38×7, 24×11, and 19×27. Have students use both strategies to estimates quotients for some division problems, such as $157 \div 23$, $246 \div 42$, and $5,512 \div 51$.

pairs   15 MIN

A Working Backward Through a Number Puzzle

Materials

- For each student: counters (optional)

NCTM Standards 1, 2, 5, 7, 8, 9, 10

Purpose To use the final number in a number puzzle to find the first number

Introduce Students should work on this activity in pairs. Explain that, unlike the puzzles that students saw in **Lesson 14.1**, the number puzzle is this activity uses pictures, not words, to describe what to do at each step. Students should use the filled-in numbers to help them interpret the pictures.

✔️ **Ongoing Assessment**

- Do students understand that they should double the value of 1 bag to find the value of 2 bags?
- Do students understand that 3 dots represent "add 3"?

Task Direct students to complete Explore: Number Puzzle Mystery.

Students should reason that the picture of the bag represents the original number, so the three steps are to double the number, add 3, and subtract the original number.

Share Students may use any strategy they wish to find the original numbers, but when

---

Chapter 14 EXPLORE
Lesson 2 Number Puzzle Mystery

Ryan discovered a number puzzle where the directions for each step are given as a picture.

		A	B	C	D	E
Step ❶	🎒	9	■	■	■	■
Step ❷	🎒🎒	?	?	?	?	?
Step ❸	🎒🎒•••	?	?	?	?	?
Step ❹	🎒•••	12	5	27	3	16

❶ What are the starting numbers for each round of this puzzle?
   2   24   0   13

❷ Describe a single step for getting from the starting number to the final number.
Add 3 to the starting number.

❸ Describe a single step for getting from the final number to the starting number.
Subtract 3 from the final number.

226 Chapter 14

Student Handbook p. 226

Differentiated Instruction

On Level To help students visualize the steps of a puzzle, provide them with manipulatives. For example, students could use envelopes or bags to represent the unknown original number and counters to represent known quantities. They could use these items to model the quantity obtained at each step.

you talk about the activity as a class, make sure you discuss how to *work backward* to find the original numbers. To do this, students need to recall that addition and subtraction "undo" each other, as do multiplication and division. The pictures indicate that the only difference between the first and fourth rows is that the number in the first row is increased by 3. Therefore, to work backward from the fourth row to the first, subtract 3.

💬 **Talk Math**

❓ The last number in a number puzzle is 20. The first number is 10. What are two ways of getting from the last number to the first? Possible answer: Subtract 10 or divide by 2.

❓ The last number in a number puzzle is 14. The first number is 9. If the last number is 21, what might the first number be? Explain your reasoning. Possible answer: 16; possible explanation: Subtract 5 from the last number to get the first number.

Use with Lesson Activity Book pp. 269–270.

B Playing *Make a Puzzle*

 pairs 15 MIN

Purpose To practice solving number puzzles using the strategy *work backward*

Goal The goal of the game is to create part of a number puzzle through random card drawings, then to complete the puzzle using problem solving strategies.

Introduce Students should play in pairs. Each student will need a copy of Activity Master: Make a Puzzle. Each pair of students will need cards cut from Activity Masters 148–149. Point out that the goal is to get back your original number, not end with a constant final number. Provide students with counters to help them during the game. Before students play the game, complete one puzzle as a class. (See About the Mathematics for an example of steps that would "undo" the beginning of a puzzle.) You might draw pictures of each step to help students follow the calculations.

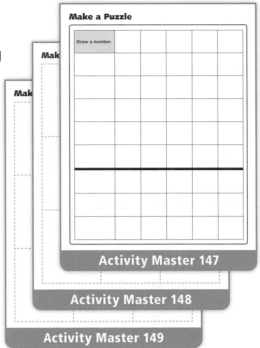

Activity Master 147

Activity Master 148

Activity Master 149

Materials
- For each student: AM147
- For each pair: AM148–AM149; counters; scissors

NCTM Standards 1, 2, 5, 7, 8, 9, 10

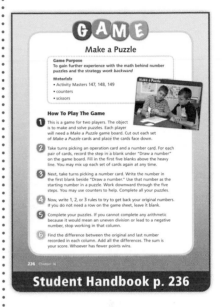

Student Handbook p. 236

How to Play

❶ Players place the Make-a-Puzzle cards with operations on them face down in one pile, and the Make-a-Puzzle cards with numbers on them face down in another pile.

❷ One player draws an operation card and a number card and records the step in the first blank of Activity Master: Make a Puzzle, beneath "Draw a number." Players take turns picking card pairs until each has written five rules in Column 1. Players may re-shuffle the cards as needed.

❸ One player now picks a number card and writes the number in the first blank beside "Draw a number." The player uses this number as the starting number in a puzzle and works through the first five steps of the puzzle. Players take turns drawing number cards and completing the five puzzle steps.

❹ Players now write up to three rules to try to get back their original numbers. Unused rows may be left blank. Players may complete one column of the puzzle to help them work out their steps.

❺ Players complete their puzzles. If a player can't complete the arithmetic in a particular column because it would require an uneven division or lead to a negative number, the player stops the computation in that column.

❻ Each player finds the difference between the original and last number recorded in each column. The sum of the five differences is the player's score.

❼ The player with the fewest points wins.

Purpose To use inverse operations to complete number puzzles

NCTM Standards 1, 2, 5, 7, 8, 9, 10

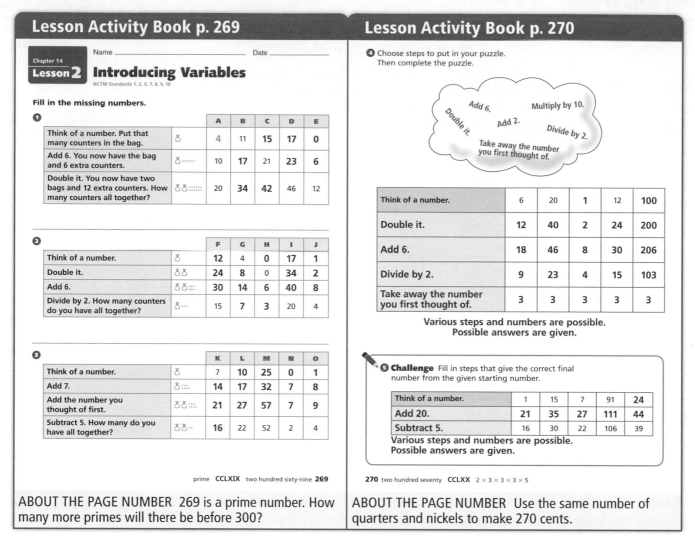

Lesson Activity Book p. 269

Name _____ Date _____

Chapter 14
Lesson 2 **Introducing Variables**
NCTM Standards 1, 2, 6, 7, 8, 9, 10

Fill in the missing numbers.

①

		A	B	C	D	E
Think of a number. Put that many counters in the bag.	⛾	4	11	15	17	0
Add 6. You now have the bag and 6 extra counters.	⛾······	10	17	21	23	6
Double it. You now have two bags and 12 extra counters. How many counters all together?	⛾⛾::::::	20	34	42	46	12

②

		F	G	H	I	J
Think of a number.	⛾	12	4	0	17	1
Double it.	⛾⛾	24	8	0	34	2
Add 6.	⛾⛾:::	30	14	6	40	8
Divide by 2. How many counters do you have all together?	⛾···	15	7	3	20	4

③

		K	L	M	N	O
Think of a number.	⛾	7	10	25	0	1
Add 7.	⛾⛾:::.	14	17	32	7	8
Add the number you thought of first.	⛾⛾::::.	21	27	57	7	9
Subtract 5. How many do you have all together?	⛾⛾··	16	22	52	2	4

prime **CCLXIX** two hundred sixty-nine **269**

ABOUT THE PAGE NUMBER 269 is a prime number. How many more primes will there be before 300?

Lesson Activity Book p. 270

④ Choose steps to put in your puzzle. Then complete the puzzle.

> Double it. Add 6. Add 2. Multiply by 10. Divide by 2. Take away the number you first thought of.

Think of a number.	6	20	1	12	100
Double it.	12	40	2	24	200
Add 6.	18	46	8	30	206
Divide by 2.	9	23	4	15	103
Take away the number you first thought of.	3	3	3	3	3

Various steps and numbers are possible. Possible answers are given.

⑤ Challenge Fill in steps that give the correct final number from the given starting number.

Think of a number.	1	15	7	91	24
Add 20.	21	35	27	111	44
Subtract 5.	16	30	22	106	39

Various steps and numbers are possible. Possible answers are given.

270 two hundred seventy **CCLXX** 2 × 3 × 3 × 3 × 5

ABOUT THE PAGE NUMBER Use the same number of quarters and nickels to make 270 cents.

Teaching Notes for LAB page 269

Have students complete the page independently or in pairs. Provide counters and scratch paper. Students are given beginnings of number puzzles, plus words and pictures to help them complete the puzzles. Most of the time, numbers other than the original number are given, so that students practice using inverse operations to work backward through a number puzzle. For example, in the first puzzle, Step 1 is "Add 6" and Step 2 is "Multiply by 2." To work backward from the third row to the second, therefore, students should divide by 2. To work backward from the second to the first row students should subtract 6.

Teaching Notes for LAB page 270

Students create and then complete their own number puzzles.

Differentiated Instruction Basic Level So that they will not have to divide odd numbers by 2, you might advise students who are having difficulty with math puzzles to make their first step "Multiply by 10" or "Double it"; or, allow them to skip the "Divide by 2" step altogether.

Differentiated Instruction Above Level Challenge students to choose steps that will always result in the same final number.

Challenge Problem The Challenge Problem contains a puzzle with some of the numbers filled in, but without descriptions of the steps. There are many ways for students to complete this puzzle. For example, Step 1 could be to add 20 and Step 2 could be to subtract 5; or Step 1 could be to add 16 and Step 2 could be to subtract 1.

Reflect and Summarize the Lesson

 Write Math

Connie made a number puzzle and had three of her friends try it. Jean chose the number 4, Sam chose 8, and Rebecca chose 3. After completing the first step of the puzzle, Jean had 12, Sam had 24, and Rebecca had 9. What was the first step of Connie's puzzle? Explain your reasoning. Possible answer: Multiply by 3; possible explanation: Each friends' final number is a multiple of 3.

Review Model

Refer students to Review Model: Using Bags and Counters, in the *Student Handbook,* p. 227, to see how they can use bags and counters to create number puzzles and to see how number puzzles work.

✔ Check for Understanding

1

2

3

4

5

6

7

8

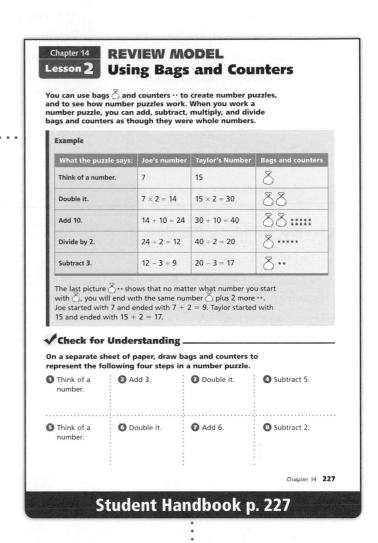

Student Handbook p. 227

Leveled Problem Solving

Kevin has 3 bags of marbles. He gets another 3 and then 2 more. He gives half the bags to Jun and 1 to Sam.

❶ Basic Level

After he gives half the bags to Jun, how many bags does Kevin have? Explain. 4; Just before he gives half to Jun, he has 8, and $8 \div 2 = 4$.

❷ On Level

How many bags does Kevin have left? Explain. 3; $3 + 3 = 6, 6 + 2 = 8, 8 \div 2 = 4, 4 - 1 = 3$.

❸ Above Level

How many marbles are in each bag if Jun gets 36 more marbles than Sam? Explain. 12; $3 + 3 = 6, 6 + 2 = 8, 8 \div 2 = 4$; He gives Jun 4 bags. $4 - 1 = 3$; Jun has 3 bags more than Sam. $36 \div 3 = 12$.

Intervention	Practice	Extension

Activity Undoing Puzzles

Give students a two-step number puzzle, such as multiply by 4 and add 3. Have a student choose a number and perform the two operations, recording the first and last numbers. Have another student undo the puzzle by recording each opposite operation. Have students determine the order for correctly undoing the puzzles. Repeat with other puzzles until students see that the order of undoing is the opposite of the order of doing.

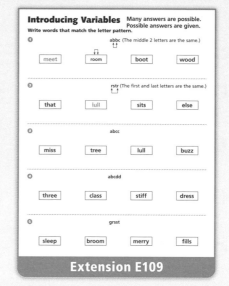

Practice P109

Extension E109

Spiral Review

Spiral Review Book page SR109 provides review of the following previously learned skills and concepts:

- reviewing the relationship between multiplication and division by writing fact families
- measuring changes in temperature in degrees Fahrenheit

You may wish to have students work with a partner to complete the page.

Spiral Review SR109

Extension Activity
Puzzle Play

Challenge students to change the Leveled Problem Solving story into a puzzle, starting with a different number of bags. They will also use that number for how many more bags Kevin gets first. Leave the remaining numbers in place and solve the problem. Have students explain why the puzzle works with either an even or an odd first number. By doubling the first number, whether even or odd, an even number is guaranteed. Adding 2 more keeps the total even so that it can be divided by 2.

Teacher's Notes 🍎

Quick Notes

More Ideas

Lesson 3 Introducing a Shorthand Notation

NCTM Standards 1, 2, 6, 7, 8, 9, 10

Lesson Planner

STUDENT OBJECTIVE ···
- To read and write symbols that describe the steps in a number puzzle

1 Daily Activities (TG p. 1099)

Open-Ended Problem Solving/Headline Story	Skills Practice and Review—Rounding in a Problem Context

2 Teach and Practice (TG pp. 1100–1103)

MATERIALS

Ⓐ **Using Large Numbers in Puzzles** (TG p. 1100)

Ⓑ **Reading and Writing Expressions with Variables** (TG p. 1101)

Ⓒ **Introducing a Shorthand Notation** (TG p. 1102)

- 📖 LAB pp. 271–272
- 📖 SH p. 228

3 Differentiated Instruction (TG p. 1104)

Leveled Problem Solving (TG p. 1104)	Practice Book P110
Intervention Activity (TG p. 1104)	Extension Book E110
Extension Activity (TG p. 1104)	Spiral Review Book SR110
Social Studies Connection (TG p. 1082)	

Lesson Notes

About the Lesson

In this lesson students meet a new, concise notation for recording steps in a number puzzle. This is particularly useful when the steps involve large numbers. Instead of drawing multiple bags, students write a number in front of a single bag. Similarly, they write a number instead of drawing counters. Then they use x to represent a bag. For example, students would represent 2 bags and 6 counters as $2x + 6$. This notation builds on the shorthand Eraser Store notation used in Chapter 3. Instead of drawing boxes to represent container types, students use standard notation, numbers, and letters.

About the Mathematics

Variables allow one to generalize mathematical ideas. For example, the expression $x + y = y + x$ states that numbers can be added in any order without affecting the sum. Similarly, variables can show the result of each step of a number puzzle for any given number.

The opposite of a variable is a constant. A number such as 3 or 1.77 is a constant because it doesn't change. If the final line of a number puzzle is constant (that is, it does not contain a variable), all starting numbers lead to the same final result.

Use with Lesson Activity Book pp. 271–272.

Developing Mathematical Language

Vocabulary: x, y, z

Even though the bag as a representation of the variable is replaced by an *x* in this lesson, you can continue to tie the symbol "*x*" to the idea of the bag by sometimes reading an expression such as $2x + 6$ as "two *x* plus six" and sometimes as "two bags and six counters." You might even sometimes read this expression as "twice the number thought of, with six added." Although any agreed-upon symbol can be used as a variable, the letters *x, y,* and *z* have been the most commonly used variables for more than three centuries; *x* is used in these lessons, as it can be introduced by erasing the top and bottom of a bag.

Familiarize students with the variables *x, y,* and *z*.

Beginning Write a number sentence on the board. Draw a bag to represent a variable. Then rewrite the number sentence using *x, y,* or *z* in place of the bag. Have students copy the number sentences.

Intermediate Write a number sentence on the board. Use a bag to represent a variable. Ask students how they could rewrite the number sentence using *x, y,* or *z*.

Advanced Have students discuss the meaning of a number sentence that uses more than one of the three variables. For example, $x + y = 7$.

Open-Ended Problem Solving

Read the Headline Story to the students. Encourage them to make imaginative statements using information from the story.

 Headline Story

> **Sophia went on a camping trip with her dad and two friends. Each person brought the same number of shirts, pants, and blankets. They had ____ shirts, ____ pants, and ____ blankets.**

Possible responses: If each person had 4 shirts, there were 16 shirts total. If each person had 3 pants, there were 12 pants. If each person had 2 blankets, there were 8 blankets. There must have been a multiple of 4 of each item. The total number of shirts, pants, and blankets must also be a multiple of 4.

Skills Practice and Review

Rounding in a Problem Context

To give students practice estimating in problem contexts, tell your class a story like the following, writing the numbers on the board:

Western County is issuing stickers to all cars of residents in the county. There are four towns in the county. Town A has 2,983 residents. Only 1,753 residents have cars, and most of them have one car. Town B has 4,024 residents, and about half of them have a car. Town C has 3,521 residents, and almost all of them have two cars. Town D has 944 residents, and 193 have a car. The county clerk needs to make a rough estimate to the nearest 1,000 of how many stickers she needs to buy.

What is a good estimate? about 11,000 stickers What if she needed to be more precise and estimate to the nearest 100 stickers? about 11,000 stickers nearest 10? about 11,000 stickers

2 | Teach and Practice

(A) Using Large Numbers in Puzzles

NCTM Standards 1, 2, 5, 7, 8, 9, 10

Purpose To motivate the use of numbers instead of counters when recording the steps of a number puzzle

Introduce Present students with a number puzzle like the following:

- Think of a number.
- Add 50.
- Double it.
- Add 48.
- Divide by 2.
- Subtract the original number.

Remind students of the pictures they have used to show the steps of a number puzzle. Ask students to describe how they would draw the first few steps of this puzzle. Draw a bag and 50 counters for the first step, 2 bags and 100 counters for the second step, and 2 bags and 148 counters for the third step.

✓ Ongoing Assessment

- Do students understand that a bag is a *variable* and can represent any number?
- Do students understand that the number of counters in a given situation is a *constant*—a specific number—and can therefore be represented by a whole number?

Task **Point out that because it will take a very long time to draw all of those counters, you would like to find an alternative ways to represent the steps. Ask students to suggest ways you might do this.** If students don't suggest it, state that instead of drawing the counters, you can simply write the number of counters.

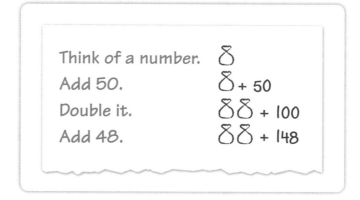

Ask students to describe how they could represent the remaining steps of the puzzle. Step 4: 1 bag + 74; Step 5: 74 To assess students' understanding of this new way of representing the steps in a puzzle, ask them to predict the final number for various starting numbers. Students should realize that because the final step of the puzzle yields 74 (without any pictures of a bag), the result of the puzzle for any starting number will always be 74. Go through the puzzle with a few numbers to demonstrate this.

💬 Talk Math

❷ How can you represent "Think of a number and add 300"? 1 bag + 300

❷ Quincy completed a puzzle, starting with one bag. For the last step, he was left with 5. What would he have been left with in the last step if he had begun with 20? Explain your reasoning. 5; Possible explanation: There are no bags in the final step, so the number at the end will be 5 no matter what number Quincy begins with.

Use with Lesson Activity Book pp. 271–272.

Reading and Writing Expressions with Variables

NCTM Standards 1, 2, 5, 7, 8, 9, 10

Purpose To motivate the use of a shorter notation for bags when recording the steps of a number puzzle

Introduce Give students a puzzle like the one at the right.

As in Activity A, ask students to describe how they would record the steps of the puzzle. Students should realize that the first step would involve drawing 200 bags.

> Think of a number.
> Multiply by 200.
> Add 20.
> Divide by 10.
> Subtract 2.
> Divide by 10.
> Subtract double the original number.

Task Point out that because it would be very time-consuming to draw 200 bags, you would like to find an alternative ways to record this step. Ask students to suggest ways you might do this. Students will likely suggest writing 200 in front of just one bag. (This notation is similar to the shorthand notation students used in Chapter 3 with the Eraser Store to represent large numbers of each type of container in a shipment.) Tell students that because bags are difficult to draw, you are no longer going to draw the top and bottom of the bag, just the x at the neck of the bag.

Have students write the shorthand notation for the remaining steps in this puzzle (shown at right). As in the previous activity, ask students to predict the final number for any given starting number. If necessary, give a few examples to demonstrate that the answer is always zero, regardless of the original number.

Think of a number:	x
Multiply by 200:	$200x$
Add 20:	$200x + 20$
Divide by 10:	$20x + 2$
Subtract 2:	$20x$
Divide by 10:	$2x$
Subtract double the original number:	0

Concept Alert

Some students may be puzzled by the fact that a bag is a variable, while the counters are not. Remind students that the bag represents any number, while the counters are always a known quantity. When you write $2x + 6$, you know that you have 6 "unbagged" counters as well as 2 bags, but you don't know how many counters are in each bag. So, while the "value" of the bag can vary depending on how many counters are in it, the value of each counter doesn't vary; it's always 1.

Finally, to make sure that students understand this new notation and are prepared for the LAB pages, ask students to give the value at various points in the puzzle for given values of x. For example, you might ask what the third row of the puzzle would be if x were 2. Students should be able to multiply 200 × 2, then add 20 to get 420.

Talk Math

❷ If x equals 5, what is the value of $x + 12$? Explain your reasoning. 17; Possible explanation: If x equals 5, then $x + 12 = 5 + 12 = 17$.

❷ If x equals 7, what is the value of $8x$? Explain your reasoning. 56; Possible explanation: If $x = 7$, then $8x = 8 \times 7 = 56$.

individuals
or pairs

🕐 **20 MIN**

Purpose To practice using clues to complete number puzzles

NCTM Standards 1, 2, 5, 7, 8, 9, 10

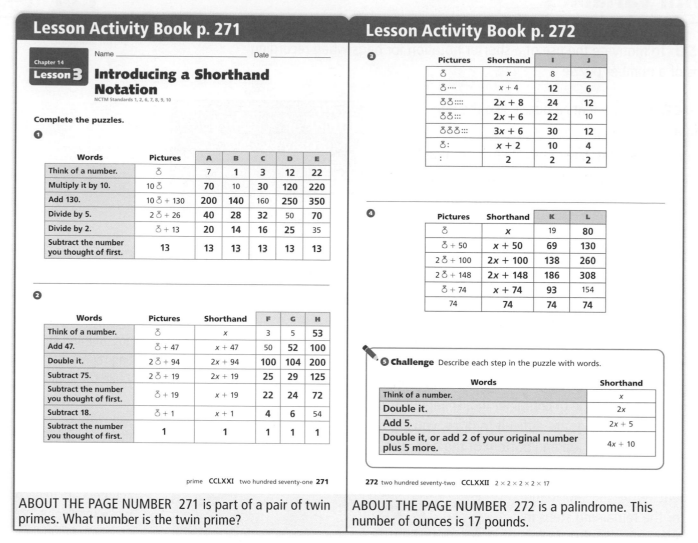

Lesson Activity Book p. 271

Name _____ Date _____

Chapter 14
Lesson 3 **Introducing a Shorthand Notation**
NCTM Standards 1, 2, 6, 7, 8, 9, 10

Complete the puzzles.

1

Words	Pictures		A	B	C	D	E
Think of a number.	♗		7	1	3	12	22
Multiply it by 10.	10 ♗		70	10	30	120	220
Add 130.	10 ♗ + 130		200	140	160	250	350
Divide by 5.	2 ♗ + 26		40	28	32	50	70
Divide by 2.	♗ + 13		20	14	16	25	35
Subtract the number you thought of first.	13		13	13	13	13	13

2

Words	Pictures	Shorthand	F	G	H
Think of a number.	♗	x	3	5	53
Add 47.	♗ + 47	x + 47	50	52	100
Double it.	2 ♗ + 94	2x + 94	100	104	200
Subtract 75.	2 ♗ + 19	2x + 19	25	29	125
Subtract the number you thought of first.	♗ + 19	x + 19	22	24	72
Subtract 18.	♗ + 1	x + 1	4	6	54
Subtract the number you thought of first.	1	1	1	1	1

prime CCLXXI two hundred seventy-one **271**

Lesson Activity Book p. 272

3

Pictures	Shorthand	I	J
♗	x	8	2
♗····	x + 4	12	6
♗♗::::	2x + 8	24	12
♗♗:::	2x + 6	22	10
♗♗♗:::	3x + 6	30	12
♗:	x + 2	10	4
:		2	2	2

4

Pictures	Shorthand	K	L
♗	x	19	80
♗ + 50	x + 50	69	130
2 ♗ + 100	2x + 100	138	260
2 ♗ + 148	2x + 148	186	308
♗ + 74	x + 74	93	154
74		74	74	74

5 Challenge Describe each step in the puzzle with words.

Words	Shorthand
Think of a number.	x
Double it.	2x
Add 5.	2x + 5
Double it, or add 2 of your original number plus 5 more.	4x + 10

272 two hundred seventy-two CCLXXII 2 × 2 × 2 × 2 × 17

ABOUT THE PAGE NUMBER 271 is part of a pair of twin primes. What number is the twin prime?

ABOUT THE PAGE NUMBER 272 is a palindrome. This number of ounces is 17 pounds.

Teaching Notes for LAB page 271

Have students complete the page individually or with partners. Words, pictures, and shorthand help students interpret each step of the puzzles. Few starting numbers are given. Instead, the values at various points in the puzzles are given, and students must determine the starting numbers in order to complete the other boxes. Make sure that students realize they should fill in the bottom row of the pictures column in both of the puzzles on this page. There are no bags left at this point so students need only write a number.

✔**Ongoing Assessment** As students work on the page, notice whether they are able to use their understanding of shorthand notation to find the starting number directly. Also, notice which students are using a guess-and-check strategy. Encourage them to try using manipulatives to work backward.

Teaching Notes for LAB page 272

Students are asked to write shorthand notation for the puzzles on this page. Pictures are provided as an aid, but they will gradually disappear in the upcoming lessons.

Challenge Problem The Challenge Problem asks students to translate the shorthand notation into words describing each step.

Reflect and Summarize the Lesson

Write Math If $3x - 12 = 24$, what is x? How do you know? 12; Possible response: $3x$ must be 36 because $36 - 12 = 24$. For $3x$ to equal 36, x must be 12.

Review Model . . . .

Refer students to Review Model: Using Shorthand Notation, in the *Student Handbook,* p. 228, to see how they can simplify recording the steps of a number puzzle.

✔ Check for Understanding

❶ A x

B $20x$

C $20x + 48$

D $10x + 24$

❷ A x

B $100x$

C $100x - 20$

D $25x - 5$

Chapter 14
Lesson 3 **REVIEW MODEL**
Using Shorthand Notation

When a number puzzle says, "Think of a number and double it," it's easy to work the puzzle with bags: 🎒🎒. But suppose the puzzle says, "Think of a number and multiply it by 50." Would you like to draw 50 bags? There's an easier way to work number puzzles.

- Use x or another variable instead of 🎒.
- Use whole numbers to represent the numbers of bags and counters.

	Bags and Counters	Shorthand Notation
Think of a number.	🎒	x
Multiply it by 8.	🎒🎒🎒🎒🎒🎒🎒🎒	$8x$
Add 14.	🎒🎒🎒🎒🎒🎒🎒🎒 ••••• ••••	$8x + 14$
Divide by 2.	🎒🎒🎒🎒 •••••• ••	$4x + 7$
Subtract 3.	🎒🎒🎒🎒 ••••	$4x + 4$

✔ Check for Understanding

Use shorthand notation to write the four steps of a number puzzle.

❶ A Think of a number.	B Multiply it by 20.	C Add 48.	D Divide by 2.
❷ A Think of a number.	B Multiply it by 100.	C Subtract 20.	D Divide by 4.

228 Chapter 14

Student Handbook p. 228

Leveled Problem Solving

Geneva brings x cookies to a party. Terrel brings twice as many as Geneva.

❶ Basic Level

What is an expression for the total number of cookies they both bring? Explain. $3x$; $2x + x = 3x$, or two of something plus one of that thing equals three of those things.

❷ On Level

If Terrel brings 18 cookies, how many cookies do Geneva and Terrel bring altogether? Explain. 27; 18 is twice 9, so Geneva brings 9, and $9 + 18 = 27$.

❸ Above Level

Eight guests each eat 3 cookies, leaving 6. How many cookies did Terrel bring? Explain. 20; $8 \times 3 = 24$, $24 + 6 = 30$, $30 \div 3 = 10$, so Geneva brought 10, and Terrel brought 2×10, or 20.

Intervention	Practice	Extension

Activity Operation Notation

Have students record the symbols for various operations that you read aloud, such as "Add 5" or "Divide by 4." For these operations, students should write "+ 5" and "÷ 4."

Then have students write their notations on the board. Discuss any variances in interpretation.

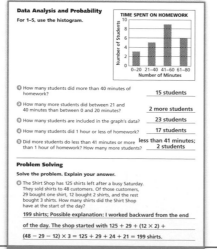

Practice P110

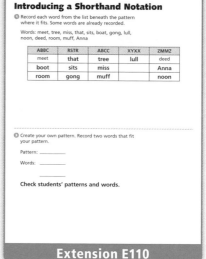

Extension E110

Spiral Review

Spiral Review Book page SR110 provides review of the previously learned skills and concepts:

• interpreting bar graphs (histograms)
• solving problems using a problem solving strategy *work backward*

You may wish to have students work with a partner to complete the page.

Spiral Review SR110

Extension Activity
Look for a Pattern

Challenge students to find a pattern in the results of a puzzle. Have them follow these steps for numbers 1–10.

a. Add 3.   **c.** Subtract 6.

b. Multiply by 4.   **d.** Divide by 2.

5, 7, 9, 11, 13, 15, 17, 19, 21, 23

Lead students to see that they can generalize the pattern. If they begin with x, they will always end with $2x + 3$. Students can verify this by using x, rather than a number, to start.

Teacher's Notes 🍎

Daily Notes . . .

More Ideas

Quick Notes

Lesson 4 Using Shorthand Notation to Complete Number Puzzles

NCTM Standards 1, 2, 6, 7, 8, 9, 10

Lesson Planner

STUDENT OBJECTIVES
- To use shorthand notation to describe steps in number puzzles and to complete number puzzles
- To make sense of number sentences with variables
- To find the value of x in number sentences

1 Daily Activities (TG p. 1107)

Open-Ended Problem Solving/Headline Story	Skills Practice and Review— Rounding to Approximate Results

2 Teach and Practice (TG pp. 1108–1111)

	MATERIALS
Ⓐ **Finding the Starting Number** (TG pp. 1108–1109)	• TR: Activity Masters, AM150–AM151
Ⓑ **Completing the Student Page** (TG p. 1110)	• base-ten blocks or counters
Ⓒ **Playing a Game:** *Equation Maze* (TG p. 1111)	• game tokens
	• 📖 LAB pp. 273–274
	• 📖 SH pp. 229, 237

3 Differentiated Instruction (TG p. 1112)

Leveled Problem Solving (TG p. 1112)	Practice Book P111
Intervention Activity (TG p. 1112)	Extension Book E111
Extension Activity (TG p. 1112)	Spiral Review Book SR111
Science Connection (TG p. 1082)	

Lesson Notes

About the Lesson

Students continue to reason about working forward and backward through number puzzles, and to apply shorthand notation to describe the steps in puzzles. They also play a game in which they use shorthand notation to determine the value of x that makes a particular number sentence true.

About the Mathematics

In this lesson, students solve equations for x. They have already been doing this in the context of number puzzles; that is, when they are told that the result of adding 3 to an unknown number is 5, they reason that the unknown number must be 2. Solving equations

may seem like a challenging activity for fourth graders. Note, however, that students solve equations here using familiar problem solving strategies such as *work backward, guess and check,* and *act it out,* rather than formal rules of algebra. Such strategies involve algebraic reasoning. For example, to solve for x in the equation $2x - 8 = 2$, students might act out ■ counters $-$ 8 counters $=$ 2 counters, concluding that $2x$ must be 10. Since $2 \times 5 = 10$, x must be 5. Alternatively, students could *guess and check,* adjusting successive guesses until they find the correct value of x.

Use with Lesson Activity Book pp. 273–274.

Developing Mathematical Language

Vocabulary: equation

The term *equation* may be new to your students. You might use it in context so that students see that it is another name for a number sentence. An *equation* shows that two quantities are equal:

$$4 + 9 = 13 \qquad x \times 5 = 20$$

An *equation* that contains a variable may be true only for certain values of the variable. For example, the *equation* $x \times 5 = 20$ is true only when $x = 4$.

Familiarize students with the term *equation.*

Beginning Tell students that another word for number sentence is *equation.* Have a student write an *equation* on the board. Then ask another student to change it so it is not an *equation.*

Intermediate Ask students what is needed to write an *equation.* Have volunteers write an *equation* on the board.

Advanced Have students discuss where they have seen an *equation* in the real world.

Open-Ended Problem Solving

Read the Headline Story to the students. Encourage them to use logical reasoning to draw conclusions about the number of laps.

 Headline Story

The coach of the soccer team explains to the players that at every practice, players must run a total of 60 laps. The more players who practice, the fewer laps each needs to run. All players must run the same number of full laps.

Possible responses: The greatest number of laps anyone might have to run is 60, if only 1 person practiced. The least is 1, if 60 or more players practiced, since each player must run the same number of full laps. If 20 players show up, each must run 3 laps.

Skills Practice and Review

Rounding to Approximate Results

As in the previous lesson, tell students a story to provide a context for making estimates. Here is another sample story:

In a food drive, students collected non-perishable items such as canned soups and vegetables. There were 4 elementary schools, 2 middle schools, and 1 high school in the town. The elementary schools collected 316, 207, 111, and 284 items respectively, the middle schools 653 and 132 items, and the high school 603 items.

Ask students to approximate the number of items contributed by elementary, middle school, and high school students. Then have them estimate the total number of items collected. Finally, ask students to make successively more precise measurements by rounding to the nearest thousand, hundred, and ten.

pairs

🕐 **15 MIN**

(A) Finding the Starting Number

Materials
- For each student: base-ten blocks or counters

NCTM Standards 1, 2, 5, 7, 8, 9, 10

✔ Ongoing Assessment

- Do students know that addition and subtraction are inverse operations, and that each undoes the other? $(4 + 7 = 11; 11 - 7 = 4)$
- Do students know that multiplication and division are inverse operations, and that each undoes the other? $(3 \times 5 = 15; 15 \div 5 = 3)$

Purpose To practice using shorthand notation to solve a number puzzle

Introduce Give each student a copy of Explore: Finding Your Number. Provide each pair of students with manipulatives such as base-ten blocks or counters to help them answer the Explore questions together.

Task Direct students to the following challenges, which appear on Explore: Finding Your Number.

❶ What number did each student think of? Betty thought of 4, Ted 11, Jun 15, and Karina 0.

❷ Use words to describe Step 1 of this number puzzle. Add 6.

❸ Use words to describe Step 2 of this number puzzle. Subtract 4.

❹ Use words to describe Step 3 of this number puzzle. Double it.

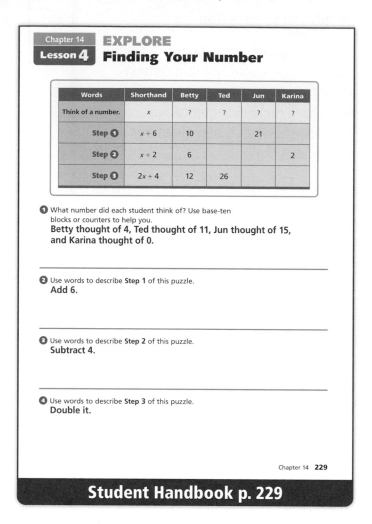

Student Handbook p. 229

Share Once students have had a chance to work through the page, invite them to explain their strategies for finding the starting numbers, and to justify why they believe their answers are correct. During the discussion, make sure students get a chance to see how several possible strategies (*act it out, guess and check, work backward*) can be used to solve the problem. If students don't spontaneously suggest these strategies, mention them and have the class apply them to the solution of the puzzle.

Write equations on the board representing students' explanations. This will allow the class to begin to see not only the expressions with variables that appear in the Explore table, but also the equations they imply.

Ted: $2x + 4 = 26$
Jun: $x + 6 = 21$
Karina: $x + 2 = 2$

To *act out* the puzzle, students can use counters to represent quantities in the table, then add, subtract, and group the counters to mirror the related shorthand expressions.

For example, to *act out* Ted's example in the fourth row of the puzzle, students can first equate $2x + 4$ to 26.

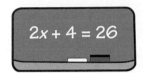

$$2x + 4 = 26$$

Next, they can count out 26 counters. From this they subtract 4 (that is, push 4 to one side), then reason that twice the unknown number remains ($2x = 26 - 4$). So, the remaining 22 items represent twice the unknown number. Those counters can be separated into two piles to show that the unknown quantity is 11.

The *guess and check* approach to Ted's example would require guessing values of x and testing them in the equation $2x + 4 = 26$. For example, a student might guess that $x = 10$, then see if $2 \times 10 + 4$ equals 26. Since $2 \times 10 + 4 = 24$, which is smaller than 26, the student would then adjust the guess upward.

Yet another approach that works well for problems like this is to *work backward* from a given number, using inverse operations. In Ted's example, we know that 26 is the last number in the puzzle. Shorthand notation tells us that the number in the last row is twice the number in the previous row. So, students can reason that the number in the next-to-last row must be 26 *divided by* 2. Continuing backward, this number, 13, is the result of subtracting 4 from the number in the previous row. Therefore, to find the number in the row above, add $4 + 13 = 17$. Finally, because the first direction in the puzzle is to add 6, students should *subtract* 6 from 17, concluding that the original number is 11.

Talk Math

❓ Jacob got 36 in Step 3 of Explore: Finding Your Number. What number did he think of? Explain how you found the answer. 16; Possible explanation: I worked backward to find the answer. The number in Step 2 is $36 \div 2 = 18$. The number in Step 1 is $18 + 4 = 22$. The number Jacob thought of is $22 - 6 = 16$.

❓ How can you use counters to find x if $2x - 3 = 11$? Possible answer: Count out 11 counters. Add 3 counters to the pile. Then divide the pile in half. The number of counters in each half, 7, is the value of x.

Purpose To practice using shorthand notation to solve number puzzles

NCTM Standards 1, 2, 5, 7, 8, 9, 10

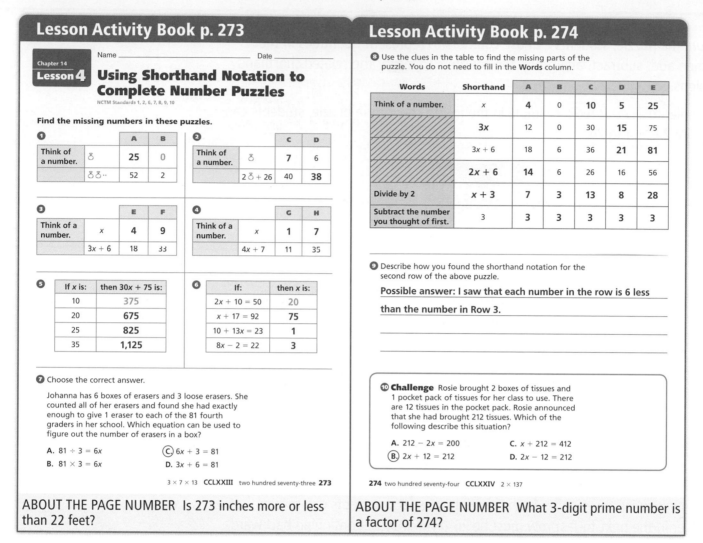

Lesson Activity Book p. 273

Chapter 14
Lesson 4 **Using Shorthand Notation to Complete Number Puzzles**

NCTM Standards 1, 2, 6, 7, 8, 9, 10

Find the missing numbers in these puzzles.

1

Think of a number.		A	B
	⚬	25	0
	⚬⚬··	52	2

2

Think of a number.		C	D
	⚬	7	6
	2⚬ + 26	40	38

3

Think of a number.		E	F
	x	4	9
	$3x + 6$	18	33

4

Think of a number.		G	H
	x	1	7
	$4x + 7$	11	35

5

If x is:	then $30x + 75$ is:
10	375
20	675
25	825
35	1,125

6

If:	then x is:
$2x + 10 = 50$	20
$x + 17 = 92$	75
$10 + 13x = 23$	1
$8x - 2 = 22$	3

7 Choose the correct answer.

Johanna has 6 boxes of erasers and 3 loose erasers. She counted all of her erasers and found she had exactly enough to give 1 eraser to each of the 81 fourth graders in her school. Which equation can be used to figure out the number of erasers in a box?

A. $81 \div 3 = 6x$ C. $6x + 3 = 81$
B. $81 \times 3 = 6x$ D. $3x + 6 = 81$

$3 \times 7 \times 13$ **CCLXXIII** two hundred seventy-three **273**

ABOUT THE PAGE NUMBER Is 273 inches more or less than 22 feet?

Lesson Activity Book p. 274

8 Use the clues in the table to find the missing parts of the puzzle. You do not need to fill in the **Words** column.

Words	Shorthand	A	B	C	D	E
Think of a number.	x	4	0	10	5	25
	$3x$	12	0	30	15	75
	$3x + 6$	18	6	36	21	81
	$2x + 6$	14	6	26	16	56
Divide by 2	$x + 3$	7	3	13	8	28
Subtract the number you thought of first.	3	3	3	3	3	3

9 Describe how you found the shorthand notation for the second row of the above puzzle.

Possible answer: I saw that each number in the row is 6 less than the number in Row 3.

10 Challenge Rosie brought 2 boxes of tissues and 1 pocket pack of tissues for her class to use. There are 12 tissues in the pocket pack. Rosie announced that she had brought 212 tissues. Which of the following describe this situation?

A. $212 - 2x = 200$ C. $x + 212 = 412$
B. $2x + 12 = 212$ D. $2x - 12 = 212$

274 two hundred seventy-four **CCLXXIV** 2×137

ABOUT THE PAGE NUMBER What 3-digit prime number is a factor of 274?

Teaching Notes for LAB page 273

Have students complete the page individually or with partners. As in the previous activity, students use shorthand notation to help them find unknown original numbers in number puzzles. Make counters available for those students who want to act out the steps.

Teaching Notes for LAB page 274

The puzzle here has fewer clues than those on LAB page 273. Students must use patterns in the numbers within the puzzle to determine the steps. They then translate the steps into shorthand notation.

Challenge Problem In the Challenge Problem, students describe the situation with an equation that they can then use to find the number of tissues in a box.

Purpose To practice finding the value of *x* in number sentences written in shorthand notation

Goal The goal of the game is to collect points by solving equations, to move on a maze to a circle with the solution of the equation, and to be the first person to reach the end of the maze.

Introduce Each pair of students will need one copy of Activity Master: Equation Maze and a set of cards cut from Activity Master: Equation Maze Cards. Each student will also need a game token.

GAME
Equation Maze

Student Handbook p. 237

Materials
• For each pair: game 2 tokens; AM150– AM151; scissors

NCTM Standards 1, 2, 5, 7, 8, 9, 10

How to Play

1 Players place the Equation Maze Cards face down in a pile between them.

2 Each player places his or her game piece at the start of the Equation Maze.

3 Players take turns picking a card from the pile and finding the value of *x* on the card.

4 If the value of *x* matches a number in a circle that is connected to the circle the player is currently in, the player moves his or her piece to that circle. If more than one connected circle contains the same number, the player can choose which direction to go in the maze. If no circles match the value of *x*, the player does not move.

5 Players continue choosing cards and moving on the maze until one player reaches the end of the maze. That player is the winner.

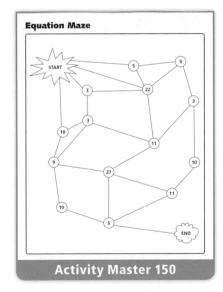

Equation Maze

Activity Master 150

Equation Maze Cards

$3x + 2 = 11$ What's *x*? **3**	$2x - 8 = 2$ What's *x*? **5**	$50 - 2x = 30$ What's *x*? **10**	$10x = 270$ What's *x*? **27**
$100 - 20x = 0$ What's *x*? **5**	$x - 2 = 10$ What's *x*? **12**	$150 - 50 = 10x$ What's *x*? **10**	$45 \div x = 5$ What's *x*? **9**
$88 - 3x = 55$ What's *x*? **11**	$9 \div x = 3$ What's *x*? **3**	$9x + 3 = 30$ What's *x*? **3**	$3x + 4 = 70$ What's *x*? **22**
$10x = 100$ What's *x*? **10**	$x = 77 \div 7$ What's *x*? **11**	$x + 73 = 100$ What's *x*? **27**	$18 - 2x = 0$ What's *x*? **9**

Activity Master 151

Reflect and Summarize the Lesson

 Write Math If $5x - 2 = 28$, what is the value of *x*? **Explain your reasoning.** 6; Possible explanation: I reasoned that if $5x - 2 = 28$, then $5x$ must be 2 greater than 28, which is 30. Then I reasoned that if $5x = 30$, *x* must equal $30 \div 5 = 6$.

Leveled Problem Solving

Jack worked 3 hours after school. He also worked on Saturday and earned $20 for the day. He earned $44 in all.

❶ Basic Level

How much did Jack earn by working after school? Explain. $24; 44 − 20 = 24.

❷ On Level

How much did Jack earn an hour when he worked after school? Explain. $8; 44 − 20 = 24, and 24 ÷ 3 = 8.

❸ Above Level

What equation describes Jack's work? Explain. $3x + 20 = 44$; You know the hours he worked, how much he made on Saturday, and how much in all. You need to find how much he earned per hour, x.

Intervention

Activity Balancing Act

Have students draw a scale with one side of an equation, such as $2x + 5 = 11$, in each pan.

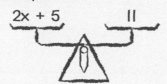

Then have students balance the scale by subtracting 5 from each side (opposite of adding 5) and then dividing by 2 (opposite of multiplying by 2). Practice with several equations.

Practice

Using Shorthand Notation to Complete Number Puzzles

Fill in the missing numbers.

		A	B	C	D	E
❶ Think of a number.	♂	12	4	0	17	1
	♂♂ ⋮⋮⋮	30	14	6	40	8

		F	G	H	I	J
❷ Think of a number.	♂	19	6	60	25	0
	♂♂ + 100	138	112	220	150	100

		K	L	M	N	O
❸ Think of a number.	x	3	1	10	9	20
	5x + 75	90	80	125	120	175

		P	Q	R	S	T
❹ Think of a number.	x	25	0	50	15	30
	3x + 150	225	150	300	195	240

Test Prep

❺ If $x = 4$, what is $3x + 18$?
A. 25
B. 28
C. 30
D. 52

❻ Explain how you found x.
Possible explanation:
I replaced x with 4 in the equation. $3 \times 4 + 18 = 12 + 18 = 30$.

Practice P111

Extension

Using Shorthand Notation to Complete Number Puzzles

Complete the puzzle.

Words	Shorthand	A	B	C	D
Think of a number.	x	10	4	14	66
Add 9.	$x + 9$	19	13	23	75
Double it.	$2x + 18$	38	26	46	150
Add the number you thought of first.	$3x + 18$	48	30	60	216
Divide by 3.	$x + 6$	16	10	20	72
Add 10.	$x + 16$	26	20	30	82
Double.	$2x + 32$	52	40	60	164
Subtract the number you thought of first.	$x + 32$	42	36	46	98
Subtract 25.	$x + 7$	17	11	21	73
Subtract the number you thought of first.	7	7	7	7	7

Extension E111

Spiral Review

Spiral Review Book page SR111 provides review of the following previously learned skills and concepts:

- practicing solving division problems
- finding rectangles with the same perimeter

You may wish to have students work with a partner to complete the page.

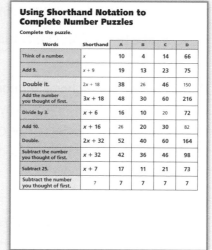

Number and Operations

Find the quotient.

❶ 6)270 45
❷ 5)480 96
❸ 4)292 73
❹ 7)406 58
❺ 15)165 11
❻ 12)228 19
❼ 3)381 127
❽ 8)696 87
❾ 9)441 49
❿ 6)582 97
⓫ 8)512 64
⓬ 7)567 81

Geometry

Draw as many rectangles as you can with the given perimeter. All possible answers are given.

⓭ 12 units
⓮ 20 units

Spiral Review SR111

Extension Activity
Working Backward

Have students find a 2-digit number by tossing a number cube twice. Tell them to write a 2-step equation whose result is that number. For example, for 26, use this format:

$$\blacksquare x + \blacksquare = 26$$

Students should use the strategy *work backward* to solve, reversing the addition or subtraction first.

Teacher's Notes 🍎

Daily Notes . . .

Quick Notes

More Ideas

Lesson 5 | Using Square Numbers to Remember Other Multiplication Facts

NCTM Standards 1, 2, 6, 7, 8, 9, 10

Lesson Planner

STUDENT OBJECTIVES ··
- To use square numbers to find related multiplication facts
- To generalize a multiplication pattern using variables

1 | Daily Activities (TG p. 1115)

| Open-Ended Problem Solving/Headline Story | Skills Practice and Review—Estimating with Compatible Numbers |

2 | Teach and Practice (TG pp. 1116–1120)

(A) Exploring Near Squares (TG pp. 1116–1117)

(B) Generalizing a Multiplication Pattern (TG p. 1118)

(C) Using Square Numbers to Remember Other Multiplication Facts (TG pp. 1119–1120)

MATERIALS

- 📖 LAB pp. 275–276
- 📖 SH pp. 230–231

3 | Differentiated Instruction (TG p. 1121)

Leveled Problem Solving (TG p. 1121)	Practice Book P112
Intervention Activity (TG p. 1121)	Extension Book E112
Extension Activity (TG p. 1121)	Spiral Review Book SR112

Lesson Notes

About the Lesson

In this lesson, students move away from number puzzles to use variables to express multiplication patterns. They find that the square of a number is one larger than the product of the number's two nearest neighbors. For example, 12 × 12 (144) is one greater than 11 × 13 (143). This pattern can be generalized, using variables instead of numbers to show that it works for all numbers. This ability to generalize is one of the main purposes of using variables.

Developing Mathematical Language

Vocabulary: dot, parentheses

To assure that the variable *x* is not confused with the multiplication symbol ×, a new symbol for multiplication, a *dot* (·), is introduced in this lesson. Students are also introduced to the use of *parentheses* in evaluating expressions. Operations in *parentheses* are performed before multiplication and division, which in turn are performed before addition and subtraction. To help students remember to perform operations within *parentheses* first, you might liken the left and right *parentheses* "( )" symbols to blinders on a horse. Until they have worked out what is between them, they cannot see anything in the world outside them!

Familiarize students with the terms *dot* and *parentheses.*

Beginning Write an expression, such as 3 × 7 + 9, on the board. Instruct students to replace the multiplication sign with a *dot* and put *parentheses* around a group of two numbers.
3 · (7 + 9) or (3 · 7) + 9

Intermediate Write an expression, such as 100 − (3 · 7 + 9), on the board. Point out the multiplication *dot* and the *parentheses.* Have students read aloud each number and symbol from left to right.

Advanced Have students explain what the *dot* and *parentheses* in a mathematical expression are used for.

Open-Ended Problem Solving

Read the Headline Story to the students. Encourage them to think of interesting scenarios that incorporate information from the story.

 Headline Story

> **Brady Elementary School has 465 students in grades K through 5. About the same number of students ride the bus as walk to school. Only 65 students ride a car to school.**

Possible responses: Less than a fifth of students ride a car to school. Almost half of the students walk to school. 400 students ride the bus or walk to school. About 200 students ride the bus and about 200 students walk. If the buses each hold 20 students and are all very full, about 10 buses are needed to take all of the students to school. If some of the buses are not full, more than 10 buses will be needed. If the buses hold 40 students and are mostly full, closer to 5 buses are needed to take students to school.

Skills Practice and Review

Estimating with Compatible Numbers

Have students use compatible numbers as an estimation strategy for solving multiplication and division problems.

Begin by writing a multiplication problem on the board that allows students to estimate the product by performing a more convenient multiplication. For example, students can use products like 19 × 11 or 20 × 11 to estimate 191 × 11. Continue with several multiplication problems, then switch to division. For example, students can estimate the quotient 960 ÷ 32 by using 9 ÷ 3 to compute 900 ÷ 30.

2 | Teach and Practice

A Exploring Near Squares

NCTM Standards 1, 2, 6, 7, 8, 9, 10

Purpose To explore a new multiplication pattern

Introduce Each student should have a copy of Explore: Products Near Square Numbers. Allow students to work individually or with partners, as they wish. Explain that in each problem, students should choose the flag with the larger area.

✓ Ongoing Assessment

• Do students recall how to multiply large numbers? If necessary, you might quickly review multiplication facts when you have a spare moment, for example, when lining up for lunch or transitioning between activities.

Task Direct students to answer the questions on the page.

❶ **Flag A:** 8 feet × 6 feet = 48 square feet
Flag B: 7 feet × 7 feet = 49 square feet Flag B is bigger.

❷ **Flag A:** 15 feet × 17 feet = 255 square feet
Flag B: 16 feet × 16 feet = 256 square feet Flag B is bigger.

❸ **Flag A:** 28 feet × 30 feet = 840 square feet
Flag B: 29 feet × 29 feet = 841 square feet Flag B is bigger.

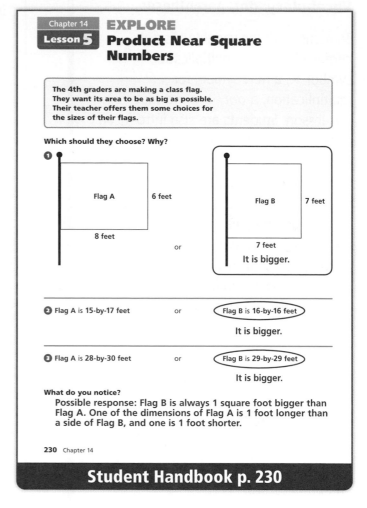

Student Handbook p. 230

What do you notice? Possible response: Flag B is always 1 square foot bigger than Flag A. One of the dimensions of Flag A is 1 foot longer than a side of Flag B, and one is 1 foot shorter.

Share After students have completed the page, bring the class together. Because students multiplied the dimensions of the flag to find each area, they should have noticed that within each pair,

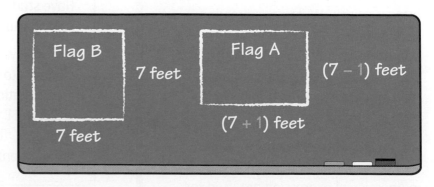

Flag B is always a square and the dimensions of Flags A and B are related: Flag A is always 1 foot shorter and 1 foot wider than Flag B.

Use with Lesson Activity Book pp. 275–276.

To make sure this is clear to all students, draw a short segment of the number line on the board, from 5 to 9, for example. Then draw curves up from the 7 and ask students for the product of 7 times itself. Fill in their response like this:

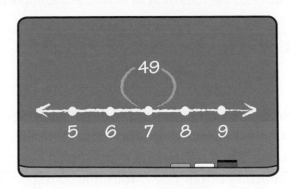

Next, ask students for the product of the two numbers on either side of 7: 6 × 8. Again draw curves up from these numbers and fill in the class's response.

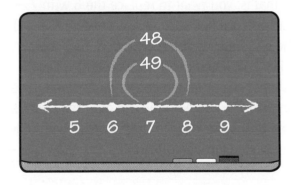

Have students describe what they notice. They should see that the product of the two numbers next to 7 is 1 less than 7 times itself.

Finally, to motivate the use of this pattern as a multiplication strategy, have students apply this pattern to a problem in which the middle number is easy to multiply by itself, but the neighbors are not so easy to multiply. For example, you might ask students to find 39 × 41. While finding this product involves many steps, finding 40 × 40 does not: 39 × 41 = 40 × 40 − 1 = 1,600 − 1 = 1,599.

💬 Talk Math

❓ Cinema East has 19 rows with 21 seats in each row. Cinema West has 20 rows with 20 seats in each row. Which theater has more seats? Explain how you can use mental math to find the answer. **Cinema West; Possible explanation: 20 × 20 is 1 bigger than 19 × 21.**

❓ Tony worked 25 hours and earned $25 per hour. Anton worked 26 hours and earned $24 per hour. Who earned more? How much more? **Tony; $1**

Teacher Story

"Students were really excited by the multiplication pattern introduced in this lesson. It made them realize that there are lots of patterns out in the world that they don't know about or that are undiscovered, and spurred them to search for patterns on their own. Some students extended the pattern from this lesson and realized that a number times itself minus 4 is equal to the product of its neighbors 2 spaces away. That is, $(x \cdot x) - 4 = (x - 2) \cdot (x + 2)$. Some students found patterns in other places, such as in the days of the week that a particular date falls on from year to year.**"**

B Generalizing a Multiplication Pattern

Purpose To use shorthand notation to record the multiplication pattern discovered in Activity A

Introduce Remind students how parentheses are used to clarify mathematical expressions. Parentheses surround operations that are to be completed first. Use an example like the following to illustrate the importance of this rule:

$$8 - 5 + 1 = 3 + 1 = 4$$
$$\text{BUT: } 8 - (5 + 1) = 8 - 6 = 2$$

Task **Draw attention to Problem 1 on Explore: Products Near Square Numbers. Ask students to give a number sentence that describes how the dimensions of Flags A and B are related.** Students should reason that they can obtain 6×8 by subtracting 1 from 7×7. Thus, the corresponding number sentence would be $(7 \times 7) - 1 = 6 \times 8$. (Alternatively, they can obtain 7×7 by adding 1 to 6×8.)

Explain that you want to rewrite this number sentence so that the 6 and the 8 are described in relation to 7; that is, you want to replace the 6 with $7 - 1$ and the 8 with $7 + 1$. The number sentence becomes $(7 \times 7) - 1 = (7 - 1) \times (7 + 1)$. Draw attention to the parentheses in the sentence. They indicate that, on the left side, 7×7 should be calculated before subtracting 1. On the right side, both $7 - 1$ and $7 + 1$ should be calculated before multiplying. (See Developing Mathematical Language for more on the use of parentheses and a fun way of remembering how they work.) Repeat this exercise with other multiplication facts. For example, students can record $(5 \times 5) - 1 = (5 - 1) \times (5 + 1)$, and $(8 \times 8) - 1 = (8 - 1) \times (8 + 1)$.

To motivate the use of variables to record this generality, tell students that the relation holds for all numbers. Have them use variables like n (which stands for "number") to say that 1 less than the square of any number equals the product of its closest neighbors. You may need to remind students that, throughout a number sentence, a variable always stands for the same number. Help students replace some of the numbers in the number sentences above with variables. For example, students could write $(n \times n) - 1 = (n + 1) \times (n - 1)$.

Finally, point out that the variable x and the multiplication symbol $\times$ can be difficult to tell apart. To avoid confusion, a dot ($\cdot$) may be used to indicate multiplication. Students can then rewrite their number sentence a final time with this new symbol: $(n \cdot n) - 1 = (n + 1) \cdot (n - 1)$.

Talk Math

❓ Are $5 - (4 - 1)$ and $(5 - 4) - 1$ the same? Explain your reasoning. No; Possible explanation: $5 - (4 - 1) = 5 - 3 = 2$. But $(5 - 4) - 1 = 1 - 1 = 0$.

❓ Jessica wrote this sentence: $5 \times x \times y = 10$. How can she rewrite the sentence to make its meaning clearer? $5 \cdot x \cdot y = 10$

Using Square Numbers to Remember Other Multiplication Facts LAB pp. 275–276

  individuals or pairs · **20 MIN**

Purpose To apply the number pattern developed in Activities A and B

NCTM Standards 1, 2, 6, 7, 8, 9, 10

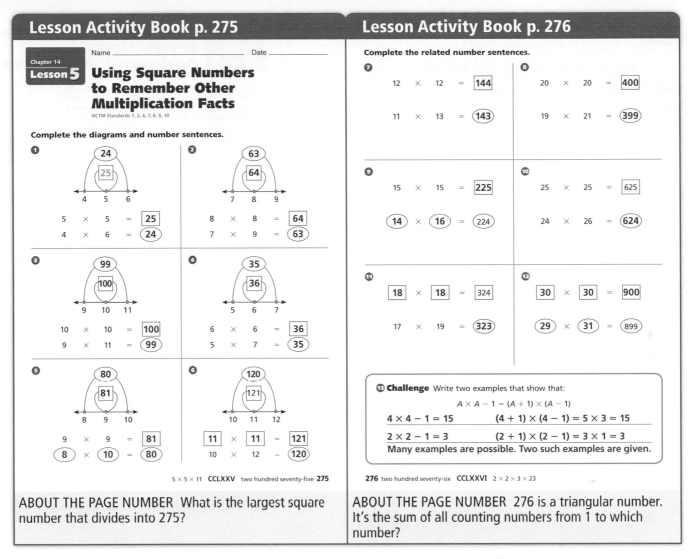

Teaching Notes for LAB page 275

Have students complete the page individually or with partners. Students continue using the relationships developed in the lesson activities. This page contains only familiar multiplication facts, allowing students to focus on recognizing and applying the squaring pattern.

Teaching Notes for LAB page 276

This page uses larger products to motivate application of the squaring pattern as a multiplication strategy. The visual aid of LAB page 275 is removed.

Challenge Problem The Challenge Problem asks students to replace variables with numbers in a number sentence to confirm that the multiplication pattern of the lesson activities is valid.

Use with Lesson Activity Book pp. 275–276.

Chapter 14 • Lesson 5 1119

Write Math

What is 89 · 91? How do you know? 8,099; Possible explanation: 89 · 91 is 1 less than 90 · 90. Since 90 · 90 is 8,100, 89 · 91 is 8,099.

Review Model

Refer students to Review Model: Applying a Squaring Pattern, in the *Student Handbook*, p. 231, to see how they can use a number pattern to help them multiply large numbers.

✓ Check for Understanding

❶ 399

❷ 1,599

❸ 6,399

❹ 9,999

❺ 1,369

❻ 2,304

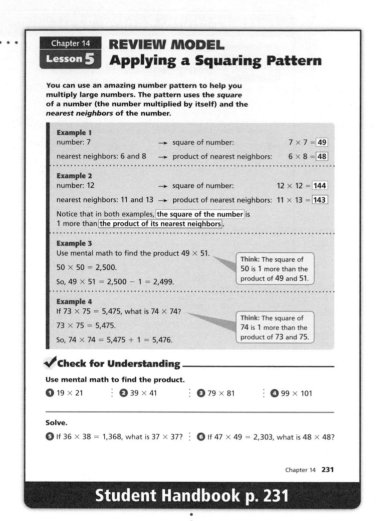

Chapter 14

Lesson 5

REVIEW MODEL
Applying a Squaring Pattern

You can use an amazing number pattern to help you multiply large numbers. The pattern uses the *square* of a number (the number multiplied by itself) and the *nearest neighbors* of the number.

Example 1
number: 7 → square of number: 7 × 7 = 49
nearest neighbors: 6 and 8 → product of nearest neighbors: 6 × 8 = 48

Example 2
number: 12 → square of number: 12 × 12 = 144
nearest neighbors: 11 and 13 → product of nearest neighbors: 11 × 13 = 143

Notice that in both examples, the square of the number is 1 more than the product of its nearest neighbors.

Example 3
Use mental math to find the product 49 × 51.
50 × 50 = 2,500.
So, 49 × 51 = 2,500 − 1 = 2,499.

Think: The square of 50 is 1 more than the product of 49 and 51.

Example 4
If 73 × 75 = 5,475, what is 74 × 74?
73 × 75 = 5,475.
So, 74 × 74 = 5,475 + 1 = 5,476.

Think: The square of 74 is 1 more than the product of 73 and 75.

✓ **Check for Understanding**

Use mental math to find the product.
❶ 19 × 21 ❷ 39 × 41 ❸ 79 × 81 ❹ 99 × 101

Solve.
❺ If 36 × 38 = 1,368, what is 37 × 37? ❻ If 47 × 49 = 2,303, what is 48 × 48?

Chapter 14 **231**

Student Handbook p. 231

3 | Differentiated Instruction

Mimi's home has 2 bedrooms. The area of one bedroom is 1 square foot greater than the area of the other.

❶ Basic Level

If the area of the smaller bedroom is 120 square feet, what could be the dimensions of the larger bedroom? Explain. Possible answer: 11 ft by 11 ft; $11 \times 11 = 121$; $121 - 1 = 120$.

❷ On Level

The larger bedroom is a square. The area of the smaller bedroom is 168 square feet. What are the dimensions of the larger bedroom? Explain. 13 ft by 13 ft; $13 \times 13 = 169$; $169 - 1 = 168$.

❸ Above Level

The larger bedroom is a square. The smaller bedroom is 14 feet by 16 feet. What are the dimensions of the larger bedroom? Explain. 15 ft by 15 ft; $14 \times 16 = 224$; $15 \times 15 = 225$; $225 - 1 = 224$.

Intervention

Activity Writing Rules

To help students with generalizations, give them situations like the following. Have them state in words the pattern relating the two quantities. Then help them write it using a variable. Have them check examples to be sure the rule works.

- Each car has 4 wheels. How many wheels are there in all? $4w$

- John has 8 fewer comics than Callie. How many does John have? $c - 8$

Practice

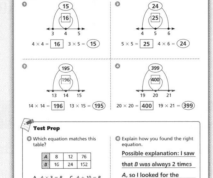

Practice P112

Extension

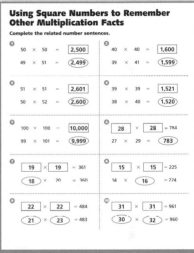

Extension E112

Spiral Review

Spiral Review Book page SR112 provides review of the previously learned skills and concepts:

- making three-dimensional figures from nets

- practicing using a ruler to measure length

You may wish to have students work with partners to complete the page.

Spiral Review SR112

Extension Activity
A Multiplication Pattern

Have students make a visual display of the relationship used in the lesson. Give students centimeter grid paper. Have them estimate the dimensions of the largest square and rectangle (with sides 1 cm greater and 1 cm less than the square) that can be drawn on the sheet. Have them draw the figures, cut them out, and label each with its length, width, and area. Students can challenge one another by showing one figure and asking a partner to name the dimensions of the other figure.

Lesson 6 Generalizing a Multiplication Problem

NCTM Standards 1, 2, 6, 7, 8, 9, 10

Lesson Planner

STUDENT OBJECTIVES
- To practice multiplication
- To continue exploring and applying the squaring multiplication pattern

1 | Daily Activities (TG p. 1123)

Open-Ended Problem Solving/Headline Story	Skills Practice and Review— Points on the Number Line

2 | Teach and Practice (TG pp. 1124–1126)

	MATERIALS
(A) **Modeling a Multiplication Pattern** (TG p. 1124)	• square tiles or counters
(B) **Drawing a Picture to Match a Multiplication Pattern** (TG p. 1125)	• graph paper • 📖 LAB pp. 277–278
(C) **Generalizing a Multiplication Pattern** (TG p. 1126)	

3 | Differentiated Instruction (TG p. 1127)

Leveled Problem Solving (TG p. 1127)	Practice Book P113
Intervention Activity (TG p. 1127)	Extension Book E113
Extension Activity (TG p. 1127)	Spiral Review Book SR113
Literature Connection (TG p. 1082)	

Lesson Notes

About the Lesson

Students continue to study the multiplication pattern of the previous lesson: a number times itself is 1 more than the product of its two neighboring numbers. Students also use manipulatives and pictures to show concretely why this pattern always holds.

About the Mathematics

As the last lesson showed, a number times itself is 1 more than the product of its nearest neighbors. This diagram illustrates the case $5 \times 5 = (6 \times 4) + 1$:

Similar patterns hold for other neighbors of squares. For example, the square of a number is 4 more than the product of the numbers 2 distant from the square:

(continued on page R9)

Use with Lesson Activity Book pp. 277–278.

Developing Mathematical Language

Vocabulary: square

To *square* a number is to multiply it by itself (e.g., 4 × 4), and the result is a *square number* (4 × 4 = 16). One reason we call these numbers *square* is that they represent the area of a geometrical *square* with whole-number side lengths. So, if the area of a *square* is 16, then each side must be 4 because the *square* of 4 is 16.

In this lesson, *square* refers only to the product of a whole number times itself. Examples of *squares* are 1, 4, 9, 16, 25, 36, and so on, because 1 × 1 = 1, 2 × 2 = 4, 3 × 3 = 9, 4 = 4 = 16, 5 × 5 = 25, 6 × 6 = 36, and so on.

Familiarize students with the term *square.*

Beginning Draw a *square* on the board and label the length and width 2. Next to the *square,* write "2 × 2 = 4, so 4 is a *square* number." Have students read the sentence aloud. Repeat with other *square* numbers through 10, allowing volunteers to write the sentences.

Intermediate List several numbers from 1 to 100 on the board. Have volunteers circle a *square* number and explain how they know it is a *square.*

Advanced Give students one-digit numbers to *square* mentally and then complete this sentence, "The *square* of ■ is ■, so ■ is a *square.*" Example: The *square* of 7 is 49, so 49 is a *square.*

Open-Ended Problem Solving

Read the Headline Story to the students. Encourage them to make imaginative statements using information from the story.

 Headline Story

Mattius and Janie are each drawing a picture. Each used a piece of paper 2 feet long and $1\frac{1}{2}$ feet wide. They oriented the pictures the same way. They want to frame the pictures in a single frame. At the frame shop, they notice that the frames' dimensions are given in inches rather than feet.

Possible responses: If they put the pictures side-by-side and don't overlap them, they will need a frame that is 2 feet by 3 feet (24 inches by 36 inches), or $1\frac{1}{2}$ feet by 4 feet (18 inches by 48 inches). They can overlap the pictures a bit and get a smaller frame.

Skills Practice and Review

Points on the Number Line

Draw a number line on the board and label it, from 2 to 5, for example. Make the line long enough (about 3 feet) so that there is room to label points between the whole numbers. Begin by having students locate and name the whole numbers on the number line. Then ask students to point to the part of the line where a number such as $2\frac{1}{2}$ or 1.1 would fall. Label these points. Then ask students to name and label points that you indicate. Be specific about where you pointing, for example saying that you are pointing exactly halfway between 2 and $2\frac{1}{2}$, so that they know to label it $2\frac{1}{4}$ or 2.25. Repeat with a segment of the number line that has large whole numbers (for example 7,437 to 7,441) and ask students to find numbers between them.

Modeling a Multiplication Pattern

Materials
- For the teacher: square tiles or counters
- For each pair: square tiles or counters

NCTM Standards 1, 2, 6, 7, 8, 9, 10

Purpose To use objects to model the squaring multiplication pattern, and to show why it works

Introduce Give each pair of students enough square tiles or counters to make a square array. For example, you might have students make a 5-by-5 array from 25 counters.

Task **Direct students to move as few tiles (or counters) as possible to make an array whose dimensions are the nearest neighbors of the length of the array–4-by-6 in this example.** Ask students how many tiles they have left over after making the new array. They should have 1 left over, because the product of the neighboring numbers is 1 less than the square number.

If necessary, demonstrate how to make the new array in as few steps as possible. For example, remove one row from the 5-by-5 array so that it now measures 4-by-5, and show how the displaced tiles can be arranged to make the new column in the 4-by-6 array. Since you removed 5 tiles but need only 4 to make the final column, 1 tile is left over.

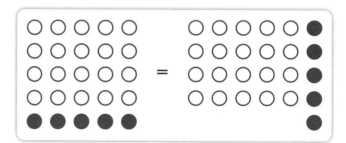

Repeat the activity with a square array of a different size.

Share Ask students to describe the patterns they see in the "before" and "after" versions of the arrays. Ask whether they think the patterns will always be seen.

💬 Talk Math

❓ Jonah built a rectangular array whose length was 2 more than its width. He wanted to use the same tiles to build a square array with sides 1 less than the length of the first array. Did he have enough tiles to do this? Explain your reasoning. No; Possible explanation: The number of tiles needed to make the square array was 1 more than the number needed to make the original rectangular array.

❓ Describe how you could make an 8-by-10 array from a 9-by-9 array. Possible description: Remove one row from the 9-by-9 array. The array now measures 8-by-9. Use the row you removed to form a column of the 8-by-9 array, making it an 8-by-10 array with a single tile left over. Remove the extra tile.

Drawing a Picture to Match a Multiplication Pattern

Purpose To confirm the squaring multiplication pattern for larger numbers

Introduce Mention that in the last activity, students used tiles or counters to build arrays and to explore the squaring multiplication pattern. Arrays would be impractical for exploring the pattern for larger numbers, however, because of the length of time they would take to build. Instead, in this activity, students will draw pictures to check the pattern for larger numbers.

Task Direct students to draw a picture to represent a large square array, measuring perhaps 30-by-30. Point out that drawing 900 dots would be tedious, and recall the area model of multiplication that students utilized in earlier lessons: all they need to do is draw a square and label each edge 30.

Ask students to give the area of this square. 900 square units Now ask how they can use this picture to help them find the area of a 29-by-31 array. Students should realize that they can remove 1 unit of length from one dimension of the square array and add 1 unit of width to this new array. Removing one unit of length removes a 1-by-30 section of the array, or an area of 30 square units. Since the array now measures 29-by-30, adding 1 unit of width requires adding a 29-by-1 section, or an area of 29 square units. Thus, the new array is 1 square unit of area smaller than the original square array.

Have students use graph paper to help them visualize this process. Students can quickly outline a 30-by-30 square array, cut off one row of the array, and use that strip to make the new column.

Share To make sure students can see that 1 square on the strip of graph paper must be removed to make the new array, ask them to explain how they carried out the activity.

Talk Math

❷ A 55-by-55 square has an area of 3,025 square units. What is the area of a 56-by-54 square? 3,024 square units

❷ The diagram shows a 7-by-9 array drawn on a piece of graph paper. One additional square has been drawn atop the first column. Describe how you could create an 8-by-8 array by making a single cut with a pair of scissors, rearranging the pieces after the cut. Possible response: Cut off the last column on the right. Turn it 90 degrees and place it atop the array, beside the single square.

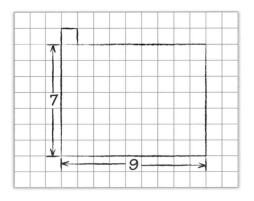

Materials
• For each student: graph paper

NCTM Standards 1, 2, 6, 7, 8, 9, 10

Differentiated Instruction

On Level You might provide students with graph paper for Activity B to help them visualize the process of changing the numbers of rows and columns in a large array. For example, they could quickly outline a 60-by-60 square array, cut one row off, and use it to make a new column. They should see that the one box remaining on the strip of graph paper must be removed to make the new array.

Generalizing a Multiplication Pattern LAB pp. 277–278

 individuals or pairs **20 MIN**

Purpose To apply and illustrate the squaring multiplication pattern

NCTM Standards 1, 2, 6, 7, 8, 9, 10

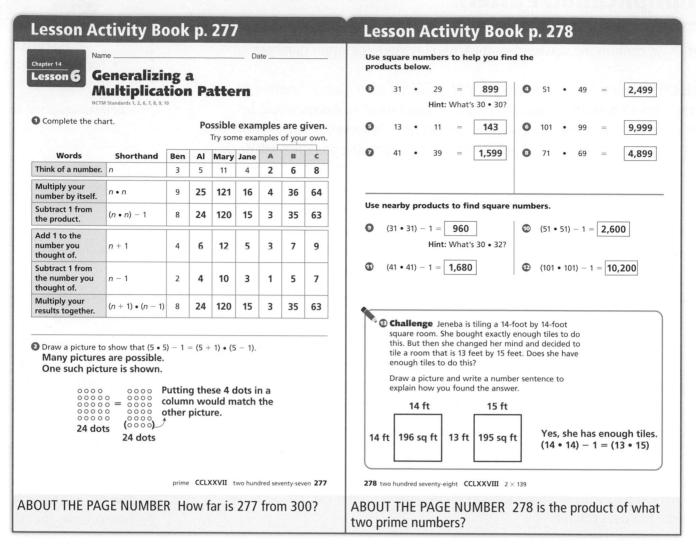

Lesson Activity Book p. 277

Chapter 14 Lesson 6 **Generalizing a Multiplication Pattern**
NCTM Standards 1, 2, 6, 7, 8, 9, 10

❶ Complete the chart.

Possible examples are given.
Try some examples of your own.

Words	Shorthand	Ben	Al	Mary	Jane	A	B	C
Think of a number.	n	3	5	11	4	2	6	8
Multiply your number by itself.	n • n	9	25	121	16	4	36	64
Subtract 1 from the product.	(n • n) − 1	8	24	120	15	3	35	63
Add 1 to the number you thought of.	n + 1	4	6	12	5	3	7	9
Subtract 1 from the number you thought of.	n − 1	2	4	10	3	1	5	7
Multiply your results together.	(n + 1) • (n − 1)	8	24	120	15	3	35	63

❷ Draw a picture to show that (5 • 5) − 1 = (5 + 1) • (5 − 1). Many pictures are possible. One such picture is shown.

Putting these 4 dots in a column would match the other picture.

24 dots = 24 dots

prime CCLXXVII two hundred seventy-seven **277**

ABOUT THE PAGE NUMBER How far is 277 from 300?

Lesson Activity Book p. 278

Use square numbers to help you find the products below.

❸ 31 • 29 = **899**
Hint: What's 30 • 30?

❹ 51 • 49 = **2,499**

❺ 13 • 11 = **143**

❻ 101 • 99 = **9,999**

❼ 41 • 39 = **1,599**

❽ 71 • 69 = **4,899**

Use nearby products to find square numbers.

❾ (31 • 31) − 1 = **960**
Hint: What's 30 • 32?

❿ (51 • 51) − 1 = **2,600**

⓫ (41 • 41) − 1 = **1,680**

⓬ (101 • 101) − 1 = **10,200**

⓭ **Challenge** Jeneba is tiling a 14-foot by 14-foot square room. She bought exactly enough tiles to do this. But then she changed her mind and decided to tile a room that is 13 feet by 15 feet. Does she have enough tiles to do this?

Draw a picture and write a number sentence to explain how you found the answer.

14 ft		15 ft	
14 ft	196 sq ft	13 ft	195 sq ft

Yes, she has enough tiles. (14 • 14) − 1 = (13 • 15)

278 two hundred seventy-eight CCLXXVIII 2 × 139

ABOUT THE PAGE NUMBER 278 is the product of what two prime numbers?

Teaching Notes for LAB page 277

Have students complete the page individually or with partners. Students tackle the squaring multiplication pattern in the now familiar format of a number puzzle. Then they draw a picture to illustrate the pattern.

Differentiated Instruction Basic Level If students struggle drawing their pictures, you might encourage them to draw pictures of the models they made in Activity A.

Teaching Notes for LAB page 278

Problems 3–8 have multiplication problems that are difficult to do without several steps of calculations. However, if students use their understanding of the squaring multiplication pattern, they can use multiples of 10 to find the products.

In Problems 9–12, students again simplify their calculations by applying the pattern, thereby taking advantage of the simple process of multiplying by multiples of 10.

Challenge Problem The Challenge Problem presents an everyday situation which students can analyze using the squaring multiplication pattern.

Reflect and Summarize the Lesson

 Write Math

How can you use the product of 20 × 22 to find the product of 21 × 21? Possible response: 20 is twice 10, so 20 × 22 is twice 10 × 22; 10 × 22 = 220, so 20 × 22 = 2 × 220 = 440; 21 × 21 is 1 more than 20 × 22, so 21 × 21 = 440 + 1 = 441.

1126 Chapter 14 • Lesson 6

Use with Lesson Activity Book pp. 277–278.

Leveled Problem Solving

A farmer fences in two pens. One is square with an area of 1,600 square feet. The other is a rectangle.

① Basic Level

What are the dimensions of the square? Explain. 40 ft by 40 ft; 40 ft × 40 ft = 1,600 sq ft.

② On Level

The area of the rectangle is 1 square foot less than the area of the square. What are its dimensions? Explain. 39 ft by 41 ft; A 39 × 41 rectangle has an area of 1,599 sq ft; 1,600 − 1,599 = 1.

③ Above Level

The area of the rectangle is 1 square foot less than the area of the square. What is the perimeter of the rectangle? Explain. 160 ft; The dimensions of the rectangle are 39 ft × 41 ft; 39 + 41 + 39 + 41 = 160.

Intervention

Activity Square Numbers Buzz

Have students stand in a circle. Tell them the first student will say 1 and the student to the right will say the next number, and so on. However, every student who gets a square number will say "buzz" instead of the number. The first 10 numbers will, therefore, be "buzz, 2, 3, buzz, 5, 6, 7, 8, buzz, 10." Have students continue through 100 (buzz).

Practice

Generalizing a Multiplication Pattern
Complete the number sentence.

① 7 • 7 = 49   6 • 8 = 48
   11 • 11 = 121   10 • 12 = 120

② (5 • 5) − 1 = 24   4 • 6 = 24
   (10 • 10) − 1 = 99   9 • 11 = 99

③ (12 • 12) − 1 = 143   11 • 13 = 143
   (15 • 15) − 1 = 224   14 • 16 = 224

④ 20 • 20 − 1 = 399   19 • 21 = 399
   60 • 60 − 1 = 3,599   59 • 61 = 3,599

Test Prep
About how long will an alligator be when it's 10 years old?
A. 10 feet   C. 6 feet
B. 8 feet   D. 2 feet

GROWTH RATE OF ALLIGATORS	
Years 1–5	1 foot per year
Years 6–15	3 inches per year

Practice P113

Extension

Generalizing a Multiplication Pattern
Complete the puzzles.

Words	Shorthand	Ben	Al	Mary	Jane
Think of a number.	n	4	3	2	5
Multiply your number by itself.	n • n	16	9	4	25
Subtract 4 from the product.	(n • n) − 4	12	5	0	21
Add 2 to your number.	n + 2	6	5	4	7
Subtract 2 from your number.	n − 2	2	1	0	3
Multiply your results together.	(n + 2) • (n − 2)	12	5	0	21

Words	Shorthand	Ben	Al	Mary	Jane
Think of a number.	n	7	4	3	5
Multiply your number by itself.	n • n	49	16	9	25
Subtract 9 from the product.	(n • n) − 9	40	7	0	16
Add 3 to your number.	n + 3	10	7	6	8
Subtract 3 from your number.	n − 3	4	1	0	2
Multiply your results together	(n + 3) • (n − 3)	40	7	0	16

Extension E113

Spiral Review

Spiral Review Book page SR113 provides review of the previously learned skills and concepts:

- exploring patterns in number puzzles
- comparing predictions with experimental results

You may wish to have students work with a partner to complete the page.

Algebra
Complete the table. Check students' work.

	Write a number between 10 and 99.	Multiply the number by 9.	Add the digits in the product.
①			
②			
③			
④			
⑤			

⑥ Describe the pattern in the third column.
The sum of the digits will always be a number that is divisible by 9.

Data Analysis and Probability
For 7–11, write the numbers 1 through 10 on slips of paper. Predict how many times the outcome will occur for this experiment: Mix up the papers, pick one, record the number, and put the paper back. Do this 10 times. Write whether your results are close to your prediction.
Possible answers are given.

⑦ a number less than 6   5 times, not close
⑧ an odd number   5 times, close
⑨ a multiple of 5   2 times, not close
⑩ a 3   1 time, not close
⑪ Why do you think the results might not match your predictions?
Possible answer: Probability experiments do not always come out the way you expect.

Spiral Review SR113

Extension Activity
Extending a Pattern

Have students draw a square on centimeter grid paper and, beside it, a rectangle with length 2 units greater than that of the square, and width 2 units less. Ask students to find and compare the areas of the figures. Have them repeat with other squares and rectangles. Ask what conclusion they can draw. The area of the square is 4 square units larger than the area of the rectangle.

Lesson 7 | Problem Solving Strategy and Test Prep

NCTM Standards 1, 2, 6, 7, 8, 9, 10

Lesson Planner

Problem Solving Strategy: Work Backward (TG pp. 1129–1130, 1132–1133)

MATERIALS

Ⓐ **Discussing the Problem Solving Strategy: Work Backward** (TG p. 1129)

Ⓑ **Solving Problems by Applying the Strategy** (TG p. 1130)

- 📖 LAB p. 279
- 📖 SH pp. 232–233

Problem Solving Test Prep (TG p. 1131)

Ⓒ **Getting Ready for Standardized Tests** (TG p. 1131)

- 📖 LAB p. 280

Lesson Notes

About Problem Solving

Problem Solving Strategy: Work Backward

In this chapter's puzzles, students used the final number and the sequence of steps to *work backward* to the starting number, undoing the steps in reverse order. Similarly, students *work backward* to solve equations like $3x - 8 = 22$. First, they add 8 to the final number, 22, then divide the sum, 30, by 3. In these and other areas, *work backward* is a strategy with extensive applications in mathematics.

Skills Practice and Review

Points on the Number Line

As in the previous lesson, draw a number line on the board, from 0 to 3, for example. Have students label the whole numbers on the line. Then ask them to indicate the locations of fractions and decimals, such as $\frac{1}{2}$ or 1.25. Label these points. Ask students to name and label other points that you indicate. Be specific about where you point, to distinguish among halves, thirds, fourths, and so on.

Problem Solving Strategy

A Discussing the Problem Solving Strategy: Work Backward

whole class 🕐 **15 MIN**

NCTM Standards 1, 2, 6, 7, 8, 9, 10

Purpose To share strategies for solving problems and focus on the problem solving strategy *work backward*

Introduce Point out that, throughout this chapter, students have been using the strategy *work backward* to solve number puzzles. Suppose, for example, that the result is 18 after your friend thinks of a number, subtracts 7, and triples it. To find the number, *work backward.* The last direction before the result, 18, was *triple it.* So, *divide by 3:* $18 \div 3 = 6$. The previous direction was *subtract 7.* So, *add 7:* $6 + 7 = 13$. Your friend's number was 13.

Problem A note on a treasure map said, "Where the island is 37 miles wide, start at its western edge. Go *x* miles east and find the treasure. If you continue east the same distance, then 5 miles more, you will reach the eastern edge of the island." How can you find the treasure?

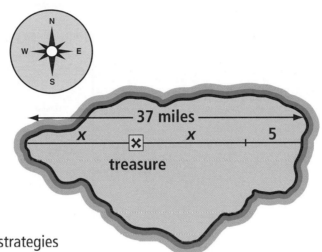

37 miles

x x 5

treasure

Share Ask students to share their strategies for solving the problem. *Work backward* is a good strategy to try, because we can write an equation to describe the location of the treasure, then solve it. Help students to see that $x + x + 5 = 37$ is such an equation. Since the distance $x + x$ is twice the distance x, the equation can also be written $2x + 5 = 37$.

To solve the equation, *work backward.* First, subtract 5 from 37: $37 - 5 = 32$. Then, divide by 2: $32 \div 2 = 16$. So, the treasure is located 16 miles from the western edge of the island.

💬 Talk Math

❷ Why did we subtract 5 and divide by 2 to solve the equation? Possible answer: To *work backward,* apply the inverse operation from the operation in the problem. So, instead of adding 5, subtract 5. Instead of multiplying by 2, divide by 2.

❷ Why can we rewrite the equation $x + x + 5 = 37$ as $2x + 5 = 37$? Possible answer: When you add a number to itself, the result is the same as multiplying the number by 2. For example, $7 + 7$ is the same as 2 times 7. So, $x + x$ is the same as 2 times x, or $2x$.

B Solving Problems by Applying the Strategy LAB p. 279

Purpose To share strategies for solving problems and focus on the problem solving strategy *work backward*

Teaching Notes for LAB page 279

Students practice the problem solving strategy *work backward* by solving each of the problems independently or in pairs. Help students get started by asking questions such as the following:

Read to Understand

What do you know? the changes in the number of marbles Lorenzo had each day from Monday through Thursday.

What do you need to find out? the number of marbles he bought on Monday.

Plan

How can you solve this problem? Think about the strategies you might use.

How could you work backward? Reverse the changes in the number of marbles he had each day, from Thursday back to Monday.

Solve

How might you work backward to solve the problem? The table shows the day-by-day changes from Monday to Thursday. Lorenzo had 14 marbles on Thursday. Since he gained 5 marbles on Wednesday, *subtract* 5: $14 - 5 = 9$. Since he gave away 3 marbles on Tuesday, *add* 3: $9 + 3 = 12$. Since he doubled the number he bought on Monday, *divide* by 2: $12 \div 2 = 6$. So, he bought 6 marbles on Monday.

Check

Look back at the original problem. Did you answer the questions that were asked? Do your answers make sense? How do you know? I can check the answer. Six marbles on Monday plus 6 more on Tuesday ($6 + 6 = 12$), minus 3 on Wednesday ($12 - 3 = 9$), plus 5 on Wednesday ($9 + 5 = 14$), gives 14 marbles on Thursday.

Students can use this method to solve the other problem on the page. Supplement the above questions with ones that are specifically tailored to Problem 2.

Lesson Activity Book p. 279

Name _____ Date _____

Chapter 14
Lesson 7 **Problem Solving Strategy**
Work Backward
NCTM Standards 1, 2, 6, 7, 8, 9, 10

Understand
Plan
Solve
Check

① On Monday, Lorenzo bought x marbles. On Tuesday, he bought the same number he bought on Monday. On Wednesday, he gave 3 marbles to his brother. On Thursday, he bought 5 more marbles, giving him a total of 14 marbles. The equation $2x - 3 + 5 = 14$ represents the number of marbles Lorenzo had on Thursday.

Fill in the table to find how many marbles Lorenzo bought on Monday.

	Shorthand	Number of Marbles
Monday	x	6
Tuesday	$2x$	12
Wednesday	$2x - 3$	9
Thursday	$2x - 3 + 5$	14

Lorenzo bought __6__ marbles on Monday.

② Jean ended up with 8 when she completed this number puzzle. What number was Jean thinking of? Fill in the table to find out.

Think of a number.	8
Double it.	16
Add 2.	18
Divide by 2.	9
Subtract 1.	8

$3 \times 3 \times 31$ **CCLXXIX** two hundred seventy-nine **279**

ABOUT THE PAGE NUMBER How can you write 279 as the product of a square number and a prime?

Reflect and Summarize the Lesson

Write Math **When might the strategy *work backward* be a good one to try to solve a problem?** Possible response: when the problem describes a series of steps from one point to another or from one time to another. To solve the problem, reverse the steps.

Problem Solving Test Prep

C Getting Ready for Standardized Tests LAB p. 280

individuals

20 MIN

Purpose To prepare students for standardized tests

NCTM Standards 1, 2, 6, 7, 8, 9, 10

Lesson Activity Book p. 280

Problem Solving Test Prep

Choose the correct answer.

❶ What is the area of the figure?

A. $16\frac{1}{2}$ square units
B. 17 square units
C. $17\frac{1}{2}$ square units
D. 18 square units

❷ Which expression has the same product as 80 × 427?

A. 800 × 42
B. 400 × 827
C. 80 × 42.7
D. 8 × 4,270

❸ Which fraction should go in the box on the number line?

$0 \quad \frac{1}{8} \quad \frac{1}{4} \quad \frac{3}{8} \quad \frac{1}{2} \quad \blacksquare \quad \frac{3}{4} \quad \frac{7}{8} \quad 1$

A. $\frac{2}{3}$
B. $\frac{5}{6}$
C. $\frac{5}{8}$
D. $\frac{6}{8}$

❹ Athena has two $\frac{1}{2}$-gallon containers and one 1-quart container of orange juice. How many 1-cup servings can she make in all?

A. 5
B. 10
C. 20
D. 24

✎ **Show What You Know**

Solve each problem. Explain your answer.

❺ Carmen has $1.43 when she gets home from school. She paid $0.35 each way on the city bus, bought lunch for $1.45, and had a snack for $0.79. How much money did she leave home with?

$4.37; $1.43 + (2 × $0.35)
+ $1.45 + $0.79 = $4.37.

❻ Curtis cut his birthday cake into equal pieces. Six pieces were eaten at the party, and half of the leftover pieces were eaten the next day. The last 3 pieces were eaten two days later. Into how many slices was the cake cut?

12 slices; 3 is half of 6. There were 6 leftover pieces.

6 + 6 = 12.

280 two hundred eighty **CCLXXX** 2 × 2 × 2 × 5 × 7

ABOUT THE PAGE NUMBER How can 280 cents be written as the sum of the same number of quarters and dimes? Quarters, dimes and nickels?

Teaching Notes for LAB page 280

The test items on this page are written in the same style and arranged in the same format as those on many state assessments. The page is cumulative and is designed for students to apply a variety of problem solving strategies, including *work backward.* Have students share the strategies they use.

The Item Analysis Chart highlights one of the possible strategies that may be used for each test item.

Show What You Know

Written Response

Direct students' attention to Problems 5 and 6. Explain that they must decide how to solve the problems. In Problem 5, the amount Carmen left home with is the sum of the amounts she spent and the amount she had left. In Problem 6, *work backward* from the last three pieces to the original number. Then have students write an explanation of how they know their answer is correct. To provide more space for students to communicate their thinking about these problems, you may wish to have them write their responses and explanations on a separate sheet of paper. Use the Scoring Rubric below to evaluate their understanding.

Item Analysis Chart

Item	Strategy
1	Make a model
2	Guess and check
3	Use logical reasoning
4	Act it out
5	Work backward
6	Work backward

Scoring Rubric

2	• Demonstrates complete understanding of the problem and chooses an appropriate strategy to determine the solution
1	• Demonstrates a partial understanding of the problem and chooses a strategy that does not lead to a complete and accurate solution
0	• Demonstrates little understanding of the problem and shows little evidence of using any strategy to determine a solution

---

Review Model...

Refer students to the Review Model: Work Backward in the *Student Handbook,* pp. 232–233 to review a model of the four steps they can use with the problem solving strategy *work backward.*

Additional problem solving practice is also provided.

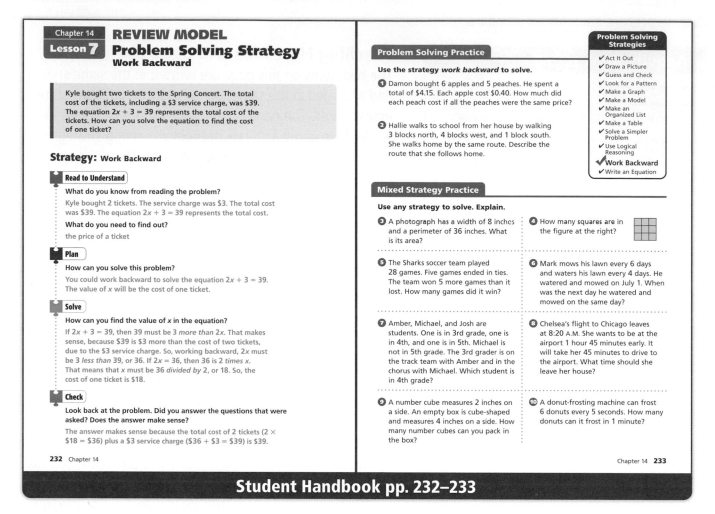

Chapter 14
Lesson 7
REVIEW MODEL
Problem Solving Strategy
Work Backward

Kyle bought two tickets to the Spring Concert. The total cost of the tickets, including a $3 service charge, was $39. The equation $2x + 3 = 39$ represents the total cost of the tickets. How can you solve the equation to find the cost of one ticket?

Strategy: Work Backward

Read to Understand

What do you know from reading the problem?
Kyle bought 2 tickets. The service charge was $3. The total cost was $39. The equation $2x + 3 = 39$ represents the total cost.

What do you need to find out?
the price of a ticket

Plan

How can you solve this problem?
You could work backward to solve the equation $2x + 3 = 39$. The value of x will be the cost of one ticket.

Solve

How can you find the value of x in the equation?
If $2x + 3 = 39$, then 39 must be 3 *more than* $2x$. That makes sense, because $39 is $3 more than the cost of two tickets, due to the $3 service charge. So, working backward, $2x$ must be 3 *less than* 39, or 36. If $2x = 36$, then 36 is 2 *times* x. That means that x must be 36 *divided by* 2, or 18. So, the cost of one ticket is $18.

Check

Look back at the problem. Did you answer the questions that were asked? Does the answer make sense?
The answer makes sense because the total cost of 2 tickets (2 × $18 = $36) plus a $3 service charge ($36 + $3 = $39) is $39.

232 Chapter 14

Problem Solving Practice

Use the strategy *work backward* to solve.

❶ Damon bought 6 apples and 5 peaches. He spent a total of $4.15. Each apple cost $0.40. How much did each peach cost if all the peaches were the same price?

❷ Hallie walks to school from her house by walking 3 blocks north, 4 blocks west, and 1 block south. She walks home by the same route. Describe the route that she follows home.

Mixed Strategy Practice

Use any strategy to solve. Explain.

❸ A photograph has a width of 8 inches and a perimeter of 36 inches. What is its area?

❹ How many squares are in the figure at the right?

❺ The Sharks soccer team played 28 games. Five games ended in ties. The team won 5 more games than it lost. How many games did it win?

❻ Mark mows his lawn every 6 days and waters his lawn every 4 days. He watered and mowed on July 1. When was the next day he watered and mowed on the same day?

❼ Amber, Michael, and Josh are students. One is in 3rd grade, one is in 4th, and one is in 5th. Michael is not in 5th grade. The 3rd grader is on the track team with Amber and in the chorus with Michael. Which student is in 4th grade?

❽ Chelsea's flight to Chicago leaves at 8:20 A.M. She wants to be at the airport 1 hour 45 minutes early. It will take her 45 minutes to drive to the airport. What time should she leave her house?

❾ A number cube measures 2 inches on a side. An empty box is cube-shaped and measures 4 inches on a side. How many number cubes can you pack in the box?

❿ A donut-frosting machine can frost 6 donuts every 5 seconds. How many donuts can it frost in 1 minute?

Problem Solving Strategies

✔ Act It Out
✔ Draw a Picture
✔ Guess and Check
✔ Look for a Pattern
✔ Make a Graph
✔ Make a Model
✔ Make an Organized List
✔ Make a Table
✔ Solve a Simpler Problem
✔ Use Logical Reasoning
✔ **Work Backward**
✔ Write an Equation

Chapter 14 **233**

Student Handbook pp. 232–233

Task Have students read the problem at the top of the Review Model page.

💬 Talk Math

❓ What do you need to find out? the price of a ticket

❓ What is the cost of two tickets without a service charge? Explain your reasoning. Possible response: $36; possible explanation: The service charge adds $3 to the total, so taking away $3 gives the total of just the two tickets.

❓ How can you find the cost of one ticket? What was the cost? by dividing the total cost of the tickets by 2; $36 ÷ 2 = $18

❓ What other strategy could you use to solve the problem? How could you use it? Possible answer: *guess and check;* possible answer: You could guess the cost of a ticket, check to see if the total cost was $39. If it wasn't, adjust your guess up or down, then check again, continuing until you find the correct price.

❶ $0.35; Possible explanation: You can *work backward* to solve the problem. The cost of apples was 6 × $0.40 = $2.40. The cost of peaches was $4.15 − $2.40 = $1.75.

Each peach cost $1.75 ÷ 5 = $0.35.

❷ 1 block north, 4 blocks east, and 3 blocks south; Possible explanation: You can *work backward* to solve the problem. Start at the end of her walk to school and reverse each stage of the trip. 1 block south reverses to 1 block north; 4 blocks west reverses to 4 blocks east; 3 blocks north reverses to 3 blocks south.

Mixed Strategy Practice

❸ 80 square inches; Possible explanation: You can *use logical reasoning* to solve the problem. Possible explanation: Half the perimeter is 18 inches, so the length is 18 − 8 = 10 inches. The area is 10 × 8 = 80 square inches.

❹ 14 squares; Possible explanation: You can *make an organized list* to solve the problem. First list the number of 3 × 3 squares (1), then the number of 2 × 2 squares (4), and finally the number of 1 × 1 squares (9). Total: 1 + 4 + 9 = 14.

❺ 14 wins; Possible explanation: You can *guess and check* to solve the problem. The team played 28 − 5 = 23 non-ties. Guess, check, and revise your guess as necessary until you find a win-loss total of 23 games with 5 more wins than losses.

❻ July 13; Possible explanation: You can *act it out* to solve the problem. List the days of July, from 1 to 31. Place two tokens, one representing mowing, one watering on July 1. Move the tokens 6 days and 4 days at a time until both land on the same date.

❼ Michael; Possible explanation: You can *use logical reasoning* to solve the problem. Neither Amber nor Michael can be in 3rd grade, so Josh is the 3rd grader. Michael is not in 5th grade so he must be in 4th grade.

❽ 5:50 A.M.; Possible explanation: You can *work backward* to solve the problem. Start at 8:20 A.M. Count backward 1 hour 45 minutes for her early arrival at the airport, then another 45 minutes for the drive.

❾ 8 cubes; Possible explanation: You can *draw a picture* or *make a model* to solve the problem. The box will hold two layers of cubes, each containing 4 cubes, for a total of 8 cubes.

❿ 72 donuts; Possible explanation: You can *use logical reasoning* to solve the problem. There are 60 seconds in a minute, and 60 ÷ 5 = 12 five-second periods in a minute. So in 1 minute the machine can frost 6 × 12 = 72 donuts.

Algebraic Thinking

NCTM Standards 1, 2, 6, 7, 8, 9, 10

Purpose To provide students with an opportunity to demonstrate understanding of Chapter 14 concepts and skills

MATERIALS
- LAB pp. 281–282
- Chapter 14 Test
  (Assessment Guide
  pp. AG117–AG118)

Chapter 14 Learning Goals and Assessment Options

These learning goals are assessed in many ways throughout the chapter. The chart below correlates each learning goal to specific formal and informal assessment options.

	Learning Goals	Lesson Number	Snapshot Assessment	Chapter Review Item Numbers	Chapter Test Item Numbers
				LAB pp. 281–282	Assessment Guide pp. AG117–AG118
14-A	Represent numbers and equations using pictures and variables	14.1–14.4	1, 2, 5, 7	1–2	1–8
14-B	Use algebra to express and apply a generalization or pattern	14.5, 14.6	3, 4, 6, 8	3–7	9–11
14-C	Apply problem solving strategies such as *work backward* to solve problems	14.7	9, 10	8	12

Snapshot Assessment

The following Mental Math and Quick Write questions and tasks provide a quick, informal assessment of students' understanding of Chapter 14 concepts, skills, and problem solving strategies.

whole class   **10 MIN**

Mental Math This oral assessment uses mental math strategies and can be used with the whole class.

❶ Express algebraically. Use *n* as the variable.
- Think of a number. *n*
- Multiply by 70. 70*n*
- Add 30. 70*n* + 30
- Divide by 10. 7*n* + 3
- Subtract 3. 7*n*
  (Learning Goal 14-A)

❷ If 3 + *w* = 7, what is *w*? 4
How do you know? Possible explanation: 3 + 4 = 7, so *w* must be 4.
- If 16 + *d* = 36, what is *d*? 20
  How do you know? Possible explanation: *d* must be 20 since 16 + 20 = 36.
- If 4*b* − 8 = 12, what is *b*? 5
  How do you know? Possible explanation: 4*b* must be 20 because 20 − 8 = 12. For 4*b* to equal 20, *b* must be 5.
  (Learning Goal 14-A)

❸ If $5 \times 5 = 25$, then what is 4×6? 24
- If $10 \times 10 = 100$, then what is 9×11? 99
- If $20 \times 20 = 400$, then what is 19×21? 399

(Learning Goal 14-B)

❹ If $12 \times 14 = 168$, then what is 13×13? 169
If $31 \times 33 = 1,023$, then what is 32×32? 1,024
Use mental math to find 29×31, and explain how you found the answer. 899. Possible explanation: I know the product will be 1 less than the product of 30×30. $30 \times 30 = 900$, so $29 \times 31 = 899$.

(Learning Goal 14-B)

Quick Write This informal written assessment can be administered to small groups or the whole class. Read each question and have the students record responses on their write-on boards. Encourage students to listen and think about the questions before responding.

❺ If $x = 5$, what is the value of $x + 17$? 22
- If $y = 12$, what is the value of $20 - y$? 8
- If $w = 6$, what is the value of $6w - 3$? 33
- If $z = 10$, what is the value of $8z - (3 \times 25)$? 5

(Learning Goal 14-A)

❻ Are $6 - (4 - 2)$ and $(6 - 4) - 2$ the same? No. Explain. Possible explanation: You must do what's inside parentheses first, so $6 - (4 - 2)$ is the same as $6 - 2$ or 4. The other expression, $(6 - 4) - 2$, is the same as $2 - 2$ or 0. 4 does not equal 0.

(Learning Goal 14-B)

❼ Tim told Peter to think of a number, multiply it by 5, and then tell him the answer. Peter said 35. Explain how Tim can figure out the number Peter started with. 7, Possible explanation: Since division is the inverse of multiplication, Tim could divide 35 by 5 to get 7.

(Learning Goal 14-A)

❽ For 4 hours, a snail moved the same distance in inches each hour. During the next hour, it moved 2 inches. It moved 18 inches in all. Write and solve an equation to find how far it moved the first hour. Explain how you solved the equation. 4 inches; Possible explanation: I used x to represent how far it moved the first hour and $4x + 2 = 18$ to represent the situation. If $4x + 2 = 18$, then $4x = 18 - 2$, or 16. If $4x = 16$, then $x = 16 \div 4$, or 4 inches.

(Learning Goal 14-B)

❾ Two friends spend $8.00 on lunch. Both had the same sandwich and milk. A sandwich costs $1.00 more than milk. How much does milk cost? How much does a sandwich cost? Use pictures, numbers, or words to explain your answer. Possible explanation: Each person spent $4.00. If a sandwich is $1.00 more than milk, then $4.00 has to be split into two parts that add to $4.00, with one part exactly $1.00 more than the other part. I know $2.50 + $1.50 = $4.00 and $2.50 is $1.00 more than $1.50. Each sandwich costs $2.50; milk costs $1.50.

(Learning Goal 14-C)

❿ John has 7 more than 3 times the number of baseball trading cards that his friend Andy has. Andy has 12 trading cards. How many cards does John have? Use pictures, numbers, or words to explain your answer. Possible explanation: John has 7 more than 3 times 12 cards. $3 \times 12 = 36$ and 7 more than 36 is 43. So, John has 43 baseball trading cards.

(Learning Goal 14-C)

Formal Assessment

Chapter Review/Assessment The Chapter 14 Review/Assessment on *Lesson Activity Book* pages 281–282 assesses students' understanding of computation in puzzles, tables, and problem solving. Students should be able to complete these pages independently.

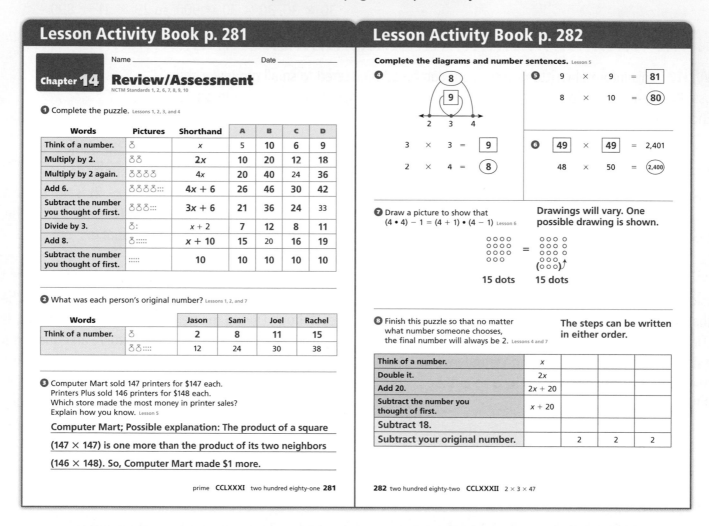

Extra Support Students who have difficulty with items on the Chapter 14 Review/Assessment may need review of the lesson where development of the concept was provided. You can use the Intervention Activity to increase students' understanding before the Chapter Test is given.

Chapter Test Use the Chapter 14 Test in the *Assessment Guide* to assess concepts, skills, and problem solving from the chapter and to prepare students for standardized tests. The Chapter Test and other test items are also available online.

Chapter Notes

Quick Notes

More Ideas

_____

_____

_____

_____

_____

_____

_____

_____

_____

_____

_____

_____

_____

_____

_____

_____

_____

_____

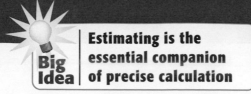

Big Idea Estimating is the essential companion of precise calculation

Estimation

About the Chapter

In this final chapter of fourth grade mathematics, students use many of the ideas, skills, and strategies they have developed over the course of the year. Estimating unites this work. Estimating is a frequent "behind the scenes" mathematical skill we rely on in daily life to make quick, approximate mental calculations. How long will it take to save enough money to buy a TV set? How long will it take to finish a science project? How many guests can we invite to our party?

Additionally, estimating strategies build on students' understanding of numbers. Estimating provides a means for quickly checking the reasonableness of computations and promotes strategic thinking and flexible computation.

Students apply estimating to a variety of everyday situations, including earning money, stocking a store, taking drinks to the beach, and measuring familiar objects. Students also use estimation to reinforce their understanding of various units of measure: How large is a cup relative to a quart, liter, or gallon? If a soccer coach brings three gallons of water to practice, has she brought enough? Is it likely that a car is six meters high? As students work problems like these, they also practice converting between different units of measure and comparing customary and metric units.

Developing Concepts Across the Grades

Topic	Prior Learning	Learning in Chapter 15	Later Learning
Measurement	• Convert between customary units of capacity • Measure and compare weights in pounds and ounces **Grade 3, Chapter 13**	• Find length, perimeter, and area using standard and non-standard units • Measure capacity and weight • Compare weights **Lessons 15.2–15.8**	• Use appropriate units and formulas to measure surface area and volume **Grade 5, Chapter 12**
Estimation	• Estimate sums and differences **Grade 3, Chapter 3**	• Review estimation strategies • Estimate length, perimeter, and area using standard and non-standard units • Estimate capacity and weight **Lessons 15.1–15.6, 15.8**	• Estimate sums and differences of mixed numbers **Grade 5, Chapter 11**
Symbolic Notation	• Find missing operation signs and numbers in addition and subtraction sentences **Grade 3, Chapter 1**	• Write equations and inequalities to match pictures about weight • Find and estimate weight from equations and inequalities **Lesson 15.8**	• Represent mathematical relationships using diagrams and equations **Grade 5, Chapter 15**

Chapter Planner

Lesson	Objectives	NCTM Standards	Vocabulary	Materials/ Resources

CHAPTER 15 World Almanac • Vocabulary • Games • Challenge
Teacher Guide pp. 1145A–1145F, Student Handbook pp. 240–241, 252–256

Lesson	Objectives	NCTM Standards	Vocabulary	Materials/ Resources
1 **Estimation Strategies** PACING 1 DAY **Teacher Guide** pp. 1146–1151 **Lesson Activity Book** pp. 283–284 **Student Handbook** Student Letter p. 239 Explore p. 242	• To review estimation strategies such as rounding and using compatible numbers • To estimate sums, differences, products, and quotients	1, 6, 7, 8, 9, 10	compatible round	**For the students:** ■ School-Home Connection, SHC57–SHC58 ■ P114, E114, SR114 **Science Connection:** **Mach Numbers** **Teacher Guide** p. 1144
2 **Estimating and Checking Length and Perimeter** PACING 1 DAY **Teacher Guide** pp. 1152–1159 **Lesson Activity Book** pp. 285–286 **Student Handbook** Explore p. 243 Review Model p. 244	• To estimate and find length, perimeter, and area using standard and non-standard units	1, 3, 4, 6, 7, 8, 9, 10	area perimeter	**For the students:** ■ Streamers or long strips of paper ■ Centimeter or meter ruler ■ P115, E115, SR115 **Literature Connection:** **The Grapes of Math** **Teacher Guide** p. 1144
3 **Designing a School** PACING 1 DAY **Teacher Guide** pp. 1160–1165 **Lesson Activity Book** pp. 287–288	• To estimate the perimeter and area of rooms and hallways on floor plans • To design floor plans to match specified perimeters or areas	1, 3, 4, 6, 7, 8, 9, 10	scale	**For the students:** ■ TR: AM152 ■ P116, E116, SR116 **Art Connection:** **Which Painting is "Bigger"?** **Teacher Guide** p. 1144
4 **Estimating and Checking Capacity** PACING 1 DAY **Teacher Guide** pp. 1166–1171 **Lesson Activity Book** pp. 289–290	• To understand the difference between volume and capacity • To estimate and measure capacity	1, 4, 6, 7, 8, 9, 10	capacity volume	**For the students:** ■ centimeter cubes and ruler (optional) ■ measuring cups and other common containers that have volume and capacity ■ base-10 blocks or other items that have volume but no (or less) capacity ■ several liter, milliliter, cup, pint, quart, and gallon containers; rice, beans, or other measurable substance ■ container from home ■ index card ■ TR: AM153 ■ P117, E117, SR117

NCTM Standards 2000
1. Number and Operations
2. Algebra
3. Geometry
4. Measurement
5. Data Analysis and Probability
6. Problem Solving
7. Reasoning and Proof
8. Communication
9. Connections
10. Representation

Key
AG: Assessment Guide
E: Extension Book
LAB: Lesson Activity Book
P: Practice Book
SH: Student Handbook
SR: Spiral Review Book
TG: Teacher Guide
TR: Teacher Resource Book

MATH GLOSSARY in **Student Handbook** p. 259

Planner (continued)

Chapter Planner *(continued)*

Lesson	Objectives	NCTM Standards	Vocabulary	Materials/Resources
5 Comparing Units of Capacity PACING 1 DAY **Teacher Guide** pp. 1172–1179 **Lesson Activity Book** pp. 291–292 **Student Handbook** Explore p. 245 Review Model p. 246	• To estimate and find capacity • To compare customary and metric units of capacity	1, 4, 6, 7, 8, 9, 10	**liter** **quart**	**For the students:** ■ Containers that students found the capacity of in Lesson 15.4 ■ index cards with the capacity of each container from Lesson 15.4 ■ P118, E118, SR118
6 Estimating and Checking Weight PACING 1 DAY **Teacher Guide** pp. 1180–1185 **Lesson Activity Book** pp. 293–294 **Student Handbook** Game p. 254	• To estimate and find weight in customary and standard units	1, 4, 6, 7, 8, 9, 10	**mass** **weight**	**For the students:** ■ scale with both grams (and kilograms) and ounces (and pounds) ■ various objects from around the room ■ calculator ■ TR: AM154 ■ P119, E119, SR119
7 Comparing Units of Weight PACING 1 DAY **Teacher Guide** pp. 1186–1193 **Lesson Activity Book** pp. 295–296 **Student Handbook** Explore p. 247 Game p. 255	• To relate pounds and kilograms • To compare weights	1, 4, 6, 7, 8, 9, 10	**kilogram** **pound**	**For the students:** ■ TR: AM155–AM156 ■ scale, kilogram weights, pound weights (optional) ■ P120, E120, SR120
8 Using Equations and Inequalities to Compute and Estimate Weight PACING 1 DAY **Teacher Guide** pp. 1194–1201 **Lesson Activity Book** pp. 297–298 **Student Handbook** Explore p. 248 Review Model p. 249	• To write equations and inequalities to match pictures about weight • To find and estimate weight from equations and inequalities	1, 2, 4, 6, 7, 8, 9, 10	**equation** **inequality**	**For the teacher:** ■ transparency of SH p. 248 **For the students:** ■ P121, E121, SR121

Planner *(continued)*

Lesson	Objectives	NCTM Standards	Vocabulary	Materials/Resources
9 **Problem Solving Strategy and Test Prep** PACING **1 DAY** **Teacher Guide** pp. 1202–1207 **Lesson Activity Book** pp. 299–300 **Student Handbook** Review Model pp. 250–251	• To practice the problem solving strategy *act it out* • To articulate the steps and strategies used to solve problems • To prepare for standardized tests	1, 2, 4, 6, 7, 8, 9, 10		
CHAPTER 15 Assessment TG pp. 1208–1211, **LAB** pp. 301–302, **AG** pp. AG121–AG124				**For the students:** ■ Chapter 15 Test pp. AG121–AG122

Planning Ahead

In **Lesson 15.4**, students will need to provide a container from home to use in an activity in which they will practice estimating capacity.

In **Lesson 15.5**, students will need containers that they brought from home to play *The Closest Estimate: Capacity.*

In **Lesson 15.6**, students will play the *The Closest Estimate: Weight.* Objects from around the classroom will be used in this game.

In **Lesson 15.7**, students will play the *Weight Match Game.* Each small group of 2–3 students will need a set of cards cut from AM155–AM156 Weight Cards I and II.

Games

Use the following games for skills practice and reinforcement of concepts.

Lesson 15.5 ▶
In *The Closest Estimate: Capacity,* students practice estimating capacity by looking at containers.

Lesson 15.6 In *The Closest Estimate: Weight,* students practice estimating the weight of an object.

Lesson 15.7 In *Weight Match,* students match equivalent pounds and kilograms.

Closest Estimate Game

Developing Problem Solvers

Open-Ended Problem Solving

The Headline Story in the Daily Activities section of every lesson provides an open-ended problem for students to complete. For each story there are many possible responses.

Headline Stories can be found on TG pages 1147, 1153, 1161, 1167, 1173, 1181, 1187, and 1195.

Leveled Problem Solving

Leveled Problem Solving provides an opportunity for students to apply learning from the lesson to a real-life situation. Problems are leveled by ability to allow students of all ability levels to become successful problem solvers. Each Leveled Problem Solving begins with a real-life scenario upon which three problems are built.

The levels of problems are:

❶ Basic Level	❷ On Level	❸ Above Level
students needing extra support	students working at grade level	students who are ready for more challenging problems

Leveled Problem Solving can be found on TG pages 1151, 1159, 1165, 1171, 1178, 1185, 1192, and 1201.

 **FOR KIDS**

The World Almanac for Kids feature is designed to stimulate student interest for the math concepts they are about to learn. Students use data to solve problems and explain solutions. The Chapter 15 Project can be found on SH pages 240–241.

Write Math Reflect and Summarize the Lesson poses a problem or question for students to think and write about. This feature can be found on TG pages 1150, 1158, 1164, 1169, 1177, 1184, 1191, 1200, and 1204.

Other opportunities to write about math can be found on LAB pages 286, 289–290, 294, 296, and 298.

Problem Solving Strategies

The focus of **Lesson 15.9** is the strategy *act it out*. However, students will use a variety of problem solving strategies as they work through the chapter. The chart below shows strategies that may be useful in completing each lesson.

Strategy	Lesson(s)	Description
✓ **Act It Out**	15.2, 15.4, 15.7, 15.8	Act it out using a non-standard unit to measure the dimensions of an object such as a door.
Guess and Check	15.6	Guess the weight of an object by estimating, then check the estimate by weighing the object on a scale.
Make a Model	15.3, 15.6	Make a scale drawing of an object to draw conclusions about relations among its dimensions.
Make a Table	15.4	Make a table to simplify the task of finding the distances a car can travel on 1, 2, 3, and more tanks of gas.
Use Logical Reasoning	15.1, 15.5, 15.6	Use logical reasoning and estimating to choose answers to multiple-choice problems without solving them.
Write an Equation	15.8	Write equations and inequalities to represent the relation between weights on a balance.

Meeting the Needs of All Learners

Differentiated Instruction

Extra Support	On Level	Enrichment
Intervention Activities TG pp. 1151, 1159, 1165, 1171, 1178, 1185, 1192, 1201	**Practice Book** pp. 114–121	**Extension Activities** TG pp. 1151, 1159, 1165, 1171, 1178, 1185, 1192, 1201
	Spiral Review Book pp. 114–121	**Extension Book** pp. 114–121
	LAB Challenge LAB pp. 284, 286, 288, 290, 292, 294, 296, 298	**LAB Challenge** LAB pp. 284, 286, 288, 290, 292, 294, 296, 298
Lesson Notes Basic Level TG pp. 1155, 1182	**Lesson Notes** On Level TG p. 1154	**Lesson Notes** Above Level TG p. 1163
Leveled Problem Solving Basic Level TG pp. 1151, 1159, 1165, 1171, 1178, 1185, 1192, 1201	**Leveled Problem Solving** On Level TG pp. 1151, 1159, 1165, 1171, 1178, 1185, 1192, 1201	**Leveled Problem Solving** Above Level TG pp. 1151, 1159, 1165, 1171, 1178, 1185, 1192, 1201

English Language Learners

Suggestions for addressing the needs of students learning English as a second language are included in the Developing Mathematical Language section at the beginning of most lessons.

ELL activities for this chapter can be found on TG pages 1147, 1153, 1161, 1167, 1173, 1181, 1187, and 1195.

The Multi-Age Classroom

Grade 3	• Students on this level should be able to complete the lessons in Chapter 15 but might need some additional practice with key concepts and skills. • Give students more practice with measurement.	See Grade 4, Intervention Activities, Lessons 15.1–15.8. See Grade 3, Lessons 10.1–10.7, 13.4–13.7.
Grade 4	• Students on this level should be able to complete the lessons in Chapter 15 with minimal adjustments.	See Grade 4, Practice pages P114–P121.
Grade 5	• Students on this level should be able to complete the lessons in Chapter 15 and to extend measurement concepts and skills. • Give students extended work with volume and surface area.	See Grade 4, Extension pages E114–E121. See Grade 5, Lessons 12.4–12.8.

Cross Curricular Connections

Science Connection

Math Concept: estimation

Mach Numbers

- Explain that scientists describe the speed of an airplane by comparing it with the speed of sound, about 760 miles per hour at sea level. This speed is called Mach 1.

- Challenge students to estimate the speed of planes traveling at different Mach speeds, such as Mach 2, Mach 3, and Mach 3.5. Mach 2: about 1,520 mi/hr; Mach 3: about 2,280 mi/hr; Mach 3.5: about 2,660 mi/hr

- Present this table.

Speed Class	Mach Number
Subsonic	Mach < 1.0
Transonic	Mach $= 1.0$
Supersonic	$1.0 <$ Mach < 5.0
Hypersonic	Mach > 5.0

- Give students various speeds in miles per hour. Have them classify the speeds using terms from the table. A plane flying 2,500 miles per hour, for example, is flying at supersonic speed.

Lesson 15.1

Art Connection

Math Concept: estimating perimeter and area

Which Painting is "Bigger"?

- Point out to students that "bigger" might have different meanings depending on what is being measured. Ask students to consider two paintings, both rectangles, hanging side by side in a museum. The dimensions of one painting are 30 inches by 12 inches, and the dimensions of the other are 20 inches by 19 inches.

- Ask students to determine which painting is bigger.

30 in. **20 in.**
12 in. **19 in.**

But first ask them to consider what "bigger" means. If they do not volunteer more than one way to think about the question, tell them that it might refer to perimeter (the frame) or to area (the entire painting). 30-in. by 12-in painting: perimeter $= (2 \times 30) + (2 \times 12) = 60 + 24 = 84$ in.; area $= 30 \times 12 = 360$ sq in.; 20-in. by 19-in. painting: perimeter $= (2 \times 20) + (2 \times 19) = 40 + 38 = 78$ in.; area $= 20 \times 19 = 380$ sq in.

Lesson 15.3

Literature Connection

Math Concept: estimation

The Grapes of Math
By Gregory Tang
Illustrated by Harry Briggs

In the Grapes of Math, guided by hints in the verses, readers find solutions to math riddles. Students estimate and make simple calculations using mental math strategies.

Lesson 15.2

School-Home Connection

A reproducible copy of the School-Home Connection letter in English and Spanish can be found in the *Teacher Resource Book* pages SHC57–SHC60.

Encourage students to play *Find Your Estimate,* found in the *Teacher Resource Book* on page SHC58, with a family member. Students will estimate capacity and weight in **Lessons 15.5** and **15.6**.

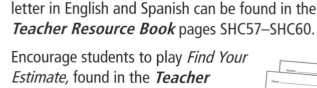

Assessment Options

There are many opportunities in *Think Math!* to assess students' understanding of concepts, skills, and problem solving. Learning Goals for Chapter 15 are provided below. The assessment options provide opportunities to evaluate whether or not students have retained learning from prior experiences. Choose the forms of assessment that best meet the needs of your students.

Chapter 15 Learning Goals

	Learning Goals	Lesson Number
15-A	Use rounding and compatible numbers to estimate solutions.	15.1
15-B	Estimate and find perimeter, area, capacity, and weight using standard and customary units.	15.2–15.4, 15.6
15-C	Convert between units of capacity and units of weight.	15.5, 15.7
15-D	Estimate weight with equations or inequalities and pictorial models.	15.8
15-E	Apply problem solving strategies such as *act it out* to solve problems.	15.9

✔ Informal Assessment

Ongoing Assessment
Provides insight into students' thinking to guide instruction (TG pp. 1156, 1168, 1175)

Reflect and Summarize the Lesson
Checks understanding of lesson concepts (TG pp. 1150, 1158, 1164, 1170, 1177, 1184, 1191, 1200, 1204)

Snapshot Assessment
Mental Math and **Quick Write**
Offers a quick observation of students' progress on chapter concepts and skills (TG pp. 1208–1209)

Performance Assessment
Provides quarterly assessment of Chapters 12–15 concepts using real-life situations
Assessment Guide
pp. AG225–AG230

✔ Formal Assessment

Standardized Test Prep
Problem Solving Test Prep
Prepares students for standardized tests
Lesson Activity Book p. 300 (TG p. 1205)

Chapter 15 Review/Assessment
Reviews and assesses students' understanding of the chapter
Lesson Activity Book pp. 301–302 (TG p. 1210)

Chapter 15 Test
Assesses the chapter concepts and skills
Assessment Guide
Form A pp. AG121–AG122
Form B pp. AG123–AG124

Benchmark 4 Assessment
Provides quarterly assessment of Chapters 12–15 concepts and skills
Assessment Guide
Benchmark 4A pp. AG125–AG132
Benchmark 4B pp. AG133–AG140

World Almanac for Kids

Use the World Almanac for Kids feature, *Bee-havior,* found on pp. 240–241 of the **Student Handbook,** to provide students with an opportunity to practice using their problem solving skills by solving real world problems.

FACT • ACTIVITY 1

❶ Possible answer: perimeter estimate: 18 cm; area estimate: 20 cm²

❷ 20 − 13 = 7 meters

❸ Possible answer: about 3.5 meters

THE WORLD ALMANAC FOR KIDS

Bee-havior

In a natural beehive, the working bees build honeycombs attached to each other from top to bottom. These honeycombs are made of beeswax and they form hexagonal cells. It takes about 15 pounds of beeswax to form the entire structure of the honeycomb. The cells of the honeycomb are used for storing honey and raising the young.

FACT • ACTIVITY 1

Look at the honeycomb.

❶ Estimate the perimeter and area of the honeycomb. Use the fact that the picture of the bee to the right of the honeycomb is 1 square centimeter.

1 cm²

For 2–3, use the drawing.

❷ How far does a bee have to fly from the beehive to reach the flowerbed?

❸ About how far is the boy from the beehive?

beehive   flowerbed   13 meters

20 meters

240 Chapter 15

Student Handbook p. 240

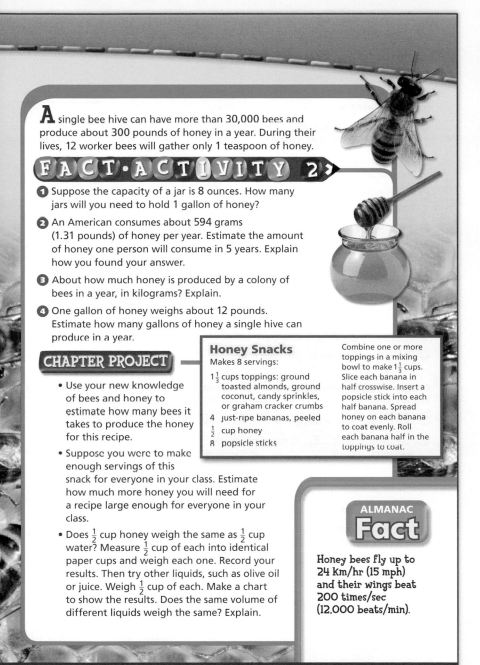

A single bee hive can have more than 30,000 bees and produce about 300 pounds of honey in a year. During their lives, 12 worker bees will gather only 1 teaspoon of honey.

FACT·ACTIVITY 2

❶ Suppose the capacity of a jar is 8 ounces. How many jars will you need to hold 1 gallon of honey?

❷ An American consumes about 594 grams (1.31 pounds) of honey per year. Estimate the amount of honey one person will consume in 5 years. Explain how you found your answer.

❸ About how much honey is produced by a colony of bees in a year, in kilograms? Explain.

❹ One gallon of honey weighs about 12 pounds. Estimate how many gallons of honey a single hive can produce in a year.

CHAPTER PROJECT

- Use your new knowledge of bees and honey to estimate how many bees it takes to produce the honey for this recipe.

- Suppose you were to make enough servings of this snack for everyone in your class. Estimate how much more honey you will need for a recipe large enough for everyone in your class.

- Does $\frac{1}{2}$ cup honey weigh the same as $\frac{1}{2}$ cup water? Measure $\frac{1}{2}$ cup of each into identical paper cups and weigh each one. Record your results. Then try other liquids, such as olive oil or juice. Weigh $\frac{1}{2}$ cup of each. Make a chart to show the results. Does the same volume of different liquids weigh the same? Explain.

Honey Snacks
Makes 8 servings:

$1\frac{1}{3}$ cups toppings: ground toasted almonds, ground coconut, candy sprinkles, or graham cracker crumbs

4 just-ripe bananas, peeled

$\frac{1}{2}$ cup honey

8 popsicle sticks

Combine one or more toppings in a mixing bowl to make $1\frac{1}{3}$ cups. Slice each banana in half crosswise. Insert a popsicle stick into each half banana. Spread honey on each banana to coat evenly. Roll each banana half in the toppings to coat.

ALMANAC Fact

Honey bees fly up to 24 km/hr (15 mph) and their wings beat 200 times/sec (12,000 beats/min).

Student Handbook p. 241

FACT·ACTIVITY 2

❶ 1 gal = 128 oz; 128 ÷ 8 = 16 jars

❷ 3 kg; Round 594 g to 600 g, then multiply by 5 years. 600 × 5 = 3,000 g = 3 kg

❸ about 150 kg; 1 lb = 2.2 kg = 2 kg; 300 ÷ 2 = 150 kg

❹ between 20 and 30 gallons (Estimate 300 ÷ 12. Possible answers: 360 ÷ 12 = 30 or 240 ÷ 12 = 20 using numbers compatible with 12)

CHAPTER PROJECT

Sample calculations:

- I found that it takes 48 teaspoons for 1 cup of honey or 24 teaspoons for $\frac{1}{2}$ cup to make the 8 servings of honey snack. Since 12 bees can produce 1 teaspoon of honey, it would take 12 × 24 = 288 bees to produce $\frac{1}{2}$ cup of honey. Estimate 12 × 24 as 10 × 25 or about 250 bees.

- Possible answer: There are 22 students in my class. The recipe is for 8 servings. I would need to make about 3 times as much (3 × 8 = 24 servings). 3 times the amount of honey is about $\frac{1}{2}$ cup × 3 = $1\frac{1}{2}$ cups.

- Possible answer: $\frac{1}{2}$ cup of different liquids weigh different amounts. Olive oil is lighter than water, and both are lighter than honey.

Vocabulary

To reinforce vocabulary concepts, invite students to complete the vocabulary activities on pp. 252–253 of the *Student Handbook.* Encourage students to record their answers in their math journals.

Many answers are possible.

12 Possible answer: *Round* the lengths of the sides of the room to *compatible* numbers. If the sides of the room are 18 feet and 24 feet, *round* each side to 20 feet. So, the perimeter would be about 80 feet and the area about 400 square feet.

13 Possible answer: I know that a liter is a little more than a quart. I can *round* 1 liter to 1 quart. If I have 12 liters, for example, I must have a little more than 12 quarts. I would guess that I have about 13 quarts.

14 Possible answer: I know that 1 kilogram is a little more than 2 pounds. I can *round* 1 kilogram to 2 pounds. If I have 8 kilograms, then I have more than 16 pounds.

Chapter **15** Vocabulary

Choose the best vocabulary term from Word List A for each sentence.

1 Numbers that are easy to compute mentally are __?__ numbers. **compatible**

2 The number of square units needed to cover a surface is the __?__ of the surface. **area**

3 The distance around a figure is the __?__ of the figure. **perimeter**

4 A metric unit for measuring capacity is the __?__. **liter**

5 A customary unit for measuring weight is the __?__. **pound**

6 A number sentence that shows that two quantities are equal is called a(n) __?__. **equation**

7 The __?__ is the measure of the amount of space a solid figure occupies. **volume**

8 The amount of matter in an object is its __?__. **mass**

9 The __?__ of an object tells how heavy it is. **weight**

Word List A

area
capacity
compatible
equation
inequality
kilogram
liter
mass
perimeter
quart
pound
round
scale
volume
weight

Complete each analogy using the best term from Word List B.

10 Quart is to __?__ as kilogram is to mass. **capacity**

11 Ruler is to inch as __?__ is to pound. **scale**

Word List B

capacity
scale
inequality

 Talk Math

Discuss with a partner what you have learned about estimation. Use the vocabulary terms *compatible* and *round*.

12 Ken's living room is a rectangle. How can you estimate its perimeter and area?

13 How can you use a liter to estimate a capacity in quarts?

14 How can you use a kilogram to estimate a weight in pounds?

252 Chapter 15

Student Handbook p. 252

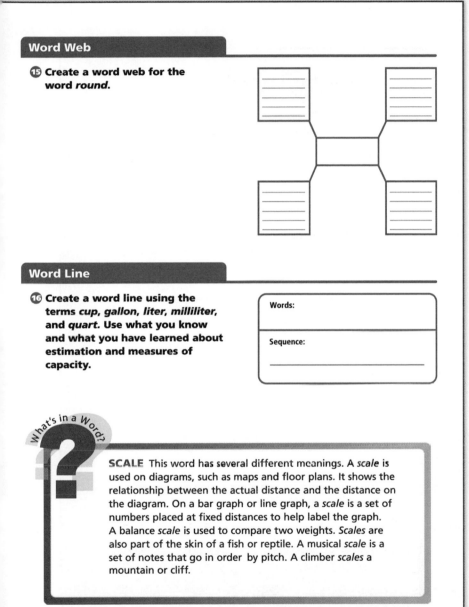

Word Web

15 Create a word web for the word *round*.

Word Line

16 Create a word line using the terms *cup*, *gallon*, *liter*, *milliliter*, and *quart*. Use what you know and what you have learned about estimation and measures of capacity.

Words:

Sequence:

What's in a Word?

SCALE This word has several different meanings. A *scale* is used on diagrams, such as maps and floor plans. It shows the relationship between the actual distance and the distance on the diagram. On a bar graph or line graph, a *scale* is a set of numbers placed at fixed distances to help label the graph. A balance *scale* is used to compare two weights. *Scales* are also part of the skin of a fish or reptile. A musical *scale* is a set of notes that go in order by pitch. A climber *scales* a mountain or cliff.

Chapter 15 **253**

Student Handbook p. 253

---

15 Many answers are possible. One example is provided.

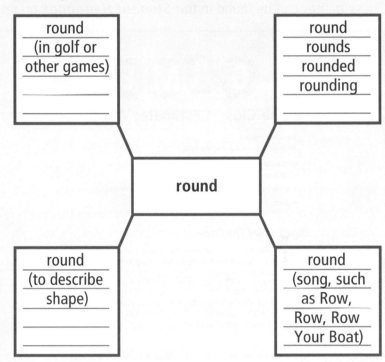

16 Many answers are possible. One example is provided.

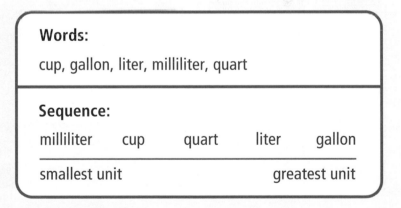

Games

Closest Estimate Game in **Lesson 15.6** provides an opportunity for students to practice estimating weight just by looking at an object that is in their classroom. *Weight Match* in **Lesson 15.7** provides an opportunity for students to use their understanding of the relationship between pounds and kilograms.

These games can be found in the *Student Handbook* on pp. 254–255.

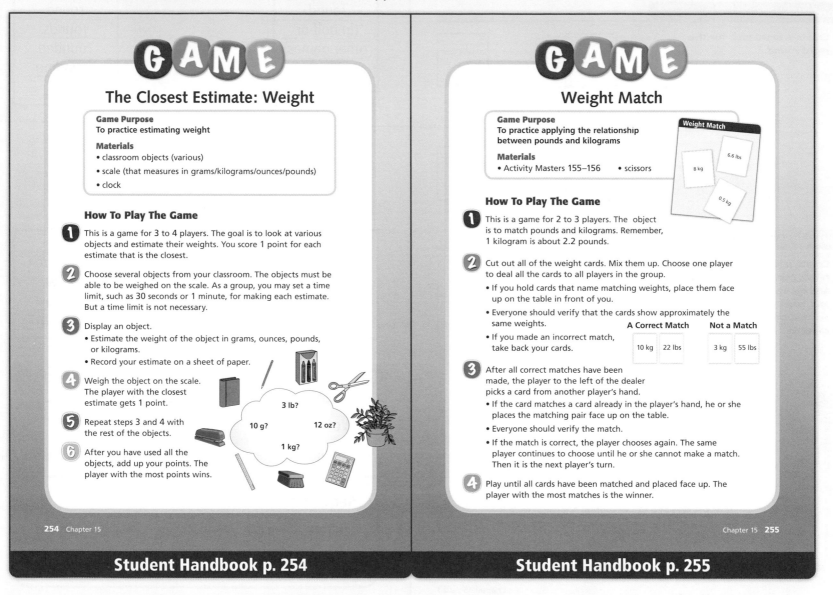

GAME

The Closest Estimate: Weight

Game Purpose
To practice estimating weight

Materials
• classroom objects (various)
• scale (that measures in grams/kilograms/ounces/pounds)
• clock

How To Play The Game

1 This is a game for 3 to 4 players. The goal is to look at various objects and estimate their weights. You score 1 point for each estimate that is the closest.

2 Choose several objects from your classroom. The objects must be able to be weighed on the scale. As a group, you may set a time limit, such as 30 seconds or 1 minute, for making each estimate. But a time limit is not necessary.

3 Display an object.
• Estimate the weight of the object in grams, ounces, pounds, or kilograms.
• Record your estimate on a sheet of paper.

4 Weigh the object on the scale. The player with the closest estimate gets 1 point.

3 lb?
10 g?
1 kg?
12 oz?

5 Repeat steps 3 and 4 with the rest of the objects.

6 After you have used all the objects, add up your points. The player with the most points wins.

254 Chapter 15

Student Handbook p. 254

GAME

Weight Match

Game Purpose
To practice applying the relationship between pounds and kilograms

Materials
• Activity Masters 155–156 • scissors

Weight Match
6.6 lbs
8 kg
0.5 kg

How To Play The Game

1 This is a game for 2 to 3 players. The object is to match pounds and kilograms. Remember, 1 kilogram is about 2.2 pounds.

2 Cut out all of the weight cards. Mix them up. Choose one player to deal all the cards to all players in the group.
• If you hold cards that name matching weights, place them face up on the table in front of you.
• Everyone should verify that the cards show approximately the same weights.
• If you made an incorrect match, take back your cards.

A Correct Match
10 kg 22 lbs

Not a Match
3 kg 55 lbs

3 After all correct matches have been made, the player to the left of the dealer picks a card from another player's hand.
• If the card matches a card already in the player's hand, he or she places the matching pair face up on the table.
• Everyone should verify the match.
• If the match is correct, the player chooses again. The same player continues to choose until he or she cannot make a match. Then it is the next player's turn.

4 Play until all cards have been matched and placed face up. The player with the most matches is the winner.

Chapter 15 255

Student Handbook p. 255

Challenge

This activity challenges students to find the amount of weight or mass that is needed to balance a scale that holds different units of measurement. This activity can be found on p. 256 of the **Student Handbook.**

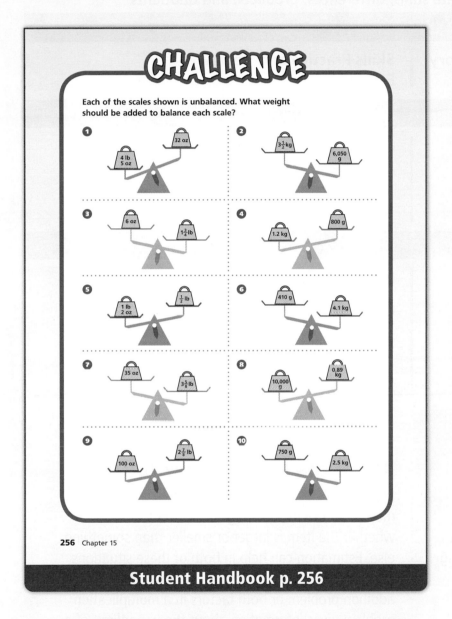

1. 2 lb 5 oz
2. 2,550 g or 2.55 kg
3. 22 oz
4. 400 g
5. 10 oz
6. 3,690 g or 3.69 kg
7. 23 oz
8. 9,110 g or 9.11 kg
9. 54 oz
10. 24,250 g or 24.25 kg

Lesson 1 Estimation Strategies

NCTM Standards 1, 6, 7, 8, 9, 10

Lesson Planner

STUDENT OBJECTIVES

- To review estimation strategies such as rounding and using compatible numbers
- To estimate sums, differences, products, and quotients

1 | Daily Activities (TG p. 1147)

| Open-Ended Problem Solving/Headline Story | Skills Practice and Review— Estimating |

2 | Teach and Practice (TG pp. 1148–1150)

A **Reading the Student Letter** (TG p. 1148)

B **Exploring Estimation** (TG p. 1149)

C **Estimation Strategies** (TG p. 1150)

MATERIALS

- 📖 LAB pp. 283–284
- 📖 SH pp. 239, 242

3 | Differentiated Instruction (TG p. 1151)

Leveled Problem Solving (TG p. 1151)	Practice Book P114
Intervention Activity (TG p. 1151)	Extension Book E114
Extension Activity (TG p. 1151)	Spiral Review Book SR114
Science Connection (TG p. 1144)	

Lesson Notes

About the Lesson

Estimation is a fitting topic to end the year because it is widely used for everyday mental computation. This first lesson draws upon such familiar situations to review strategies of estimating. Students use rounding and compatible numbers to estimate answers.

In future lessons within this chapter, there are items to be brought from home. Each student will need to bring in a container of any size for **Lesson 15.4**. The teacher will need liter, milliliter, cup, pint, quart, and gallon containers for **Lessons 15.4** and **15.5** and a scale for **Lesson 15.6**.

About the Mathematics

Sometimes knowing the approximate size of an item may be sufficient. One might also want to know whether the item is larger or smaller than something else. Estimation can help in both of these situations. For example, rounding up both addends in an addition problem or both factors in a multiplication problem gives information about the upper limit of a reasonable answer. However, to estimate a quotient, it may not be helpful to round up both numbers. In this case, rounding the larger number up and the smaller number down would give an upper limit on the quotient.

Use with Lesson Activity Book pp. 283–284.

Developing Mathematical Language

Vocabulary: compatible, round

Compatible numbers are numbers that are used in mental computations. *Compatible* numbers do not have to result in an exact answer. They may be used to provide an estimate. Frequently, but not always, *compatible* numbers are multiples of 10. Sometimes *compatible* numbers are numbers that add to a multiple of 10 or 100, such as 275 + 125, or numbers that work well for division. For example, to estimate 437 ÷ 93, the *compatible* numbers could be 450 ÷ 90. Students might find it easy to associate *compatible* with personal friendships.

Familiarize students with the terms *compatible* and *round*.

Beginning Point out that *rounding* numbers changes one or more place values to zero. Make the connection between a round shape and a zero.

Intermediate Have a student write the name of a food on the board. Have students name foods that are *compatible* or not *compatible* with that food.

Advanced Have students think of a friend. Ask students to describe, without identifying the friend, what makes that person *compatible*.

Open-Ended Problem Solving

Read the Headline Story to the students. Encourage them to use logical reasoning to draw conclusions about the car wash.

 Headline Story

> **Ms. Jenkins' class held a car wash. Students charged $2.25 for cars and $3.50 for vans. The proceeds were distributed equally to four different charities.**

Possible response: The number of cents in the total proceeds must be a multiple of 25. For washing 20 cars, the class would earn $45.00. If they washed 10 vans they would earn $35. If they washed 22 cars and 12 vans, they would earn $49.50 from the cars and $35 + $7 for the vans, for a total of $91.50. Each charity would get more than $20.

Skills Practice and Review

Estimating

Have students practice using both rounding and compatible numbers as estimation strategies. Ask students to use each strategy at least once for each operation. You might also ask students to say whether their estimates are more or less than the exact answer.

Begin by writing an addition problem on the board, such as 129 + 217. Ask for an estimate of the sum. Possible strategies: 129 + 200 (rounding); 130 + 220 (compatible numbers). For a subtraction problem you might write 168 − 88. Possible strategies: 170 − 90 (rounding); 160 − 80 (the ones digits are the same). For multiplication you might write 191 × 11. Possible strategies for forming the basis of the estimated product: 200 × 10 (rounding); 19 × 11 (compatible numbers); 20 × 11 (compatible numbers). For division you might write 960 ÷ 32. Possible strategies: 960 ÷ 30 (rounding); 900 ÷ 30 (compatible numbers).

NCTM Standards 1, 6, 7, 8, 9, 10

(A) Reading the Student Letter

Purpose To review the purpose of estimating and the principal estimating strategies

Introduce Briefly discuss the topics of this chapter with your class. Remind students that many problems they encounter in school and in everyday life do not require exact answers; estimations are often enough.

Concept Alert

When students use rounding to estimate, they must pay attention to whether an estimate makes sense. For example, when presented with a problem like 443 + 19, students might estimate the sum as 400 + 20 = 420, which doesn't make sense since the estimate is smaller than one of the addends. Students should evaluate the reasonableness of their estimates, just as they use estimates to evaluate the reasonableness of exact answers.

Task Have students read the Student Letter with you. Ask them to think about answers to the questions. You may want to have them jot down their ideas, for use in the ensuing discussion.

Share Ask students to describe estimation methods that they recall. Some may remember that they can round numbers to the nearest 10, 100, 1,000, and so on, to estimate sums, differences, products, or quotients. For example, estimate 873 ÷ 9, students might round 873 to 900; the quotient is about 90.

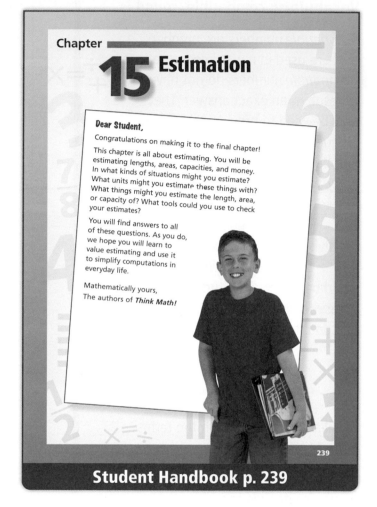

Chapter

15 Estimation

Dear Student,

Congratulations on making it to the final chapter!

This chapter is all about estimating. You will be estimating lengths, areas, capacities, and money. In what kinds of situations might you estimate? What units might you estimate these things with? What things might you estimate the length, area, or capacity of? What tools could you use to check your estimates?

You will find answers to all of these questions. As you do, we hope you will learn to value estimating and use it to simplify computations in everyday life.

Mathematically yours,
The authors of *Think Math!*

239

Student Handbook p. 239

Similarly, they may rely on facts that involve smaller numbers to estimate answers to problems. For example, to find 1,265 × 81, students can use 12 × 8 to estimate the product as 96,000. Because the class will practice these strategies in the lesson, there is no need to discuss them extensively at this point.

💬 Talk Math

❓ Hans works for Mr. Siple as a gardener. He is paid $8 per hour. At the end of each week, Hans tells Mr. Siple how many hours he has worked. Should he estimate the number of hours or figure out the exact number? Explain your reasoning. figure out the exact number; Possible explanation: An employer expects to pay an employee working by the hour for the exact number of hours the employee worked.

❓ Meg has $8 in her purse. She plans to eat lunch in a restaurant but wants to make sure that she can pay for her meal. She knows what she wants to eat and the approximate cost of each item. Should she estimate the cost of the meal or should she figure it out exactly? Explain your reasoning. estimate; Possible explanation: She can approximate the cost of the meal closely enough to judge whether she has enough money.

Use with Lesson Activity Book pp. 283–284.

pairs

⏱ **20 MIN**

Purpose To practice using estimation

Introduce Give each student a copy of Explore: The Lemonade Stand. Encourage students to use estimation as they work on the page. Students should work with partners.

Task Direct students to read about the lemonade stand and to answer the questions at the bottom of the page.

Share After students have worked through the page, bring the class together to discuss their strategies. For the first question, instead of finding an exact answer, students may reason that in order for five people to each get $4, there must be a total of $20 available. However, both $8.15 and $9.65 are less than $10, so their sum must be less than $10 + $10 − 20.

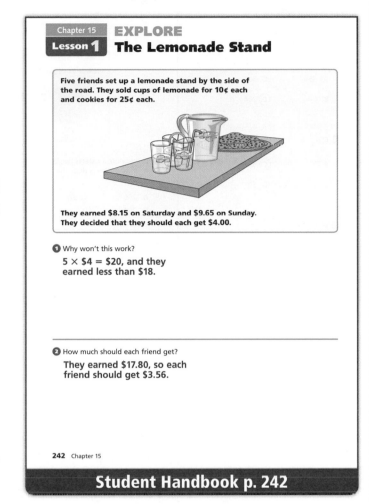

Chapter 15
Lesson 1 **EXPLORE**

The Lemonade Stand

Five friends set up a lemonade stand by the side of the road. They sold cups of lemonade for 10¢ each and cookies for 25¢ each.

They earned $8.15 on Saturday and $9.65 on Sunday. They decided that they should each get $4.00.

❶ Why won't this work?
5 × $4 = $20, and they earned less than $18.

❷ How much should each friend get?
They earned $17.80, so each friend should get $3.56.

242 Chapter 15

Student Handbook p. 242

During the discussion, make sure that the estimating strategies of rounding and using compatible numbers are brought up. For example, in the first problem students might have rounded $8.15 to $8 and $9.65 to $10 to see that the amount of money earned was less than $20. In the second problem, they might have used the division facts of 15 ÷ 5 and 20 ÷ 5 to estimate that the amount each friend should get would be between $3 and $4. They could also reason that because the total amount of money earned was almost exactly midway between $15 and $20, the amount each friend received should be almost exactly midway between $3 and $4.

💬 **Talk Math**

❷ Explain how you could estimate how much more the friends earned on Sunday than they earned on Saturday. Possible explanation: Round Saturday's amount down to $8 and Sunday's up to $10; $10 − $8 = $2.

❷ About how much more would the friends have had to earn on Sunday so that each could have gotten $5. Explain. Possible estimate: $2; possible explanation: I rounded $17.80, the total for Saturday and Sunday, up to $18. They would have needed to earn about $20 − $18 = $2 more on Sunday.

Purpose To practice using estimating to answer multiple-choice questions

NCTM Standards 1, 6, 7, 8, 9, 10

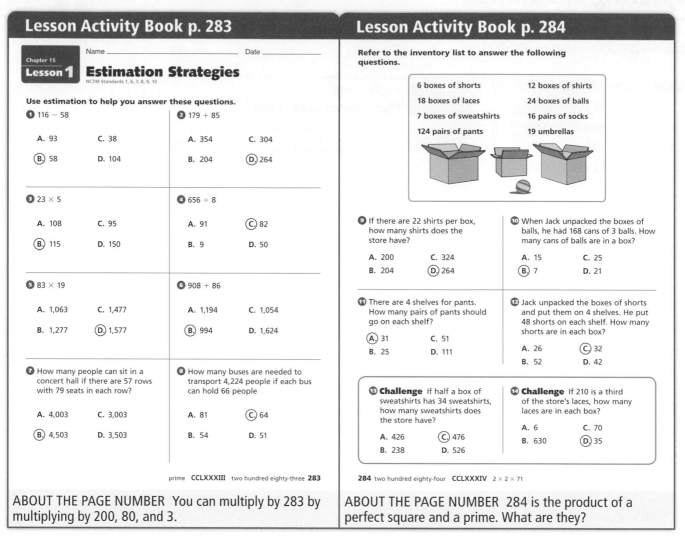

Lesson Activity Book p. 283

Chapter 15
Lesson 1 **Estimation Strategies**
NCTM Standards 1, 6, 7, 8, 9, 10

Name _____ Date _____

Use estimation to help you answer these questions.

1 116 − 58

 A. 93 C. 38
 B. 58 D. 104

2 179 + 85

 A. 354 C. 304
 B. 204 D. 264

3 23 × 5

 A. 108 C. 95
 B. 115 D. 150

4 656 ÷ 8

 A. 91 C. 82
 B. 9 D. 50

5 83 × 19

 A. 1,063 C. 1,477
 B. 1,277 D. 1,577

6 908 + 86

 A. 1,194 C. 1,054
 B. 994 D. 1,624

7 How many people can sit in a concert hall if there are 57 rows with 79 seats in each row?

 A. 4,003 C. 3,003
 B. 4,503 D. 3,503

8 How many buses are needed to transport 4,224 people if each bus can hold 66 people

 A. 81 C. 64
 B. 54 D. 51

prime CCLXXXIII two hundred eighty-three **283**

Lesson Activity Book p. 284

Refer to the inventory list to answer the following questions.

6 boxes of shorts   12 boxes of shirts
18 boxes of laces   24 boxes of balls
7 boxes of sweatshirts   16 pairs of socks
124 pairs of pants   19 umbrellas

9 If there are 22 shirts per box, how many shirts does the store have?

 A. 200 C. 324
 B. 204 D. 264

10 When Jack unpacked the boxes of balls, he had 168 cans of 3 balls. How many cans of balls are in a box?

 A. 15 C. 25
 B. 7 D. 21

11 There are 4 shelves for pants. How many pairs of pants should go on each shelf?

 A. 31 C. 51
 B. 25 D. 111

12 Jack unpacked the boxes of shorts and put them on 4 shelves. He put 48 shorts on each shelf. How many shorts are in each box?

 A. 26 C. 32
 B. 52 D. 42

13 Challenge If half a box of sweatshirts has 34 sweatshirts, how many sweatshirts does the store have?

 A. 426 C. 476
 B. 238 D. 526

14 Challenge If 210 is a third of the store's laces, how many laces are in each box?

 A. 6 C. 70
 B. 630 D. 35

284 two hundred eighty-four CCLXXXIV 2 × 2 × 71

ABOUT THE PAGE NUMBER You can multiply by 283 by multiplying by 200, 80, and 3.

ABOUT THE PAGE NUMBER 284 is the product of a perfect square and a prime. What are they?

Teaching Notes for LAB page 283

Have students work on the page individually or with partners. Students use estimation to help them answer multiple-choice questions. There are many strategies they can use. For example, they can compute the ones digit of an answer, then scan the choices in search of one that ends with the same digit. Encourage students to estimate the answers, as practice for multiple-choice tests that have time constraints that encourage the use of efficient strategies.

Teaching Notes for LAB page 284

The problems are given in a context and therefore require students to choose the appropriate operation for each situation. The questions also provide practice in ignoring extraneous information and heeding only the relevant information in a problem.

Challenge Problem These problems are similar to the other problems on the page, except that they require students to reason with fractions as well as whole numbers.

Reflect and Summarize the Lesson

Write Math

Describe two different ways to estimate this difference: 1,892 − 722. Possible response: One way is to round 1,892 to 1,900 and 722 to 700. Estimate: 1,900 − 700 = 1,200. Another way is to use compatible numbers. I subtracted 19 − 7 to find the number of hundreds in the answer, 12. So, my estimate was 1,200.

Leveled Problem Solving

Ms. Thomas buys 28 packages of stickers for her class. Each package costs $1.99.

❶ Basic Level

About how much does she pay for the stickers in all? Explain. About $60; round 28 to 30 and $1.99 to $2.00; $30 \times 2 = 60$.

❷ On Level

Each package has 32 stickers. About how many stickers are there in all? Explain. About 900; round 28 to 30 and 32 to 30; $30 \times 30 = 900$.

❸ Above Level

Ms. Thomas has $60 to pay for the stickers. Does she have enough? Explain. Yes; Rounding 28 up to 30 and $1.99 up to $2.00 shows that the estimate will be an overestimate, so she has enough.

Intervention

Activity Rounding to Estimate

Provide an addition or subtraction problem for students to estimate, such as $376 + 233$. Guide students through rounding each number to the same place value. Direct the students to cover all digits to the right of the place value they are rounding to and then uncover the next number to the right to see whether they should round up or just drop those digits to the right. Finally, have students add or subtract. Provide practice with several examples.

Practice

Estimation Strategies

Compare. Use <, >, or =. Hint: Estimate!

$320 \times 8 \,(>)\, 180 \times 10$	$16 \times 9 \,(>)\, 24 \times 4$
$70 \times 9 \,(=)\, 90 \times 7$	$93 \times 15 \,(<)\, 24 \times 100$
$108 \times 22 \,(>)\, 250 \times 8$	$99 \times 19 \,(<)\, 20 \times 100$
$61 \times 8 \,(>)\, 52 \times 9$	$53 \times 8 \,(>)\, 101 \times 3$
$104 \times 19 \,(<)\, 206 \times 15$	$272 \times 5 \,(>)\, 201 \times 5$
$199 \times 8 \,(>)\, 147 \times 6$	$189 \times 12 \,(>)\, 206 \times 9$
$98 \times 15 \,(<)\, 198 \times 10$	$89 \times 9 \,(<)\, 11 \times 99$

Test Prep

1 gallon = 4 quarts

How many quarts in 10 gallons?
A. $2\frac{1}{2}$ (L.) 4U
B. 20   D. 160

How many gallons in 20 quarts?
(A.) 5   C. 40
B. 10   D. 80

Practice P114

Extension

Estimation Strategies

These division problems have remainders. Estimate their quotients. Several estimates are possible. One such estimate is given.

$23 \div 3 = \blacksquare$	$23 \div 4 = \blacksquare$	$23 \div 5 = \blacksquare$
Estimate: __8__	Estimate: __6__	Estimate: __5__
$5\,\overline{)\,24}$	$3\,\overline{)\,25}$	$3\,\overline{)\,40}$
Estimate: __5__	Estimate: __8__	Estimate: __13__
$38 \div 7 = \blacksquare$	$25 \div 7 = \blacksquare$	$41 \div 7 = \blacksquare$
Estimate: __5__	Estimate: __4__	Estimate: __6__
$7\,\overline{)\,62}$	$9\,\overline{)\,62}$	$9\,\overline{)\,87}$
Estimate: __9__	Estimate: __7__	Estimate: __10__

Extension E114

Spiral Review

Spiral Review Book page SR114 provides review of the following previously learned skills and concepts:

- using rounding and compatible numbers to estimate missing factors and quotients
- predicting the results of an experiment by calculating the likelihood of particular events

You may wish to have students work with a partner to complete the page.

Number and Operations

Use rounding or compatible numbers to estimate the missing factor or quotient. Possible answers are given.

$39 \times \boxed{20} = 792$	$\boxed{8}$ $78\overline)639$	$18 \times \boxed{20} = 379$
$\boxed{90}$ $6\overline)532$	$\boxed{40}$ $22\overline)812$	$51 \times \boxed{10} = 486$
$\boxed{50}$ $37\overline)1,835$	$82 \times \boxed{3} = 252$	$63 \times \boxed{80} = 4,776$

Data Analysis and Probability

Write the probability as a fraction.

For 10–12, use this experiment: One card is picked from a deck of ten cards numbered 2 to 11.

an even numbered card	$\frac{5}{10}$, or $\frac{1}{2}$
a number that is a multiple of 3	$\frac{3}{10}$
a number that is a factor of 12	$\frac{4}{10}$, or $\frac{2}{5}$

For 13–15, use this experiment: One marble is picked from a bag containing 5 red, 3 blue, 1 green, and 1 yellow.

a marble that is not red	$\frac{5}{10}$, or $\frac{1}{2}$
a marble that is either green or yellow	$\frac{2}{10}$, or $\frac{1}{5}$
a marble that is not blue	$\frac{7}{10}$

Spiral Review SR114

Extension Activity
Test Maker

Challenge small groups of students to write four multiple-choice estimation problems, one for each operation—addition, subtraction, multiplication, and division. Direct students to give one correct and three incorrect answer choices for each problem. The incorrect choices should show mistakes students might make with the problems. Then have the groups share their work, explaining which mistakes the incorrect answer choices show.

Lesson 2 Estimating and Checking Length and Perimeter

NCTM Standards 1, 3, 4, 6, 7, 8, 9, 10

Lesson Planner

STUDENT OBJECTIVE ·
- To estimate and find length, perimeter, and area using standard and non-standard units

1 | Daily Activities (TG p. 1153)

Open-Ended Problem Solving/Headline Story	Skills Practice and Review— Converting Between Units of Length

2 | Teach and Practice (TG pp. 1154–1158)

	MATERIALS
Ⓐ **Estimating Perimeter and Area** (TG pp. 1154–1155)	• streamers or long strips of paper
Ⓑ **Finding Perimeter and Area** (TG p. 1156)	• centimeter or meter ruler
Ⓒ **Estimating and Checking Perimeter and Area** (TG p. 1157)	• LAB pp. 285–286 • SH pp. 243–244

3 | Differentiated Instruction (TG p. 1159)

Leveled Problem Solving (TG p. 1159)	Practice Book P115
Intervention Activity (TG p. 1159)	Extension Book E115
Extension Activity (TG p. 1159)	Spiral Review Book SR115
Literature Connection (TG p. 1144)	

Lesson Notes

About the Lesson

Students continue to estimate in this lesson, but now do so in the context of perimeter and area. They use standard metric units and non-standard units, such as pencils, to estimate the dimensions of a rectangular object. Then they estimate its perimeter and area. As students estimate and find these measurements, they also have an opportunity to apply estimation strategies of the previous lesson. That is, they can round or use compatible numbers to estimate the number of units in a measurement.

Use with Lesson Activity Book pp. 285–286.

Developing Mathematical Language

Vocabulary: area, perimeter

In this lesson, students convert between units of measurement. Different numbers are used to describe the same measurement. Stress the importance of always recording the unit of measurement; recording only the number is not an adequate answer. As students estimate *perimeter* and *area,* remind them that *perimeter,* whether an actual measurement or an estimate, is a linear measurement, while *area* is a measurement in square units.

Encourage students to develop a sense of the relative sizes of units of *area.* Compare the *area* of the school playground with a square mile—the playground is smaller—and a square inch—the playground is much larger. Students should begin to see that the smaller the measuring tool or unit, the greater the number of units needed.

Familiarize students with the terms *area* and *perimeter.*

Beginning Draw a rectangle on the board. Have a student shade its *area.* Have another student draw over its *perimeter.*

Intermediate Have students tell whether measuring the length of a fence around a garden would be measuring the *area* or *perimeter.*

Advanced Have students explain the difference between the *area* and the *perimeter* of the playground.

Open-Ended Problem Solving

Read the Headline Story to the students. Encourage them to make interesting statements using information from the story.

 Headline Story

Our class invited 58 third graders to a play. We arranged the room to provide lots of room in front for the actors, and lots for the audience. The classroom is 30 feet by 25 feet. We had 30 chairs that are each 18 inches wide.

Possible response: To fit an entire class of actors, the performance space should be about half the classroom. So, the "stage" could be about 30-by-12 feet or 25-by-15 feet. The area of the stage could be about 350 square feet. If we left a small gap between the stage and the audience, there would be enough room to put a row or two of chairs fairly close together, and still leave floor space where the rest of the kids could sit. If each chair takes up about a 2-by-3 foot space, there would be room for almost 60 chairs in 350 square feet. That would mean that there should be room for 30 chairs and for the remaining 28 kids to sit on the floor.

Skills Practice and Review

Converting Between Units of Length

Give students a measurement in yards, feet, or inches and ask for the corresponding measurement in other units. For example, if you give a length of 16 inches, students can convert this to 1 foot and 4 inches. Also give measurements that combine different units. For example, if you say that the length of the room is 3 yards, 2 feet, and 3 inches, students can convert this to 8 feet and 3 inches, or 135 inches. Next, repeat with metric units of length. For example, 250 centimeters would convert to 2.5 meters.

pairs · 15 MIN

A Estimating Perimeter and Area

NCTM Standards 1, 3, 4, 6, 7, 8, 9, 10

Purpose To practice estimating perimeter and area

Possible Discussion

Students may wonder why they would need to estimate perimeter or area. You might encourage students to discuss why estimating perimeter or area might be a useful skill. At the most basic level, estimating measurements allows one quickly to see if an actual measurement makes sense. Sometimes a space is not precisely a shape whose perimeter or area can be found easily. In such an instance, estimating is a good approach. People also estimate the sizes of rooms, furniture, and posters to decide how to set up and decorate their homes, classrooms, and offices. In the next lesson, students will have a chance to use these estimating skills to design the layout of a school.

Differentiated Instruction

On Level Have students think of other situations where they might estimate a perimeter or area, so they can understand the value of estimating in their everyday experiences. Students should list these examples on a piece of paper. Encourage students to list as many situations as possible.

Introduce Give each student a copy of Explore: Estimating Perimeter page. Students should work in pairs. Explain that they will be using two unusual units to estimate a measurement someone might want to know in an everyday situation.

Task **Direct students to read the information at the top of the page and then answer the questions below.** Students first consider how to estimate the perimeter of the door in the non-standard units using Paul's height and pencils. Then they use the given information about Paul's height in meters and the length of a pencil in centimeters to evaluate a set of perimeter estimates. This evaluation requires not only translating each estimate from the non-standard unit into a standard unit, but also converting between standard units to compare these estimates directly.

Chapter 15
Lesson 2
EXPLORE
Estimating Perimeter

Paul Perimeter is $1\frac{1}{4}$ meters tall. His pencil is a little more than 10 centimeters long.

Paul is going to glue a border around the sides of his door. He is trying to find the door's perimeter to figure out how much border he needs.

❶ How can Paul use his height to estimate the perimeter in meters?
Possible answer: He can estimate the height of the door as $1\frac{1}{2}$ or 2 times his height, and the width of the door as a little less than his height.

❷ How can Paul use his pencil to estimate the perimeter of the door in centimeters?
Possible answer: He might estimate about 25 pencils in the door's height and about 10 pencils in its width.

❸ Would these two estimates of the door's perimeter make sense? Why or why not?

    4 times Paul's height   100 pencils

No; Possible answer: 100 pencils is about 1,000 centimeters, or 10 meters, while 4 times Paul's height is about 5 meters.

Chapter 15 **243**

Student Handbook p. 243

❶ How can Paul use his height to estimate the perimeter in meters? Possible response: He can estimate the height of the door as $1\frac{1}{2}$ or 2 times his height, and the width of the door as a little less than his height.

❷ How can Paul use his pencil to estimate the perimeter in centimeters? Possible response: He might estimate about 25 pencils in the door's height and about 10 pencils in its width.

❸ Would these two estimates of the door's perimeter make sense? Why or why not?

    4 times Paul's height   100 pencils

Possible response: No; 100 pencils is about 1,000 centimeters, or 10 meters, while 4 times Paul's height is about 5 meters.

Use with Lesson Activity Book pp. 285–286.

Share Once students have worked through the page, have them share their ideas on how they can use Paul's height and the length of a pencil to estimate the perimeter. Students should reason that multiple copies of each unit could be lined up along the sides of the door. If multiple copies are not available, the top of a unit could be marked on the door. One end of the unit could then be moved to the mark, repeating this process until the measurement is complete.

Ask students how they can convert Paul's estimated height into meters and the estimated number of pencils into centimeters. Students should realize that since Paul's height represents about $1\frac{1}{4}$ meter, they should repeatedly add his height in their estimated measurement. Similarly, they should multiply the number of pencils in their estimates by 10 centimeters to find the number of centimeters in their estimate.

Finally, ask for ideas on how students can use their estimates of the dimensions of the door to estimate its area. Students should remember that the area of a rectangle is the product of its length and its width. So, the approximate area of the door is the product of the approximate number of meters or centimeters in its height and the approximate number of meters or centimeters in its width. Have students estimate the door's area. Because the estimated dimensions of the door in meters may contain fractions, remind students that they can round these numbers to the nearest whole numbers to help them estimate the product.

Talk Math

❶ A pencil is about 4 paper clips long. A rug is about 40 pencils long. About how long is the rug in paper clips? Explain your reasoning. about 160 paper clips; Possible explanation: Every pencil in the estimate of the rug's length equals about 4 paper clips, so the length is about $40 \times 4 = 160$ paper clips.

❷ Jake said that his father was about 20 bananas tall. Did his estimate make sense? Explain your reasoning. Possible answer: no; possible explanation: A banana is about $\frac{1}{2}$ foot long, so 20 bananas is about half of 20 feet, or 10 feet. It is unlikely that Jake's dad is 10 feet tall.

Differentiated Instruction

Basic Level To students who are still struggling to understand why the product of the dimensions of a rectangular region equals its area, you might give graph paper with which to represent such a region. By counting the enclosed squares, students can verify that multiplying the length by the width is simply a faster way of counting the squares.

Teacher Story

❝I held a contest for the students in my class, in which I had them estimate the perimeters and areas of the surfaces of their desks. The person whose estimates came closest to the exact answers we found by using a ruler to measure the desks, was allowed to be my co-teacher for the math lesson the next day. Since it was the end of the year, I used this motivation to keep students interested in the lesson.❞

B Finding Perimeter and Area

Materials

- For the teacher: streamers or long strips of paper
- For each student: centimeter or meter ruler, scrap paper

NCTM Standards 1, 3, 4, 6, 7, 8, 9, 10

✓ Ongoing Assessment

- Do students recall what they learned about area and perimeter in Chapter 5 and measurement strategies in Chapter 9? This lesson provides an opportunity for you to see how well students have maintained what they learned. For example, you might see if students are still measuring the four sides of a rectangular object to find its perimeter, or whether they realize they can find the perimeter by doubling the combined lengths of two adjacent sides. Similarly, you might see if students remember that they can multiply the dimensions of a rectangle to find its area. If any students are using inefficient strategies for finding perimeter and area at this point, have others describe their more efficient strategies.

Purpose To find the perimeter and area of a door

Introduce Give each pair of students a centimeter or meter ruler. Remind them that in the last activity, they explored strategies for estimating perimeters and areas.

Task **Direct each pair of students to find the perimeter of the door.** Make sure that students record their results on scrap paper so they can report back to the class. If you have a pair who can work quietly, you might let them measure a closed door in the hallway, so that the whole class is not crowded around one door.

Share Once students have measured the door and calculated its perimeter, have them read their measurements aloud. Students may be surprised to find that different pairs of students found different measurements, even though all were using equivalent rulers. You might briefly discuss some of the causes for these discrepancies. For example, if students did not line up their rulers precisely at the ends of their previous measurement, small differences in measurements might have accumulated. Ask students to share their strategies for finding the perimeter. Make sure that the idea of measuring one long side of the door and one short side, then doubling the sum of these measurements, is brought up as a labor-saving strategy.

Task **Direct each pair to find the area of the door.** As in Activity A, students should multiply the length of the door by its width to find the area in square centimeters or square meters. You might have students compare their estimates of the area of the imaginary door in Activity A to the area of the real door here.

End this activity by using students' measurements to make a border on the classroom door, as Paul intended to do in Activity A. Pick one set of measurements and have a few students cut streamers or strips of paper that match these measurements. The degree to which the completed border fits the door can serve as a further check of the accuracy of the chosen students' measurements.

💬 Talk Math

❓ Toni was measuring a length of fabric. Instead of lining up her ruler with the mark from the previous measurement, she overlapped the ruler.

By her measurements, the fabric was 12 feet long. Was the actual length greater than or less than 12 feet? Explain your reasoning. less than; Possible explanation: The drawing shows that what Toni would have measured as 2 feet was actually less than 2 feet. So her measurement was greater than the actual measurement, and the actual length was less than hers.

❓ A door had a height of 8 feet and a perimeter of 22 feet. What was its width? Explain how you found the answer. 3 feet; Possible explanation: height + width = $\frac{1}{2} \times 22 = 11$ feet. So the width is 11 feet − 8 feet = 3 feet.

Purpose To practice estimating perimeter and area

NCTM Standards 1, 3, 4, 6, 7, 8, 9, 10

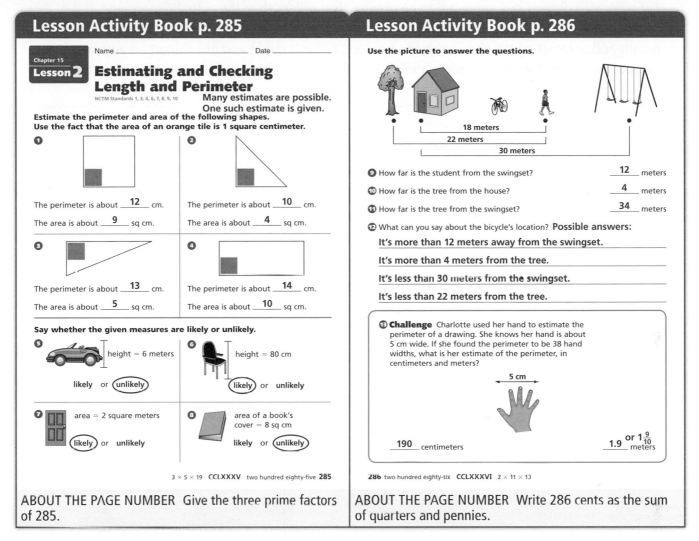

Lesson Activity Book p. 285

Name _____ Date _____

Chapter 15
Lesson 2

Estimating and Checking Length and Perimeter

NCTM Standards 1, 3, 4, 6, 7, 8, 9, 10

Many estimates are possible. One such estimate is given.

Estimate the perimeter and area of the following shapes. Use the fact that the area of an orange tile is 1 square centimeter.

1 The perimeter is about __12__ cm.
The area is about __9__ sq cm.

2 The perimeter is about __10__ cm.
The area is about __4__ sq cm.

3 The perimeter is about __13__ cm.
The area is about __5__ sq cm.

4 The perimeter is about __14__ cm.
The area is about __10__ sq cm.

Say whether the given measures are likely or unlikely.

5 height = 6 meters
likely or (unlikely)

6 height = 80 cm
(likely) or unlikely

7 area = 2 square meters
(likely) or unlikely

8 area of a book's cover = 8 sq cm
likely or (unlikely)

3 × 5 × 19 CCLXXXV two hundred eighty-five **285**

Lesson Activity Book p. 286

Use the picture to answer the questions.

18 meters
22 meters
30 meters

9 How far is the student from the swingset? __12__ meters

10 How far is the tree from the house? __4__ meters

11 How far is the tree from the swingset? __34__ meters

12 What can you say about the bicycle's location? **Possible answers:**

It's more than 12 meters away from the swingset.

It's more than 4 meters from the tree.

It's less than 30 meters from the swingset.

It's less than 22 meters from the tree.

13 Challenge Charlotte used her hand to estimate the perimeter of a drawing. She knows her hand is about 5 cm wide. If she found the perimeter to be 38 hand widths, what is her estimate of the perimeter, in centimeters and meters?

5 cm

__190__ centimeters

__1.9__ or $1\frac{9}{10}$ meters

286 two hundred eighty-six CCLXXXVI 2 × 11 × 13

ABOUT THE PAGE NUMBER Give the three prime factors of 285.

ABOUT THE PAGE NUMBER Write 286 cents as the sum of quarters and pennies.

Teaching Notes for LAB page 285

Have students complete the page individually or with partners. The top of the page provides a picture of a tile with sides that are 1 cm long. This will give students a sense of the size of the unit they are using to estimate. The bottom of the page gives measurements that students must label as reasonable or unreasonable. You may need to point out to students that they are not deciding if a measurement is possible or impossible, only whether it is likely or unlikely.

Students can use the picture of the tile to help them estimate the area and perimeter of each of these figures. Some students may simply look at the given unit and mentally visualize how many tiles would fit along each edge or within the given space. Others may draw additional squares of similar sizes to help them. You might also make white Cuisenaire® cubes available to help students make their estimations.

Teaching Notes for LAB page 286

Students solve problems to determine distances between given objects.

Challenge Problem Students translate a non-standard unit into centimeters and meters. The answers to Problem 12 and to this problem may vary slightly since exact measurements are not given.

Reflect and Summarize the Lesson

Write Math

How could you estimate the area of a non-rectangular region? Possible response: If the region was nearly rectangular in shape, I could estimate the longest and widest dimensions of the region, and then find their product. I might add or subtract an amount, depending on whether my estimated dimensions appeared to be greater than or less than the actual dimensions. If the region was closer in shape to that of a triangle, I could find the product of the estimated greatest length and greatest width, then halve the product. Again, I might add or subtract an amount, depending on whether my estimated dimensions appeared to be greater than or less than the actual dimensions.

Review Model

Refer students to Review Model: Finding Perimeter and Area in the **Student Handbook,** p. 244, to see how they can determine the perimeter and area of a rectangle.

✔ **Check for Understanding**

❶ 16 in.; 15 sq in.

❷ 16 cm; 12 sq cm

❸ 22 ft; 24 sq ft

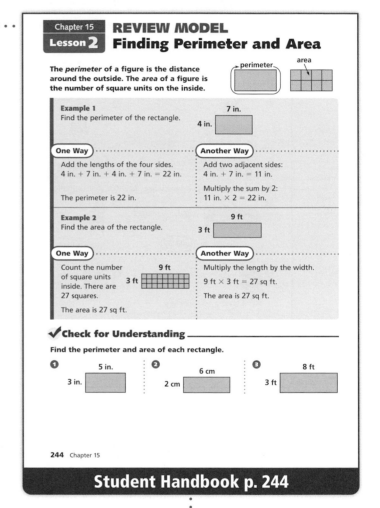

Use with Lesson Activity Book pp. 285–286.

3 | Differentiated Instruction

Jin wants to use 1-cm-square tiles to cover the top of a jewelry box he made. He can cut some tiles if necessary.

❶ Basic Level

The top of the box is a rectangle 9 cm by 12 cm. Are 100 tiles enough? Explain. No; The area is 9×12, or 108, and $108 > 100$.

❷ On Level

The top of the box is a rectangle $8\frac{1}{2}$ cm by 13 cm. Are 100 tiles enough? Explain. No; If he rounds $8\frac{1}{2}$ to 8, $8 \times 13 = 104$ sq cm, and $104 > 100$.

❸ Above Level

The top of the box is a rectangle $7\frac{1}{2}$ cm by $12\frac{1}{2}$ cm. Are 100 tiles enough? Explain. Yes; $8 \times 13 = 104$ and is an overestimate, but $7 \times 13 = 91$; $100 - 91 > 104 - 100$.

Intervention	Practice	Extension

Activity Classroom Estimates

Have students estimate the perimeter and area of various classroom objects, such as a window, wall, door, desktop, tile, podium, or box. Have students determine whether their estimates are high or low. Then measure the item to determine the actual perimeter and area. Have students compare their estimates with the actual measures.

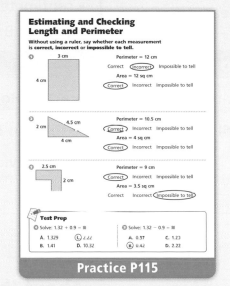

Practice P115

Extension E115

Spiral Review

Spiral Review Book page SR115 provides review of the following previously learned skills and concepts:

- labeling points on a coordinate grid using coordinates

- reading and writing symbols that describe the steps in a number puzzle

You may wish to have students work with a partner to complete the page.

Spiral Review SR115

Extension Activity
Estimating Distances

Have small groups of students line up four objects, A, B, C, and D. Have them measure and record the distances from A to B, B to C, and C to D. Make a diagram showing the distances between the objects and the total distance A to D. Direct groups to exchange diagrams. Have each group estimate the actual distances between the objects based on the diagram and then compare their estimates with the original measurements.

Lesson 3 Designing a School

NCTM Standards 1, 3, 4, 6, 7, 8, 9, 10

Lesson Planner

- To estimate the perimeter and area of rooms and hallways on floor plans
- To design floor plans to match specified perimeters or areas

1 | Daily Activities (TG p. 1161)

Open-Ended Problem Solving/Headline Story	Skills Practice and Review— Estimating Area

2 | Teach and Practice (TG pp. 1162–1164)

MATERIALS

Ⓐ **Designing a School** (TG pp. 1162–1163)

Ⓑ **Applying Estimating and Measuring** (TG p. 1164)

- TR: Activity Master, AM152
- centimeter ruler
- 📖 LAB pp. 287–288

3 | Differentiated Instruction (TG p. 1165)

Leveled Problem Solving (TG p. 1165)	Practice Book P116
Intervention Activity (TG p. 1165)	Extension Book E116
Extension Activity (TG p. 1165)	Spiral Review Book SR116
Art Connection (TG p. 1144)	

Lesson Notes

About the Lesson

This lesson gives students an opportunity to apply the estimating and measuring skills they reviewed in the previous lesson. Working in small groups, students design a school with a given number of rooms of specified approximate sizes. As they do this, they use rounding and compatible numbers to estimate areas, to judge whether there is sufficient space for a certain room. They also explore ways in which area and perimeter change as the shape of a room changes. There are items to be brought from home for future lessons within this chapter. Each student will need to bring in a container of any size for **Lesson 15.4**. The teacher will need liter, milliliter, cup, pint, quart, and gallon containers for **Lessons 15.4–15.5** and a scale for **Lesson 15.6.**

About the Mathematics

In this lesson, students work with floor plans that represent larger spaces. They use a scale to translate floor plan measurements into real-life measurements. Students use proportions to apply the scale. For example, if 1 centimeter on paper represents 4 meters in reality, then 5 centimeters on paper represents 20 meters. (See Possible Discussion for more on reading a scale.)

Developing Mathematical Language

Vocabulary: scale

Students will use a *scale* for their drawings in this lesson. They will see a *scale* for weighing items in **Lesson 15.6.** We spell and pronounce both words the same way, but they mean different things. This is not surprising, as many math terms have been adapted from everyday language. You might challenge students to recall other math terms used in everyday language.

Students will begin to develop the concept of proportion by using a *scale,* such as 1 centimeter = 4 meters, in a floor plan. Students experienced *scale* in the previous lesson when they converted between units.

Familiarize students with the term *scale.*

Beginning Show students a map. Have them point out the *scale.*

Intermediate Tell students that a *scale* is given on a map or floor plan. Present pairs of units that students might see on a map, and have students take turns creating *scales.*

Advanced Have students discuss what *scale* might be used on a map of your state.

Open-Ended Problem Solving

Read the Headline Story to the students. Encourage them to use logical reasoning to draw conclusions about the school.

 Headline Story

At Eli's school, the two kindergarten classrooms are bigger than the two 1st grade classrooms, which are bigger than the two 2nd, 3rd, 4th, and 5th grade classrooms. The art room is bigger than each kindergarten room. The cafeteria is a little bigger than the art room. The gym is the biggest room. The total area is 1,000 sq. m.

Possible response: The school could be 20-by-50 m or 25-by-40 m. The gym could have an area of 100 sq m. If it did, the cafeteria might be 80 sq m, the art room 75 sq m, the 2nd–5th grade classrooms 60 sq m each, the 1st grade classrooms 65 sq m, and the kindergarten rooms 67 sq m, a total of 999 sq m. These possibilities leave no room for hallways, bathrooms, offices, or other rooms.

Skills Practice and Review

Estimating Area

Explain that you will draw a rectangle on the board that represents a much larger area in real life. Label the length and width with numbers that are difficult to multiply together mentally, but that are close to numbers that can simplify the mental computation, for example, 58 inches and 48 inches. Students can round these dimensions to 60 and 50 inches to estimate the area as 3,000 square inches. Continue with other rectangles, varying the units.

30 MIN

A Designing a School

Materials

- For each group of 2–4 students: AM152

NCTM Standards 1, 3, 4, 6, 7, 8, 9, 10

Purpose To make a scale drawing

Introduce
Explain to the class that they have been hired by the school district to design a school. In this activity, working in small groups, they will show how they would do this.

Go over the specifications of the design and write them on the board for easy reference. The school needs:

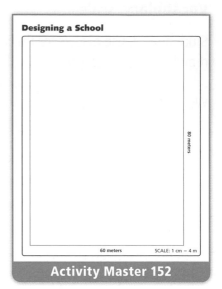

Designing a School

80 meters

60 meters   SCALE: 1 cm = 4 m

Activity Master 152

Possible Discussion

The floor plans that students create during this lesson are scaled down to fit the page. It would be impractical to draw a building plan on paper the same size as the land on which the building would be built! Point out that the dimensions given are not actual measurements, since 60 meters is more than half a football field. Each centimeter on the page stands for a much longer length in real life—4 meters, to be exact. So, 1 square centimeter on the plan represents $4 \times 4 = 16$ square meters in real life.

In order to avoid messy calculations, the majority of students will probably not draw their floor plans exactly according to this scale. Since proportional reasoning of this sort is not the focus of the lesson, there is no need to require it of your students.

- 6 classrooms, each with an area of approximately 30 square meters
- a cafeteria that will hold at least 75 students
- a gym with a perimeter of about 100 meters
- hallways to allow passage from one place to another within the school

Provide each group of 2–4 students with a copy of Activity Master: Designing a School, and a centimeter ruler. You may need to explain the "scale" of 1 centimeter = 4 meters, which may be an unfamiliar concept to students. (See Possible Discussion for more on discussing the scale.)

Task
Direct students to make a drawing of the school, following the guidelines you have written on the board. Before they begin, you may want to have students share a few ideas about how they will go about designing the school using the given specifications. For example, you might ask the class what dimensions a classroom might have if its area is about 30 square meters, or what the dimensions of the gym might be if its perimeter is about 100 meters. classroom: Possible dimensions: 5 meters by 6 meters; gym: possible dimensions: 30 meters by 20 meters

Allow students to work as a group for about 15 minutes to sketch a design of the school. Expect them to make mistakes and to need multiple copies of the Activity Master.

Use with Lesson Activity Book pp. 287–288.

Share After students have designed their schools, bring the class together to share the designs. As groups present their sketches, ask them to verify that the specifications have been met. For example, you might ask students for the dimensions of the cafeteria, to make sure that 75 students can comfortably fit in it along with tables and chairs. (The cafeteria should probably have an area of at least 60 square meters.) You also might also ask students to explain how they used the ruler to measure the desired lengths on the sketch. For example, to make a room that is 20 meters long, they should have drawn a length of 5 centimeters on the sketch.

Talk Math

? A drawing of a tree has a scale of 1 centimeters = 3 meters. In real life, the tree is 30 meters tall. How tall should the drawing of the tree be? Explain your reasoning. 10 centimeters; Possible explanation: Each 3 meters of the tree measures 1 centimeter on the drawing. The tree has $30 \div 3 = 10$ three-meter sections. Each of those 10 sections measures 1 centimeter on the drawing, making a total of 10 centimeters.

? A drawing of a ship has a scale of 1 centimeter = 6 meters. The drawing is 8 centimeters long. How long is the ship? Explain your reasoning. 48 meters; Possible explanation: Each 1 centimeter on the drawing represents 6 meters of the ship. There are 8 such 1-centimeter sections on the drawing. So, the ship must be $8 \times 6 = 48$ meters long.

Teacher Story

"One of my groups of students finished their school plan before the others, so I suggested that they add bathrooms to their drawing. This was challenging because the scale of the floor plan forced the bathrooms to be small. Still, the students enjoyed making their plan more "real." Another group asked if they could save their sketch and then color it and make it more detailed later. I thought that was a great idea. The sketch was so nice by the time it was finished it that I displayed it on the wall."

Differentiated Instruction

Above Level Have more advanced students draw their floor plans exactly to scale. For example, if they want to make a wall 5 meters long, they would have to measure exactly 1.25 centimeters on the floor plan

Purpose To apply estimation and measurement skills

NCTM Standards 1, 3, 4, 6, 7, 8, 9, 10

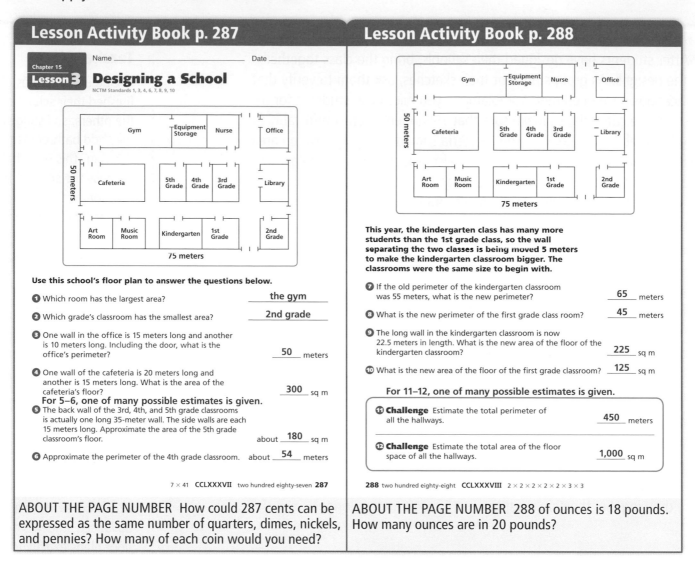

Lesson Activity Book p. 287

Name _____ Date _____

Chapter 15
Lesson 3 **Designing a School**
NCTM Standards 1, 3, 4, 6, 7, 8, 9, 10

[Floor plan diagram: 50 meters (height), 75 meters (width)]
- Gym | Equipment Storage | Nurse | Office
- Cafeteria | 5th Grade | 4th Grade | 3rd Grade | Library
- Art Room | Music Room | Kindergarten | 1st Grade | 2nd Grade

Use this school's floor plan to answer the questions below.

❶ Which room has the largest area? _the gym_

❷ Which grade's classroom has the smallest area? _2nd grade_

❸ One wall in the office is 15 meters long and another is 10 meters long. Including the door, what is the office's perimeter? _50_ meters

❹ One wall of the cafeteria is 20 meters long and another is 15 meters long. What is the area of the cafeteria's floor? _300_ sq m

For 5–6, one of many possible estimates is given.

❺ The back wall of the 3rd, 4th, and 5th grade classrooms is actually one long 35-meter wall. The side walls are each 15 meters long. Approximate the area of the 5th grade classroom's floor. about _180_ sq m

❻ Approximate the perimeter of the 4th grade classroom. about _54_ meters

7 × 41 **CCLXXXVII** two hundred eighty-seven **287**

ABOUT THE PAGE NUMBER How could 287 cents can be expressed as the same number of quarters, dimes, nickels, and pennies? How many of each coin would you need?

Lesson Activity Book p. 288

[Floor plan diagram: 50 meters (height), 75 meters (width)]
- Gym | Equipment Storage | Nurse | Office
- Cafeteria | 5th Grade | 4th Grade | 3rd Grade | Library
- Art Room | Music Room | Kindergarten | 1st Grade | 2nd Grade

This year, the kindergarten class has many more students than the 1st grade class, so the wall separating the two classes is being moved 5 meters to make the kindergarten classroom bigger. The classrooms were the same size to begin with.

❼ If the old perimeter of the kindergarten classroom was 55 meters, what is the new perimeter? _65_ meters

❽ What is the new perimeter of the first grade class room? _45_ meters

❾ The long wall in the kindergarten classroom is now 22.5 meters in length. What is the new area of the floor of the kindergarten classroom? _225_ sq m

❿ What is the new area of the floor of the first grade classroom? _125_ sq m

For 11–12, one of many possible estimates is given.

⓫ **Challenge** Estimate the total perimeter of all the hallways. _450_ meters

⓬ **Challenge** Estimate the total area of the floor space of all the hallways. _1,000_ sq m

288 two hundred eighty-eight **CCLXXXVIII** 2 × 2 × 2 × 2 × 2 × 3 × 3

ABOUT THE PAGE NUMBER 288 of ounces is 18 pounds. How many ounces are in 20 pounds?

Teaching Notes for LAB page 287

Have students complete the page individually or in pairs. Students continue to apply their estimation and measurement skills. The page asks students to estimate and compare the perimeters and areas of various rooms in a school whose floor plan is shown. You might need to point out that Problem 2 specifically asks for the *classroom* with the smallest area, not just any room with the smallest area.

Teaching Notes for LAB page 288

Challenge Problem Students estimate the perimeters and areas of the hallways. Because there are several hallways, keeping track of the different parts of their estimates can be tricky, and students will likely use a variety of strategies. For example, some may see that there are two hallways that run the width of the building and two that almost run the length of the building, and conclude that they can use the dimensions of the school to make their estimates. Others may compare parts of the hallways to other rooms in the school whose areas or perimeters they already know.

Reflect and Summarize the Lesson

 Write Math

A rectangular room in an office building measures about 22 feet by about 29 feet. What is the approximate perimeter of the room? What is the approximate area? Explain your reasoning. Possible answers: perimeter: about 100 feet; area: about 600 square feet; Possible explanation: The room measures about 20 feet by 30 feet. Its perimeter is about 2 × (20 + 30) = 2 × 50 = 100 feet. Its area is about 20 × 30 = 600 square feet.

Leveled Problem Solving

A drawing shows three classrooms side-by-side along a wall.
1 inch on the drawing represents 8 feet in the school.

❶ Basic Level

If the drawing is 9 inches long, what is the total length of the three classrooms? Explain. 72 ft; Since 1 in. represents 8 ft, 9 in. represents 9×8, or 72 ft

❷ On Level

Each room is 20 feet wide. How wide are the rooms in the drawing? Explain. $2\frac{1}{2}$ in.; Since 1 in. represents 8 ft, 2 in. represents 16 ft, and $\frac{1}{2}$ in. represents 4 ft; $2 + \frac{1}{2} = 2\frac{1}{2}$.

❸ Above Level

Each room is 24 feet long and 20 feet wide. What is the perimeter of the rooms on the drawing? Explain. 23 in.; $3 \times 24 = 72$ ft, $2 \times 72 = 144$, $144 \div 8 = 18$ in.; $2 \times 20 = 40$ and $40 \div 8 = 5$; $18 + 5 = 23$.

Intervention

Activity On the Grid

Have each student draw a large rectangle on centimeter grid paper to represent a room. Give students a scale such as 1 centimeter = 3 feet. Have students estimate the perimeter and area of the room their rectangle represents. Have volunteers present their diagrams and explain how they found the perimeter and the area.

Practice

Practice P116

Extension

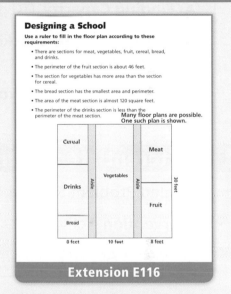

Extension E116

Spiral Review

Spiral Review Book page SR116 provides review of the following previously learned skills and concepts:

- converting among ounces, pounds, and tons
- solving problems using the strategy *draw a picture*

You may wish to have students work with a partner to complete the page.

Spiral Review SR116

Extension Activity
Floor Plans

Create or copy from a real estate advertisement a simple home floor plan. The plan should have room dimensions. Give a copy of the floor plan to each small group of students. Have them answer questions such as the following:

- What is the area of the largest room? What is its perimeter?
- List the bedrooms in order from least area to greatest area. Do the same for the perimeter. Are the two lists the same? Do they have to be the same?

Lesson 4 Estimating and Checking Capacity

NCTM Standards 1, 4, 6, 7, 8, 9, 10

Lesson Planner

STUDENT OBJECTIVE ·
- To estimate and measure capacity

1 | Daily Activities (TG p. 1167)

Open-Ended Problem Solving/Headline Story	Skills Practice and Review— Estimating and Finding Volume

2 | Teach and Practice (TG pp. 1168–1170)

Ⓐ **Finding Capacity** (TG p. 1168)

Ⓑ **Estimating and Checking Capacity** (TG p. 1169)

Ⓒ **Solving Problems Involving Capacity** (TG p. 1170)

MATERIALS

- TR: Activity Master, AM153
- milliliter, liter, cup, pint, quart, and gallon containers; measurable substance such as rice or dried beans; index card
- calculators
- 📖 LAB pp. 289–290

3 | Differentiated Instruction (TG p. 1171)

Leveled Problem Solving (TG p. 1171)	Practice Book P117
Intervention Activity (TG p. 1171)	Extension Book E117
Extension Activity (TG p. 1171)	Spiral Review Book SR117

Lesson Notes

About the Lesson

Continuing their study of estimation, students turn to estimating capacities of containers. They also find exact capacities using multiple copies of a standard unit, such as a liter or cup. On the LAB pages, they combine estimating capacity with problem solving skills and checking for reasonableness.

About the Mathematics

While both capacity and volume are related to the amount of space within an object, capacity is the amount an object can hold, while volume is the amount of space the object occupies. So, a hollow three-dimensional shape has capacity (because it can be filled with air, rice, water, and so on) as well as volume (because it takes up space). Nevertheless, solid three-dimensional shapes are generally considered to have volume but not capacity.

Use with Lesson Activity Book pp. 289–290.

Developing Mathematical Language

Vocabulary: capacity, volume

Capacity is the amount a container can hold, whereas *volume* is the amount of space a container takes up. The subtle difference is that an object can have *volume* whether it is solid, like a brick, or empty, like a corrugated box. The box, however, also has *capacity* because things can be placed inside it. The brick does not have *capacity* because it is solid. Discuss these differences between *capacity* and *volume,* but do not require students to understand the subtle differences between them.

Familiarize students with the terms *capacity* and *volume*.

Beginning Tell students that the word *volume* has more than one meaning. They probably have seen a *volume* knob on a television or CD player. The spelling and pronunciation are the same; but *volume* on a television refers to sound, while the *volume* of an object is how much space it takes up.

Intermediate Have students name containers that have *capacity*. Have students then name something that might fill each container.

Advanced Ask students to explain how they know something has *volume*.

Open-Ended Problem Solving

Read the Headline Story to the students. Encourage them to think of imaginative ways to draw conclusions about the relay race.

 Headline Story

> **The Field Day relay race required team members to take turns filling 8-ounce cups with water, running to the other side of the field trying not to spill the water, and dumping the cups into 5-gallon buckets. The first team to fill its bucket to the 4-gallon mark won the race. Each team had 10 students.**

Possible response: If each student on a team made one trip to the bucket and didn't spill any water, the team would have 80 ounces of water in the bucket, which is 10 cups, 5 pints, 2.5 quarts, or just over half of a gallon of water. Therefore, each team member will likely need to make at least 8 trips to the bucket.

Skills Practice and Review

Estimating and Finding Volume

Materials
• centimeter cubes

Provide students with centimeter cubes. Hold up a small box and ask students to use their cubes as guides for estimating its volume. Check students' estimates by filling the box with cubes and having the class count the number of centimeter cubes you used. Pass out small boxes (or other objects that have tops and can be filled) to pairs of students. Have them estimate and then measure the volumes of these objects as closely as possible. If there is time, pairs can switch objects with neighbors and work with new volumes.

A Finding Capacity

Materials

- For the class: milliliter, liter, cup, pint, quart, and gallon containers; measurable substance such as rice or dried beans
- For each student: container from home; index card

NCTM Standards 1, 4, 6, 7, 8, 9, 10

Purpose To find the capacity of an object

Introduce Students should have brought containers from home for this activity. If any have forgotten to do so, pair them with other students. Have students write their names on their containers, or tape to them pieces of paper with their names on them.

To help students with their work, show them standard measurement containers, including milliliter, liter, cup, pint, quart, and gallon containers. Place these in one part of the room so that students can access them during the activity. Ask students for ideas on how they can use the standard containers to find the capacities of their own. Students should remember from Chapter 9 that they can fill any combination of standard containers with rice, beans, water, or other substances, then empty them into their own containers until they are filled. Caution students to use either metric or customary units, rather than some combination of the two, to find the capacities of their containers. Make sure that some students measure in metric units, others in customary units.

✓ Ongoing Assessment

- Do students have a sense of the relative sizes of the units of capacity? While the exact relationships among the units may be difficult for students to remember, they should have a sense of their relative sizes. Before students find the capacities of their containers, you might first ask them to make rough estimates of the capacities, to see if their ideas about the unit sizes are accurate.

Task **Direct students to find the capacities of their containers.** Give the class about ten minutes to complete the activity. Then give students index cards on which to record their names and the capacities of their containers. Collect and save the cards and containers for use in the game in the next lesson.

💬 Talk Math

❓ Sandi has a 1-gallon container. How many cups of water will it take to fill the container? Explain your reasoning. 16 cups; Possible explanation: There are 4 quarts in a gallon. Each quart is equivalent to 4 cups. So it will take $4 \times 4 = 16$ cups of water to fill the container.

❓ Mike found that it took 4 pints of liquid to fill his container. What was the capacity of his container in gallons? Explain your reasoning. $\frac{1}{2}$ gallon; Possible explanation: There are 8 pints in a gallon, so Mike's container held $\frac{4}{8}$ or $\frac{1}{2}$ gallon.

Possible Discussion

Because both volume and capacity measure three-dimensional attributes, students may wonder why volume is measured in cubic units, while capacity does not appear to be. You might explain that units of capacity are words that indicate cubic measurements.

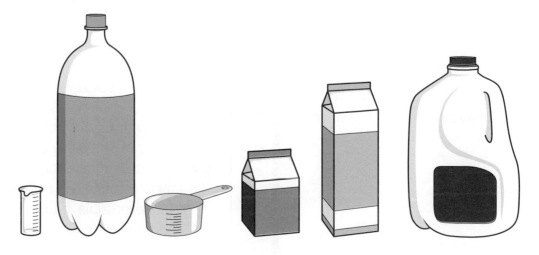

Use with Lesson Activity Book pp. 289–290.

Purpose To practice finding and estimating capacity

NCTM Standards 1, 4, 6, 7, 8, 9, 10

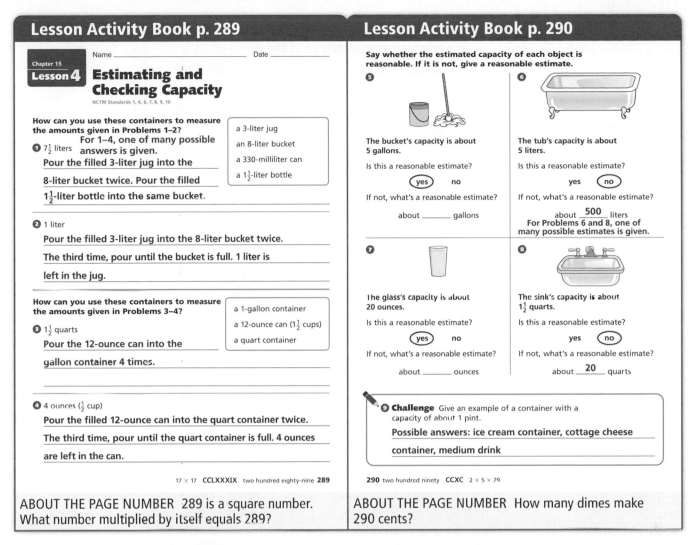

Teaching Notes for LAB page 289

Have students work on the page individually or with partners. Students are asked to use containers with given capacities to find other capacities. More than one container (but not necessarily all of them) is usually needed to find the required capacity in each problem. For example, three of the four containers are needed in Problem 1. (The 330-milliliter can is not.)

If students struggle to remember the relation between customary units of capacity, you might write "16 cups = 4 quarts = 1 gallon" on the board.

Teaching Notes for LAB page 290

Students estimate capacity to evaluate the reasonableness of a given capacity for a given container.

Challenge Problem The Challenge Problem asks students to give an example of an everyday item that has a capacity of about a pint.

C Solving Problems Involving Capacity

Materials
- For each student: AM153
- For the class: calculators

NCTM Standards 1, 3, 4, 6, 7, 8, 9, 10

Purpose To solve problems involving car gas mileage

Introduce Hand out Activity Master: Distances Between Cities. Have students read the problem as a class. Discuss possible strategies. Students might think about making a table that would show the distance Betsy's family could travel on one, two, three, or more tanks of gas.

12 gallons × 25 miles per gallon = 300 miles per tank

Number of tanks	1	2	3	4
Total miles	300	600	900	1,200

Distances Between Cities

Chicago
350 miles — Cleveland
130 miles
Pittsburgh
250 miles
Boston
210 miles
New York
110 miles
Philadelphia
130 miles
Washington D.C.

Betsy's family is going to take a driving trip from her house in Boston to visit friends in Washington D.C., driving through New York City and Philadelphia to get there.

① If their car holds 12 gallons of gasoline and they can travel 25 miles for each gallon, how many times will they have to stop to fill the tank traveling from Boston to Washington?

② How many times will they need to stop if they continue on to Pittsburgh?

③ What if they go all the way to Chicago?

Activity Master 153

Teacher Story

"I made a project of the travel problem in Activity C, having my students plan an imagined trip to visit friends or relatives. Some students calculated not only the distances they would need to travel, but also the times the trips would take, and the cost of the gas. Since students enjoyed choosing routes for their trips, I brought in maps and had them estimate distances."

Task After you have discussed possible approaches to the problem, have students work in small groups to answer the questions. Make calculators available to simplify students' calculations.

① If their car holds 12 gallons of gasoline and they can travel 25 miles for each gallon, how many times will they have to stop to fill the tank traveling from Boston to Washington? distance Boston–Washington: 210 + 110 + 130 = 450 miles; They can travel 300 miles on one tank, so they will need to stop once to fill up before they reach Washington.

② How many times will they need to stop if they continue on to Pittsburgh? distance Boston–Pittsburgh: 450 + 250 = 700 miles; They can travel 600 miles on two tanks, so they will need to stop twice.

③ What if they go all the way to Chicago? distance Boston–Chicago: 700 + 130 + 350 = 1,180 miles; They can travel 900 miles on three tanks, so they will need to stop three times.

💬 Talk Math

❓ Between Boston and Washington, the car traveled at an average speed of 50 miles per hour. How long did the trip take? Explain your reasoning. 7 hours; 450 miles ÷ 50 miles per hour = 7 hours

❓ It took 8 hours to travel from Pittsburgh to Chicago. What was the car's average rate of speed? Explain. 60 miles per hour; distance =130 + 350 = 480 miles; 480 miles ÷ 8 hours = 60 miles per hour

Reflect and Summarize the Lesson

 Write Math

Stan had a 50-milliliter container. He filled it ten times and emptied the contents into a larger container, filling it completely. What was the capacity of the larger container in liters? Explain. 0.5 liter; Possible explanation: The capacity of the larger container was 50 × 10 = 500 milliliters. There are 1,000 milliliters in a liter. Since 500 is half of 1,000, the larger container had a capacity of 0.5 liter.

Use with Lesson Activity Book pp. 289–290.

3 | Differentiated Instruction

Leveled Problem Solving

Suppose you have a 2-quart container and a 5-quart container. You also have as much water as you need.

① Basic Level

Could you measure 4 quarts? Explain. Yes; Fill the 2-qt container and pour it into the 5-qt; fill the 2-qt again and pour it into the 5-qt; there are 4 quarts in the 5-qt container.

② On Level

Could you measure 3 quarts? Explain. Yes; Fill the 5-qt container, and then fill the 2-qt container from the 5-qt container; there are 3 quarts left in the 5-qt container.

③ Above Level

Could you measure 1 quart? Explain. Yes; Fill the 2-qt, pour it into the 5-qt, and repeat; fill the 2-qt a third time, and fill the 5-qt from it; there will be 1 quart left in the 2-qt container.

Intervention	Practice	Extension

Activity Capacity Measures

Encourage students to name as many customary and metric capacity measures as they can think of until they have named milliliter, liter, cup, pint, quart, and gallon. Then have students help you list the measures in order from least to greatest horizontally on the board. Display the appropriate container under each measure. Then point to one, and have students approximate the number of pints, quarts, or cups it contains.

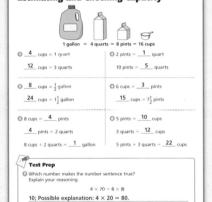

Practice P117

Extension E117

Spiral Review

Spiral Review Book page SR117 provides review of the following previously learned skills and concepts:

- finding the value of *x* in number sentences
- graphing measurement data

You may wish to have students work with a partner to complete the page.

Spiral Review SR117

Extension Activity
Order These

Have students work in small groups, using the containers they brought for the lesson. Have them use the sand or rice to order their containers from least capacity to greatest. When groups are finished, have one representative from each group explain to the class how they decided on the order

---

Lesson 5 | Comparing Units of Capacity

NCTM Standards 1, 4, 6, 7, 8, 9, 10

Lesson Planner

STUDENT OBJECTIVES
- To estimate and find capacity
- To compare customary and metric units of capacity

1 | Daily Activities (TG p. 1173)

Open-Ended Problem Solving/Headline Story	Skills Practice and Review— Finding a Container's Capacity

2 | Teach and Practice (TG pp. 1174–1177)

MATERIALS

Ⓐ **Comparing Units of Capacity** (TG p. 1174)

Ⓑ **Playing a Game: *The Closest Estimate: Capacity*** (TG p. 1175)

Ⓒ **Relating Units of Capacity** (TG p. 1176)

- containers that students found the capacity of in Lesson 15.4; index cards recording the capacity of each container from Lesson 15.4
- sheet of paper
- 📖 LAB pp. 291–292
- 📖 SH pp. 245–246

3 | Differentiated Instruction (TG p. 1178)

Leveled Problem Solving (TG p. 1178)	Practice Book P118
Intervention Activity (TG p. 1178)	Extension Book E118
Extension Activity (TG p. 1178)	Spiral Review Book SR118

Lesson Notes

About the Lesson

Students compare capacities in this lesson. The comparisons are complicated by the fact that they are made between capacities measured in customary units, such as gallons, and others measured in metric units, such as liters. Students also play a game where they use their knowledge of the approximate size of each unit of capacity to generate a reasonable estimate of the capacity of a container.

About the Mathematics

In the previous lessons of this chapter, estimating was presented as a strategy to aid computation. For example, for the sum 203 + 187, students could estimate that the answer would be about 400. In this lesson, estimating has a slightly different flavor. It is used to approximate a visual representation of a quantity. Both ways of using estimating are used in everyday life.

 Use with Lesson Activity Book pp. 291–292.

Developing Mathematical Language

Vocabulary: liter, quart

A *quart* is a little less than a *liter.* A *quart* is a customary unit of capacity, while a *liter* is a metric unit of capacity. Metric measures are commonly used throughout the world. Customary measures are used mostly in the United States. However, U.S. containers include both measures on product labels. Students should be able to relate *quarts* and *liters* and know that a *liter* is slightly more than a *quart.*

Familiarize students with the terms *liter* and *quart.*

Beginning Show students a *liter* container and a *quart* container. Demonstrate the relationship between a *liter* and a *quart* by filling the *liter* container with water and pouring the water into the *quart* container. Show students that there is still some water left in the *liter* container, so a *liter* is a little bit larger than a *quart.*

Intermediate Have students name products that are measured in *quarts* and *liters.*

Advanced Have students write a sentence using each term, *quart* and *liter.*

Open-Ended Problem Solving

Read the Headline Story to the students. Encourage them to use logical reasoning to draw conclusions about the number of marbles in the jar.

 Headline Story

> June guessed there were about 200 marbles in a jar. When she started counting, she counted 70 marbles and saw that the jar was almost half empty.

Possible response: There were fewer than 200 marbles in the jar. There were probably about 150 marbles in the jar because half of 150 is 75, and 70 marbles was a little less than half. 200 is a reasonable estimate of the number of marbles in the jar.

Skills Practice and Review

Finding a Container's Capacity

Display a container and ask students to describe how they would find its capacity. They should realize that they could pour standard units of capacity into the container, counting units until the container is full. Invite a student to do this to find container's capacity. To prepare for the game in this lesson, first ask students to estimate the capacity of the container, so that they can assess the reasonableness of their estimate. Repeat this activity with other containers as time allows. Make sure to use both metric (milliliters or liters) and customary (ounces, cups, pints, quarts, or gallons) units of capacity.

individuals or
whole class

10 MIN

Ⓐ Comparing Units of Capacity

NCTM Standards 1, 4, 6, 7, 8, 9, 10

Purpose To review the relative sizes of capacity units

Introduce Students should work in pairs. Give each student a copy of Explore: Comparing Liters and Gallons.

Task Challenge students to answer the questions on the Explore page. Students can use common sense to answer the first question. To answer Questions 2 and 3, they must reason more abstractly, using their knowledge of the relation between units of capacity to compare capacities.

Share After students have worked through the page, discuss it as a class. Ask students to share how they used estimation to help them complete the page. They could have used estimation in Problem 2, reasoning that, because 4 liters is a little more than 4 quarts, it is also a little more than 1 gallon. In Problem 3,

Possible Discussion

Students have learned that a quart is a little less than a liter. They may be wondering how much less. In fact, the difference is quite small. One liter is about 1.056 quarts, which is usually rounded to 1.06 quarts. The difference becomes more important as the numbers of liters and quarts increase. For example, 10 liters is about 10.6 quarts, a difference of 2 cups.

Chapter 15
Lesson 5

EXPLORE
Comparing Liters and Gallons

Felisha is going to the beach and wants to bring lots of water with her. She has two water coolers. One of the coolers holds 1 gallon and the other holds 4 liters.

❶ What can Felisha do to figure out which cooler holds more water?
Possible answer: She can fill one container and then pour into the other container. If it doesn't completely fill the new container, it is smaller. If it overflows the new container, it is bigger.

❷ Felisha just remembered that 1 liter is a little bit more than 1 quart. How can this help her decide which cooler is bigger?
Possible answer: Because 4 quarts equal 1 gallon, 4 liters must be more than a gallon.

❸ Felisha changed her mind. She wants to bring lemonade instead of water to the beach. To make lemonade, she mixes one lemonade packet with 8 cups of water. About how many packets should she use to make enough lemonade to fill the larger cooler? Explain your reasoning.
Two packets, because 16 cups equal 1 gallon, and 4 liters is just a little more than 1 gallon.

Chapter 15 **245**

Student Handbook p. 245

---

they could have reasoned that, because 16 cups equals 1 gallon, about 2 packets would be needed to make 4 liters of lemonade.

💬 Talk Math

❓ There are 6 micas in a kez. A dib is a little bigger than a mica. Would you estimate that there are more or less than 6 dibs in a kez? Explain your reasoning. less than; Possible explanation: If a dib is a little bigger than a mica, then 6 dibs are bigger than 6 micas, which is a kez. If 6 dibs are bigger than a kez, there must be fewer than 6 dibs in a kez.

❓ Which is bigger, a cup or 250 milliliters? Explain your reasoning. 250 milliliters; Possible explanation: A liter is a little more than a quart, so $\frac{1}{4}$ liter, or 250 milliliters, is a little more than $\frac{1}{4}$ quart, which is a cup.

Playing *The Closest Estimate: Capacity*

Purpose To practice estimating capacity

Goal Working in teams, students look at containers and estimate their capacities. The team whose estimates are most consistently closest to the exact capacities wins the game.

Introduce For this game, you will need the containers that students brought from home for **Lesson 15.4,** along with the index cards that students used to record the capacities of the containers. Place the containers on your desk or somewhere where the class can see them as you hold them up.

Students play the game in teams of 4 to 6. Each team needs a piece of paper.

How to Play

❶ Display a container.

❷ Allow teams to consult for one minute to formulate their best estimates for the capacity of the container. Remind students that they can estimate in cups, pints, quarts, gallons, or liters, but that they should use only one unit in their estimates.

❸ After one minute, instruct teams to write down their estimates, and to note whether their measures are in customary or metric units.

❹ Have a member of each team state the team's estimate. Then reveal the measured capacity of the container. The team whose estimate is closest to the measured capacity gets 1 point.

❺ Repeat Steps 1 through 4 using the other containers. Teams must alternate the system of measurement they use to make their estimates. If they use metric units for one estimate, they must use customary for the next; if they use customary units for one estimate, they must use metric for the next.

❻ When you have displayed all the containers, you may declare the team with the most points the winner.

❼ Have students re-measure the capacity of each container. This will help them refine their ideas about the relative sizes of the units of capacity.

Materials
- For each student: containers that students found the capacity of in Lesson 15.4; index cards with the capacity of each container from Lesson 15.4
- For each team: sheet of paper

NCTM Standards 1, 4, 6, 7, 8, 9, 10

Teacher Story

❝My students seemed to have trouble coming up with reasonable estimates during the game. So, after the closest estimate was determined, we used standard measurement tools to find the capacity of the container. This provided another illustration of the relative sizes of the units.❞

✔ Ongoing Assessment

- Do students understand the relative sizes of the units of capacity? Their responses while playing *The Closest Estimate: Capacity* can help you find out. For example, if students guess that a small container could hold a gallon, their mental representations of this unit are probably too large. Similarly, if they say that a large container could hold only a few cups, their images of a cup are likely too small.

Purpose To compare units of capacity

NCTM Standards 1, 4, 6, 7, 8, 9, 10

Lesson Activity Book p. 291

Chapter 15
Lesson 5 **Comparing Units of Capacity**
NCTM Standards 1, 4, 6, 7, 8, 9, 10

Name _____ Date _____

Use estimation to help you compare these capacities.

① 18×16 gallons $<$ 19×16 gallons

② 67×8 cups $>$ 66×4 pints

③ 74×19 liters $>$ 74×19 quarts

④ 83×4 quarts $<$ 87×1 gallon

⑤ 38×27 pints $<$ 38×14 quarts

⑥ 22×82 cups $<$ 21×22 quarts

Answer the questions.

⑦ The soccer coach brought 2 gallons of water to the game and the assistant coach brought 1 gallon of fruit juice. The drinks were shared equally among the 24 kids on the team. How many cups could each player have?

3 gallons × 16 = 48 cups, so each player gets 2 cups.

⑧ Before driving 456 miles to grandpa's house, Jen's mom filled the car with gas. The car holds 18 gallons of gas. If the car uses 10 gallons to go 240 miles, will Jen's mom need to fill the car with gas again during the drive? If so, how much more gas will she need? If not, how much will they have left in the tank?

10 gallons go 240 miles, so 1 gallon goes 24 miles.

The remaining 8 gallons need to go 216 miles.

8 × 24 = 192, so they need 1 more gallon of gas.

3×97 CCXCI two hundred ninety-one **291**

ABOUT THE PAGE NUMBER How many yards are 291 feet?

Lesson Activity Book p. 292

Compare. Use <, >, or =.

⑨ $\frac{1}{2}$ gallon $>$ 2 pints

⑩ 1.1 gallon $>$ 4 quarts

⑪ 4.5 quarts $>$ $\frac{3}{4}$ gallon

⑫ $\frac{10}{10}$ pints $<$ 10 cups

⑬ $\frac{7}{8}$ gallon $>$ 10 cups

⑭ 3 liters $>$ 2 quarts

⑮ 5 cups $=$ $2\frac{1}{2}$ pints

⑯ 4 pints $<$ $3\frac{1}{2}$ liters

⑰ 1.7 liters $>$ 5.07 cups

⑱ $\frac{3}{4}$ cup $<$ $\frac{3}{4}$ pint

⑲ 7.5 cups $<$ $\frac{6}{12}$ gallon

⑳ 987.5 ml $<$ $\frac{1}{2}$ gallon

㉑ $\frac{5}{6}$ quart $>$ 0.5 liter

㉒ 24 cups $=$ 1.5 gallons

㉓ **Challenge** Fill in the blanks to make the statements true.

$67 \times$ __**32**__ cups = 8 quarts $\times 67$

2.5 pints $\times 17 =$ __**5**__ cups $\times 17$

$\frac{1}{2}$ gallon + 2 cups = __**4.5**__ pints + 1 cup
or $4\frac{1}{2}$

$\frac{9}{10}$ pint > __$\frac{1}{4}$__ cups

Many answers are possible. Answer must be less than $\frac{9}{20}$.

292 two hundred ninety-two CCXCII $2 \times 2 \times 73$

ABOUT THE PAGE NUMBER 292 is a palindrome. Is it even or odd? What is it divisible by?

Teaching Notes for LAB page 291

Have students work on the page individually or with partners.

Students use the relation between units of capacity, as well as their estimating skills, to compare various capacities. Then they answer questions involving comparing units of capacity.

No computations are required. Instead, students use their knowledge of units of capacity and of multiplication to find which is the larger quantity.

Teaching Notes for LAB page 292

Students continue to compare capacities, but now use non-whole numbers of units.

Challenge Problem The Challenge Problem asks students to fill in the numbers of units of capacity that make given equations true.

Reflect and Summarize the Lesson

Write Math
If a jug holds about 4 liters, about how many pints will it hold? Explain your reasoning.
Possible estimate: about 8 pints; possible explanation: 4 liters is a little more than 4 quarts. Since there are 2 pints in a quart, 4 liters is a little more than 4 × 2 pints, or 8 pints.

Review Model . . . .

Refer students to Review Model: Comparing Units of Capacity in the *Student Handbook,* p. 246, to see how they can compare units of capacity in the metric and customary systems of measurement.

✔ Check for Understanding

❶ 4 cups

❷ 3 pints

❸ 2 quarts

❹ 4 cups

❺ 5 cups

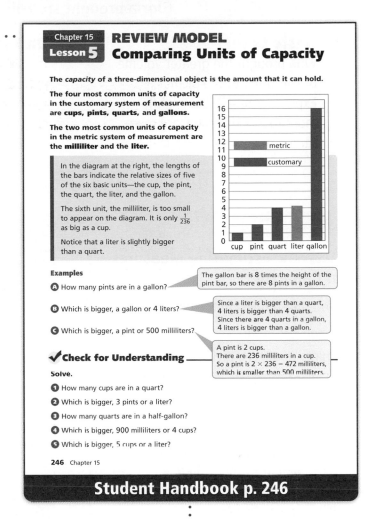

Student Handbook p. 246

Leveled Problem Solving

Emmit brought six 1-quart bottles of soft drink to a picnic.
Gloria brought six 1-liter bottles.

❶ Basic Level

Who brought the greater volume of soft drink to the picnic? Explain. Gloria; 1 L is slightly more than 1 qt, so 6 L are more than 6 qt.

❷ On Level

The six 1-quart bottles were used to fill drinking cups that each held 1 cup. How many cups could be filled? Explain. 24 cups; 1 qt = 4 c, and $6 \times 4 = 24$.

❸ Above Level

The 1-liter bottles filled cups that each held $\frac{1}{4}$ liter. Which held more, a 1-cup drinking cup or a $\frac{1}{4}$-liter drinking cup? Explain. $\frac{1}{4}$-L cup; 1 L > 1 qt, so $\frac{1}{4}$ L > $\frac{1}{4}$ qt, or 1 c.

Intervention	Practice	Extension

Activity Estimating Measures of Capacity

Write these rules on the board:

To convert from:
- pints to quarts, divide by 2;
- gallons to quarts, multiply by 4;
- cups to quarts, divide by 4;
- pints to quarts, divide by 2.

Then have students use the table to estimate how many liters various containers hold, given their customary measures.

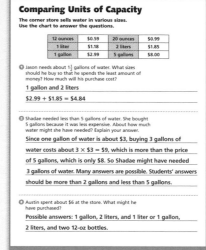

Practice P118

Extension E118

Spiral Review

Spiral Review Book page SR118 provides review of the following previously learned skills and concepts:

- using place value to compare and order numbers through millions
- describing attributes of prism and pyramids

You may wish to have students work with a partner to complete the page.

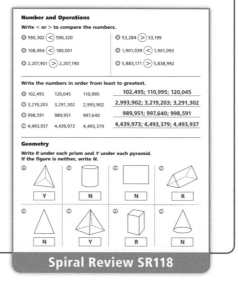

Spiral Review SR118

Extension Activity
Same Capacity?

Give each pair of students three sheets of paper. Have them make one cylinder by taping the longer side (without overlapping) to itself and the other by taping the shorter side to itself. Ask them to predict which cylinder will have the greater capacity. Have students stand the cylinders in a box and use rice or sand to compare the capacities. Then repeat the experiment, cutting the remaining sheet of paper in half to create two more cylinders. Have students create a table to display their results.

Teacher's Notes 🍎

Daily Notes . . .

Quick Notes

More Ideas

Lesson 6 Estimating and Checking Weight

NCTM Standards 1, 4, 6, 7, 8, 9, 10

Lesson Planner

STUDENT OBJECTIVE ··
- To estimate and find weight in customary and standard units

1 | Daily Activities (TG p. 1181)

| Open-Ended Problem Solving/Headline Story | Skills Practice and Review— Weight Versus Mass |

2 | Teach and Practice (TG pp. 1182–1184)

MATERIALS

Ⓐ **Weight Scavenger Hunt** (TG p. 1182)

Ⓑ **Playing a Game: *The Closest Estimate: Weight*** (TG p. 1183)

Ⓒ **Estimating and Checking Weight** (TG p. 1184)

- TR: Activity Master, AM154
- various objects from around the room
- gram/kilogram/ounce/pound scale
- sheet of paper
- 📖 LAB pp. 293–294
- 📖 SH p. 254

3 | Differentiated Instruction (TG p. 1185)

Leveled Problem Solving (TG p. 1185)	Practice Book P119
Intervention Activity (TG p. 1185)	Extension Book E119
Extension Activity (TG p. 1185)	Spiral Review Book SR119

Lesson Notes

About the Lesson

Students continue estimating, but focus on estimating weight in customary and standard units. As in the previous lesson, estimating is based on visual information and is separate from any computation. Using estimating this way helps students to develop a sense of the size of the units for measuring weight.

Developing Mathematical Language

Vocabulary: mass, weight

Though we commonly use *mass* and *weight* interchangeably, they are technically different. *Weight* fluctuates from place to place. An object that weighs 100 pounds in a valley weighs less on top of a mountain. However, its *mass* is the same no matter where the object is.

Familiarize students with the terms *mass* and *weight*.

Beginning Have students name units of *mass* and units of *weight* that they are familiar with.

Intermediate Have students name items that have a *weight* of more than 1 pound but less than 10 pounds.

Advanced Have students write a sentence comparing the *weight* and the *mass* of a object on Earth and on the moon. Remind students that items are 6 times heavier on Earth than on the moon.

1 | Daily Activities

Open-Ended Problem Solving

Read the Headline Story to the students. Encourage them to think of creative ways for Jana to find the weight of her suitcase.

 Headline Story

Jana is going on a trip and she is allowed only 30 pounds of luggage on the airplane. She wants to figure out the weight of her suitcase to make sure it isn't too heavy. The problem is that her suitcase doesn't fit on her scale.

Possible response: Jana can weigh herself and then weigh herself holding the suitcase, then find the difference to determine the weight of the suitcase. If Jana weighs 118 pounds with the suitcase and 90 pounds without it, then the suitcase weighs $118 - 90 = 28$ pounds. If Jana and the suitcase weigh 136 pounds, then the suitcase weighs 46 pounds, 16 pounds too heavy to go on the plane.

Skills Practice and Review

Weight Versus Mass

Ask students to explain the difference between weight and mass. They should remember from **Chapter 9** that mass is the amount of stuff that something is made from, while weight is how heavy it is. Tell students that on the Moon, objects weigh about one-sixth their weight on Earth, on Jupiter about 300 times their weight on Earth. Give students various weights and masses on Earth, the Moon, and Jupiter. Ask for the corresponding weights and masses in the other places. For example, tell students that a cat has a weight and mass of 6 kilograms on Earth. Ask for its weight and mass on the Moon and on Jupiter. The masses are the same on the Moon and on Jupiter. On the Moon, the weight of the cat is $6 \div 6 = 1$ kilogram, while on Jupiter its weight would be $6 \times 300 = 1,800$ kilograms.

2 | Teach and Practice

(A) Weight Scavenger Hunt

Materials
- For the teacher: gram/kilogram/ounce/pound scale
- For each student: AM154

NCTM Standards 1, 4, 6, 7, 8, 9, 10

Differentiated Instruction

Basic Level If students struggle to find objects of certain weights during the scavenger hunt, you might arrange a collection of objects whose weights approximate those in the scavenger hunt. Have the students try to match the objects to the weights on the page.

Purpose To use estimating to identify objects of given weights

Introduce Students should work with partners. Before beginning the activity, quickly review the relative sizes of the various units students have used to measure weight. You might list the units from smallest to largest on the board: gram, ounce, pound, kilogram, ton. Then you might hold up an object, such as a pencil, and ask students if they think its weight is closer to a gram or an ounce. ounce Once the class has a sense of the approximate weight that each unit measures, give each student a copy of Activity Master: Scavenger Hunt.

Activity Master 154

Task **Direct students to search the room for objects whose weights match the clues on the page, and to record one object for each clue.** Students should use estimation to choose their objects, not direct measurement on a scale. Be sure the class understands that for some weights, there may be many objects that could be listed, while for others there may be few. In any case, there is no "right" answer for any of the given weights, rather a variety of possible answers.

Share After students have scavenged the room for a few minutes, gather them to share their answers with the class. As students mention the objects that they found, ask them to place the items on a scale and evaluate whether they match the clues. Once an object is found that approximates the weight given in the clue, invite students to record this object in the proper sections of their Activity Masters. This will provide them with a reference for that particular weight. If there are weights that no one was able to match, share the answers from your copy of the Activity Master.

 Talk Math

❓ Would you expect an object that weighs about a pound to be heavier or less heavy than an object that weighs about a kilogram? Explain your reasoning. less heavy; Possible explanation; A kilogram is heavier than a pound, so an object that weighs a pound will be less heavy than an object that weighs a kilogram.

❓ An object weighs a little more than an ounce. Which is a better estimate of the number of such objects you would need to make a pound, 5, 10, or 100? Explain your reasoning. 10; Possible explanation: 5 objects would probably weigh between 5 and 10 ounces; 10 objects would weigh between 10 and 20 ounces; 100 objects would weigh between 100 and 200 ounces. Since there are 16 ounces in one pound, the best estimate of the number of objects needed to make a pound is 10.

B Playing *The Closest Estimate: Weight*

 small groups

 15 MIN

Purpose To practice estimating weight

Goal Working in teams, students look at various objects and estimate their weights. The team whose estimates are consistently closest to the exact weights wins the game.

Introduce Now that students have been reminded of the sizes of various weight units, they play a variation of the game introduced in the previous lesson. This time the game is played in the context of weight rather than capacity. Use various objects from the classroom, preferably different ones from those that were used in the previous activity. Students play in teams of 4 to 6. Each team needs a sheet of paper.

How to Play

❶ Display an object.

❷ Allow teams to consult for one minute to formulate their best estimates for the weight of the object. Remind students that they can estimate in grams, ounces, pounds, or kilograms, but that they should only use one unit in their estimates.

❸ After one minute, instruct teams to write down their estimates.

❹ Have a member of each team state the team's estimate. Then weigh the object on the scale. Give the weight in whatever units are necessary for students to decide which team's estimate is closest to the measured weight. That team receives 1 point.

❺ Repeat steps 1 through 4 with the other objects.

❻ When you have displayed all the objects, you may declare the team with the most points the winner.

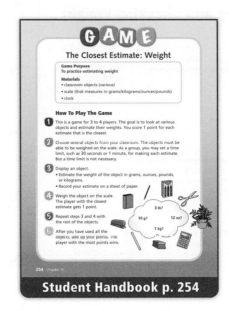

Student Handbook p. 254

Materials
- For the teacher: various objects from around the room; scale
- For each team: sheet of paper

NCTM Standards 1, 4, 6, 7, 8, 9, 10

C Estimating and Checking Weight LAB pp. 293–294

individuals
or pairs

20 MIN

Purpose To use estimation to reason about situations involving weight

NCTM Standards 1, 4, 6, 7, 8, 9, 10

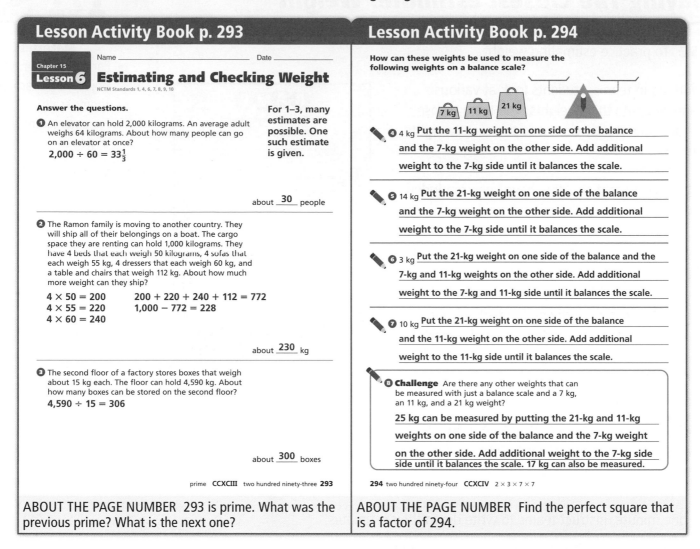

Lesson Activity Book p. 293

Name _____ Date _____

Chapter 15
Lesson 6 **Estimating and Checking Weight**
NCTM Standards 1, 4, 6, 7, 8, 9, 10

Answer the questions.

For 1–3, many estimates are possible. One such estimate is given.

❶ An elevator can hold 2,000 kilograms. An average adult weighs 64 kilograms. About how many people can go on an elevator at once?

2,000 ÷ 60 = 33⅓

about __30__ people

❷ The Ramon family is moving to another country. They will ship all of their belongings on a boat. The cargo space they are renting can hold 1,000 kilograms. They have 4 beds that each weigh 50 kilograms, 4 sofas that each weigh 55 kg, 4 dressers that each weigh 60 kg, and a table and chairs that weigh 112 kg. About how much more weight can they ship?

4 × 50 = 200   200 + 220 + 240 + 112 = 772
4 × 55 = 220   1,000 − 772 = 228
4 × 60 = 240

about __230__ kg

❸ The second floor of a factory stores boxes that weigh about 15 kg each. The floor can hold 4,590 kg. About how many boxes can be stored on the second floor?

4,590 ÷ 15 = 306

about __300__ boxes

prime CCXCIII two hundred ninety-three **293**

ABOUT THE PAGE NUMBER 293 is prime. What was the previous prime? What is the next one?

Lesson Activity Book p. 294

How can these weights be used to measure the following weights on a balance scale?

[7 kg] [11 kg] [21 kg]

❹ 4 kg Put the 11-kg weight on one side of the balance and the 7-kg weight on the other side. Add additional weight to the 7-kg side until it balances the scale.

❺ 14 kg Put the 21-kg weight on one side of the balance and the 7-kg weight on the other side. Add additional weight to the 7-kg side until it balances the scale.

❻ 3 kg Put the 21-kg weight on one side of the balance and the 7-kg and 11-kg weights on the other side. Add additional weight to the 7-kg and 11-kg side until it balances the scale.

❼ 10 kg Put the 21-kg weight on one side of the balance and the 11-kg weight on the other side. Add additional weight to the 11-kg side until it balances the scale.

❽ **Challenge** Are there any other weights that can be measured with just a balance scale and a 7 kg, an 11 kg, and a 21 kg weight?
25 kg can be measured by putting the 21-kg and 11-kg weights on one side of the balance and the 7-kg weight on the other side. Add additional weight to the 7-kg side side until it balances the scale. 17 kg can also be measured.

294 two hundred ninety-four CCXCIV 2 × 3 × 7 × 7

ABOUT THE PAGE NUMBER Find the perfect square that is a factor of 294.

Teaching Notes for LAB page 293

Have students complete the page individually or with partners. To solve the word problems on the page, students should not find the exact number of people that will fit in the elevator, the exact number of kilograms that the shipment can have, or the exact number of boxes. Instead, though it is not stated explicitly, they should solve by estimating. Doing so, rather than calculating exact answers, mirrors the way such problems would be handled in everyday situations. All reasonable answers should be accepted.

Teaching Notes for LAB page 294

Students are asked to write about ways they can find certain weights using a balance scale and three given weights.

Be sure students understand that a scale balances when the weights on both sides are equal.

Challenge Problem The Challenge Problem asks students to search for additional weights that can be measured on a balance scale, using the three weights from the previous problems on the page.

Reflect and Summarize the Lesson

 Write Math **What units would you use to approximate the weight of a piece of paper? the weight of a table? the weight of a house?** Many answers are possible, including the following: A piece of paper can be estimated in grams or ounces, a table in kilograms or pounds, and a house in tons.

Leveled Problem Solving

Will has 3-lb, 5-lb, and 7-lb weights. Using a balance scale, he wants to fill empty bags with sand to make new weights.

❶ Basic Level

Can he make a 15-lb weight? Explain. Yes; Put all 3 weights on one side of the scale, put the empty bag on the other side, and fill it until the scale balances.

❷ On Level

Can he make a 2-lb weight? Explain. Yes; Put the 5-lb weight on one side and put the 3-lb weight on the other with an empty bag. Fill the bag until the scale balances.

❸ Above Level

Can he make a 9-lb weight? Explain. Yes; Put the 5-lb and 7-lb weights on one side and put the 3-lb weight on the other side with an empty bag. Fill the bag until the scale balances.

Intervention

Activity Visual Comparisons

Write the customary units of weight on the board, *pound* and *ounce*. Draw a line segment next to *ounce* to represent the unit one ounce. Have students estimate how long the line segment would be for the unit *pound*. 16 times as long Repeat the activity for gram and kilogram. 1,000 times as long

Practice

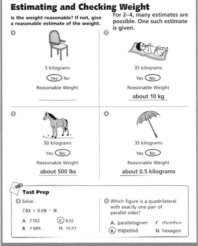

Practice P119

Extension

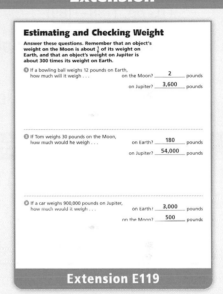

Extension E119

Spiral Review

Spiral Review Book page SR119 provides review of the following previously learned skills and concepts:

- estimating and finding length, perimeter, and area using standard and non-standard units.
- solving problems using the strategy *work backward.*

You may wish to have students work with a partner to complete the page.

Spiral Review SR119

Extension Activity
A Weighty Activity

Have students bring a variety of the same type of item to class (e.g., fruits, small toys, and so on), or prepare groups of different small classroom objects (e.g., groups of 1 marker, 1 crayon, 1 base-ten block, and so on). Give each group of students a balance scale. Challenge the groups to order the items they have from least to greatest weight by using only the balance scale. When the groups have finished, each should explain the strategy they used.

Lesson 7 Comparing Units of Weight

NCTM Standards 1, 4, 6, 7, 8, 9, 10

Lesson Planner

STUDENT OBJECTIVES
- To relate pounds and kilograms
- To compare weights

1 | Daily Activities (TG p. 1187)

Open-Ended Problem Solving/Headline Story	Skills Practice and Review— Converting Units of Weight

2 | Teach and Practice (TG pp. 1188–1191)

A Comparing Units of Weight (TG pp. 1188–1189)

B Playing a Game: *Weight Match* (TG p. 1190)

C Relating Units of Weight (TG p. 1191)

MATERIALS

- TR: Activity Masters, AM155–AM156
- scale, kilogram weights, pound weights (all optional)
- calculators
- LAB pp. 295–296
- SH pp. 247, 255

3 | Differentiated Instruction (TG p. 1192)

Leveled Problem Solving (TG p. 1192)	Practice Book P120
Intervention Activity (TG p. 1192)	Extension Book E120
Extension Activity (TG p. 1192)	Spiral Review Book SR120

Lesson Notes

About the Lesson

In this lesson, students relate standard units of weight to customary units. They find that one kilogram is a little more than 2 pounds. They then use this relation to estimate the weight measurement in one unit converted from the measurement stated in terms of another unit. They also order a collection of weights by size.

Use with Lesson Activity Book pp. 295–296.

Developing Mathematical Language

Vocabulary: kilogram, pound

Loosely, 1 *kilogram* weighs about 2.2 *pounds*. Students might understand that 1 ounce is $\frac{1}{16}$ *pound,* 1 gram is $\frac{1}{1,000}$ *kilogram,* and 1 milligram is $\frac{1}{1,000,000}$ *kilogram.* It is more important at this level, however, for students to understand relative weights than to make exact computations.

Familiarize students with the terms *kilogram* and *pound.*

Beginning Help students write a list of items that weigh less than a *kilogram.*

Intermediate Have students write a sentence using the word *kilogram.*

Advanced Have students compare a *kilogram* to a *pound.*

Open-Ended Problem Solving

Read the Headline Story to the students. Encourage them to think of interesting statements to make about Jason's and Rosa's comments.

 Headline Story

> Jason said that a gallon of milk weighed 8 pounds. Rosa said that a gallon of milk weighed 3.5 kilograms.

Possible response: Since 1 kilogram is a little more than 2 pounds, 3.5 kilograms and 8 pounds are pretty close (though not exactly the same). Pounds and kilograms are both units for measuring weight. Milk weighs about the same as water, and a liter of water weighs 1 kilogram. Since there are a little less than 4 liters in a gallon, the weight of 3.5 kilograms for a gallon of milk makes sense.

Skills Practice and Review

Converting Units of Weight

Write a weight in tons on the board. Ask students how many pounds and how many ounces it is. If necessary, remind students that there are 2,000 pounds in a ton and 16 ounces in a pound. To provide estimating practice, you might first have students estimate the number of ounces in the measurement, rather than multiply the number of tons by 32,000, or the number of pounds by 16. Repeat this activity with a weight in pounds or ounces. Have students convert the measure to the other customary units. Take care in choosing the numbers of pounds or ounces for conversion. For example, 70 ounces is difficult to convert to pounds because neither 8 nor 16 divides it evenly. Instead, choose measurements such as 80 ounces or 88 ounces, which convert to 5 pounds and $5\frac{1}{2}$ pounds respectively.

2 | Teach and Practice

A Comparing Units of Weight

Materials

- For the teacher: scale, kilogram weights, pound weights (all optional)
- For students: calculators

NCTM Standards 1, 4, 6, 7, 8, 9, 10

Purpose To compare kilograms and pounds

Introduce Students should work in pairs. Give each student a copy of Explore: Comparing Pounds and Kilograms. Explain that by studying a series of pictures of a scale and answering the accompanying questions, students will work out the relation between pounds and kilograms. Have calculators available for students who wish to use them.

Task Direct students to work with their partners to answer the questions on the page.

❶ What does this scale tell Jean?

The kilogram weight far outweighs the pound weight, so 1 kilogram is more than 1 pound.

❷ What does this scale tell her? The kilogram weight outweighs two 1-pound weights, but not by much, so 1 kilogram is a little more than 2 pounds.

❸ What does this scale tell her? The kilogram weight is lighter than 3 1-pound weights, so 1 kilogram is less than 3 pounds.

❹ What does this scale tell her? Use a calculator to approximate the relation between pounds and kilograms. 5 kilograms is about 11 pounds. To find the number of pounds in 1 kilogram, divide 11 by 5: 11 ÷ 5 = 2.2, so 1 kilogram is about 2.2 pounds.

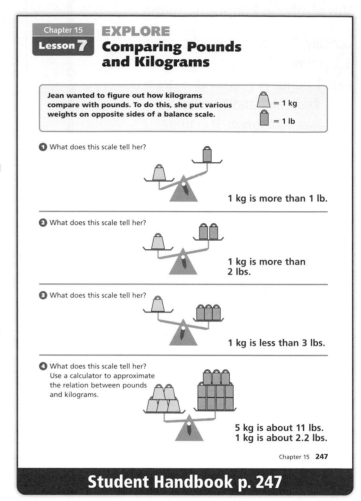

Chapter 15
Lesson 7

EXPLORE
Comparing Pounds and Kilograms

Jean wanted to figure out how kilograms compare with pounds. To do this, she put various weights on opposite sides of a balance scale.

= 1 kg
= 1 lb

❶ What does this scale tell her?

1 kg is more than 1 lb.

❷ What does this scale tell her?

1 kg is more than 2 lbs.

❸ What does this scale tell her?

1 kg is less than 3 lbs.

❹ What does this scale tell her? Use a calculator to approximate the relation between pounds and kilograms.

5 kg is about 11 lbs.
1 kg is about 2.2 lbs.

Chapter 15 **247**

Student Handbook p. 247

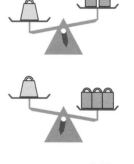

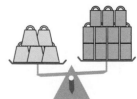

Students should find that one kilogram is more than 2 pounds but less than 3 pounds, and that 5 kilograms is almost exactly 11 pounds. Thus, one kilogram is much closer to 2 pounds than to 3 pounds.

Share After students have worked through the page on their own, ask them to share their answers and to explain and justify their reasoning. Have your students demonstrate each of the Explore problems with a scale and with kilogram and pound weights. During the discussion, make sure that students reach the conclusion that a kilogram is just a little more than 2 pounds, and is in fact close to 2.2 pounds.

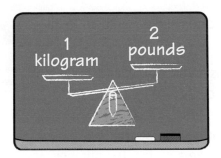

💬 Talk Math

❷ A scale has 10 kilograms on one side and 22 pounds on the other. Are the pans about equally balanced, or is one side considerably heavier than the other? Explain your reasoning. about equally balanced; Possible explanation: Since 1 kilogram is about 2.2 pounds, 10 kilograms is about $2.2 \times 10 = 22$ pounds. So, the two sides have about the same weight.

❷ A "stone" is a unit of weight equal to 14 pounds. Estimate the number of kilograms in a stone. Explain how you made your estimate. Possible estimate: 6 kilograms; possible explanation: Since 1 kilogram is slightly more than 2 pounds, 6 kilograms is slightly more than $6 \times 2 = 12$ pounds, or about 14 pounds.

Concept Alert

In previous lessons, students learned that a kilogram is heavier than a pound. When they relate the two units in this lesson, however, they may be perplexed to find that although a kilogram is more than a pound, the number of kilograms in a given weight is less than the number of pounds. Equally confusing, perhaps, may be the fact that 60 kilograms, for example, is heavier than 100 pounds. To explain these seeming contradictions, you might turn to more familiar contexts. For example, you could point out that 1 foot–a longer unit than an inch–equals 12 inches, and that 2 hours is more than 80 minutes, because an hour is much longer than a minute.

B Playing *Weight Match*

Materials
- For each group of 2–3 students: AM155–AM156

NCTM Standards 1, 4, 6, 7, 8, 9, 10

Purpose To practice applying the relation between pounds and kilograms

Goal Players attempt to make matches choosing cards that show weights in both pounds and kilograms. The player who makes the most matches is the winner.

Introduce Each group of 2 or 3 students needs a complete set of cut-out Activity Masters: Weight Cards I and Weight Cards II. Remind students of the basic relation between pounds and kilograms: 1 kilogram is about 2.2 pounds.

How to Play

❶ One player shuffles the cards and deals them to all players in the group.

❷ If any players have cards naming matching weights, they place the cards face up on the table where all players can see them. The other players should verify that the cards show approximately the same weights. (To make a match, the number of pounds should be a little more than twice the number of kilograms, but less than two and a half times the number of kilograms.) If any matches are incorrect, players take them back into their hands.

❸ After all correct matches have been placed down, the player to the left of the dealer picks a card from another player's hand. If the card matches a card in the player's hand, the player places the matching pair face up on the table. Again, the other players check the match. If it is, the player chooses again, continuing until he or she fails to choose a match. Play then passes to the next player.

❹ Players take turns choosing cards and putting down matches until all cards have been paired and placed on the table.

❺ The player with the most matches is the winner.

Student Handbook p. 255

Weight Cards I

1 kg	2 kg	3 kg	4 kg
5 kg	6 kg	7 kg	8 kg
9 kg	10 kg	0.5 kg	1.5 kg
25 kg	50 kg	100 kg	5.5 kg

Activity Master 155

Weight Cards II

2.2 lbs	4.4 lbs	6.6 lbs	8.8 lbs
11 lbs	13.2 lbs	15.4 lbs	17.6 lbs
19.8 lbs	22 lbs	1.6 lbs	3.8 lbs
55 lbs	110 lbs	220 lbs	12.6 lbs

Activity Master 156

C Relating Units of Weight LAB pp. 295–296

Purpose To relate metric and customary units of weight

NCTM Standards 1, 4, 6, 7, 8, 9, 10

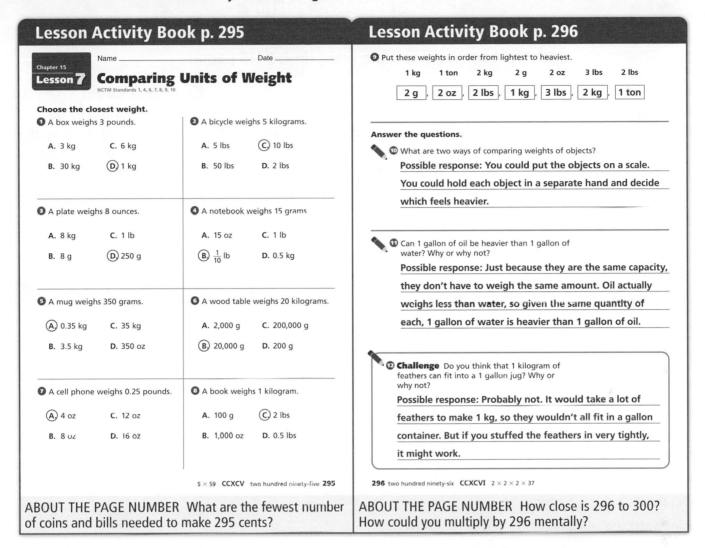

Lesson Activity Book p. 295

Chapter 15
Lesson 7 **Comparing Units of Weight**
NCTM Standards 1, 4, 6, 7, 8, 9, 10

Name _____ Date _____

Choose the closest weight.

1 A box weighs 3 pounds.

   A. 3 kg   C. 6 kg

   B. 30 kg   (D.) 1 kg

2 A bicycle weighs 5 kilograms.

   A. 5 lbs   (C.) 10 lbs

   B. 50 lbs   D. 2 lbs

3 A plate weighs 8 ounces.

   A. 8 kg   C. 1 lb

   B. 8 g   (D.) 250 g

4 A notebook weighs 15 grams

   A. 15 oz   C. 1 lb

   (B.) $\frac{1}{10}$ lb   D. 0.5 kg

5 A mug weighs 350 grams.

   (A.) 0.35 kg   C. 35 kg

   B. 3.5 kg   D. 350 oz

6 A wood table weighs 20 kilograms.

   A. 2,000 g   C. 200,000 g

   (B.) 20,000 g   D. 200 g

7 A cell phone weighs 0.25 pounds.

   (A.) 4 oz   C. 12 oz

   B. 8 oz   D. 16 oz

8 A book weighs 1 kilogram.

   A. 100 g   (C.) 2 lbs

   B. 1,000 oz   D. 0.5 lbs

5 × 59 CCXCV two hundred ninety-five **295**

Lesson Activity Book p. 296

9 Put these weights in order from lightest to heaviest.

   1 kg   1 ton   2 kg   2 g   2 oz   3 lbs   2 lbs

   2 g , 2 oz , 2 lbs , 1 kg , 3 lbs , 2 kg , 1 ton

Answer the questions.

10 What are two ways of comparing weights of objects?

Possible response: You could put the objects on a scale. You could hold each object in a separate hand and decide which feels heavier.

11 Can 1 gallon of oil be heavier than 1 gallon of water? Why or why not?

Possible response: Just because they are the same capacity, they don't have to weigh the same amount. Oil actually weighs less than water, so given the same quantity of each, 1 gallon of water is heavier than 1 gallon of oil.

12 Challenge Do you think that 1 kilogram of feathers can fit into a 1 gallon jug? Why or why not?

Possible response: Probably not. It would take a lot of feathers to make 1 kg, so they wouldn't all fit in a gallon container. But if you stuffed the feathers in very tightly, it might work.

296 two hundred ninety-six CCXCVI 2 × 2 × 2 × 37

ABOUT THE PAGE NUMBER What are the fewest number of coins and bills needed to make 295 cents?

ABOUT THE PAGE NUMBER How close is 296 to 300? How could you multiply by 296 mentally?

Teaching Notes for LAB page 295

Have students complete the page individually or with partners. Students relate pounds, kilograms, and other units of weight. In each problem, they choose the weight that most closely matches an object's given weight. Some problems offer choices that are exact matches of the given weights; others offer good estimates.

Teaching Notes for LAB page 296

Students order several measurements given in different units, and explain how to compare weights.

Challenge Problem The Challenge Problem asks students to reason about the relation between weight and capacity. Accept any answers that show sound reasoning about the distinctions between the two.

Reflect and Summarize the Lesson

Write Math **A book weighs about 10 pounds. About how many kilograms does it weigh? Explain your reasoning.** Possible answer: a little more than 4 kilograms; possible explanation: 1 kilogram is a little more than 2.2 pounds, so 4 kilograms is a little more than 8.8 pounds, or about 9 pounds. Since 9 is not quite 10, the answer must be a little more than 4 kilograms.

Leveled Problem Solving

Paulo fills his backpack with books. He stands on a scale with the backpack, and the scale shows 115 pounds.

❶ Basic Level

If Paulo weighs 95 pounds, how much does the backpack filled with books weigh? Explain.
20 lb; 115 − 95 = 20.

❷ On Level

If Paulo weighs 95 pounds, about how many kilograms does the backpack weigh? Explain.
About 9 kg; 115 − 95 = 20 lb; each kilogram is a little more than 2 pounds but less than $2\frac{1}{2}$ pounds.

❸ Above Level

If Paulo weighs 95 pounds, about how many grams does the backpack weigh? Explain.
About 9,000 g; 115 − 95 = 20 lb; 20 lb is about 9 kg, and 9 kg × 1,000 = 9,000 g.

Intervention	Practice	Extension

Intervention

Activity Weight Benchmarks

Have students copy this table.

Object	Approximate Weight
Large bag of rice	1 kilogram
Two medium apples	1 pound
1 U.S. dollar bill	1 gram
5 new pencils	1 ounce
1 drop of water	1 milligram

Then have them use these benchmarks to estimate weights of various objects.

Practice

Comparing Units of Weight

❶ Put these weights in order from lightest to heaviest.

40 kg	1 kg	75 lb	100 g	1 lb	12 oz	3 tons
100 g	12 oz	1 lb	1 kg	75 lbs	40 kg	3 tons

Fill in each blank with a reasonable unit.

❷ An elephant weighs about 2 _____ tons _____

❸ An adult weighs about 70 _____ kilograms _____

❹ A newborn baby weighs about 7 _____ pounds _____

❺ A birthday card weighs about 1 _____ ounce _____

❻ A box of cereal weighs about 1 _____ pound _____

Test Prep

❼ Which number makes the number sentence true?

$36 \times 81 = 36 \times 80 + \blacksquare$

A. 30   **B.** 36   C. 80   D. 81

Practice P120

Extension

Comparing Units of Weight

Write the name of an object that weighs close to the given weight.

Many answers are possible. One such answer is given.

❶ 100 grams	small pad of paper
❷ 12 ounces	glass of water
❸ 1 pound	loaf of bread
❹ 10 pounds	empty suitcase with wheels
❺ 100 pounds	middle school student
❻ 10 kilograms	backpack stuffed with books
❼ 70 kilograms	adult
❽ 100 kilograms	filled bookshelf
❾ 1 ton	car
❿ 5 tons	truck

Extension E120

Spiral Review

Spiral Review Book page SR120 provides review of the following previously learned skills and concepts:

- adding and subtracting decimals in the context of finding distances
- solving problems using the strategy *look for a pattern*

You may wish to have students work with a partner to complete the page.

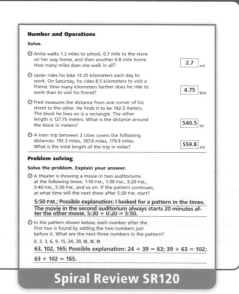

Number and Operations

Solve.

❶ Anita walks 1.2 miles to school, 0.7 mile to the store on her way home, and then another 0.8 mile home. How many miles does she walk in all?   **2.7** mi

❷ Javier rides his bike 13.25 kilometers each day to work. On Saturday, he rides 8.5 kilometers to visit a friend. How many kilometers farther does he ride to work than to visit his friend?   **4.75** km

❸ Fred measures the distance from one corner of his street to the other. He finds it to be 142.5 meters. The block he lives on is a rectangle. The other length is 127.75 meters. What is the distance around the block in meters?   **540.5** m

❹ A train trip between 3 cities covers the following distances: 192.3 miles, 187.6 miles, 179.9 miles. What is the total length of the trip in miles?   **559.8** mi

Problem solving

Solve the problem. Explain your answer.

❺ A theater is showing a movie in two auditoriums at the following times: 1:10 P.M., 1:30 P.M., 3:20 P.M., 3:40 P.M., 5:30 P.M., and so on. If the pattern continues, at what time will the next show after 5:30 P.M. start?

5:50 P.M.; Possible explanation: I looked for a pattern in the times. The movie in the second auditorium always starts 20 minutes after the other movie. 5:30 + 0:20 = 5:50.

❻ In the pattern shown below, each number after the first two is found by adding the two numbers just before it. What are the next three numbers in the pattern?

0, 3, 3, 6, 9, 15, 24, 39, ■, ■, ■

63, 102, 165; Possible explanation: 24 + 39 = 63; 39 + 63 = 102; 63 + 102 = 165.

Spiral Review SR120

Extension Activity
Cereal Conversions

Ask each student to bring an empty cereal box of any size to class. Have students work in small groups. Taking turns, each student tells the weight of his or her box in one type of unit (customary or metric) and challenges the other group members to estimate the weight in the other type of unit. When all students have presented their cereal boxes and discussed the results, have a representative of each group describe to the class the strategies they used.

Teacher's Notes 🍎

Daily Notes . . .

More Ideas

🗒 **Quick Notes**

Lesson 8 Using Equations and Inequalities to Compute and Estimate Weight

NCTM Standards 1, 2, 4, 6, 7, 8, 9, 10

Lesson Planner

STUDENT OBJECTIVES
- To write equations and inequalities to match pictures about weight
- To find and estimate weight from equations and inequalities

1 | Daily Activities (TG p. 1195)

Open-Ended Problem Solving/Headline Story	Skills Practice and Review— Estimating Weight

2 | Teach and Practice (TG pp. 1196–1200)

	MATERIALS
Ⓐ **Using Information From Scales to Estimate and Find Weight** (TG pp. 1196–1197)	• transparency of SH p. 248 (optional)
Ⓑ **Writing Equations to Match Pictures** (TG p. 1198)	• 📖 LAB pp. 297–298
	• 📖 SH pp. 248–249
Ⓒ **Using Variables to Compute and Estimate Weight** (TG p. 1199)	

3 | Differentiated Instruction (TG p. 1201)

Leveled Problem Solving (TG p. 1201)	Practice Book P121
Intervention Activity (TG p. 1201)	Extension Book E121
Extension Activity (TG p. 1201)	Spiral Review Book SR121

Lesson Notes

About the Lesson

In this lesson, students find and estimate weight in a new way. They look at pictures of balance scales with known weights on one side and unknown weights (hidden in bags) on the other. Depending on whether the scale is balanced or not, they either find exactly or estimate the unknown weight. They also write equations and inequalities to match the pictures.

About the Mathematics

Balance scales are designed to weigh exactly. Of course, though we say "exact," we realize that no measurement can be completely exact. In any event, when a scale is balanced, the weights on both sides can be said to be equal. If we know the weight on one side, we can determine the weight on the other. When a scale is not balanced, we can still garner approximate information about the

(continued on page R10)

Developing Mathematical Language

Vocabulary: equation, inequality

Any two objects can be the same size, or one can be larger or smaller than the other. The relationship between same-size objects or groups of objects can be represented by an *equation* with an equal sign (=) between the two amounts. The relationship between objects of different sizes can be represented by an *inequality* with an *inequality* symbol (> or <) between the two amounts. To help students differentiate between the two *inequality* symbols, have them think of alligator jaws that open up to the larger number and arrowheads that point to the smaller number.

Familiarize students with the terms *equation* and *inequality.*

Beginning Write the words *equal* and *equation* on the board. Have students circle the parts of the words that are the same. Point out that an *equation* always has an equal sign.

Intermediate Ask students how they can tell whether a number sentence is an *equation* or an *inequality.*

Advanced Write an expression on the board. Have students explain how to change the expression into an *inequality.*

Open-Ended Problem Solving

Read the Headline Story to the students. Encourage them to think of imaginative statements to make about the weights the ships can carry.

 Headline Story

> **Ship A can hold ■ tons. Ship B holds twice as many tons. Ship C holds 2,000 tons less than Ship B. Ship D holds half as many tons as Ship C. Ship E holds 5,000 tons more than Ship D.**

Possible response: If Ship A holds 5,000 tons, Ship B will hold 10,000 tons, Ship C 8,000 tons, Ship D 4,000 tons, and Ship E 9,000 tons. Ship D will hold the least amount of weight, Ship B the greatest amount. If Ship A holds 20,000 tons, Ship B will hold 40,000 tons, Ship C 38,000 tons, Ship D 19,000 tons, and Ship E 24,000 tons. Ship D will hold the least amount of weight, Ship B the greatest amount. If Ship A holds only 1 ton, Ship B will hold 2 tons, Ship C 0 tons, Ship D 0 tons, and Ship E 5,000 tons. Now Ships C and D will hold the least amount of weight and Ship E the greatest.

Skills Practice and Review

Estimating Weight

Materials
• Scale

Hold up a familiar object, a hardcover book, for example, and ask students to estimate its weight. (A book is likely to weigh somewhere between 1 and 3 pounds, or between 0.5 kg and about 1.5 kg.) After students make their estimates, check the weight on a scale. Continue with other objects, such as a paperback book, a marshmallow, a shoe, or a pencil. Ask students to make some of their estimates in metric units and some in customary units.

pairs

15 MIN

NCTM Standards 1, 2, 4, 6, 7, 8, 9, 10

A Using Information From Scales to Estimate and Find Weight

Purpose To practice estimating and calculating unknown weights

Introduce Students should work with partners on this activity. Give each student a copy of Explore: Mystery Bags. Explain that students will be using pictures of balance scales to estimate or find unknown weights.

Teacher Story

"I decided to set up a balance scale in my classroom with visible weights on one side and other weights, hidden in bags, on the other side. After students concluded what they could about the weight in each bag, we opened the bag to verify our conclusions. Acting out the situation helped students to understand the estimating strategy presented in the lesson."

Task Direct students to work with their partners to answer the questions on the page.

❶ 8 boxes balance a $\frac{1}{2}$-pound weight. What weight could be in each box? Why do you think so?

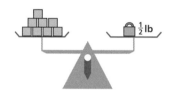

1 ounce; Possible explanation: The scale is balanced. Because 8 ounces equal half a pound and there are 8 boxes, each box must hold 8 ÷ 8 = 1 ounce.

❷ 3 bags are heavier than 3 kilograms.

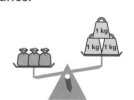

3 bags are a little lighter than 5 kilograms.

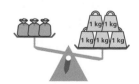

What weight could be in each bag? Why do you think so? Many answers are possible. One possible answer: 3 pounds; Possible explanation: Three bags would weigh 9 pounds, and 9 pounds is more than 3 kilograms but less than 5 kilograms.

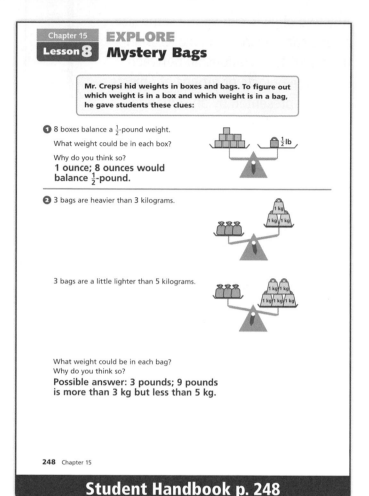

Chapter 15 **EXPLORE**

Lesson 8 **Mystery Bags**

Mr. Crepsi hid weights in boxes and bags. To figure out which weight is in a box and which weight is in a bag, he gave students these clues:

❶ 8 boxes balance a $\frac{1}{2}$-pound weight.

What weight could be in each box?

Why do you think so?
1 ounce; 8 ounces would balance $\frac{1}{2}$-pound.

❷ 3 bags are heavier than 3 kilograms.

3 bags are a little lighter than 5 kilograms.

What weight could be in each bag?
Why do you think so?
Possible answer: 3 pounds; 9 pounds is more than 3 kg but less than 5 kg.

248 Chapter 15

Student Handbook p. 248

Use with Lesson Activity Book pp. 297–298.

In Problem 2, students see that three of the mystery weights together weigh more than 3 kilograms but less than 5 kilograms. They can use the pictures to *estimate* the weight hidden in each bag. Students may reason that the weight in each bag must be more than 1 kilogram but less than 2 kilograms. If students remember that 1 kilogram is a little more than 2 pounds, they may reason that the hidden weight is about 3 pounds.

Share Ask students to share their strategies for answering the questions. Have them explain what each picture told them, and whether they needed all the pictures to answer the questions. Also, ask students why they could find an exact weight in Problem 1 but only an estimate of the weight in Problem 2. This discussion should prepare students for writing equations to describe these pictures in the next activity.

Talk Math

❷ A scale balances with 4 bags on one side and 1 pound on the other. What weight could be in each bag? Why do you think so? 4 ounces; Possible explanation: 1 pound is 16 ounces, which is divided among 4 bags. So, each bag must contain $16 \div 4 = 4$ ounces.

❷ 4 bags are heavier than 10 kilograms but lighter than 13 kilograms. What weight could be in each bag? Why do you think so? Many answers are possible. One possible answer: 6 pounds; Possible explanation: 4 bags must weigh about 12 kilograms, so one bag must weigh about $12 \div 4 = 3$ kilograms, or 6 pounds.

B **Writing Equations to Match Pictures**

Materials

• For the teacher: transparency of Explore: Mystery Bags (optional)

NCTM Standards 1, 2, 4, 6, 7, 8, 9, 10

Purpose To convert problem situations into equations and inequalities with variables

Introduce Students should remember what an equation is from Chapter 14, where they wrote equations to describe parts of a number puzzle. Nevertheless, remind them that an equation is a number sentence with variables. If you have a transparency of Explore: Mystery Bags, display the first picture. Otherwise, sketch the picture on the board.

Task **Challenge students to help you write an equation to describe the picture.** The picture shows a balanced scale. A weight of 8 boxes on the left equals a weight of $\frac{1}{2}$ pound on the right. Because the weights are equal, we can let x represent the weight of a box and write an *equation* to describe the picture:

$$8x = \tfrac{1}{2} \text{ lb}$$

From the previous activity, students know that x is equal to 1 ounce, so they have already solved this equation: $x = 1$ oz.

The second scale is not balanced. Therefore, we must write an *inequality* to describe the picture:

$$3x > 3 \text{ kg}$$

Students can use similar reasoning to write an inequality to describe the third picture:

$$3x < 5 \text{ kg}$$

Finally, have students compare the weight hidden in a box to the weight hidden in a bag. Although students do not know the exact weight in a bag, they can still say that there is more weight in a bag than in a box, because 1 bag is more than 1 kilogram, which is more than 1 ounce.

Talk Math

❓ A balanced scale has 5 boxes on the left and 20 pounds on the right. What equation can you write to describe the situation? What is the solution of the equation? How did you find the solution? $5x = 20$; $x = 4$ pounds; Possible explanation: I looked for a number which, when multiplied by 5, gave the product 20. That number is 4.

❓ An unbalanced scale has 4 bags on the left and 10 kilograms on the right. The 4 bags are slightly heavier than the 10 kilograms. What inequality can you write to describe the situation? $4x > 10$ kg

Using Variables to Compute and Estimate Weight LAB pp. 297–298

Purpose To use pictures and equations to find unknown weights

NCTM Standards 1, 2, 4, 6, 7, 8, 9, 10

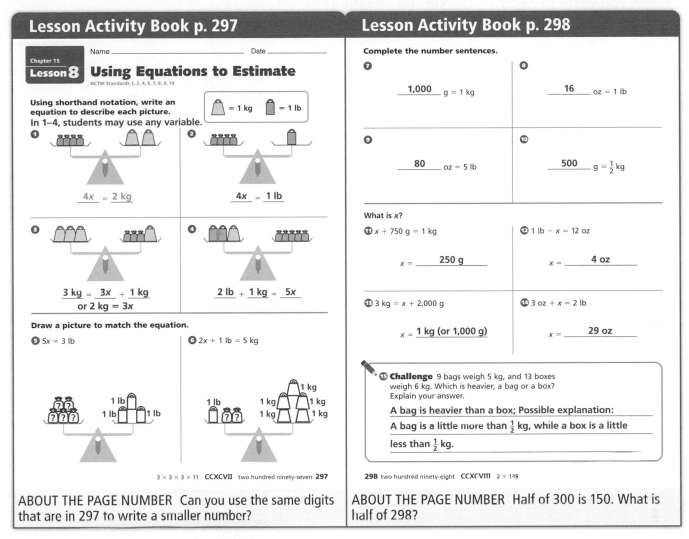

Lesson Activity Book p. 297

Name _____ Date _____

Chapter 15
Lesson 8 Using Equations to Estimate
NCTM Standards 1, 2, 4, 6, 7, 8, 9, 10

Using shorthand notation, write an equation to describe each picture. In 1–4, students may use any variable.

⬜ = 1 kg   🔲 = 1 lb

1 $4x = 2$ kg

2 $4x = 1$ lb

3 3 kg $= 3x + 1$ kg
or 2 kg $= 3x$

4 2 lb $+ 1$ kg $= 5x$

Draw a picture to match the equation.

5 $5x = 3$ lb

6 $2x + 1$ lb $= 5$ kg

3 × 3 × 3 × 11   CCXCVII   two hundred ninety-seven   **297**

ABOUT THE PAGE NUMBER Can you use the same digits that are in 297 to write a smaller number?

Lesson Activity Book p. 298

Complete the number sentences.

7 $1,000$ g $= 1$ kg

8 16 oz $= 1$ lb

9 80 oz $= 5$ lb

10 500 g $= \frac{1}{2}$ kg

What is x?

11 $x + 750$ g $= 1$ kg
$x =$ 250 g

12 1 lb $- x = 12$ oz
$x =$ 4 oz

13 3 kg $= x + 2,000$ g
$x =$ 1 kg (or $1,000$ g)

14 3 oz $+ x = 2$ lb
$x =$ 29 oz

15 Challenge 9 bags weigh 5 kg, and 13 boxes weigh 6 kg. Which is heavier, a bag or a box? Explain your answer.

A bag is heavier than a box; Possible explanation:
A bag is a little more than $\frac{1}{2}$ kg, while a box is a little less than $\frac{1}{2}$ kg.

298 two hundred ninety-eight   CCXCVIII   2 × 149

ABOUT THE PAGE NUMBER Half of 300 is 150. What is half of 298?

Teaching Notes for LAB page 297

Have students work on the page individually or with partners. At the top of the page, students write equations to describe pictures. They may use any variables that they choose in their equations. The answers given use the variable x, but students might use other letters or shapes. At the bottom of the page, students draw pictures to match given equations.

Teaching Notes for LAB page 298

Students are asked to find exact missing weights. They can use estimation to check that their answers make sense.

Challenge Problem The Challenge Problem can be solved by estimating the approximate weight of a bag or a box. Students are discouraged from finding exact weights because the numbers chosen are inconvenient.

Reflect and Summarize the Lesson

Write Math A balanced scale has 3 identical boxes on the left and 12 kilograms on the right. When the 3 boxes are transferred to the left side of another scale, the boxes are heavier than the 20 pounds on the right side of the scale. What equation can you write to describe the first situation? What inequality can you write to describe the second situation? $3x = 12$ kg; $3x > 20$ lb

Review Model . . . .

Refer students to Review Model: Writing Equations and Inequalities in the *Student Handbook*, p. 249, to see how they can use equations and inequalities to represent the relation between weights on a scale.

✔ Check for Understanding

❶ $3x = 9$ kg

❷ $8x < 24$ oz

❸ 40 oz $= 2\frac{1}{2}$ lb

❹ 5 lb > 2 kg

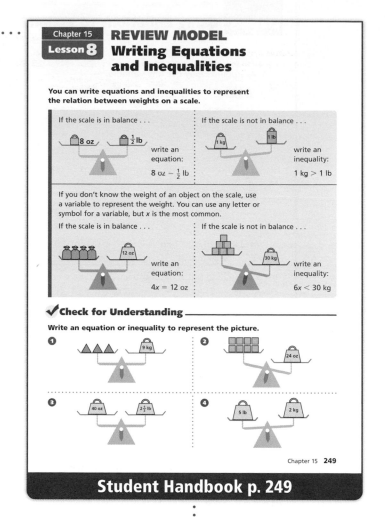

Student Handbook p. 249

Leveled Problem Solving

Dana puts 6 identical bags on one side of a balance scale and three 1-kg weights on the other. The scale balances.

❶ Basic Level

What is the weight of each bag in kilograms? Explain $\frac{1}{2}$ kg; 2 bags would balance 1 kg, so each bag is equivalent to $\frac{1}{2}$ kg.

❷ On Level

Write an equation with a variable that describes what is on the scale. Explain. $6x = 3$; If the variable is x, then there is 6 times that weight, or $6x$, on one side, and 3 kg on the other.

❸ Above Level

Dana takes 1 bag off the scale. Write an inequality to explain what the scale shows now. Explain. $3 \text{ kg} > 5x$; The three 1-kg weights are heavier than the 5 bags.

Intervention	**Practice**	**Extension**

Activity Balancing Act

Place an unequal number of counters on two sides of a balance scale. Have a student write a related inequality on the board. Under the inequality, write a related equation. For example, if the inequality is $4 < 11$, the equation might be $n + 4 = 11$ or $4 = 11 - n$. Then have a student add or remove counters to get the scale to balance. Invite students to continue with other groups of counters.

Using Equations to Estimate

Solve.

❶ If 7 bags weigh 15 kilograms, is 1 bag more than 2 kilograms? (Yes) No

❷ If 7 bags weigh 15 kilograms, are 10 bags more than 17 kilograms? (Yes) No

❸ If 6 bags weigh 10 kilograms, are 10 bags more than 20 kilograms? Yes (No)

❹ If 10 bags weigh 5 kilograms, is 1 bag more than 1 kilogram? Yes (No)

❺ If 15 bags weigh 13 kilograms, are 21 bags more than 25 kilograms? Yes (No)

Test Prep

❻ If $y = 3x - 18$ and $x = 12$, what is y? Explain how you found the answer.

18; Possible explanation: I replaced x in the equation $y = 3x - 18$ with 12. So, $y = 3 \times 12 - 18 = 36 - 18 = 18$.

Practice P121

Using Equations to Estimate

Solve.

❶ If 8 bags weigh 10 kg and 7 boxes weigh 11 kg, which is heavier, a bag or a box? _____ box

❷ If 12 bags weigh 20 kg and 15 boxes weigh 30 kg, which is heavier, a bag or a box? _____ box

❸ If 21 bags weigh 15 lb and 19 boxes weigh 16 lb, which is heavier, a bag or a box? _____ box

❹ If 5 bags weigh 6 lb and 6 boxes weigh 5 lb, which is heavier, a bag or a box? _____ bag

❺ If 16 bags weigh 4 lb and 24 boxes weigh 8 lb, which is heavier, a bag or a box? _____ box

❻ If 10 bags weigh 9 lb and 11 boxes weigh 10 lb, which is heavier, a bag or a box? _____ box

Extension E121

Spiral Review

Spiral Review Book page SR121 provides review of the following previously learned skills and concepts:

- generalizing a multiplication pattern using variables

- converting between inches, feet, and yards and thereby practicing multiplication and division

You may wish to have students work with a partner to complete the page.

Algebra

Find the products.

❶ $12 \times 12 =$ **144**   ❹ $14 \times 14 =$ **196**

$11 \times 13 =$ **143** $13 \times 15 =$ **195**

❷ $21 \times 21 =$ **441**   ❺ $16 \times 16 =$ **256**

$20 \times 22 =$ **440** $15 \times 17 =$ **255**

❸ $31 \times 31 =$ **961**   ❻ $25 \times 25 =$ **625**

$30 \times 32 =$ **960** $24 \times 26 =$ **624**

❹ $27 \times 27 =$ **729**   ❼ $42 \times 42 =$ **1,764**

$26 \times 28 =$ **728** $41 \times 43 =$ **1,763**

❺ $36 \times 36 =$ **1,296**   ❽ $53 \times 53 =$ **2,809**

$35 \times 37 =$ **1,295** $52 \times 54 =$ **2,808**

Measurement

Write the equivalent measure.

❶ 48 inches = **4** feet   ❼ 3 yard = **108** inches

❷ 6 feet = **72** inches   ❽ 60 inches = **5** feet

❸ 96 inches = **8** feet   ❾ 35 feet = **420** inches

❹ 11 yards = **396** inches   ❿ 39 feet = **13** yards

❺ 132 inches = **11** feet   ⓫ 252 inches = **7** yards

Spiral Review SR121

Extension Activity
Balancing Equations

Direct small groups of students to create diagrams of equations and inequalities depicting a balance scale. Have them draw several metric or customary weights (kilograms or pounds) on one side of the scale, and several identical unknowns on the other. The scale can, but does not have to, balance. For each diagram, have them write the corresponding equation or inequality. Students can then estimate the weights of each unknown using the picture and equation or inequality.

Lesson 9 Problem Solving Strategy and Test Prep

NCTM Standards 1, 2, 4, 6, 7, 8, 9, 10

Lesson Planner

STUDENT OBJECTIVES ·
- To practice the problem solving strategy *act it out*
- To articulate the steps and strategies used to solve problems
- To prepare for standardized tests

Problem Solving Strategy: Act It Out (TG pp. 1203–1204, 1206–1207)

MATERIALS

Ⓐ **Discussing the Problem Solving Strategy: Act It Out** (TG p. 1203)

Ⓑ **Solving Problems by Applying the Strategy** (TG p. 1204)

-  LAB p. 299
- 📖 SH pp. 250–251

Problem Solving Test Prep (TG p. 1205)

Ⓒ **Getting Ready for Standardized Tests** (TG p. 1205)

- LAB p. 300

Lesson Notes

About Problem Solving

Problem Solving Strategy: Act It Out

Throughout this chapter students have estimated lengths, areas, capacities, and weights. To check their estimates, they sometimes acted out measurement strategies. This lesson focuses on the problem solving strategy *act it out,* and does so both in the context of measurement and outside that context.

Skills Practice and Review

Points on the Number Line

Draw a short segment of a number line on the board, from 11 to 15, for example. Make the line long enough so there is room for labeling points between whole numbers. State a number containing a fraction or a decimal that lies on the line. Have a student point to and label the approximate spot on the line where the number would fall. Next, indicate a spot on the line and ask a student to identify the approximate point you are pointing to. Be as clear as possible about the location of the point on the line. Repeat with other numbers and points.

Use with Lesson Activity Book pp. 299–300.

Problem Solving Strategy

(A) Discussing the Problem Solving Strategy: Act It Out

NCTM standards 1, 4, 6, 7, 8, 9, 10

Purpose To share strategies for solving problems and focus on the problem solving strategy *act it out.*

Introduce Remind students that throughout this chapter, they have used scales and pictures of scales to estimate, compare, check, and calculate weights. To perform any such activity is to *act it out.* You may wish to draw a parallel between *acting it out* to solving a math problem and performing a scientific experiment to collect data. Both are hands-on activities that look at how something works in real-life rather than in theory.

Problem Mark has 7 coins in his pocket. All are the same type (pennies, nickels, dimes, quarters, or half dollars). Together they weigh 35 grams. He wrote the equation $7x = 35$ grams to describe the situation. How can you find out which type of coin he has, and use the answer to solve the equation?

Share Ask students to share their strategies for solving the problem. *Act it out* is a good strategy to try, because you can use weights, coins, and a balance scale to find which type of coin, in a group of 7, weighs 35 grams.

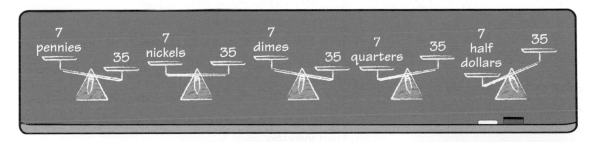

The balanced scale, second from the left above, shows that 7 nickels weigh 35 grams. The scale at the right shows that 1 nickel weighs 5 grams. So the solution to the equation $7x = 35$ grams is $x = 5$ grams.

Talk Math

- ❓ What equation or inequality could you write to describe the picture of 7 dimes above? the picture of 7 quarters? $7x < 35$ grams; $7x > 35$ grams

- ❓ What other strategy could you use to solve the equation $7x = 35$ grams? Possible answer: *guess and check*

Solving Problems by Applying the Strategy LAB p. 299

Purpose To share strategies for solving problems and focus on the problem solving strategy *act it out.*

Teaching Notes for LAB page 299

Students practice the problem solving strategy *act it out* by solving each of the problems independently or in pairs. Help students get started with Problem 1 by asking questions such as the following:

Read to Understand

What do you need to find out? whether 27¢, 30¢, 11¢, and 37¢ can be made exactly using only 3¢ and 7¢ stamps

Plan

How can you solve this problem? Think about the strategies you might use.

How could you act out the problem? Possible answer: Take three cards that say "3 cents" on them and three that say "7 cents" on them. Give them to six students and have them arrange themselves in different combinations. You might instead want to assign an "arranger" role to an additional student, who groups students to represent different total values.

Solve

What are the results when you *act it out?* You could put three students with 7¢ stamps and two students with 3¢ stamps together to make 27¢ of postage. You could put three students with 7¢ stamps and three students with 3¢ stamps together to make 30¢, which is 3¢ more than 27¢. Similarly, you could add one more student with a 7¢ stamp to the 30¢ group to make 37¢. There is no way to arrange the students to make 11¢.

Check

Look back at the original problem. Did you answer the questions that were asked? Do your answers make sense? How do you know?

Students can use this method to solve the other problem on the page. Supplement the above questions with ones that are specifically tailored to Problem 2.

Lesson Activity Book p. 299

Name _____ Date _____

Chapter 15
Lesson 9 **Problem Solving Strategy**
Act It Out
NCTM Standards 1, 2, 4, 6, 7, 8, 9, 10

Understand
Plan
Solve
Check

❶ Xavier has several 3¢ stamps and 7¢ stamps in his desk drawer. He has weighed several letters and knows what postage each one needs. Can he use only the stamps he already has and put the exact postage on each letter?

A

yes (three 7¢ stamps + two 3¢ stamps)

27¢

B

no

11¢

C

yes (ten 3¢ stamps, or three 7¢ stamps + three 3¢ stamps)

30¢

D

yes (one more 7¢ stamp than the stamps used to make 30¢)

37¢

❷ Sally is taller than Jake and Laura. Miguel is taller than Jake but shorter than Laura. Selby is shorter than Jake. Robert is taller than Sally. Put these six students in order from shortest to tallest.

Selby , Jake , Miguel , Laura , Sally , Robert

13 × 23   **CCXCIX**   two hundred ninety-nine **299**

ABOUT THE PAGE NUMBER To add this number, add 300 and then take away 1.

Reflect and Summarize the Lesson

Write Math

What advantage does solving a problem by *acting it out* with other students have over solving the problem alone? Possible response: Group members can put their ideas together to see solutions that none might have seen working alone.

Use with Lesson Activity Book pp. 299–300.

Problem Solving Test Prep

(C) Getting Ready for Standardized Tests LAB p. 300

Purpose To prepare students for standardized tests

NCTM standards 1, 4, 6, 7, 8, 9, 10

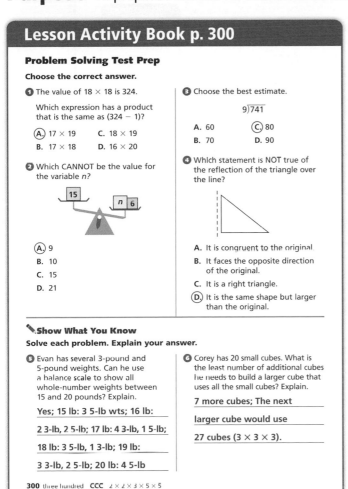

Lesson Activity Book p. 300

Problem Solving Test Prep

Choose the correct answer.

1 The value of 18 × 18 is 324.

Which expression has a product that is the same as (324 − 1)?

(A.) 17 × 19   C. 18 × 19

B. 17 × 18   D. 16 × 20

2 Which CANNOT be the value for the variable *n*?

[balance scale: 15 | n 6]

(A.) 9
B. 10
C. 15
D. 21

3 Choose the best estimate.

9)741

A. 60   (C.) 80
B. 70   D. 90

4 Which statement is NOT true of the reflection of the triangle over the line?

[triangle figure]

A. It is congruent to the original.
B. It faces the opposite direction of the original.
C. It is a right triangle.
(D.) It is the same shape but larger than the original.

Show What You Know

Solve each problem. Explain your answer.

5 Evan has several 3-pound and 5-pound weights. Can he use a balance scale to show all whole-number weights between 15 and 20 pounds? Explain.

Yes; 15 lb: 3 5-lb wts; 16 lb:

2 3-lb, 2 5-lb; 17 lb: 4 3-lb, 1 5-lb;

18 lb: 3 5-lb, 1 3-lb; 19 lb:

3 3-lb, 2 5-lb; 20 lb: 4 5-lb

6 Corey has 20 small cubes. What is the least number of additional cubes he needs to build a larger cube that uses all the small cubes? Explain.

7 more cubes; The next

larger cube would use

27 cubes (3 × 3 × 3).

300 three hundred   CCC   2 × 2 × 3 × 5 × 5

ABOUT THE PAGE NUMBER 300 is a triangular number: 1 + 2 + ... + 24. It has a horizontal line of symmetry.

Teaching Notes for LAB page 300

The test items on this page are written in the same style and arranged in the same format as those on many state assessments. The page is cumulative and is designed for students to apply a variety of problem solving strategies, including *act it out*. Have students share the strategies they use.

The Item Analysis Chart below highlights one of the possible strategies that may be used for each test item.

Show What You Know

Short Response

Direct students' attention to Problems 5 and 6. Explain that they must decide how to solve the problems. They can act out Problem 5 using 3-penny and 5-penny stacks to represent the weights. They can act out Problem 6 using inch cubes or centimeter cubes. Then have students write an explanation of how they know their answer is correct. To provide more space for students to communicate their thinking about these problems, you may wish to have them write their responses and explanations on a separate sheet of paper. Use the Scoring Rubric below to evaluate their understanding.

Item Analysis Chart

Item	Strategy
1	Guess and check
2	Act it out
3	Solve a simpler problem
4	Draw a picture
5	Act it out
6	Act it out

Scoring Rubric

2	• Demonstrates complete understanding of the problem and chooses an appropriate strategy to determine the solution
1	• Demonstrates a partial understanding of the problem and chooses a strategy that does not lead to a complete and accurate solution
0	• Demonstrates little understanding of the problem and shows little evidence of using any strategy to determine a solution

Review Model

Refer students to the Problem Solving Strategy Review Model: *Act It Out* in the **Student Handbook,** pp. 250–251, to review a model of the four steps they can use with problem solving strategy *act it out.*

Additional problem solving practice is also provided.

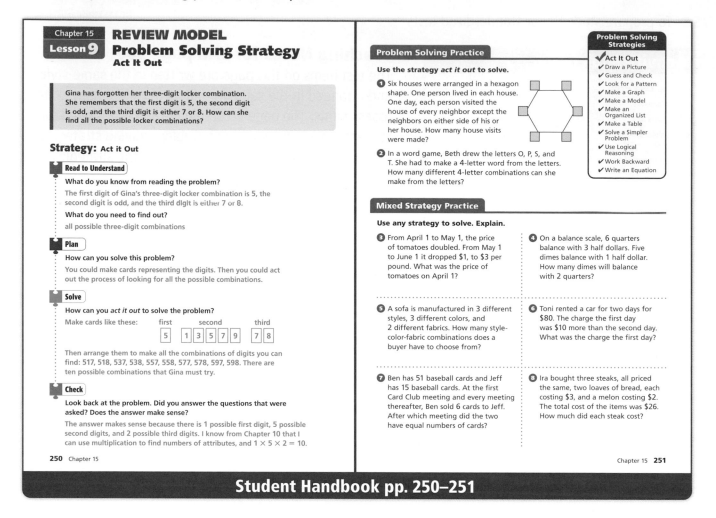

Student Handbook pp. 250–251

Task Have students read the problem at the top of the Review Model page. Then discuss.

💬 Talk Math

❓ How can Gina open the lock? Possible answer: by finding all possible three-digit combinations, and trying each until one opens the lock

❓ When arranging cards to act out the problem, how can you be sure you find every combination? Possible answer: The first number must be 5. Combine it first with 1 and then each of the two possible third numbers, 7 and 8. Then pair it with 3, along with 7 and 8. Follow with 5 along with 7 and 8, 7 along with 7 and 8, and 9 along with 7 and 8.

Problem Solving Practice

1. 18; Possible explanation: You can *act it out* to solve the problem. Place six objects in the shape of a hexagon, and move each to the houses that are not beside it, keeping track of the total number of moves.

2. 24; Possible explanation: You can *act it out* to solve the problem. Write the letters O, P, T, and S on four cards, one letter to a card. Then arrange the cards in all possible four-letter combinations.

Mixed Strategy Practice

3. \$2 per pound; Possible explanation: You can *work backward* to solve the problem. To find the May 1 price, add $\$3 + \$1 = \$4$. To find the April 1 price, divide by 2: $\$4 \div 2 = \$2$.

4. 5 dimes; Possible explanation: You can *act it out* to solve the problem. Balance a ruler on a pencil. Find how many dimes will balance 2 quarters. Or *use logical reasoning*: If 6 quarters balance 3 half dollars, 2 quarters balance 1 half dollar, which balances 5 dimes.

5. 18 combinations: Possible explanation: You can *make an organized list* to solve the problem. Let S1, S2, and S3 represent the styles, C1, C2, and C3 the colors, and F1 and F2 the fabrics. List all possible style-color-fabric combinations of the symbols.

6. \$45; Possible explanation: You can *guess and check* to solve the problem. Guess different possible first-day charges and see whether the second-day charge is \$10 less. If it is not, adjust your guess and check again.

7. the third meeting; Possible explanation: You can *make a table* to solve the problem. For each meeting decrease the number in Ben's row by 6. Increase the number in Jeff's row by 6.

Meeting	1	2	3
Ben	$51 - 6 = 45$	$45 - 6 = 39$	$39 - 6 = 33$
Jeff	$15 + 6 = 21$	$21 + 6 = 27$	$27 + 6 = 33$

8. \$6; Possible explanation: You can *work backward* from the total price to solve the problem. The three steaks must have cost \$26 − \$2 (melon) − \$6 (2 loaves of bread), or \$18. $\$18 \div 3$ steaks $= \$6$.

Estimation

NCTM Standards 1, 2, 4, 6, 7, 8, 9, 10

Purpose To provide students with an opportunity to demonstrate understanding of Chapter 15 concepts and skills

MATERIALS

• LAB pp. 301–302
• Chapter 15 Test
(Assessment Guide pp. AG121–AG122)

Chapter 15 Learning Goals and Assessment Options

These learning goals are assessed in many ways throughout the chapter. The chart below correlates each learning goal to specific formal and informal assessment options.

	Learning Goals	Lesson Number	Snapshot Assessment	Chapter Review Item Numbers	Chapter Test Item Numbers
				LAB pp. 301–302	Assessment Guide pp. AG121–AG122
15-A	Use rounding and compatible numbers to estimate solutions.	15.1	1, 5, 8, 9	1–4	1–4
15-B	Estimate and find perimeter, area, capacity, and weight using standard and customary units.	15.2–15.4, 15.6	2, 10	5–8	5–8
15-C	Convert between units of capacity and units of weight.	15.5, 15.7	3, 6	9–16	9–11
15-D	Estimate weight with equations or inequalities and pictorial models.	15.8	4, 7	18–19	12–13
15-E	Apply problem solving strategies such as *act it out* to solve problems.	15.9	11, 12	17	14

Snapshot Assessment

The following Mental Math and Quick Write questions and tasks provide a quick, informal assessment of students' understanding of Chapter 15 concepts, skills, and problem solving strategies.

whole class 10 MIN

Mental Math This oral assessment uses mental math strategies and can be used with the whole class.

❶ Describe two different ways to estimate this difference: 1,969 − 813. Possible answer: One way is to round 1,969 to 2,000 and round 813 to 800, then subtract 2,000 − 800 = 1,200. Another way is to use compatible numbers. Subtract 20 − 8 to find the number of hundreds in the answer, 12. My answer is 1,200.
(Learning Goal 15-A)

❷ Estimate the perimeter of your desk, using the length of your pencil. Answers will vary, depending upon desk size; accept reasonable answers; allow for different pencil lengths.

Is the estimate reasonable?

• Area of a 7-foot square is 100 square feet. no
• 3 books weigh 100 pounds. no
• 15 paper clips weigh 10 grams. yes
(Learning Goal 15-B)

3 Which is bigger?
- a quart or a liter liter
- 5 pints or 2 liters 5 pints
- 3 quarts or 1 gallon 1 gallon
(Learning Goal 15-C)

4 A scale balances with 12 pounds on one side and 4 boxes on the other. How much does each box weigh? How do you know? 3 pounds; Possible explanation: $12 \div 4 = 3$, so there must be 3 pounds in each box.
(Learning Goal 15-D)

Quick Write This informal written assessment can be administered to small groups or the whole class. Read each question and have the students record responses on their write-on boards. Encourage students to listen and think about the questions before responding.

5 What numbers would you use in estimating the sum of $14.79 + $32.13? Possible answer: $15 + $32
(Learning Goal 15-A)

6 Which is bigger, 2 liters or $\frac{1}{2}$ gallon? 2 liters
Which is bigger, a kilogram or a pound? 1 kilogram
(Learning Goal 15-C)

7 2 pouches are heavier than 75 grams, but less than 100 grams. What weight could be in each pouch? Possible answer: 40 grams; accept anything between 38 grams and 49.5 grams.
(Learning Goal 15-D)

8 Use compatible numbers to estimate the sum of $30 + 52 + 70 + 13$. Explain your reasoning. Possible explanation: Add $30 + 70 = 100$ since they are compatible; round 52 to 50 and 13 to 10; add $50 + 10 = 60$. Now add 100 and 60 for an estimate of 160.
(Learning Goal 15-A)

9 Mr. Frank's class collects 316 cans for the fund raiser. Mr. Rush's class collects 472 cans, and Miss Long's class collects 380 cans. Estimate how many cans are collected. Use pictures, numbers, or words to explain your answer. Possible estimate: Round 316 to 300, round 472 to 500, round 380 to 400, then add $300 + 500 + 400 = 1,200$.
(Learning Goal 15-A)

10 A rectangular outdoor field measures about 37 meters by about 49 meters. What is the approximate perimeter of the field? Explain your reasoning. Possible answer: Round 37 to 40 and round 49 to 50. Add $40 + 40 + 50 + 50 = 180$ meters.
(Learning Goal 15-B)

11 Morey has $63.00. He wants to buy as many model cars as he can. If each car costs $8.75, about how many cars can he buy? Use pictures, numbers, or words to explain your answer. 7; Possible explanation: round $8.75 to $9.00. There are 7 groups of $9.00 in $63.00.
(Learning Goal 15-E)

12 A balanced scale has 3 yellow bags on the left and 5 red bags on the right. Find one solution for how much each yellow bag weighs and how much each red bag weighs. Use metric weight. Use pictures, numbers, or words to explain your answer. Possible answer: Each yellow bag weighs 5 g and each red bag weighs 3 g; $3 \times 5 = 15$ g for yellow, and $5 \times 3 = 15$ g for red.
(Learning Goal 15-E)

Formal Assessment

Chapter Review/Assessment The Chapter 15 Review/Assessment on *Lesson Activity Book* pages 301–302 assesses students' understanding of computation in puzzles and tables and problem solving. Students should be able to complete these pages independently.

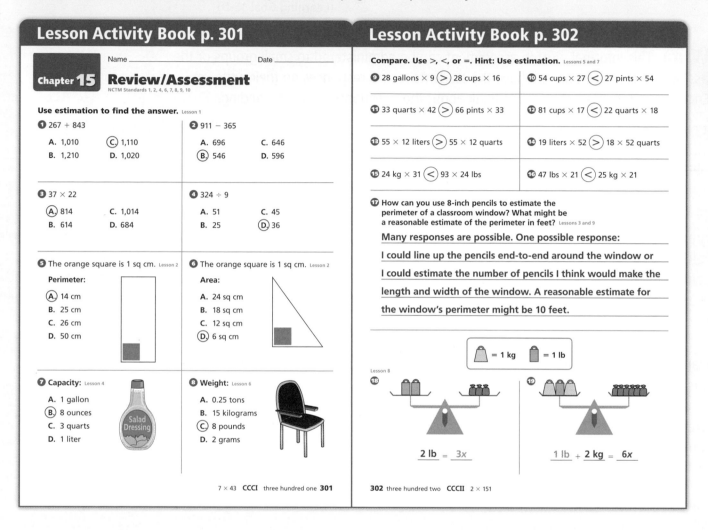

Lesson Activity Book p. 301

Name _____ Date _____

Chapter 15 Review/Assessment
NCTM Standards 1, 2, 4, 6, 7, 8, 9, 10

Use estimation to find the answer. Lesson 1

1 267 + 843
  A. 1,010   **C.** 1,110
  B. 1,210   D. 1,020

2 911 − 365
  A. 696   C. 646
  B. 546   D. 596

3 37 × 22
  A. 814   C. 1,014
  B. 614   D. 684

4 324 ÷ 9
  A. 51   C. 45
  B. 25   **D.** 36

5 The orange square is 1 sq cm. Lesson 2
  Perimeter:
  A. 14 cm
  B. 25 cm
  C. 26 cm
  D. 50 cm

6 The orange square is 1 sq cm. Lesson 2
  Area:
  A. 24 sq cm
  B. 18 sq cm
  C. 12 sq cm
  D. 6 sq cm

7 Capacity: Lesson 4
  A. 1 gallon
  B. 8 ounces
  C. 3 quarts
  D. 1 liter

8 Weight: Lesson 6
  A. 0.25 tons
  B. 15 kilograms
  C. 8 pounds
  D. 2 grams

7 × 43 **CCCI** three hundred one **301**

Lesson Activity Book p. 302

Compare. Use >, <, or =. Hint: Use estimation. Lessons 5 and 7

9 28 gallons × 9 ⊙> 28 cups × 16

10 54 cups × 27 ⊙< 27 pints × 54

11 33 quarts × 42 ⊙> 66 pints × 33

12 81 cups × 17 ⊙< 22 quarts × 18

13 55 × 12 liters ⊙> 55 × 12 quarts

14 19 liters × 52 ⊙> 18 × 52 quarts

15 24 kg × 31 ⊙< 93 × 24 lbs

16 47 lbs × 21 ⊙< 25 kg × 21

17 How can you use 8-inch pencils to estimate the perimeter of a classroom window? What might be a reasonable estimate of the perimeter in feet? Lessons 3 and 9

Many responses are possible. One possible response:

I could line up the pencils end-to-end around the window or

I could estimate the number of pencils I think would make the

length and width of the window. A reasonable estimate for

the window's perimeter might be 10 feet.

= 1 kg   = 1 lb

Lesson 8

18 **2 lb** = **3x**

19 **1 lb** + **2 kg** = **6x**

302 three hundred two **CCCII** 2 × 151

Extra Support Students who have difficulty with items on the Chapter 15 Review/Assessment may need review of the lesson where development of the concept was provided. You can use the Intervention Activity to increase students' understanding before the Chapter Test is given.

Chapter Test Use the Chapter 15 Test in the *Assessment Guide* to assess concepts, skills, and problem solving from the chapter and to prepare students for standardized tests. The Chapter Test and other test items are also available online.

Chapter Notes

 Quick Notes

More Ideas

Table of Measures

METRIC	CUSTOMARY
LENGTH	
1 centimeter (cm) = 10 millimeters (mm)	1 foot (ft) = 12 inches (in.)
1 decimeter (dm) = 10 centimeters	1 yard (yd) = 3 feet, or 36 inches
1 meter (m) = 100 centimeters (cm)	1 mile (mi) = 1,760 yards, or 5,280 feet
1 kilometer (km) = 1,000 meters	
CAPACITY	
1 liter (L) = 1,000 milliliters (mL)	1 tablespoon (tbsp) = 3 teaspoons (tsp)
	1 cup (c) = 8 fluid ounces (fl oz)
	1 pint (pt) = 2 cups
	1 quart (qt) = 2 pints
	1 gallon (gal) = 4 quarts
MASS/WEIGHT	
1 gram (g) = 1,000 milligrams (mg)	1 pound (lb) = 16 ounces (oz)
1 kilogram (kg) = 1,000 grams	1 ton (T) = 2,000 pounds

METRIC-CUSTOMARY COMPARISONS

Length: 1 meter is a little more than 1 yard (1 meter is about 1.09 yards)

Capacity: 1 liter is a little more than 1 quart (1 liter is about 1.06 quarts)

Mass/Weight: 1 kilogram is about 2.2 pounds

TIME	MONEY
1 minute (min) = 60 seconds (sec)	1 penny = 1 cent (¢)
1 hour (hr) = 60 minutes	1 nickel = 5 cents
1 day = 24 hours	1 dime = 10 cents
1 week (wk) = 7 days	1 quarter = 25 cents
1 year (yr) = 12 months (mo), or about 52 weeks	1 half dollar = 50 cents
1 year = 365 days	1 dollar ($) = 100 cents
1 leap year = 366 days	

SYMBOLS

$<$	is less than	°	degree	$^{-}8$	negative 8
$>$	is greater than	°F	degrees Fahrenheit	(2,3)	ordered pair (x,y)
$=$	is equal to	°C	degrees Celsius	%	percent
$\neq$	is not equal to	$^{+}8$	positive 8		

FORMULAS

Perimeter of polygon = sum of length of sides

Perimeter of rectangle $P = (2 \times l) + (2 \times w)$
$= 2 \times (l + w)$

Perimeter of square $P = 4 \times s$

Area of rectangle $A = l \times w$

Volume of rectangular prism $V = l \times w \times h$

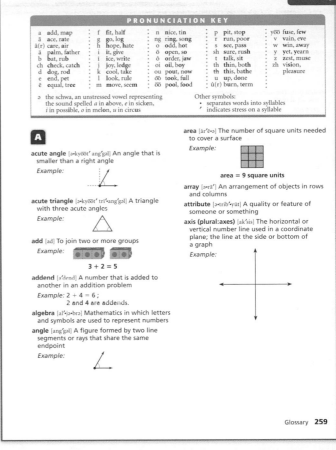

PRONUNCIATION KEY

a	add, map	f	fit, half	n	nice, tin	p	pit, stop	yōō	fuse, few
ā	ace, rate	g	go, log	ng	ring, song	r	run, poor	v	vain, eve
â(r)	care, air	h	hope, hate	o	odd, hot	s	see, pass	w	win, away
ä	palm, father	i	it, give	ō	open, so	sh	sure, rush	y	yet, yearn
b	bat, rub	ī	ice, write	ô	order, jaw	t	talk, sit	z	zest, muse
ch	check, catch	j	joy, ledge	oi	oil, boy	th	thin, both	zh	vision,
d	dog, rod	k	cool, take	ou	pout, now	th	this, bathe		pleasure
e	end, pet	l	look, rule	ōō	took, full	u	up, done		
ē	equal, tree	m	move, seem	ōō	pool, food	û(r)	burn, term		

ə the schwa, an unstressed vowel representing the sound spelled *a* in *above*, *e* in *sicken*, *i* in *possible*, *o* in *melon*, *u* in *circus*

Other symbols:
• separates words into syllables
ʹ indicates stress on a syllable

A

acute angle [ə·kyōōt′ ang′gəl] An angle that is smaller than a right angle

Example:

acute triangle [ə·kyōōt′ trī′ang′gəl] A triangle with three acute angles

Example:

add [ad] To join two or more groups

Example:

$3 + 2 = 5$

addend [aʹdend] A number that is added to another in an addition problem

Example: $2 + 4 = 6$;
2 and 4 are addends.

algebra [al′·jə·brə] Mathematics in which letters and symbols are used to represent numbers

angle [ang′gəl] A figure formed by two line segments or rays that share the same endpoint

Example:

area [âr′ē·ə] The number of square units needed to cover a surface

Example:

area = 9 square units

array [ə·rā′] An arrangement of objects in rows and columns

attribute [ə·trib′·yūt] A quality or feature of someone or something

axis (plural:axes) [ak′sis] The horizontal or vertical number line used in a coordinate plane; the line at the side or bottom of a graph

Example:

B

bar graph [bär graf] A graph that uses bars to show data

base [bās] A number used as a repeated factor

Example: $8^3 = 8 \times 8 \times 8$. The base is 8.

base-seven [bās sev′ən] A place value system in which the greatest single-digit number is 6

base-ten [bās ten] see base-ten system

base-ten system [bās ten sis′təm] A place value system in which numbers are expressed using the numerals 0 to 9 and successive powers of 10

C

capacity [kə·pas′ə·tē] The amount a container can hold when filled

centimeter (cm) [sän′tə·mē′·tər] A metric unit for measuring length or distance
100 centimeters = 1 meter

Example:

1 centimeter

certain [sûr′tən] An event is certain if it will always happen

chart [chärt] Any display of data

column [ko·ləm] A vertical line in an array

Example:

↓column
○○○○
○○○○
○○○○
○○○○
○○○○
○○○○

combine [kəm·bīn′] To put together

comma [kom′ə] The symbol used in large numbers to separate the hundreds from the thousands, the thousands from the millions, and so on

Example:

125,452,300

↓
Commas

commutative property [kə·myōō′tə·tiv prop′ər·tē] The property that states that when the order of addends or factors is changed, the sum or product is the same

Example: $9 + 4 = 4 + 9$.
$6 \times 3 = 3 \times 6$

compare [kəm·pâr′] To describe whether numbers are equal to, less than, or greater than each other

compatible numbers [kəm·pad′ə·bə] num′bərz] Numbers that are easy to compute mentally

Example: Estimate $4,126 \div 8$.
Think: 40 and 8 are compatible numbers.
$4,126 \div 8$

$4,000 \div 8 = 500$

So, $4,126 \div 8$ is about 500.

congruent [kən·grōō′ənt] Having the same size and shape

Example:

coordinate plane [kō·ôr′də·nət plān] A plane formed by two intersecting and perpendicular number lines called axes

Example:

---

coordinates [kō·ôr′də·nāts] The numbers in an ordered pair

Example:

The coordinates of A are (1, 3).
The coordinates of B are (ˉ4, ˉ3).

cubic [kyū′·bik] Relating to a cube

cup (c) [kup] A customary unit used to measure capacity

Example: 8 ounces = 1 cup

D

data [dā′tə] Information collected about people or things

decimal point [des′ə·mal point] A symbol used to separate dollars from cents in money, and the ones place from the tenths place in decimal numbers

decimal portion [des′ə·mal pôr′shən] Digits to the right of a decimal point

Example: 3.76

decimal sums [des′ə·mal sums] The result of adding decimal numbers

degree (°) [di·grē′] The unit used for measuring temperatures

denominator [di·nä′mə·nā′·tər] The number below the bar in a fraction that tells how many equal parts are in the whole

Example: $\frac{3}{4}$ ← denominator

diagonal [dī·ag′·ə·nal] A line that connects two opposite corners of a figure

diagram [dī′·ə·gram] A drawing that can be used to represent a situation

digit [di′·jət] Any one of the ten symbols 0, 1, 2, 3, 4, 5, 6, 7, 8, 9 used to write numbers

dimension [də·men′shən] A measure in one direction

distance [dis′·təns] A measure of the length between two points

distributive property [di·stri′byə·tiv prä′·pər·tē] The property that states that multiplying a sum by a number is the same as multiplying each addend by the number and then adding the products

Example: $5 \times (10 + 6) = (5 \times 10) + (5 \times 6)$

divide [də·vīd′] To separate into equal groups

Example:
○ ○ ○ ○ ○
○ ○ ○ ○ ○

$10 \div 5 = 2$

divided by [də·vī·did bī] The term used to show the operation of division is to be used on a variable

dividend [di′·və·dend] The number that is to be divided in a division problem

Example: $36 \div 6$; $6\overline{)36}$; The dividend is 36.

division [də·vi′·zhən] The process of sharing a number of items to find how many groups can be made or how many items will be in each group; the opposite operation of multiplication

divisor [də·vī′·zər] The number that divides the dividend

Example: $15 \div 3$; $3\overline{)15}$; The divisor is 3.

dollar notation [dol′·ər nō·tā′·shən] An application of the decimal system where places have the same value as in the decimal system, although they are read differently

Example: $4.25
four dollars and twenty-five cents

dot [dot] A symbol used to represent multiplication

E

edge [ej] The line segment where two or more faces of a solid figure meet

Example:

 edge

eighth [ātth] The term to describe each of eight fractional parts

Example:

endpoint [end∆•point]The point at the end of a line segment

Example:

endpoint

equal (=) [ΠΛ•kwəl]A symbol used to show that two amounts have the same value

Example: 384 = 384

equation [i•kwΣΖhən] A number sentence which shows that two quantities are equal

Example: 4 + 5 = 9

equilateral triangle [Π-kwəlaΔtə•rəl trnΔang•əl] A triangle with 3 equal, or congruent, sides

Example: 6 cm 6 cm 6 cm

equivalent [Π-kwivΔΔlənt] Having the same value or naming the same amount

estimate [esΔtə•mΣt]verbTo find an answer that is close to the exact amount

estimate [esΔtə•mət]nounA number close to an exact amount

F

face [fΣs] A polygon that is a flat surface of a solid figure

Example:

 face

fact family [fakt famΔəΠ]A set of related multiplication and division, or addition and subtraction, equations

Examples: 7 × 8 = 56; 8 × 7 = 56
56 ÷ 7 = 8; 56 ÷ 8 = 7

factor [fakΔtə] A number multiplied by another number to find a product

factor pairs [fakΔtə pΣrs]Factors that are paired within a fact family

fifth [fifth] The term to describe each of five fractional parts

Example:

flipping [fliΔ•ping]Moving a figure to a new position by flipping the figure over a line

Example:

foot (ft) [f%ot] A customary unit used for measuring length or distance

fourth [fôrth] The term to describe each of four fractional parts

Example:

fraction [frakΔshən] A number that names a part of a whole or part of a group

function [fungkΔ•shən]A relationship between two quantities in which one quantity depends on the other

G

gallon (gal) [gaΔlən] A customary unit for measuring capacity

Example: 4 quarts = 1 gallon

greater than (>) [grāΔtər than] A symbol used to compare two quantities, with the greater quantities given first

Example: 6 > 4

greatest [grāΔtist] The largest of something

grid [grid] Evenly divided and equally spaced squares on a figure or flat surface

H

height [hīt] The length of a perpendicular from the base to the top of a plane figure or solid figure

Example:

 height

hexagon [hekΔsə•gän] A polygon with six sides

Examples:

horizontal line [hôrΔə•zon΄təl lin] A line drawn in a left-right direction

Examples: 0 1 2 3 4 5 6 7 8
horizontal

how many [hou menΔē] What the top number of a fraction shows

hundredth [hanΔdrədth] One of one hundred equal parts

Example:

hundredth

I

impossible [im•päΔsə•bəl] Never able to happen

inch (in.) [inch] A customary unit used for measuring length or distance

Example: ← 1 inch →

inequality [in•i•kwolΔə•tē] A mathematical sentence that shows two expressions do not represent the same quantity

Example: 4 < 9 − 3

intersecting lines [in•tər•sekΔting linz] Lines that cross each other at exactly one point

Example:

inverse operations [inΔvərs ä•pə•rāΔshənz] Operations that undo each other. Addition and subtraction are inverse operations. Multiplication and division are inverse operations.

Example: 5 + 4 = 9, so 9 − 4 = 5
3 × 4 = 12, so 12 ÷ 4 = 3

isosceles triangle [i•säΔsə•lēz triΔang•əl] A triangle with two equal, or congruent sides

Example: 10 in. 10 in.
7 in.

K

kilogram (kg) [kiΔlə•gram] A metric unit for measuring mass

Example: 1 kilogram = 1,000 grams

L

least [lēst] The smallest of something

left [left] A direction found by referring to the left side of the body

leftover [leftΔ•ō•vər] The extra numbers that cannot be divided evenly in a division problem

length [lenkth] The measure of a side of a figure

less than (<) [les than] A symbol used to compare two numbers, with the lesser number given first

Example: 3 < 7

likely [līkΔlΠ]Having a greater than even chance of happening

line [līn] A straight path of points in a plane that continues without end in both directions with no endpoints

Example: ← S T →

line of symmetry [līn ov simΔə•trΠ] A line that separates a figure into two congruent parts

Example:

line segment [līn segΔmənt]A part of a line that includes two points called endpoints and all the points between them

Example: A B

liter (L) [lēΔtər]A metric unit for measuring capacity

Example: 1 liter = 1,000 milliliters

lower [louΔər] A location in reference to being below something else

M

mass [mas] The amount of matter in an object

median [mēΔdΠ•ən]The middle number in an ordered set of data

meter (m) [mēΔtər]A metric unit for measuring length or distance

Example: 100 centimeters = 1 meter

meter stick [mēΔtər stik]A tool used to measure length in centimeters and meters

metric system [metΔrik sisΔtəm]A measurement system that measures length in millimeters, centimeters, meters, and kilometers; capacity in liters and milliliters; mass in grams and kilograms; and temperature in degrees Celsius

middle [midΔ•əl] A place in the center

milliliter (mL) [milΔə•lΠ•tər] A metric unit for measuring capacity

Example: 1,000 milliliters = 1 liter

minus [miΔnəs] A sign indicating subtraction

missing factor [misΔing fakΔtər]Unknown factors in a number sentence

Example: 6 × ___ = 18
18 ÷ 6 = ___
The missing factor is 3

mode [mōd] The number(s) or items(s) that occur most often in a set of data

multi-digit number [mulΔti dijΔit numΔ•bər] A number that has more than one digit

multiple [mulΔtə•pəl] The product of a given whole number and another whole number

multiplication [mul•tə•plāΔkΣΔshən] A process to find the total number of items in equal-sized groups, or to find the total number of items in a given number of groups when each group contains the same number of items; multiplication is the inverse of division

multiply [mulΔtə•plī] To find the total number of items in equal-sized groups, or to find the total number of items in a given number of groups with each group contains the same number of items

Example:

3 × 4 = 12

N

negative [neΔgə•tiv] All the numbers to the left of zero on the number line; negative numbers are less than zero

negative number [negΔ•ə•tiv numΔ•bər] Any number less than zero

Example:

-8 -7 -6 -5 -4 -3 -2 -1 0 1 2 3 4 5 6 7 8
The red numbers
are negative numbers.

net [net] A two-dimensional pattern that can be folded to make a three-dimensional figure

Example:

ninth [ninth] The term to describe each of nine fractional parts

Example:

non-decimal portion [nonΔ desΔ•ə•məl pórΔ•shən] The portion of a number that is to the left of a decimal

Example: 53.76

numerator [nōōΔmə•rā•tər] The number above the bar in a fraction that tells how many equal parts of the whole are being considered

Example: $\frac{2}{3}$ ← numerator

O

obtuse angle [äb•tōōs΄ angΔəl] An angle that is larger than a right angle but smaller than a straight angle

Example:

obtuse triangle [äb•tōōs΄ triΔang•əl] A triangle with one obtuse angle

Example:

operations [op•ə•rāΔshəns] Addition, subtraction, multiplication, and division

Example: operation signs: +, −, ×, ÷

order of operations [órΔdər ov op•ə•rāΔshəns] Rules for performing operations in mathematical phrases with more than one operation

ordered pair [órΔdərd pär] A pair of numbers used to locate a point on a coordinate grid. The first number tells how far to move horizontally, and the second number tells how far to move vertically

origin [órΔ•jən] The point where the the x-axis and the y-axis in the coordinate plane intersect, (0,0)

outcome [outΔkum] A possible result of an experiment